SOCIOLOGY
93/94

Twenty-Second Edition

Annual Editions
A Library of Information from the Public Press

Editor

Kurt Finsterbusch
University of Maryland, College Park

Kurt Finsterbusch received his bachelor's degree in history from Princeton University in 1957, and his bachelor of divinity degree from Grace Theological Seminary in 1960. His Ph.D. in sociology, from Columbia University, was conferred in 1969. He is the author of several books, including *Understanding Social Impacts* (Sage Publications, 1980), *Social Research for Policy Decisions* (Wadsworth Publishing, 1980, with Annabelle Bender Motz), and *Organizational Change as a Development Strategy* (Lynne Rienner Publishers, 1987, with Jerald Hage). He is currently teaching at the University of Maryland, College Park, and, in addition to serving as editor for *Annual Editions: Sociology*, he is also coeditor for The Dushkin Publishing Group's *Taking Sides: Clashing Views on Controversial Social Issues.*

Cover illustration by Mike Eagle

The Dushkin Publishing Group, Inc.
Sluice Dock, Guilford, Connecticut 06437

The Annual Editions Series

Annual Editions is a series of over 55 volumes designed to provide the reader with convenient, low-cost access to a wide range of current, carefully selected articles from some of the most important magazines, newspapers, and journals published today. Annual Editions are updated on an annual basis through a continuous monitoring of over 300 periodical sources. All Annual Editions have a number of features designed to make them particularly useful, including topic guides, annotated tables of contents, unit overviews, and indexes. For the teacher using Annual Editions in the classroom, an Instructor's Resource Guide with test questions is available for each volume.

VOLUMES AVAILABLE

Africa
Aging
American Government
American History, Pre-Civil War
American History, Post-Civil War
Anthropology
Biology
Business Ethics
Canadian Politics
China
Commonwealth of Independent States
Comparative Politics
Computers in Education
Computers in Business
Computers in Society
Criminal Justice
Drugs, Society, and Behavior
Dying, Death, and Bereavement
Early Childhood Education
Economics
Educating Exceptional Children
Education
Educational Psychology
Environment
Geography
Global Issues
Health
Human Development
Human Resources
Human Sexuality
India and South Asia

International Business
Japan and the Pacific Rim
Latin America
Life Management
Macroeconomics
Management
Marketing
Marriage and Family
Microeconomics
Middle East and the Islamic World
Money and Banking
Nutrition
Personal Growth and Behavior
Physical Anthropology
Psychology
Public Administration
Race and Ethnic Relations
Social Problems
Sociology
State and Local Government
Third World
Urban Society
Violence and Terrorism
Western Civilization, Pre-Reformation
Western Civilization, Post-Reformation
Western Europe
World History, Pre-Modern
World History, Modern
World Politics

Library of Congress Cataloging in Publication Data
Main entry under title: Annual Editions: Sociology. 1993/94.
    1. Sociology—Periodicals. 2. United States—Social Conditions—1960—Periodicals.
I. Finsterbusch, Kurt, *comp.* II. Title: Sociology.
ISBN 1–56134–214–9   301′.05   72–76876
HM1.A76

Twenty-Second Edition

Printed in the United States of America

To the Reader

In publishing ANNUAL EDITIONS we recognize the enormous role played by the magazines, newspapers, and journals of the *public press* in providing current, first-rate educational information in a broad spectrum of interest areas. Within the articles, the best scientists, practitioners, researchers, and commentators draw issues into new perspective as accepted theories and viewpoints are called into account by new events, recent discoveries change old facts, and fresh debate breaks out over important controversies.

Many of the articles resulting from this enormous editorial effort are appropriate for students, researchers, and professionals seeking accurate, current material to help bridge the gap between principles and theories and the real world. These articles, however, become more useful for study when those of lasting value are carefully *collected, organized, indexed,* and *reproduced* in a *low-cost format,* which provides easy and permanent access when the material is needed. That is the role played by *Annual Editions.* Under the direction of each volume's *Editor,* who is an expert in the subject area, and with the guidance of an *Advisory Board,* we seek each year to provide in each *ANNUAL EDITION* a current, well-balanced, carefully selected collection of the best of the public press for your study and enjoyment. We think you'll find this volume useful, and we hope you'll take a moment to let us know what you think.

The 1990s inherit from the 1980s crises, changes, and challenges. Crime is running rampant. The public is demanding more police, more jails, and tougher sentences, but less government spending. The economy suffers from foreign competition, trade deficits, budget deficits, and economic uncertainties. Government economic policies seem to create almost as many problems as they solve. Laborers, women, blacks, and many other groups complain of injustices and victimization. The use of toxic chemicals has been blamed for increases in cancer, sterility, and other diseases. Marriage and the family have been transformed, in part, by the women's movement, and in part by the stress caused by current conditions for women to combine family and careers. Schools, television, and corporations are commonly vilified. Add to this the problems of population growth, ozone depletion, and the greenhouse effect, and it is easy to despair.

The present generation may be the one to determine the course of history for the next 200 years. Great changes are taking place and new solutions are being sought where old answers no longer work. The issues the current generation faces are complex and must be interpreted within a sophisticated framework. The sociological perspective provides such a framework. The articles that follow should help you develop the sociological perspective, which will enable you to determine how the issues of the day relate to the way society is structured. They will provide not only information, but also models of interpretation and analysis which will guide you as you form your own views.

Annual Editions: Sociology 93/94 emphasizes social change, institutional crises, and prospects for the future. It provides an intellectual preparation for acting for the betterment of humanity in times of crucial change. The sociological perspective is needed more than ever as humankind tries to find a way to peace, prosperity, health, and well-being that can be maintained for generations in an improving environment. The obstacles that lie in the path of these important goals seem to increase yearly. The goals of this edition are to communicate to students the excitement and importance of the study of the social world, and to provoke interest in and enthusiasm for the study of sociology.

Annual Editions depends upon reader response to develop and change. You are encouraged to return the article rating form at the back of the book with your opinions about existing articles, recommendations of articles you think have sociological merit for subsequent editions, and advice on how the anthology can be made more useful as a teaching and learning tool.

Kurt Finsterbusch
Editor

Contents

Introduction

Two selections introduce the role of the sociologist and the discipline of sociology.

Unit 1

Culture

Seven selections consider American values and life-styles, cultural changes, and primitive and unusual cultures.

The concepts in bold italics are developed in the article. For further expansion please refer to the Topic Guide, the Index, and the Glossary.

Unit

2

Socialization, Biology, Social Control, and Deviance

Six articles examine the effects of social influences on childhood, personality, and human behavior with regard to the socialization of the individual.

Unit 3

Groups and Roles in Transition

Seven articles discuss some of the social roles and
group relationships that are in transition in today's
society. Topics include primary and secondary groups
and the reevaluation of social choices.

The concepts in bold italics are developed in the article. For further expansion please refer to the Topic Guide, the Index, and the Glossary.

Unit 4

Stratification and Social Inequalities

Six selections discuss the social stratification and inequalities that exist in today's society with regard to the rich, the poor, blacks, and women.

Unit 5

Social Institutions in Crisis and Change

Eleven articles examine several social institutions that are currently in crisis. Selections focus on the political, economic, and social spheres, as well as the overall state of the nation.

The concepts in bold italics are developed in the article. For further expansion please refer to the Topic Guide, the Index, and the Glossary.

The concepts in bold italics are developed in the article. For further expansion please refer to the Topic Guide, the Index, and the Glossary.

Unit 6

Social Change and the Future

Five selections discuss the impact that technology, environmental degradation, and changing social values will have on society's future.

Topic Guide

This topic guide suggests how the selections in this book relate to topics of traditional concern to students and professionals involved with the study of sociology. It is useful for locating articles that relate to each other for reading and research. The guide is arranged alphabetically according to topic. Articles may, of course, treat topics that do not appear in the topic guide. In turn, entries in the topic guide do not necessarily constitute a comprehensive listing of all the contents of each selection.

TOPIC AREA	TREATED IN:	TOPIC AREA	TREATED IN:
Bureaucracy	33. From Ouagadougou to Cape Canaveral 35. Paradigms for Postmodern Managers	Economy	31. Real Economy 36. Is America on the Way Down? 44. Post-Capitalist World
Children/Childhood	8. Mountain People 10. Childhood Through the Ages 11. Guns and Dolls 12. Is TV Ruining Our Children? 16. Breakup of the Family	Education	11. Guns and Dolls 38. Stand and Deliver
		Euthanasia	22. Dignity, Choice, and Care
Community	3. Tyranny of Choice 5. Fragmenting of America 9. Tribal Wisdom 15. Way Out of the Morass 20. 'They Can't Stop Us Now'	Family/Marriage	8. Mountain People 10. Childhood Through the Ages 16. Breakup of the Family 17. Can We Talk? 28. Global War Against Women
Competition	31. Real Economy 36. Is America on the Way Down?	Handicapped	21. "Sociology of Acceptance"
Crime	13. Crime Pays 14. Nature of the Beast 15. Way Out of the Morass	Individualism	3. Tyranny of Choice 5. Fragmenting of America 9. Tribal Wisdom
Culture	3. Tyranny of Choice 5. Fragmenting of America 6. Upbeat Generation 7. Blame It on Feminism 8. Mountain People 9. Tribal Wisdom 11. Guns and Dolls 17. Can We Talk? 18. Time for Men 37. Possible to Be Pro-Life and Pro-Choice?	Integration	5. Fragmenting of America
		Law Enforcement	13. Crime Pays 14. Nature of the Beast
		Leadership	27. Why Women Aren't Making It to the Top
		Life-Styles	3. Tyranny of Choice 4. Workers of the World, Unwind 8. Mountain People 9. Tribal Wisdom
Death	22. Dignity, Choice, and Care	Market	30. Jihad vs. McWorld 31. Real Economy 44. Post-Capitalist World
Democracy	30. Jihad vs. McWorld		
Demography	29. Life on the Brink 37. Possible to Be Pro-Life and Pro-Choice? 40. Population Explosion	Marriage	See Family/Marriage
		Media	12. Is TV Ruining Our Children?
Discrimination	7. Blame It on Feminism 21. "Sociology of Acceptance" 25. Crisis of Shattered Dreams 26. Thinking Beyond Race 27. Why Women Aren't Making It to the Top 28. Global War Against Women	Organizations	33. From Ouagadougou to Cape Canaveral 35. Paradigms for Postmodern Managers
		Political/ Government	23. Upside-Down Welfare 24. Poverty Industry 25. Crisis of Shattered Dreams 32. Big Messes 33. From Ouagadougou to Cape Canaveral 34. Money Changes Everything 39. America's Holy War
Drugs	15. Way Out of the Morass		
Ecology/ Environment	8. Mountain People 40. Population Explosion 42. Rural Populations and the Global Environment	Population Growth	29. Life on the Brink 40. Population Explosion 42. Rural Populations and the Global Environment

TOPIC AREA	TREATED IN:	TOPIC AREA	TREATED IN:
Poverty	8. Mountain People 24. Poverty Industry 29. Life on the Brink 40. Population Explosion	**Socialization**	10. Childhood Through the Ages 11. Guns and Dolls 12. Is TV Ruining Our Children? 17. Can We Talk?
Race/Ethnic Relations	25. Crisis of Shattered Dreams 26. Thinking Beyond Race	**Sociological Perspective**	1. Invitation to Sociology
Religion	39. America's Holy War	**Technology**	5. Fragmenting of America 37. Possible to Be Pro-Life and Pro-Choice?
Roles	10. Childhood Through the Ages 11. Guns and Dolls 18. Time for Men		43. Communication Networks 44. Post-Capitalist World
Science/Knowledge	1. Invitation to Sociology 2. Real Patriots Ask Questions 33. From Ouagadougou to Cape Canaveral 44. Post-Capitalist World	**Tribalism**	30. Jihad vs. McWorld
		Underclass	23. Upside-Down Welfare 24. Poverty Industry
Sex Roles	7. Blame It on Feminism 11. Guns and Dolls 17. Can We Talk? 18. Time for Men 27. Why Women Aren't Making It to the Top	**Unemployment**	*See* Work/Unemployment
		Upper Class	23. Upside-Down Welfare
		Urban	19. Second Coming of the Small Town
Sexism	7. Blame It on Feminism 14. Nature of the Beast	**Values**	3. Tyranny of Choice 4. Workers of the World, Unwind 5. Fragmenting of America 6. Upbeat Generation 7. Blame It on Feminism 8. Mountain People 9. Tribal Wisdom 16. Breakup of the Family 18. Time for Men 37. Possible to Be Pro-Life and Pro-Choice?
Social Change	4. Workers of the World, Unwind 5. Fragmenting of America 6. Upbeat Generation 7. Blame It on Feminism 8. Mountain People 10. Childhood Through the Ages 16. Breakup of the Family 21. "Sociology of Acceptance" 22. Dignity, Choice, and Care 25. Crisis of Shattered Dreams 26. Thinking Beyond Race 27. Why Women Aren't Making It to the Top 32. Big Messes 37. Possible to Be Pro-Life and Pro-Choice? 43. Communication Networks 44. Post-Capitalist World		
		Violence	13. Crime Pays
		Welfare	15. Way Out of the Morass 23. Upside-Down Welfare 24. Poverty Industry
		Women	7. Blame It on Feminism 11. Guns and Dolls 17. Can We Talk? 27. Why Women Aren't Making It to the Top 28. Global War Against Women
Social Class/ Stratification	23. Upside-Down Welfare 24. Poverty Industry 26. Thinking Beyond Race	**Work/ Unemployment**	4. Workers of the World, Unwind 31. Real Economy 41. Immigrants
Social Control	13. Crime Pays 14. Nature of the Beast		
Social Movements	7. Blame It on Feminism		
Social Relationships	3. Tyranny of Choice 5. Fragmenting of America 7. Blame It on Feminism 8. Mountain People 16. Breakup of the Family 17. Can We Talk? 18. Time for Men 26. Thinking Beyond Race 28. Global War Against Women		

Introduction

Sociology is both the scientific study of society and social behavior and a method by which ordinary people strive to understand what is happening to them and their society. The need for such understanding is urgent at the present historical moment. Change has become so rapid that most people are bewildered and amazed by events over the past two decades: the energy crisis transformed global economics; new technologies changed the workplace; the communist world is becoming radically reorganized; and a complex, interdependent world means that the changes in one country cause changes in other countries.

Most people today are associated with large, complex, and impersonal organizations, which often do not treat us very well. Universities frequently herd students through large classes and seldom create truly joyful intellectual work. The medical system extorts stupendous fees from patients, making them feel like victims. The tobacco industry enthusiastically markets its highly addictive and harmful drug that endangers the health of hundreds of thousands of Americans every year. Corporations close factories in New England and open factories in Taiwan. American banks invest in the Japanese industries that are invading the American market. Our personal worlds are deeply affected and often quite negatively by remote forces and decisions of large organizations. We feel powerless.

Nevertheless, unprecedented opportunities to build a better world and improve the quality of life for many people lie ahead. The study of sociology can help students figure out how society works and what they can do to change it by developing a sociological imagination and sociological perspective. The article by Peter L. Berger in this introductory section focuses on the common occurrences of everyday life. The author challenges the student to use the sociological perspective to "see," in daily events, the sociological truths that most people miss. Carl Sagan and Ann Druyan demonstrate the importance of asking questions, challenging accepted notions for science, and obtaining a true understanding of the functioning of society.

Looking Ahead: Challenge Questions

How can sociology contribute to one's understanding of the contemporary world?

In what ways can the sociological imagination become a significant factor in political policies?

Can sociology contribute to personal growth?

Invitation to Sociology
A Humanistic Perspective

Peter L. Berger

. . . The sociologist, then, is someone concerned with understanding society in a disciplined way. The nature of this discipline is scientific. This means that what the sociologist finds and says about the social phenomena he studies occurs within a certain rather strictly defined frame of reference. One of the main characteristics of this scientific frame of reference is that operations are bound by certain rules of evidence. As a scientist, the sociologist tries to be objective, to control his personal preferences and prejudices, to perceive clearly rather than to judge normatively. This restraint, of course, does not embrace the totality of the sociologist's existence as a human being, but is limited to his operations *qua* sociologist. Nor does the sociologist claim that his frame of reference is the only one within which society can be looked at. For that matter, very few scientists in any field would claim today that one should look at the world only scientifically. The botanist looking at a daffodil has no reason to dispute the right of the poet to look at the same object in a very different manner. There are many ways of playing. The point is not that one denies other people's games but that one is clear about the rules of one's own. The game of the sociologist, then, uses scientific rules. As a result, the sociologist must be clear in his own mind as to the meaning of these rules. That is, he must concern himself with methodological questions. Methodology does not constitute his goal. The latter, let us recall once more, is the attempt to understand society. Methodology helps in reaching this goal. In order to understand society, or that segment of it that he is studying at the moment, the sociologist will use a variety of means. Among these are statistical techniques. Statistics can be very useful in answering certain sociological questions. But statistics does not constitute sociology. As a scientist, the sociologist will have to be concerned with the exact significance of the terms he is using. That is, he will have to be careful about terminology. This does not have to mean that he must invent a new language of his own, but it does mean that he cannot naively use the language of everyday discourse. Finally, the interest of the sociologist is primarily theoretical. That is, he is interested in understanding for its own sake. He may be aware of or even concerned with the practical applicability and consequences of his findings, but at that point he leaves the sociological frame of reference as such and moves into realms of values, beliefs and ideas that he shares with other men who are not sociologists. . . .

We would say then that the sociologist (that is, the one we would really like to invite to our game) is a person intensively, endlessly, shamelessly interested in the doings of men. His natural habitat is all the human gathering places of the world, wherever men come together. The sociologist may be interested in many other things. But his consuming interest remains in the world of men, their institutions, their history, their passions. And since he is interested in men, nothing that men do can be altogether tedious for him. He will naturally be interested in the events that engage men's ultimate beliefs, their moments of tragedy and grandeur and ecstasy. But he will also be fascinated by the commonplace, the everyday. He will know reverence, but this reverence will not prevent him from wanting to see and to understand. He may sometimes feel revulsion or contempt. But this also will not deter him from wanting to have his questions answered. The sociologist, in his quest for understanding, moves through the world of men without respect for the usual lines of demarcation. Nobility and degradation, power and obscurity, intelligence and folly—these are equally *interesting* to him, however unequal they may be in his personal values or tastes. Thus his questions may lead him to all possible levels of society, the best and the least known places, the most respected and the most despised. And, if he is a good sociologist, he will find himself in all these places because his own questions have so taken possession of him that he has little choice but to seek for answers.

It would be possible to say the same things in a lower key. We could say that the sociologist, but for the grace of his academic title, is the man who must listen to gossip despite himself, who is tempted to look through keyholes, to read other people's mail, to open closed cabinets. Before some otherwise unoccupied psychologist sets out now to construct an aptitude test for sociologists on the basis of sublimated voyeurism, let us quickly say that we are speaking merely by way of analogy. Perhaps some little boys consumed with curiosity to watch their maiden aunts in the bathroom later become inveterate sociologists. This is quite uninteresting. What interests us is the curiosity that grips any sociologist in front of a closed door behind which there are human voices. If he is a good sociologist, he will want to open that door, to understand these voices. Behind each closed door he will anticipate some new facet of human life not yet perceived and understood.

The sociologist will occupy himself with matters that others regard as too sacred or as too distasteful for dispassionate investigation. He will find rewarding the company of priests or of prostitutes, depending not on his personal preferences but on the questions he happens to be asking at the moment. He will also concern himself with matters that others may find much too boring. He will be interested in the human interaction that goes with warfare or with great intellectual discoveries, but also in the relations between people employed in a restaurant or between a group of little girls playing with their dolls. His main focus of attention is not the ultimate significance of what men do, but the action in itself, as another example of the infinite richness of human conduct. . . .

Any intellectual activity derives excitement from the moment it becomes a trail of discovery. In some fields of learning this is the discovery of worlds previously unthought and unthinkable. This is the excitement of the astronomer or of the nuclear physicist on the antipodal boundaries of the realities that man is capable of conceiving. But it can also be the excitement of bacteriology or geology. In a different way it can be the excitement of the linguist discovering new realms of human expression or of the anthropologist exploring human customs in faraway countries. In such discovery, when undertaken with passion, a widening of awareness, sometimes a veritable transformation of consciousness, occurs. The universe turns out to be much more wonder-full than one had ever dreamed. The excitement of sociology is usually of a different sort. Sometimes, it is true, the sociologist penetrates into worlds that had previously been quite unknown to him—for instance, the world of crime, or the world of some bizarre religious sect, or the world fashioned by the exclusive concerns of some group such as medical specialists or military leaders or advertising executives. However, much of the time the sociologist moves in sectors of experience that are familiar to him and to most people in his society. He investigates communities, institutions and activities that one can read about every day in the newspapers. Yet there is another excitement of discovery beckoning in his investigations. It is not the excitement of coming upon the totally unfamiliar, but rather the excitement of finding the familiar becoming transformed in its meaning. The fascination of sociology lies in the fact that its perspective makes us see in a new light the very world in which we have lived all our lives. This also constitutes a transformation of consciousness. Moreover, this transformation is more relevant existentially than that of many other intellectual disciplines, because it is more difficult to segregate in some special compartment of the mind. The astronomer does not live in the remote galaxies, and the nuclear physicist can, outside his laboratory, eat and laugh and marry and vote without thinking about the insides of the atom. The geologist looks at rocks only at appropriate times, and the linguist speaks English with his wife. The sociologist lives in society, on the job and off it. His own life, inevitably, is part of his subject matter. Men being what they are, sociologists too manage to segregate their professional insights from their everyday affairs. But it is a rather difficult feat to perform in good faith.

The sociologist moves in the common world of men, close to what most of them would call real. The categories he employs in his analyses are only refinements of the categories by which other men live—power, class, status, race, ethnicity. As a result, there is a deceptive simplicity and obviousness about some sociological investigations.

One reads them, nods at the familiar scene, remarks that one has heard all this before and don't people have better things to do than to waste their time on truisms—until one is suddenly brought up against an insight that radically questions everything one had previously assumed about this familiar scene. This is the point at which one begins to sense the excitement of sociology.

Let us take a specific example. Imagine a sociology class in a Southern college where almost all the students are white Southerners. Imagine a lecture on the subject of the racial system of the South. The lecturer is talking here of matters that have been familiar to his students from the time of their infancy. Indeed, it may be that they are much more familiar with the minutiae of this system than he is. They are quite bored as a result. It seems to them that he is only using more pretentious words to describe what they already know. Thus he may use the term "caste," one commonly used now by American sociologists to describe the Southern racial system. But in explaining the term he shifts to traditional Hindu society, to make it clearer. He then goes on to analyze the magical beliefs inherent in caste tabus, the social dynamics of commensalism and connubium, the economic interests concealed within the system, the way in which religious beliefs relate to the tabus, the effects of the caste system upon the industrial development of the society and vice versa—all in India. But suddenly India is not very far away at all. The lecture then goes back to its Southern theme. The familiar now seems not quite so familiar any more. Questions are raised that are new, perhaps raised angrily, but raised all the same. And at least some of the students have begun to understand that there are functions involved in this business of race that they have not read about in the newspapers (at least not those in their hometowns) and that their parents have not told them—partly, at least, because neither the newspapers nor the parents knew about them.

It can be said that the first wisdom of sociology is this—things are not what they seem. This too is a deceptively simple statement. It ceases to be simple after a while. Social reality turns out to have many layers of meaning. The discovery of each new layer changes the perception of the whole.

Anthropologists use the term "culture shock" to describe the impact of a totally new culture upon a newcomer. In an extreme instance such shock will be experienced by the Western explorer who is told, halfway through dinner, that he is eating the nice old lady he had been chatting with the previous day—a shock with predictable physiological if not moral consequences. Most explorers no longer encounter cannibalism in their travels today. However, the first encounters with polygamy or with puberty rites or even with the way some nations drive their automobiles can be quite a shock to an American visitor. With the shock may go not only disapproval or disgust but a sense of excitement that things can *really* be that different from what they are at home. To some extent, at least, this is the excitement of any first travel abroad. The experience of sociological discovery could be described as "culture shock" minus geographical displacement. In other words, the sociologist travels at home—with shocking results. He is unlikely to find that he is eating a nice old lady for dinner. But the discovery, for instance, that his own church has considerable money invested in the missile industry or that a few blocks from his home there are people who engage in cultic orgies may not be drastically different in emotional impact. Yet we would not want to imply that sociological discoveries are always or even usually outrageous to moral sentiment. Not at all. What they have in common with exploration in distant lands, however, is the sudden illumination of new and unsuspected facets of human existence in society. This is the excitement and, as we shall try to show later, the humanistic justification of sociology.

People who like to avoid shocking discoveries, who prefer to believe that society is just what they were taught in Sunday School, who like the safety of the rules and the maxims of what Alfred Schuetz has called the "world-taken-for-granted," should stay away from sociology. People who feel no temptation before closed doors, who have no curiosity about human beings, who are content to admire scenery without wondering about the people who live in those houses on the other side of that river, should probably also stay away from sociology. They will find it unpleasant or, at any rate, unrewarding. People who are interested in human beings only if they can change, convert or reform them should also be warned, for they will find sociology much less useful than they hoped. And people whose interest is mainly in their own conceptual constructions will do just as well to turn to the study of little white mice. Sociology will be satisfying, in the long run, only to those who can think of nothing more entrancing than to watch men and to understand things human. . . .

The connection between the method of science and the Bill of Rights

---

Real Patriots Ask Questions

Carl Sagan
and Ann Druyan

Pulitzer Prize-winner Carl Sagan teaches science at Cornell University. Ann Druyan is Secretary of the Washington-based Federation of American Scientists. This article is the basis of a keynote address presented by Dr. Sagan at the annual meeting of the American Bar Association. Exercising their First Amendment freedoms, the authors have organized three large protests against continued nuclear weapons testing by the United States and have participated in scores of other peaceful demonstrations. They are married and have two children.

A FEW YEARS AGO, WE were at a dinner in Peredelkino, a village outside Moscow where Communist Party officials, retired generals and a few favored intellectuals have their summer homes. The air was electric with the prospect of new freedoms—especially the right to speak your mind, even if the government doesn't like what you're saying.

But, despite *glasnost*, there were widespread doubts. Would those in power really allow their critics to be heard? Would freedom of speech, of assembly, of the press, of religion, really be permitted? Would people inexperienced with freedom be able to bear its burdens?

Some of these Soviet citizens had fought—for decades and against long odds—for the freedoms that most Americans take for granted; indeed, they had been inspired by the American experiment, a real-world demonstration that nations could survive and prosper with these freedoms intact. They even were considering the possibility that prosperity was *due to* freedom—that, in an age of high technology and swift change, the two rise or fall together.

There were many toasts, as there always are at dinners in the USSR. The most memorable was given by a world-famous Soviet novelist. He stood up, raised his glass, looked us in the eye and said, "To the Americans. They have a little freedom." He paused, then added: "And they know how to keep it."

Do we?

Science may be hard to understand. It may challenge cherished beliefs. In the hands of politicians or industrialists, it may lead to weapons of mass destruction and grave threats to the environment.

But one thing you have to say about science: It delivers the goods. If you want to know when the next eclipse of the Sun will be, you might try magicians and mystics, but you'll do much better with scientists. They can tell you within a fraction of a second when an eclipse will happen decades or centuries in the future, how long it'll last and where on Earth you should be standing to get a

> *If we can't
> think for ourselves,
> if we're unwilling
> to question authority,
> then we are just
> putty in the hands
> of those in power.*

good look. If you want to know the sex of your unborn child, you can consult astrologers or plumb-bob danglers all you want, but they'll be right, on average, only one time in two. If you want real accuracy, try science.

What is the secret of its success? Partly, it's this: There is a built-in error-correcting machinery. There are no forbidden questions in science, no matters too sensitive or delicate to be probed, no sacred truths. There is an openness to new ideas combined with the most rigorous, skeptical scrutiny of all ideas, a sifting of the wheat from the chaff. Arguments from authority are worthless. It makes no difference how smart, august or beloved you are. You must prove your case in the face of determined, expert criticism. Diversity and debate between contending views are valued.

Scientific findings and theories are routinely subjected to a gantlet of criticism—oral defenses of doctoral theses, debates at scientific meetings, university colloquia punctuated by withering questions, anonymous reviews of papers submitted to scientific journals, refutations and rebuttals. There is a reward structure built into science for finding errors: The more basic and fundamental the error exposed, and the more widely accepted it was, the greater is the reward.

This may sound messy and disorderly. In a way, it is. Science is far from perfect. It's just the most successful method known, by far, to understand the world. The discipline of science is hard; scientists, being human, don't always follow the methods of science themselves. Like other people, they don't especially enjoy having their favorite ideas challenged. But they recognize it as the cost of getting to the truth. And the truth—rather than the confirmation of their preconceptions—is what they're after.

Wherever possible, scientists experiment. They do not trust what is intuitively obvious. That the Earth is flat was once obvious. That heavier bodies fall faster was once obvious. That blood-sucking leeches cure disease was once obvious. That some people are naturally and by divine decree slaves was once obvious. That the Earth is at the center of the Universe was once obvious. The truth may be puzzling or counterintuitive; it may contradict deeply held prejudices. But, as the history of both science and politics has amply demonstrated, preferring comfortable error to the hard truth is, sooner or later, disastrous.

At another dinner in another city, many decades ago, the physicist Robert W. Wood was asked to respond to the toast, "To physics and metaphysics." By "metaphysics," people then meant something like philosophy, or truths you could recognize just by thinking about them. Wood answered along these lines:

The physicist has an idea. The more he thinks it through, the more sense it seems to make. He goes to the scientific literature, and the more he reads, the more promising the idea seems. Thus prepared, he devises an experiment to test the idea out. The experiment is painstaking. Many possibilities are checked. The accuracy of measurement is refined. At the end of all this work, however, the idea is shown to be worthless. The physicist discards it, frees his mind from the clutter of error and moves on to something else. The difference between physics and metaphysics, Wood concluded, is that the metaphysicist has no laboratory.

Now, humans are not electrons or laboratory rats. But every act of Congress, every Supreme Court decision, every National Security Directive of the President is an experiment. Every change in economic policy, every increase in funding for Head Start, every toughening of criminal sentences is an experiment. Communism in Eastern Europe, the Soviet Union and China was an experiment. Japan and West Germany investing a great deal in science and technology and next to nothing on defense was an experiment. Ideas can be tested.

Some of the opponents of the U.S. Constitution insisted that it would never work; that a republican form of government spanning a continent with "such dissimilar climates, economies, morals, politics and peoples," as George Clinton of New York said, was impossible; that such a government and such a Constitution, as Patrick Henry of Virginia declared, "contradicts all the experience of the world." The experiment was tried anyway.

Even a casual scrutiny of history reveals that we humans have a sad tendency to make the same mistakes again and again. Having power tends to corrupt us. We're afraid of strangers or anybody who's a little different from us. When we get scared, we start pushing people around. We have readily accessible buttons that release powerful emotions when pressed. We can be manipulated into utter senselessness by clever politicians. Give us the right kind of leader, and we'll gladly do just about anything he wants—even things we know to be wrong. The framers of the Constitution were students of history. In recognition of the human condition, they sought to invent a machine that would keep us free in spite of ourselves.

Thomas Jefferson, who had written the Declaration of Independence, had little to do with the Constitution; as it was being formulated, he was abroad, serving as America's ambassador to France. When he read its provisions, he was very pleased, with two reservations: One was that there was no limit on the number of terms the President could serve. This, Jefferson feared, was a way for a President to become a king, in fact if not in law. The other major deficiency was the absence of a bill of rights. The citizen—the average person—was insufficiently protected, Jefferson thought, from the inevitable abuses of those in power.

In 1791, with James Madison playing a leading role, the first ten amendments were added to the Constitution. From the beginning, they were called the Bill of Rights. The Constitution, the Bill of Rights and the subsequent amendments were a new force in the world—a government with a written set of rules that distribute political power among the various segments of the society, with specific machinery not just vaguely allowing but actually protecting the expression of unpopular ideas. It was a machine of government designed to correct itself—like the evolutionary process, adapting to changing environments.

The Constitution is a daring and courageous document because it allows for continuous change—even of the form of government itself—if the people so wish. Because no one is wise enough to foresee which ideas may prove useful and answer urgent societal needs—even if they've been counterintuitive and disquieting in the past—it guarantees the fullest and freest expression of views.

There is, of course, a price. Most of us are for freedom of expression when there's a danger that our own views will be suppressed. We're not all that upset, though, if views we hate encounter a little censorship here and there. But within certain narrowly circumscribed limits—Justice Holmes' example was causing panic by falsely crying "fire" in a crowded theater—great liberties are permitted in America:

• Even if they mock Judaeo-Christian-Islamic values—even if they ridicule everything most of us hold dear—devil-worshipers (if there are any) are entitled to practice their religion, so long as they break no law.
• Those who oppose abortion are free to picket the abortion clinics and to display pictures of mangled fetuses, as long as their protest remains peaceful and nonobstructive. The fact that those who come to have abortions understandably do not wish to see these pictures is insufficient grounds for banning the demonstration.
• A purported scientific article asserting the "superiority" of one race over another may not be censored by the government, no matter how pernicious it is; the cure for a fallacious argument is a better argument, not the suppression of ideas.
• Individuals are free, if they wish, to praise the lives and politics of such undisputed mass murderers as Adolf Hitler and Josef Stalin. Even detestable opinions have a right to be heard.

9

Aliens And Sedition

The ink was barely dry on the Bill of Rights before politicians found a way to subvert it—by cashing in on fear and patriotic hysteria. In 1798, the ruling Federalist Party knew that the button to push was prejudice. Exploiting tensions between France and the U.S., and a widespread fear that French and Irish immigrants were somehow intrinsically unfit to be Americans, the Federalists passed a set of laws that have come to be known as the Alien and Sedition Acts.

One law upped the residency requirement for citizenship from five to 14 years. (Citizens of French and Irish origin usually voted for the opposition, Jefferson's Democratic-Republican Party.)

The Alien Act gave President John Adams the power to deport any foreigner who aroused his suspicions. Making the President nervous, said a member of Congress, "is the new crime." Jefferson believed the Alien Act had been framed explicitly to expel C. F. Volney, the French historian; Pierre Samuel du Pont de Nemours, patriarch of the famous chemical family; and the British scientist Joseph Priestley, the discoverer of oxygen. In Jefferson's view, these were just the sort of people America needed.

The Sedition Act made it unlawful to publish "false or malicious" criticism of the government or to inspire oppostion to any of its acts. Some two dozen arrests were made, 10 people were convicted and many more were censored or intimidated into silence. The act attempted, Jefferson said, "to crush all political opposition by making criticism of Federalist officials or policies a crime."

In the first week of Jefferson's Presidency, he began pardoning every victim of the Sedition Act because, he said, it was as contrary to the spirit of American freedoms as if Congress had ordered us all to fall down and worship a golden calf. By 1802, none of the Alien and Sedition Acts remained on the books.

From across 200 years, it's hard to recapture the frenzied mood that made the French and the "wild Irish" seem so grave a threat that we were willing to surrender our most precious freedoms. But that's how it always works. It always seems an aberration later, but by then we're in the grip of the next prejudice.

Those who seek power at any price detect a societal weakness, a fear that they can ride into office. It could be ethnic differences, as it was then, or perhaps different amounts of melanin in the skin; different philosophies or religions; or maybe it's drug use, violent crime, economic crisis or "desecration" of the flag.

Whatever the problem, the quick fix is generally to shave a little freedom off the Bill of Rights. Yes, in 1942, Japanese-Americans were protected by the Bill of Rights, but we locked them up—after all, there was a war on. Yes, there are prohibitions against unreasonable search and seizure, but we have a war on drugs. Yes, there's freedom of speech, but we don't want foreign authors here, spouting alien ideologies, do we? The pretexts change from year to year, but the result remains the same: concentrating more power in fewer hands and suppressing diversity, even though it's central to our future.

When permitted to listen to alternative opinions and engage in substantive debate, people have been known to change their minds. It can happen. For example, Hugo Black, in his youth, was a member of the Ku Klux Klan; but he later became a Supreme Court justice and was one of the leaders in the historic Supreme Court decisions, partly based on the 14th Amendment, that affirmed the civil rights of all Americans: It was said that when he was a young man, he dressed up in white robes and scared black folks; when he got older, he dressed up in black robes and scared white folks.

In matters of criminal justice, the Bill of Rights recognizes the temptation that may be felt by police, prosecutors and the judiciary to intimidate witnesses and expedite punishment. The criminal-justice system is fallible: Innocent people might be punished for crimes they did not commit; governments are perfectly capable of framing those who, for reasons unconnected with the purported crime, they do not like. So the Bill of Rights protects defendants. A kind of cost-benefit analysis is made. The guilty may on occasion be set free so that the innocent will not be punished. This is not only a moral virtue; it also inhibits the misuse of the criminal-justice system to suppress unpopular opinions or despised minorities.

New ideas, and creativity in general, always represent a kind of freedom—a breaking out from previous hobbling constraints. Freedom is a prerequisite for science—which is one reason the Soviet Union could not remain a totalitarian state and be competitive in science and technology.

The Constitution was, in a way, a product of the scientific revolution. Once you questioned the prevailing religious insistence that the Earth did not turn, why should you accept the repeated assertions by many religions that God sent kings to rule over us? In the 17th century, it was easy to whip English and Colonial juries into a frenzy over this impiety or that heresy. They were willing to torture people to death for their beliefs. By the late 18th century, they weren't so sure.

The Bill of Rights decoupled religion from the state, in part because so many religions were steeped in an absolutist frame of mind—each convinced that it alone had a monopoly on the truth and therefore eager for the state to impose this truth on others. Often, the leaders and practitioners of absolutist religions couldn't see the middle ground or realize that the truth might draw upon and embrace apparently contradictory doctrines.

The framers of the Bill of Rights had before them the example of England, where the ecclesiastical crime of heresy and the secular crime of treason had become nearly indistinguishable. Many of the early Colonists had come to America fleeing religious persecution, although some of them were perfectly happy nonetheless to persecute other people for *their* beliefs. The Founders of our nation recognized that a close relation between the government and any of the quarrelsome religions would be fatal to free inquiry.

Now, it's no good to have such rights if they're not used—a right of free speech when no one contradicts the government, freedom of the press when no one is willing to ask the tough questions, a right of assembly when there are no protests, universal suffrage when less than half of the electorate votes, and so on. Use 'em or lose 'em.

Due to the foresight of the framers of the Bill of Rights, it's hard to bottle up free speech. School library committees, the immigration service, the police, the FBI—or the ambitious politician looking to score cheap votes—may attempt it from time to time, but sooner or later the cork usually pops. The Constitution is, after all, the law of the land, and public officials are sworn to uphold it. However, through lowered educational standards, declining intellectual competence, diminished zest for debate and social sanctions against skepticism, our liberties can be slowly eroded and our rights subverted.

The Founders understood this well: "The time for fixing every essential right on a legal basis is while our rulers are honest, and ourselves united," said Thomas Jefferson. "From the conclusion of this [Revolutionary] war we shall be going downhill. It will not then be necessary to resort every moment to the people for support. They will be forgotten, therefore, and their rights disregarded. They will forget themselves but in the sole faculty of making money, and will never think of uniting to effect a due respect for their rights. The shackles, therefore, which shall not be knocked off at the conclusion of this war will remain on us long, will be made heavier and heavier, 'til our rights shall revive or expire in a convulsion."

Education about the value of free speech and the other freedoms reserved by the Bill of Rights, about what happens when you don't have them, about how to exercise and protect them, is an essential part of being an American. If we can't think for ourselves, if we're unwilling to question authority, then we're just putty in the hands of those in power. But if the citizens are educated and form their own opinions, then those in power work for *us*.

In his famous little book, *On Liberty*, John Stuart Mill argued that silencing an opinion is "a peculiar evil." If the opinion is right, we are robbed of the "opportunity of exchanging error for truth"; and if it's wrong, we are deprived of a deeper understanding of the truth in "its collision with error." If we know only our own side of the argument, we hardly know even that; it becomes stale, soon learned only by rote, untested, a pallid and lifeless truth. Mill also wrote, "If society lets any considerable number of its members grow up as mere children, incapable of being acted on by rational consideration of distant motives, society has itself to blame."

And Jefferson said the same thing more strongly, drawing the connection between science, which the Founders greatly admired, and freedom: "If a nation expects to be both ignorant and free in a state of civilization, it expects what never was and never will be." In a letter to Madison, he continued the thought: "A society that will trade a little liberty for a little order will lose both, and deserve neither."

We suggest that a good way to celebrate this 200th anniversary of the Bill of Rights is to rededicate ourselves to the habits of free inquiry, skeptical scrutiny, exposure of government actions to public view and support for the right to express all opinions—including, especially, those we find personally distasteful. In a democracy, opinions that upset everyone are sometimes exactly what we need. We should be teaching our children the scientific method and the Bill of Rights.

We Americans were once legendary for our inventiveness. We were considered disarmingly original, audacious, able to do the impossible. This is, by and large, not a description of the United States today. We must make sure our children understand why the vigorous exercise of our civil liberties is essential —not just to retain what freedoms we have, freedoms celebrated and envied in countries we were once taught to think of as our adversaries, but also to preserve and invigorate our nation's soul.

Culture

- **American Values and Life-Styles (Articles 3–5)**
- **Cultural Changes (Articles 6 and 7)**
- **Primitive and Unusual Cultures (Articles 8 and 9)**

The ordinary, everyday objects of living and the daily routines of life provide a structure to social existence that is regularly punctuated by festivals and celebrations. Both the routine and special times are the "stuff" of culture, for culture is the sum total of all the pieces of one's social inheritance. Culture includes language, tools, values, habits, literature, and art.

Because culture is often overlooked and taken for granted, it is useful to pause and reflect upon the shared beliefs and relationships that form the foundations of group life. In a similar way, an examination of exotic and different cultures is valuable in helping us recognize how cultural assumptions affect all facets of life. A great deal can be learned by observing how other people treat their elderly or raise their young. Moreover, through such observations, individuals can recognize how misunderstandings begin, and can appreciate the problems of maintaining cultural continuity in a rapidly changing environment. Through an awareness of culture, people begin to "know" themselves, for culture lies at the heart of their personal and collective identities. Culture is one of the most powerful and important concepts in sociology.

The first three articles in this section take a look at American culture and discuss the impacts of important cultural traits that have not been sufficiently recognized. Steven Waldman's analysis of the abundance of the material culture in America develops the thesis that Americans have too much choice. We might be proud of the fact that Russian leaders have often demonstrated their desire to go on an American shopping spree, but Waldman examines the consequences of so much choice and discovers many negatives in the list. Probably his main complaint is that it is frustrating and makes once-simple actions complex and confusing, but he also points to consequences such as the erosion of commitment, much waste of time, worsening quality of decisions, political alienation, psychic stress, and reduced social bonding. Juliet Schor points to another assault on the psyches of Americans. She discusses the large increase in work time (an increase of 163 annual hours from 1969 to the present) and a one-third decline in leisure time. These tighter time constraints negatively impact on marriages, families, child care, and on workers' health. Increased work hours may not even increase productivity, which is their justification.

Next, Robert Samuelson discusses the fragmentation of society, which is a theme that dovetails with the previous two articles. His emphasis, however, is on the causes of this fragmentation rather than the consequences of it.

The next set of articles focus on cultural changes. The previous articles also involved cultural changes but these changes were largely a result of larger technological, business, and other forces. The next two articles, however, deal with changes that arise more in the cultural sphere. Alan Deutschman discusses the culture and values of those people in their twenties. Susan Faludi responds to the cultural backlash to the women's movement and discusses the changes in female sex roles brought about by the women's movement and the difficulties women have in meeting both career and family goals under current arrangements.

The last two articles deal with primitive cultures that are under considerable stress today. Specific cultures are shaped by the conditions of life. When those conditions change, the culture will also change over time. Colin Turnbull looks at an African tribe that was moved off its original land and was forced to live in a harsh environment. Literally all aspects of life changed for the tribe's members, in a disturbingly sinister way. The experiences of this tribe lead Turnbull to question some of the individualistic tendencies of America.

David Maybury-Lewis challenges our sense of cultural superiority by demonstrating the wisdom of tribal patterns compared to our modern life-styles. Tribal societies value people, but modern societies value things. The reader probably will not abandon his or her life-style after reading this article, but he or she should have a lot more respect for tribal societies.

Looking Ahead: Challenge Questions

What do you think are the core values in American society?

What are the strengths and weaknesses of cultures that emphasize either cooperation or individualism?

What are the boundaries of a culture? How does one cross over boundaries?

What is the relationship between culture and identity?

What might a visitor from a primitive tribe describe as shocking and barbaric about American society?

A consumer revolts.

THE TYRANNY OF CHOICE

Steven Waldman

STEVEN WALDMAN is a Washington correspondent for *Newsweek*.

Why did I nearly start crying the last time I went to buy socks? I'd stopped in a store called Sox Appeal, the perfect place, one might imagine, to spend a pleasant few minutes acquiring a pair of white athletic socks. After a brief visit to the men's dress sock department—dallying with more than 300 varieties, among them products embroidered with bikini-clad women, neckties, flowers, Rocky and Bullwinkl, and elegant logos such as "The Gold Bullion Collection: Imported" and "D'zin Pour Homme"—I finally made it into the athletics section. Here, the product-option high was even headier. Past the "Hypercolor" socks that change hue, combination "sport-and-dress" white socks, and "EarthCare" environmentally safe socks (which, unfortunately, boast of decomposing easily) were hosiery for every sport: racquetball, running, walking, cycling, hiking, basketball, and aerobics. I needed help.

"What if I play racquetball occasionally and run occasionally and walk sometimes, but don't want to get a different sock for each one?" I asked the saleswoman. She wrinkled her nose: "It's really a matter of personal preference." Did she have any standard-issue white tube socks? The nose-wrinkle again. "Well, yeah, you *could* get those, but ... " I started reading the backs of the boxes, elaborately illustrated with architects' renderings of the stress points in the "Cushion-Engineered (TM) Zone Defense." After briefly contemplating the implications of the Cross-Training Sock—"Shock-Woven elastic arch brace contours to arch, providing additional support and normal articulation of the bones in the foot, while keeping sock migration minimal"—I spent another five minutes studying shapes (anklet, crew, or quarter) and manufacturers, and grabbed a Cross Trainer, two walkers, and, in an environmental guilt-spasm, one pair of the EarthCare.

Since that day, the sock metaphor has crept constantly into my mind—and not just when I'm buying consumer products. At work I pick through dozens of options on my cafeteria insurance benefits plan. At the doctor's I'm offered several possible treatments for a neck problem and no real way to decide. At the video rental store I end up renting four movies even though I'll watch only one. Choices proliferate everywhere. My mental "tilt" light flashes continuously. I keep thinking that the more choices there are, the more wrong choices there are—and the higher the odds I'll make a mistake.

The topic of how much freedom freedom brings has fascinated philosophers throughout the ages. But when Sartre urged man to embrace and acknowledge his own power to choose, he did not have in mind figuring out the difference between hair conditioner, rejuvenator, reconstructor, and clarifier. So far, public debate on choice has been limited to just two realms: abortion and, more recently, public schools. But we're in the midst of a choice explosion that is much further reaching.

Think it over. A typical supermarket in 1976 had 9,000 products; today it has more than 30,000. The average produce section in 1975 carried sixty-five items; this summer it carried 285. (Kiwi has hit the top 20 list.) A Cosmetic Center outside Washington carries about 1,500 types and sizes of hair care products. The median household got six TV stations in 1975. Thanks to deregulation of the cable TV industry, that family now has more than thirty channels. The number of FM radio stations has doubled since 1970. A new religious denomination forms every week. (The 1980s brought us major additions such as the Evangelical Presbyterian Church and smaller groups such as the Semjase Silver Star Center, which follows the Twelve Bids from Patule that were given by extraterrestrial Space Brothers to Edmund "Billy" Meier.) In 1955 only 4 percent of the adult population had left the faith of their childhood. By 1985 one-third had. In 1980, 564 mutual funds existed. This year there are 3,347.

There has been a sharp rise in the number of people choosing new faces. More than twice as many cosmetic surgery operations were performed in the 1980s than in the 1970s, estimates the American Academy of Cosmetic Surgery. In the past decade a new periodical was born every day. Some have perished, but the survivors include: *Elvis International Forum, Smart Kids* (recent cover headline: "Should Babies Learn to Read?"), *American Handgunner, Triathlete, Harley Women, Log Home Living, Musclecar Classics,* and (my favorite) *Contemporary Urology.*

The growth of variety predates this recession, will continue after it, and, to a large extent, has persisted during it. *New Product News* reports that despite the depressed economy 21 percent more new products were introduced in supermarkets and drug stores in 1991 than the year before. Obvious benefits abound, of course, and not just for people with money. Telephone deregulation has made it cheaper to stay in touch with faraway friends; periodical proliferation meant I had *Fantasy Baseball* magazine to help me prepare for Rotisserie draft day; increased social tolerance has allowed more people (including me) to marry outside their faith or ethnic group; low sodium orange juice means people with high blood pressure can drink it (and it has increased juice sales); more cosmetics mean black women have shades that match their complexions. And so on. And in the words of Morris Cohen, a professor at the Wharton Business School: "If you're overwhelmed by the sock store, don't go there anymore." The beauty of the free market, he explains, is that each individual can select which options to exploit and which to ignore.

But Cohen's rational approach fails to account for how the mind actually processes all this variety. In fact, choice can be profoundly debilitating. It forces us to squander our time, weakens our connections to people and places, and can even poison our sense of contentedness. What follows is a simple checklist—take your pick—of the drawbacks of our new way of choosing.

Choice Erodes Commitment. The same psychological dynamic that has led to a decline in brand loyalty can operate on more important decisions. The more options we have, the more tenuous our commitment becomes to each one. The compulsion to take inventory of one's wants and continually upgrade to a better deal can help explain everything from the rise of the pathological channel switcher who can never watch one TV show straight through to staggering divorce rates and employer-employee disloyalty. Baseball players have never had as many career options as they do now. As a result, sportswriter Thomas Boswell notes, the slightest sign of trouble leads the player or team to try someplace or someone better, producing many "insincere love affairs and very few committed marriages." Sound familiar? Yes, even the infamous male commitment problem results in part from the same thinking. I recently married a wonderful woman, but only after several years of embarrassingly tortured contemplation of what kind of "options" I might be foreclosing. There are, after all, 9,538,000 unmarried females aged 24-39, each with the potential to be more "perfect" than the one before.

Choice Takes Too Much Time. Taken individually, most choices are manageable and, for some sector of the population, a pleasure. Stereo buffs love being able to select the finest woofers. But spend the optimal amount of time on each decision and pretty soon you run out of life. It's not surprising, then, that people feel more rushed than they used to. John P. Robinson, a professor of sociology at the University of Maryland who studied time diaries in 1965, 1975, and 1985, believes we feel harried partly because so much of our free time is absorbed by the process of deciding what to do with it. For all consumers, some time is simply wasted, not in figuring out which options suit them best but rather which distinctions matter. Before you can compare breakfast cereals' bran content you have to figure out if bran is really healthful. Should one care if a hair dryer has higher wattage? Are disposable diapers really worse for the environment than cloth? Being an educated consumer is a full-time job. You need to subscribe to several consumer magazines to do it properly. But which magazine to choose?

Choice Awakens Us to Our Failings. Choice-making lays claim to an expanding portion of our mental energy because the perceived consequences of making the wrong selection keep growing. Under cafeteria insurance plans, if you choose to forgo the dismemberment benefits in favor of extra teeth cleanings, you have no one to blame after an accident but yourself. Each time I checked off a box on my benefit election form I flashed forward to some weepy scene when I had to explain to my wife why I had decided to consign us to poverty and despair. When the company dictated my dental plan I could at least curse the Bosses for their gross disregard of dental self-esteem and go about adapting to the situation. Arbitrariness had its comforts.

Similarly, before the mid-1970s, people had little choice about how to invest their money. If inflation eroded their savings accounts, they were at least suffering, along with others, from the cruelty of an irresistible outside force. Today the availability of hundreds of possible investment "products" means everyone is fully capable of doing much worse than her neighbor. The wealthy try to solve that problem by spending still more money to hire financial advisers, only to confront a new set of worries about whether they have selected the best one. For the financially strapped, the anxiety can grow even more intense: the fewer dollars you have the more consequential each mistake becomes. Even when the stakes are small, we live in constant fear of being a Bad Consumer, which in a consumer-oriented society translates roughly into "sucker."

Choice Leads to Inept Consumption. The more choice available, the more information a consumer must have to make a sensible selection. When overload occurs, many simply abandon the posture of rational Super-Consumer. Warning labels on products have become so common that many shoppers simply ignore them all, including the important ones. Several friends have confessed that the selection of car models—591 and rising—has become so dizzying that they tossed aside *Con-*

sumer Reports and relied entirely on the recommendation of a friend. Some become so paralyzed by the quest for the better deal that they postpone decisions indefinitely, while others become so preoccupied with absorbing the new features touted by a manufacturer that they forget to consider the basics. After all the fretting over the migration patterns of the socks, I took them home and found them to be quite fluffy and supportive, but the wrong size.

Consumers may be better informed than they were two decades ago, but salespeople have more tools with which to fight back. I spent three days studying up for a trip to Circuit City to buy a CD player. Despite having read several magazine and newspaper articles, I was, within minutes, putty in the salesman's hands. When I asked for a particular model, he rolled his eyes and laughed, "You must have gotten that from *Consumer Reports*." With a simple well-timed chuckle he made me doubt my entire research regimen. He then battered me with a flurry of techno-terms and finally moved in for the kill by giving me an audio comparison test between two different systems that sounded exactly alike. My resistance was exhausted, so I bought the system he suggested, which, of course, cost more than I had intended to spend.

Choice Causes Political Alienation. Voters don't necessarily have more choices than they used to—an increase in primaries and referenda having been offset by the influence of incumbency and money—but the *way* voters choose has changed dramatically. As a result of the weakening of political parties, voting behavior now closely resembles the consumption of products. The biggest political group is not Democrats or Republicans, but "independents," shopper-equivalents who've dropped brand loyalty in favor of product-by-product analysis. Last century two-thirds of voters went straight party line; in 1980 two-thirds split tickets. In theory, this means voters carefully weigh the candidate's policies, character, and history. In reality, it's nearly impossible to sort through a candidate's "stands" on the "issues" from a blizzard of untrustworthy ads, a newspaper editorial, or a blip on the TV news. Was he the one who wants a revolving loan fund for worker retraining or the one who gives flag burners early parole? No wonder voters, like shoppers, act impulsively or vote according to the wisdom of their favorite interest group. Many who vote for ballot initiatives or lower offices simply follow the recommendation of the local newspaper, which is like buying a car on the word of the local auto columnist. When I was voting absentee in New York I selected judicial candidates on the basis of gender and race since I knew little else about them. The ultimate political choice overload came in California in 1990, when voters received a 222-page ballot pamphlet to help them decide among twenty-eight initiatives.

Candidates have responded to the rise of the consumer-voter by turning to marketing professionals who've only made the voters' dilemma worse. In the 1950s political consultants were advertising men who selected a candidate attribute and then sold it, the way an automaker

might remind consumers of a large car's natural advantages, like spaciousness and safety. Political consulting has evolved, though. Candidates now rely heavily on market researchers—i.e., the pollsters—trying less to determine what part of their essence they should highlight than what they should become to match voters' desires. Sometimes that means candidates become more responsive to public thinking, but more often it means politicians forget to consult (or have) their own core beliefs. Witness the breathtaking spectacle of pro-life pols who once assailed the supreme immorality of baby-killing quickly becoming pro-choice because of the supreme importance of polls. This "politics as consumption" (in the phrase of University of Rochester professor Robert Westbrook) seems to produce more gelatinous politicians—precisely the sort that voters have the hardest time judging.

Choice Erodes the Self. In theory, choice enables an individual to select the car, money market fund, or spouse that expresses herself most precisely. But if choice is self-definition, more choices mean more possible definitions. Kenneth Gergen, a professor of psychology at Swarthmore, argues in his new book, *The Saturated Self,* that the postmodern personality becomes "populated" with growing numbers of "selves" as it's bombarded by an ever increasing number of potential relationships from TV, travel, telephones, faxes, computers, etc. From an insecure sense of self, you then spiral toward what Gergen calls "multiphrenia," in which the besieged, populated self frantically flails about trying to take advantage of the sea of choices. This condition may never merit its own telethon, but as choices increase so do the odds that multiphrenia will strike, leaving the scars of perpetual self-doubt. It's why the people who work hardest to improve their appearance never seem to feel much better than before they sampled the offerings of the Self-Perfection Industry (exercise videos, customized makeup, cosmetic surgery, health food). They become like politicians with their own private pollsters; the quest to re-create virtually supplants whatever person was once there.

Choice Reduces Social Bonding. The proliferation of choice helps cause, and results from, another trend—social fragmentation. Together they ensure that Americans share fewer and fewer common experiences. A yuppie diet bears less and less resemblance to that of a lower-income family. I don't even know who's on the Wheaties box anymore because my cereal is located about ninety feet down the aisle. As marketers divide us into increasingly narrow segments, we inevitably see ourselves that way too. When there was one movie theater in a neighborhood, everyone sat under the same roof and watched the same film. Video rental stores enable you to be a movie junkie without ever having to sit next to another human being. Three decades ago, even when everyone was sitting in their own homes they were at least all watching "Gunsmoke." Today's viewing public scatters to its particular demographic niche on the cable dial.

Even the spiritual realm has evolved like a supermarket. "It has become a consumer-oriented, highly fragmented religious marketplace," says David Roozen, director of the Hartford Seminary for Social and Religious Research. In a buyer's market, the individual can select the religious institution with which he or she is most comfortable. But as each generation discards the nasty (or difficult) parts of the faith, religious traditions decay. Moreover, instead of integrating people of different backgrounds under the same theological roof, denominations sprout to appeal to smaller groups of like-minded people. (If, for example, you decide the followers of the teachings of Billy Meier's Space Brothers aren't your kind of people, you can turn to the Universe Society Church, which observes the wisdom of Fahsz, an extraterrestrial contacted by someone named Hal Wilcox.) The comedian Emo Philips tells a joke about discovering similarities in religious backgrounds with someone he just met. "I said [are you] Protestant or Catholic? He said, 'Protestant.' I said, 'Me Too! What franchise?' He says, 'Baptist.' I said, 'Me too! Northern Baptist or Southern Baptist?' He says, 'Southern Baptist.' I said, 'Me Too!'" The two go back and forth in this vein. Finally, Emo asks, "'Northern conservative fundamentalist Baptist Great Lakes Region Council of 1879 or Northern conservative fundamentalist Baptist Great Lakes Region Council of 1912?' And he says 'Northern conservative fundamentalist Baptist Great Lakes Region Council of 1912.' And I said, 'Die Heretic!'"

How can we adapt to this world of choice? Some steps are being taken for us. The Food and Drug Administration recently announced rules to standardize product labels that should simplify our task in the supermarket. Some school districts have required uniforms in order to curb the clothing competition that has led to killings over sneakers. Regulatory agencies could further help by simply banning products they consider unsafe, rather than slapping on warning labels that force us to perform quickie risk assessment studies. The market itself will develop some innovations to help us cope. "Price clubs" have sprouted up in which customers shop at huge warehouses stocked with just a few brands, but very low prices. Bicycle stores now offer "hybrids" for those who can't decide between mountain, city, touring, and racing. But the general trend remains overwhelmingly toward market fragmentation.

Dealing with an abundance of choices mostly requires a mental reorientation. Choice overload helped me finally understand what was so offensive about the stereotypical yuppie obsession with "quality," of which I have often been guilty. It's not that some coffee beans aren't, in fact, more flavorful than others, it's that people who spend so much of their lives thinking about small differences become small people.

Imagine instead a world in which we used our choice brain lobes for the most important decisions and acted more arbitrarily on the rest. Perhaps you might select a brand name and buy all its products for the next four years, scheduling Choice Day during non-presidential election years. Or you might embrace the liberating powers of TV commercials. As everyone knows, ads brainwash us into choosing products through insidious appeals to sex or other animal urges. But sometimes it feels good to let an ad take us by the hand. A few years ago I had an epiphany while deciding what to eat for dinner. I looked in the refrigerator, thought about nearby restaurants and markets, and grew puzzled. Just then an ad came on the TV for Burger King, featuring a luscious Whopper with fake charcoal stripes painted with perfect symmetry across the juicy meat. I put on my coat and immediately walked, zombielike, to the nearby Burger King and ordered a Whopper. I found it exhilarating, because I knew it wasn't the behavior of a rational economic player, and that it didn't matter.

As the Twelve Steppers say, we must acknowledge our powerlessness. We cannot knowledgeably make even a fraction of the appropriate choices available. Say it out loud. Today I will make several wrong choices. Now, whether you've selected an inferior vacuum cleaner, bought the large soda when the jumbo was a better deal, or accidentally prayed to the wrong god—forgive yourself. If we took some joy in being bad choosers, or at least placed less value on being stellar consumers of unimportant things, we would be training ourselves to accept a few extra drops of imperfection in our lives. Somehow, that would seem more like progress than having the choice between polypropylene arch brace contours and a solar-powered argyle.

Workers of the World, Unwind

Juliet B. Schor

Juliet B. Schor is an associate professor of economics at Harvard University. She has written The Overworked American: The Unexpected Decline of Leisure *(Basic Books, copyright 1991)—from which this article is adapted.*

In the last 20 years, the amount of time Americans spend at their jobs has risen steadily. Each year the change has been small, amounting to about nine hours, or slightly more than one additional day of work. But the accumulated increase over two decades is substantial. Today's work year of 1,949 hours is 163 hours—almost a month—longer than in 1969.

Not surprisingly, as work rises, leisure falls. People report nationwide that their leisure time has declined by as much as a third since the early 1970s. According to one survey, Americans have only 16$^{1}/_{2}$ hours of leisure a week after taking care of the obligations of job and household.

The leisure crunch didn't have to happen. Whenever productivity grows, we are presented with the possibility of receiving either more free time or more money—and since 1948, the productivity of the U.S. worker has more than doubled. In other words, we could now produce our 1948 standard of living (measured in marketed good services) in less than half the time it took in that year. We could have chosen a four-hour day. Or a working year of six months. Or each worker in the United States could now be taking every other year off from work, with pay. Some economists in the 1950s even predicted

that today's standard retirement age would be 38.

But between 1948 and the present, we did not use any of the "productivity dividend" to reduce hours. Although productivity grew rapidly—at about 3 percent a year—in the first two decades after 1948, work hours have held steady. Since 1969, productivity growth has been slower, averaging just over 1 percent a year. Yet hours have risen markedly.

What went wrong? Why has leisure been such a conspicuous casualty of prosperity? Much of the answer lies in our insidious cycle of "work-and-spend."

We don't have to work ourselves to death. Government, business, and individuals can take action to balance labor with leisure, while actually boosting productivity.

In its starkest terms, the cycle operates like this: Employers ask for long hours from employees. They do so in part because long-hour jobs pay more and thus are more desirable to workers, who will labor more productively to keep them. Also, the fewer workers a firm needs to hire, the less it has to spend on fringe benefits. The high pay, in turn, creates a high level of consumption. People buy houses and go into debt; luxuries become necessities; Smiths keep up with Joneses—and workers accept, or even ask for, longer hours so they can go on spending. Work-and-spend has become a powerful dynamic keeping us from a more relaxed and leisured way of life.

RISING HOURS FOR FULLY EMPLOYED U.S. WORKERS

HOURS WORKED PER YEAR

Although the work week hasn't grown much in 20 years, the number of work weeks in a year has. The figures are the author's estimates based on the Bureau of Labor Statistics Current Population Survey. They exclude unemployed and underemployed workers.

	1969	1987	Increase
All workers	1,786	1,949	163
Men	2,054	2,152	98
Women	1,406	1,711	305

HOURS WORKED PER WEEK

	1969	1987	Increase
All workers	39.8	40.7	0.9
Men	43.0	43.8	0.8
Women	35.2	37.0	1.8

WEEKS WORKED PER YEAR

	1969	1987	Increase
All workers	43.9	47.1	3.2
Men	47.1	48.5	1.4
Women	39.3	45.4	6.1

HOURS WORKED PER YEAR IN MANUFACTURING

Not only do European factory workers put in shorter hours than their U.S. counterparts, but their work-load has been steadily shrinking.

	1970	1979	1989
Belgium	1,870	1,638	1,572
Canada	1,918	1,859	1,887*
Denmark	1,829	1,639	1,595
France	1,872	1,712	1,610
Germany (West)	1,889	1,717	1,603
Italy	1,905	1,738	1,858
Japan	2,269	2,159	2,155
Netherlands	1,893	1,669	1,592
Norway	1,794	1,572	1,614
Sweden	1,744	1,513	1,539
U.K.	1,939**	1,886	1,856
U.S.	1,913	1,907	1,951

*1988   ** 1971

Chart Source (Bottom): Bureau of Labor Statistics

If hours keep rising, it's hard to see how we can solve the accompanying crises of family—the problems of child care and the strains of marriage—or the adverse health effects of stress and overwork. And then there's the health of the environment: further rounds of work-and-spend will only multiply the amount of natural resources we use up and pollutants we spew out.

Can America Afford Less Work?

Not everyone accepts the need for more leisure. A 1989 letter from work-time expert William McGaughey, Jr., to 300 business leaders advocating a shorter work week failed to yield a single favorable response. This reply from the CEO of one Fortune 500 company was typical: "My view of the world, our country, and our country's needs is diametrically opposite of yours. I cannot imagine a shorter work week. I can imagine a longer one both in school and at work if America is to be competitive in the first half of the next century." In one *Fortune* poll, three-quarters of CEOs took the view that competing with the Japanese will require them to "push their managers harder." Its fierce opposition even to unpaid parental leave suggests that business thinks it can't afford any concessions.

Of course, employers have been sounding the alarm of foreign competition for at least a century and a half. In 1830, New York employers opposed the 10-hour day on grounds that it would allow foreigners to undersell them. Their laborers put forth the other point of view, in a debate that has changed little since then. An article in *The Working Man's Advocate* asked: "Are we to slave 13 or 14 hours a day, because the Manchester spinner or the Birmingham blacksmith so slaves?"

In fact, the vast majority of America's competitors work far less than we do. When business executives claim that Americans must work harder, they show selective vision, looking only East, to Japan or South Korea. In Japan, not only do half the workers pass up vacation time but many work a six-day week. In manufacturing—the sector where most foreign competition takes place—Japanese workers put in six weeks more each year than do their counterparts in the United States. But U.S. workers are already doing eight weeks more than their French and western German peers and eleven more than Swedes. The West Europeans have managed to maintain their standard of living, cutting neither wages nor time off.

Discrepancies in work time are often cited as if they were proof enough that the U.S. must replicate Japanese ways. But the economics of competition is not the economics of mimicry. It's more complex. First, we must be clear about what business leaders are asking for. If it's more hours at existing pay, then it is merely a roundabout way of reducing workers' wages. While lower wages help competitiveness in the short term, in the long run they can boomerang, as declining wages lead to declining productivity, through diminished incentives to invest, lower employee morale, and higher turnover. The game of lowering wages can get insidious. Once the highest in the world, U.S. manufacturing wages have fallen substantially for a decade, and now rank below many West European nations. How far down should they go? Korea, Brazil, and India are growing competitors. If corporations demand a decline to the poverty wages paid in such countries, should American workers simply accede?

What we should learn from the Japanese, and from our own history, is not the need to reduce wages, or raise hours, but the importance of productivity. In the international market, what matters in the long run is not how many hours one works but how productively one works them. If an American can produce an equivalent computer in fewer hours than a Japanese (at a comparable wage rate), then that computer will sell,

Technology and Time

IN the beginning, most of the U.S. labor force was involved in producing food. More than 7 out of every 10 people had agricultural jobs as late as 1830, the year Cyrus McCormick demonstrated his mechanical reaper and ushered in a new age of productivity improvement that has had a profound effect on the nation's employment needs.

After McCormick's reaper, which made it possible to harvest grain five times faster, other technological improvements—notably steam-powered tractors—promoted steady growth in farm productivity. Thus, while the total U.S. labor force quadrupled between 1820 and 1900, the portion of people employed in agriculture dropped by almost half, down to 37 percent. Today, thanks to continued technological advances such as electrification, synthetic fertilizers, and powerful combines, agricultural workers make up only about 3 percent of the work force, even though the country's population has tripled since the turn of the century.

As these changes occurred, the "surplus" workers were able to move into the growth industries of the day: manufacturing and construction. Blue-collar employment, as a fraction of the labor force, grew steadily until it peaked in the mid-1950s.

Since then, modern industrial technologies have become established. Numerically controlled machine tools, introduced in the 1950s, permit a single operator to run several machines simultaneously. With computers, shop-floor personnel are less machine operators and more machine monitors. Programmable machines, intelligent sensors, and computerized warehousing and inventory control, among other technologies, have automated many processes.

Although manufacturing output has grown rapidly since the 1950s, the number of blue-collar manufacturing workers has stayed relatively stable. This is partly because of a surge in imports in the past 10 years, but mainly the result of the enormous productivity-enhancing effects of modern technologies.

In recent decades, the fastest expansion has occurred in white-collar employment, particularly among clerical workers. Yet the U.S. Bureau of Labor Statistics (BLS) projects much slower growth for clerical workers over the next decade because much of the work these people do can be mechanized. Consider, for example, the use of automatic teller machines for bank transactions, automatic analyzers in laboratories, and computerized plotters for engineering drawings.

Modern technologies also enable professional and managerial workers to take over some of the work previously relegated to subordinates. This article is a good example: I wrote and printed it on a word processor and faxed it to an editor, all without a secretary. While such technological change means that secretaries can do other work and be more productive, in many offices it also means that the clerical work force has ceased to grow.

How can we avoid creating large numbers of displaced workers? In the past, declines in work time helped to absorb the large productivity gains generated by new technology. The average work day dropped from as much as 15 hours in the nineteenth century to less than 8. The standard work week is five days today instead of the six or more that were typical several generations ago. And holidays and vacations, rare a century ago, are common now.

But since the 1950s, technology-driven productivity gains have not translated into significant reductions in individuals' work time. The situation can only get worse as "running lean and mean" becomes the operating philosophy of U.S. industry and individuals' work loads grow while companies "downsize."

A better approach is to employ more people who work less. We need to return to some successful strategies of the past: investing in education to provide the skilled work force needed by modern workplaces, paying higher wages to maintain buying power, and using some of the wealth generated by technology to enable people to work less time at higher hourly wages.

—*By DENNIS CHAMOT (The author is executive assistant to the president of the Department for Professional Employees at the AFL-CIO.)*

whether the American works a 50- or a 40- or a 30-hour week. And efficient production itself will yield rising wages, as the cases of Japan and Korea reveal. Instead of pushing their employees' standard of living even farther down the global hierarchy, U.S. management should be figuring out how to make the hours they buy more productive.

The irony of corporate America's position is that in Japan excessive hours are a serious problem. Consider the white-collar "salarymen," who adhere to grueling schedules in a pressure-cooker environment. They face arduous commutes, an extended work day, and obligatory "after work" socializing. They are strongly discouraged from taking their vacations. In recent years, Japan's vibrant economy has brought overtime hours near their all-time high. The result: untold numbers of workers have become victims of "karoshi," or "death by overwork." Otherwise perfectly healthy, they keel over at their desks, usually after a prolonged stretch of overtime or a particularly high-pressure deal.

Significantly, a recent Japanese government study found that the nation's productivity, despite its high growth, is lower than that of other advanced countries in part because the working hours are too long. (According to the most recent figures, U.S. labor productivity is a third higher than Japan's.) And there is now considerable pressure in Japan to reduce work time. The government has made 1,800 hours a national goal, which, if achieved, would put Japanese hours below those of the United States. And according to a 1985 opinion poll, most young Japanese workers frown on overtime and would probably rather work less than earn more.

To increase work hours in the name of economic success would be sheer folly. Those who call for America to replicate the Japanese work culture have forgotten that the point of economic success is to make possible a good life. Besides, some shorter-hour schedules can actually raise productivity. For example, many people are more productive on Monday, the first day of the week. An arrangement such as job sharing can boost productivity by creating two "Mondays."

But most surprising is the evidence that under certain conditions a shorter work day will not necessarily reduce output, and can even raise it. When the Kellogg Co. made its historic switch to a six-hour day in 1930, it was searching for a strategy to cope with the unemployment of the Depression. To their surprise, managers found that workers were 3 to 4 percent more productive. The workers were pleased, preferring the quicker pace but shorter hours. And management was pleased as well. According to W.K. Kellogg, "The efficiency and morale of our employees is so increased, the accident and insurance rates are so improved, and the unit cost of production is so lowered that we can afford to pay as much for six hours as we formerly paid for eight."

PAID VACATION IN EUROPEAN COUNTRIES

COUNTRY	BY LAW	BY CONTRACT
Austria	5 weeks	Same
Belgium	4 weeks	5 weeks
Denmark	—	5 weeks
Finland	5 weeks	5 to 6 weeks
France	5 weeks	5 to 6 weeks
Germany	3 weeks	5½ to 6 weeks
Greece	4 weeks	Same
Iceland	4 weeks, 4 days	Same
Ireland	3 weeks	Approx. 4 weeks
Italy	—	4 to 6 weeks
Luxembourg	5 weeks	25 to 30 days
Malta	4 weeks	Same
Netherlands	4 weeks	4 to 5 weeks
Norway	4 weeks 1 day	Same
Portugal	30 civil days	4½ to 5 weeks
Spain	30 civil days	4½ to 5 weeks
Sweden	5 weeks	5 to 8 weeks
Switzerland	4 weeks	4 to 5 weeks
U.K.	—	4 to 6 weeks

Chart Source: European Trade Union Institute

While U.S. workers average two weeks' paid vacation a year (and the Japanese take only a week and a half), Europeans enjoy at least a month off.

Contemporary evidence tells a similar story. When the Medtronic Corp. in Minneapolis decided to give its employees 40 hours' pay for 36 hours' work, it hired no additional personnel but found that output increased. On balance, the company saved money. Ideal Industries, a small family-owned business in Chicago, shifted to a four-day, 38-hour week—also at 40 hours' pay. Again, productivity did not decline, but absenteeism did. At the United Services Automobile Association insurance company in Texas, sales were up, even though personnel hours were down. Efficiency and morale improved, turnover and error rates declined. These experiences have been repeated in other U.S. companies, as well as in foreign firms. A British study of a variety of companies reached similar conclusions. Far from being costly, nearly all these work-week reductions paid for themselves, even when workers' incomes were held steady.

One reason is that when hours are shorter, workers can physically and mentally sustain more intense effort. Another is that the work day gets compressed. The typical work day contains unproductive time, either scheduled (such as official break and meal times) or unscheduled (such as gatherings around the water cooler). As Chris Nyland, an economist at Australia's University of Wollongong, has argued, when management cuts the work week, what actually shrinks is often these idle periods. Higher morale is another factor. Workers appreciate a company's willingness to schedule fewer hours (a move that, in effect, raises hourly pay). As a result, they conduct more personal business on their own time and show up for work more regularly.

Historically, the working day has been "too long" in the sense that fatigue has impaired effectiveness. Each time the work day was reduced—first to ten hours in the mid-nineteenth century and then to eight after World War I—productivity rose. A shift to six or seven hours could have a similar effect. The problem is that management has always been resistant to lowering hours, on the grounds of cost. But now, as in the past, its calculus is too narrow.

Toward a Saner Lifestyle

Despite the many benefits of shorter working hours, some people are skeptical of Americans' ability to use leisure time. Work may be bad, but perhaps leisure isn't all it's cracked up to be either. According to Brookings Institution economist Gary Burtless, "Most Americans who complain they enjoy too little leisure are struggling to find a few extra minutes to watch Oprah Winfrey and *L.A. Law*." Will free time be "wasted" in front of the tube or at the mall? What will we do with all that leisure? Won't people just acquire second jobs? These are serious questions, embodying two main objections. The first is that people prefer work, or if they don't they should. The second is that leisure time is wasted time that is neither valued nor valuable.

It's always possible that the urge to work is irrepressible. In the 1950s, after Akron rubber workers had won a six-hour day, many of the men at Firestone—perhaps one in five—also drove cabs, cut hair, or sold insurance. Some observers concluded from this experience that American workers do not want, or cannot handle, leisure time. If they are right, so be it—if the chance to work shorter hours, when fairly presented, is not appealing, then people will not take it. But before we accept the Akron experience as definitive, it may be worth asking *why* so many took a second job.

The male rubber workers were reasonably well paid by the blue-collar standards of the day, and many of their wives worked. They did not labor out of sheer economic necessity. Very likely they were driven more by a cultural imperative—the one that says men with leisure are lazy. It is significant that women rubber workers did not seek a second paycheck.

Today there are signs that this cultural imperative is weakening. Perhaps most important is the transformation of sex roles. Women have taken up more responsibility for breadwinning. And men are more comfortable around the house. In a recent *Time* magazine poll of men between the ages of 18 and 24, nearly half said

---

Americans are accused of wasting free time in front of the tube, but people could just be too tired after work to engage in active leisure.

---

they would like to stay home and raise their children. The ethos of "male sacrifice" is disappearing: fewer people believe that being a "real man" entails self-denial and being the family provider.

The traditional work ethic is also undergoing transformation. Commitment to hard work retains its grip on the American psyche. But ideas of what work is and what it is for are changing. The late 1960s and the 1970s witnessed the rise of what some have called "post-materialist values"—desires for personal fulfillment, self-expression, and meaning. Throughout the industrialized world, a culture shift occurred as young people especially began demanding satisfying work. Even the burst of old-style materialism during the 1980s did not permanently dislodge what now looks like a long-term trend. People are expecting more from work than a paycheck and more from life than what 1950s culture offered.

Of course, the skeptics who cite heavy television viewing or excessive shopping have a point. But it may be that work itself has been eroding our ability to benefit from leisure time. People could just be too tired after work to engage in active leisure. According to a 1986 Gallup poll, the most popular ways to spend an evening are all low-energy choices: television, resting, and reading. Perhaps not coincidentally, the globe's only other rich industrialized country with longer hours than the United States—namely, Japan—is also the only nation to watch more television. Many potentially satisfying leisure activities are off limits because they take too much time: participating in community theater, seriously taking up a sport or a musical instrument, getting involved with a church or a community organization. In the leisure time available to us, there's less of interest to do. So to derive the full benefits of free time, we may just need more of it.

A final impediment to using leisure is the growing connection between free time and spending money. Private corporations have dominated the leisure "market," encouraging us to think of free time as a consump-

tion opportunity. Vacations, hobbies, popular entertainment, eating out, and shopping itself are costly forms of leisure. How many of us, if asked to describe an ideal weekend, would choose activities that cost nothing? How resourceful are we about doing things without spending money? A successful movement to enhance free time will have to address this dynamic head on. Governments and communities will need to subsidize more affordable leisure activities, from the arts to parks to adult education. We need a conscious effort to reverse the "commodification of leisure."

The transformation in people's relationship with their work must therefore be not only economic and social but cultural and psychological. On all these fronts there are some hopeful signs. Some forward-looking companies have been waking up to the realities of their employees' lives. Wells Fargo gives personal-growth leaves, Xerox offers social-service sabbaticals. Job sharing is possible at a growing number of companies, including Hewlett Packard, Black & Decker, TRW Vidar, and Levi-Strauss. Control Data has a flourishing part-time program that includes benefits. Anna Roddick, founder of the Body Shop grooming-aid chain, gives her employees a half-day off each week with pay to engage in volunteer activities. While the number of innovative corporations is still small, it is rising.

And there is growing public awareness of the need for change. For the first time since such surveys have been systematically conducted, a majority of Americans report that they are willing to relinquish income to gain more family and personal time. In a 1989 poll conducted for Robert Half International, a California firm, almost two-thirds said they would prefer to give up some of their salary, by an average amount of 13 percent; fewer than a quarter were unwilling to give up any money at all. Although this is just one study, its findings are intriguing; they offer hope that Americans may be ready to change their overly demanding work lives.

Timely Innovations

Despite the actions of a few enlightened companies, recent history shows that increased leisure is likely to be opposed by most businesses. More free time will not result from market forces or the munificence of technology. It will come only when people devise specific ways to achieve it.

The idea of establishing a right to free time is not as utopian as it sounds. The state has regulated working hours since the colonial period, and has legislated the right to free time in the form of legal holidays—not to mention the social security system, which assumes that workers have a right to leisure toward the end of their lives. What I propose is the extension of this right—so that everyone can enjoy free time while they are still young and throughout their lives.

To gain this right—to reduce the reliance on long hours—it will be necessary to break the work-and-spend cycle. That means first of all that the incentives for employers to demand long hours will have to be weakened. Second, employees will need opportunities to convert work into free time instead of money. Through a number of relatively simple changes in work laws, it should be possible to accomplish both aims without causing U.S. productivity to suffer.

One group of workers for whom structural reforms are necessary are those paid on salary rather than by the hour. Since salaried workers don't qualify for overtime, companies have an incentive to squeeze as many hours out of these employees as they can. To put the brakes on this practice, firms should have to pay for what they now receive courtesy of their salaried work force; they ought to be required to attach a standard schedule to every job. Along with annual pay, each position would also have an explicit number of hours—for example, a nine-to-six schedule—and a specified number of holidays, vacation and personal days, and sick days. Ideally, the firm would designate an annual total of hours and allow flexible scheduling within it.

Of course, many salaried positions already have official weekly hours, even if they're not adhered to. And paid time off is almost always specified in advance. But standard hours would be a departure in many of the longest-hour fields, such as finance, consulting, upper administration and management, and law. While employers could set any amount of hours as the standard, they could only request—not demand—that an employee work extra hours, and the worker would have to be compensated for them.

This system would not be a cure-all for the excessive hours of some occupations. But competition for personnel may discourage employers from setting very long days. If a prospective trainee at Salomon Brothers were asked to guarantee 80 hours and Goldman, Sachs sets 70, the former would be at a disadvantage. For those employees who *want* their time, the standardization of hours could help them get it.

When workers do put in extra hours, the company should compensate them with time, not money. The idea is to transform overtime into "comp" time. An extra hour worked today would yield an extra hour of paid time off in the future. Workers would be able to bank their overtime hours to take longer vacations, go on sabbatical, or switch to part-time work at full-time pay. This arrangement would not only reduce the total number of hours worked but also make jobs much more flexible. It would become far easier to go to school, be a parent, or do volunteer work while carrying a full-time job. Of course, there may be limitations on scheduling time off. Existing practices involving comp time or programs of voluntary work reduction usually have some restrictions such as prior notification and management approval. But where both sides have shown flexibility and goodwill, these limitations have not been onerous.

Employers will favor some things about this proposal and not others. Payment by comp time means that workers are remunerated for extra hours at their regular wage rate, rather than time and a half. Employers will like this. But it also means companies will have to expand their staffs to make up for the additional time off. They will not like that, in part because of the fringe benefits they will have to provide. I suspect employers will be still more averse to the idea of associating standard hours with all salaried jobs. Despite the flexibility built into the proposal (they can choose any level of standard hours and adjust it frequently), they will complain that it is an unnecessary intrusion on their prerogatives. But management has sounded this refrain over many successful benefits in the past.

Meanwhile, many hourly workers would bitterly oppose the elimination of overtime pay, at least at the beginning. Overtime is the only way they can earn high, or even livable, incomes—a circumstance that has turned more than a few into slaves to their jobs. But here the solution should be livable wages, not unlivable schedules.

The idea that jobs pay more where overtime is available is to some extent an illusion. A recent study by Stephen J. Trejo, an economist at the University of California, Santa Barbara, shows that workers who get overtime receive lower hourly wages, as firms "undo" some of the effect of the overtime premium. If this research is correct, it is likely that hourly wages would rise in response to the elimination of overtime.

Another much-needed change is to make part-time work more feasible. At the moment, most part-time positions are low-pay, low-mobility, and largely without benefits. The impediments for professionals and managers are especially difficult; in many places, part-time is tantamount to career suicide.

Some simple reforms would smooth the way for part-time work. A first, crucial step is to eliminate the fringe benefits penalty. Part-time workers would receive a share of health insurance, pension benefits, and other fringes, prorated by their hours of work. They would also get the option to go to full coverage at their own expense. A second option is to institute job sharing, in which two people split one position's fringe benefits, responsibility, work, and pay. Each of these changes would reduce biases toward long-hour jobs.

Trading Future Income for Time Off

To sever the link between pay raises and increased consumption, we must exploit the psychological difference between income that is already being spent and income that is merely expected. According to most surveys, people cling tenaciously to their current paycheck, unwilling or unable to trade it for time. But polls also indicate strong sentiment for using *future* income to fund additional time off. Suppose companies were required by law to give people a choice between raises and free time.

The company would announce the percentage pay increase it plans to give each group of employees. Then it would calculate equivalent hours of time off. The employee could decide among the alternatives—from the extremes of all pay or all time, to various fractional splits in between. The company could offer different forms of time off (reductions in daily hours, part-time schedules, or additional vacation or personal days). Free time could be accumulated from year to year.

How would this choice work out if it were available today? There are two key parameters: the rate of income growth the company is willing to provide, and the fraction of increased income that workers designate toward free time. Let's assume the former is 2 percent plus an adjustment for inflation, and the latter is 100 percent. Then, about a decade from now, the average work year will have fallen from 1,949 hours to 1,600 hours a year. If a firm offered faster income growth—4 percent a year—annual hours could drop to 1,300, allowing workers to go to school one semester a year, take a four-month vacation, or work a five-hour day.

If it sounds too good to be true, remember that in this example purchasing power is completely stagnant. People who go 100 percent toward free time for 10 years will experience no increase whatsoever in their material standard of living. Purchasing power will keep up with inflation, but not exceed it. If you can be content tomorrow with the amount you consume today, however,

---

A majority of Americans surveyed say they are willing to relinquish income to gain more family and personal time.

---

then trading off future income can be a blessing.

How many people would actually choose to forgo future income? Survey data give some idea. In a 1978 Department of Labor survey, 84 percent of workers say they would choose to trade off *some* future income—with almost half opting for a 100 percent tradeoff. The Robert Half poll mentioned earlier asked people which of two career paths they would choose—one enabling them to schedule their own full-time work hours and have more leisure time to spend with their families, but with slower career advancement, or one with rigid work hours and less attention to family, but faster career advancement. Nearly eight out of ten preferred the path with more time. Indeed, large majorities of both men and women (74 percent and 82 percent) chose this option. And although 34 percent said they would be "likely to accept a promotion involving greater responsibility if it meant spending less time with

family," 55 percent said they would not. Of course, there is no guarantee that people would act as they say they would. But even if participation were lower, the program would still have a major impact on work time.

There would be hard-core resisters. This country has plenty of workaholics—people for whom work is an escape, an obsession, or, if they have nothing better to do, the default option—who will not be interested in my proposal. There are others for whom money is everything, who will take the highest-paying job they can find, regardless of its working hours, stress level, effect on their family life, or social implications. And among the male population, many are ensnared in the traditional breadwinner role, as well as by the tendency of our culture to equate self-worth with job and pay.

Nevertheless, the idea of giving up money for time might become more palatable to such workers as their colleagues spread the word about their newfound leisure—and happiness. A case in point is a group of overtime-loving workers in a British shoe factory. When hard times hit, the plant went into work sharing, and employees who had chased after all the extra hours they could get—including Sundays and holidays—now found themselves with time on their hands.

One worker reported: "Bit by bit, there was an unbelievable phenomenon of physical recuperation. The idea of money really lost its intensity. I don't mean it had disappeared, but eventually even the blokes with families to look after said, 'It's better now than before.' It's true that we lost a good deal of money [25 percent of former income] . . . but, quite soon, only one or two of the blokes minded.

"It was about now that . . . friendships began: we were now able to go beyond political conversation, and we managed to talk about love, impotence, jealousy, family life. . . . It was also at this time that we realized the full horror of working in the factory on Saturday afternoons or evenings. Before, the blokes had put up with it, but now we were once again learning the meaning of the word living."

Of course, the wages of many Americans are so low, or their conditions of employment so precarious, that they cannot afford to give up any income—present or future. And their ranks are swelling. Nearly a third of all U.S. workers currently earn wages that, on a full-time schedule, are insufficient to lift them out of poverty. Millions can make ends meet only through overtime, moonlighting, and multi-earner families. And many are unable to make ends meet at all.

The danger of increasing leisure time voluntarily is that it could replace inequality of income with inequality of time. The poorest third would work just as many hours as ever—or more, as more work became available—while the top two-thirds would gradually become a leisured class. The people who would gain free time would be those who already had the financial resources that make it possible: education, homes, and a bank account. They would be mainly white and mainly upper and middle class.

Ultimately, solving inequality of time means redressing the underlying inequality of income—say, by raising the minimum wage and reducing the large differences in pay that exist within most companies. But in the meantime, there are other ways poorer workers can gain more leisure time. In addition to *voluntary* increases, I advocate *mandatory* increases in free time. The United States stands out among rich countries in its failure to ensure basic rights to vacation or parental leaves. What about government-mandated four-week paid vacations for all employees, independent of length of service? Or six-month paid parental leaves, financed through the social security system? These would be a step in the right direction.

My proposals also run the risk of reproducing inequalities of gender. The suggestions themselves—such as making part-time work more desirable or allowing people to trade off income for time—are gender-neutral. But without change in underlying gender roles, women will be more likely to take advantage of them. If this occurs, it will perpetuate women's responsibility for housework and childcare. Therefore, feminists' continuing efforts to equalize the division of labor within the family are crucial to the larger success of my proposed reforms. If men take considerably more responsibility for children and housework—as many now say they want to—then they too will want to opt for working patterns that are compatible with family duties. In that event, the proposals would help undermine rigid gender roles, by making shared parenting and two-career families more feasible.

If men and women work together and demand a right to time from their employers and government, the nation might at last be able to slow down, unwind, and start enjoying the time dividend that modern technology and values make more feasible than ever.

The Fragmenting of America

Our fragmented society exalts freedom. But it also sacrifices a larger sense of belonging.

Robert J. Samuelson

Robert J. Samuelson is a columnist for Newsweek *and* The Washington Post.

Who would have thought that the three major television networks could be toppled from their pedestals? But they have been. Between 1975 and 1990, their share of the prime-time television audience has fallen from 93 percent to 64 percent. It could go lower. Little wonder that network executives whine about how poor and beleaguered they've become. In an odd way, I mourn their plight.

Network dominance never consistently provided quality programming. But it did give us something that's now slipping away: shared experience and a sense of community. People in the 1950s watched *The Honeymooners*. In the 1970s they watched *All in the Family*. As the television audience scatters to its many new choices—dozens of cable channels, VCR tapes, computer games—we're losing that. It wouldn't matter much, if the networks' eclipse were an isolated phenomenon. But it isn't. It's part of what I call the fragmenting of America.

If you examine recent economic and social trends, you will find that they emphasize (and sometimes exaggerate) our differences. By contrast, the great economic and social trends of the early post-World War II era, perhaps through the mid-1960s, emphasized and nurtured our similarities. The growing awareness of differences is a constant theme in today's politics. It underlies the raging debate over "multiculturalism." There is more to it, though, than race or immigration.

The fragmenting of America builds isolation and makes more of everyday life alien.

We have a deeper sense of accumulating differences. At some level, we don't like it. This explains a barely concealed public hunger for things that remind us of a common national heritage or destiny. Ronald Reagan was so popular in part because he spoke above a splintered society to give voice to traditional (for some, merely nostalgic) values. This hunger also explains why the Persian Gulf war, once won, made most Americans feel good.

When I say that economic and social forces are fragmenting us, here's what I mean:

Technology: In the 1950s and 1960s, television gave us universal entertainment. The explosion in long-distance telephone service shrank distances. So did construction of interstate highways and the expansion of air travel.

Now, technology transforms the "mass market" into endless "niche markets." Computers slice us by income, age, education, and purchasing patterns into market "segments." Cable television and direct mail cater to our micro tastes.

Economic equality: There's less of it. We are more a society of haves and have-nots. Until the early 1970s, family income rose rapidly and its distribution became more even. Between 1959 and 1973, the poverty rate dropped from 22.4 percent to 11.1 percent. In 1989 it was 12.8 percent. It's not just income but also the availability of health insurance and pension benefits that's becoming less equal. Coverage, once expanding, now isn't.

Regional convergence: "Rolling recession" has become part of our vocabulary. In the 1980s, regions suffered severe slumps at different times. First the Rust Belt and the Farm Belt. Then the Oil Patch. And now the Northeast. Until the 1980s, regional per capita incomes were converging. Between 1950 and 1980, the South's income rose from 69 percent to 86 percent of the national average. In the '80s, the gap among regional incomes widened.

Life styles: Everyone knows that the "traditional" two-parent family with children is on the wane. Marrying later, divorcing more often, and living longer, Americans have created new life styles, subcultures, and market niches. In 1960, 74 percent of households were married couples, and 44 percent were couples with children. By 1990, the same groups were 56 percent and 26 percent of the total.

Immigration: The huge influx of Hispanic and Asian immigrants (legal and illegal) beginning in the 1970s has literally changed the face of America. In the 1980s, the Hispanic population of Los Angeles County—to take one example—increased by nearly 1.3 million, reports *American Demographics* magazine.

To the list, I'd also add the mere passage of time. In the 1950s and early 1960s, all adult Americans had lived through two great traumas: the Great Depression and World War II. They affected everyone powerfully. Today's Americans,

spanning at least three generations, no longer have common, anchoring experiences of such intensity. Each has its own: For the baby-boomers, it was Vietnam. The generation gap has become the generations' gaps.

In some ways, the forces pulling America together in the early postwar period was unrepresentative of the economic and social tensions typical of U.S. history. In the 1920s, immigration was a great source of conflict. Nor was the "traditional" family so traditional. It was less prevalent before World War II than in the 1950s. We have reverted to a more normal state. Political calm was shattered in the 1960s by Vietnam and civil rights. Though less dramatic, the changes since then have quietly segregated us. A lot of little things have pulled us apart by creating many more separate worlds in which we all live.

We celebrate diversity and individuality. We also crave a sense of nation and community. The unifying forces of the early postwar era involved social and political conformity ("bad" in our individualistic culture), but they also created consensus ("good" in a society that values compromise). Consensus is more elusive now. Too many groups move in different directions, preoccupied by different problems and navigating by different reference points. Politicians survive by offending no one, doing nothing, and disappointing almost everyone.

Our fragmented society exalts freedom and expands consumer choice. But it also sacrifices a larger sense of belonging. The less we have in common, the more we seek out people just like us. This isn't evil. It's human nature. But it isn't necessarily good, either. It builds isolation and makes more of everyday life strange and alien. There's no conspiracy here. It's history. The television networks' decline is a small part of the story. Their eclipse is probably inevitable and maybe desirable. Or maybe not. Someday, we may yearn for a bit more of *The Honeymooners*.

THE UPBEAT GENERATION

Surprise! A FORTUNE poll says working Americans in their 20s are optimistic about their careers and financial prospects. They expect to live just as well as their parents.

Alan Deutschman

COMPARING themselves with their parents, they think it's going to be harder for them to own a house. Harder to achieve financial security. Harder to provide for a family. Or to have enough leisure time—not that they can ever really have enough. What about making a lasting marriage? Harder. Paying for a child's college education? Don't even think about it.

They are the twentysomethings, and despite the powerful obstacles in the way of their upward mobility, they are a remarkably buoyant bunch. They, too, believe in the American dream—but in an end-of-the-century version.

For all the tough sledding they see ahead, 89% of young working Americans in their 20s are optimistic about their own careers and financial prospects in the next decade. A stunning 43% are *very* optimistic. Ninety-two percent think they live as well as or better than their parents did at the same age. When they reach middle age, this group expects to live at least as well as mom and dad do in *their* middle age. These are some of the findings of a nationwide poll of 500 21- to 29-year-olds who have been in the labor force at least a year, conducted for FORTUNE by the opinion research firm Clark Martire & Bartolomeo. Admittedly, their upbeat attitude may stem from the fact that they have already found jobs.

Even so, you might be thinking: What are these kids smoking? Sorry, baby-boomers, that was *your* generation. Drugs are a major threat to the American way of life, say 81% of the twentysomethings. They are pretty downbeat on America too. Only 31% think the U.S. will have a more important role in the world in the next ten years, and 55% are pessimistic about the nation's economic prospects over the decade.

So what explains their optimism, their seemingly naive faith in the inevitability of

REPORTER ASSOCIATE *Kate Ballen*

their own progress in a darkening world? The short answer: a different view of the American dream. Only 21% say the most important measure of living the good life is financial success, and a scant 4% believe that the criterion is owning a home. The rest are more concerned with the acquisition of intangibles—a rich family or spiritual life, a rewarding job, the chance to help others, and the opportunity for leisure and travel or for intellectual and creative enrichment. By these yardsticks, the young people figure they'll come out way ahead of mom and dad. They say it will be easier for them to lead interesting

Q: Do you think you live better than your parents did at your age?		Q: When you are middle-aged, do you expect to live better than your parents did at middle age?	
A:	**%**	**A:**	**%**
Better	63	Better	51
About same	29	About same	40
Not as well	8	Not as well	9

SAMPLING ERROR: PLUS OR MINUS 4.5%.

lives, to find enjoyment and accomplishment in their work, and to achieve personal fulfillment.

Granted, the overall zeitgeist in the U.S. has been moving in this same direction. In a Roper poll taken three years ago, more Americans said leisure rather than work was the "important thing" in their lives, for the first time since 1975. The baby-busters' attitudes are partly a reaction against the workaholism of the preceding generation, but even the aging boomers have been mellowing a bit.

Douglas Coupland, 30, author of the 1991 novel *Generation X*, cynically explains this shift in the national mind-set as the philosophy of *lessness*, "whereby one rec-

onciles oneself with diminishing expectations of material wealth." But most twentysomethings aren't suffering from diminished expectations. Even though they esteem *wa*—the Japanese term for harmony—over wealth, they confidently expect to garner a fair amount of wealth too.

This is the "but not for me" generation—things may be tough all over, but *I* won't be affected. They don't make any connection between their pessimistic outlook for the overall economy and their optimism about their own well-being. For example, they believe that today a family of four needs $57,000 a year on average to live comfortably—that's 37% above the national median. Moreover, they confidently predict they will have a family income of, on average, $76,900 (in today's dollars) when they are 40. The reality is that not many will pull it off: Today only 10% of people filing income-tax returns earn $70,000 or more.

FORTUNE's poll was conducted in late April and amplified with follow-up interviews of 20 of the survey's 500 participants. What follows are some voices of today's young employees, neighbors, taxpayers, and voters. They are not running the country yet, but they will be—assuming they are up to the job—after the baby-boomers get their turn.

What is most reassuring about this generation is their appreciation of the fact that they live better now than their parents did at the same age. They recognize the sacrifices their parents made, and they are thankful for them. Twentysomethings know they grew up in relative prosperity if only because they remember the stories of struggle and hard times endlessly retold by parents who started out with much less. Call it the Mario Cuomo my-father's-bleeding-feet phenomenon.

Jim Malin, 29, a seventh-grade English teacher in Worland, Wyoming, recalls that his father had to quit medical school during the Depression and ended up working 34 years as a postman. Ronnie Nelson, 27, of Greensboro, North Carolina, enlarges on the theme: "Both sets of my grandparents were farmers, and my parents had to grow up through the Depression. My father served in World War II. When I was growing up, compared to them it was a piece of cake." Adds Robby Patterson, 29, a pipe fitter from Newport, Arkansas: "I remember my dad telling me about the first time he saw a TV. I grew up with one." And unlike her parents, "at least we don't have an outhouse," says Sabre Taylor, 24, an assistant loan officer from Miller, Missouri.

Moreover, their parents, whose Depression-inspired thrift enabled them to accumulate considerable savings, have the wherewithal to help the kids financially now—paying for college, cars, and even condos—or later, by leaving them money. Tim Ring, 29, an engineer at Pratt & Whitney in West Palm Beach, Florida, tells how his father got out of the service in 1960 and left his native Ohio at age 21 to start from scratch in Florida. Says Ring: "It was rough for him, not having a steady income. At that age I was still living at home, going to college, had a nice car, could do what I wanted and spend what I wanted."

Ramon Guerra's father was a house painter and now owns a construction company and a bar-and-grill in Portland, Oregon. "My parents struggled for a lot of things and did their best to make sure I didn't have to struggle," says Guerra, 26, a sales supervisor for a regional bakery. "They were very helpful financially. When they were my age, their parents didn't have that luxury. Times were much tougher for the whole family." Five years ago Guerra's parents co-signed his mortgage on a $48,000 three-bedroom house near the home where he grew up.

Twentysomethings say their lives have also been enriched by opportunities to travel that their parents never had. They are the children of the jet age: fare deregulation genus, economy-class species. Rather than succumbing to societal pressure to find a serious job after college, stick with it, and build a career, legions of these young adults guiltlessly view their jobs as interludes between far-off adventures. Later this year Michael Konyk, 23, plans to quit the University Inn in West Lafayette, Indiana, where he is a sous-chef, to explore either the East or the West Coast, before heading off to work in Ukraine, where his parents came from. "I need change," he says. "I love change. It stimulates me."

Konyk typifies the enhanced sense of freedom, of possibilities, of control over decisions that will shape their lives that characterizes this generation. The men, many of whom have parents or older brothers who were drafted, are grateful that they haven't been forced to go to war. The women came of age in a time of vastly expanded possibilities for them. "I have a lot more choices and more opportunities now than my mom had when she was younger," says Lynette Harkleroad, 23, who works at a Wal-Mart in Altus, Oklahoma. Her mother was a homemaker in Edmon, Pennsylvania, near Pittsburgh.

Dan Quayle notwithstanding, young people feel they are no longer as stigmatized for what were once derided as "alternative lifestyles." Bonnie Rucker, 26, is an unmarried mother of a 6-year-old son. Says she: "Raising a child alone has been hard in every way—mentally, emotionally, and physically. But it's worth it." Rucker clerks at the 7-Eleven in Vinton, Virginia, and her mother, who lives a couple of doors away, watches the boy day or night, depending on Rucker's shift.

Even if their view of their situation today vs. that of their parents at a similar age is realistic, the twentysomethings are astoundingly blithe about the future. Why do they assume they will continue to prosper despite a slower-growth economy? It turns out that they are pinning their hopes on two forces: favorable demographics and education. Births in the United States dropped off a cliff after 1964, the last year of the baby boom, producing fewer new entrants for today's labor market. Says Ronnie Nelson, who operates a four-color printing press at L&E Packaging in Greensboro, North Carolina: "I see plenty of opportunity to move up in the company because of the age of some of the people who are now doing the management jobs and upper-level jobs. They are getting close to retirement age, and there aren't many baby-boomers to replace them. I'll have a pretty good leg up on the people they hire after me."

In their eyes, education is an even more powerful propellant for upward mobility. Many young people stayed in school longer than their parents did—31% of our sample completed some college, typically receiving two-year associate degrees from community colleges. Another 33% hold four-year or graduate degrees. They speak of learning both as the key to economic advancement and as an enriching influence that opened new realms of lasting interest for them. Michael Konyk minored in anthropology at Purdue University while equipping himself to rattle those pots and pans with a degree in consumer food science. "College really opens your mind," he says. "I was granted an education, and my parents were really supportive. They let my mind grow and wander. It's really rare that I'm bored."

DESPITE the lackluster economy, youngsters who have carefully eyed the job market and trained themselves for the workplace are taking advantage of what Peter Morrison, a demographer at Rand Corp., calls "the pervasive shortage of skills." Wendy Leonard, 22, made sure to take business and computer courses when she was in high school in Wake Forest, North Carolina. There she mastered Lotus 1-2-3 and several word-processing systems, and learned to program in Cobol. "I knew that computers were what I needed," she says. Leonard recently landed a clerical position at Lambert's Cable Splicing Co. in Henderson, North Carolina, which installs cable for the phone company. "There are a lot of jobs out here, and we don't have the qualified people to fill them," she says.

Bill Bommer, 25, who teaches organizational behavior at the Indiana University business school, says, "I ask my students to imagine if they didn't go to college, what

Q: Compared with your parents, how easy will it be for you to ...

A:	Easier %	Harder %	Same %
Lead an interesting life	45	10	45
Find enjoyment and accomplishment in your work	40	13	47
Move up in a company	38	39	23
Find personal fulfillment	30	16	54
Enjoy a high quality of life	28	27	45
Own a single-family home	26	57	17
Own a business	25	55	20
Achieve financial security	24	54	22
Have enough leisure time	23	50	27
Provide for a family	22	51	27
Have a lasting marriage	20	43	37
Pay for child's college education	14	77	9

they'd be doing—and nobody can even imagine it." But the reality is that even with only a high school education, twentysomethings believe they can reach positions of considerable independence and responsibility by dint of conscientious effort. While she was in high school, Lynette Harkleroad worked part time at the McDonald's in Leechburg, Pennsylvania. When the Air Force stationed her husband, Jeffery, in Altus, her letter of recommendation from the fast-food chain got her a job at Wal-Mart, where she has worked for the past four years. She started out as a checker, then became a Universal Product Code clerk—scanning items, making sure the prices on the labels were right. Two years ago she was promoted to department manager in charge of greeting cards.

As they push to exceed their parents' attainments, Americans are more likely to return to school later in life. During the 1980s, U.S. colleges and universities saw an influx of so-called nontraditional students older than the usual 18- to 24-year-olds. Harkleroad will likely be one of this crowd. She plans to use her Wal-Mart profit sharing—which could be worth about $10,000 when it fully vests in three years—to pay for an 18-month or two-year degree, then to become a medical secretary. Similarly, Bonnie Rucker is thinking about going back to school to study to be a paramedic: "I like the business field, but there's only so far you can go with it," she says. "I want to get into a worthwhile position—something that makes me feel good about myself." She hopes to attend a community college in Virginia for the training she needs.

I F MORE EDUCATION and better demographics don't fully explain the under-30s' sanguine view of the long run, then perhaps the explanation is heredity. As Alexis de Tocqueville discovered a century and a half ago, a mania for self-improvement is an integral part of the collective American psyche. "Without optimism, you don't have anything," says Bonnie Rucker, who currently earns $6.05 an hour.

That optimism is reinforced by their experience in the labor force. The under-30 set is surprisingly content with their work: 80% are satisfied with the progress of their careers so far, 81% consider themselves very or extremely productive, and 62% have already discovered what they want to do for a career. An impressive 85% say their attitude toward their jobs has stayed the same or become more positive since they began working full time. When asked how they feel on a typical day at work, the No. 1 answer was "respected" (cited by 86% of those polled). Other top responses: "happy" (85%) and "accomplished" (82%). Only 19% felt "exploited" or "depressed."

The most important aspect of a job is "a company or supervisor who treats you with respect as an individual," followed by job security. Security probably ranks so high because the young people entered the work force during a time of redundancy, recession, and restructuring. Some of Tim Ring's acquaintances at Pratt & Whitney, which has a lot of defense business, were laid off as a result of Pentagon cutbacks. Ring is well aware that he was spared largely because he works on the space shuttle rather than a military contract.

"It's hard to get a full-time job here," says Lisa Guagliano, 22, who works two night shifts a week as a nurse trainee at Millard Fillmore Hospital in Buffalo. "They've cut a lot of positions and have lots of part-timers. It's really hard to get into the department you want." Positions are filled based on experience and seniority, and Guagliano must compete with legions of nurses in their 30s and 40s. She wants to specialize in cardiology and hopes to get the training and experience she needs from a stint in the Army as soon as she passes her licensing exams early next year: "I'm young—what's four to six years?"

Typical of many baby-busters, Guagliano wants a career where she can make a contribution to society. She decided to become a nurse because she was hospitalized at age 3 for kidney problems caused by exposure to toxic waste when her family lived near Love Canal. She was in and out of hospitals until she was a teenager, and she says, "Medicine looked like it would be really rewarding. Nurses saved my life on several occasions."

Layoffs at big companies are encouraging more and more young workers to gravitate to smaller outfits. A recent survey of college students by Right Associates, a Philadelphia consulting firm, found that 32% prefer to work for companies with 100 or fewer employees, vs. 23% in 1990.

Consider the case of Ronnie Nelson, the printing press operator at L&E Packaging, which makes tags and labels for clothes such as Levi's jeans and Lacoste shirts. He worked for seven years in the same job at a division of giant Avery Dennison, the office products manufacturer that went through a big restructuring last year. Four months ago he followed his former boss to L&E. "It's been a pretty bad situation in the printing industry," he says. "A lot of companies have folded—and a lot have so much overhead they can't make the profit they need." He says his positive attitude toward work "has 100% to do with" being at a smaller, more competitive concern.

On average these folks work a 45-hour week, and they'd like to cut that back to 39. Only 18% say they work harder than their parents did. But if they are really so upbeat about their work, why do they shrink from putting in long hours? Isn't work supposed to be the "hedonism of the middle class," as essayist Barbara Ehrenreich wrote in *Fear of Falling*? Not necessarily. Twentysomethings want the job to be satisfying but not to dominate their existence. "I'm not going to work my life away," says Lynette Harkleroad. "My family and I come before work does. I'll be at work when they need me, but I'm not going to die there."

Sure, work can be fun, but so is softball. A lot of young people sound like Ronnie Nelson. In one breath he says, "The easiest way to have an interesting life is to be happy with what you do." Then in the next, "I play a lot of golf and softball. I don't have to have the extra money to make my life interesting."

To the younger generation, "having a good time" is a legitimate goal. Four nights a week Lisa Guagliano hangs out at the Pleasure Dome, a huge bar and mecca for the younger crowd in Niagara Falls. There she competes in bikini contests or dons a Velcro-covered suit and hurls herself at a Velcro wall where, miraculously, she sticks. She peels herself off and hops into a translucent spaceball, a plastic sphere that spins and simulates the giddy feeling of space flight. Sometimes, before she heads to the Dome, she goes bungee jumping, bouncing on an elastic cord while hanging over a cliff near Niagara Falls. "It's the world's biggest thrill," she says. The biggest? "Well, pretty close."

W HEN THIS GROUP is asked which is more important to them, their personal lives or their careers, the former wins hands down—64% to 36%. Not surprisingly, one-third consider a rich family life as defining the good life. They herald a back-to-basics movement: Once again, marriage is for keeps. Although they acknowledge that it's gotten harder to make a union endure in a high-pressure, two-paycheck world, 94% expect to get married (or already are) and 87% plan to be married only once. And they want to spend plenty of time with their kids. Many saw their parents break up when the divorce boom began in

Q: The most important measure of living the good life is ...

A:	%
A rich family life	33
Financial success and security	21
A rich spiritual life	16
Having a rewarding job/career	10
Helping others	6
The opportunity for leisure and travel	6
Owning a home	4
Intellectual/creative enrichment	3

the 1970s. Work was all to a generation that knew what it was like to be out of work. Family is all to a generation that knows what divorce is.

They see marriage more as a source of companionship and support and less as a response to economic necessity or societal pressure. "My parents didn't have a lot of common interests," says Beth Nielsen, 29, who lives with her husband, Todd, a lawyer, in Creston, Iowa. "My dad was a sportswriter for the Creston *News Advertiser*, gone four or five nights a week. He worked so much that when I was younger, I don't remember taking family vacations together." Beth would like to have three children and thinks that the holidays and three-month summer vacations she enjoys as a substitute grade-school teacher will make it easy for her to spend time with them.

In contrast to her mother, who married at 19, Beth was 27 when she wed, and she and Todd share a number of interests. Both are laid back and enjoy golf, tennis, and jazz. "We're very much alike," she says. "When my parents married, I don't think people thought about finding someone who was like themselves. In the long run our relationship will be much richer."

Buying a home has always been the natural next step for married couples starting a family. It still is. Jim and Kim Malin, who are both English teachers, together earn about $49,000 annually. They have two daughters, Maggie, 6, and Katie, 2, and in 1990 they bought a $70,000 house in Worland, Wyoming. This year Ronnie Nelson and his wife, Kelly, plan to break ground on a three-bedroom ranch-style house on an acre of land in Greensboro, North Carolina. Total cost: $84,000.

Because Americans are getting married later and later—45% of men and 31% of women are still single at 29—some are tempted to buy a house before tying the knot. Tim Ring, who is single, is trying to buy a house and needs to come up with a $10,000 down payment to qualify for a $100,000 mortgage. He has money put by but figures he'll have to tap into the company savings plan, which is really meant for retirement. Like 57% of his age cohort, Ring thinks it will be harder for him to own a single-family home than it was for his parents. After all, they bought their first house with $250 down.

But owning a home is no longer the cornerstone of the American dream. House lust smacks of the sort of conspicuous materialism that baby-busters dislike. Though renters Beth and Todd Nielsen plan to buy a house once Beth gets a full-time position, "no matter what we buy or whatever we do, we won't be any happier than we are now," she says. "If we're not happy now, buying those things isn't going to make us happy."

On balance, the twentysomethings sometimes appear to represent a sort of existential cocooning or failure to engage the real world. They have never been up against a big challenge, like a war. The Persian Gulf conflict is already fading from memory: Only 31% of this generation say that global political and military unrest is a big threat to the American way of life.

"People my own age kind of make me nervous," says Jim Malin. "We haven't had our moral fiber tested as much as the people who came before us. We never lived through a draft. What would we do? Would we turn and run?" His father served with the Navy in Manila during World War II; his mother fled the Netherlands when her hometown was destroyed by the Nazis; one of his brothers fought in Vietnam.

Unlike the Sixties youth movement, which cohered around an us vs. them view of adults, today's young people have an odd and disturbing disdain for their own generation, perhaps revealing an insidious sense of discomfort or uncertainty about their own beliefs. For instance, consider their views on their own work ethic. They admit, a little self-righteously, that their career success takes a back seat to their personal fulfillment, but now listen to their voices as angst-filled generational self-criticism sets in. "I'm not really sure about the work ethic of people my age," says Jim Malin. "Today, if you ask someone to take out the garbage, it's like asking them to swim across the Atlantic." Adds Ramon Guerra: "Everyone wants to be there on payday but doesn't want to work all week."

Wayne's World, the popular film based on a series of TV sketches, may speak for some of these folks. Wayne and Garth are 20-ish and still live with their parents, amusing themselves while failing to "get a life." Wayne collects hairnets and name tags from his various short-lived factory jobs. Now switch from *Wayne's World* back to the real world and listen to Ramon Guerra: "Most of my buddies from high school haven't changed a lot—they go from job to job and wait to party on the weekend. Just making enough money to pay the rent and get by, not too worried about the future. I'm pretty much the only one in my circle who's married with children."

Nor is the under-30 set particularly interested in keeping up with the news. A 1990 Times Mirror study, *The Age of Indifference*, found that this generation "knows less, cares less, and reads newspapers less" than any generation in the past five decades. Only 30% of 21- to 34-year-olds said they "read a newspaper yesterday" and 41% said they "watched TV news yesterday." Says Malin: "I'm afraid that people my age and younger seem real apathetic about what's going on in the world. A lot of them don't ever look at the front page of the newspaper and kind of forget what's going on outside of their lives."

Their attitudes toward national and world affairs spring from personal experience and direct observation. "I have a hard time understanding spending billions and billions on defense and then having education cutbacks," says Ronnie Nelson, whose wife, Kelly, teaches disabled children.

Tim Ring belongs to the 8% sliver who are very optimistic about the U.S. economy, and his attitude springs directly from his experiences at work. He earns around $30,000 a year at the Pratt & Whitney plant in West Palm Beach testing and developing high pressure oxygen turbopumps for the space shuttle's main engine. "I see the latest in American technology in my job. I deal with engineers who have graduated from the top universities across the nation. I just see how brilliant and knowledgeable Americans can be when they want to be. I don't see the Japanese sending astronauts up into space."

But certain laments came up again and again in the interviews: America is going downhill. We spend too much on defense, not enough on education; too much on foreign aid, not enough on domestic problems like homelessness and hunger.

"Bush hasn't done a very good job—he's more interested in foreign affairs than here where we're at," says Bonnie Rucker. "People are going hungry in our own country." Echoes Lynette Harkleroad: "We give a lot of money to foreign countries for stupid reasons, and we don't take care of those problems in our own country." These people can see homeless families and drug sales in their own towns, but abstract issues such as foreign trade are hard to grasp.

Twentysomethings' disdain for their own generation is exceeded only by their antipathy toward the baby-boomers, whom they see as over-the-top materialists and remiss parents. For the most part, busters are not afflicted by what novelist Coupland called "boomer envy." Only 24% say that status or prestige is a "very important" aspect of a job. More attribute high importance to "working with people you like" (70%) than to salary (58%).

Ronnie Nelson, like 78% of his age cohort, says he wouldn't want to be like the baby-boomers: "The only thing the people I know in that generation—like my brother, Mike, who's 39—seem to be concerned with is having money. Not so much with being happy with what you do—just making the money. I really don't want to wake up in the morning and say, 'I don't want to go to work today, but the money's really good.' I want to say, 'I'm ready to go to work, and the money's decent.'"

This is a generation that values solid family lives, recognizes they are the beneficiaries of parents who had it tough, and feels they are treated with respect on a typical workday. Their heads are a little mixed up maybe, but their hearts are sure in the right place.

Blame it on Feminism

What's wrong with women today? Too much equality.

Susan Faludi

To Be A Woman In America at the Close of the twentieth century—what good fortune. That's what we keep hearing, anyway. The barricades have fallen, politicians assure us. Women have "made it," Madison Avenue cheers. Women's fight for equality has "largely been won," *Time* magazine announces. Enroll at any university, join any law firm, apply for credit at any bank. Women have so many opportunities now, corporate leaders say, that they don't really need opportunity policies. Women are so equal now, lawmakers say, that they no longer need an Equal Rights Amendment. Women have "so much," former president Ronald Reagan says, that the White House no longer needs to appoint them to high office. Even American Express ads are saluting a woman's right to charge it. At last, women have received their full citizenship papers.

And yet . . .

Behind this celebration of the American woman's victory, behind the news, cheerfully and endlessly repeated, that the struggle for women's rights is won, another message flashes: You may be free and equal now, but you have never been more miserable.

This bulletin of despair is posted everywhere—at the newsstand, on the TV set, at the movies, in advertisements and doctors' offices and academic journals. Professional women are suffering "burnout" and succumbing to an "infertility epidemic." Single women are grieving from a "man shortage." The *New York Times* reports: Childless women are "depressed and confused" and their ranks are swelling. *Newsweek* says: Unwed women are "hysterical" and crumbling under a "profound crisis of confidence." The health-advice manuals inform: High-powered career women are stricken with unprecedented outbreaks of "stress-induced disorders," hair loss, bad nerves, alcoholism, and even heart attacks. The psychology books advise:

Independent women's loneliness represents "a major mental-health problem today." Even founding feminist Betty Friedan has been spreading the word: She warns that women now suffer from "new problems that have no name."

How can American women be in so much trouble at the same time that they are supposed to be so blessed? If women got what they asked for, what could possibly be the matter now?

The prevailing wisdom of the past decade has supported one, and only one, answer to this riddle: It must be all that equality that's causing all that pain. Women are unhappy precisely because they are free. Women are enslaved by their own liberation. They have grabbed at the gold ring of independence, only to miss the one ring that really matters. They have gained control of their fertility, only to destroy it. They have pursued their own professional dreams—and lost out on romance, the greatest female adventure. "Our generation was the human sacrifice" to the women's movement, writer Elizabeth Mehren contends in a *Time* cover story. Baby-boom women, like her, she says, have been duped by feminism: "We believed the rhetoric." In *Newsweek*, writer Kay Ebeling dubs feminism the "Great Experiment That Failed" and asserts, "Women in my generation, its perpetrators, are the casualties."

In the eighties, publications from the *New York Times* to *Vanity Fair* to *The Nation* have issued a steady stream of indictments against the women's movement, with such headlines as "WHEN FEMINISM FAILED" or "THE AWFUL TRUTH ABOUT WOMEN'S LIB." They hold the campaign for women's equality responsible for nearly every woe besetting women, from depression to meager savings accounts, from teenage suicides to eating disorders to bad complexions. The *Today* show says women's liberation is to blame for bag ladies. A guest columnist in the *Baltimore Sun* even proposes that feminists produced the rise in slasher movies. By making the "violence" of abortion more acceptable, the author reasons, women's-rights activities made it all right to show graphic murders on screen.

At the same time, other outlets of popular culture have been forging the same connection: In Hollywood films, of which *Fatal Attraction* is only the most famous, emancipated women with condominiums of their own slink wild-eyed between bare walls, paying for their liberty with an empty bed, a barren womb. "My biological clock is ticking so loud it keeps me awake at night," Sally Field cries in the film *Surrender,* as, in an all-too-common transformation in the cinema of the eighties, an actress who once played scrappy working heroines is now showcased groveling for a groom. In prime-time television shows, from *thirtysomething* to *Family Man,* single, professional, and feminist women are humiliated, turned into harpies, or hit by nervous breakdowns; the wise ones recant their independent ways by the closing sequence. In popular novels, from Gail Parent's *A Sign of the Eighties* to Stephen King's *Misery,* unwed women shrink to sniveling spinsters or inflate to firebreathing she-devils; renouncing all aspirations but marriage, they beg for wedding bands from strangers or swing axes at reluctant bachelors. Even Erica Jong's high-flying independent heroine literally crashes by the end of the decade, as the author supplants *Fear of Flying's* saucy Isadora Wing, an exuberant symbol of female sexual emancipation in the seventies, with an embittered careerist-turned-recovering-"codependent" in *Any Woman's Blues*—a book that is intended, as the narrator bluntly states, "to demonstrate what a dead end the so-called sexual revolution had become and how desperate so-called free women were in the last few years of our decadent epoch."

Popular psychology manuals peddle the same diagnosis for contemporary female distress. "Feminism, having promised her a stronger sense of her own identity, has given her little more than an identity *crisis,* the best-selling advice manual *Being a Woman* asserts. The authors of the era's self-help classic, *Smart Women/Foolish Choices,* proclaim that women's distress was "an unfortunate consequence of feminism" because "it created a myth among women that the apex of self-realization could be achieved only through autonomy, independence, and career."

In the Reagan and Bush years, government officials have needed no prompting to endorse this thesis. Reagan spokeswoman Faith Ryan Whittlesey declared feminism a "straitjacket" for women, in one of the White House's only policy speeches on the status of the American female population—entitled "Radical Feminism in Retreat." The U.S. attorney general's Commission on Pornography even proposed that women's professional advancement might be responsible for rising rape rates: With more women in college

and at work now, the commission members reasoned in their report, women just have more opportunities to be raped.

Legal scholars have railed against the "equality trap." Sociologists have claimed that "feminist-inspired" legislative reforms have stripped women of special "protections." Economists have argued that well-paid working women have created a "less stable American family." And demographers, with greatest fanfare, have legitimated the prevailing wisdom with so-called neutral data on sex ratios and fertility trends; they say they actually have the numbers to prove that equality doesn't mix with marriage and motherhood.

Finally, some "liberated" women themselves have joined the lamentations. In *The Cost of Loving: Women and the New Fear of Intimacy,* Megan Marshall, a Harvard-pedigreed writer, asserts that the feminist "Myth of Independence" has turned her generation into unloved and unhappy fast-trackers, "dehumanized" by careers and "uncertain of their gender identity." Other diaries of mad Superwomen charge that "the hardcore feminist viewpoint," as one of them puts it, has relegated educated executive achievers to solitary nights of frozen dinners and closet drinking. The triumph of equality, they report, has merely given women hives, stomach cramps, eye "twitching" disorders, even comas.

But what "equality" are all these authorities talking about?

If American women are so equal, why do they represent two-thirds of all poor adults? Why are more than 70 percent of full-time working women making less than twenty-five thousand dollars a year, nearly double the number of men at that level? Why are they still far more likely than men to live in poor housing, and twice as likely to draw no pension? If women "have it all," then why don't they have the most basic requirements to achieve equality in the work force: unlike that of virtually all other industrialized nations, the U.S. government still has no family-leave and child-care programs.

If women are so "free," why are their reproductive freedoms in greater jeopardy today than a decade earlier? Why, in their own homes, do they still shoulder 70 percent of the household duties—while the only major change in the last fifteen years is that now men *think* they do more around the house? In thirty states, it is still generally legal for husbands to rape their wives; and only ten states have laws mandating arrest for domestic violence—even though battering is the leading cause of injury to women (greater than rapes, muggings, and auto accidents combined).

The word may be that women have been "liberated," but women themselves seem to feel otherwise. Repeatedly in national surveys, majorities of women say they are still far from equality. In poll after poll in the decade, overwhelming majorities of women said they need equal pay and equal job opportunities, they need an Equal Rights Amendment, they need the right to an abortion without government interference, they need a federal law guaranteeing maternity leave, they need decent child-care services. They have none of these. So how exactly have women "won" the war for women's rights?

Seen against this background, the much bally-hooed claim that feminism is responsible for making women miserable becomes absurd—and irrelevant. The afflictions ascribed to feminism, from "the man shortage" to "the infertility epidemic" to "female burnout" to "toxic day care," have had their origins not in the actual conditions of women's lives but rather in a closed system that starts and ends in the media, popular culture, and advertising—an endless feedback loop that perpetuates and exaggerates its own false images of womanhood. And women don't see feminism as their enemy, either. In fact, in national surveys, 75 to 95 percent of women credit the feminist campaign with *improving* their lives, and a similar proportion say that the women's movement should keep pushing for change.

If the many ponderers of the Woman Question really wanted to know what is troubling the American female population, they might have asked their subjects. In public-opinion surveys, women consistently rank their own *inequality*, at work and at home, among their most urgent concerns. Over and over, women complain to pollsters of a lack of economic, not marital, opportunities; they protest that working men, not working women, fail to spend time in the nursery and the kitchen. It is justice for their gender, not wedding rings and bassinets, that women believe to be in desperately short supply.

As the last decade ran its course, the monitors that serve to track slippage in women's status have been working overtime. Government and private surveys are showing that women's already vast representation in the lowliest occupations is rising, their tiny presence in higher-paying trade and craft jobs stalled or backsliding, their minuscule representation in upper management posts stagnant or falling, and their pay dropping in the very occupations where they have made the most "progress."

In national politics, the already small numbers of women in both elective posts and political appointments fell during the eighties. In private life, the average amount that a divorced man paid in child support fell by about 25 percent from the late seventies to the mid-eighties (to a mere $140 a month). And government records chronicled a spectacular rise in sexual violence against women. Reported rapes more than doubled from the early seventies—at nearly twice the rate of all other violent crimes and four times the overall crime rate in the United States.

The truth is that the last decade has seen a powerful counterassault on women's rights, a backlash, an attempt to retract the handful of small and hard-won victories that the feminist movement did manage to win for women. This counterassault is largely insidious: in a kind of pop-culture version of the big lie, it stands the truth boldly on its head and proclaims that the very steps that have elevated women's position have actually led to their downfall.

The backlash is at once sophisticated and banal, deceptively "progressive" and proudly backward. It deploys both the "new" findings of "scientific research" and the dime-store moralism of yesteryear; it turns into media sound bites both the glib pronouncements of pop-psych trend-watchers and the frenzied rhetoric of New Right preachers. The backlash has succeeded in framing virtually the whole issue of women's rights in its own language. Just as Reaganism shifted political discourse far to the right and demonized liberalism, so the backlash convinced the public that women's "liberation" was the true contemporary American scourge—the source of an endless laundry list of personal, social, and economic problems.

But what has made women unhappy in the last decade is not their "equality"—which they don't yet have—but the rising pressure to halt, and even reverse, women's quest for that equality. The "man shortage" and the "infertility epidemic" are not the price of liberation; in fact, they do not even exist. But these chimeras are part of a relentless whittling-down process—much of it amounting to outright propaganda—that has served to stir women's private anxieties and break their political wills. Identifying feminism as women's enemy only furthers the ends of a backlash against women's equality by simultaneously deflecting attention from the backlash's central role and recruiting women to attack their own cause.

Some social observers may well ask whether the current pressures on women actually constitute a backlash—or just a continuation of American society's long-standing resistance to women's equal rights. Certainly hostility to female independence has always been with us. But if fear and loathing of feminism is a sort of perpetual viral condition in our culture, it is not always in an acute stage; its symptoms subside and resurface periodically. And it is these episodes of resurgence, such as the one we face now, that can accurately be termed "backlashes" to women's advancement. If we trace these occurrences in American history, we find such flare-ups are hardly random; they have always been triggered by the perception—accurate or not—that women are making great strides. These outbreaks are backlashes because they have always arisen in reaction to women's "progress," caused not simply by a bedrock of misogyny but by the specific efforts of contemporary women to improve their status, efforts that have been interpreted time and again by men—especially men grappling with real threats to their economic and social well-being on other fronts—as spelling their own masculine doom.

The most recent round of backlash first surfaced in the late seventies on the fringes, among the evangelical Right. By the early eighties, the fundamentalist ideology had shouldered its way into the White House. By the mid-eighties, as resistance to women's rights acquired political and social acceptability, it passed into the popular culture. And in every case, the timing coincided with signs that women were believed to be on the verge of a breakthrough.

Just when women's quest for equal rights seemed closest to achieving its objectives, the backlash struck it down. Just when a "gender gap" at the voting booth surfaced in 1980, and women in politics began to talk of capitalizing on it, the Republican party elevated Ronald Reagan and both political parties began to shunt women's rights off their platforms. Just when support for feminism and the Equal Rights Amendment reached a record high in 1981, the amendment was defeated the following year. Just when women were starting to mobilize against battering and sexual assaults, the federal government cut funding for battered-women's programs, defeated bills to fund shelters, and shut down its Office of Domestic Violence—only two years after opening it in 1979. Just when record numbers of younger women were supporting feminist goals in the mid-eighties (more of them, in fact, than older women) and a majority of all women were calling themselves feminists, the media declared the advent of a younger "postfeminist generation" that supposedly reviled the women's movement. Just when women racked up their largest percentage ever supporting the right to abortion, the U.S. Supreme Court moved toward reconsidering it.

In other words, the antifeminist backlash has been set off not by women's achievement of full equality but by the increased possibility that they might win it. It is a preemptive strike that stops women long before they reach the finish line. "A backlash may be an indication that women really have had an effect," feminist psychiatrist Dr. Jean Baker Miller has written, "but backlashes occur when advances have been small, before changes are sufficient to help many people. . . . It is almost as if the leaders of backlashes use the fear of change as a threat before major change has occurred." In the last decade, some women did make substantial advances before the backlash hit, but millions of others were left behind, stranded. Some women now enjoy the right to legal abortion—but not the forty-four million women, from the indigent to the military worker, who depend on the federal government for their medical care. Some women can now walk into high-paying professional careers—but not the millions still in the typing pools or behind the department-store sales counters. (Contrary to popular myth about the "have-it-all" baby-boom women, the largest percent-

age of women in this generation remain in office support roles.)

As the backlash has gathered force, it has cut off the few from the many—and the few women who have advanced seek to prove, as a social survival tactic, that they aren't so interested in advancement after all. Some of them parade their defection from the women's movement, while their working-class peers founder and cling to the splintered remains of the feminist cause. While a very few affluent and celebrity women who are showcased in news stories boast about going home to "bake bread," the many working-class women appeal for their economic rights—flocking to unions in record numbers, striking on their own for pay equity, and establishing their own fledgling groups for working-women's rights. In 1986, while 41 percent of upper-income women were claiming in the Gallup poll that they were not feminists, only 26 percent of low-income women were making the same claim.

Women's advances and retreats are generally described in military terms: battles won, battles lost, points and territory gained and surrendered. The metaphor of combat is not without its merits in this context, and, clearly, the same sort of martial accounting and vocabulary is already surfacing here. But by imagining the conflict as two battalions neatly arrayed on either side of the line, we miss the entangled nature, the locked embrace, of a "war" between women and the male culture they inhabit. We miss the reactive nature of a backlash, which, by definition, can exist only in response to another force.

In times when feminism is at a low ebb, women assume the reactive role—privately and, most often, covertly struggling to assert themselves against the dominant cultural tide. But when feminism itself becomes the tide, the opposition doesn't simply go along with the reversal: it digs in its heels, brandishes its fists, builds walls and dams. And its resistance creates countercurrents and treacherous undertows.

The force and furor of the backlash churn beneath the surface, largely invisible to the public eye. On occasion in the last decade, they have burst into view. We have seen New Right politicians condemn women's independence, antiabortion protesters firebomb women's clinics, fundamentalist preachers damn feminists as "whores." Other signs of the backlash's wrath, by their sheer brutality, can push their way into public consciousness for a time—the sharp increase in rape, for example, or the rise in pornography that depicts extreme violence against women.

More subtle indicators in popular culture may receive momentary, and often bemused, media notice, then quickly slip from social awareness: A report, for instance, that the image of women on prime-time TV shows has suddenly degenerated. A survey of mystery fiction finding the numbers of tortured and mutilated female characters mysteriously multiplying. The puzzling news that, as one commentator put it, "so many hit songs have the B word [bitch] to refer to women that some rap music seems to be veering toward rape music." The ascendancy of violently misogynist comics like Andrew Dice Clay, who calls women "pigs" and "sluts," or radio hosts like Rush Limbaugh, whose broadsides against "femi-Nazi" feminists helped make his syndicated program the most popular radio talk show in the nation. Or word that, in 1987, the American Women in Radio and Television couldn't award its annual prize to ads that feature women positively: it could find no ad that qualified.

These phenomena are all related, but that doesn't mean they are somehow coordinated. The backlash is not a conspiracy, with a council dispatching agents from some central control room, nor are the people who serve its ends often aware of their role; some even consider themselves feminists. For the most part, its workings are encoded and internalized, diffuse and chameleonic. Not all of the manifestations of the backlash are of equal weight or significance, either; some are mere ephemera thrown up by a culture machine that is always scrounging for a "fresh" angle. Taken as a whole, however, these codes and cajolings, these whispers and threats and myths, move overwhelmingly in one direction: they try to push women back into their "acceptable" roles—whether as Daddy's girl or fluttery romantic, active nester or passive love object.

Although the backlash is not an organized movement, that doesn't make it any less destructive. In fact, the lack of orchestration, the absence of a single string-puller, only makes it harder to see—and perhaps more effective. A backlash against women's rights succeeds to the degree that it appears *not* to be political, that it appears not to be a struggle at all. It is most powerful when it goes private, when it lodges inside a woman's mind and turns her vision inward, until she imagines the pressure is all in her head, until she begins to enforce the backlash, too—on herself.

In the last decade, the backlash has moved through the culture's secret chambers, traveling through passageways of flattery and fear. Along the way, it has adopted disguises: a mask of mild derision or the painted face of deep "concern." Its lips profess pity for any woman who won't fit the mold, while it tries to clamp the mold around her ears. It pursues a divide-and-conquer strategy: single versus married women, working women versus homemakers, middle versus working class. It manipulates a system of rewards and punishments, elevating women who follow its rules, isolating those who don't. The backlash remarkets old myths about women as new facts and ignores all appeals to reason. Cornered, it denies its own existence, points an accusatory finger at feminism, and burrows deeper underground.

Backlash happens to be the title of a 1947 Hollywood movie in which a man frames his wife for a murder he's committed. The backlash against women's rights works in much the same way: its rhetoric charges feminists with all the crimes it perpetrates. The backlash line blames the women's movement for the "feminization of poverty"—while the backlash's own instigators in Washington have pushed through the budget cuts that have helped impoverish millions of women, have fought pay-equity proposals, and undermined equal-opportunity laws. The backlash line claims the women's movement cares nothing for children's rights—while its own representatives in the capital and state legislatures have blocked one bill after another to improve child care, slashed billions of dollars in aid for children, and relaxed state licensing standards for day-care centers. The backlash line accuses the women's movement of creating a generation of unhappy single and childless women—but its purveyors in the media are the ones guilty of making single and childless women feel like circus freaks.

To blame feminism for women's "lesser life" is to miss its point entirely, which is to win women a wider range of experience. Feminism remains a pretty simple concept, despite repeated—and enormously effective—efforts to dress it up in greasepaint and turn its proponents into gargoyles. As Rebecca West wrote sardonically in 1913, "I myself have never been able to find out precisely what feminism is: I only know that people call me a feminist whenever I express sentiments that differentiate me from a doormat."

The meaning of the word feminism has not really changed since it first appeared in a book review in *The Athenaeum* on April 27, 1895, describing a woman who "has in her the capacity of fighting her way back to independence." It is the basic proposition that, as Nora put it in Ibsen's *A Doll's House* a century ago, "Before everything else I'm a human being." It is the simply worded sign hoisted by a little girl in the 1970 Women's Strike for Equality: "I AM NOT A BARBIE DOLL." Feminism asks the world to recognize at long last that women aren't decorative ornaments, worthy vessels, members of a "special-interest group." They are half (in fact, now more than half) of the national population, and just as deserving of rights and opportunities, just as capable of participating in the world's events, as the other half. Feminism's agenda is basic: It asks that women not be forced to "choose" between public justice and private happiness. It asks that women be free to define themselves—instead of having their identity defined for them, time and again, by their culture and their men.

The fact that these are still such incendiary notions should tell us that American women have a way to go before they enter the promised land of equality.

The Mountain People

Colin M. Turnbull

Anthropologist Colin M. Turnbull, author of The Forest People *and* The Lonely Africans, *went to study the Ik of Uganda, who he believed were still primarily hunters, in order to compare them with other hunting-and-gathering societies he had studied in totally different environments. He was surprised to discover that they were no longer hunters but primarily farmers, well on their way to starvation and something worse in a drought-stricken land.*

In what follows, there will be much to shock, and the reader will be tempted to say, "how primitive, how savage, how disgusting," and, above all, "how inhuman." The first judgments are typical of the kind of ethno- and egocentricism from which we can never quite escape. But "how inhuman" is of a different order and supposes that there are certain values inherent in humanity itself, from which the people described here seem to depart in a most drastic manner. In living the experience, however, and perhaps in reading it, one finds that it is oneself one is looking at and questioning; it is a voyage in quest of the basic human and a discovery of his potential for inhumanity, a potential that lies within us all.

Just before World War II the Ik tribe had been encouraged to settle in northern Uganda, in the mountainous northeast corner bordering on Kenya to the east and Sudan to the north.

Until then they had roamed in nomadic bands, as hunters and gatherers, through a vast region in all three countries. The Kidepo Valley below Mount Morungole was their major hunting territory. After they were confined to a part of their former area, Kidepo was made a national park and they were forbidden to hunt or gather there.

The concept of family in a nomadic society is a broad one; what really counts most in everyday life is community of residence, and those who live close to each other are likely to see each other as effectively related, whether there is any kinship bond or not. Full brothers, on the other hand, who live in different parts of the camp may have little concern for each other.

It is not possible, then, to think of the family as a simple, basic unit. A child is brought up to regard any adult living in the same camp as a parent, and age-mate as a brother or sister. The Ik had this essentially social attitude toward kinship, and it readily lent itself to the rapid and disastrous changes that took place following the restriction of their movement and hunting activities. The family simply ceased to exist.

It is a mistake to think of small-scale societies as "primitive" or "simple." Hunters and gatherers, most of all, appear simple and straightforward in terms of their social organization, yet that is far from true. If we can learn about the nature of society from a study of small-scale societies, we can also learn about human relationships. The smaller the society, the less emphasis there is on the formal system and the more there is on interpersonal and intergroup relations. Security is seen in terms of these relationships, and so is survival. The result, which appears so deceptively simple, is that hunters frequently display those characteristics that we find so admirable in man: kindness, generosity, consideration, affection, honesty, hospitality, compassion, charity. For them, in their tiny, close-knit society, these are necessities for survival. In our society anyone possessing even half these qualities would find it hard to survive, yet we think these virtues are inherent in man. I took it for granted that the Ik would possess these same qualities. But they were as unfriendly, uncharitable, inhospitable and generally mean as any people can be. For those positive qualities we value so highly are no longer functional for them; even more than in our own society they spell ruin and disaster. It seems that, far from being basic human qualities, they are luxuries we can afford in times of plenty or are mere mechanisms for survival and security. Given the situation in which the Ik found

themselves, man has no time for such luxuries, and a much more basic man appears, using more basic survival tactics.

Turnbull had to wait in Kaabong, a remote administration outpost, for permission from the Uganda government to continue to Pirre, the Ik water hole and police post. While there he began to learn the Ik language and became used to their constant demands for food and tobacco. An official in Kaabong gave him, as a "gift," 20 Ik workers to build a house and a road up to it. When they arrived at Pirre, however, wages for the workers were negotiated by wily Atum, "the senior of all the Ik on Morungole."

The police seemed as glad to see me as I was to see them. They hungrily asked for news of Kaabong, as though it were the hub of the universe. They had a borehole and pump for water, to which they said I was welcome, since the water holes used by the Ik were not fit for drinking or even for washing. The police were not able to tell me much about the Ik, because every time they went to visit an Ik village, there was nobody there. Only in times of real hunger did they see much of the Ik, and then only enough to know that they were hungry.

The next morning I rose early, but even though it was barely daylight, by the time I had washed and dressed, the Ik were already outside. They were sitting silently, staring at the Land Rover. As impassive as they seemed, there was an air of expectancy, and I was reminded that these

were, after all, hunters, and the likelihood was that I was their morning's prey. So I left the Land Rover curtains closed and as silently as possible prepared a frugal breakfast.

Atum was waiting for me. He said that he had told all the Ik that Iciebam [friend of the Ik] had arrived to live with them and that I had given the workers a "holiday" so they could greet me. They were waiting in the villages. They were very hungry, he added, and many were dying. That was probably one of the few true statements he ever made, and I never even considered believing it.

There were seven villages in all. Village Number One was built on a steep slope, and even the houses tilted at a crazy angle. Atum rapped on the outer stockade with his cane and shouted a greeting, but there was no response. This was Giriko's village, he said, and he was one of my workers.

"But I thought you told them to go back to their villages," I said.

"Yes, but you gave them a holiday, so they are probably in their fields," answered Atum, looking me straight in the eye.

At Village Number Two there was indisputably someone inside, for I could hear loud singing. The singing stopped, a pair of hands gripped the stockade and a craggy head rose into view, giving me an undeniably welcoming smile. This was Lokelea. When I asked him what he had been singing about, he answered, "Because I'm hungry."

Village Number Three, the smallest of all, was empty. Village Number Four had only 8 huts, as

against the 12 or so in Lokelea's village and the 18 in Giriko's. The outer stockade was broken in one section, and we walked right in. We ducked through a low opening and entered a compound in which a woman was making pottery. She kept on at her work but gave us a cheery welcome and laughed her head off when I tried to speak in Icietot. She willingly showed me details of her work and did not seem unduly surprised at my interest. She said that everyone else had left for the fields except old Nangoli, who, on hearing her name mentioned, appeared at a hole in the stockade shutting off the next compound. Nangoli mumbled toothlessly at Losike, who told Atum to pour her some water.

As we climbed up to his own village, Number Five, Atum said that Losike never gave anything away. Later I remembered that gift of water to Nangoli. At the time I did not stop to think that in this country a gift of water could be a gift of life.

Atum's village had nearly 50 houses, each within its compound within the stout outer stockade. Atum did not invite me in.

A hundred yards away stood Village Number Six. Kauar, one of the workers, was sitting on a rocky slab just outside the village. He had a smile like Losike's, open and warm, and he said he had been waiting for me all morning. He offered us water and showed me his own small compound and that of his mother.

Coming up from Village Number Seven, at quite a respectable speed, was a blind man. This was Logwara, emaciated but alive and remarkably active. He had heard us and had come to greet me, he said, but he added the inevitable demand for tobacco in the same breath. We sat down in the open sunlight. For a brief moment I felt at peace.

After a short time Atum said we should start back and called over his shoulder to his village. A muffled sound came from within, and he said, "That's my wife, she is very sick—and hungry." I offered to go and see her, but he shook his head. Back at the Land Rover I gave Atum some food and some aspirin, not knowing what else to give him to help his wife.

I was awakened well before dawn by the lowing of cattle. I made an extra pot of tea and let Atum distribute it, and then we divided the workers into two teams. Kauar was to head the team building the house, and Lokelatom, Losike's husband, was to take charge of the road workers.

While the Ik were working, their heads kept turning as though they were expecting something to happen. Every now and again one would stand up and peer into the distance and then take off into the bush for an hour or so. On one such occasion, after the person had been gone two hours, the others started drifting off. By then I knew them better; I looked for a wisp of smoke and followed it to where the road team was cooking a goat. Smoke was a giveaway, though, so they economized on cooking and ate most food nearly raw. It is a curious hangover from what must once have been a moral code that Ik will offer food if surprised in the act of eating, though they now go to enormous pains not to be so surprised.

I was always up before dawn, but by the time I got up to the villages they were always deserted. One morning I followed the little *oror* [gulley] up from *oror a pirre ï* [Ravine of Pirre] while it was still quite dark, and I met Lomeja on his way down. He took me on my first illicit hunt in Kidepo. He told me that if he got anything he would share it with me and with anyone else who managed to join us but that he certainly would not take

anything back to his family. "Each one of them is out seeing what he can get for himself, and do you think they will bring any back for me?"

Lomeja was one of the very few Ik who seemed glad to volunteer information. Unlike many of the others, he did not get up and leave as I approached. Apart from him, I spent most of my time, those days, with Losike, the potter. She told me that Nangoli, the old lady in the adjoining compound, and her husband, Amuarkuar, were rather peculiar.

They helped each other get food and water, and they brought it back to their compound to eat together.

I still do not know how much real hunger there was at that time, for most of the younger people seemed fairly well fed, and the few skinny old people seemed healthy and active. But my laboriously extracted genealogies showed that there were quite a number of old people still alive and allegedly in these villages, though they were never to be seen. Then Atum's wife died.

Atum told me nothing about it but kept up his demands for food and medicine. After a while the beady-eyed Lomongin told me that Atum was selling the medicine I was giving him for his wife. I was not unduly surprised and merely remarked that

that was too bad for his wife. "Oh no," said Lomongin, "she has been dead for weeks."

It must have been then that I began to notice other things that I suppose I had chosen to ignore before. Only a very few of the Ik helped me with the language. Others would understand when it suited them and would pretend they did not understand when they did not want to listen. I began to be forced into a similar isolationist attitude myself, and although I cannot say I enjoyed it, it did make life much easier. I even began to enjoy, in a peculiar way, the company of the silent Ik. And the more I accepted it, the less often people got up and left as I approached. On one occasion I sat on the *di* [sitting place] by Atum's rain tree for three days with a group of Ik, and for three days not one word was exchanged.

The work teams were more lively, but only while working. Kauar always played and joked with the children when they came back from foraging. He used to volunteer to make the two-day walk into Kaabong and the even more tiring two-day climb back to get mail for me or to buy a few things for others. He always asked if he had made the trip more quickly than the last time.

Then one day Kauar went to Kaabong and did not come back. He was found on the last peak of the trail, cold and dead. Those who found him took the things he had been carrying and pushed his body into the bush. I still see his open, laughing face, see him giving precious tidbits to the children, comforting some child who was crying, and watching me read the letters he carried so lovingly for me. And I still think of him probably running up that viciously steep mountainside so he could break his time record and falling dead in his pathetic prime because he was starving.

Once I settled down into my new home, I was able to work more effectively. Having recovered at least some of my anthropological detachment, when I heard the telltale rustling of someone at my stockade, I merely threw a stone. If when out walking I stumbled during a difficult descent and the Ik shrieked with laughter, I no longer even noticed it.

Anyone falling down was good for a laugh, but I never saw anyone actually trip anyone else. The adults were content to let things happen and then enjoy them; it was probably conservation of energy. The children, however, sought their pleasures with vigor. The best game of all, at this time, was teasing poor little Adupa. She was not so little—in fact she should have been an adult, for she was nearly 13 years old—but Adupa was a little mad. Or you might say she was the only sane one, depending on your point of view. Adupa did not jump on other people's play houses, and she lavished enormous care on hers and would curl up inside it. That made it all the more jump-on-able. The other children beat her viciously.

Children are not allowed to sleep in the house after they are "put out," which is at about three years old, four at the latest. From then on they sleep in the open courtyard, taking what shelter they can against the stockade. They may ask for permission to sit in the doorway of their parents' house but may not lie down or sleep there. "The same thing applies to old people," said Atum, "if they can't build a house of their own and, of course, *if* their children let them stay in their compounds."

I saw a few old people, most of whom had taken over abandoned huts. For the first time I realized that there really was starvation and saw why I had never known it before: it was confined to the aged. Down in Giriko's village the old ritual priest, Lolim, confidentially told me that he was sheltering an old man who had been refused shelter by his son. But Lolim did not have enough food for himself, let alone his guest; could I . . . I liked old Lolim, so, not believing that Lolim had a visitor at all, I brought him a double ration that evening. There was a rustling in the back of the hut, and Lolim helped ancient Lomeraniang to the entrance. They shook with delight at the sight of the food.

When the two old men had finished eating, I left; I found a hungry-looking and disapproving little crowd clustered outside. They muttered to each other about wasting food. From then on I brought food daily, but in a very short time Lomeraniang was dead, and his son refused to come down from the village above to bury him. Lolim scratched a hole and covered the body with a pile of stones he carried himself, one by one.

Hunger was indeed more severe than I knew, and, after the old people, the children were the next to go. It was all quite impersonal—even to me, in most cases, since I had been immunized by the Ik themselves against sorrow on their behalf. But Adupa was an exception. Her madness was such that she did not know just how vicious humans could be. Even worse, she thought that parents were for loving, for giving as well as receiving. Her parents were not given to fantasies. When she came for shelter, they drove her out; and when she came because she was hungry, they laughed that Icien laugh, as if she had made them happy.

Adupa's reactions became slower and slower. When she managed to find food—fruit peels, skins, bits of bone, half-eaten berries—she held it in her hand and looked at it with wonder and delight. Her playmates caught on quickly; they put tidbits in her way and watched her simple drawn little face wrinkle in a smile. Then as she raised her hand to her mouth, they set on her with cries of excitement, fun and laughter, beating her savagely over the head. But that is

not how she died. I took to feeding her, which is probably the cruelest thing I could have done, a gross selfishness of my part to try to salve my own rapidly disappearing conscience. I had to protect her, physically, as I fed her. But the others would beat her anyway, and Adupa cried, not because of the pain in her body but because of the pain she felt at the great, vast, empty wasteland where love should have been.

It was *that* that killed her. She demanded that her parents love her. Finally they took her in, and Adupa was happy and stopped crying. She stopped crying forever because her parents went away and closed the door tight behind them, so tight that weak little Adupa could never have moved it.

The Ik seem to tell us that the family is not such a fundamental unit as we usually suppose, that it is not essential to social life. In the crisis of survival facing the Ik, the family was one of the first institutions to go, and the Ik as a society have survived.

The other quality of life that we hold to be necessary for survival—love—the Ik dismiss as idiotic and highly dangerous. But we need to see more of the Ik before their absolute lovelessness becomes truly apparent.

In this curious society there is one common value to which all Ik hold tenaciously. It is *ngag*, "food." That is the one standard by which they measure right and wrong, goodness and badness. The very word for "good" is defined in terms of food. "Goodness" is "the possession of food," or the "*individual* possession of food." If you try to discover their concept of a "good man," you get the truly Icien answer: one who has a full stomach.

We should not be surprised, then, when the mother throws her child out at three years old. At that age a series of *rites de passage* begins. In this environment a child has no chance of survival on his own until he is about 13, so children form age bands. The junior band consists of children between three and seven, the senior of eight- to twelve-year-olds. Within the band each child seeks another close to him in age for defense against the older children. These friendships are temporary, however, and inevitably there comes a time when each turns on the one that up to then had been the closest to him; that is the *rite de passage,* the destruction of that fragile bond called friendship. When this has happened three or four times, the child is ready for the world.

The weakest are soon thinned out, and the strongest survive to achieve leadership of the band. Such a leader is eventually driven out, turned against by his fellow band members. Then the process starts all over again; he joins the senior age band as its most junior member.

The final *rite de passage* is into adulthood, at the age of 12 or 13. By then the candidate has learned the wisdom of acting on his own, for his own good, while acknowledging that on occasion it is profitable to associate temporarily with others.

One year in four the Ik can count on a complete drought. About this time it began to be apparent that there were going to be two consecutive years of drought and famine. Men as well as women took to gathering what wild fruits and berries they could find, digging up roots, cutting grass that was going to seed, threshing and eating the seed.

Old Nangoli went to the other side of Kidepo, where food and water were more plentiful. But she had to leave her husband, Amuarkuar, behind. One day he appeared at my *odok* and asked for water. I gave him some and was going to get him food when Atum came storming over and argued with me about wasting water. In the midst of the dispute Amuarkuar quietly left. He wandered over to a rocky outcrop and lay down there to rest. Nearby was a small bundle of grass that evidently he had cut and had been dragging painfully to the ruins of his village to make a rough shelter. The grass was his supreme effort to keep a home going until Nangoli returned. When I went over to him, he looked up and smiled and said that my water tasted good. He lay back and went to sleep with a smile on his face. That is how Amuarkuar died, happily.

There are measures that can be taken for survival involving the classical institutions of gift and sacrifice. These are weapons, sharp and aggressive. The object is to build up a series of obligations so that in times of crisis you have a number of debts you can recall; with luck one of them may be repaid. To this end, in the circumstances of Ik life, considerable sacrifice would be justified, so you have the odd phenomenon of these otherwise singularly self-interested people going out of their way to "help" each other. Their help may very well be resented in the extreme, but is done in such a way that it cannot be refused, for it has already been given. Someone may hoe another's field in his absence or rebuild his stockade or join in the building of a house.

The danger in this system was that the debtor might not be around when collection was called for and, by the same token, neither might the creditor. The future was too uncertain for this to be anything but one additional survival measure, though some developed it to a fine technique.

There seemed to be increasingly little among the Ik that could by any stretch of the imagination be called social life, let alone social organization. The family does not hold itself together; economic interest is centered on as many stomachs as there are people; and cooperation is merely a device for furthering an interest that is consciously selfish. We often do the same thing in our so-called "altruistic" practices, but we tell ourselves it is for the good of others. The Ik have dispensed with the myth of altruism. Though they have no centralized leadership or means of physical coercion, they do hold together with remarkable tenacity.

In our world, where the family has also lost much of its value as a social unit and where religious belief no longer binds us into communities, we maintain order only through coercive power that is ready to uphold a rigid law and through an equally rigid penal system. The Ik, however, have learned to do without coercion, either

spiritual or physical. It seems that they have come to a recognition of what they accept as man's basic selfishness, of his natural determination to survive as an individual before all else. This they consider to be man's basic right, and they allow others to pursue that right without recrimination.

In large-scale societies such as our own, where members are individual beings rather than social beings, we rely on law for order. The absence of both a common law and a common belief would surely result in lack of any community of behavior; yet Ik society is not anarchical. One might well expect religion, then, to play a powerful role in Icien life, providing a source of unity.

The Ik, as may be expected, do not run true to form. When I arrived, there were still three ritual priests alive. From them and from the few other old people, I learned something of the Ik's belief and practice as they had been before their world was so terribly changed. There had been a powerful unity of belief in Didigwari—a sky god—and a body of ritual practice reinforcing secular behavior that was truly social.

Didigwari himself is too remote to be of much practical significance to the Ik. He created them and abandoned them and retreated into his domain somewhere in the sky. He never came down to earth, but the *abang* [ancestors] have all known life on earth; it is only against them that one can sin and only to them that one can turn for help, through the ritual priest.

While Morungole has no legends attached to it by the Ik, it nonetheless figures in their ideology and is in some ways regarded by them as sacred. I had noticed this by the almost reverential way in which they looked at it—none of the shrewd cunning and cold appraisal with which they regarded the rest of the world. When they talked about it, there was a different quality to their voices. They seemed incapable of talking about Morungole in any other way, which is probably why they talked about it so very seldom. Even that weasel Lomongin became gentle the only time he talked about it to me. He said, "If Atum and I were there, we would not argue. It is a good place." I asked if he meant that it was full of food. He said yes. "Then why do Ik never go there?" "They do go there." "But if hunting is good there, why not live there?" "We don't hunt there, we just go there." "Why?" "I told you, it is a good place." If I did not understand him, that was my fault; for once he was doing his best to communicate something to me. With others it was the same. All agreed that it was "a good place." One added, "That is the Place of God."

Lolim, the oldest and greatest of the ritual priests, was also the last. He was not much in demand any longer, but he was still held in awe, which means kept at a distance. Whenever he approached a *di*, people cleared a space for him, as far away from themselves as possible. The Ik rarely called on his services, for they had little to pay him with, and he had equally little to offer them. The main things they did try to get out of him were certain forms of medicine, both herbal and magical.

Lolim said that he had inherited his power from his father. His father had taught him well but could not give him the power to hear the *abang*—that had to come from the *abang* themselves. He had wanted his oldest son to inherit and had taught him everything he could. But his son, Longoli, was bad, and the *abang* refused to talk to him. They talked instead to his oldest daughter, bald Nangoli. But there soon came the time when all the Ik needed was food in their stomachs, and Lolim could not supply that. The time came when Lolim was too weak to go out and collect the medicines he needed. His children all refused to go except Nangoli, and then she was jailed for gathering in Kidepo Park.

Lolim became ill and had to be protected while eating the food I gave him. Then the children began openly ridiculing him and teasing him, dancing in front of him and kneeling down so that he would trip over them. His grandson used to creep up behind him and with a pair of hard sticks

drum a lively tattoo on the old man's bald head.

I fed him whenever I could, but often he did not want more than a bite. Once I found him rolled up in his protective ball, crying. He had had nothing to eat for four days and no water for two. He had asked his children, who all told him not to come near them.

The next day I saw him leaving Atum's village, where his son Longoli lived. Longoli swore that he had been giving his father food and was looking after him. Lolim was not shuffling away; it was almost a run, the run of a drunken man, staggering from side to side. I called to him, but he made no reply, just a kind of long, continuous and horrible moan. He had been to Longoli to beg him to let him into his compound because he knew he was going to die in a few hours, Longoli calmly told me afterward. Obviously Longoli could not do a thing like that: a man of Lolim's importance would have called for an enormous funeral feast. So he refused. Lolim begged Longoli then to open up Nangoli's *asak* for him so that he could die in *her* compound. But Longoli drove him out, and he died alone.

Atum pulled some stones over the body where it had fallen into a kind of hollow. I saw that the body must have lain parallel with the *oror*. Atum answered without waiting for the question: "He was lying looking up at Mount Meraniang."

Insofar as ritual survived at all, it could hardly be said to be religious, for it did little or nothing to bind Icien society together. But the question still remained: Did this lack of social behavior and communal ritual or religious expression mean that there was no community of belief?

Belief may manifest itself, at either the individual or the communal level, in what we call morality, when we behave according to certain principles supported by our belief even when it seems against our personal interest. When we call ourselves moral, however, we tend to ignore that ultimately our morality benefits us even as individuals, insofar as we are social individuals and live in a

society. In the absence of belief, law takes over and morality has little role. If there was such a thing as an Icien morality, I had not yet perceived it, though traces of a moral past remained. But it still remained a possibility, as did the existence of an unspoken, unmanifest belief that might yet reveal itself and provide a basis for the reintegration of society. I was somewhat encouraged in this hope by the unexpected flight of old Nangoli, widow of Amuarkuar.

When Nangoli returned and found her husband dead, she did an odd thing: she grieved. She tore down what was left of their home, uprooted the stockade, tore up whatever was growing in her little field. Then she fled with a few belongings.

Some weeks later I heard that she and her children had gone over to the Sudan and built a village there. This migration was so unusual that I decided to see whether this runaway village was different.

Lojieri led the way, and Atum came along. One long day's trek got us there. Lojieri pulled part of the brush fence aside, and we went in and wandered around. He and Atum looked inside all the huts, and Lojieri helped himself to tobacco from one and water from another. Surprises were coming thick and fast. That households should be left open and untended with such wealth inside . . . That there should have been such wealth, for as well as tobacco and jars of water there were baskets of food, and meat was drying on racks. There were half a dozen or so compounds, but they were separated from each other only by a short line of sticks and brush. It was a village, and these were homes, the first and last I was to see.

The dusk had already fallen, and Nangoli came in with her children and grandchildren. They had heard us and came in with warm welcomes. There was no hunger here, and in a very short time each kitchen hearth had a pot of food cooking. Then we sat around the central fire and talked until late, and it was another universe.

There was no talk of "how much better it is here than there"; talk revolved around what had happened on the hunt that day. Loron was lying on the ground in front of the fire as his mother made gentle fun of him. His wife, Kinimei, whom I had never seen even speak to him at Pirre, put a bowl of fresh-cooked berries and fruit in front of him. It was all like a nightmare rather than a fantasy, for it made the reality of Pirre seem all the more frightening.

The unpleasantness of returning was somewhat alleviated by Atum's suffering on the way up the stony trail. Several times he slipped, which made Lojieri and me laugh. It was a pleasure to move rapidly ahead and leave Atum gasping behind so that we could be sitting up on the *di* when he finally appeared and could laugh at his discomfort.

The days of drought wore on into weeks and months and, like everyone else, I became rather bored with sickness and death. I survived rather as did the young adults, by diligent attention to my own needs while ignoring those of others.

More and more it was only the young who could go far from the village as hunger became starvation. Famine relief had been initiated down at Kasile, and those fit enough to make the trip set off. When they came back, the contrast between them and the others was that between life and death. Villages were villages of the dead and dying, and there was little difference between the two. People crawled rather than walked. After a few feet some would lie down to rest, but they could not be sure of ever being able to sit up again, so they mostly stayed upright until they reached their destination. They were going nowhere, these semianimate bags of skin and bone; they just wanted to be with others, and they stopped whenever they met. Perhaps it was the most important demonstration of sociality I ever saw among the Ik. Once they met, they neither spoke nor did anything together.

Early one morning, before dawn, the village moved. In the midst of a hive of activity were the aged and crippled, soon to be abandoned, in danger of being trampled but seemingly unaware of it. Lolim's widow, Lo'ono, whom I had never seen before, also had been abandoned and had tried to make her way down the mountainside. But she was totally blind and had tripped and rolled to the bottom of the *oror a pirre'i;* there she lay on her back, her legs and arms thrashing feebly, while a little crowd laughed.

At this time a colleague was with me. He kept the others away while I ran to get medicine and food and water, for Lo'ono was obviously near dead from hunger and thirst as well as from the fall. We treated her and fed her and asked her to come back with us. But she asked us to point her in the direction of her son's new village. I said I did not think she would get much of a welcome there, and she replied that she knew it but wanted to be near him when she died. So we gave her more food, put her stick in her hand and pointed her the right way. She suddenly cried. She was crying, she said, because we had reminded her that there had been a time when people had helped each other, when people had been kind and good. Still crying, she set off.

The Ik up to this point had been tolerant of my activities, but all this was too much. They said that what we were doing was wrong. Food and medicine were for the living, not the dead. I thought of Lo'ono. And I thought of other old people who had joined in the merriment when they had been teased or had a precious morsel of food taken from their mouths. They knew that it was silly of them to expect to go on living, and, having watched others, they knew that the spectacle really was quite funny. So they joined in the laughter. Perhaps if we had left Lo'ono, she would have died laughing. But we prolonged her misery for no more than a few brief days. Even worse, we reminded her of when things had been different, of days when children had cared for parents and parents for children. She was already dead, and we made her unhappy as well. At the time I was sure we were right, doing the only "human" thing. In a way we *were*—we were making life more comfortable for ourselves. But now I wonder if the Ik way was not right, if I too should not have laughed as Lo'ono flapped about, then left her to die.

Ngorok was a man at 12. Lomer, his older brother, at 15 was showing signs of strain; when he was carrying a load, his face took on a curious expression of pain that was no physical pain. Giriko, at 25 was 40, Atum at 40 was 65, and the very oldest, perhaps a bare 50, were centenarians. And I, at 40, was younger than any of them, for I still enjoyed life, which they had learned was not "adult" when they were 3. But they retained their will to survive and so offered grudging respect to those who had survived for long.

Even in the teasing of the old there was a glimmer of hope. It denoted a certain intimacy that did not exist between adjacent generations. This is quite common in small-scale societies. The very old and the very young look at each other as representing the future and the past. To the child, the aged represent a world that existed before their own birth and the unknown world to come.

And now that all the old are dead, what is left? Every Ik who is old today was thrown out at three and has survived, and in consequence has thrown his own children out and knows that they will not help him in his old age any more than he helped his parents. The system has turned one full cycle and is now self-perpetuating; it has eradicated what we know as "humanity" and has turned the world into a chilly void where man does not seem to care even for himself, but survives. Yet into this hideous world Nangoli and her family quietly returned because they could not bear to be alone.

For the moment abandoning the very old and the very young, the Ik as a whole must be searched for one last lingering trace of humanity. They appear to have disposed of virtually all the qualities that we normally think of as differentiating us from other primates, yet they survive without seeming to be greatly different from ourselves in terms of behavior.

Their behavior is more extreme, for we do not start throwing our children out until kindergarten. We have shifted responsibility from family to state, the Ik have shifted it to the individual.

It has been claimed that human beings are capable of love and, indeed, are dependent upon it for survival and sanity. The Ik offer us an opportunity for testing this cherished notion that love is essential to survival. If it is, the Ik should have it.

Love in human relationships implies mutuality, a willingness to sacrifice the self that springs from a consciousness of identity. This seems to bring us back to the Ik, for it implies that love is self-oriented, that even the supreme sacrifice of one's life is no more than selfishness, for the victim feels amply rewarded by the pleasure he feels in making the sacrifice. The Ik, however, do not value emotion above survival, and they are without love.

But I kept looking, for it was the one thing that could fill the void their survival tactics had created; and if love was not there in some form, it meant that for humanity love is not a necessity at all, but a luxury or an illusion. And if it was not among the Ik, it meant that mankind can lose it.

The only possibility for any discovery of love lay in the realm of interpersonal relationships. But they were, each one, simply alone, and seemingly content to be alone. It was this acceptance of individual isolation that made love almost impossible. Contact, when made, was usually for a specific practical purpose having to do with food and the filling of a stomach, a single stomach. Such contacts did not have anything like the permanence or duration required to develop a situation in which love was possible.

The isolation that made love impossible, however, was not completely proof against loneliness. I no longer noticed normal behavior, such as the way people ate, running as they gobbled, so as to have it all for themselves. But I did notice that when someone was making twine or straightening a spear shaft, the focus of attention for the spectators was not the person but the action. If they were caught watching by the one being watched and their eyes met, the reaction was a sharp retreat on both sides.

When the rains failed for the second year running, I knew that the Ik as a society were almost certainly finished and that the monster they had created in its place, that passionless, feelingless association of individuals, would spread like a fungus, contaminating all it touched. When I left, I too had been contaminated. I was not upset when I said good-bye to old Loiangorok. I told him I had left a sack of *posho* [ground corn meal] with the police for him, and I said I would send money for more when that ran out. He dragged himself slowly toward the *di* every day, and he always clutched a knife. When he got there, or as far as he could, he squatted down and whittled at some wood, thus proving that he was still alive and able to do things. The *posho* was enough to last him for months, but I felt no emotion when I estimated that he would last one month, even with the *posho* in the hands of the police. I underestimated his son, who within two days had persuaded the police that it would save a lot of bother if he looked after the *posho*. I heard later that Loiangorok died of starvation within two weeks.

So, I departed with a kind of forced gaiety, feeling that I should be glad to be gone but having forgotten how to be glad. I certainly was not thinking of returning within a year, but I did. The following spring I heard that rain had come at last and that the fields of the Ik had never looked so prosperous, nor the country so green and fertile. A few months away had refreshed me, and I wondered if my conclusions had not been excessively pessimistic. So, early that summer, I set off to be present for the first harvests in three years.

I was not surprised too much when two days after my arrival and installation at the police post I found Logwara, the blind man, lying on the roadside bleeding, while a hundred yards up other Ik were squabbling over the body of a hyena. Logwara had tried to get there ahead of the others to grab the meat and had been trampled on.

First I looked at the villages. The lush outer covering concealed an inner decay. All the villages were like this to some extent, except for Lokelea's. There the tomatoes and pumpkins were carefully pruned and cleaned, so that the fruits were larger and healthier. In what had been my own compound the shade trees had been cut down for firewood, and the lovely hanging nests of the weaver birds were gone.

The fields were even more desolate. Every field without exception had yielded in abundance, and it was a new sensation to have vision cut off by thick crops. But every crop was rotting from sheer neglect.

The Ik said that they had no need to bother guarding the fields. There was so much food they could never eat it all, so why not let the birds and baboons take some? The Ik had full bellies; they were good. The *di* at Atum's village was much the same as usual, people sitting or lying about. People were still stealing from each other's fields, and nobody thought of saving for the future.

It was obvious that nothing had really changed due to the sudden glut of food except that interpersonal relationships had deteriorated still further and that Icien individualism had heightened beyond what I thought even Ik to be capable of.

The Ik had faced a conscious choice between being humans and being parasites and had chosen the latter. When they saw their fields come alive, they were confronted with a problem. If they reaped the harvest, they would have to store grain for eating and planting, and every Ik knew that trying to store anything was a waste of time. Further, if they made their fields look too promising, the government would stop famine relief. So the Ik let their fields rot and continued to draw famine relief.

The Ik were not starving any longer; the old and infirm had all died the previous year, and the younger survivors were doing quite well. But the famine relief was administered in a way that was little short of criminal. As before, only the young and well were able to get down from Pirre to collect the relief; they were given relief for those who could not come and told to take it back. But they never did—they ate it themselves.

The facts are there, though those that can be read here form but a fraction of what one person was able to gather in under two years. There can be no mistaking the direction in which those facts point, and that is the most important thing of all, for it may affect the rest of mankind as it has affected the Ik. The Ik have "progressed," one might say, since the change that has come to them came with the advent of civilization to Africa. They have made of a world that was alive a world that is dead—a cold, dispassionate world that is without ugliness because it is without beauty, without hate because it is without love, and without any realization of truth even, because it simply is. And the symptoms of change in our own society indicate that we are heading in the same direction.

Those values we cherish so highly may indeed be basic to human society but not to humanity, and that means that the Ik show that society itself is not indispensable for man's survival and that man is capable of associating for purposes of survival without being social. The Ik have replaced human society with a mere survival system that does not take human emotion into account. As yet the system if imperfect, for although survival is assured, it is at a minimal level and there is still competition between individuals. With our intellectual sophistication and advanced technology we should be able to perfect the system and eliminate competition, guaranteeing survival for a given number of years for all, reducing the demands made upon us by a social system, abolishing desire and consequently that ever-present and vital gap between desire and achievement, treating us, in a word, as individuals with one basic individual right—the right to survive.

Such interaction as there is within this system is one of mutual exploitation. That is how it already is with the Ik. In our own world the mainstays of a society based on a truly social sense of mutuality are breaking down, indicating that perhaps society as we know it has outworn its usefulness and that by clinging to an outworn system we are bringing about our own destruction. Family, economy, government and religion, the basic categories of social activity and behavior, no longer create any sense of social unity involving a shared and mutual responsibility among all members of our society. At best they enable the individual to survive as an individual. It is the world of the individual, as is the world of the Ik.

The sorry state of society in the civilized world today is in large measure due to the fact that social change has not kept up with technological change. This mad, senseless, unthinking commitment to technological change that we call progress may be sufficient to exterminate the human race in a very short time even without the assistance of nuclear warfare. But since we have already become individualized and desocialized, we say that extermination will not come in our time, which shows about as much sense of family devotion as one might expect from the Ik.

Even supposing that we can avert nuclear holocaust or the almost universal famine that may be expected if population keeps expanding and pollution remains unchecked, what will be the cost if not the same already paid by the Ik? They too were driven by the need to survive, and they succeeded at the cost of their humanity. We are already beginning to pay the same price, but we not only still have the choice (though we may not have the will or courage to make it), we also have the intellectual and technological ability to avert an Icien end. Any change as radical as will be necessary is not likely to bring material benefits to the present generation, but only then will there be a future.

The Ik teach us that our much vaunted human values are not inherent in humanity at all but are associated only with a particular form of survival called society and that all, even society itself, are luxuries that can be dispensed with. That does not make them any less wonderful, and if man has any greatness, it is surely in his ability to maintain these values, even shortening an already pitifully short life rather than sacrifice his humanity. But that too involves choice, and the Ik teach us that man can lose the will to make it. That is the point at which there is an end to truth, to goodness and to beauty, an end to the struggle for their achievement, which gives life to the individual and strength and meaning to society. The Ik have relinquished all luxury in the name of individual survival, and they live on as a people without life, without passion, beyond humanity. We pursue those trivial, idiotic technological encumbrances, and all the time we are losing our potential for social rather than individual survival, for hating as well as loving, losing perhaps our last chance to enjoy life with all the passion that is our nature.

Tribal wisdom

Is it too late for us to reclaim the benefits of tribal living?

David Maybury-Lewis

Tribal people hold endless fascination for us moderns. We imagine them as exotics trapped in a lyrical past, or as charming anachronisms embarking on the inevitable course toward modernity. What few of us realize is that tribal peoples have not tried (and failed) to be like us, but have actually chosen to live differently. It is critical that we examine the roads they took that we did not; only then can we get a clear insight into the choices we ourselves make and the price we pay for them—alienation, loneliness, disintegrating families, ecological destruction, spiritual famishment. Only then can we consider the possibility of modifying some of those choices to enrich our lives.

In studying tribal societies, as I have for 30 years, we learn that there is no single "tribal" way of life—I use the word here as a kind of shorthand to refer to small-scale, preindustrial societies that live in comparative isolation and manage their affairs without a central authority such as the state. But however diverse, such societies do share certain characteristics that make them different from "modern" societies. By studying the dramatic contrasts between these two kinds of societies, we see vividly the consequences of modernization and industrialization. Modernization has changed our thinking about every facet of our lives, from family relationships to spirituality to our importance as individuals. Has ours been the road best traveled?

Strange relations

The heart of the difference between the modern world and the traditional one is that in traditional societies people are a valuable resource and the interrelations between them are carefully tended; in modern society things are the valuables and people are all too often treated as disposable.

In the modern world we shroud our interdependency in an ideology of independence. We focus on individuals, going it alone in the economic sphere, rather than persons, interconnected in the social sphere. As French anthropologist Marcel Mauss put it, "It is our Western societies that have recently turned man into an economic animal." What happened?

A truly revolutionary change—a social revolution centering on the rights of the individual—swept Western Europe during the Renaissance and eventually came to dominate and define the modern world. While traditional societies had denounced individualism as anti-social, in Western Europe a belief in the rights and dignity of the individual slowly came to be regarded as the most important aspect of society itself.

The glorification of the individual, this focus on the dignity and rights of the individual, this severing of the obligations to kin and community that support and constrain the individual in traditional societies—all this was the sociological equivalent of splitting the atom. It unleashed the human energy and creativity that enabled people to make extraordinary technical advances and to accumulate undreamed-of wealth.

But we have paid a price for our success. The ever-expanding modern economy is a driven economy, one that survives by creating new needs so that people will consume more. Ideally, under the mechanics of this system, people should have unlimited needs so that the economy can expand forever, and advertising exists to convince them of just that.

The driven economy is accompanied by a restless and driven society. In the United States, for example, the educational system teaches children to be competitive and tries to instill in them the hunger for personal achievement. As adults, the most driven people are rewarded by status. Other human capabilities—for kindness, generosity, patience, tolerance, cooperation, compassion—all the qualities one might wish for in one's family and friends, are literally undervalued: Any job that requires such talents usually has poor pay and low prestige.

The tendency of modern society to isolate the individual is nowhere more clearly evident than in the modern family. In the West we speak of young people growing up, leaving their parents, and "starting a family." To most of the world, including parts of Europe, this notion seems strange. Individuals do not start families, they are born into them and stay in them until death or even beyond. In those societies you cannot leave your family without becoming a social misfit, a person of no account.

When the modern system works, it provides a marvelous release for individual creativity and emotion; when it does not, it causes a lot of personal pain and social stress. It is, characteristically, an optimistic system, hoping for and betting on the best. In contrast, traditional societies have settled for more cautious systems, designed to make life tolerable and to avoid the worst. Americans, in their version of the modern family, are free to be themselves at the risk of ultimate loneliness. In traditional family systems the individual may be suffocated but is never unsupported. Is there a middle way?

Finding that middle way is not a problem that tribal societies have to face, at least not unless they find

In traditional societies, people are valuable; in modern society, things are the valuables.

their way of life overwhelmed by the outside world. They normally get on with the business of bringing up children against a background of consensus about what should be done and how, which means that they can also be more relaxed about who does the bringing up. Children may spend as much time with other adults as they do with their parents, or, as in the Xavante tribe of central Brazil, they may wander around in a flock that is vaguely supervised by whichever adults happen to be nearby. As soon as Xavante babies are old enough to toddle, they attach themselves to one of the eddies of children that come and go in the village. There they are socialized by their peers. The older kids keep an eye on the younger ones and teach them their place in the pecking order. Of course there are squabbles and scraps, and one often sees a little child who has gotten the worst of it wobbling home and yelling furiously. The child's parents never do what parents in our society often do—go out and remonstrate with the children in an attempt to impose some kind of adult justice (often leaving the children with a burning sense of unfairness). Instead they simply comfort the child and let her return to the fold as soon as her bruised knee or battered ego permits. At the same time, there is never any bullying among the Xavante children who are left to police themselves.

The Xavante system represents an informal dilution of parents' everyday responsibilities. In many societies these responsibilities are formally transferred to other relatives. In the Pacific Islands, for example, it is quite common for children to be raised by their parents' kin. Among the Trobriand Islanders, this is seen as useful for the child, since it expands his or her network of active kin relationships without severing ties to the biological parents. If children are unhappy, they can return to their true parents. If they are contented, they remain with their adoptive parents until adulthood.

Tribal societies also differ from the modern in their approach to raising teenagers. The tribal transition to maturity is made cleanly and is marked with great ceremony. In Western societies families dither over their often resentful young, suggesting that they may be old enough but not yet mature enough, mature enough but not yet secure enough, equivocating and putting adolescents through an obstacle course that keeps being prolonged.

Tribal initiation rites have always held a special interest for outside observers, who have been fascinated by their exotic and especially by their sexual aspects. It is the pain and terror of such initiations that make the deepest impression, and these are most frequently inflicted on boys, who are in the process of being taken out of the women's world and brought into that of the men. Some Australian Aboriginal groups peel the penis like a banana and cut into the flesh beneath the foreskin. Some African groups cut the face and forehead of the initiate in such a way as to leave deep scars.

Circumcision is, of course, the commonest of all initiation procedures. Its effect on the boy is, however, intensified in some places by an elaborate concern with his fortitude during the operation. The Maasai of East Africa, whose *moran* or warriors are world famous as epitomes of courage and bravado, closely watch a boy who is being circumcised for the slightest sign of cowardice. Even an involuntary twitch could make him an object of condemnation and scorn.

The tribal initiation gives girls a strong sense of the powers of women.

Initiation rituals are intended to provoke anxiety. They act out the death and rebirth of the initiate. His old self dies, and while he is in limbo he learns the mysteries of his society—instruction that is enhanced by fear and deprivation and by the atmosphere of awe that his teachers seek to create. In some societies that atmosphere is enhanced by the fact that the teachers are anonymous, masked figures representing the spirits. The lesson is often inscribed unforgettably on his body as well as in his mind. Later (the full cycle of ceremonies may last weeks or even months) he is reborn as an adult, often literally crawling between the legs of his sponsor to be reborn of man into the world of men.

Girls' initiation ceremonies are as dramatically marked in some societies as those of boys. Audrey Richards' account of the *chisungu,* a month-long initiation ceremony among the Bemba of Zambia, describes the complex ritual that does not so much add to the girl's practical knowledge as inculcate certain attitudes— a respect for age, for senior women and men, for the mystical bonds between husband and wife, for what the Bemba believe to be the dangerous potentials of sex, fire, and blood. The initiate learns the secret names of things and the songs and dances known only to women. She is incorporated into the group of women who form her immediate community, since this is a society that traces descent in the female line and a husband moves to his wife's village when they marry. Western writers tend to assume that it is more important for boys to undergo separation from their mothers as they mature than it is for girls. But the Bemba stress that mothers must surrender their daughters in the *chisungu* to the community at large (and to the venerable mistress of ceremonies in particular) as part of a process through which they will eventually gain sons-in-law.

The ceremony Richards observed for the initiation of three girls included 18 separate events, some 40 different pottery models (shaped for the occasion and destroyed immediately afterward), nearly a hundred songs, and numerous wall paintings and dances, all used to instruct the girls in their new status. All of this represents a large investment of time and resources. The initiation gives girls a strong sense of the solidarity and powers of women in a society that also stresses male authority and female submissiveness.

Ever since the influential work of Margaret Mead, there has been a tendency in the West to assume that, if growing up is less stressful in tribal societies, it is because they are less puritanical about sex. The modern world has, however, undergone a sexual revolution since Mead was writing in the 1930s and 1940s, and it does not seem to have made growing up much easier. I think that, in our preoccupation with sex, we miss the point. Take the case of tribal initiations. They not only make it clear to the initiates (and to the world at large) that they are now mature enough to have sex and to have children; the clarity also serves to enable the individual to move with a fair degree of certainty through clearly demarcated stages of life.

A moral economy
Since earliest times, the exchange of gifts has been the central mechanism through which human beings relate to one another. The reason is that the essence of a gift is obligation. A person who gives a gift compels the recipient either to make a return gift or to reciprocate in some other way. Obligation affects the givers as well. It is not entirely up to them whether or when to bestow a gift. Even in the modern world, which prides itself on its pragmatism, people are expected to give gifts on certain occasions—at weddings, at childbirth, at Christmas, and so on. People are expected to invite others to receive food and drink in their houses and those so invited are expected to return the favor.

In traditional societies, it is gifts that bond people to one another and make society work. It follows that in such societies a rich person is not somebody who accumulates wealth in money and goods but rather somebody who has a large network of people beholden to him. Such networks are the instrument through which prominent people can demonstrate their prestige. They are also the safety net that sees an individual through the crises of life.

In modern societies these networks have shrunk, just as the family continues to shrink. There are fewer and fewer people to whom we feel obligated and, more ominously, fewer and fewer who feel obligated to us. When we think of a safety net, when our politicians speak of it, we refer to arrangements made by abstract entities— the state, the corporation, the insurance company, the pension fund—entities we would not dream of giving presents to; entities we hope will provide for us (and fear they will not).

Traditional societies operate a moral economy, that is, an economy permeated by personal and moral considerations. In such a system, exchanges of goods in the "market" are not divorced from the personal relationships between those who exchange. On the contrary, the exchanges define those relationships. People who engage in such transactions select exchange partners who display integrity and reliability so that they can go back to them again and again. Even when cash enters such an economy, it does not automatically transform it. People still look for just prices, not bargain prices, and the system depends on trust and interdependence. In traditional societies the motto is "seller beware," for a person who gouges or shortchanges will become a moral outcast, excluded from social interaction with other people.

An ecology of mind
The sense of disconnection so characteristic of modern life affects not only the relations between people but equally importantly the relations between people and their environment. As a result, we may be gradually making the planet uninhabitable. The globe is warming up and is increasingly polluted. We cannot take fresh air or clean water for granted anymore. Even our vast oceans are starting to choke on human garbage. The rain forests are burning. The ozone layer is being depleted at rates that constantly exceed our estimates.

How have we come to this? A hundred years ago science seemed to hold such promising possibilities. But the scientific advances of the 19th century were built

Gift exchanges form the safety net that sees an individual through life's crises.

on the notion that human beings would master nature and make it produce more easily and plentifully for them. Medieval Christianity also taught that human beings, although they might be sinners, were created in God's image to have dominion over this earth. Whether human dominion was guaranteed by the Bible or by science, the result was the same—the natural world was ours to exploit.

Tribal societies, by contrast, have always had a strong sense of the interconnectedness of things on this earth and beyond. For example, human beings have, for the greater part of the history of our species on this earth, lived by hunting and gathering. Yet peoples who lived by hunting and gathering did not—and do not to this day—consider themselves the lords of creation. On the contrary, they are more likely to believe in (and work hard to maintain) a kind of reciprocity between human beings and the species they are obliged to hunt for food.

The reciprocity between hunter and hunted is elaborately expressed in the ideas of the Makuna Indians of southeastern Colombia. The Makuna believe that human beings, animals, and all of nature are parts of the same One. Their ancestors were fish people who came ashore along the rivers and turned into people. Out of their bodies or by their actions these ancestors created everything in the world, the hills and forests, the animals and the people. They carved out river valleys by pushing their sacred musical instruments in front of them.

People, animals, and fish all share the same spiritual essence and so, the Makuna say, animals and fish live in their own communities, which are just like human communities. They have their chiefs, their shamans, their dance houses, birth houses, and "waking up houses" (places where they originally came into being as species). They have their songs and dances and their material possessions. Above all, animals and fish are just like humans because they wear ritual ornaments, consume spirit foods—coca, snuff, and the hallucinogenic brew called *yage*—and use the sacred *yurupari* instruments in their ceremonies. When shamans blow over coca, snuff, and other spirit foods during human ceremonies, they are offering them to the animal people. When human beings dance in this world, the shaman invites the animal people to dance in theirs. If humans do not dance and shamans do not offer spirit food to the animal people, the animals will die out and there will be no more game left in this world.

Thus when the fish are spawning, they are actually dancing in their birth houses. That is why it is particularly dangerous to eat fish that have been caught at the spawning places, for then one eats a person who is ceremonially painted and in full dance regalia. A human being who does this or enters a fish house by mistake will sicken and die, for his soul will be carried away to the houses of the fish people.

Tribal people maintain a reciprocity with the species they must hunt for food.

It is clear that Makuna beliefs have specific ecological consequences. The sacredness of salt licks and fish-spawning places, the careful reciprocity between humans and their fellow animals and fish, all mediated by respected shamans, guarantee that the Makuna manage their environment and do not plunder it. The Swedish anthropologist Kaj Arhem, an authority on the Makuna, describes their ecological practices and cosmological speculations as an "ecosophy," where the radical division between nature and culture, humans and animals—so characteristic of Western thought—dissolves.

Arhem suggests that we need an ecosophy of our own, imbued with moral commitment and emotional power, if we are to protect the resources on which we depend and ensure not only our own survival but also that of our fellow creatures on this earth.

We, on the other hand, tend to forget our environment except when we want to extract wealth from it or use it as the backdrop for a scenic expedition. Then we take what we want. There is no compact, none of the reciprocity so characteristic of tribal societies. For the most part we mine the earth and leave it, for we do not feel we belong to it. It belongs to us. This rootlessness and the waste that goes with it are particularly shocking to traditional societies.

The Indians of the western United States were outraged by the way in which the invaders of their territories squandered the resources that they themselves used so sparingly. The Indians on the plains lived off the buffalo, killing only as many as they needed and using every bit of the dead animals. They ate the meat, made tents and clothes from the hides, and used the bones to make arrow straighteners, bows, mallets, even splints for setting fractures. They made butter from the marrow fat and cords from the sinews. When the white buffalo hunters came, it was more than an invasion. It was a sacrilege. These men slaughtered the herds with their powerful rifles, often taking only the tongue to eat and leaving the rest of the animal to rot.

The deep sadness of the Indians over this slaughter was expressed in a speech attributed to Chief Seattle, after whom the city of Seattle is named, believed to have been delivered in 1854 to an assembly of tribes preparing to sign away their lands under duress to the white man. Some contend the speech was actually written by a Texas speechwriter in 1971. Whatever their origin, these moving words convey an environmental and spiritual ethic that most tribal people share. They speak as much to us about our own predicament as they did to Chief Seattle's fellow chiefs about their defeated civilization. "What is man without the beasts?" he asked. "If all the beasts were gone, man would die from a great loneliness of spirit. For whatever happens to the beasts, soon happens to man. All things are connected. . . . We know that the white man does not understand our ways. One portion of the land is the same to him as the next, for he is a stranger who comes in the night and takes from the land whatever he needs. The earth is not his brother, but his enemy, and when he has conquered it, he moves on. He leaves his fathers' graves behind, and he does not care. He kidnaps the earth from his children. He does not care. His fathers' graves and his children's birthright are forgotten. He treats his mother, the earth, and his brother, the sky, as things to be bought, plundered, sold like sheep or bright beads. His appetite will devour the earth and leave behind only a desert."

Touching the timeless

Modern society is intensely secular. Even those who regret this admit it. Social theorists tend to assume that modernization is itself a process of secularization that has not only undermined people's religious beliefs but has also deprived them of their spirituality. In the industrial nations of the West many of the people who believe in God do not expect to come into close contact with the divine, except after death—and some of them are not too sure about it even then.

Indeed, it seems that those who live in the secular and industrialized West are already searching for ways to fill the vacuum in their lives left by "organized" religion and the numbing delights of mass society. We live in a world that prides itself on its modernity yet is hungry for wholeness, hungry for meaning. At the same time it is a world that marginalizes the very impulses that might fill this void. The pilgrimage toward the divine, the openness to knowledge that transcends ordinary experience, the very idea of feeling at one with the universe are impulses we tolerate only at the fringes of our society.

It seems that we denigrate our capacity to dream and so condemn ourselves to live in a disenchanted world. Shorn of the knowledge that we are part of something greater than ourselves, we also lose the sense of responsibility that comes with it. It is this connectedness that tribal societies cherish. Yet for modern society, this is a bond we cannot bring ourselves to seek. But if we do not listen to other traditions, do not even listen to our inner selves, then what will the future hold for our stunted and overconfident civilization?

The tightrope of power

Meanwhile, this civilization of ours, at once so powerful and so insecure, rolls like a juggernaut over societies that have explored the very solutions that might help us save ourselves. We do so in the name of progress, insisting all too often that we offer science, truth, plenty, and social order to peoples who lack these things. Yet the contrast between tribal societies and the centralized states that prey on them is not one of order and disorder, violence and peace. It is instead a contrast between societies in which no one has a monopoly on the legitimate use of force and others in which those rights are vested in a state. The 20th century has been one of the bloodiest in history, not only because of the wars between countries employing weapons of mass destruction but also because modern technology has been used by ruthless rulers to cow their own subjects. Hitler and Stalin are only the most notorious examples of dictators who directed violence against their own people in the name of the state. There are literally scores of shooting wars going on at the moment, most of them between states and their own subjects.

The state guarantees order, or is supposed to. Force, the monopoly of the government, is applied massively but, once the system is in place, relatively invisibly. Its victims are hidden in concentration camps or banished to Siberias. In many places today, the victims simply disappear.

It seems that people will often acquiesce in despotism for fear of anarchy. Recent history seems to indicate that the most advanced countries are more afraid of anarchy than they are of oppression. The Russians, whose whole history is a struggle to create order on the open steppes of Eurasia, have a fear of disorder (which they call *besporyadok*, the condition of not being "lined up") that has frequently led them to accept tyranny. At the other extreme, the United States, whose whole history is a determination to avoid despotism, allows more internal chaos than most other industrial nations. It values individual freedom to the point of allowing private citizens to own arsenals of weapons and puts up with a rate of interpersonal violence that would be considered catastrophic in other countries.

It seems that human beings are everywhere searching for the right balance between the mob and the dictator, between chaos and tyranny, between the individual and society. Industrial societies give a monopoly of power to the state in exchange for a guarantee of peace. We take this social order for granted to the extent that we tend to assume that there is anarchy and perpetual warfare in tribal societies. What we do not realize is that such societies are acutely conscious of the fragility of the social order and of the constant effort needed to maintain it. Paradoxically, the people who live in societies that do not have formal political institutions are more political than those who do since it is up to each individual to make sure that the system works, indeed to ensure that the system continues to exist at all. Tribal people avoid the perils of anarchy only through constant and unremitting effort.

Elijah Harper, an Ojibwa-Cree who is a member of parliament in the Canadian province of Manitoba, contrasted the democratic procedures of the native Canadians he represented with those of the Canadian government that was trying to push through a revision of Canada's constitution. The new constitution was designed to respond to Quebec's demand to be considered a distinct society within Canada, with appropriate protection for its own language and culture. Harper used parliamentary procedure to block the constitutional change, on the grounds that native Canadians had been asking for similar consideration for years without getting a hearing. A new round of discussions concerning the revision of Canada's constitution is now taking place and this time the rights of Canada's "first nations," the aboriginal peoples, are also on the agenda.

The Canadian crisis makes clear what is only dimly perceived in other countries, namely that the destiny of the majority in any state is intimately linked to the fate of its minorities. The failure of the first attempt to change their constitution has forced Canadians to think about what kind of society they want theirs to be. These are the same questions that the Aborigines are trying to put on the Australian agenda and that the Indians are forcing Brazilians to think about as they protest against the rape of Amazonian regions.

It is not only in authoritarian states that questions arise about how people within a state are allowed to go about their business. The dramatic events in Eastern Europe, however, have led some people to think so. Once the heavy hand of Communist dictatorship was lifted, the nations of Eastern Europe started to unravel. Old ethnic loyalties surfaced and ethnic rivalries threaten to dismember one nation after another. The problem in Eastern Europe is not that it is made up of more peoples than states, but rather that the states have not been successful in working out political solutions that could enable those peoples to live together amicably. But neither do democratic regimes find it easy to create more imaginative solutions that allow diverse groups of people to live together.

The reason for this failure is that such solutions require us to have a different idea of the state, a kind of new federalism which, after the manner of the League of the Iroquois, permits each people in the nation to keep its council fire alight. This requires more than rules; it requires commitment. The Great Law of the Iroquois was remarkable because it was a constitution that had the force of a religion. People were willing, indeed eager, to subscribe to it because they saw it and revered it as the source of peace. Is it too much to hope that in a world riven with ethnic conflict we might search for political solutions more energetically than we have in the past? That we will not continue to expect strong states to iron out ethnicity, even if it means wiping out the "ethnics"? A new federalism is in our own interest, for it offers the hope of peace and the prospect of justice. Nations that trample on the rights of the weak are likely to end up trampling on everybody's rights. As we wring our hands over the fate of tribal peoples in the modern world, we would do well to remember John Donne's words: "Never send to know for whom the bell tolls; it tolls for thee."

Serious consideration of tribal ways of life should lead us to think carefully and critically about our own. What would it take for us to try to live in harmony with nature or to rehumanize our economic systems? How can we mediate between the individual and the family, between genders and generations? Should we strive for a less fragmented view of physical reality or of our place in the scheme of things? These questions revolve around wholeness and harmony, around tolerance and pluralism. The answers are still emerging, but they too are variations on a grand theme that can be summed up in E. M. Forster's famous phrase: "Only connect." The project for the new millennium will be to re-energize civil society, the space between the state and the individual where those habits of the heart that socialize the individual and humanize the state flourish.

Socialization, Biology, Social Control, and Deviance

- Childhood and Influences on Personality and Behavior (Articles 10–12)
- Crime, Social Control, and Law Enforcement (Articles 13–15)

Belonging is as essential to human survival as breathing. Recent studies confirm the threat to health and well-being caused by social isolation. Learning how to belong is one of the most fundamental lessons of socialization; it is a lifelong process of adapting to others and learning what is the expected behavior in particular situations. Through contact with others, one gains self-knowledge. Socialization may take place in many contexts. The most basic socialization takes place in the family, but churches, schools, communities, the media, and workplaces also play major roles in the process.

This section contains articles that deal with the conditions of childhood and both the negative and positive socialization of children. In the first article, Elin McCoy reveals that parents were callous and indifferent toward children hundreds of years ago. Before the eighteenth century, many children were punished severely for trifling offenses, many died in their first year, and many spent little time with their parents.

The next article analyzes some of the factors that shape us. Many biological differences between males and females are identified in the article "Guns and Dolls." This article focuses on the impact of differential socialization on sex role differences.

Another major socializing influence on children is television. Richard Zoglin discusses the impact of television on children's development, including poorer school performance and violence. An average work year is 2,000 hours and the average child will spend 5,000 passive hours watching television before she or he begins school.

Crime is a leading concern of Americans and law enforcement efforts are being strengthened. Some zones in certain cities are almost completely lawless. News reports are filled with stories of murders. In the next article, "Crime Pays, But So Does Imprisonment," Morgan Reynolds contends that the high crime rate in the United States is caused by the very low average expected prison terms served for various crimes. When the costs of crime to the criminal rise, then the crime rate will drop significantly, because crime will no longer pay.

The last two articles focus on other actions that are problems of social control and, in their severe forms, are serious crimes. Anita Hill presents an overview of the problem of sexual harassment today. The problem is not well understood by most people, which adds to the problem. Finally, the social problems that most people have given up on are discussed and the solutions to drug use, teen pregnancy, and welfare is presented. Here is good news where bad news has dominated.

Looking Ahead: Challenge Questions

How can the ways in which children are socialized in America be improved?

Why is socialization a lifelong process?

What are the principal factors that make people what they are?

How are girls socialized differently from boys?

What traditional American norms are no longer widely honored?

What are some reasons for the increase of crime in the United States?

Unit 2

Childhood Through the Ages

Elin McCoy

Elin McCoy is the author of "The Incredible Year-Round Playbook" (Random House).

A gentleman-in-waiting and the nurse of little Comte de Marle often amused themselves tossing the swaddled infant back and forth across the sill of an open window. One day one of them failed to catch him, and the infant landed on a stone step and died.

The surgeon of the newborn Louis XIII cut the "fiber" under his tongue a few days after he was born, believing that if it remained uncut, Louis would be unable to suck properly and would eventually stutter.

These aren't atypical examples of child rearing in the past. Recent historical research indicates that for most of the past 2,500 years, childhood was a brief, grim period in most people's lives, especially when judged against contemporary views of child rearing.

A new field—family history.

Through a new field of historical research, known as family history, we now know that family life and childhood in the previous centuries were startlingly different from what most people, including historians, had imagined them to be. Scores of historians are currently probing such questions as: How were children treated in the past? What concept of childhood did people have in different centuries? How important were children to their parents? Is there such a thing as "instinctual" parental behavior? What do the prevailing child-rearing beliefs and practices of the past tell us about the political, social and psychological ideals of society? And what kind of adults resulted from such child-rearing practices?

"Family history is the most explosive field of history today," says Professor Lawrence Stone—director of Princeton University's Shelby Cullom Davis Center for Historical Studies—whose 1977 book, *The Family, Sex and Marriage in England 1500–1800,* came out in an abridged paperback last year. "In the 1930s only about 10 scholarly books and articles on the family and childhood in history were published each year, but, incredibly, between 1971 and 1976 over 900 important books and articles were published on that subject, just covering America, England, and France." Two scholarly journals devoted to the subject were also started in the 1970s.

Why, suddenly, have so many historians focused on the family? "A whole series of contemporary anxieties has contributed to this new interest," explains Professor Stone. "General anxiety about the state of the family and whether it's breaking down, concern about the rising divorce rate, anxieties about current permissiveness in raising children, and concern about what effects women's liberation will have on children, the family, and society. And underlying all of these anxieties are two questions: Are we really doing so badly? Was it better in the past?"

In addition, two other trends in historical research have focused attention on childhood and the family. The first is social historians' growing interest in the daily lives of ordinary people in history, which has meant a greater concern with children, parenting, marriage, disease, death, and aging. The second is historians' recent efforts to employ psychological concepts as a research tool in order to understand human motivations and experiences in the past.

Although all family historians agree that child-rearing patterns influence what happens in history, they disagree about how much and in what precise ways the treatment of children shapes history. Some researchers in the field, like Lloyd deMause, founder of *The Journal of Psychohistory: A Quarterly Journal of Childhood and Psychohistory,* go so far as to say that, in deMause's words, "child-rearing practices have been *the* central force for change in history." Along with some other psychohistorians, deMause believes that "if you want to understand the causes of historical events like the growth of Nazism, you have to look at how the children who became Nazis as adults were treated as children." But many scholars have reservations about attributing the character of a society solely to the relations between parents and children, pointing out that these relations must be understood in the context of the society as a whole and that such factors as economics must also be taken into account.

Surprising discoveries.

Family historians have recently exploded many long-standing myths about childhood and the nature of the family throughout history. It's now clear that the functions and structure of the family have changed continuously over the years and that a variety of family types coexisted in each historical period in different regions and classes. Scholars have found, surprisingly, that the prevailing family mode in America today (the small nuclear family of parents and children living apart from other relatives)—a structure that is under much attack—is not as new to our culture as they had previously thought. Even as long ago as thirteenth-century England, as many as half of all families consisted of only a mother and/or father and two to three children. In fact, the large, loving extended families we tend to picture, with eight to ten children and several generations of relatives living under the same roof, were more the exception than the rule, even in Colonial America.

According to Professor Tamara Hareven—founder and head of the first History of the Family program in the country, at Clark University in Worcester, Massachusetts, and founding editor of the *Journal of Family History*—one of the great surprises for today's historians was "finding out that in the past, the concept of childhood and children was not the same in all centuries, classes, and countries. While the middle classes were 'discovering' childhood and becoming interested in children" she explains, "the working classes still regarded children as small adults with the same responsibilities. And in the past, childhood as we know it lasted for a much shorter time." In medieval England, for example, children as young as seven were sent to live in other households as apprentices, and for peasant children, childhood was even briefer—they joined their parents to work in the fields as soon as they could.

Infants were regarded in medieval times as unimportant, unformed animals, in the sixteenth century as "exasperating parasites," and even as late as the seventeenth century they were not seen as individuals with their own identities. Children were considered interchangeable, and frequently were given the same name as an older sibling who had died. Small children were not even viewed as interesting; Montaigne, the French essayist, summed up the prevailing attitudes of a few hundred years ago when he dismissed infants as having "neither movement in the soul, nor recognizable form in the body by which they could render themselves lovable."

Scholars tell us that infants and small children were important only insofar as they could benefit their parents. Considered possessions with no individual rights, they were used to further adult aims, and they ended up as security for debts, as ways of increasing property holdings through arranged marriages, as political hostages, and even as slaves sold for profit.

Infancy in the past.

Throughout history, parents' treatment of infants and very small children has been characterized by psychological coldness and physical brutality that horrify most of us today. But this behavior becomes at least comprehensible when we realize some of the conditions of people's lives. The physical realities of life were oppressive. And there were severe parental limitations as well: in addition to being influenced by unscientific medical knowledge and religious views about the nature of man, most adults had to concentrate so much of their energy on mere survival that they had little time to care for or worry about infants and small children. Abusive and violent behavior was common among adults, and, therefore, not looked on with disapproval when it appeared in the treatment of children.

In view of the following facts, consider what your experience as a parent and your child's experience as an infant would have been if you had lived prior to the eighteenth century.

Your child probably wouldn't have been wanted. Lack of birth control meant that having children was not a choice. For poverty-stricken peasants, an infant meant another mouth to feed—and food was precious—as well as interference with the mother's role as a worker whose contribution was necessary to the family's ability to survive. In all classes, the high risk of maternal mortality made the birth of a child a traumatic event. Even in the relatively healthy conditions enjoyed by the inhabitants of Plymouth Colony, 20 percent of women died from causes related to childbirth (compared with under 1 percent today), and in seventeenth-century England and France, the rates were much higher. It's no wonder that most children were probably unwanted. In fact, Professor Stone suggests that the availability of birth control was probably one of the necessary conditions for the increase in affection for children that began in England and America in the eighteenth century.

Your infant would have had a good chance of dying before his or her first birthday. In medieval England and seventeenth-century France, for example, between 20 and 50 percent of all infants died within the first year after birth. Complications of childbirth, prematurity, diseases such as smallpox and the plague, and generally unsanitary living conditions, as well as such customs as baptism in icy water in freezing churches, took a heavy toll among vulnerable newborns. America was healthier for infants—in Plymouth Colony, infant mortality was only 10 to 15 percent (which is still ten times higher than it is in America today). The likelihood that one's infants would die discouraged parents from investing much affection or interest in them and from regarding them as special, unique individuals until it appeared more certain that they might live to adulthood.

Illegitimate infants and infants of poverty-stricken parents (and parents who felt they already had enough children) were often the victims of infanticide through deliberate murder, abandonment, or neglect. In ancient Greece, for example, infants who seemed sickly or didn't have a perfect shape or cried too much or too little were "exposed," or abandoned to die, a decision that was made by the father shortly after birth. In mid-eighteenth-century England, so many babies—both legitimate and illegitimate—were abandoned to die in the streets of cities and towns that the first foundling home established in London received several thousand babies a year. In early America, infanticide seems to have affected only illegitimate children.

If you were well-off, your baby probably would have been breast-fed by someone else. In spite of the fact that all medical advice since Roman times had stressed that babies breast-fed by their own mothers had a better chance of survival, for eighteen centuries any woman who could afford it sent her infant to a wet nurse.

Recuperation from a difficult childbirth prevented some women from breast-feeding, but many others thought it too demanding, especially since it was customary for infants to breast-feed for as long as two years. Also, many husbands would not allow their wives to breast-feed, partly because medical opinion held that women who were breast-feeding should not engage in sexual intercourse.

Underlying these reasons may have been parents' desire to distance themselves emotionally from their infants.

In Renaissance Italy, middle-class infants were delivered to the *bália*, or wet nurse, immediately after baptism—two or three days after birth—and, if they survived, remained there for two years. Rarely did mothers visit their infants, and thus a baby was returned home at the end of that time to a stranger.

Although some wet nurses moved in with the family, most women left their babies at the wet nurse's home, where the child was often neglected and starved because wet nurses commonly took on too many babies in order to make more money. Frequently wet nurses ran out of milk, and infants had to be sent to a series of different nurses and thus were deprived even of a single surrogate mother.

The first groups of middle-class women to change this 1,800-year-old pattern on a large scale were the Puritans in the seventeenth century. Eventually, in the eighteenth century, there was a widespread cult of maternal breast-feeding in both America and England. Scholars have suggested that this shift may have contributed substantially to the shift in parental feelings for infants that began in the eighteenth century; certainly it reduced infant mortality.

Your infant would have spent little time with you. In the past, parents spent much less time with their children than even working parents do today and clearly did not feel the need to arrange supervision for them. Peasants and women commonly left their infants and toddlers alone all day at home while they worked elsewhere. In one area of England during the thirteenth century, for example, half the infant deaths involved infants in cradles being burned while no one was home. Unsupervised toddlers frequently wandered off and drowned. In the middle and upper classes, parental neglect took the form of turning toddlers over to the servants to raise.

Your infant would have been swaddled in tightly bound cloths from birth to as old as eight months. Emotional distancing, economic necessity, and faulty medical knowledge are also evident in another common practice—swaddling. In England this practice continued up to the eighteenth century; in France, the nineteenth century; and in Russia, into the twentieth century. Kept in tightly bound bandages, swaddled infants were totally isolated from their surroundings for the first four months or so. After that, only their legs were bound. They couldn't turn their heads, suck their own thumbs for comfort, or crawl. Swaddling that

was too tight occasionally caused suffocation. Although doctors advocated changing the infant two or three times a day, this apparently was uncommon, and even Louis XIII developed severe rashes because of his swaddling bands.

Medical reasons for the practice included the beliefs that if free, the infant might tear off his ears or scratch out his eyes, that swaddling was necessary to keep infants warm in cold, draughty cottages, houses and castles, and that it ensured that the infant's pliable limbs would grow straight so he would be able to stand erect. Even when the swaddling bands were removed from their legs, children were not allowed to crawl "like an animal," but were forced to stand with the help of bizarre contraptions. Convenience was another reason for swaddling: it caused infants to sleep more and cry less, so they could be

Mother's helper: The "roundabout" was a 19th-century gadget designed to keep baby out of mother's way. But it sacrificed a freedom of movement that today we know is crucial to a child's development.

left for long periods of time while mothers worked. Also, swaddled infants were easier to carry and could even be hung on a peg on the wall out of the way.

Your infant or child would probably have received harsh beatings regularly—from you or a servant—even for such "normal" behavior as crying or wanting to play. For many centuries, discipline and teaching of the infant and young child concentrated on "breaking the child's will," which meant crushing all assertiveness and instilling complete obedience. This was accomplished through physical and psychological maltreatment that today we would consider "child abuse." Susanna Wesley, mother of John Wesley, the founder of the Methodist Church, records her treatment of her children: "When turned a year old, and some before, they were taught to fear the rod and cry softly." Louis XIII was whipped every morning, starting at the age of two, simply for being "obstinate," and was even whipped on the day of his coronation at the age of nine. The Puritans believed that "the newborn babe is full of the stains and pollutions of sin" and saw the first strivings of a one- and two-year-old to independence—which we now recognize as essential to a child's growing mastery of himself and understanding of the world—as a clear manifestation of that original sin. It was considered the duty of parents to use physical harshness and psychological terrorization—locking children in dark closets for an entire day or frightening them with tales of death and hellfire, for example—to wipe this sin out.

These child-rearing practices, as well as the difficult realities of life in the past, had important psychological effects on children's development. According to Professor Stone, the isolation, sensory deprivation, and lack of physical closeness that resulted from swaddling; the absence of a mother because of death in childbirth or the practice of wet-nursing; the common experience for small children of losing parents and siblings; and the suppression of self-assertion through whipping and other fear-producing techniques all resulted in an "adult world of emotional cripples."

A change for the better.

In the late seventeenth and eighteenth centuries, many of these child-rearing practices began to change among wealthy merchants and other groups in the upper middle classes of England and America. Some changes can be traced to the Puritans, who, even though they advocated harsh disciplinary measures, focused a new attention on children and the importance of their upbringing. By the late eighteenth century, among some groups, methods of contraception were available, swaddling had been abandoned, maternal breast-feeding had become the fashion, and "breaking the will" had given way to affection and a degree of permissiveness that seems extraordinary even by today's standards. In England the indulgent Lord Holland, for example, intent on gratifying his little son Charles's every whim, allowed him to jump and splash in the large bowl of cream intended for dessert at a grand dinner while the guests, a group of foreign ministers, looked on. Many adults feared the effect on society when these spoiled children reached maturity. And in fact, many of them did spend their lives in lifelong dissipation and often became followers of evangelical religions. While the Victorian era varied from harsh to permissive in the treatment of children, by the end of the nineteenth century the child-oriented family became a reality for all classes in Western society.

What it all means for us.

Were childhood and family life better in the past? The answer—obviously—is a resounding no. One is tempted to agree with Lloyd deMause that "the history of childhood is a nightmare from which we have only recently begun to awaken."

Nevertheless, Professor Hareven feels that there were some good aspects to childhood in the past, which we can learn from today. "Children were not so segregated from adults and responsibility," she points out. "The historical record shows children grew up in households that included servants, other workers employed by the family, lodgers, visiting relatives, and siblings of widely differing ages, as well as parents. They were exposed to a greater variety of adult roles than children usually are today and they interacted with a greater variety of people of all ages. They also knew more about their parents' work. And unlike today, children were working, contributing members of families and the society from an early age—as they are in contemporary China. Today's child-oriented family and the postponement of responsibility and work limit children's experience. The models are there in history for us to borrow and shape to today's ideals."

Historical research on childhood helps us view our own ideas about parenthood from a perspective in which it is clear that there are no absolutes. The new facts that are available to us show that assumptions behind child rearing change and that what we think of as parents' "instincts" actually depend on the beliefs and experiences of their society. The possessiveness and affection toward infants, which we take for granted, is a recent development. Even the "maternal instinct" to breast-feed one's own child was not instinctive for many women for over 1,800 years.

Family history also gives us an informative view of family structure. Those who are worried about the high divorce rate and the effect of parental separation on children, for example, should realize that in the past, approximately the same percentage of families were separated—only it was by the death of one of the parents instead of by divorce.

Although problems with child

"The Human Comedy": That's the name of this 19th-century sketch—but the partially-swaddled child, left alone hanging on a wall, isn't finding anything in his situation to laugh about.

rearing will probably always be with us, the very existence of family history means that we have come to the point where we are much more self-conscious about how we raise children, and, in turn, this may help us to be more thoughtful about the way we treat them. By examining childhood in the past, we become aware that our own attempts to do things differently—"nonsexist" child rearing, co-parenting, and different mixes of permissiveness and discipline—may have profound effects on society. If we can avoid the mistakes of the past, borrow what was good, and continue to examine our own aims and practices, the society our children make may be a better one than ours.

Guns and Dolls

Alas, our children don't exemplify equality any more than we did. Is biology to blame? Scientists say maybe—but parents can do better, too.

LAURA SHAPIRO

Meet Rebecca. She's 3 years old, and both her parents have full-time jobs. Every evening Rebecca's father makes dinner for the family—Rebecca's mother rarely cooks. But when it's dinner time in Rebecca's dollhouse, she invariably chooses the Mommy doll and puts her to work in the kitchen.

Now meet George. He's 4, and his parents are still loyal to the values of the '60s. He was never taught the word "gun," much less given a war toy of any sort. On his own, however, he picked up the word "shoot." Thereafter he would grab a stick from the park, brandish it about and call it his "shooter."

Are boys and girls *born* different? Does every infant really come into the world programmed for caretaking or war making? Or does culture get to work on our children earlier and more inexorably than even parents are aware? Today these questions have new urgency for a generation that once made sexual equality its cause and now finds itself shopping for Barbie

clothes and G.I. Joe paraphernalia. Parents may wonder if gender roles are immutable after all, give or take a Supreme Court justice. But burgeoning research indicates otherwise. No matter how stubborn the stereotype, individuals can challenge it; and they will if they're encouraged to try. Fathers and mothers should be relieved to hear that they do make a difference.

Biologists, psychologists, anthropologists and sociologists have been seeking the origin of gender differences for more than a century, debating the possibilities with increasing rancor ever since researchers were forced to question their favorite theory back in 1902. At that time many scientists believed that intelligence was a function of brain size and that males uniformly had larger brains than women—a fact that would nicely explain men's pre-eminence in art, science and letters. This treasured hypothesis began to disintegrate when a woman graduate student compared the cranial capacities of a group of male scientists with those of female college students; several women came out ahead of the men,

Girls' cribs have pink tags and boys' cribs have blue tags; mothers and . . .

GIRLS

NEWBORNS

BOYS

. . . fathers should be on the alert, for the gender-role juggernaut has begun

and one of the smallest skulls belonged to a famous male anthropologist.

Gender research has become a lot more sophisticated in the ensuing decades, and a lot more controversial. The touchiest question concerns sex hormones, especially testosterone, which circulates in both sexes but is more abundant in males and is a likely, though unproven, source of aggression. To postulate a biological determinant for behavior in an ostensibly egalitarian society like ours requires a thick skin. "For a while I didn't dare talk about hormones, because women would get up and leave the room," says Beatrice Whiting, professor emeritus of education and anthropology at Harvard. "Now they seem to have more self-confidence. But they're skeptical. The data's not in yet."

Some feminist social scientists are staying away from gender research entirely— "They're saying the results will be used against women," says Jean Berko Gleason, a professor of psychology at Boston University who works on gender differences in the acquisition of language. Others see no reason to shy away from the subject. "Let's say it were proven that there were biological foundations for the division of labor," says Cynthia Fuchs Epstein, professor of sociology at the City University of New York, who doesn't, in fact, believe in such a likelihood. "It doesn't mean we couldn't do anything about it. People can make from scientific findings whatever they want." But a glance at the way society treats those gender differences already on record is not very encouraging. Boys learn to read more slowly than girls, for instance, and suffer more reading disabilities such as dyslexia, while girls fall behind in math when they get to high school. "Society can amplify differences like these or cover them up," says Gleason. "We rush in reading teachers to do remedial reading, and their classes are almost all boys. We don't talk about it, we just scurry around getting them to catch up to the girls. But where are the remedial math teachers? Girls are *supposed* to be less good at math, so that difference is incorporated into the way we live."

No matter where they stand on the question of biology versus culture, social scientists agree that the sexes are much more alike than they are different, and that variations within each sex are far greater than variations between the sexes. Even differences long taken for granted have begun to disappear. Janet Shibley Hyde, a professor of psychology at the University of Wisconsin, analyzed hundreds of studies on verbal and math ability and found boys and girls alike in verbal ability. In math, boys have a moderate edge; but only among highly precocious math students is the disparity large. Most important, Hyde found that verbal and math studies dating from the '60s and '70s showed greater differences than more recent research. "Parents may be making more efforts to tone down the stereotypes," she says. There's also what academics call "the file-drawer effect." "If you do a study that shows no differences, you assume it won't be published," says Claire Etaugh, professor of psychology at Bradley University in Peoria, Ill. "And until recently, you'd be right. So you just file it away."

The most famous gender differences in academics show up in the annual SAT results,

which do continue to favor boys. Traditionally they have excelled on the math portion, and since 1972 they have slightly outperformed girls on the verbal side as well. Possible explanations range from bias to biology, but the socioeconomic profile of those taking the test may also play a role. "The SAT gets a lot of publicity every year, but nobody points out that there are more women taking it than men, and the women come from less advantaged backgrounds," says Hyde. "The men are a more highly selected sample: they're better off in terms of parental income, father's education and attendance at private school."

Another longstanding assumption does hold true: boys tend to be somewhat more active, according to a recent study, and the difference may even start prenatally. But the most vivid distinctions between the sexes don't surface until well into the preschool years. "If I showed you a hundred kids aged 2, and you couldn't tell the sex by the haircuts, you couldn't tell if they were boys or girls," says Harvard professor of psychology Jerome Kagan. Staff members at the Children's Museum in Boston say that the boys and girls racing through the exhibits are similarly active, similarly rambunctious and similarly interested in model cars and model kitchens, until they reach first grade or so. And at New York's Bank Street preschool, most of the 3-year-olds clustered around the cooking table to make banana bread one recent morning were boys. (It was a girl who gathered up three briefcases from the costume box and announced, "Let's go to work.")

By the age of 4 or 5, however, children start to embrace gender stereotypes with a determination that makes liberal-minded parents groan in despair. No matter how careful they may have been to correct the disparities in "Pat the Bunny" ("Paul isn't the *only* one who can play peekaboo, *Judy* can play peekaboo"), their children will delight in the traditional male/female distinctions preserved everywhere else: on television, in books, at day care and preschool, in the park and with friends. "One of the

things that is very helpful to children is to learn what their identity is," says Kyle Pruett, a psychiatrist at the Yale Child Study Center. "There are rules about being feminine and there are rules about being masculine. You can argue until the cows come home about whether those are good or bad societal influences, but when you look at the children, they love to know the differences. It solidifies who they are."

Water pistols: So girls play dolls, boys play Ghostbusters. Girls take turns at hopscotch, boys compete at football. Girls help Mommy, boys aim their water pistols at guests and shout, "You're dead!" For boys, notes Pruett, guns are an inevitable part of this developmental process, at least in a television-driven culture like our own. "It can be a cardboard paper towelholder, it doesn't have to be a miniature Uzi, but it serves as the focus for fantasies about the way he is going to make himself powerful in the world," he says. "Little girls have their aggressive side, too, but by the time they're socialized it takes a different form. The kinds of things boys work out with guns, girls work out in terms of relationships— with put-downs and social cruelty." As if to underscore his point, a 4-year-old at a recent Manhattan party turned to her young hostess as a small stranger toddled up to them. "Tell her we don't want to play with her," she commanded. "Tell her we don't like her."

Once the girls know they're female and the boys know they're male, the powerful stereotypes that guided them don't just disappear. Whether they're bred into our chromosomes or ingested with our cornflakes, images of the aggressive male and the nurturant female are with us for the rest of our lives. "When we see a man with a child, we say, 'They're playing'," says Epstein. "We never say, 'He's nurturant'."

The case for biologically based gender differences is building up slowly, amid a great deal of academic dispute. The theory is that male and female brains, as well as bodies, develop differently according to the amount of testosterone circulating around the time of birth. Much of the evidence rests on animal studies showing, for instance, that brain cells from newborn mice change their shape when treated with testosterone. The male sex hormone may also account for the different reactions of male and female rhesus monkeys, raised in isolation, when an infant monkey is placed in the cage. The males are more likely to strike at the infant, the females to nurture it. Scientists disagree—vehemently—on whether animal behavior has human parallels. The most convincing human evidence comes from anthropology, where cross-cultural studies consistently find that while societies differ in their predilection toward violence, the males in any given society will act more aggressively than the females. "But it's very important to emphasize that by aggression we mean only physical violence," says Melvin Konner, a physician and anthropologist at Emory University in Atlanta. "With competitive, verbal or any other form of aggression, the evidence for gender differences doesn't hold." Empirical findings (i.e., look around you) indicate that women in positions of corporate, academic or political power can learn to wield it as aggressively as any man.

Apart from the fact that women everywhere give birth and care for children, there is surprisingly little evidence to support the notion that their biology makes women kinder, gentler people or even equips them specifically for motherhood. Philosophers—and mothers, too—have taken for granted the existence of a maternal "instinct" that research in female hormones has not conclusively proven. At most there may be a temporary hormonal response associated with childbirth that prompts females to nurture their young, but that doesn't explain women's near monopoly on changing diapers. Nor is it likely that a similar hormonal surge is responsible for women's tendency to organize the family's social life or take up the traditionally underpaid "helping" professions—nursing, teaching, social work.

Studies have shown that female newborns cry more readily than males in response to the cry of another infant, and that small girls try more often than boys to comfort or help their mothers when they appear distressed. But in general the results of most research into such traits as empathy and altruism do not consistently favor one sex or the other. There is one major exception: females of all ages seem better able to "read" people, to discern their emotions, without the help of verbal cues. (Typically researchers will display a picture of someone expressing a strong reaction and ask test-takers to identify the emotion.) Perhaps this skill—which in evolutionary terms would have helped females survive and protect their young—is

the sole biological foundation for our unshakable faith in female selflessness.

Infant ties: Those who explore the unconscious have had more success than other researchers in trying to account for male aggression and female nurturance, perhaps because their theories cannot be tested in a laboratory but are deemed "true" if they suit our intuitions. According to Nancy J. Chodorow, professor of sociology at Berkeley and the author of the influential book "The Reproduction of Mothering," the fact that both boys and girls are primarily raised by women has crucial effects on gender roles. Girls, who start out as infants identifying with their mothers and continue to do so, grow up defining themselves in relation to other people. Maintaining human connections remains vital to them. Boys eventually turn to their fathers for self-definition, but in order to do so must repress those powerful infant ties to mother and womanhood. Human connections thus become more problematic for them than for women. Chodorow's book, published in 1978, received national attention despite a dense, academic prose style; clearly, her perspective rang true to many.

Harvard's Kagan, who has been studying young children for 35 years, sees a different constellation of influences at work. He speculates that women's propensity for caretaking can be traced back to an early awareness of their role in nature. "Every girl knows, somewhere between the ages of 5 and 10, that she is different from boys and that she will have a child—something that everyone, including children, understands as quintessentially natural," he says. "If, in our society, nature stands for the giving of life, nurturance, help, affection, then the girl will conclude unconsciously that those are the qualities she should strive to attain. And the boy won't. And that's exactly what happens."

Kagan calls such gender differences "inevitable but not genetic," and he emphasizes—as does Chodorow—that they need have no implications for women's status, legally or occupationally. In the real world, of course, they have enormous implications. Even feminists who see gender differences as cultural artifacts agree that, if not inevitable, they're hard to shake. "The most emancipated families, who really feel they want to engage in gender-free behavior toward their kids, will still encourage boys to be boys and girls to be girls," says Epstein of CUNY. "Cultural constraints are acting on you all the time. If I go to buy a toy for a friend's little girl, I think to myself, why don't I buy her a truck? Well, I'm afraid the parents wouldn't like it. A makeup set would really go against my ideology, but maybe I'll buy some blocks. It's very hard. You have to be on the alert every second."

In fact, emancipated parents have to be on

GIRLS

All children have to deal with aggression: girls wield relationships as...

6-7 YEARS

BOYS

...weapons, while boys prefer to brandish water pistols.

the alert from the moment their child is born. Beginning with the pink and blue name tags for newborns in the hospital nursery—I'M A GIRL/I'M A BOY—the gender-role juggernaut is overwhelming. Carol Z. Malatesta, associate professor of psychology at Long Island University in New York, notes that baby girls' eyebrows are higher above their eyes and that girls raise their eyebrows more than boys do, giving the girls "a more appealing, socially responsive look." Malatesta and her colleagues, who videotaped and coded the facial expressions on mothers and infants as they played, found that mothers displayed a wider range of emotional responses to girls than to boys. When the baby girls displayed anger, however, they met what seemed to be greater disapproval from their mothers than the boys did. These patterns, Malatesta suggests, may be among the reasons why baby girls grow up to smile more, to seem more sociable than males, and to possess the skill noted earlier in "reading" emotions.

The way parents discipline their toddlers also has an effect on social behavior later on. Judith G. Smetana, associate professor of education, psychology and pediatrics at the University of Rochester, found that mothers were more likely to deal differently with similar kinds of misbehavior depending on the sex of the child. If a little girl bit her friend and snatched a toy, for instance, the mother would explain why biting and snatching were unacceptable. If a boy did the same thing, his mother would be more likely to stop him, punish him and leave it at that. Misbehavior such as hitting in both sexes peaks around the age of 2; after that, little boys go on to misbehave more than girls.

Psychologists have known for years that boys are punished more than girls. Some have conjectured that boys simply drive their parents to distraction more quickly; but as Carolyn Zahn-Waxler, a psychologist at the National Institute of Mental Health, points out, the difference in parental treatment starts even before the difference in behavior shows up. "Girls receive very different messages than boys," she says. "Girls are encouraged to care about the problems of others, beginning very early. By elementary school, they're showing more caregiver behavior, and they have a wider social network."

Children also pick up gender cues in the process of learning to talk. "We compared fathers and mothers reading books to children," says Boston University's Gleason. "Both parents used more inner-state words, words about feelings and emotions, to girls than to boys. And by the age of 2, girls are using more emotion words than boys." According to Gleason, fathers tend to use more directives ("Bring that over here") and more threatening language with their sons than their daughters, while mothers' directives take more polite forms ("Could you bring that to me, please?"). The 4-year-old boys and girls in one study were duly imitating their fathers and mothers in that very conversational pattern. Studies of slightly older children found that boys talking among themselves use more threatening, commanding, dominating language than girls, while girls emphasize agreement and mutuality. Polite or not, however, girls get interrupted by their parents more often than boys, according to language studies—and women get interrupted more often than men.

Despite the ever-increasing complexity and detail of research on gender differences, the not-so-secret agenda governing the discussion hasn't changed in a century: how to understand women. Whether the question is brain size, activity levels or modes of punishing children, the traditional implication is that the standard of life is male, while the entity that needs explaining is female. (Or as an editor put it, suggesting possible titles for this article: "Why Girls Are Different.") Perhaps the time has finally come for a new agenda. Women, after all, are not a big problem. Our society does not suffer from burdensome amounts of empathy and altruism, or a plague of nurturance. The problem is men—or more accurately, maleness.

"There's one set of sex differences that's ineluctable, and that's the death statis-

tics," says Gleason. "Men are killing themselves doing all the things that our society wants them to do. At every age they're dying in accidents, they're being shot, they drive cars badly, they ride the tops of elevators, they're two-fisted hard drinkers. And violence against women is incredibly pervasive. Maybe it's men's raging hormones, but I think it's because they're trying to be a *man*. If I were the mother of a boy, I would be very concerned about societal pressures that idolize behaviors like that."

Studies of other cultures show that male behavior, while characteristically aggressive, need not be characteristically deadly. Harvard's Whiting, who has been analyzing children cross-culturally for half a century, found that in societies where boys as well as girls take care of younger siblings, boys as well as girls show nurturant, sociable behavior. "I'm convinced that infants elicit positive behavior from people," says Whiting. "If you have to take care of somebody who can't talk, you have to learn empathy. Of course there can be all kinds of experiences that make you extinguish that eliciting power, so that you no longer respond positively. But on the basis of our data, boys make very good baby tenders."

In our own society, evidence is emerging that fathers who actively participate in raising their children will be steering both sons and daughters toward healthier gender roles. For the last eight years Yale's Pruett has been conducting a groundbreaking longitudinal study of 16 families, representing a range of socioeconomic circumstances, in which the fathers take primary responsibility for child care while the mothers work full time. The children are now between 8 and 10 years old, and Pruett has watched subtle but important differences develop between them and their peers. "It's not that they have conflicts about their gender identity—the boys are masculine and the girls are feminine, they're all interested in the same things their friends are," he says. "But when they were 4 or 5, for instance, the stage at preschool when the boys leave the doll corner and the girls leave the block corner, these children didn't give up one or the other. The boys spent time playing with the girls in the doll corner, and the girls were building things with blocks, taking pride in their accomplishments."

Little footballs: Traditionally, Pruett notes, fathers have enforced sex stereotypes more strongly than mothers, engaging the boys in active play and complimenting the girls on their pretty dresses. "Not these fathers," says Pruett. "That went by the boards. They weren't interested in bringing home little

footballs for their sons or little tutus for the girls. They dealt with the kids according to the individual. I even saw a couple of the mothers begin to take over those issues— one of them brought home a Dallas Cowboys sleeper for her 18-month-old. Her husband said, 'Honey, I thought we weren't going to do this, remember?' She said, 'Do what?' So that may be more a function of being in the second tier of parenting rather than the first."

As a result of this loosening up of stereotypes, the children are more relaxed about gender roles. "I saw the boys really enjoy their nurturing skills," says Pruett. "They knew what to do with a baby, they didn't see that as a girl's job, they saw it as a human job. I saw the girls have very active images of the outside world and what their mothers were doing in the workplace—things that become interesting to most girls when they're 8 or 10, but these girls were interested when they were 4 or 5."

Pruett doesn't argue that fathers are better at mothering than mothers, simply that two involved parents are better than "one and a lump." And it's hardly necessary for fathers to quit their jobs in order to become more involved. A 1965-66 study showed that working mothers spent 50 minutes a day engaged primarily with their children, while the fathers spent 12 minutes. Later studies have found fathers in two-career households spending only about a third as much time with their children as mothers. What's more, Pruett predicts that fathers would benefit as much as children from the increased responsibility. "The more involved father tends to feel differently about his own life," he says. "A lot of men, if they're on the fast track, know a lot about competitive relationships, but they don't know much about intimate relationships. Children are experts in intimacy. After a while the wives in my study would say, 'He's just a nicer guy'."

Pruett's study is too small in scope to support major claims for personality development; he emphasizes that his findings are chiefly theoretical until more research can be undertaken. But right now he's watching a motif that fascinates him. "Every single one of these kids is growing something," he says. "They don't just plant a watermelon seed and let it die. They're really propagating things, they're doing salad-bowl starts in the backyard, they're breeding guinea pigs. That says worlds about what they think matters. Generativity is valued a great deal, when both your mother and your father say it's OK." Scientists may never agree on what divides the sexes; but someday, perhaps, our children will learn to relish what unites them.

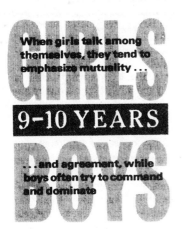

When girls talk among themselves, they tend to emphasize mutuality . . .

9-10 YEARS

. . . and agreement, while boys often try to command and dominate

Is TV Ruining Our Children?

Reforms are at hand, but the way kids grow up has already been profoundly changed

By RICHARD ZOGLIN

Behold every parent's worst nightmare: the six-year-old TV addict. He watches in the morning before he goes off to school, plops himself in front of the set as soon as he gets home in the afternoon and gets another dose to calm down before he goes to bed at night. He wears Bart Simpson T shirts, nags Mom to buy him Teenage Mutant Ninja Turtles toys and spends hours glued to his Nintendo. His teacher says he is restless and combative in class. What's more, he's having trouble reading.

Does this creature really exist, or is he just a paranoid video-age vision? The question is gaining urgency as the medium barges ever more aggressively into children's lives. Except for school and the family, no institution plays a bigger role in shaping American children. And no institution takes more heat. TV has been blamed for just about everything from a decrease in attention span to an increase in street crime. Cartoons are attacked for their violence and sitcoms for their foul language. Critics ranging from religious conservatives to consumer groups like Action for Children's Television have kept up a steady drumbeat of calls for reform.

Last week Congress took a small step toward obliging. Legislators sent to President Bush a bill that would set limits on commercial time in children's programming (a still generous 10½ minutes per hour on weekends and 12 minutes on weekdays). The bill would also require stations to air at least some educational kids' fare as a condition for getting their licenses renewed. Bush has argued that the bill infringes on broadcasters' First Amendment rights, but (unlike President Reagan, who vetoed a similar measure two years ago) he is expected to allow it to become law.

Yet these mild efforts at reform, as well as critics' persistent gripes about the poor quality of children's TV, skirt the central issue. Even if the commercialism on kidvid were reined in, even if local stations were persuaded to air more "quality" children's fare, even if kids could be shielded from the most objectionable material, the fact remains that children watch a ton of TV. Almost daily, parents must grapple with a fundamental, overriding question: What is all that TV viewing doing to kids, and what can be done about it?

Television has, of course, been an inseparable companion for most American youngsters since the early 1950s. But the baby boomers, who grew up with Howdy Doody and Huckleberry Hound, experienced nothing like the barrage of video

> **"Television exposes kids to behavior that adults spent centuries trying to hide from children."**

images that pepper kids today. Cable has vastly expanded the supply of programming. The VCR has turned favorite shows and movies into an endlessly repeatable pastime. Video games have added to the home box's allure.

The average child will have watched 5,000 hours of TV by the time he enters first grade and 19,000 hours by the end of high school—more time than he will spend in class. This dismayingly passive experience crowds out other, more active endeavors: playing outdoors, being with friends, reading. Marie Winn, author of the 1977 book *The Plug-In Drug,* gave a memorable, if rather alarmist, description of the trance-like state TV induces: "The child's facial expression is transformed. The jaw is relaxed and hangs open slightly; the tongue rests on the front teeth (if there are any). The eyes have a glazed, vacuous look . . ."

Guided by TV, today's kids are exposed to more information about the world around them than any other generation in history. But are they smarter for it? Many teachers and psychologists argue that TV is largely to blame for the decline in reading skills and school performance. In his studies of children at Yale, psychologist Jerome Singer found that kids who are heavy TV watchers tend to be less well informed, more restless and poorer students. The frenetic pace of TV, moreover, has seeped into the classroom. "A teacher who is going into a lengthy explanation of an arithmetic problem will begin to lose the audience after a while," says Singer. "Children are expecting some kind of show." Even the much beloved *Sesame Street* has been criticized for reinforcing the TV-inspired notion that education must be fast paced and entertaining. Says Neil Postman, communications professor at New York University and author of *Amusing Ourselves to Death:* "*Sesame Street* makes kids like school only if school is like *Sesame Street.*"

Televised violence may also be having an effect on youngsters. Singer's research has shown that prolonged viewing by children of violent programs is associated with more aggressive behavior, such as getting into fights and disrupting the play of others. (A link between TV and violent crime, however, has not been clearly established.) Other studies suggest that TV viewing can dampen kids' imagination. Patricia Marks Greenfield, a professor of psychology at UCLA, conducted experiments in which several groups of children were asked to tell a story about the Smurfs. Those who were shown a Smurfs TV cartoon beforehand were less "creative" in their storytelling than kids who first played an unrelated connect-the-dots game.

But the evidence is flimsy for many popular complaints about TV. In a 1988 report co-authored for the U.S. Department of Education, Daniel Anderson, professor of psychology at the University of Massachusetts in Amherst, found no convincing evidence that TV has a "mesmerizing effect" on children, overstimulates them or reduces their attention span. In fact, the report asserted, TV may actually increase attention-focusing capabilities.

Nor, contrary to many parents' fears, have the new video technologies made matters worse. Small children who repeatedly watch their favorite cassettes are, psychologists point out, behaving no differently from toddlers who want their favorite story read to them over and over. (The VCR may actually give parents *more* control over their kids' viewing.) Video games may distress adults with their addictive potential, but researchers have found no exceptional harm in them—and even some possible benefits, like improving hand-eye coordination.

Yet TV may be effecting a more profound, if less widely recognized, change in the whole concept of growing up. Before the advent of television, when print was the predominant form of mass communication, parents and teachers were able to control just what and when children learned about the world outside. With TV, kids are plunged into that world almost instantly.

In his 1985 book, *No Sense of Place,* Joshua Meyrowitz, professor of communication at the University of New Hampshire, points out that TV reveals to children the "backstage" activity of adults. Even a seemingly innocuous program like *Father Knows Best* showed that parents aren't all-knowing authority figures: they agonize over problems in private and sometimes even conspire to fool children. "Television exposes kids to behavior that adults spent centuries trying to hide from children," says Meyrowitz. "The average child watching television sees adults hitting each other, killing each other, breaking down and crying. It teaches kids that adults don't always know what they're doing." N.Y.U.'s Postman believes TV, by revealing the "secrets" of adulthood, has virtually destroyed the notion of childhood as a discrete period of innocence. "What I see happening is a blurring of childhood and adulthood," he says. "We have more adultlike children and more childlike adults."

What all this implies is that TV's impact is pervasive and to a large extent inevitable. That impact cannot be wished away; all that can be done is to try to understand and control it. Reforms of the sort Congress has enacted are a salutary step. Networks and stations too—though they are in the business of entertainment, not education—must be vigilant about the content and commercialization of kids' shows.

The ultimate responsibility still rests with parents. The goal should not be—cannot be—to screen out every bad word or karate chop from kids' viewing, but rather to make sure TV doesn't crowd out all the other activities that are part of growing up. These counterbalancing influences—family, friends, school, books—can put TV, if not out of the picture, at least in the proper focus.   —*Reported by William Tynan/New York*

CRIME PAYS, BUT SO DOES IMPRISONMENT

Morgan O. Reynolds
Texas A & M University

America is burdened by an appalling amount of crime. Even though the crime rate is not soaring as it did during the 1960s and 1970s, we still have more crimes per capita than any other developed country.

- Every year nearly 6 million people are victims of violent crimes – murder, rape, robbery or assault.[1]

- Another 29 million Americans each year are victims of property crimes – arson, burglary and larceny-theft.[2]

- There is a murder every 25 minutes, a rape every six minutes, a robbery every minute and an aggravated assault every 35 seconds.[3]

- There is a motor vehicle theft every 22 seconds, a burglary every ten seconds, and a larceny-theft every four seconds.[4]

Although the number of crimes reported to the police each year has leveled off somewhat in the 1980s, our crime rate today is still enormously high – 411 percent higher, for example, than it was in 1960.

Why is there so much crime?

The Expected Punishment for Committing a Crime

The economic theory of crime is a relatively new field of social science. According to this theory, most crimes are not irrational acts. Instead, crimes are freely committed by people who compare the expected benefits of crime with the expected costs. The reason we have so much crime is that, for many people, the benefits outweigh the costs. For some people, a criminal career is more attractive than their other career options. Put another way, the reason we have so much crime is that crime pays.

Because criminals and potential criminals rarely have accurate information about the probabilities of arrest, conviction and imprisonment, a great deal of uncertainty is involved in the personal assessment of the expected punishment from committing crimes. Individuals differ in skill and intellect. The more skillful and more intelligent criminals have better odds of committing successful crimes. Some people overestimate their probability of success, while others underestimate theirs.

Despite the element of subjectivity, the economic theory of crime makes one clear prediction: Crime will increase if the

expected cost of crime to criminals declines. This is true for "crimes of passion" as well as economic crimes such as burglary or auto theft. The less costly crime becomes, the more often people fail to control their passions.

The economic theory of crime is consistent with public opinion,[5] and with the perceptions of potential criminals.[6] It is supported by considerable statistical research.[7] According to the theory, the amount of crime is inversely related to expected punishment. What follows is a brief summary of the punishment criminals can expect.

Expected Time in Prison

What is the expected punishment for committing major types of serious crime in the United States today? As Table I shows, the expected punishment is shockingly low.

- Even for committing the most serious crime – murder – an individual can expect to spend only 2.3 years in prison.

- On the average, an individual who commits an act of burglary can expect to spend only 7.1 days in prison.

- Someone considering an auto theft can expect to spend only 6.3 days in prison.

Note: Table I does not show the length of time prisoners actually stay in prison. On the average, people sent to prison remain there for 17 months. Expected time in prison is the actual time adjusted for the probabilities of arrest, prosecution, conviction and imprisonment. Expected time in prison takes into account the fact that more than 98 percent of all crimes do not result in any prison time served.[8]

The Decline in Expected Imprisonment and the Rise in Crime

If the numbers in Table I appear low, the full reality may be worse. On the average, those crimes with the longest expected prison terms (murder, rape, robbery and assault) are the crimes least frequently committed, comprising only about 10 percent of all serious crime. The remaining 90 percent carry an expected prison term of only a few days.

When expected punishment is weighted by the frequency of types of crimes, the picture is even more shocking: On the average, a perpetrator of a serious crime in the United States can expect to spend about eight days in prison. Table II shows how this overall expectation has changed over time.

- Since the early 1950s, the expected punishment for committing a serious crime in the United States (measured in terms of expected time in prison) has been reduced by two-thirds.

My thanks to Dr. John Goodman, President, National Center for Policy Analysis, Dallas, Texas, for his help on this paper and his permission to reprint material from NCPA Report No. 149. Author.

CRIME AND PUNISHMENT

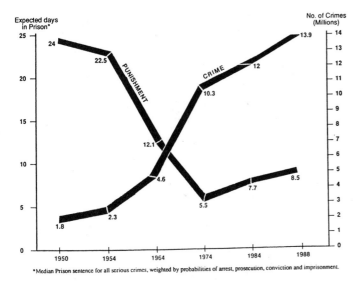

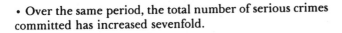

*Median Prison sentence for all serious crimes, weighted by probabilities of arrest, prosecution, conviction and imprisonment.

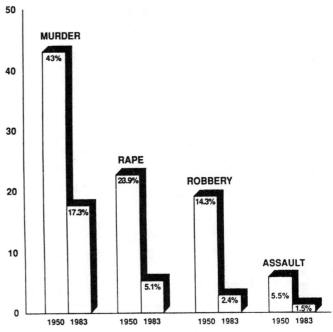

- Over the same period, the total number of serious crimes committed has increased sevenfold.

The "Prices" We Charge for Crime

It is virtually impossible to prevent people from committing crimes. The most that the criminal justice system can do is impose punishment after the crime has been committed. People are largely free to commit almost any crime they choose. What the criminal justice system does is construct a list of prices (expected punishments) for various criminal acts. People commit crimes so long as they are willing to pay the prices society charges, just as many of us might risk parking or speeding tickets.

Viewed in this way, the expected prison sentences listed in Table I are the prices we charge for various crimes. Thus, the price of murder is about 2.3 years in prison; the price of burglary is 7.7 days; the price for stealing a car is 4.2 days. Since these prices are so low, it is small wonder so many people are willing to pay them.

Calculating the Expected Punishment for Crime

Five adverse events must occur before a criminal actually ends up in prison. The criminal must be arrested, indicted, prosecuted, convicted and sent to prison. As a result, the expected punishment for crime depends upon a number of probabilities: The probability of being arrested, given that a crime is committed; the probability of being prosecuted, given an arrest; the probability of conviction, given prosecution; and the probability of being sent to prison, given a conviction. As Table III shows, the overall probability of being punished is the result of multiplying four probabilities.

Even if each of the separate probabilities is reasonably high, their product can be quite low. For example, suppose that each of these probabilities were 0.5. That is, one-half of crimes result in an arrest, one-half of arrests lead to prosecution, one-half of prosecutions lead to a conviction, and one-half of convictions lead to a prison term. In this case, the overall probability that a criminal will spend time in prison is only 6.25 percent.

Table III also depicts recent probabilities in the case of burglary. Note that burglars who are sent to prison stay there

for about 17 months, on the average. (In Texas burglars serve a median sentence of 8 months). But someone considering an act of burglary will surely be influenced by the fact that the probability of being arrested is only 14 percent. Although the probabilities of prosecution and conviction following an arrest are high, the criminal's probability of going to prison is less than one in three after being convicted. When all factors are

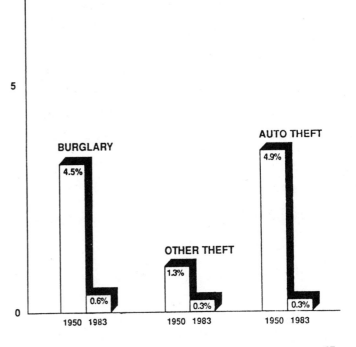

TABLE I

EXPECTED PUNISHMENT FOR POTENTIAL CRIMINALS

Crime	Expected Time in Prison[1]
Murder	2.3 years
Rape	3.5 months
Robbery	36.0 days
Arson	17.1 days
Aggravated Assault[2]	13.2 days
Burglary[3]	7.1 days
Motor Vehicle Theft	6.3 days
Larceny/Theft[4]	1.8 days

[1]Based on the probabilities of arrest, prosecution, conviction and imprisonment.

[2]The FBI defines "aggravated assault" as an unlawful attack by one person on another for the purpose of inflicting severe or aggravated bodily injury, usually accompanied by the use of a weapon or by means likely to produce death or great bodily harm.

[3]Burglary is the unlawful entry of a structure to commit a felony or theft.

[4]Larceny-theft is the unlawful taking, carrying, leading, or riding away of property from the possession or constructive possession of another.

Source: Appendix A, Table A-5

TABLE III

CALCULATING THE EXPECTED PUNISHMENT FOR POTENTIAL CRIMINALS

Expected Time in Prison = Probability of arrest x Probability of prosecution, given arrest

x Probability of conviction, given prosecution x Probability of imprisonment, given conviction

x median sentence

Example: Expected Punishment for Burglary

Expected Time in Prison = 14% (Probability of arrest) x 88% (Probability of prosecution, given arrest)

x 81% (Probability of conviction, given prosecution) x 28% (Probability of imprisonment, given conviction)

x 1/2 (Adjustment for unreported crimes)[1] x 17 months (median sentence)

= 7.1 days

[1] Approximately one-half of all burglaries are not reported to the police. Law enforcement agencies "clear" (or solve) an offense when at least one person is arrested, charged with the offense and turned over for prosecution.

Source: Appendix A. Table A-5

taken into account (including the probability that the crime will never be reported), the overall probability that a burglar will end up in prison is less than one percent. The expected punishment prior to committing the crime is only 7.1 days.

Probability of Arrest

Table IV shows the proportion of crimes "cleared by arrest," whether or not the individual was indicted and convicted. The striking fact about Table IV is the degree to which arrest rates have declined over the past 40 years, even for the most serious crimes. For example:

- Since 1950, the probability of being arrested after committing a murder has fallen by 25 percent.
- The probability of arrest for rapists has fallen 35 percent, for robbers 42 percent and for burglars 53 percent.

On the average, during the 1980s, only about 21 percent of all crimes in the United States were cleared by arrest. In Japan, by contrast, the clearance-by-arrest rate is 50 percent. Moreover, Japan with a population of 122 million has fewer

TABLE II

THE DECLINE IN EXPECTED PUNISHMENT FOR ALL SERIOUS CRIMES

Year	Expected Time in Prison
1950	24.0 days*
1954	22.5 days
1964	12.1 days
1974	5.5 days
1984	7.7 days
1988	8.5 days*

*NCPA estimates, based on incomplete data.

Source: Appendix A, Table A-1

TABLE IV

PERCENT OF CRIMES CLEARED BY ARREST

Crime	1950	1988
Murder	94.0%	70.0%
Rape	80.0	52.1
Robbery	44.0	25.6
Aggravated Assault	77.0	56.8
Burglary	29.0	13.5
Larceny/Theft	22.0	19.7

Source: Appendix A, Table A-2

TABLE V

**PERCENT OF CRIMES WHICH
RESULT IN A PRISON SENTENCE**

Crime	1950	1983
Murder	43.0%	17.3%
Rape	23.9	5.1
Robbery	14.3	2.4
Aggravated Assault	5.5	1.5
Burglary	4.5	0.6
Larceny/Theft	1.3	0.3
Motor Vehicle Theft	4.9	0.3

Source: Federal Bureau of Investigation, *Crime in the United States, Uniform Crime Reports for the United States* (Washington, DC: U.S. Dept. of Justice, 1988) and Bureau of Justice, *Bulletin* NCJ-110331, April 1988.

---

murders each year than New York City with a population of seven million.[9]

Probability of Prosecution, Conviction and Imprisonment

Although there are 13 million arrests each year in the United States, including 2.8 million for serious (Index) crimes,[10] annual admissions to prison only topped 200,000 in 1986. In other words, only eight of every 100 arrests for Index crimes results in imprisonment after defense attorneys, prosecutors and courts complete their work.

Overall Probability of Going to Prison

A criminal's overall probability of imprisonment has fallen dramatically since 1950. As Table V shows:
- Since 1950, the percent of crimes resulting in a prison sentence has declined by at least 60 percent for every major category of crime.
- This includes a 60 percent drop for murder, a 79 percent decrease for rape, an 83 percent reduction for robbery and a 94 percent plunge for auto theft.

Unreported Crimes

Based on the number of crimes reported to the police, 1.66 percent of all serious crimes are punished by imprisonment; therefore 98.34 percent of serious crimes are not. According to the National Crime Survey, however, only 37 percent of serious crimes are actually reported. If there are two unreported crimes for every one reported, then the overall probability of going to prison for the commission of a serious crime falls to about 0.61 percent (.37 x 1.66%). This amounts to one prison term for every 164 felonies committed.

• • •

Conclusion

While crime continues on the high plateau, there are grounds for optimism. The number of young males began to decline in the 1980s and will continue to do so through the 1990s. Further, the odds of imprisonment for a serious offense increased in the 1980s as legislators responded to the public's "get tough" attitude. Yet we remained plagued with crime rates (per capita) triple those of the 1950s.

What can be done to build on this relatively promising recent trend? At a minimum the analysis in this report suggests three things. First, the U.S. Supreme Court should continue to reestablish the rule of law by restricting application of the exclusionary rule and other expansions of criminal privileges inherited from the Warren Court. Second, the public sector must continue raising the odds of imprisonment toward those of the 1950s in order to improve personal security. Deterrence of criminals implies building prisons and reducing prison costs by privatization. Third, the laws hampering productive employment of prisoners must be relaxed to take full advantage of the benefits of privatization.

Note: Nothing written here should be construed as necessarily reflecting the views of the National Center for Policy Analysis or as an attempt to aid or hinder the passage of any bill before Congress.

• • •

Notes

1. Based on the National Crime Survey conducted annually by the U.S. Bureau of Census for the Bureau of Justice Statistics.
2. *Ibid.*
3. Federal Bureau of Investigation, *Crime in the United States, Uniform Crime Reports for the United States* (Washington, DC: U.S. Dep. of Justice, 1988).
4. *Ibid.*
5. As Harvard political scientist James Q. Wilson wrote, "The average citizen thinks it is obvious that people have discovered it is easier to get away with it." James Q. Wilson, *Thinking About Crime,* Revised Ed. (New York: Basic Books, 1983), p. 117.
6. "The risks posed by the criminal enforcement system are notoriously low," writes economist Kip Vicusi, "and data show that youthful criminals knew it." W. Kip Viscusi, "The Risks and Rewards of Criminal Activity: A Comprehensive Test of Criminal Deterrence," *Journal of Labor Economics,* Vol. 4, No. 3, 1986, pp. 317–340.
7. *Ibid.* See also the earlier surveys of the literature in Gordon Tullock, "Does Punishment Deter Crime?" *The Public Interest,* 36, Summer 1974, pp. 103–111; and Morgan O. Reynolds, *Crime by Choice* (Dallas: Fisher Institute, 1985), Ch. 12.
8. The method for calculating expected time in prison is shown in Table III below.
9. Reynolds, "Crime by Choice," p. 32.
10. The FBI began defining serious offenses as Index offenses in 1929 Serious offenses consist of the violent crimes of murder, non-negligent manslaughter, rape, robbery and aggravated (severe) assault plus the property crimes of burglary, larceny/theft and motor vehicle theft. By Congressional mandate, arson was added as the eighth Index offense in 1979.

THE NATURE OF THE BEAST

Anita Hill

The response to my Senate Judiciary Committee testimony has been at once heartwarming and heart-wrenching. In learning that I am not alone in experiencing harassment, I am also learning that there are far too many women who have experienced a range of inexcusable and illegal activities—from sexist jokes to sexual assault—on the job.

My reaction has been to try to learn more. As an educator, I always begin to study an issue by examining the scientific data—the articles, the books, the studies. Perhaps the most compelling lesson is in the stories told by the women who have written to me. I have learned much; I am continuing to learn; I have yet ten times as much to explore. I want to share some of this with you.

"The Nature of the Beast" describes the existence of sexual harassment, which is alive and well. A harmful, dangerous thing that can confront a woman at any time.

What we know about harassment, sizing up the beast:

Sexual harassment is pervasive . . .

1. It occurs today at an alarming rate. Statistics show that anywhere from 42 to 90 percent of women will experience some form of harassment during their employed lives. At least one percent experience sexual assault. But the statistics do not fully tell the story of the anguish of women who have been told in various ways on the first day of a job that sexual favors are expected. Or the story of women who were sexually assaulted by men with whom they continued to work.

2. It has been occurring for years. In letters to me, women tell of incidents that occurred 50 years ago when they were first entering the workplace, incidents they have been unable to speak of for that entire period.

3. Harassment crosses lines of race and class. In some ways, it is a creature that practices "equal opportunity" where women are concerned. In other ways it exhibits predictable prejudices and reflects stereotypical myths held by our society.

We know that harassment all too often goes unreported for a variety of reasons . . .

1. Unwillingness (for good reason) to deal with the expected consequences;

2. Self-blame;

3. Threats or blackmail by coworkers or employers;

4. What it boils down to in many cases is a sense of powerlessness that we experience in the workplace, and our acceptance of a certain level of inability to control our careers and professional destinies. This sense of powerlessness is particularly troubling when one observes the research that says individuals with graduate education experience more harassment than do persons with less than a high school diploma. The message: when you try to obtain power through education, the beast harassment responds by striking more often and more vehemently.

That harassment is treated like a woman's "dirty secret" is well known. We also know what happens when we "tell." We know that when harassment is reported the common reaction is disbelief or worse . . .

1. Women who "tell" lose their jobs. A typical response told of in the letters to me was: I not only lost my job for reporting harassment, but I was accused of stealing and charges were brought against me.

2. Women who "tell" become emotionally wasted. One writer noted that "it was fully eight months after the suit was conducted that I began to see myself as alive again."

3. Women who "tell" are not always supported by other women. Perhaps the most disheartening stories I have received are of mothers not believing daughters. In my kindest moments I believe that this reaction only represents attempts to distance ourselves from the pain of the harassment experience. The internal response is: "It didn't happen to me. This couldn't happen to me. In order to believe that I am protected, I must believe that it didn't happen to her." The external response is: "What did you do to provoke that kind of behavior?" Yet at the same time that I have been advised of hurtful and unproductive reactions, I have also heard stories of mothers and daughters sharing their experiences. In some cases the sharing allows for a closer bonding. In others a slight but cognizable mending of a previously damaged relationship occurs.

> *How do we turn rage into energy? Through the power of women working together.*

What we are learning about harassment requires recognizing this beast when we encounter it, and more. It requires looking the beast in the eye.

We are learning painfully that simply having laws against harassment on the books is not enough. The law, as it was conceived, was to provide a shield of protection for us. Yet that shield is failing us: many fear reporting, others feel it would do no good. The result is that less than 5 percent of women victims file claims of harassment. Moreover, the law focuses on quid pro quo, but a recent New York *Times* article quoting psychologist Dr. Louise Fitzgerald says that this makes up considerably less than 5 percent of the cases. The law needs to be more responsive to the reality of our experiences.

As we are learning, enforcing the law alone won't terminate the problem. What we are seeking is equality of treatment in the workplace. Equality requires an expansion of our attitudes toward workers. Sexual harassment denies our treatment as equals and replaces it with treatment of women as objects of ego or power gratification. Dr. John Gottman, a psychologist at the University of Washington, notes that sexual harassment is more about fear than about sex.

Yet research suggests two troublesome responses exhibited by workers and by courts. Both respond by . . .

1. Downplaying the seriousness of the behavior (seeing it as normal sexual attraction between people) or commenting on the sensitivity of the victim.

2. Exaggerating the ease with which victims are expected to handle the behavior. But my letters tell me that unwanted advances do not cease—and that the message was power, not genuine interest.

We are learning that many women are angry. The reasons for the anger are various and perhaps all too obvious . . .

1. We are angry because this awful thing called harassment exists in terribly harsh, ugly, demeaning, and even debilitating ways. Many believe it is criminal and should be punished as such. It is a form of violence against women as well as a form of economic coercion, and our experiences suggest that it won't just go away.

2. We are angry because for a brief moment we believed that if the law allowed for women to be hired in the workplace, and if we worked hard for our educations and on the job, equality would be achieved. We believed we would be respected as equals. Now we are realizing this is not true. We have been betrayed. The reality is that this powerful beast is used to perpetuate a sense of inequality, to keep women in their place notwithstanding our increasing presence in the workplace.

What we have yet to explore about harassment is vast. It is what will enable us to slay the beast.

Research is helpful, appreciated, and I hope will be required reading for all legislators. Yet research has what I see as one shortcoming: it focuses on our reaction to harassment, not on the harasser. How we enlighten men who are currently in the workplace about behavior that is beneath our (and their) dignity is the challenge of the future. Research shows that men tend to have a narrower definition of what constitutes harassment than do women. How do we expand their body of knowledge? How do we raise a generation of men who won't need to be reeducated as adults? We must explore these issues, and research efforts can assist us.

What are the broader effects of harassment on women and the world? Has sexual harassment left us unempowered? Has our potential in the workplace been greatly damaged by this beast? Has this form of economic coercion worked? If so, how do we begin to reverse its effects? We must begin to use what we know to move to the next step: what we will do about it.

How do we capture our rage and turn it into positive energy? Through the power of women working together, whether it be in the political arena, or in the context of a lawsuit, or in community service. This issue goes well beyond partisan politics. Making the workplace a safer, more productive place for ourselves and our daughters should be on the agenda for each of us. It is something we can do for ourselves. It is a tribute, as well, to our mothers—and indeed a contribution we can make to the entire population.

I wish that I could take each of you on the journey that I've been on during all these weeks since the hearing. I wish that every one of you could experience the heartache and the triumphs of each of those who have shared with me their experiences. I leave you with but a brief glimpse of what I've seen. I hope it is enough to encourage you to begin—or continue and persist with—your own exploration. And thank you.

This article is based on remarks delivered by Anita Hill (professor of law, University of Oklahoma) as part of a panel on sexual harassment and policymaking at the National Forum for Women State Legislators convened by the Center for the American Woman and Politics (CAWP) late last year. Other panel members were Deborah L. Rhode, professor of law at Stanford; Susan Deller Ross, professor of law and director of the Sex Discrimination Clinic at Georgetown University Law School; and Kimberle Williams Crenshaw, professor of law at UCLA. A transcript of the entire proceedings (the largest meeting of elected women ever held) is available from CAWP, Eagleton Institute of Politics, Rutgers University, New Brunswick, New Jersey 08901.

A Way Out of the Morass

YES, SOME SOLUTIONS WORK. BUT CAN WE IMPLEMENT THEM BROADLY?

The problems are starting to look intractable. The government says that 1991's poverty rate hit 14.2%, a 30-year high. Unemployment among black men is double that for whites. There's an explosion in births to unmarried girls. More teenage ghetto males die from gunshots than from all natural causes combined. Emergency room visits for drug overdoses are rising.

Spurred by the twin demons of economic and social decay, the damage spreads in ever-widening circles. As decent-paying, low-skilled jobs disappear and real wages fall, ghetto kids are robbed both of necessities and of any sense of the value of work. Children of highly stressed or drug-addicted parents do poorly in school or drop out, sabotaging their futures. Daughters of long-term welfare mothers line up for the dole. Another lost generation starts its downward spiral, saddling America with billions in costs that displace investment and damage U.S. competitiveness.

But if cost is the issue, how can America, with its jumbo deficit, afford to fix these problems? The answer lies not in just spending more but rather in redirecting resources. Many of the expensive policies of recent years—filling prisons, for instance—have produced a meager return, despite some short-term benefits. More promising programs, by contrast, do better, sometimes at no higher cost. "Research and experience explode the myth that nothing works," says Lisbeth B. Schorr, director of Harvard University's Project on Effective Services and author of *Within Our Reach: Breaking the Cycle of Disadvantage*.

The strategies that work share a common philosophy. They assume that, in most cases, what seem to be isolated problems are really interrelated. "If people have a drug problem, you can't deal with their joblessness by only giving them training," says Mitchell S. Rosenthal, president of Phoenix House, a private agency that rehabilitates drug abusers. The most successful programs view social ills as interwoven, requiring a more comprehensive solution than traditionally has been tried.

In stressing prevention over punishment, these projects resemble some Great Society programs of the 1960s. But there's one crucial difference. In contrast to the government-as-savior approach, many modern programs are joint public-private ventures. Their aim is not only to rescue but to empower, to make the disadvantaged responsible for their kids, their neighborhoods, their lives. It's an up-by-your-bootstraps approach for a financially strapped era.

CRIME. Few approaches to social ills have proved less effective than the assault on violent crime. The 1980s solution was to build more prisons—$37 billion worth—doubling the number of state and federal beds to 625,000. But that "hasn't worked," declares Lynn A. Curtis, president of the Milton S. Eisenhower Foundation, a private group that has taken over the functions of President Johnson's National Commission on the Causes & Prevention of Violence. The ranks of prisoners, including those in local jails, rose 138% in the 1980s, to 747,00. But violent crime still rose 35%.

What works better? One answer can be found in the Bronx in New York. There, a group called the Argus Community provides residential and day programs for 17- to 21-year olds, most of whom have been involved with drug dealing and other criminal activity. Without help, many might land in prison or die in street wars. To avoid that, Argus has its kids work toward a general educa-

THE HIGH COST OF DRUG ABUSE

It costs $3,000 to $14,600, depending on the type of therapy, to get a drug abuser to stop. But that pales beside the potential costs of doing nothing:

AIDS	★*Intravenous drug use accounts for one-third of the more than 1 million people who are now HIV-positive. Average long-term cost of caring for a person with AIDS: $60,000*
CRACK BABIES	★*More than 550,000 drug-exposed babies are born each year. Median daily hospital costs: $5,500. Total cost of care for each year's newborns until age 1: $51 million*
PRISONS	★*Nearly 50% of federal inmates and 70% of state inmates have a history of drug abuse, and 50% of federal prisoners are serving time for drug-related crimes. Average yearly cost of incarceration: $16,946*
FOSTER KIDS	★*Drug abuse accounts for a 29% increase in the number of children placed in foster care—from 280,000 in 1987 to 360,000 in 1989. Annual cost of care: up to $36,000*

DATA: HOUSE SELECT COMMITTEE ON NARCOTICS ABUSE & CONTROL

tion diploma in small classes where relationships with teachers are much closer than in big high schools. "Everyone here acts like a family," says Alita Bruce, 19, who quit her Harlem high school in the 10th grade. Argus counselors teach punctuality and good attendance, and try to boost self-esteem. College grads from the neighborhood, the counselors are living proof that the ghetto can be overcome. "That makes a huge difference," says Argus Executive Director Elizabeth L. Sturz.

Government-funded audits required by the federal Job Training Partnership Act found that of the 65 Argus adolescents who took part in the JTPA program last year, 100% had clean criminal records through the year, and 87% were placed in training-related jobs. Argus, financed with private, federal, and state funds, spends $15,000 a person, one-seventh the cost of a new prison bed.

A preventive vs. punitive philosophy also characterizes a positive trend in police work. Community policing "doesn't see crime as a compartmentalized problem but as a result of many problems," says Chief David Mitchell in Prince Georges County, Md. He was assigned 22 officers as troubleshooters in a few key neighborhoods. They combat drugs not just by making arrests, but by calling crews to condemn dilapidated buildings or clean up garbage-strewn areas that attract dealers. They've reduced afternoon crime by working with schools to keep students in class and by getting older neighbors to watch latchkey kids, who are on their own after school.

As a result, residents are more likely to work with cops. Since July, 1991, violent crime has dropped by 15% and drug-related calls by 20% in community policing areas. Mitchell, who plans to expand the program fivefold by 1995, sees one more benefit: Cleaning up and uniting the community will make it easier to recruit businesses—creating jobs for otherwise trouble-prone youth.

DRUGS. As with crime, the effort to stop drug use has been a defensive fight. Washington spends a record $12 billion a year in the drug wars: two-thirds for law enforcement to choke supply, one-third for education and treatment to combat demand. The emphasis should be reversed, argue experts such as Dr. Herbert D. Kleber, vice-president of Columbia University's Center on Addiction & Substance Abuse. Although overall

AN OUNCE OF PREVENTION IS WORTH A POUND OF CARE

TYPE OF CARE/PROGRAM	FUTURE SAVING PER $1 OF INVESTMENT NOW
IMMUNIZATION AGAINST CHILDHOOD DISEASES	*$10 in future medical costs*
PRENATAL CARE FOR LOW-INCOME WOMEN	*$3.38 in health care in baby's first year*
JOB CORPS TRAINING FOR DISADVANTAGED YOUTHS	*$1.45 in crime, drug abuse, and welfare costs*
PRESCHOOL EDUCATION	*$4.75 in special education, public assistance, and crime*
EMPLOYMENT TRAINING FOR WELFARE MOTHERS	*$3 in welfare costs*

DATA: COMMITTEE FOR ECONOMIC DEVELOPMENT, U.S. SENATE, MANPOWER DEMONSTRATION RESEARCH CORP., BW

drug use in the U.S. is down, hard-core use is rising: Emergency room overdose cases rose 12% in the six months ending in April, 1991. Prevention is the way to halt that trend, Kleber believes. But, he notes, weaning addicts wins fewer votes than prosecuting drug lords does: "No one ever lost an election because they didn't vote for expanding treatment."

As a result, adds Kleber, a former top official at the National Drug Policy Office, 700,000 addicts a year can't get treatment. Providing it would cost $1.2 billion annually, but that would be well spent. Each dollar in treatment saves $11.54 in costs such as prisons and lost productivity, according to the National Association of State Alcohol & Drug Abuse Directors. A study financed by the National Institute on Drug Abuse of 10,000 individuals in residential, outpatient, and methadone programs found that these methods significantly reduced heroin and cocaine use. Up to five years after treatment, fewer than 20% of the clients were using any drug except marijuana, and the proportion of clients committing predatory crimes was less than one-half of pretreatment levels.

Disadvantaged youths who abuse drugs wreak the most social havoc, so there's a big payoff in helping them. Phoenix House's Rosenthal says residential treatment works particularly well. His group's 18-month program of counseling, education, job training, and recreation helps youths build the self-esteem and self-control they need to kick drugs, finish school, and hold jobs. The yearly cost per kid is $14,000-plus. But Rosenthal claims the results are worth it. More than 90% of his graduates have remained drug-free, law-abiding, and employed—up to seven years after leaving.

Other programs also are trying to lessen drug abuse by attacking the root causes. One, funded in 13 cities by the Robert Wood Johnson Foundation, is called Fighting Back. It brings together police, schools, business, and neighborhood leaders to help cut drug demand. Fighting Back's fledgling program in Newark, N.J., starts with recreational activities at churches and schools to keep kids occupied. Mothers who need drug treatment get child-care vouchers. The foundation has set up a $1 million fund to stimulate economic development, figuring that drug traffic rarely flourishes on busy streets. And Fighting Back is prodding tenants to push courts to evict drug dealers from private housing. "We're trying to create an environment where people believe they can save their neighborhoods," says Irene L. James, director of the Newark effort.

TEEN PREGNANCY. Both drugs and crime are side effects of poverty, which is worsened by a stunning increase in births to unmarried teens. In 1989, some 67% of U.S. teen births were to single mothers, vs. 30% in 1970. Washington spent $25 billion in 1990 on families begun by teen parents. This paid for benefits such as welfare, food stamps, and nutrition programs.

Some experts attribute this escalating problem on the declining economic fortunes of young men: If fathers can't support a family, mothers see little need to marry. Others believe that the culture—changing views on sex, divorce, and parenthood—is partly to blame. In any case, most experts agree that the teens most likely to get pregnant have low self-esteem and no realistic goals.

Several projects are starting to remedy this. In New York, a pregnancy prevention program for 12- to 17-year-olds run by a nonprofit group called Girls Inc. teaches younger teens to become more assertive and helps older ones develop career plans. With greater skills and a sense of self-confidence, participants are half as likely to initiate sexual activity, according to a Girls Inc. study that ran from 1985 to 1987.

WELFARE. Those positive results have important economic implications, since unmarried teen mothers are swelling the welfare rolls. While many use welfare for a shorter time, some 25%—most of them high school dropouts—depend on it for more than 10 years, says Harvard public policy professor David T. Ellwood. How to help this group shake free has been the focus of years of debate. In 1988, Congress passed the Family Support Act, which gave states the power—and matching funds—to set up job-training and placement programs for welfare recipients. But this "workfare" initiative has been disappointing: Many financially strapped states haven't come up with their share for matching grants. Only 53% of the available $1 billion in federal funds has been used. And only 500,000 of the 4.8 million welfare recipients nationwide are in FSA programs now.

Beyond that, such tinkering with the welfare system doesn't address a big problem: For too many low-skilled women, welfare and its accompanying benefits—subsidized child care and Medicaid—pay more than any job they can get. One proposed solution is to abolish welfare, replacing it with a "family security program," as Harvard sociologist Theda R. Skocpol calls it. Her idea, still

embryonic, is to fold cash supports for the poor into a universal social insurance that gives every family affordable health and child care. She would also replace the current tax deduction for dependents with a refundable tax credit. This would give families that earn too little to owe any tax a cash payment.

So that the entire burden wouldn't fall on government, Skocpol adds, such a program would beef up efforts to find absent fathers. Those who are unemployed would get job training and placement. Those who work would have to pay child support. The plan would also make up the difference between what a father could afford and a minimum federal standard. An unlikely team—liberal Thomas J. Downey (D-N.Y.) and conservative Henry J. Hyde (R-Ill.)—have authored a bill to set up such a system, though its chances of passage aren't clear. By putting more of the onus on fathers, they say, the plan could reduce the number of out-of-wedlock pregnancies.

Some 40 states have tried to discourage welfare dependency by freezing or restricting payments. But punitive plans aren't ideal for instilling responsibility. So, Senator David L. Boren (D-Okla.) has introduced a bill that would require recipients, except for those with young children, to work—and would set up a Community Works Project Administration to provide jobs. Such a program would likely be better than current workfare, which only requires recipients to sign up for training or placement. A Boren aide says the cost of the new proposal would exceed Washington's projected welfare tab over the next five years by $8 billion, or 13%. Still, mandatory work might cut down on single

motherhood and give welfare children better role models—first steps toward snapping the cycle of welfare dependency.

FAMILY SERVICES. If a comprehensive approach is to work, Washington has to overhaul the way it delivers services. A family that needs prenatal care, nutrition, Head Start, counseling, housing, and job training faces a formidable array of programs, each with its own rules. "A family could be going to 18 agencies," says Marion W. Pines, a senior policy fellow at Johns Hopkins University.

Some states are starting to coordinate services. Family Partnership in Frederick, Md., is a one-stop center for family services such as literacy education, training, career planning, Head Start, and child care. "They give me help on parenting issues and emotional support, and have put me in touch with financial support," says Karen Spain, 37, a divorced mother of two. Even better, Washington could create a national youth coordinator—sort of a poverty czar—to evaluate programs, publicize effective ones, and streamline the way agencies cooperate.

After years of trial-and-error, experts have learned a great deal about what does and does not alleviate social problems. What is needed now is to replicate on a broad scale the programs with proven records. Politically, of course, it's still more appealing to crack down on drug kingpins and welfare queens and battle crime in the streets. But in the long run, prevention is a far better alternative than living with an unworkable status quo.

By Susan B. Garland, with Christina Del Valle in Washington

Groups and Roles in Transition

- Male/Female Relations and Family Dynamics (Articles 16–18)
- Community Living and Action (Articles 19 and 20)
- Changing Definitions of Disability and Dying (Articles 21 and 22)

Primary groups are small, intimate, spontaneous, and personal. In contrast, secondary groups are large, formal, and impersonal. Often primary groups are formed within a factory, school, or business. Primary groups are the main source that the individual draws upon in developing values and an identity. The family, couples, gangs, cliques, teams, and small tribes or rural villages are examples of primary groups. Secondary groups include most of the organizations and bureaucracies in a modern society, and carry out most of its instrumental functions.

Urbanization, geographic mobility, centralization, bureaucratization, and other aspects of modernization have had an impact on the nature of groups, the quality of the relationships between people, and individuals' feelings of belonging. The family, in particular, is undergoing radical transformation. The greatly increased participation of women in the paid labor force and increased careerism among women have caused severe strains between their work and family roles.

In the first subsection of this unit, various aspects of the changes in sex roles that have taken place in the last three decades are discussed. The changes have been profound and the adjustments for many have been difficult. David Popenoe has written a book on the breakup of the family, the thesis of which is presented in the first article. He relates the problems of the family to social changes in the society, but Peggy Taylor, in the following article, relates them to severe communication problems between spouses due to very different socialization patterns for males and females. An aspect of the sex role problem that receives little attention is what is happening to men. Andrew Kimbrell shows that most men are not "masculine" in the ideal sense. They are subordinated at work and unable to adequately provide for their families. He presents social changes that would address their needs.

The next subsection deals with community living and community action. The most popular style of living place for Americans is the small town, vastly preferred over the suburb, farm or city. Andres Duany and Elizabeth Plater-Zyberk explain this finding by pointing out the failings of suburbs, which are caused mainly by zoning.

Until recently the community or the neighborhood were major foci for sociological research because they were the important context for people's lives. Today people's social ties are less community- or neighborhood-based. Nevertheless, social disorganization is so great in some parts of many cities that community vitality must be regained or life becomes terror, despair, and defeat. Community is difficult to create, however, when couples are so busy and social life is not geographically based. David Osborne provides an example of community building. He describes the wonderful accomplishments of the people of a public housing project who have taken over its management, cleaned it up, made it safe, and launched programs to improve the lives of the residents.

The last subsection deals with changing attitudes toward disabilities and handling death and dying. Howard Schwartz argues that people with disabilities have achieved a high level of social acceptance and in some ways are valued more highly than persons who are non-disabled. Public opinion has improved considerably in recent years, as Schwartz demonstrates in his study of attitudes toward a physically disabled person being the subject of a *Playboy* photo layout. His analysis has implications for the sociology of deviance.

The painful issues of dying that advances in modern medicine have created are discussed in "Dignity, Choice, and Care." Today we are confronted with the shocking question "Is it good to let people die and bad to let them live?" Should death be helped along? Some say that life is sacred and should be protected at all costs. Others talk about dying with dignity. Death has become an ideological problem.

Looking Ahead: Challenge Questions

How can women balance family and career? What changes are needed in the work world to accommodate two-career families? How can these changes be brought about?

How satisfactory are traditional male roles? How realistic is the masculine ideal?

Is power and competition the key to the world of men?

What factors are needed to make self-help work? Why are disadvantaged groups so infrequently mobilized?

What factors create community? How can they be brought into being under today's conditions? What are the impediments to community?

How do people with disabilities want to be treated? Why have attitudes toward them improved substantially?

Is there a point where death is good and not bad? If yes, where is that point? What actions are permissible at that point, and who should decide on those actions? What are the dangers of such policies?

BREAKUP OF THE FAMILY:
Can We Reverse the Trend?

"What is needed is a new social movement [that stresses] . . . a lasting, monogamous, heterosexual relationship which includes the procreation of children."

David Popenoe

Dr. Popenoe, Associate Dean for the Social Sciences, Rutgers University, New Brunswick, N.J., is the author of Disturbing the Nest: Family Change and Decline in Modern Societies.

AS a social institution, the family has been "in decline" since the beginning of world history. It gradually has been becoming weaker through losing social functions and power to other institutions such as church, government, and school. Yet, during the past 25 years, family decline in the U.S., as in other industrialized societies, has been both steeper and more alarming than during any other quarter-century in our history. Although they may not use the term decline, most scholars now agree—though for many this represents a recent change of viewpoint—that the family has undergone a social transformation during this period. Some see "dramatic and unparalleled changes," while others call it "a veritable revolution."

I believe, in short, that we are witnessing the end of an epoch. Today's societal trends are bringing to a close the cultural dominance of the traditional nuclear family—one situated apart from both the larger kin group and the workplace, and focused on procreation. It consists of a legal, lifelong, sexually exclusive, heterosexual, monogamous marriage, based on affection and companionship, in which there is a sharp division of labor (separate spheres), with the female as full-time housewife and the male as primary provider and ultimate authority. Lasting for only a little more than a century, this family form emphasized the male as "good provider," the female as "good wife and mother," and the paramount importance of the family for childbearing. (Of course, not all families were able to live up to these cultural ideals.) During its heyday, the terms family, home, and mother ranked extraordinarily high in the hierarchy of cultural values.

In certain respects, this family form reached its apogee in the middle of the 20th century. By the 1950's—fueled in part by falling maternal and child mortality rates, greater longevity, and a high marriage rate—a larger percentage of children than ever before were growing up in stable, two-parent families. Similarly, this period witnessed the highest-ever proportion of women who married, bore children, and lived jointly with their husbands until at least age 50.

In the 1960's, however, four major social trends emerged to signal a widespread "flight" from both the ideal and the reality of the traditional nuclear family: rapid fertility decline, the sexual revolution, the movement of mothers into the labor force, and the upsurge in divorce. None of these changes was new to the 1960's; each represents a tendency that already was in evidence in earlier years. What happened in the 1960's was a striking acceleration of the trends, made more dramatic by the fact that, during the 1950's, they had leveled off and, in some cases, even reversed direction.

First, fertility declined in the U.S. by almost 50% between 1960 and 1989, from an average of 3.7 children per woman to only 1.9. Although births have been diminishing gradually for several centuries (the main exception being the two decades following World War II), the level of fertility during the past decade was the lowest in U.S. history and below that necessary for the replacement of the population.

A growing dissatisfaction with parenthood is now evident among adults in our culture, along with a dramatic decrease in the stigma associated with childlessness. Some demographers predict that 20-25% of today's young women will remain completely childless, and nearly 50% will be either childless or have only one offspring.

Second, the sexual revolution has shattered the association of sex and reproduction. The erotic has become a necessary ingredient of personal well-being and fulfillment, both in and outside of marriage, as well as a highly marketable commodity. The greatest change has been in the area of premarital sex. From 1971 to 1982 alone, the proportion of unmarried females in the U.S. aged 15-19 who engaged in premarital sexual intercourse jumped up from 28 to 44%. This behavior reflects a widespread change in values; in 1967, 85% of Americans condemned premarital sex as morally wrong, compared to 37% in 1979.

The sexual revolution has been a major contributor to the striking increase in unwed parenthood. Nonmarital births jumped from five percent of all births in 1960 (22% of black births) to 22% in 1985 (60% of black births). This is the highest rate of nonmarital births ever recorded in the U.S.

Third, although unmarried women long have been in the labor force, the past quarter-century has witnessed a striking movement into the paid work world of married women with children. In 1960, only 19% of married women with children under the age of six were in the labor force (39% with children between six and 17); by 1986, this figure had climbed to 54% (68% of those with older children).

Fourth, the divorce rate in the U.S. over the past 25 years (as measured by the number of divorced persons per 1,000 married persons) has practically quadrupled, going from 35 to 130. This has led many to refer to a divorce revolution. The probability that a marriage contracted today will end in divorce ranges from 44 to 66%, depending upon the method of calculation.

These trends signal a widespread retreat from the traditional nuclear family in its dimensions of a lifelong, sexually exclusive unit, focused on children, with a division of labor between husband and wife. Unlike most previous change, which reduced family functions and diminished the importance of the kin group, that of the past 25 years has tended to break up the nucleus of the family unit—the bond between husband and wife. Nuclear units, therefore, are losing ground to single-parent households, serial and step-families, and unmarried and homosexual couples.

The number of single-parent families, for example, has grown sharply—the result not only of marital breakup, but also of marriage decline (fewer persons who bear children are getting married) and

widespread male abandonment. In 1960, only nine percent of U.S. children under 18 were living with a lone parent; by 1986, this figure had climbed to nearly one-quarter of all children. (The comparable figures for blacks are 22 and 53%.) Of children born during 1950-54, only 19% of whites (48% of blacks) had lived in a single-parent household by the time they reached age 17. For children born in 1990, however, the figure is projected to be 70% (94% for blacks).

The psychological character of the marital relationship also has changed substantially over the years. Traditionally, marriage has been understood as a social obligation—an institution designed mainly for economic security and procreation. Today, marriage is understood mainly as a path toward self-fulfillment. One's self-development is seen to require a significant other, and marital partners are picked primarily to be personal companions. Put another way, marriage is becoming deinstitutionalized. No longer comprising a set of norms and social obligations that are enforced widely, marriage today is a voluntary relationship that individuals can make and break at will. As one indicator of this shift, laws regulating marriage and divorce have become increasingly more lax.

As psychological expectations for marriage grow ever higher, dashed expectations for personal fulfillment fuel our society's high divorce rate. Divorce also feeds upon itself. With more divorce, the more "normal" it becomes, with fewer negative sanctions to oppose it and more potential partners available. In general, psychological need, in and of itself, has proved to be a weak basis for stable marriage.

Trends such as these dramatically have reshaped people's lifetime connectedness to the institution of the family. Broadly speaking, the institution of the family has weakened substantially over the past quarter-century in a number of respects. Individual members have become more autonomous and less bound by the group, and the latter has become less cohesive. Fewer of its traditional social functions are now carried out by the family; these have shifted to other institutions. The family has grown smaller in size, less stable, and with a shorter life span; people are, therefore, family members for a smaller percentage of their lives. The proportion of an average person's adulthood spent with spouse and children was 62% in 1960, the highest in our history. Today, it has dropped to a low of 43%.

The outcome of these trends is that people have become less willing to invest time, money, and energy in family life. It is the individual, not the family unit, in whom the main investments increasingly are made.

These trends are all evident, in varying degrees, in every industrialized Western society. This suggests that their source lies not in particular political or economic systems, but in a broad cultural shift that has accompanied industrialization and urbanization. In these societies, there clearly has emerged an ethos of radical individualism in which personal autonomy, individual rights, and social equality have gained supremacy as cultural ideals. In keeping with these ideals, the main goals of personal behavior have shifted from commitment to social units of all kinds (families, communities, religions, nations) to personal choices, lifestyle options, self-fulfillment, and personal pleasure.

Social consequences

How are we to evaluate the social consequences of recent family decline? Certainly, one should not jump immediately to the conclusion that it is necessarily bad for our society. A great many positive aspects to the recent changes stand out as noteworthy. During this same quarter-century, women and many minorities clearly have improved their status and probably the overall quality of their lives. Much of women's status gain has come through their release from family duties and increased participation in the labor force. In addition, given the great emphasis on psychological criteria for choosing and keeping marriage partners, it can be argued persuasively that those marriages today which do endure are more likely than ever before to be true companionships that are emotionally rewarding.

This period also has seen improved health care and longevity, as well as widespread economic affluence that has produced, for most people, a material standard of living that is historically unprecedented. Some of this improvement is due to the fact that people no longer are dependent on their families for health care and economic support or imprisoned by social class and family obligation. When in need, they now can rely more on public care and support, as well as self-initiative and self-development.

Despite these positive aspects, the negative consequences of family decline are real and profound. The greatest negative effect of recent trends, in the opinion of nearly everyone, is on children. Because they represent the future of a society, any negative consequences for them are especially significant. There is substantial, if not conclusive, evidence that, partly due to family changes, the quality of life for children in the past 25 years has worsened. Much of the problem is of a psychological nature, and thus difficult to measure quantitatively.

Perhaps the most serious problem is a

weakening of the fundamental assumption that children are to be loved and valued at the highest level of priority. The general disinvestment in family life that has occurred has commonly meant a disinvestment in children's welfare. Some refer to this as a national "parent deficit." Yet, the deficit goes well beyond parents to encompass an increasingly less child-friendly society.

The parent deficit is blamed all too easily on newly working women. Yet, it is men who have left the parenting scene in large numbers. More than ever before, fathers are denying paternity, avoiding their parental obligations, and absent from home. (At the same time, there has been a slow, but not offsetting, growth of the "house-father" role.)

The breakup of the nuclear unit has been the focus of much concern. Virtually every child desires two biological parents for life, and substantial evidence exists that childrearing is most successful when it involves two parents, both of whom are strongly motivated to the task. This is not to say that other family forms can not be successful, only that, as a group, they are not as likely to be so. This also is not to claim that the two strongly motivated parents must be organized in the patriarchal and separate-sphere terms of the traditional nuclear family.

Regardless of family form, there has been a significant change over the past quarter-century in what can be called the social ecology of childhood. Advanced societies are moving ever further from what many hold to be a highly desirable child-rearing environment, one consisting of a relatively large family that does a lot of things together, has many routines and traditions, and provides a great deal of quality contact time between adults and children; regular contact with relatives, active neighboring in a supportive neighborhood, and contact with the adult world of work; little concern on the part of children that their parents will break up; and the coming together of all these ingredients in the development of a rich family subculture that has lasting meaning and strongly promulgates such values as cooperation and sharing.

Agendas for change

What should be done to counteract or remedy the negative effects of family decline? This is the most controversial question of all, and the most difficult to answer. Among the agendas for change that have been put forth, two extremes stand out as particularly prominent in the national debate. The first is a return to the structure of the traditional nuclear family characteristic of the 1950's; the second is the development of extensive governmental policies.

Aside from the fact that it probably is impossible to return to a situation of an earlier time, the first alternative has major drawbacks. It would require many women to leave the workforce and, to some extent, become "de-liberated," an unlikely occurrence indeed. Economic conditions necessitate that even more women take jobs, and cultural conditions stress ever greater equality between the sexes.

In addition to such considerations, the traditional nuclear family form, in today's world, may be fundamentally flawed. As an indication of this, one should realize that the young people who led the transformation of the family during the 1960's and 1970's were brought up in 1950's households. If the 1950's families were so wonderful, why didn't their children seek to emulate them? In hindsight, the 1950's seem to have been beset with problems that went well beyond patriarchy and separate spheres. For many families, the mother-child unit had become increasingly isolated from the kin group, the neighborhood and community, and even from the father, who worked a long distance away. This was especially true for women who were fully educated and eager to take their place in work and public life. Maternal childrearing under these historically unprecedented circumstances became highly problematic.

Despite such difficulties, the traditional nuclear family is still the one of choice for millions of Americans. They are comfortable with it, and for them it seems to work. It is reasonable, therefore, at least not to place roadblocks in the way of couples with children who wish to conduct their lives according to the traditional family's dictates. Women who freely desire to spend much of their lives as mothers and housewives, outside of the labor force, should not be penalized economically by public policy for making that choice. Nor should they be denigrated by our culture as second-class citizens.

The second major proposal for change that has been stressed in national debate is the development of extensive governmental programs offering monetary support and social services for families, especially the new "non-nuclear" ones. In some cases, these programs assist with functions these families are unable to perform adequately; in others, the functions are taken over, transforming them from family to public responsibilities.

This is the path followed by the European welfare states, but it has been less accepted by the U.S. than by any other industrialized nation. The European welfare states have been far more successful than the U.S. in minimizing the negative economic impact of family decline, especially children. In addition, many European nations have established policies making it much easier for women (and increasingly men) to combine work with childrearing. With these successes in mind, it seems inevitable that the U.S. will (and I believe should) move gradually in the European direction with respect to family policies, just as we are now moving gradually in that direction with respect to medical care.

There are clear drawbacks, however, in moving too far down this road. If children are to be served best, we should seek to make the family stronger, not to replace it. At the same time that welfare states are minimizing some of the consequences of decline, they also may be causing further breakup of the family unit. This phenomenon can be witnessed today in Sweden, where the institution of the family probably has grown weaker than anywhere else in the world. On a lesser scale, it has been seen in the U.S. in connection with our welfare programs. Fundamental to successful welfare state programs, therefore, is keeping uppermost in mind that the ultimate goal is to strengthen families.

While each of the above alternatives has some merit, I suggest a third one. It is premised on the fact that we can not return to the 1950's family, nor can we depend on the welfare state for a solution. Instead, we should strike at the heart of the cultural shift that has occurred, point up its negative aspects, and seek to reinvigorate the cultural ideals of family, parents, and children within the changed circumstances of our time. We should stress that the individualistic ethos has gone too far, that children are getting woefully short-changed, and that, over the long run, strong families represent the best path toward self-fulfillment and personal happiness. We should bring again to the cultural forefront the old ideal of parents living together and sharing responsibility for their children and for each other.

What is needed is a new social movement whose purpose is the promotion of families and their values within the new constraints of modern life. It should point out the supreme importance to society of strong families, while at the same time suggesting ways they can adapt better to the modern conditions of individualism, equality, and the labor force participation of both women and men. Such a movement could build on the fact that the overwhelming majority of young people today still put forth as their major life goal a lasting, monogamous, heterosexual relationship which includes the procreation of children. It is reasonable to suppose that this goal is so pervasive because it is based on a deep-seated human need.

The time seems ripe to reassert that strong families concerned with the needs of children are not only possible, but necessary.

Can We Talk?

Why do so many women say that men don't tell them anything, but just lecture and criticize? Why do so many men say that women nag them and waste their time with small talk? A sociolinguist offers provocative insights into male-female communication.

Peggy Taylor

A New Age Journal Interview with Deborah Tannen

Imagine attempting to negotiate the tortuous twists and turns of a relationship with a partner who was raised speaking a different language and hewing to a different value system and world view from your own. It'd be tough, wouldn't it? Yet according to sociolinguist Deborah Tannen, that's exactly what millions of exasperated American men and women are doing every day.

In her provocative new best-selling book, *You Just Don't Understand: Women and Men in Conversation,* Tannen argues that much of the male-female strife with which all of us are so achingly familiar can be traced back to the fact that boys and girls grow up in essentially different cultures. By the time they become men and women—and begin interacting in relationships—they possess radically divergent styles of communication and conversation. As a result, transacting everything from which restaurant to go to for dinner to the very future of a relationship can and often does end up mired in misunderstanding, frustration, and conflict. And partners blame themselves—and each other—when they might more profitably be trying to understand their mate's words and behavior, much as they would try to decode a foreign visitor's halting English. "Talk between women and men is cross-cultural communication," Tannen writes. "If we recognize and understand the differences between us, we can take them into account, adjust to and learn from each other's styles."

Tannen, forty-five, a professor of linguistics at Georgetown University, has been studying the intricacies of everyday conversation for the better part of two decades. As a scholar, she says she is well aware of the dangers of painting with too broad a brush. Certainly all of us know men and women who defy any number of gender stereotypes. Yet, she asserts, the risk involved in ignoring sex differences is greater than the danger in naming them.

"Sweeping something big under the rug doesn't make it go away," she writes. "Denying real differences can only compound the confusion that is already widespread in this era of shifting and reforming relationships between women and men."

NEW AGE JOURNAL: *How did you get interested in studying the dynamics of male-female communication?*

DEBORAH TANNEN: While I was doing research for a book about everyday conversation, I was invited to study a series of videotapes that psychologist Bruce Dorval had made of males and females, ranging from seven years old to twenty-five, talking to their best friends of the same gender. I had intended to use the tapes to study the use of repetition in conversation. But instead, as I watched them back to back, I wound up being stunned by the differences between the males and females. It was overwhelming.

What kinds of differences did you see?

The first thing that struck me was their physical alignment. The girls would face each other physically and look directly at each other, while the boys sat parallel or at angles and didn't look directly at each other. The girls responded very conge-

nially to the request that they just sit and talk to each other; the boys, on the other hand, were extremely uncomfortable—as if they were being asked to do something bizarre. The youngest boys, for example, kept saying things like, "I can't wait till we play games. What games does he have?" And, "Do you want to come over to my house and ride my bike?" They kept talking about a time that they could *do* something. The overall topics they talked about were also completely different. The girls quickly settled on talking about the problems of one girl and then went on talking about that. This happened with all the different age groups. The boys jumped from topic to topic. They didn't talk about any one topic for more than just a few turns. Suddenly it struck me: These kids are growing up in different worlds.

In your book you characterize the boy's world as dominated by a hierarchical social order where you're either one up or one down. Girls, on the other hand, live in a network of social connections, where intimacy and community are paramount. How does this affect our way of communicating?

For males, conversation is the way you negotiate your status in the group and keep people from pushing you around; you use talk to preserve your independence. Females, on the other hand, use conversation to negotiate closeness and intimacy; talk is the essence of intimacy, so being best friends means sitting and talking. For boys, activities, doing things together, are central. Just sitting and talking is not an essential part of friendship. They're friends with the boys they do things with.

Reprinted from *New Age Journal,* November/December 1990, pp. 31-33, 60-64, 107-108.

So what implications does this hold for us as adults?

It causes a lot of friction and confusion in adult relationships. What happens is that the same situation can have a very different meaning depending on whether you are looking at it from the female perspective—connection and intimacy—or from the male perspective of relative dominance; i.e., who's one up, who's one down.

Can you give some examples?

OK, let's take the issue of asking for directions. Men generally don't want to stop to ask for directions and women do. Women can't understand why men don't want to do it. To women, asking for directions means having a fleeting connection with a stranger. That's a positive thing. You don't lose anything. But for a man, it means you're putting yourself "one down" to a stranger, and that's very uncomfortable. As an extension of that, men assume that if the person they're asking doesn't know, he's going to tell them the wrong thing, since admitting ignorance would put him "one down." Women think if the person doesn't know, he'll simply say so.

Another example comes from a story about my parents. While I was working on my research for this book, I would periodically ask them to tell me about their most recent arguments. One time my father said that my mother had recently noticed that he was holding his arm funny, so she asked him what was wrong. When he told her it was hurting him, she asked, "For how long?" He said, "About two weeks." And she said, "Go ahead, treat me like a stranger." I instinctively understood my mother's feeling about it, but I hadn't a clue why my father wouldn't have told her. So I asked him. "Well I guess from the beginning men learn to be protective of women," he told me. That was the biggest nonsequitur I had ever heard! What did that have to do with telling her that his arm hurt? He explained, "Well, if I tell her about something that's bothering me, then she worries. So why should I worry her? It might be nothing and go away."

I've since heard from other men that they don't tell their wives things because they don't want to worry them. And yet for women, not being told something is the very worst thing. They see it as a big rejection, because for women, intimacy is telling secrets, and if you withhold something, you're not as intimate as they'd like.

Male and female sales people provide another example. Women often feel that if they go to buy a computer or something from a male, he gives information in a way that makes them feel stupid, using terms they don't understand. And if they tell him they don't understand, then he acts like they're even stupider. Many male sales people tend to use information to establish a one-up position. Women sales people, on the other hand, don't tend to use the information they know to make themselves feel better. In fact, they seem to feel best if they can help you know as much as they do.

After reading a draft of my book, a male colleague of mine went to a conference and then told me he suddenly understood what women are doing when they give talks. A woman who was giving a paper at the conference kept saying, "Do you understand? Do you follow me?" And he said it blew his mind that her main concern really was that the audience understand her. When he gives a paper, he said, he's not concerned with that; he's concerned that no one in the audience be able to stand up and put him down once he stops talking. He's covering his ass (*laughs*). Whether or not people understand what he's talking about is way down on his list of priorities.

This makes men seem awfully foolish.

(*Laughs*). That's because you're a woman. Now, here is the stand that I take. Men live in a world where people *are* in fact trying to put them down. So that perspective makes sense to them. The women's world is not like that, so it doesn't make sense to us.

What are the most common conflicts that couples run into as a result of trying to communicate across this gender gap?

The biggest complaint I hear from women is that their partners don't talk or listen to them. Women are seeking that certain kind of conversation that they feel is the essence of closeness and intimacy; that kind where I tell you everything that's on my mind and discuss everything with you. Men don't have those kinds of conversations, so they don't know what women are trying to get at. They can't figure out what women want from them. They feel that women just go on and on about nothing (*laughs*). So we have the scenario where the woman's trying to talk, and the guy's got the newspaper in front of his face because he feels there's nothing to talk about.

A central area of confusion for couples involves what I call "troubles talk." For women, talking about troubles is the essence of connection. I tell you my troubles, you tell me your troubles, and we're close. Men, however, hear troubles talk as a request for advice, so they respond with a solution.

Here's a typical example: A taxi driver was telling me about communication with his wife. "What she says doesn't make any sense," he told me. When I asked for an example, he said, "OK, she says all of a sudden, apropos of nothing, 'What should my brother do?' " And he said to me, "Her brother's thirty-five. Why should I give him advice?" Now, advice had nothing to do with it for her, I'm sure. She just wanted to start a certain kind of conversation. She wanted to talk about things. But he heard it as, "I want you to give my brother advice."

So if a woman is having a problem and she starts talking about it, she's looking for something different than a man might be looking for?

I think so. I think for most men, talking about the problem is wallowing in it and makes them feel worse. For women, talking about it makes them feel better, because it makes them feel connected to someone; they don't feel alone with their problems.

So even if a solution isn't arrived at, that's not the point?

Right. It's not only not the point, but it gets in the way, because if she wants to keep talking about it and he comes in with a solution, then there's nothing more to talk about. One woman told me that when she talks to her partner about a problem and he just moves in with a solution, she feels he's diminishing her problem. I told her that he is, but from his vantage point that's a nice thing to do.

Why is that?

This is well illustrated by Dorval's tape of tenth-grade boys talking to each other. Each one is talking about his own problems and dismissing the other's problems as if to imply, "You shouldn't feel bad, because your problem isn't so bad." The boys seemed to be very happy with that.

What kinds of complaints do you hear from men about women?

The most common one is that women complain all the time and don't want to do anything about it: "She asks for my advice and then she doesn't want to take it." Men misunderstand the ritual nature of women's complaining. She'll tell about a trouble, and he'll tell her how to fix it. Because he really thinks that she's asked for advice, he's frustrated that she won't take it. I often hear things like, "My wife complains and complains about her job. And then I say, 'If you hate your job so much, why don't you quit?' Then she'll say, 'Huh? I love my job.' " Just because she's complaining doesn't mean that she hates it. But a man assumes that she does—because *he* wouldn't complain that way unless he really *did* hate his job.

So the most common problem is that men don't want to talk and women want to talk all the time—

At home.

At home?

Yes. It's not that women talk more than men overall; it's that women talk more *at home* since talk, for them, is a way of creating intimacy. Since men regard talk as a means to negotiate status, they often see no need to talk at home. But they talk more in public situations with people they know less well. At a meeting, when questions are solicited from the floor, it is almost always a man who speaks first. When the phones are opened on a radio talk show, the vast majority of calls are from men, who are more likely to speak at length, giving introductions to their questions (if they have any), and addressing multiple topics.

Another common cause of frustration between couples is that when women are focusing on intimacy or connection, men often feel like they're being pushed around.

Can you give an example of that?

An example I give in the book is a common one. It involves a woman who won't make plans without checking them first with her husband. He, on the other hand, simply reports his own plans to her as a fait accompli. "Why don't you tell your friends you need to check with me?" she says. To which he replies, "I can't tell my friends that I need to ask my wife for permission." Thus, the same act—checking plans with a spouse—connotes very different things for husband and wife. For her, it simply means, "We are connected to each other."

And for him?

It means, "one up, one down." Having to check reminds a man of being a child. Unlike women, men have a gut-level resistance to doing what they're told, to doing what someone expects them to do.

Here's another example. It's a bit explosive because it has to do with sleeping with other women. But I think the way they talk about it is significant. A woman told me that she was living with a man

and they had an understanding that they wouldn't hurt each other *and* they wouldn't limit each other's freedom. So he starts sleeping with other women and she registers a complaint. "This is hurting me, and we agreed not to hurt each other." And he says, "But you're limiting my freedom." And she says, "Well, how can you keep doing it when you know it makes me feel so bad?" And he says, "You're manipulating me."

When I heard that, I thought, There's something so universal about this; I mean I've heard this kind of thing so many times. Men feeling that women are manipulating them, because women want men to do what we want. We want them *to want* to do what we want, because that's what *we* do. If a woman perceives that something she's doing is really hurting a man, she wants to stop doing it. If she perceives that he really wants her to do something, she wants to do it. So she thinks that that's love and he should feel the same way toward her. But men have a gut-level resistance to doing what they're told, to doing what someone expects them to do. It's the opposite response of what women have.

I think men might beg to differ with that point.

I actually haven't heard men disagreeing with that. They have told me that it seems right to say that men are sensitive to being told what to do, so if they feel somebody's telling them what to do, they want to resist. Now, certainly there are men who are very eager to please their wives—I would not want to say that that's never the case. But if a man is going to be touchy, it's more likely to go in that direction. Whereas if a woman is insecure, she's more likely to go in the other direction, be super-accommodating.

And where does that tendency to accommodate stem from?

Once again, I trace it back to the way girls and boys talk among their friends. In the girls' groups, there's a great premium put on being agreeable and being the same.

And the boys—

Resist doing what they're told. Because to them, being given orders, being told to do something, means the other person is dominant and they don't want to be dominated. So I think much of what comes off as men dominating women is really men's response to the fear of being dominated. Women don't see that because it's not a threat that their antennae are tuned to. Instead, they're watching for any sign that

someone might be pushing them away. Men worry about being pushed around; women, about being pushed away.

So it sounds like you're saying that in a classic domestic squabble such as a woman asking her mate to take out the garbage, there's likely to be two very different agendas going on. The woman who's asking her mate to help out probably thinks, What's the big deal? It'll just take a minute. But for the man it may really be a big deal.

I think so. As in, "Uh oh, she's telling me what to do. If I hop to, I'm subordinate here." It's an alignment that's being established: I'm one down and I'm being told what to do. Whereas for her, it's just one request. She's thinking of it as if they're on equal footing and no one is one up or one down.

This is the sort of thing that I think comes out so clearly in the research on kids. And here it's Marjorie Harness Goodwin's research that's so crucial. She's an anthropologist who hung around with the kids in her Philadelphia neighborhood for a year and half, recording everything they said. She found that boys give orders as a way of gaining social status. The high-status boys gave orders just to maintain their dominance, not because they particularly needed the thing done. And the boys who were being told what to do were low status, by virtue of doing what they were told. So men's response makes sense in the context of the social groups they grew up in.

Girls, on the other hand, are egalitarian. No one is giving orders; people are making suggestions and the group tends to take up those suggestions.

Egalitarian sounds so good. What's the dark side to the way young girls relate?

It's that if a girl does something the other girls don't like, she'll be criticized, or even ostracized. That's why when I talk about this, some men say to me, Well, obviously the boys' way is better because look at what bitches girls are. And what do girls put other girls down for? For standing out, for seeming better than the others. Goodwin has two examples of girls who got ostracized—one because she was wearing clothes that were better than the other girls', the other because she skipped a grade of school and she boasted about it. I mean, really—no wonder people talk about women's fear of success!

So you're saying the female mode prevents excellence?

It prevents *displaying* it.

That wouldn't seem to bode well for

women's prospects in male-dominated fields like business or politics.

Well, what's so depressing is that women are in a double bind. If we talk in ways expected of women, we're thought incompetent, yet if we talk in ways expected of men, we're called bitches. This doesn't leave a lot of options. And of course there are women who are succeeding, and we all succeed somewhat, but it is frustrating. But as more women get into these fields, things have got to get better.

One thing that's encouraging is that I've heard from management consultants that there's a kind of movement out there toward what might be called a feminine managerial style. That is, managing by consensus rather than fiat. I think the fact that Americans are giving more respect to the Japanese is going to be a factor, too, because what I refer to as women's style is close in many ways to the Japanese way of doing business. A lot of men call in to talk shows that I'm on and say, "Well obviously women's ways are ridiculous and men's ways are better because who would want to spend all this time talking about personal things before you get down to business?" And I tell them, "If you're doing business with a Japanese businessman, then the woman's way is going to work much better, and your way isn't going to get you anywhere." It's definitely characteristic of the Japanese style to make sure there's a personal relationship as a foundation for doing business. And to be indirect: not to get right to the point.

Are you saying women typically communicate more indirectly than men in our culture?

Well, not across the board. If you ask, for example, about what's bothering you—how do you *feel*?—then women will be more direct. But I think men are more direct when it comes to making decisions about what to do.

In relationships, too?

Yes. Something I hear a lot is that women feel men make all the decisions and don't take their wishes into account. This problem often can be traced to conversations in which a woman tries to start a discussion by asking a question. For example, a couple's driving in a car, and the woman says, "Would you like to stop for a drink?" The man replies, "No." And that's the end of that. She then feels, "He doesn't care what I want. He's not interested." She thinks he should have responded by asking her what she wanted. Then they could talk about it and come to a decision by consensus. But he took the question literally. Later, when he finds out that she's

annoyed, he feels that he's being manipulated: "You didn't tell me what you wanted, and now you're mad at me because you didn't get it. Why don't you just tell me what you want in the first place?" In fact she did try to tell him but she didn't get to, because her way of starting the negotiation got short-circuited.

In reading parts of your book it's hard not to think that the female modes of interaction are in some sense superior. Do men feel slighted by your work?

Not at all. The reaction I've gotten from men has been very enthusiastic. I think men in particular are relieved to see a woman writing about this phenomenon in a way that doesn't *blame* them. A lot of self-help books—and by the way, I feel strongly that mine is *not* one—imply that there's something wrong with men because they don't communicate like women.

And you don't think so?

I think it's crucial to realize that if the vast majority of men act like this starting from as early as two-and-a-half to three years old, there's a limit to how much you can say their behavior is pathological. We might say that men would be better off if they were different, but we don't want to say that they're sick.

That intimate talk is a healthier way of communicating?

Right. Now I know that there is some research that says that if people talk about their problems they get better sooner—they don't grieve as long and things like that—and I don't want to question those findings. But after all, there are entire cultures where no one, man or woman, would ever talk openly about their problems; are we going to say those cultures are sick? Of course, that doesn't mean that people can't change if they want to.

Except that, for the last twenty years at least, women have been trying very hard to get men to change toward what you might call a more female style of communication—with what seems like limited success.

There's always going to be a few men who come over. Talking more intimately is a learnable skill, as we've seen from the encounter groups and sensitivity-training movement of the '60s. But you're right; it hasn't affected many men, and it certainly hasn't broken through to the mainstream.

My husband, for example, likes to sit and talk with his friends about whatever's on his mind. And he always laments how hard it is to find other men who are willing to do that.

So it's going to be a good, long time before

the sexes reach common ground. That's pretty discouraging.

Well, yes and no. Certainly a lot of profound unhappiness is caused by these differences; after all, there's nothing more deeply distressing than to have your fundamental intent misunderstood by the person you're closest to. On the other hand, if women can begin to understand that intimate talk doesn't have the same meaning to a man as it does to them—and men can begin to understand women's need to share and connect—then maybe at least people can avoid the feeling that something is terribly wrong with their relationships. Realizing that a partner's behavior is not his or her individual failing, but a normal expression of gender, lifts this burden of blame and disappointment. Understanding gender differences in ways of communication is the first step toward change.

And what comes next?

From there, there are two options: Make adjustments, or learn to accept. Clearly the choice will depend on the individuals involved. If you're with a person who's amenable to negotiation, then I think the ideal thing is for each person to give a little. Some men have learned over time the kinds of stories their wives want to hear, and they've learned to come home and tell them. Now, they'll probably never do it exactly the way the woman would like, but it's closer. And then other women just accept that they're not going to get the kind of intimate communication they want from their husband, and don't take it as a tremendous failure of the relationship. "I'd rather he talk to me that way, but he doesn't," they say, in effect. "I'll get it from my friends."

If the men and women of our generation have already been polarized to some extent, what about our children? Can we raise them to break down the barriers?

I think what parents can do is limited. But again, I think awareness is the most important thing. That doesn't mean trying to make sons like daughters and daughters like sons. Rather, it means instilling a flexibility and mutual respect in children of both genders. That would be the ideal.

Is there a larger metaphor in your plea for understanding and tolerance between the sexual "cultures"?

Yes, I definitely see it as part and parcel of the larger cross-cultural perspective. What I'm ultimately advocating, in a sense, is respect for diversity—of all sorts.

A time for men to pull together

A manifesto for the new politics of masculinity

ANDREW KIMBRELL · SPECIAL TO UTNE READER

Andrew Kimbrell is an attorney and policy director for the Foundation on Economic Trends in Washington, D.C. (although the views expressed here do not necessarily reflect those of the foundation). His work has appeared in Harper's, *the* Washington Post, *and the* New York Times. *He's interested in hearing from people with ideas about a national Men's Action Network. Write to him c/o Utne Reader.*

"Our civilization is a dingy ungentlemanly business; it drops so much out of a man."
—Robert Louis Stevenson

Men are hurting—badly. Despite rumors to the contrary, men as a gender are being devastated physically and psychically by our socioeconomic system. As American society continues to empower a small percentage of men—and a smaller but increasing percentage of women—it is causing significant confusion and anguish for the majority of men.

In recent years, there have been many impressive analyses documenting the exploitation of women in our culture. Unfortunately, little attention has been given to the massive disruption and destruction that our economic and political institutions have wrought on men. In fact, far too often, men as a gender have been thought of as synonymous with the power elite.

But thinking on this subject is beginning to change. Over the last decade, men have begun to realize that we cannot properly relate to one another, or understand how some of us in turn exploit others, until we have begun to appreciate the extent and nature of our dispossessed predicament. In a variety of ways, men across the country are beginning to mourn their losses and seek solutions.

This new sense of loss among men comes from the deterioration of men's traditional roles as protectors of family and the earth (although not the sole protectors)—what psychologist Robert Mannis calls the *generative* potential of men. And much of this mourning also focuses on how men's energy is often channeled in the direction of destruction—both of the earth and its inhabitants.

The mission of many men today—both those involved in the men's movement and others outside it—is to find new ways that allow men to celebrate their generative potential and reverse the cycle of destruction that characterizes men's collective behavior today. These calls to action are not abstract or hypothetical. The oppression of men, especially in the last several decades, can be easily seen in a disturbing upward spiral of male self-destruction, addiction, hopelessness, and homelessness.

While suicide rates for women have been stable over the last 20 years, among men—especially white male teenagers—they have increased rapidly. Currently, male teenagers are five times more likely to take their own lives than females. Overall, men are committing suicide at four times the rate of women. America's young men are also being rav-

Most men lead powerless, subservient lives in the factory or office.

aged by alcohol and drug abuse. Men between the ages of 18 and 29 suffer alcohol dependency at three times the rate of women of the same age group. More than two-thirds of all alcoholics are men, and 50 percent more men are regular users of illicit drugs than women. Men account for more than 90 percent of arrests for alcohol and drug abuse violations.

A sense of hopelessness among America's young men is not surprising. Real wages for men under 25 have actually declined over the last 20 years, and 60 percent of all high school dropouts are males. These statistics, added to the fact that more than 400,000 farmers have lost their land in the last decade, account in part for the increasing rate of unemployment among men, and for the fact that more than 80 percent of America's homeless are men.

The stress on men is taking its toll. Men's life expectancy is 10 percent shorter than women's, and the incidence of stress-related illnesses such as heart disease and certain cancers remains inordinately high among men.

And the situation for minority men is even worse. One out of four black men between the ages of 20 and 29 is either in jail, on probation, or on parole—ten times the proportion for black women in the same age range. More black men are in jail than in college, and there are 40 percent more black women than black men studying in our nation's colleges and universities. Homicide is the leading cause of death among black males ages 15 to 24. Black males have the lowest life expectancy of any segment of the American population. Statistics for Native American and Hispanic men are also grim.

Men are also a large part of the growing crisis in the American family. Studies report that parents today spend 40 percent less time with their children than did parents in 1965, and men are increasingly isolated from their families by the pressures of work and the circumstances of divorce. In a recent poll, 72 percent of employed male respondents agreed that they are "torn by conflict" between their jobs and the desire to be with their families. Yet the average divorced American man spends less than two days a month with his children. Well over half of black male children are raised without fathers. While the trauma of separation and divorce affects all members of a family, it is especially poignant for sons: Researchers generally agree that boys at all ages are hardest hit by divorce.

The enclosure of men

The current crisis for men, which goes far beyond statistics, is nothing new. We have faced a legacy of loss, especially since the start of the mechanical age. From the Enclosure Acts, which forced families off the land in Tudor England, to the ongoing destruction of indigenous communities throughout the Third World, the demands of the industrial era have forced men off the land, out of the family and community, and into the factory and office. The male as steward of family and soil, craftsman, woodsman, native hunter, and fisherman has all but vanished.

As men became the primary cog in industrial production, they lost touch with the earth and the parts of themselves that needed the earth to survive. Men by the millions—who long prided themselves on their husbandry of family, community, and land—were forced into a system whose ultimate goal was to turn one man against another in the competitive "jungle" of industrialized society. As the industrial revolution advanced, men lost not only their independence and dignity, but also the sense of personal creativity and responsibility associated with individual crafts and small-scale farming.

The factory wrenched the father from the home, and he often became a virtual nonentity in the household. By separating a man's work from his family, industrial society caused the permanent alienation of father from son. Even when the modern father returns to the house, he is often too

Men cannot understand how we exploit others until we look at the nature of our own oppression.

tired and too irritable from the tensions and tedium of work in the factory or corporation to pay close attention to his children. As Robert Bly, in his best-selling book *Iron John* (1990, Addison-Wesley), has pointed out, "When a father, absent during the day, returns home at six, his children receive only his

Four men, one boy, and a rusty tractor

A love story about men

In his fine poem "Axe Handles," Gary Snyder provides a counterpoint to the view that men exist in complete emotional isolation from one another. Snyder takes teaching his son to make a new axe handle as a metaphor for the connection between generations of men. The handle of the working axe serves as a model for the new handle it fashions, just as a father teaches and molds a son. The axe is an apt symbol, with both a constructive and a destructive aspect. A father's influence may be felt in many ways as well; through affection and involvement at one moment and through absence and disregard at another. Either instance shapes a son. Snyder's description reminds us that connections occur on many levels, some spoken, others not. We are unfair to ourselves if we only think of what is missing and ignore the bonds that are there.

TOOLS, AND WORK WITH MY MALE RELATIVES, WAS ONE STEP FOR ME into the world of men. When we went to visit either grandfather, there was always a job or two on the farm that couldn't be put off for our visit. The more solitary tasks of tending livestock or doing field-work on the tractor had their pleasure, but there was a particular joy in shared work. Perhaps because of the isolation in which they spent much of their lives, the men I knew relished a chance to spend time together, even if it meant work.

One summer afternoon, my father, uncle, and grandfather were trying to mount the sickle bar on the tractor to cut weeds out in the back pasture. I was there as an observer, too young then for this kind of work. A nut had rusted tight on a threaded stud. My grandfather sweated and struggled, finally rounding the nut through his attempts to get it off. Vise grips slipped and penetrating oil didn't seem to make a difference. I alternated between throwing sticks for the dog and watching.

"Damn," my grandfather said, finally. It was not a word I had ever heard him say. The men stopped to confer.

"I don't know if we're going to get it."

"We could knock that nut off with a chisel," my father said.

"Might take the stud with it," my uncle said. "Then where would we be?"

A neighbor who lived down the road a mile came by on his way into town. He pulled his pickup into the barn lot and up under the tree where we were working.

"Looks like a convention," he said. "Can't resist watching other people work."

"Give us a hand, Dave," my grandfather said. "We're stuck with this nut here."

"Yeah, I've got a stuck nut, too," Dave said, moving his hand toward his groin. There was a different tone to this remark than the talk before. My father and uncle were laughing but my grandfather glanced over at me.

"Watch it," he said to Dave. "The boy."

"Sorry," Dave said.

"Don't worry," my father said. "It's okay."

"Probably too many city fellas working on this," Dave said. Both my father and my uncle had left the farm for lives in the city. "Let a farmer get on this job, right Ralph?" Dave winked at my grandfather as he picked up a wrench.

They finally got the mower to work that day. Dave knew a trick that broke the nut loose, I think. There was laughter about putting one over on the "city boys." A few years later I learned to run that mower, first sitting with my grandfather on the high seat, then driving the tractor alone. What I remember most, though, is the feeling of that afternoon: standing in the shade of the burr oak in the barnyard, happy to be out with the men, feeling how physical they were, smelling the sweat and machinery, laughing at the teasing that went back and forth, wishing I was old enough to help.

It is important to draw a distinction between intimacy and bonding. Intimacy involves the open sharing of inner thoughts, feelings, vulnerabilities. Bonding is not so conscious or spoken a thing. I don't know if there was much intimacy between the men I love in my family. I don't think there was. Opening your deepest emotions did not come easily in the rural life of Missouri—especially for men. But the absence of openly shared love didn't mean it wasn't there.

—*Eric McCollum*
North American Review

Excerpted with permission from the literary journal North American Review *(Dec. 1990). Subscriptions: $14/yr. (4 issues) from North American Review, University of Northern Iowa, Cedar Falls, IA 30614. Back issues: $4 from same address.*

temperament, and not his teaching." The family, and especially sons, lose the presence of the father, uncle, and other male role models. It is difficult to calculate the full impact that this pattern of paternal absence has had on family and society over the last several generations.

While the loss of fathers is now beginning to be discussed, men have yet to fully come to terms with the terrible loss of sons during the mechanized wars of this century. World War I, World War II, Korea, and Vietnam were what the poet Robert Graves called "holocausts of young men." In the battlefields of this century, hundreds of millions of men were killed or injured. In World Wars I and II—in which more than 100 million soldiers were casualties—most of the victims were teenage boys, the average age being 18.5 years.

Given this obvious evidence of our exploitation, it is remarkable that so few men have acknowledged the genocide on their gender over the last century—much less turned against those responsible for this vast victimization. Women have increasingly identified their oppression in society; men have not. Thankfully, some men are now working to create a movement, or community, that focuses on awareness and understanding of men's loss and pain as well as the potential for healing. Because men's oppression is deeply rooted in the political and economic institutions of modern society, it is critical that awareness of these issues must be followed by action: Men today need a comprehensive political program that points the way toward liberation.

Lost in the male mystique

Instead of grieving over and acting on our loss of independence and generativity, modern men have often engaged in denial—a denial that is linked to the existence of a "male mystique." This defective mythology of the modern age has created a "new man." The male mystique recasts what anthropologists have identified as the traditional male role throughout history—a man, whether hunter-gatherer or farmer, who is steeped in a creative and sustaining relationship with his extended family and the earth household. In the place of this long-enduring, rooted masculine role, the male mystique has fostered a new image of men: autonomous, efficient, intensely self-interested, and disconnected from community and the earth.

The male mystique was spawned in the early days of the modern age. It combines Francis Bacon's idea that "knowledge is power" and Adam Smith's view that the highest good is "the individual exerting himself to his own advantage." This power-oriented, individualistic ideology was further solidified by the concepts of the survival of the fittest and the ethic of efficiency. The ideal man was no longer the wise farmer, but rather the most successful man-eater in the Darwinian corporate jungle.

The most tragic aspect of all this for us is that as the male mystique created the modern power elite, it destroyed male friendship and bonding. The male mystique teaches that the successful man is competitive, uncaring, unloving. It celebrates the ethic of isolation—it turns men permanently against each other in the tooth and claw world of making a living. As the Ivan Boesky-type character in the movie *Wall Street* tells his young apprentice, "If you need a friend, get a dog."

The male mystique also destroys men's ties to the earth. It embodies the view of 17th century British philosopher John Locke that "[l]and that is left wholly to nature is called, as indeed it is, waste."

A sustainable relationship with the earth is sacrificed to material progress and conspicuous consumption.

Ironically, men's own sense of loss has fed the male mystique. As men become more and more powerless in their own lives, they are given more and more media images of excessive, caricatured masculinity with which to identify. Men look to manufactured macho characters from the Wild West, working-class America, and modern war in the hope of gaining some sense of what it means to be a man. The primary symbols of the male mystique are almost never caring fathers, stewards of the land, or community organizers. Instead, over several decades these aggressively masculine figures have evolved from the Western independent man (John Wayne, Gary Cooper) to the blue-collar

Men as a gender are being devastated by our socioeconomic system.

macho man (Sly Stallone and Robert DeNiro) and finally to a variety of military and police figures concluding with the violent revelry of *Robocop*.

Modern men are entranced by this simulated masculinity—they experience danger, independence, success, sexuality, idealism, and adventure as voyeurs. Meanwhile, in real life most men lead powerless, subservient lives in the factory or office—frightened of losing their jobs, mortgaged to the gills, and still feeling responsible for supporting their families. Their lauded independence—as well as most of their basic rights—disappear the minute they report for work. The disparity between their real lives and the macho images of masculinity perpetrated by the media confuses and confounds many men. In his book *The Men from the Boys*, Ray Raphael asks, "But is it really that manly to wield a jackhammer, or spend one's life in the mines? Physical labor is often mindless, repetitive, and exhausting.... The workers must be subservient while on the job, and subservience is hard to reconcile with the masculine ideal of personal power."

Men can no longer afford to lose themselves in denial. We need to experience grief and anger over our losses and not buy into the pseudo-male stereotypes propagated by the male mystique. We are not, after all, what we are told we are.

At the same time, while recognizing the pervasive victimization of women, we must resist the view of some feminists that maleness itself, and not the current systems of social control and production, is primarily responsible for the exploitation of women. For men who are sensitive to feminist thinking, this view of masculinity creates a confusing and debilitating double bind: We view ourselves as oppressors yet experience victimization on the personal and social level. Instead of blaming maleness, we must challenge the defective mythology of the male mystique. Neither the male mystique nor the denigration of maleness offers hope for the future.

Fortunately, we may be on the verge of a historic shift in male consciousness. Recently, there

---

The male mystique teaches that the successful man is competitive, uncaring.

---

has been a rediscovery of masculinity as a primal creative and generative force equal to that of the recently recognized creative and nurturing power of the feminine. A number of thinkers and activists are urging men to substitute empathy for efficiency, stewardship for exploitation, generosity for the competitiveness of the marketplace.

At the forefront of this movement have been poet Robert Bly and others working with him: psychologist James Hillman, drummer Michael Meade, Jungian scholar Robert Moore. Bly has called for the recognition and reaffirmation of the "wild" man. As part of Bly's crusade, thousands of men have come together to seek a regeneration of their sexuality and power, as they reject the cerebral, desiccated world of our competitive corporate culture. Another compelling analysis is that of Jungian therapist Robert Mannis, who has called for a renewal of the ethic of "husbandry," a sense of masculine obligation involved with generating and maintaining a stable relationship to one's family and to the earth itself. And a growing number of men are mounting other challenges to the male mystique. But so far, the men's movement has remained primarily therapeutic. Little effort has been made to extend the energy of male self-discovery into a practical social and political agenda.

A manifesto for men

AS MANY OF US COME TO MOURN THE LOST FATHERS AND SONS OF THE last decades and seek to re-establish our ties to each other and to the earth, we need to find ways to change the political, social, and economic structures that have created this crisis. A "wild man" weekend in the woods, or intense man-to-man discussions, can be key experiences in self-discovery and personal empowerment. But these personal experiences are not enough to reverse the victimization of men. As the men's movement gathers strength, it is critical that this increasing sense of personal liberation be channeled into political action. Without significant changes in our society there will only be continued hopelessness and frustration for men. Moreover, a coordinated movement pressing for the liberation of men could be a key factor in ensuring that the

struggle for a sustainable future for humanity and the earth succeeds.

What follows is a brief political platform for men, a short manifesto with which we can begin the process of organizing men as a positive political force working for a better future. This is the next step for the men's movement.

Fathers and children

Political efforts focusing on the family must reassert men's bonds with the family and reverse the "lost father" syndrome. While any long-term plan for men's liberation requires significant changes in the very structure of our work and economic institutions, a number of intermediate steps are possible: We need to take a leadership role in supporting parental leave legislation, which gives working parents the right to take time from work to care for children or other family members. And we need to target the Bush administration for vetoing this vital legislation. Also needed is pro-child tax relief such as greatly expanding the young child tax credit, which would provide income relief and tax breaks to families at a point when children need the most parental care and when income may be the lowest.

We should also be in the forefront of the movement pushing for changes in the workplace including more flexible hours, part-time work, job sharing, and home-based employment. As economic analyst William R. Mattox Jr. notes, a simple step toward making home-based employment more viable would be to loosen restrictions on claiming home office expenses as a tax deduction for parents. Men must also work strenuously in the legal arena to promote more liberal visitation rights for non-custodial parents and to assert appropriateness of the father as a custodial parent. Non-traditional family structures should also be given more recognition in our society, with acknowledgment of men's important roles as stepfathers, foster fathers, uncles, brothers, and mentors. We must seek legislative ways to recognize many men's commitments that do not fit traditional definitions of family.

Ecology as male politics

A sustainable environment is not merely one issue among others. It is the crux of all issues in our age, including men's politics. The ecological struggles of our time offer a unique forum in which men can express their renewed sense of the wild and their traditional roles as creators, defenders of the family, and careful stewards of the earth.

The alienation of men from their rootedness to the land has deprived us all of what John Muir called the "heart of wilderness." As part of our efforts to re-experience the wild in ourselves, we should actively become involved in experiencing the wilderness first hand and organize support for the protection of nature and endangered species. Men should also become what Robert Bly has called "inner warriors" for the earth, involving themselves in non-violent civil disobedience to protect wilderness areas from further destruction.

An important aspect of the masculine ethic is defense of family. Pesticides and other toxic pollutants that poison our food, homes, water, and air

Men should be in the forefront of the movement pushing for changes in the workplace— flexible hours, job-sharing, part-time work.

represent a real danger, especially to children. Men need to be adamant in their call for limitations on the use of chemicals.

Wendell Berry has pointed out that the ecological crisis is also a crisis of agriculture. If men are to recapture a true sense of stewardship and husbandry and affirm the "seedbearing," creative capacity of the male, they must, to the extent possible, become involved in sustainable agriculture and organic farming and gardening. We should also initiate and support legislation that sustains our farming communities.

Men in the classrooms and community

In many communities, especially inner cities, men are absent not only from homes but also from the schools. Men must support the current efforts by black men's groups around the country to implement male-only early-grade classes taught by men. These programs provide role models and a surrogate paternal presence for young black males. We should also commit ourselves to having a far greater male presence in all elementary school education. Recent studies have shown that male grade school students have a higher level of achievement when they are taught by male teachers. Part-time or full-time home schooling options can also be helpful in providing men a great opportunity to be teachers—not just temperaments—to their children.

We need to revive our concern for community. Community-based boys' clubs, scout troops, sports leagues, and big brother programs have achieved significant success in helping fatherless male children find self-esteem. Men's groups must work to strengthen these organizations.

Men's minds, men's bodies, and work

Men need to join together to fight threats to male health including suicide, drug and alcohol abuse, AIDS, and stress diseases. We should support active prevention and education efforts aimed at these deadly threats. Most importantly, men need to be leaders in initiating and supporting holistic and psychotherapeutic approaches that directly link many of these health threats to the coercive nature of the male mystique and the current economic system. Changes in diet, reduction of drug and alcohol use, less stressful work environments, greater

nurturing of and caring for men by other men, and fighting racism, hopelessness, and homelessness are all important, interconnected aspects of any male health initiative.

Men without hope or homes

Men need to support measures that promote small business and entrepreneurship, which will allow more people to engage in crafts and human-scale, community-oriented enterprises. Also important is a commitment to appropriate, human-scale technologies such as renewable energy sources. Industrial and other inappropriate technologies have led to men's dispossession, degradation—and increasingly to unemployment.

A related struggle is eliminating racism. No group of men is more dispossessed than minority men. White men should support and network with African-American and other minority men's groups. Violence and discrimination against men because of their sexual preference should also be challenged.

Men, who represent more than four-fifths of the homeless, can no longer ignore this increasing social tragedy. Men's councils should develop support groups for the homeless in their communities.

The holocaust of men

As the primary victims of mechanized war, men must oppose this continued slaughter. Men need to realize that the traditional male concepts of the noble warrior are undermined and caricatured in the technological nightmare of modern warfare. Men must together become prime movers in dismantling the military-industrial establishment and redistributing defense spending toward a sustainable environment and protection of family, school, and community.

Men's Action Network

No area of the men's political agenda will be realized until men can establish a network of activists to create collective action. A first step might be to create a high-profile national coalition of the men's councils that are growing around the country. This coalition, which could be called the Men's Action Network (MAN), could call for a national conference to define a comprehensive platform of men's concerns and to provide the political muscle to implement those ideas.

A man could stand up

The current generation of men face a unique moment in history. Though often still trapped by economic coercion and psychological co-option, we are beginning to see that there is a profound choice ahead. Will we choose to remain subservient tools of social and environmental destruction or to fight for rediscovery of the male as a full partner and participant in family, community, and the earth? Will we remain mesmerized by the male mystique, or will we reclaim the true meaning of our masculinity?

There is a world to gain. The male mystique, in which many of today's men—especially the most politically powerful—are trapped, is threatening the family and the planet with irreversible destruction. A men's movement based on the recovery of masculinity could renew much of the world we have lost. By changing types of work and work hours, we could break our subordination to corporate managers and return much of our work and lives to the household. We could once again be teaching, nurturing presences to our children. By devoting ourselves to meaningful work with appropriate technology, we could recover independence in our work and our spirit. By caring for each other, we could recover the dignity of our gender and heal the wounds of addiction and self-destruction. By becoming husbands to the earth, we could protect the wild and recover our creative connections with the forces and rhythms of nature.

Ultimately we must help fashion a world without the daily frustration and sorrow of having to view each other as a collection of competitors instead of a community of friends. We must celebrate the essence and rituals of our masculinity. We can no longer passively submit to the destruction of the household, the demise of self-employment, the disintegration of family and community, and the desecration of our earth.

Shortly after the First World War, Ford Madox Ford, one of this century's greatest writers, depicted 20th century men as continually pinned down in their trenches, unable to stand up for fear of annihilation. As the century closes, men remain pinned down by an economic and political system that daily forces millions of us into meaningless work, powerless lives, and self-destruction. The time has come for men to stand up.

The second coming of the small town

Fed up with suburban sprawl, Americans want to walk again

Andres Duany and Elizabeth Plater-Zyberk

This essay is based on a lecture that Andres Duany delivered at the Harvard Graduate School of Design in November 1990.

Three years ago, Dade County, Florida, sentenced itself to the absurd fate of perpetual urban adolescence. Responding to a state mandate, the county government adopted a package of "balanced growth" measures, conceding that traffic congestion and growing demands on the public purse for roads and other infrastructure had made it impossible for the city of Miami to grow any further in the old way. Most citizens were pleased.

The reaction against growth has become a nationwide phenomenon. This is unprecedented. Never before in American history has growth been so unwelcome. What is responsible for this bizarre antipathy is not growth itself but the particular kind of growth we have in the United States. Suburban sprawl is cancerous growth rather than healthy growth, and it is destroying our civic life.

Americans are only beginning to understand that this is so. The credit for this change belongs partly to the environmental movement, which has persuaded most Americans of the need to stop ravaging the landscape and polluting the atmosphere with ever more roads and cars.

Suburbanites sense what is wrong with the places they inhabit. The classic suburb is less a community than an agglomeration of houses, shops, and offices connected to one another by cars, not by the fabric of human life. The only public space is the shopping mall, which in reality is only quasi-public, given over almost entirely to commercial ends. The structure of the suburb tends to confine people to their houses and cars.

Is there an alternative? There is, and it is close at hand: the traditional American town. This is not a radical idea—far from it. When the Gallup organiza-tion asked Americans in 1989 what kind of place they would like to live in, 34 percent chose a small town. Only 24 percent chose a suburb, 22 percent a farm, and 19 percent a city. One hardly needs an opinion poll to discover the allure of towns. The market reveals it. Americans have shown over and over again that they will pay premium prices to live in the relatively few traditional towns that remain, places such as Marblehead, Massachusetts, Princeton, New Jersey, and Oak Park, Illinois.

All of the elements of the traditional town exist in the modern American suburb. For various historical reasons, though, they have been improperly assembled. There are housing "clusters," office "parks," and shopping "centers." These elements have the makings of a great cuisine, but they have never been properly combined. It is as if we were expected to eat, rather than a completed omelet, first the eggs, then the cheese, and then the green peppers. The omelet has not been allowed to become the sum of its parts.

The tragedy is that we could have been building towns during the 1970s and '80s. But all of that wonderful growth has been wasted, and it is doubtful that we will ever see anything like it again in our lifetimes. Misguided planning, not rapacious real-estate developers, is chiefly to blame for this gross miscarriage of growth. Left to their own devices, developers would have every incentive to build towns. Traditional towns are less expensive. Because these towns are more compact than sprawl, the cost of land, streets, water and sewer lines, and other infrastructure is lower.

All of our recent suburban development occurred under the dominion of Euclidean zoning—zoning that requires the rigid segregation of housing, commerce, and industry. This approach to zoning is a residue of the industrial revolution, which made it seem desirable to move people's homes away from the dark satanic mills. Such distancing is no longer necessary, of course, since most contemporary office parks and electronics plants make extraordinarily benign neighbors.

There are people alive today who have never even laid eyes on the alternative to suburbia—people, in other words, who have never seen a real town. Authentic urban experience has become such a rarity that many places have become tourist attractions simply by virtue of being real towns. Visitors drive hundreds of miles to spend a weekend in places like Sonoma,

California, just for the sake of experiencing the pleasures of small-town living.

This also explains the success of Disneyland and Disney World. Visitors do not spend as much time on the rides as they do wandering along Main Street, USA, and through the international villages of Epcot, getting the civic kicks that they cannot get at home.

One of the great mysteries of the American suburb is this: How, with such low-density development, have we produced such extraordinarily high traffic? How have we achieved the traffic of a metropolis and the culture of a cow town? That, too, has been accomplished by the miraculous tool of postwar urban planning: the collector street, festooned with its variety of pods—shopping centers, office parks, schools, and residential areas—each with an independent connection to the collector. This arrangement guarantees that nobody can go to lunch, go shopping, or get to work or school without driving. In Orlando, Florida, it has been estimated that each single-family house generates an average of 13 car trips a day and thus vast amounts of pollution.

Building more highways to reduce traffic congestion is an exercise in futility. Whenever it is done, more people take to their cars, and before long the roads are as clogged as ever. We cannot continue to spend as extravagantly on roads as we did during the postwar decades of affluence. We must revert to planning approaches from the days when America was a poorer but smarter nation. The only permanent solution to the traffic problem is to bring housing, shopping, and workplaces within walking distance.

Reducing dependence on the auto would also help solve the problem of affordable housing. At the

To reduce traffic, shopping, work, and housing must be within walking distance.

Massachusetts Institute of Technology, architects are going to great lengths to find ways to make housing cheaper, developing prefabricated components, spacing wall studs further apart, and using rubber hoses for plumbing. In the end, all of these efforts do not add up to very much—perhaps a $10,000 or $20,000 savings. Nothing can be done for housing costs that rivals making it possible for a family to get by with one less car. The second or third car, so necessary in today's suburb, costs about $5,000 *annually* to operate. That is a highly leveraged sum, large enough to supply the payments on a $54,000 mortgage at 10 percent.

The tyranny of the auto reaches into every corner of American life. The auto's worst victims, however, are the very young and the very old. The suburb is poorly suited to the elderly. A suburbanite who loses his or her driver's license—perhaps because of failing eyesight—ceases to be a viable citizen. That person cannot go shopping, visit friends, or get to the doctor's office. He cannot take care of himself. In a town, he can. He may be too old to drive, but he is not too old to walk.

Children are the other great victims of the suburbs. Families move to the suburbs precisely because suburbs are supposed to be "good for the kids." And the fresh air and open spaces *are* good for them. Suburban sprawl is not. Children in the postwar suburbs are kept in an unnaturally extended state of isolation and dependence because they live in places designed for cars rather than people.

The school is the social center of the child's life, but the routine of the typical suburban school is governed by the school bus. The children are bused in at eight o'clock in the morning and most of them are bused home at three o'clock, regardless of what they are doing, warehoused in front of television sets until their parents come home from work. If the parents do not want their children to lead that kind of life, one of them (usually the mother) has to stay home to take care of them. And that often amounts to little more than exchanging a career for a new job as an unpaid chauffeur. Imagine how the lives of children would change if the suburban house and yard were assembled in the form of a traditional neighborhood so that kids could visit friends, go out for a hamburger, or walk to a library on their own.

All of us suffer. The eight-hour workday was the great victory of the past century, but we have squandered our gains by expanding our commuting time. Instead of spending two more hours a day with our families and friends, or forging bonds of community over the backyard fence or at the town hall, we have chosen to spend them competing with our fellow citizens for that scarce commodity called asphalt. Now, do you know that if you commute an hour a day to work and an hour back, which is perfectly normal in the suburbs, you're spending 500 hours a year in the car? That's the equivalent of 62.5 workdays or 12.5 work weeks.

Americans are ready for the return of the town. The signs of a revival of interest in community on a smaller scale are everywhere. In major cities, police officers are deserting their patrol cars and walking the sidewalks, not just responding to crises but actually getting to know the people on their beats. Los Angeles yuppies by the thousands are leaving the city's sprawl for the more traditional neighborhoods of Portland and Seattle.

Building real towns will require changing master plans, codes, road-building standards, and, above all, attitudes. The mindless administration of rules enshrining the unwisdom of the past half century must cease; the reign of the traffic engineers must end. Americans need to be reacquainted with their small-town heritage and to be persuaded of the importance of protecting the human habitat every bit as rigorously as the natural habitat. Architects and planners and developers can be leaders and educators, but ordinary citizens will have to insist that the happiness of people finally takes precedence over the happiness of cars, that the health of communities takes precedence over the unimpeded flow of traffic.

'THEY CAN'T STOP US NOW'

Kimi Gray and the other residents of D.C.'s Kenilworth-Parkside complex have overcome poverty, crime, drugs and innumerable layers of public housing bureaucracy—not to mention charges that they're just cogs in Jack Kemp's propaganda machine. Their goal? To take control of their own lives

DAVID OSBORNE

David Osborne is the author of Laboratories of Democracy, *which examined social and economic policy innovations in state government in the 1980s.*

IT WAS AUTUMN 1986, AND AFTER THREE YEARS OF WAITing, Kimi Gray was about to get her first glimpse of the city's plans to renovate her home. In 1983, the federal Department of Housing and Urban Development had awarded the city a grant to modernize the 464-unit Kenilworth-Parkside public housing complex in Northeast Washington. After dragging its feet for years, the city had hired an architectural firm. But when Kimi and her staff had asked to meet with the firm to explain what they wanted done—as required by HUD—the architects had repeatedly demurred. It wasn't time yet, they said. They weren't ready. Apparently, they did not relish the prospect of planning a major renovation project with a roomful of poor black women.

Finally they had agreed to a meeting. As they unfolded their sketches and presented their plans, Kimi's anger grew. Where were the plans for a new heating plant? What about the underground water pipes that kept bursting? What about the plumbing? These were pretty colored drawings, but they were fluff. They had nothing to do with Kenilworth's real problems.

Michael Price was the first to speak. A decade earlier, Price had been a high school dropout, hanging out on the streets. Kimi had convinced him to go back to school, then sent him to college through her College Here We Come program. Now a professional architect, he was repaying his debt, helping the Resident Management Corp. negotiate the renovation plans.

Price asked about the heating plant, the plumbing, the pipes.

"I was shocked, because they knew that half of that stuff I would catch," he says. "I guess they banked on me just letting it ride—being polite and not saying anything. But I got quite angry."

Other residents picked up on his anger. Finally, their board chairman stood up and walked slowly to the front of the room. "No hard feelings against you all," Kimi said, "but your supervisors sent you down here to get your asses kicked. And that's exactly what we're going to do tonight." She proceeded to take apart the drawings in harsh language and great detail. Other residents joined in.

After 45 minutes, Kimi entertained a motion to adjourn. "You just pack up and go home," she told the architects. "We'll deal with it."

And deal with it they did. Kimi went to HUD and demanded that the agency refuse to reimburse the $500,000 the city had already paid the architects. By failing to consult with the tenants, she argued, the architects had broken their contract. HUD agreed, and the city was out $500,000.

'It's Economics, That's What It's All About'

It was not the first time the irresistible force of Kimi Gray had met the immovable object of the city bureaucracy. And it was not the first time the irresistible force had won.

A massive figure with short cropped hair, large earrings and several pounds of jewelry around her neck and wrists, Kimi—as virtually everyone calls her—patrols the Kenilworth-Parkside development like a mother bear circling her cubs. Her voice erupts out of her slow-moving body like a volcano: one moment soft and low, the next exploding in a shout, the next dissolving in deep, rich laughter.

Sitting at her desk or behind the wheel of her ubiquitous van, wearing her jewelry and her bright yellow dresses, she brings the full force of her personality to bear on everyone who crosses her path.

Whether it is a child who needs discipline: "What you doing, girl? Why aren't you in school?"

Or an employee who deserves her praise: "I want to thank you so much, Lonnie. I understand the parade was *excellent.*"

Or a teenager with a wad of bills: "Little boys went out two Sundays ago, they came back, they had a knot. I said, 'Where's that money from, boy?' They say, 'Kimi, we worked!' They go over to the Eastern Market and sell tie-dye shirts they made—they work about three or four hours, they make about $75 or $80."

Or a D.C. police officer who neglected to invite her to his backyard barbecue: "Okay, do me a favor. You put a message on the board, in dark Magic Marker print. Tell him I got a CONTRACT on his head, for not inviting me to his damn cookout Saturday! And tell him I say when he gets off work at 3:30, report to my office! Immediately! Underline immediately!" Her voice returns to velvet: "Thank you, my love. Bye bye."

Kimi's desk sits where a receptionist would normally be, right by the front door, so the residents can always find her. Her assistants work upstairs, away from the constant stream of visitors. They field the calls, slip her messages, bring her paperwork to sign between sentences. This is a woman who has won award after award, who has been invited to the White House, who has preached her message from Paris to Seoul. But when a resident comes in, she drops everything.

"The only way that you'll truly get my time is getting me away from this property," she tells the public housing director of Alaska, who wants her help. " 'Cause if a resident walks through this door with me, I don't care who's here, he's my first priority. And I won't try and make believe it's no different, okay?" Reporters wait hours for an interview, weeks for a return phone call. Jack Kemp recently waited an hour and a half for a photo session at her office; finally, he gave up.

Somehow, through it all, things get done. It is easy to exaggerate the accomplishments of Kenilworth-Parkside, and Kimi Gray's supporters have often done so. Kenilworth residents are still poor: Many are single mothers, some are on welfare. Drug use is still widespread. This is still public housing, and though the grass gets cut, it still has that public housing shagginess around the edges. Twenty-five percent of the rent money still goes uncollected. All that said, there is no denying that a remarkable transformation has taken place.

The drug dealers who once used Kenilworth-Parkside as an open-air market are gone.

Teenage pregnancies have fallen.

Residents who once lived with gunfire now walk the project streets in safety. The crime rate has fallen from 12 to 15 reported crimes a month—one of the highest levels in the city—to 2, according to the police.

In the 15 years since Kimi founded College Here We Come, according to her records, more than 600 residents have gone to college. In the previous 15 years, two had.

In 1986, the accounting firm Coopers & Lybrand released an audit of Kenilworth-Parkside. During the four years that Kenilworth had been managed by its tenants, the firm reported, rent collections increased 77 percent—seven times the increase at public housing citywide. Vacancy rates fell from 18 percent—then the citywide average—to 5.4 percent. The Kenilworth-Parkside Resident Management Corp. helped at least 132 residents get off welfare: It hired 10 as staff and 92 to run the businesses it started, while its employment office found training and jobs for 30 more. (Others received part-time jobs.)

Overall, Coopers & Lybrand estimated, four years of resident management had saved the city at least $785,000. If trends continued over the next six years, it would save $3.7 million more. (The federal government would reap additional savings.)

Since the Coopers & Lybrand audit, a complete renovation of Kenilworth has begun under HUD's normal renovation program. (Hence only about 70 units are now occupied; more than 300 families have been temporarily relocated.) The most amazing moment will come next year, if the renovation is completed on schedule: The residents will buy the development from the city for $1. A community of 3,000, once characterized largely by families on welfare, will have become a community of homeowners, the majority of whom work.

It is an incredible story, but not a unique one. Residents in a handful of other public housing complexes around the nation have similar stories to tell. They are testaments to the power of empowerment—vivid demonstrations of what happens when ownership of public services is pulled out of the hands of bureaucrats and put in the hands of those receiving the services. They are living proof that when people are treated as clients for whom decisions must be made, they will learn dependency; but when they are given control over their destinies, they will learn independence.

These stories are also tales of salvation through self-help, rather than salvation through politics. "Self-sufficiency" is the driving theme at Kenilworth-Parkside; one hears the phrase constantly, from all sides. "It's economics, that's what it's all about," says Kimi Gray. "We can talk racism and all this and that, but it's economics. If you got some money, you can buy a lot of this stuff we're talking about begging for, okay?"

Finally, the story of tenant management and tenant ownership is a story of extraordinary political role reversals. Empowerment of poor people was a theme close to the heart of the New Left, carried forward into populist citizens' organizations with fanciful acronyms: ACORN, COPS, BUILD. But in Washington, conservatives like Jack Kemp and Stuart Butler, director of domestic policy studies at the Heritage Foundation, led the charge for tenant management and ownership—and they convinced Ronald Reagan and George Bush to come along.

Low-income housing activists have supported tenant management for two decades. But when Reagan and then-Congressman Kemp picked up the cause—and added the wrinkle of *selling* public housing to its tenants—red flags went up throughout the liberal community. Reagan cut federal funding for low-income housing from $24 billion to $8 billion a year. He slowed construction of public housing from more than 30,000 units a year to fewer than 5,000. And Jack Kemp voted with him. To many liberals, Kemp's talk of tenant management, his constant invocation of Kenilworth-Parkside and Kimi Gray, are political cover for a devastating retreat from federal commitments to the poor. Worse, they say, proposals to sell public housing to tenants are a ploy to get the federal government out of the housing business.

"Mr. Bush projects a gentler, kinder nation," says Maxine Green, chairperson of the National Tenants Organization. "Fine. Let the tenants have a kinder, gentler position, with the funds that are required to make that kind of a nation. But don't go into the capital, where you have 59 public housing developments, and sing about one.

"Kimi Gray was an active member of the National Tenants Organization," Green adds. "I give myself credit for sitting with her and giving her a direction. And now Kimi has joined, to my understanding, the Heritage Foundation."

A lifelong Democrat, Kimi does not let such suspicions worry her. She is a savvy politician who uses her relationship with Jack Kemp to the advantage of her residents—just as she does her relationship with Democrat Marion Barry. She understands that Kemp and Barry will use her in turn. (Kemp is so eager to be identified with Gray and tenant management that his staff volunteered an interview for this article without being asked.)

For Kimi Gray, economic self-sufficiency for her residents overrides all other goals. "I've been approached by some people who say, 'Well, Kimi, now you're a Republican,'" she explains. "And I say, 'No, I'm a dollar bill. And on each bill there's a different president. My family was poor when we had Roosevelt in the White House, we were poor when we had Kennedy, we were poor when we had Nixon and Ford and Carter. And we're no richer now.'"

'The System Penalizes Performance'

Kimi Odesser Houston was born January 1, 1945. She was raised in the Frederick Douglass public housing project in Southeast Washington by her mother and grandmother. Her father died when she was 7.

"Odesser's my grandmother's name," Kimi says. "She and I did not see eye to eye, not one day of her life. Now I know why, because we are identical. She was a strong-willed old southern lady who had a lot of morals and principles, and she didn't tolerate bad behavior.

"When I was young my grandma told me, 'No, babe, you cannot be *as good as* him, you gotta be *better* than he is.' When I ran track, I didn't want to run with the girls, 'cause I knew I could beat them. I wanted to run against the boys, okay? You can't be as good as them, you got to be better than them—as long as you keep thinking that way, that's what you'll be. And that's what I tell all my kids."

Kimi was an organizer from the start. In first grade, she got her first formal assignment: Her teacher made her substitute teacher—"and I just took over." When she was 11, she was elected citywide chairman of the youth section of the Junior Police and Citizen Corps.

But Kimi's energy was not always channeled into civic duty. "I put the J in juvenile delinquent myself," she says today. When she was 14, she had her first child. When she was 16, expecting her third, she married. At 19, with five children, she separated from her husband and went on welfare. She was 21 and miserable, living with her five children in a tiny apartment, when she got an apartment at Kenilworth. It was "1966, December the third, on a Wednesday," she says. "That's how happy I was to get this unit out here."

A complex of 37 low-rise buildings, Kenilworth-Parkside is sandwiched between the Anacostia River and I-295 hard by the Maryland line. It opened in 1959, about the time public housing began its downward spiral. The federal program had been launched during the New Deal as transitional housing for working people who hit hard times. Once constructed, units were not subsidized: Local public housing authorities charged enough rent to cover their operating costs. They screened carefully, and their standards were rigid. Parents had to be married. Many authorities excluded people on welfare. And if residents found better jobs and could afford to move out, they had to.

The program worked well for two decades, but during the boom times of the 1950s, the middle class headed for the suburbs, working families moved out of public housing, and poor migrants from the South poured in. Urban renewal hastened the process: When redevelopment agencies needed to move poor people out of the way of their bulldozers, they pressured the housing authorities to take them—regardless of their incomes, moral standards or presence on the welfare rolls.

Public housing's new residents were poorer; many had trouble coping with life in urban high-rise apartments; and many were black—which often meant they were ignored. Yet as this radically different population moved in, few housing authorities did anything to address its problems.

Meanwhile, early public housing developments were beginning to exhaust their 30-year life cycles. Yet because tenants' incomes were falling behind expenses, housing authorities were burning up the reserves they needed for renovation. When they raised rents to cope with the squeeze, Congress slapped them back, limiting rents to 25 percent of family income.

Soon Congress had to provide an operating subsidy. With Washington making up the difference between expenses and income, local housing authorities now had little incentive to run businesslike operations. If they saved money or increased their income, Washington gave them smaller subsidies. As a spokesman for the Council of Large Public Housing Authorities put it, "The system penalizes performance." To make matters worse, until 1980, Congress provided no capital budget to finance renovation.

Welfare policy also undermined public housing. Congress decided to deny welfare to most families if the father was present—which drove many fathers away. Meanwhile, welfare mothers in public housing got subsidized rent, which meant that if they left welfare to work, their rent often tripled or quadrupled.

In some cities, including New York, dedicated housing authorities made the program work against all odds. But in others, many of the largest, most congested public housing developments sank into a vicious cycle of drugs, crime, violence, teenage pregnancy and welfare dependency. The crisis earned its most enduring symbol in 1972, when the St. Louis housing authority quit trying to rescue a 15-year-old, 43-building development called Pruitt-Igoe, and simply blew it up.

In Washington, the housing authority lost virtually all ability to respond to its 50,000 customers. The director of a 1987 blue ribbon commission that investigated the system described it to The Washington Post as "total chaos." Drugs and crime were rampant; half the residents were not paying rent; repairs were so slow that the vacancy rate was approaching 20 percent; and the vast majority of eviction notices were never even served. Then-public housing director Alphonso Jackson described an agency riddled with employees "who are not capable of doing their jobs," property managers who "just sat in their offices all day," engineers who were "creating havoc in our boiler rooms" and administrators who regularly submitted reports full of inaccurate data.

College Here We Come

KIMI GRAY STARTED ORGANIZING VIRTUALLY THE DAY SHE arrived at Kenilworth-Parkside. She got training and then a job with a federally funded social services organization, working with delinquent youth. (Today, her only income is from her $22,000-a-year job with the D.C. Department of Recreation as a counselor to troubled youth. She receives no salary as Kenilworth board chairman and says she donates all speaking honoraria to College Here We Come.) In the early '70s, she began trying to breathe new life into Kenilworth's moribund residents council. Then in 1974, "Some students came to me and said, 'Miss Kimi, we want to go to college.' What the hell did I know about going to college? Well, I've always worked with young people—always—because they have their dreams, and they're our future. So I said, 'Let me check it out.' "

With help from the local Community Action agency and the city's resident services staff, she gathered information on colleges and financial aid and set up a regular Tuesday meeting with the kids. Soon she and her helpers were tutoring them, bringing in black college graduates to talk, drumming up scholarship money, helping kids find summer and part-time jobs and helping them fill out applications.

With the money from their jobs, the students opened bank accounts. After all the scholarships and loans and work-study jobs had been hustled, if a student still needed $600 or $1,000, College Here We Come kicked in the rest—much of it raised from bake sales and raffles.

To make the program intriguing, Kimi took her students out to play tennis, had birthday parties for them and took them on weekend trips to visit colleges. "That brought about a lot of unity among them," she says, "till it became a family. So we went through the winter and the summer together, and when it was time for our first group to go away, we cried. The hardest job was us departing from one another. When you would go to the bus station, we all would pile in the car."

When kids started actually leaving for college, word spread quickly: "Man, this stuff is real! People really going to college! These children couldn't believe that. Poor people, from public housing, their mothers on welfare, absent fathers, going to college?

"Seventeen kids went to school the first August. That first semester when they came back, we must not have slept for two days. They had so much to tell us. Kids were out West, down South, up North, they were everywhere. They couldn't believe it! They were sharing experiences: 'Well, let me tell you about this!' 'Well, did you know this?' 'Well, it's nothing like this.' "

Nine of the original 17 graduated, and four went on to graduate school. Of the 600 Kimi says have gone to college since, she guesses 75 percent have graduated. (There is no way to independently verify such numbers, and Kimi has been known to exaggerate. But graduates of the program back up the figures.)

Whatever the numbers, College Here We Come is clearly an in thing to do at Kenilworth. Even 16-year-old boys who hang out on street corners look up to those in the program. Every year, Kimi asks graduates to come back and share their experiences with the younger kids. "That's all I ask of 'em: 'Come back and share something. Pass it on.' "

Michael Price was in one of the early groups. When Kimi first asked him what he wanted to do with his life, he told her he wanted to go back to school and become a draftsman. "No," she said. "You don't want to be a draftsman. You want to be an architect. That's where the money is." She helped him earn his high school degree, then sent him off to Paine College in Georgia. He lasted a semester.

"Kimi was very disappointed and angry at me," Price remembers. "But during the winter of '77, I said, 'Look, I want to try it again.' " This time he attended Elizabeth City State University in North Carolina. After a shaky start, he earned a high enough grade point average to transfer to the architecture program at Howard University.

"It was difficult," he says. "I'd call Kimi, and sometimes I'd cry, and she'd cuss me out. She'd tell me, 'Yeah, you're not going to succeed. You're not going to make it.' I'd be so angry, I'd sit back down at my drawing board, at 3 o'clock in the morning, and I'd say, 'I'm going to make it. You think I'm going to quit, but I'm not.' She used reverse psychology on me, and it worked.

"At other times, she would be just as gentle as could be.

She'd say, 'I know it's hard, but you gotta hang in there, Mike. You know what our dream is.' " From the beginning, she had told him, "'Mike, you go to school and become the architect, and I'll stay home and do the legwork, and together we're going to do Kenilworth.' And we did it." After five years as an architect—including his stint at Kenilworth—Price is now a construction superintendent for the Temple Group Inc. "I just thank God that Kimi was there for me," he says. "She's a beautiful person." He pauses, and laughs. "And she can be a *dangerous* person."

The Force of Peer Pressure

DESPITE THE STUDENTS' SUCCESS, CONDITIONS WERE STILL going downhill at Kenilworth. The resident council seized on a HUD program through which a private management company ran the project, but things went from bad to worse. The roofs started to leak. There was no grass left, no fences. Rubbish was rarely picked up; rats infested the buildings. Drug dealers were common, and the management company put a bulletproof barrier around its office. For three years, residents often went without heat or hot water.

Not long after Mayor Marion Barry took office in 1979, Kimi told him her residents wanted to manage Kenilworth themselves. He agreed. The tenants wrote their own constitution and bylaws, their own personnel and policy procedures, their own job descriptions. The bureaucrats "*could not* believe it," Kimi says. "Public housing residents? I said, 'The worst it can do is have wrong grammar in it.' But at least we would understand and we would know clearly what was in it, right? So therefore we could enforce what we knew we had written." Besides, if HUD wrote it, there would be 10 lawyers in the room, writing "rules for things that don't even exist."

Knowing tenant management was on the way, Kimi says, the private management company left Kenilworth-Parkside on December 31, 1981. "It was the coldest winter since 1949," she remembers. "I'll never forget it: We were having a New Year's Eve party, and it seemed like every pipe on our property started bursting. The Lord had seen fit for us to take on this, and He said, 'I'll really give you a challenge.' " It was the perfect metaphor for the way D.C. spends money on public housing—people shivering while hot water ran down the middle of the street.

The residents patched the pipes with rubber hoses, put their own staff in place and got the housing authority to start replacing pipes. On March 1, 1982, the Kenilworth-Parkside Resident Management Corp.—a nonprofit organization—signed a contract to manage the property. Its elected board of residents, chaired by Kimi Gray, held monthly meetings of all tenants. They hired and trained residents to manage the property and do the maintenance. In what Kimi dubbed a "Bring the Fathers Out of the Closets" campaign, they hired absentee fathers. They set up fines for violating the rules—littering, loitering in hallways, sitting on fences, not cutting your grass—and created a system of elected building captains and court captains to enforce them. They created mandatory Sunday classes to teach housekeeping, budgeting, home repair and parenting. And they began to bend the force of peer pressure toward their own ends.

"The only way you can make a change is through peer pressure," says Kimi. "Rules can't be enforced if you have to go through judiciary proceedings." For instance, "If your momma was a bad housekeeper, and if her stove broke down, we would put the old dirty range out in front of her house, so everybody could see it. Leave it there *all day long*. Go get the brand-new stove, in the carton so everybody could see it, have it brought down, but not to your house." Instead it would go to a good housekeeper, whose old stove would go to the bad housekeeper. "Now when your momma learns to keep the stove clean, she'll get a brand-new one."

The Resident Management Corp. limited use of the day-care center to mothers who worked, went to school or were in training. As demand rose, they trained residents to provide day-care in their apartments. They had their college students do a "needs survey" to find out what people wanted. Based on the results, they created an after-school homework and tutorial program for kids whose mothers worked full time. They set up courses to help adults get their high school degrees. They contracted with a doctor and a dentist to set up part-time office hours and make house calls at the development. They set up an employment office to help people find training and jobs. And they began to create their own businesses, to keep money and jobs within the community.

The first was a shop to replace windows, screens and doors, owned by a young man who could neither read nor count. In return for a start-up loan from the resident council, he trained 10 students, who went on to market their skills elsewhere in Washington. The board fired the garbage collection service and contracted with another young man, on condition he hire Kenilworth-Parkside residents. At one time or another over the next five years, Kenilworth had a cooperative store, a snack bar, two laundromats, a beauty salon, a barber shop, a clothes boutique, a thrift shop, a catering service, a moving company, and a construction company that helped renovate vacant apartments. All employed residents, and all were required to hire young people to work with the adults. Before relocation of several thousand residents during the renovation shut most of the businesses down, 120 residents had jobs at Kenilworth-Parkside.

Gradually, maintenance improved as well. If something needed repairing, the managers and maintenance men lived on the property. "It has to be someone who's there all the time, on the property," says Renee Sims, head teacher at the Learning Center. "Because if you have someone outside managing it, and a pipe bursts over the weekend, you're not going to get it done."

Kimi and her managers estimate that in 1982, when they took over, less than half the rent was being collected. There was no heat or hot water, few other services, and people had caught on that if they didn't pay, there were no penalties. Resident manager Gladys Roy and her assistants began going door to door, serving 30-day eviction notices. They explained that if people didn't pay the rent, they couldn't afford the repairs people needed. If people did not have the cash, they worked out payment plans or collected what they could. As services improved and the managers kept up their door-to-door rounds, rent collections gradually improved. They were up to 75 percent by late 1987, according to Dennis Eisen, a real estate consultant hired to prepare a financial plan for tenant ownership.

'My Fear Was Drugs and Crime'

Denise Yates moved to Kenilworth with her parents in 1979. She was 22, unmarried, with one child. Their new apartment was "depressing," she says. "The roof leaked terribly. There was no heat for weeks at a time, no hot water. The grounds weren't kept up. Cars were parked up on your lawn. There were burglaries, there were rapes, there were drugs, there were shootouts. The person who lived there before was selling drugs out of the house, so we had a problem with people constantly knocking on the door at night."

Yates had never lived in public housing, never been on welfare. Now she was doing both: "Sitting at home, nothing to

Kenilworth-Parkside and the Politics of Public Housing

THE DAY KENILWORTH-PARKSIDE RESIDENTS ANNOUNCED the deal designed to turn them into homeowners, Jesse Jackson and D.C. Del. Walter Fauntroy held a "counter event." Though the sale would not take place for another two years, the Reagan administration had scheduled the announcement for 10 days before the 1988 election.

"This administration is having a housing press conference instead of a housing policy," Jackson declared. "My fear is that an uncritical media will let them have this photo opportunity and escape responsibility for the fact that they have cut the federal housing budget by 75 percent, at a time when 7.7 million people are in inadequate housing, when 5.4 million needy families receive no housing assistance, when 3 million to 5 million Americans are homeless."

So it was that Jackson, the Democrat most admired by poor blacks, and Fauntroy, the Democratic sponsor of a bill enabling Kenilworth residents to buy their homes, came together to denounce the sale. If ever one scene could capture the bizarre politics surrounding Kimi Gray and Kenilworth-Parkside, it happened on that chilly October afternoon. Few issues so disorient the political gyroscopes of Washingtonians as tenant management and ownership of public housing.

Neither issue is new. Tenants in Boston's Bromley-Heath project pioneered tenant management back in 1973, after crime got so bad that stores wouldn't deliver and taxis wouldn't drive into the area. Residents of St. Louis's Cochran Gardens tried it three years later. Born of crisis, both efforts achieved startling results: Crime rates dropped, vacant apartments were renovated, jobs were created, and residents were hired. Today, 13 public housing developments are managed by their residents.

Local housing authorities have been selling units to tenants even longer. Most such "turnkey" sales have involved single-family homes or small apartment buildings, sold to handpicked tenants with decent incomes; efforts to sell larger complexes have generally failed. There have been exceptions: Louisville recently sold a 100-unit complex to its residents as condos. But most turnkey sales of large projects have faltered because the tenants did not go through the process of organizing and taking control of their community.

"The psychological transformation doesn't happen when today I'm a renter and tomorrow I'm an owner," says David Freed, a consultant who specializes in low-income tenant buyouts. "It happens when there is a process that renters go through together, and there is a change in people's view of themselves and their neighbors. I see it again and again: It's that conversion experience."

The Kimi Grays of the world understand this. Several years ago, Robert Woodson of the National Center for Neighborhood Enterprise asked public housing tenant leaders to draw up a list of policy changes that would remove barriers to their success. Based on that list, they developed seven amendments to federal housing legislation. Woodson took them to then-U.S. Rep. Jack Kemp and recruited Fauntroy to co-sponsor the bill. Their 1987 legislation specifically targeted the transformation process: It gave resident councils the right to manage their own developments; it gave them priority for HUD renovation grants; it set up procedures by which they could buy their projects after three years of successful self-management; and it appropriated $5 million to train residents in self-management at 50 projects.

As HUD secretary, Kemp says, he would like to provide training grants to several hundred more groups during the next four years, help perhaps 50 of them begin managing their own developments and see perhaps half of those push on to financial ownership. He has already persuaded President Bush to support a $44 million home-ownership fund to help this "urban homesteading" along.

"I'm not suggesting that we're going to force it down people's throats, or that everybody should be treated in exactly the same manner," Kemp says. "But I at least want the opportunity out there for everybody." He promises to support the kinds of subsidies provided at Kenilworth-Parkside.

Kemp's strategy has sown confusion and anger among liberals, who often find their enthusiasm for tenant empowerment overwhelmed by their distrust of conservative motives. Liberal critics articulate three basic criticisms of the strategy:

1. **It won't work.** Specifically, critics argue that management of large properties is too difficult for most tenants; that ownership is too expensive for the poor; and that there are too few leaders like Kimi Gray to make it widely replicable.

This line of reasoning simply misses the point, supporters retort. Yes, self-management is difficult, they agree, but where tenants do not want management responsibilities, other tactics are available: Some resident councils have significant input into housing authority decisions; some hire and fire their own private management companies; some create partnerships with private management firms. The point is to empower residents, by whatever means they choose.

When tenants are powerless, advocates argue, they become dependent. "Bureaucratic, command-control approaches transfer the will for self-achievement away from local people, to bureaucracies," says Robert Woodson. Look at most D.C. public housing projects: Residents have no power to police their communities to enforce standards of behavior, to evict criminals. If someone deals drugs out of the apartment next door, they can complain, but the system rarely responds. So they give up.

As with self-management, empowerment advocates do not argue that ownership is for all tenants; even Kemp envisions a limited number of sales. They understand that most tenant groups could not afford to pay even the operating expenses on their apartments. But as Robert Woodson and Kimi Gray point out, resident management corporations do not just do housing; they do *economic development*. They create jobs, provide training and raise incomes. Where they succeed, ownership can become realistic.

Are there enough Kimi Grays out there to replicate the Kenilworth-Parkside story a thousand times? Woodson points out that every vital organization—whether Kenilworth-Parkside or IBM—owes its start to a strong leader. So why not create more opportunities in poor communities, and see how many leaders emerge?

2. **The dwindling stock of public housing should be preserved for the poor.** At the insistence of liberals, the Kemp-Fauntroy bill required that housing authorities replace any unit sold with a new unit of public housing. It also stipulated that any unit later resold had to go—for a limited price—to a low-income person, a resident management corporation or a housing authority. Some liberal critics want more, insisting that if buyers rise to middle-income status, they be forced to sell and move out.

In fact, tenants are no longer evicted from public housing when their incomes rise—their rents simply go up, remaining at 30 percent of their incomes. So even under current circumstances, some units are "lost" to middle-income people. But even if this were not the case, supporters ask, what is wrong with "losing" public housing units, if the people in them make the jump into the middle class? Public housing and welfare operate as traps, creating powerful incentives to remain poor and dependent. Should they not be redesigned to function as ladders out of poverty?

Besides, doesn't the current system guarantee the loss of thousands of units every year? Today, 78,000 of the nation's 1.4 million public housing units are vacant, ripe for decay and eventual destruction. Many will be lost forever—added to the thousands already "deprogrammed."

What we need, argues Woodson, is a new system: "If 20 percent of public housing was under the management of residents, we could save $5 billion a year."

"We are dealing with social behavior," adds Bertha Gilkey, who led the tenant takeover at Cochran Gardens. "You can spend $22 million on fixing up those buildings. You can spend $32 million. But unless you change the behavior of the people who live there, they're still going to tear them up." If Gilkey's experience is any indication, empowering tenants can not only change that behavior, it can actually *increase* the supply of low-income housing. Cochran Gardens has already developed 1,300 units of new housing, in partnership with private development firms.

3. **Unless it is accompanied by significant new funding for low-income housing, the Reagan-Bush embrace of Kimi Gray is a political sideshow designed to distract voters from the appalling homelessness that is the real result of conservative housing policy.** Gordon Cavanaugh, a spokesman for the Coalition of Large Public Housing Authorities, pulls no punches: "I think the conservative agenda is ending public ownership of public housing, and they cloak that agenda in the rhetoric of empowerment. I mean, this is the same crowd that killed HUD's 235 program, which was designed to subsidize low-income people into ownership. This is the same administration that is trying to kill the Farmers Home program that does much the same thing. Why wouldn't I be skeptical about what we're about here? We've had an administration which for eight years fought to kill all the programs that provided low-income home ownership, and all during that time we had this thing waved in our faces."

Jack Kemp responds that many federal housing programs deserved to be eliminated, because—like public housing—they flushed enormous sums down the toilet. "But what I want to do is not just curse the darkness," he is quick to add. "I want to light some candles." And candles, he agrees, cost money.

This is Kemp's quandary: Until George Bush is willing to propose significant new funding for urban homesteading, Kemp will face a political stalemate. Liberals will continue to distrust conservatives because they have gutted funding for housing. Conservatives will continue to distrust liberals because they are unwilling to restructure programs that waste billions of dollars every year. To break the logjam, Bush will have to demonstrate a commitment to both restructuring *and* investment. Kemp understands this, and says he has made it plain to the president. "The jury's out," he acknowledges, "but I'm confident we can get a program."—D.O.

look forward to but the monthly check. I knew I was worth more than that." A high school graduate and a good typist, she enrolled in a shorthand program to become a steno clerk. She took a civil service exam. And then she waited. No job offer came from the city, and when she looked elsewhere she could find nothing.

"When we moved into public housing," she says, "my fear was drugs and crime." Her fears came true when one of her sisters was raped. "From that point on, all our thoughts were negative. We basically stayed to ourselves." She was afraid to let her kids—she had two now—play outside alone, because of the drug dealers. She was trapped.

In 1982, the Resident Management Corp. hired Denise as a clerk typist. She began to understand that she was not alone, and she began to find her voice. BY 1985, she had been promoted to assistant manager. But the job did nothing to change her fears: If anything, the drug dealing intensified. Hundreds of dealers lined Quarles Street every night, selling to people who pulled off I-295, a block away. Mothers kept their children barricaded indoors.

Many of the worst offenders lived at Kenilworth. "These guys were not cream puffs," says Sgt. Robert L. Prout Jr. of the Sixth District police. "We had people here wanted for bank robbery, very serious crimes. And we were somewhat reluctant to come over here because the citizens were hostile to the police."

Even when they came, they had trouble making a dent in the drug problem. "Drug dealers are a lot smarter than we give them credit for," says Prout. "What they would do is stash their drugs in various locations. We would confront them, and they wouldn't have any drugs on them."

Finally Kimi called a meeting and invited the police. At first, most residents wouldn't come. "They thought if the police were there, the people that attended were gonna snitch on other residents, or on kids of other residents, and get them arrested," says Prout. "It took a long time for them to develop confidence in us."

The residents first asked for foot patrols at Kenilworth. Then they suggested a temporary station—a trailer—right on the grounds. The police agreed. "By putting guys over there, on a regular basis, they began slowly to develop a sense of trust in us," Prout explains. "And they began to give us information. At first it was channeled through Miss Roy or Kimi or one of the other people who worked for her. Then it became a thing where people were not afraid to be seen talking to us right on the street. We would tell them who we were looking for. And little by little, people would call up on the phone and give us information, and we'd come over. We would ask the residents to tell us where the stash was—if it's in a trash can, or hanging from a tree, or whatever. And they would. And now it's got to the point where we have mothers that have sons that if they're wanted for something, they'll pick up the phone and call us."

Kimi remained the role model. She turned in anyone who was selling drugs—even members of her beloved College Here We Come. Her own son was arrested for dealing in Southwest D.C. "I'm not cold, now, I'm a loving mother," she says. "But my son was 26, living in his own apartment, and he chose that as his way of life. After I spent my money to send him to college for two years, he decided that he wanted to be a hustler. So I figured he must have wanted to go to jail to see what that experience was like too. He's home now. Don't smoke, drink or nothing, works two jobs. He learned his lesson. The best thing I think I did was I didn't cater to him while he was incarcerated. I was hurt. But my momma and my grandma always said to me, 'You make your bed hard, you got to lay in it.' "

Every household in which someone was dealing got a 30-day eviction notice. The message was for the others: "Put him out, or lose your place." If nothing happened, "We got with the attorney down at the Housing Department, and we wore 'em to death, till we got them to take our cases to court. Now once we got to court, we were all right, because we would take residents with us down to court to say, 'No, your honor, that fella cannot stay in our community any longer.' " Four families were evicted, Kimi says. "That's all it took. People seen, 'Hey, they serious.' "

Evictions did not stop the dealers who lived elsewhere, of course. Finally, in 1984, the residents decided to confront them head on. "We got together and we marched," says Denise Yates. "Day after day, and in the evening too. We marched up and down the street with our signs. We had the police back us. Maybe half the community would march. A lot of teenagers and little kids, in addition to mothers."

At first the dealers assumed it was a temporary nuisance. But after several weeks of disrupted business, they began to drift away. That was the turning point. Today "there's very little crime" at Kenilworth, says Prout. "We have almost no break-ins. We still have a little minor drug traffic. What that is, that's your 15- and 16-year-olds that still live here, who try to do what they say their friends do. But it's nothing like it was."

Making the change was not easy. Residents were threatened. Someone cut the brake lines in Kimi's car, put sugar in her gas tank, slashed her tires. "They cut the brand-new tires," Kimi says. "That's when I got angry. I knew the guy that was the main guy, that I figured paid somebody to do it. I said, 'You went a tad too goddam far! You know how much those four tires cost me to go on that van? More than the damn van cost!' I said, 'Now I'm goin' to cut your damn tires up!' " For good measure, she threatened to send her brother, who stands 6-foot-3, to call. "And he's been nice to me ever since"—until he left for jail, that is.

Kimi's confidence rubbed off. "When people saw she didn't show any fear of being seen with the police, or riding through the neighborhood with us, then they more or less followed suit," says Prout.

The lesson is clear: The police can make raid after raid, but only if a community decides to take responsibility for its own safety can the police be truly effective. "We tell them, 'The police can't be here all the time,' " says Prout. " 'You live here, you know more about what goes on, you know who does what. It's just a matter of whether you want your community, or whether you want them to have your community.' "

Carrots and Sticks

Weeding out drug dealers is not the same as ending drug abuse, of course. Dr. Alice Murray, a psychologist who runs Kenilworth's Substance Abuse Prevention project ("SAP, because you're a sap if you take drugs") believes that "a large percentage of the families" still at Kenilworth have at least one family member with a drug problem. She helps an average of two people a month get into treatment. "Crack is the problem at the moment," she says. "They experiment with it for six months, and then they're really into it. It is highly addictive."

Murray and her staff of six have a budget of $300,000 from the city. They attack the drug problem in a dozen different ways. Narcotics Anonymous meets every noon. A "Chief Executive Officers" program puts young mothers through 15 weeks of training—three days a week, six hours a day—in everything from child rearing to personal responsibility. The Teen Council (a youth version of the Residents Council) operates a Youth

Enterprise Program—"to get young people to understand how they can take their skills of hustling on the street and use them in a positive way, the way people make money in America." In addition to running their tie-dye clothing business, the kids design, produce and sell greeting cards, and they bake and sell cookies. They are paid wages, returning the rest of their earnings to the program.

During the summer, Murray's staff operates two "academies," one for 5- to 9-year-olds, another for teenagers. "We call it an academy, not a camp, because though it's play, we want

How Not to Manage Public Housing

Getting accurate information from the city about Kenilworth-Parkside's finances is a bit like getting a straight answer from the Cheshire Cat. The D.C. Department of Public and Assisted Housing (DPAH), which runs Washington's 59 public housing projects, makes Alice's Wonderland look absolutely straightforward. How much of Kenilworth's operating expenses are covered by rental income? DPAH doesn't know. "We looked for that," says Alphonso Jackson, who ran DPAH for 18 months before leaving last December in frustration. (He now runs the Dallas Housing Authority.) "Those records were nowhere to be found."

DPAH does not keep separate accounts for each of its public housing developments, so it cannot say how much rent is coming from each. You want to know how much resident management at Kenilworth has saved (or cost) the city? Sorry, DPAH doesn't know. You want to compare expenses and rental income at Kenilworth with those at other developments? "I think even the GAO gave up on that," says Valerie Holt, DPAH's deputy director for finance and subsidized housing. (The General Accounting Office is conducting a study of Kenilworth-Parkside for the Senate Subcommittee on Housing and Urban Affairs.)

Within the fog of nonexistent and often-conflicting numbers, however, a few things are clear:

•DPAH signs an annual contract under which the Kenilworth-Parkside Resident Management Corp. handles all expenses save utilities. In 1987 and 1988, DPAH provided just over $1 million a year.

•DPAH in turn receives an operating subsidy from HUD. Again, it is impossible to isolate Kenilworth's share from that of the 58 other projects. But when HUD required a figure in planning for the sale of Kenilworth, Jackson "guesstimated" it at $1.7 million to $1.8 million. He added that DPAH absorbed about a third of the total in overhead.

•Several programs at Kenilworth are subsidized separately. For instance, the Substance Abuse Prevention project receives $300,000 a year, half from DPAH, half from another city agency.

•DPAH has received roughly $23 million from HUD to renovate Kenilworth-Parkside under the federal modernization program. This translates into nearly $50,000 per unit—double the average cost in neighboring Baltimore, though the renovation required may be less extensive there. The whopping price tag has led some critics to charge that the Reagan administration shoveled money to Kenilworth far in excess of what other projects received. The administration did insist that a renovation grant go to Kenilworth to support tenant management and to pave the way for ownership. But the cost per unit is so high mainly because DPAH manages renovation so ham-handedly. Other DPAH renovation projects have cost even more—and contractors' bids today are coming in at *$80,000* to *$90,000* per unit.

According to virtually all knowledgeable observers, DPAH is a textbook case of how not to manage public housing. "I've been chairman of the Committee on Housing and Economic Development since 1981," says D.C. Council member Charlene Drew Jarvis. "Since then, there have been eight heads of the department. The department has suffered from a lack of continuity of leadership, a problem with timely contracting, a relative absence of contract monitoring and an absence of skilled workers. The simple tracking of work orders has even been a problem."

The problems were exacerbated in Kenilworth's case, Jarvis adds, by "tension" between DPAH and HUD after HUD insisted that a renovation grant go to Kenilworth.

"They said to me, 'This wasn't one we'd planned to do, so we'll just have to get to it when we do,' " explains Margaret White, manager of HUD's D.C. field office. "We could not get the housing authority to send the paperwork to us. It was as though there was a concerted effort to delay, to drag it out, to obfuscate, to pull red herrings across the trail."

White, as it happens, was on temporary reassignment as this article went to press, pending the investigation of management failures in *her* office. Part of the nationwide HUD scandal probe, the D.C. investigation focuses on the theft by private escrow agents of proceeds from the sale of foreclosed properties. So far, it is unrelated to public housing.

Still, if one did want to examine problems in D.C. public housing, DPAH would be an obvious place to start. The problems at Kenilworth have been endless.

After two years of inaction by DPAH, leaking roofs threatened to make Kenilworth unsalvageable. To save it, White finally ordered that the roofs be done separately, driving costs up. Then the architects' drawings turned out to be "inadequate," to use Jackson's phrase, because "DPAH did not hold the architects and engineering firms accountable." While units stood vacant, pipes and other equipment were vandalized. DPAH finally fired the original contractor, and HUD has threatened to do the same with the second. With so many complications, the original $13.2 million renovation grant ran out, and DPAH went back to HUD for $9 million more.

"My honest perspective on it," says Jackson, "is that it was incompetence on the part of DPAH that took so long to get that project started. What I had in D.C. was unorganized chaos."

Roland Turpin, who succeeded Jackson at DPAH a few months ago, declined to be interviewed for this story. Instead, he provided a statement: "We are fully aware that there are problems, but we are firmly committed to this home ownership conversion for the residents of Kenilworth-Parkside, and we'll do whatever is appropriate to see that it becomes a reality."

Meanwhile, most Kenilworth residents are stuck in other public housing projects, where they were relocated several years ago. "I tell you, every time I ride by that place, I get totally infuriated," says for Kenilworth resident and architect Michael Price. "The people downtown go home every night to their plush homes in the suburbs or wherever, and the residents are in housing projects like Kenilworth was back in the 1970s. They weathered that storm, and it's not fair for them to be moved into a brand-new storm. The people in that bureaucracy ought to be horsewhipped."

—D.O.

them to maintain their academic skills," Murray explains. Virtually all the children at Kenilworth participate. They play, do arts and crafts, take trips, work on academics and receive substance abuse education—all with a heavy stress on emotional and family health.

Other efforts include a mandatory eight-hour substance abuse prevention program for new residents; counseling for addicts and their families; referrals to in-patient and out-patient care; follow-up with families after treatment; a program to help parents work with the public schools; and a teen pregnancy prevention program.

"What we're working for is a change of behavior and attitude," says Murray. In the case of teen pregnancy, it appears to be working. Accurate numbers are hard to come by at Kenilworth (when asked how much welfare dependency had been reduced, for instance, Kimi Gray and her top two managers gave wildly different figures). But all sources agree that teenage pregnancy—once the norm—has dropped significantly.

"One of the things that this community has brought back is a kind of old-fashioned shunning," says Murray, "a way of saying, 'This behavior we will not tolerate. Should it happen, then we put you through all the services, but we don't expect it to happen ever again.' It's done in a very kind and gentle and loving way, but there's shame when it occurs—which is not the case in the outside community."

By shunning negative behavior, supporting constructive behavior and offering treatment for people with drug problems, Kenilworth's leaders are trying to build a viable culture. It is a constant effort, using both carrots and sticks. Mothers turn children in for drug dealing: College Here We Come attends every high school graduation to cheer its members on.

"Development begins with a belief system," says Robert Woodson, whose National Center for Neighborhood Enterprise has worked with Kenilworth since 1981. "What Kimi and other tenant leaders have done is just self-confidence, and they've passed that self-confidence on to others. Only when you overcome the crisis of self-confidence can opportunity make a difference in your life. But we act with programs as if opportunity carries with it elements of self-confidence. And it does not."

This is where ownership comes in. Kimi and her colleagues believe that when they become property owners, the process of building self-confidence and opportunity will take another quantum leap. Late next year, if the schedule holds, the last family will move back into the renovated development (courtesy of a HUD grant of roughly $23 million). Not only that, they will own the place. The experience cannot help but send a powerful message.

It will not be easy. It costs close to $400 per unit per month simply to maintain and operate the complex. Federal subsidies will continue for five more years, probably somewhere between $1.2 million and $1.7 million a year, but that will not be enough. At some point, the Resident Management Corp. plans to sell

shares in a limited equity co-op for perhaps $10,000 per unit—though details are still sketchy and no one knows what kind of down payment, if any, will be required. The residents also hope to borrow $1.75 million, to put in air conditioning, dishwashers, a community cafeteria, tennis courts, racquetball courts, a locker room and a swimming pool. Financial plans are still extremely tentative. But one recent version called for Kenilworth to raise rent collections from 75 percent to 92.5 percent by 1995, drive residents' average income ($10,200 by 1987, at least for reported income) up 6 percent annually and put $500,000 of the HUD subsidy in the bank every year—just to stay afloat when the subsidy ends.

The strategy is ambitious and the assumptions optimistic, but according to experts on co-op conversions, it is not impossible. It will require a more businesslike operation, particularly when Kenilworth becomes dependent on bankers rather than bureaucrats. "It will require strong property management, fiscal oversight and also very good tenant education," says David Freed, a real estate consultant who specializes in low-income co-op conversions in D.C. "The key to good cooperative ownership conversion is the quality of the leadership. And they have superb leadership."

'The Door Is Open'

Kimi Gray is not worried about whether her residents will be able to afford ownership. She's got bigger plans than that.

There's the reverse commute program—from inner city to suburbs—that she's working on with a grant from the Department of Transportation. And the shopping mall she wants to build next to Kenilworth. And the self-help credit union, and the industrial facility and the construction company. There are two buildings she is trying to buy and renovate—to train her construction company and house her college students. There's a building she plans to put up for senior citizens. And there are the condos she wants to develop, so the most successful Kenilworth residents can move up without leaving the community.

On a recent Monday, Kimi spent an entire afternoon at the D.C. Department of Public and Assisted Housing—cajoling the director, talking to his lawyer, rounding up the right people and shepherding them back to the director's office, all to get title to land Kenilworth will own in a year anyway, so she can start building her senior housing now. After three hours of tireless and expert manipulation, she still did not have what she wanted.

"You know," she said as she left the building, "every time I get the runaround, I think about the same thing. They have to deal with me, 'cause I've got all this publicity, and this is how they treat me. How the hell do you think they treat Mrs. Jones?"

There is no time to be bitter, however, There is too much to do. It is 1989, and the dam is finally breaking. "Folk want freedom," Kimi says, as she climbs back into her van and heads for one more meeting. "Folk want power. The door is open—they can't stop us now."

Further Thoughts on a "Sociology of Acceptance" for Disabled People

Howard D. Schwartz

HOWARD D. SCHWARTZ is professor of sociology at Radford University.

Social scientists studying the relationship between people with disabilities and the larger society, in recent years and with increasing intensity, have been waging a frontal assault against the dominant conceptual model of disability as deviance. A central tenet of the critics is that the deviance perspective leads to a predetermined view of people with disabilities as negatively valued by, and socially isolated from, the rest of society.

To be found among the growing number of critical voices are Robert Bogdan and Steven Taylor (1987) who call for the development of a "sociology of acceptance" through which to view people with disabilities. In proposing this, Bogdan and Taylor do not totally reject the deviance approach. Rather, they point to the need for adding a complementary perspective to accommodate those instances when the disabled person is accepted rather than rejected by others. While this contention seems legitimate and important, the informality of their presentation makes their argument less persuasive than it might be.

In the first place, and Bogdan and Taylor recognize this, the supporting data they present are less than satisfactory. Drawn ad hoc from their 15 years of clinical work in human services, the evidence is more suggestive than confirmatory regarding societal acceptance of people with disabilities.

Second, the authors talk about two different accepting public postures without, unfortunately, providing anything more than a preliminary discus-

> **There is clear evidence of a change toward a far more favorable public opinion of the disabled.**

sion of either posture or the difference between them. On the one hand, they speak of the kind of acceptance found in the seminal work of Nora Groce's *Everyone Here Spoke Sign Language* (1985). Analyzing the position of the deaf in the community of Martha's Vineyard up to the first part of this century, Groce concludes that "they were just like everyone else" (which is, in fact, the title of the first chapter). In a community where everyone was bilingual in English and sign language, the deaf were simply seen as equal to the hearing, no better, no worse.

On the other hand, Bogdan and Taylor consider acceptance in terms of disabled persons being viewed by others as "special, more interesting, more stimulating, more challenging, more appreciative." The example of a caseworker and his mentally retarded client is used to show the disabled person in this favored-status role. After a while, the caseworker came to value as special his disabled friend's candor, which included the ability to express feelings and show emotions.

For conceptual clarity, the term *acceptance* will be used here to define relationships between disabled and able-bodied persons in which all partici-

pants are viewed as equals. The term *advocacy* will be employed where those with disabilities are given favored status. It thus becomes the positive counterpart of rejection in a continuum of public postures that includes rejection, acceptance, and advocacy.

With these comments about the Bogdan and Taylor argument in mind, what emerges from the recent empirical research, including my own, is admittedly limited, but clear evidence of a change toward a far more favorable public opinion of disabled persons.

EVIDENCE FOR A "SOCIOLOGY OF ACCEPTANCE"

In 1986, in a paper that received considerable attention, Katz, Kravetz, and Karlinsky reported the results of a study comparing the attitudes of high school seniors in Berkeley, Calif., toward disabled and nondisabled people. According to the authors, what was notable about the study results was that they were not consistent with those of many earlier research results, since they seemed "to imply that the disabled person is viewed more positively than the nondisabled one in the United States."

The students had been presented with videotapes of a man who was variously identified as being a civilian or in the military, disabled or able-bodied. The respondents rated, on intelligence, vocational (work) competence, morality, and sociability, the individual that they viewed. After an overall rating score was calculated for each student, it was found that the average score for the disabled person was significantly higher than the average score for the ablebodied one.

The researchers speculate that an explanation of their results might be found in the unique nature of Berkeley. As an archtypical academic environment, it contains a substantial disabled population affected by mainstreaming and other educational innovations aimed at changing public attitudes toward persons with a disability. Consequently, "the nondisabled population is exposed to persons with disabilities who cope and live within the community" and "get to know them and their abilities beyond the disability."

While Katz and his colleagues are correct in their assessment of the atypical character of their study findings, they are not the only ones to have identified public advocacy of disabled people. Several studies, also using student respondents, have found that, on several key dimensions, disabled people are rated higher than the ablebodied as potential employees.

In one study, Siegfried and Toner (1981) asked college students to rate two target subjects: a potential co-worker and a potential supervisor. One-half of the students thought these people were disabled due to an automobile accident, and the other half were presented with the identical description except that there was no mention of a disability. For 11 of the 16 dependent measures, covering a wide range of work-related behaviors (e.g., professional competence, missing work, successful performance, and ability to travel), the disabled and able-bodied target subjects were rated equally. On those five factors for which significant differences were found, the disabled person was rated higher. He or she was seen as more likely to be approached with a personal problem, more likely to be asked a favor of, less likely to upset co-workers, and less likely to need special assistance.

In a similar vein, in a study published earlier by Krefting and Brief (1976), college students rated a disabled person (a paraplegic using a wheelchair) equal to an ablebodied person on most job-related measures, but higher on work motivation and likelihood of being a long-term employee.

THE *PLAYBOY* STUDY

My own research, carried out in the fall of 1987, can now be added to this body of literature (Schwartz, 1988). While similar to the aforementioned studies in its use of student respondents, a wheelchair-user target subject, and the same kind of experimental technique, it differed in an important way. The target subject was neither a military man nor a potential employee, but Ellen Stohl, the first disabled woman to be the subject of a *Playboy* (1987) photo layout.

As explained in the story accompanying the pictures, Ms. Stohl, who had a spinal-cord injury, offered to pose for *Playboy* as a way of demonstrating that people with disabilities can also be sexy. In the letter in which she asked the magazine for the opportunity to pose, she wrote, "Sexuality is the hardest thing for disabled persons

---

Several studies have found that the disabled are rated higher than the ablebodied as potential employees.

---

to hold onto," and that she wanted to "teach society that being disabled does not make a difference."

Irving Kenneth Zola (1987), a sociologist writing about disability in America, views "the right to be sexy" as a central item on the agenda related to the psychological and social liberation of people with disabilities. Harlan Hahn (1988) has touched on the same issue in his article, "Can Disability Be Beautiful?" Nevertheless, there seem to be limited opportunities for disabled people to assert their claim to sexuality, particularly through the media of popular culture. The *Playboy* article is unique in providing such a forum. It also offered the possibility of research to ascertain how, in a sexual context, the public evaluates the disabled person compared to the ablebodied one, and the disabled versus the ablebodied person's "right to be sexy."

The study was carried out at a medium-sized state university in Virginia, with a total enrollment of about 8,000. The majority of students come from urban centers within a 500-mile radius of the university such as Washington, D.C., with about one-third coming from more rural areas in the general vicinity of the university. Ten percent are from out of state.

The respondents were all of the students taking introductory sociology. Each student was shown one of two pictures of Ellen Stohl that had appeared in *Playboy*: one showed Stohl's face in closeup and shoulder partially bare; the other, providing a higher level of sexual display, had a partially-nude Stohl sitting on a couch with her legs tucked under her and wearing a negligee open in the front exposing a breast and her midriff. An additional aspect of the research design was that each student was given only one of two versions of whichever picture he or she received. An ablebodied version included, along with the picture, a biographical sketch which noted that Stohl was a college student and that the pictures had appeared in a national magazine with a readership of over 3 million. A second, disabled version had the identical biography except that Stohl was identified as spinal-cord injured, and a smaller picture of her fully clothed in a wheelchair was presented along with the larger picture. The analysis centered on comparing, for each picture, the responses of the students receiving the two versions.

The almost 700 respondents (80 students who had seen the pictures in *Playboy* or had heard about them were excluded) were asked to look at the photo of Stohl and rate her on six personal characteristics and on six factors concerned with conjectured success-failure or satisfaction-dissatisfaction in present or future life situations.

Regardless of the picture seen (the specific picture viewed had no effect in any of the comparisons), the disabled Stohl was rated equal to the ablebodied Stohl on sociability, intelligence, physical attractiveness, and the likelihood of having a fulfilling life.

Most interestingly, for five of the eight dependent measures for which a significant difference was found, Stohl was rated higher when presented as disabled than when presented as able-bodied. When identified as spinal-cord injured, she was seen as having greater strength of character, sensitivity to others, and competence at work, more likelihood of being a good parent, and less likelihood of getting divorced. The disabled Stohl's perceived relative superiority on these factors seems to confirm the finding of the previously cited studies which used the same or similar dependent measures that a disabled person is seen as better than one who is not disabled. Put another way, there is the strong hint of the disabled person's being viewed as a "paragon of virtue."

For two of the three measures on which the disabled Stohl was rated lower—the likelihood of getting married and satisfaction with life—the differences, while statistically significant, were so small as to be negligible. On the third, sexual appeal (the only measure to show a gender difference), the women saw no difference between the disabled and ablebodied Stohl while the men favored the latter. Yet, as far as the response of the male students is concerned, this is somewhat misleading. In fact, while both the men and women rated the disabled Stohl's sexual appeal as very high, the men rated it higher than the women did. In absolute terms, the men rated Stohl when disabled as "very sexually appealing," the second highest response on the 6-point Likert item.

Taken together, the ratings on sexual appeal and the equal ratings on physical attractiveness lead us to conclude that disability did very little, if anything, to diminish Stohl's physical appeal in the eyes of respondents.

In addition to rating Stohl on this array of measures, respondents were asked, "In your opinion, was it appropriate for this woman to pose for this picture?" (The respondents could answer "yes," "no," or "undecided".) The results show unequivocally that it was deemed more appropriate for the disabled Stohl to pose.

In all but one group comparison (over 80 percent of the men who viewed Stohl's face in closeup approved of her posing), a significantly higher percentage of those who saw the disabled Stohl approved of her posing. For example, of those shown the partially-nude picture, 55 percent with the disabled version approved compared to 36.4 percent with the ablebodied version. For men alone, the corresponding percentages were 75 percent versus 52.1 percent, and for women, 43.2 percent to 30.6 percent.

THE RIGHT TO BE SEXY
Analysis of the open-ended responses of those who, upon viewing the disabled Stohl, approved of her posing

can better help us to understand the distinction between acceptance and advocacy of the disabled person's "right to be sexy." Grouping respondents according to the reasons given for approval allows us to differentiate those reasons in terms of whether they are likely to lead to one or the other positive postures.

Acceptance would seem to be a logical outcome of the responses of two groups. The first group gave what might be called "disabled-blind" explanations ("Why not? An honest way to make a dollar"). The common factor here was the absence of any recognition of the disability. A second group did take account of Stohl's disability,

---

Educational institutions may now constitute enabling environments.

---

couching their approval in terms of the very basic theme of equal rights ("She has as much right as anyone to pose for this picture").

Advocacy would likely follow from the responses of three other groups. A good number of respondents saw Stohl as an example or role model representing to the public and/or other disabled people the ability of the disabled to succeed in endeavors in which they have not, historically, had the opportunity to participate ("Maybe her doing so will show other handicapped people that they are beautiful and show the general public the same. Good for her"). The responses of a second group expressed admiration for the disabled person having to overcome much more than others to achieve a goal ("With her disability it is a great step and very courageous. She is doing things in her life."). The underlying theme in the responses of the third group was the unique social-psychological benefits that a disabled person would derive from this experience ("If it makes her feel more 'complete' or happier why not?").

Assuming that the above speculation about the link between response type and the two positive public postures has validity, the difference between acceptance and advocacy is that in the case of advocacy there exists the perception of a greater urgency, sali-

ence, or merit related to the disabled person's "right to be sexy." This is most evident in the statements of those students who held a double standard, resulting in a type of "reverse discrimination" on behalf of the disabled. As one respondent put it, "Normally, I'm *very* against people posing in these pornographic pictures, but in this case I feel she made a statement that she is comfortable with, and I can't help but admire her reasons for it. She's trying to convey that handicapped people can be human, they are sexually attractive, and they are in control of their lives."

DISABLED PERSONS IN SOCIETY
The data presented provide support, and the beginnings of an empirical database, for social scientists like Bogdan and Taylor, who insist that there is a need to augment the conceptual and theoretical arsenal used in assessing the role of disability and disabled people in society. The finding of overwhelmingly favorable student attitudes toward an individual who uses a wheelchair raises doubts about the relevance of the deviance perspective to specific instances of disability. Maybe most striking is the absence in my research of any evidence of what Hahn has argued is discrimination toward disabled people based on aesthetic criteria. Not only was the disabled Stohl seen as physically attractive as her ablebodied counterpart, but also her disability did not lead to the imputation of "sexlessness," a causal sequence taken as a given in the literature. Quite to the contrary, the disabled Stohl was perceived as a woman with considerable sexual appeal.

Exploration of the origins and implications of the view of the disabled individual as a "paragon of virtue" is called for. Bogdan and Taylor see this perception as arising from the particular character of a specific one-to-one relationship between a disabled and nondisabled individual. While they may be correct on this score, the new research points to the existence of a more generalized notion that may involve a cultural stereotyping of disabled people in this way. Future research can provide important answers as to why they are seen as more likely to fulfill normatively-defined role obligations in circumstances ranging from friend to parent, spouse and employee. It is worth cautioning that, although obviously there is nothing inherently wrong with being viewed as a good person, there is always the possibility that this kind of stereotype could lead to unrealistic and unfair expectations concerning what disabled people are like and how they are likely to behave.

The limited purview of the studies presented precludes any grandiose claims about how far society has come in the way it perceives and treats people with disabilities. For example, the target subjects were all physically-disabled wheelchair users. And the literature shows that, in general, the physically disabled evoke more positive reactions from ablebodied people than do those with emotional and cognitive impairments (Bordieri and Drehmer, 1987). Despite this, the data presented do underscore the need to refrain from viewing all disabled people as occupying a unitary social status. One would hope that a new generation of writers will avoid describing all those with disabilities as "stigmatized" (Goffman, 1963) or as "outsiders" inhabiting the "other side" (Becker, 1963, 1964). It is time for works of quality that deal with how the various public postures—that is, rejection, acceptance, and advocacy—are distributed over the broad range of disabled persons.

A theoretical perspective that needs to be exploited in the future is one implied by Bogdan and Taylor and explicated most clearly by those taking a "minority group" approach to disabled people. It would replace the focus on disabled versus nondisabled individuals with one on disabling and enabling environments. The research cited here suggests that, as with the contexts of family and friends discussed by Bogdan and Taylor, educational institutions may now constitute enabling environments.

This was a position taken by Katz and his colleagues to explain the Berkeley high school students' favorable perception of disabled people. It is also compatible with my impression of the social milieu at the site of my study. There, over the last decade, disabled people have become an increasingly visible and prominent segment of the campus community.

Student attitudes in the studies discussed may also be a consequence of a more favorable climate toward disabled people in the society at large. In this regard, I cannot help but make mention of the recent, and very striking, events that took place at Gallaudet University in the spring of 1988. The unexpected force of public support—both immediate and seemingly unanimous—for the student body seeking deaf leadership may have been the critical factor in the swift capitulation of the powers-that-were. As the board of trustees' choice for the presidency of the university declared when she resigned, "I was swayed by the groundswell across the nation that it is time for a deaf president."

Finally, something must be said about the relevance of what has been discussed to the very practical issue of the employment of the disabled. When *Playboy* decided to publish pictures of Ellen Stohl, the mass media reported that the editorial staff was strongly divided on the wisdom of that decision and that those who held the negative opinion felt that the public was not ready for it. As my data show, they needn't have worried. Moreover, insofar as employers are reluctant to hire disabled people for fear of an unaccepting public, the data from all four studies show that they may be misreading public opinion. The dissemination

of social scientific research and perspectives relating to the acceptance and advocacy of people with disabilities would seem an important step in any process that is to have the capability of leading to their full integration into the larger society.

REFERENCES

Becker, Howard S., *Outsiders: Studies in the Sociology of Deviance* (New York: The Free Press. 1963).
___. *The Other Side: Perspectives on Deviance* (New York: The Free Press, 1964).
Bogdan, Robert and Steven Taylor, "Toward a Sociology of Acceptance: The Other Side of the Study of Deviance," *Social Policy* (Fall 1987), pp. 34-39.
Bordieri, James W. and David E. Drehmer, "Attribution of Responsibility and Predicted Social Acceptance of Disabled Workers," *Rehabilitation and Counseling Bulletin* (June 1987), pp. 219-26.
Groce, Nora, *Everyone Here Spoke Sign Language: Hereditary Deafness on Martha's Vineyard* (Cambridge: Harvard University Press, 1985).
Goffman, Erving, *Stigma: Notes on the Management of Spoiled Identity* (Englewood Cliffs, NJ: Prentice-Hall, 1963).
Hahn, Harlan, "Can Disability be Beautiful?" *Social Policy* (Winter 1988), pp. 26-31.
Katz, Shlomo, Shlomo Kravetz, and Mickey Karlinsky, "Attitudes of High School Students in the United States Regarding Disability: A Replication of an Israeli Study," *Rehabilitation Counseling Bulletin* (December 1986), pp. 102-9.
Krefting, Linda A. and Arthur P. Brief, "The Impact of Applicant Disability on Evaluative Judgments in the Selection Process," *Academy of Management Journal* (December 1976), pp. 675-80.
"Meet Ellen Stohl," *Playboy* (July 1987), pp. 16-18.
Schwartz, Howard D., "Disability and Sexual Display: Empirical Evidence of Public Advocacy for Disabled People and the Disabled Person's Right to be 'Sexy.'" Paper presented at the annual meeting of the American Sociological Association, Atlanta, August 28, 1988.
Siegfried, William D. and Ignatius J. Toner, "Students' Attitudes toward Physical Disability in Prospective Co-Workers and Supervisors," *Rehabilitation Counseling Bulletin* (September 1987), pp. 20-25.
Zola, Irving Kenneth, "Neither Defiant nor Cheering," *Disability Rag* (September/October 1987), pp. 16-18.

Dignity, Choice, And Care

William McCord

William McCord is professor of sociology at the City University of New York. He is author of Voyages to Utopia; Paths to Progress; *and* The Dawn of the Pacific Century *(published by Transaction). He is clerk of the Connecticut Valley Quarterly Meeting of Friends.*

The rationally planned suicide of Arthur Koestler in 1990, the huge sales of Derek Humphry's *Final Exit,* and the defeat of Initiative 119 in 1991 in the State of Washington, and the indictment for murder of Jack Kervorkian in 1992 are events that have evoked a thoughtful and deeply troubled response in the American public. They touch directly on two fundamental issues: Does man have a right to choose his own death? Should doctors or the state assist in carrying out this ultimate choice?

Death, particularly when it occurs by one's own hand, has long been taboo in America; surrounded by shame, hidden by the cosmetic care of morticians, and disguised by the gentle euphemisms of pastors. Now, like the closely related issue of abortion, the subject of suicide has been exposed to public debate. The advance of medical technology and the 1974 decision by the Supreme Court in the landmark case of Karen Ann Quinlan have transformed a private matter of assisted suicide into a public forum on the sanctity of life, the duties of physicians, and the limits on self-determination.

In the wake of the Quinlan decision, twenty-eight states have ruled that patients have the right to refuse life-sustaining treatment. Nine states now specifically allow the withdrawal of artificial feeding from patients in a vegetative state, allowing them to starve to death. In 1991, a federal law required that all patients admitted to any hospital for any reason must be asked if they want to plan for their death by filling out a "living will."

Neo-conservatives have tried to draw a fine line between withholding treatment and assisting others to commit suicide in a different fashion. In practice, this distinction has increasingly lost its meaning. What in fact is the difference between a doctor who starves his patient to death and one who prescribes a dose of Seconal with the warning that a gram will result in death? Most reasonable people will recognize that pulling the plug on a machine or allowing a patient to purchase a lethal dose of morphine for self-administration are both forms of "active" assistance and have the same result.

What is at issue today is who has the right to decide on ending life and what should be the safeguards surrounding this decision. Current American law is of little help in resolving such issues. Some states carry laws on their books punishing the act of suicide as a "crime." Others are silent on the issue, and still others would label those who assist in another's death as "murderers." In Michigan, as one blatant example of the law's ambiguity, the State Supreme Court in 1920 upheld the murder conviction of a man who placed poison within reach of his dying wife (*People v. Campbell*). Yet sixty-three years later, a Michigan appellate court ignored this precedent and dismissed a murder charge against a man who gave a gun to a person who later killed himself. In 1991, Michigan reversed itself once again by indicting Kevorkian for murder because he put his "suicide machine" at the disposal of two women who suffered from incurable diseases. Even the prosecution acknowledged that the patients themselves had pressed the button that triggered their death.

Voters in Washington decided to put the matter of assisted suicide on a democratic ballot. In 1991, citizens of Washington considered a legislative proposition unlike any ever debated by Americans. Initiative 119 asked: "Shall adult patients who are in a medically terminal condition be permitted to request and receive from a physician aid-in-dying?" The initiative required that adults could request aid-in-dying only after two physicians certified that they were mentally competent, terminally ill, and had less than six months to live; two independent witnesses had to certify the patient's

From *Society*, Vol. 29, No. 5, July/August 1992, pp. 20-24. Copyright © 1992 by Transaction, Inc. Reprinted by permission.

condition. The initiative forced voters to choose between the various "right-to-life" and "pro-choice" arguments as they apply to death. How volatile this issue is was illustrated by the fact that 61 percent of state residents favored the initiative before the vote. When it actually came before them, however, 54 percent voted "no."

Some orthodox Christians and Jews who normally take a conservative stance in politics and on social issues welcomed the Washington vote. Perhaps their most definitive statement, "Always to Care, Never to Kill: A Declaration on Euthanasia," came from the Ramsey Colloquium of the New York-based Institute on Religion and Public Life. The colloquium consists of Jewish and Christian theologians and ethicists who meet periodically to consider questions of religion and public policy. Their manifesto first appeared in *The Wall Street Journal* on November 27, 1991 and subsequently in *First Things* in February 1992. The authors come from a cross section of the nation and include Midge Decter, Rabbi Marc Gellman, Russell Hittinger of the Catholic University of America, and Richard John Neuhaus.

The eloquent manifesto welcomed the decision of Washington state to "turn back a measure that would have extended the permission to kill" and affirmed that "we must learn again the wisdom that teaches us always to care, never to kill." The signatories warned that "euthanasia is an extension of the license of kill." They predicted that "once we cross the boundary between killing and allowing to die, there will be no turning back."

The authors based their opposition to suicide and assisted suicide on four grounds:

Religious: As Christians and Jews, say the authors, "We have learned to think of human life—our own and that of others—as both gift and trust. . . We are never to 'solve' the problem of suffering by eliminating those who suffer."

Moral: "To treat our life as a 'thing' that we can authorize another to terminate is profoundly dehumanizing. . . If life is a thing that can be renounced or taken at will, the moral structure of human community, understood as a community of persons, is shattered."

Political: With the founders of our nation, the signers of the declaration held that life is an inalienable right that cannot be given away. "Except when government exercises its duty to protect citizens against force and injustice, or when it punishes evildoers, it may not presume for itself an authority over human life."

Institutional: To blur the distinction between healing and killing would inevitably push doctors further to engage in the killing of people who are not termi-nally ill or competent to give their consent. "Legalized euthanasia would inevitably require the complicity of physicians." This well-reasoned and deeply felt, if mistaken, appeal deserves serious consideration by those who regard death with dignity and choice as a civilized option for mankind.

Religious Wisdom: It is a matter of deep controversy whether the Judeo-Christian tradition sanctions the preservation of life above all other possible goods. The fact is that the orthodox traditions have often allowed killing—including suicide—in the service of some higher goal. Among Jews, the mass suicide at Masada in defiance of Roman oppression is now celebrated as a glorious event. Among Christians, the other-worldliness of the Pauline tradition sometimes led early converts into an epidemic of suicide. Tertullian describes how entire Christian villages would implore a Roman proconsul to grant them the privilege of martyrdom. Lucian told of Christians who gave themselves up to be slain in eager anticipation of eternal salvation.

Orthodox traditions have often allowed killing in the service of a higher goal.

Contemporary Christians can dismiss these early activities as aberrations and they can reasonably argue that dogmatic justification of some forms of killing—capital punishment and "just" wars, for example—are grave misinterpretations of Jesus' commands. Clearly Jesus never instructed mankind to cling to life at all cost. He enjoined man to love God and to love his neighbor as himself. In themselves, these two commandments do not logically condemn suicide or assisted suicide. In fact, a death with dignity, if undertaken in a spirit of compassion, could be the ultimate fulfillment of these injunctions. Jesus' acceptance of his crucifixion testifies to his conscious willingness to sacrifice his own life for a higher purpose.

Life is a gift. It may also become an intolerable burden. Dalton Trumbo makes this clear in his classic account *Johnny Got His Gun*. In this novel, "Joe" goes off to war in a burst of patriotism. He is grievously wounded but his brain still functions. The doctors exhibit him in a box as a triumph of medical science. Joe can communicate with the world only by tapping out messages in Morse code which at first are not recognized. A nurse finally understands his pleas but her superiors refuse to hear them. At the end, Joe asks: "Why didn't they kill him? Why didn't they put an end to his suffering? Why should he be a prisoner? He had committed no crime. What right had they to keep him? What possible reason could they have to be so inhuman to him?" Which action would be more in accord with the Christian doctrine of compassion and human dignity: To leave Joe in torment or to accept his cry for release?

Moral Wisdom: Our ethical tradition includes not only Immanuel Kant and Albert Schweitzer who condemned suicide, but a lineage of thinkers from Socrates through Epictetus to Shakespeare and Nietzsche who have affirmed man's privilege of selecting his own death a voluntary, rational, and compassionate ending chosen not by accident but by lucid free choice. The Stoic tradition particularly stresses that man has the prerogative of a humane and dignified termination of life chosen courageously and with deliberate self-control.

The act of suicide, if undertaken with dignity and autonomy, can augment the moral bonds that tie men together.

Following Epictetus, the Stoics sought to rid themselves of "the fetters of the wretched body" and to assert their will "against kings or thieves who, by controlling men's bodies, try to dictate their fate." The Stoics and the Epicureans believed that men should make the final choice about their destinies with dignity and fortitude. "Remember," Epictetus wrote, "the door is open. . . Depart instead of staying to moan."

More recently, Friedrich Nietzsche deplored the "unfree, coward's death" that most men, trapped in contemptible conditions at the wrong time and deceived by a slave's morality, must endure. Instead, he celebrated "free death." "From love of life," Nietzsche argued, "one should deserve a different death: free, conscious, without accident, without ambush."

In contemporary times, those who contemplate asserting control over suffering and dying contend that the possibility of rational suicide preserves man's fragile dignity in the face of brutal circumstances. Indeed, they point out that one of man's unique and defining attributes is his ability to foresee, to contemplate, and potentially to control the circumstances of his own death; it is this noble quality that sets him apart from all other animals. Rather than degenerating helplessly, the ill person can choose the timing, the setting, and the conditions of death. He or she may prepare friends and family for the end, make reasonable provisions for the welfare of others, complete worldly duties, and take leave of loved ones in a dignified, truly human manner.

By affirming his uniquely human capacity to mediate and mold death, man enhances his threatened self-determination in the face of a merciless fate. A death with dignity is the final proof of man's independence and self control; an affirmation of man's ultimate liberty and his last infusion of meaning into an often formless reality. If suicide and assisted suicide were allowed, would this shatter the moral structure of human community, as the neo-conservatives argue? Hardly. Our experience with ancient civilizations and our own indicates that the act of suicide, if undertaken with dignity and autonomy, can augment the moral bonds that tie men together.

In Japan, the honorable practice of *hara-kiri* morally linked the person to his fellows and to the emperor. It was an ultimate affirmation of loyalty and moral responsibility. Among the pre-modern Eskimos, the elderly or sick ended their lives gracefully as a way of preserving the community against the threats of a harsh environment. In Confucian China, *sze-chien*, or sending a "death memorandum" to an evil emperor, was a noble way for imperial scholars to assert their moral judgment. In the time of the megalomaniac Empress Wu, for instance, the highest officials sent her a message imploring her to do what was right. After insuring the receipt of their advice, the scholars ate their last supper with their families, gave them final instructions, and dressed themselves in the proper official robes with great calm and dignity. They then committed suicide.

In contemporary times, the experience of those nations that have given assisted suicide wide latitude must also be considered. The example of the Netherlands is particularly relevant. The practice of assisted suicide is more open and extensive in there than anywhere else in the modern world. Although Dutch law still formally forbids assisted suicide, authorities and doctors have long chosen to ignore the anachronistic mandate. According to a government report, 25,300 cases of assisted suicide occur each year in Holland. This represents 19.4 percent of all deaths. There are 13,691 cases where an overdose of morphine or the withdrawal of life-sustaining treatment brings about death. Carlos S. Gomez, in his study *Regulating Death*, suggests that there are no rigid rules governing the Dutch system. Contrary to neo-conservative claims, the Netherlands has not collapsed as a moral society because of this practice. While one might wish for changes in the law and stricter regulation, the Dutch approach has met with wide public approval and has not led to a devaluation of human life per se.

Political Wisdom:The Founding Fathers did indeed recognize life as an inalienable right. They also proclaimed, however, that the rights to liberty and the pursuit of happiness as equally important gifts bestowed by "Nature and Nature's God." The real political question is how to balance these rights. To acknowledge that the state has the authority to kill evildoers, as the neo-conservatives affirm, already relativizes the claim to the sanctity of human life. They grant the state a permit to kill. One may disagree with their point of view but the fact remains that under certain circumstances they are willing to let the state exercise its power over the individual. Those who defend assisted suicide believe that there is a strong case for arguing that the state should abstain from interference in this final decision. They argue that choices made by rational, consenting people in the "pursuit of happiness" should be acknowledged as a proper way of asserting their liberty. The state should not interfere. To give the state the authority to block these freely made choices is to presume an ultimate power it does not have in our political tradition.

Institutional Wisdom: Neo-conservatives fear that physicians will be corrupted by assisting in suicide. They affirm a distinction between killing and allowing to die. Alas, as anyone who has witnessed the "pulling of the plug" knows, this is a spurious distinction. Letting a person die of thirst, starvation, or asphyxiation is an active decision on the part of the physician. Withholding of treatment can cause agonizing pain. The physician is often more directly involved in killing the person in such cases than when he places a vial of sleeping pills at a patient's bedside and leaves the ultimate decision to him.

The real issue is whether it is the patient or the doctor who makes the final decision. Physicians should not be in charge of the actual death since their oath requires them to prolong life. If they are allowed to shorten life, patients will receive an ambiguous message: How can they be sure of the doctor's intentions? In general, physicians should not be directly involved in ending life, certainly less so than they are now in the termination of feeding without the patient's consent or, indeed, in capital punishment. Certainly, too, physicians must avoid involvement in euthanasia. In this matter, neo-conservatives make a crucial mistake in not distinguishing between euthanasia and assisted suicide. Euthanasia involves taking the patient's life with or without consent in the name of some higher goal. Assisted suicide is the act of allowing the patient to carry out his own decision by providing him with the means for ending his life.

It would be dangerous if our society became involved in active euthanasia, such as was practiced in Nazi Germany. Admittedly, an argument could be made that some human beings, incapable of choice, should be granted a "gentle death." Katie Letcher Lyle has described such an instance in the case of "Henry" in her article "A Gentle Way to Die" *(Newsweek,* March 2, 1992). Henry is a retarded dangerous person who makes life unlivable for others. Ejected from the facility where he lived, Henry faces "either a drugged hell of an existence behind bars; or, more likely, de-institutionalization, street life, an agonizing death in a filthy alley." Rather than those alternatives, Lyle advocates euthanasia and finds it "disgraceful, as well as ironic, that we cannot bring ourselves to treat our fellow humans as humanely as we treat our pets."

Acknowledging that the state has the authority to kill relativizes the claim to the sanctity of human life.

To kill Henry would violate all major religious and ethical cannons for we would take the choice out of his own hands and arrogate it to ourselves. This cannot be allowed. It opens the door for the state to decide who is fit to live and, by involving physicians, would undoubtedly subvert the medical profession. We must say no to euthanasia while affirming a patient's right to assisted suicide.

Safeguards to Assisted Suicide

When we consider assisted suicide as a public policy, we must also insure that safeguards against abuses are in place. Three considerations should dominate the discussion of public policy: 1) Does the action enhance the dignity of the person? 2) Is it the result of the person's self-determination? 3) Does it reflect compassion for the person and others?

In California and other states to follow, the clash over current medical and legal arrangements for death will undoubtedly raise stark questions:

Should those who are afflicted with serious conditions but are not near death be allowed to limit their lives? Proponents contend that people who are still able to choose despite being physically helpless (such as paraplegics) and those who are diagnosed as being on the brink of an inexorable decline (such as Alzheimer patients) should be allowed to consider suicide as a viable possibility.

Opponents contend that such a concession would open the door for the mentally unstable, the temporarily depressed, or the immature to end their lives. People who pass through a period of depression often entertain the idea of suicide but will reject it when they are properly sedated or treated. Similarly, a large proportion of American teen-agers—roughly one in twelve high school students—say that they tried to commit suicide.

The physician should be a counselor, not the one making the decision.

To guard against the possibility of unrestrained suicide, public policy should provide that only mature, mentally competent adults with acceptable reasons are allowed to make the decision after a waiting period. Before a person's request for aid in dying is approved by a public body, it would be wise to have psychiatrists consult with the patient and explore all options. While such an approach would screen out the majority of the disturbed, impetuous, harassed, or temporarily dejected, it would allow those who anticipate a life of misery to choose death with dignity.

What if a doctor makes a mistake? Inevitably, a physician may make the wrong diagnosis or a "miracle" may occur. Conceivably, a new treatment could result in unexpected cures. This is unquestionably one of the great risks of medical practice and it suggests again that the role of the physician should be minimized. The doctor should be an expert counselor but not the person who controls the decision. The burden of choice must be born by the patient; the exercise of an individual's autonomy should be that person's sole responsibility. If rational suicide were allowed, would the elderly or ill choose it simply to spare their families?

Possibly. Such self-sacrifice should not be categorized as necessarily evil, but it must not be undertaken lightly. As in other cases, a frank, open, and loving consultation between patient and family should precede any action.

What of the grim possibility that someone, even a family member, might push the patient to suicide? Is it possible that a murder could be hidden as suicide? This could happen, as it does today. The Dutch experience, however, indicates that legitimizing rational suicide does not increase this possibility. With the safeguards proposed, even in Initiative 119, it seems reasonable to suppose that the chances of an "involuntary" suicide or murder masked as suicide would actually decrease.

Is the hospice movement not a better alternative to rational suicide? Certainly, it provides an important alternative and a humane mode of coping with death under circumstances of relatively little pain. Whether it is better to perish slowly, benumbed by morphine cocktails, however, as opposed to being allowed to choose the mode, manner, and time of one's death is a matter best left to individual discretion.

Failure to decide these issues because of personal or social anguish over "contemplating the unthinkable" will continue to burden many people with humiliating debilities, pointless suffering, and meaningless "final exits." Sensible provisions for rational suicide governed by principles of self-determination, dignity, and compassion offer mankind the possibility of ending a life that has become so unacceptable as to require no further deeds or days. Thus, for defenders of rational suicide as well as for the ancient Stoics, the image of perfect nobility is the person lovingly doing his duty to others and meeting death with pride and freedom and courage. For doctors, the guideline should be: Always to care, with dignity and choice.

Stratification and Social Inequalities

- **Fortunes of Income Classes and Welfare (Articles 23 and 24)**
- **Racial Inequalities (Articles 25 and 26)**
- **Sex Inequalities (Articles 27 and 28)**

People are ranked in many different ways: by physical strength, education, wealth, or other characteristics. Those who are rated highly usually enjoy special privileges and opportunities. They often have power over others, special status, and prestige. The differences among people constitute their life chances, or the probability that an individual or group will be able to obtain the valued and desired goods in a society. These differences are referred to as stratification, or the system of structured inequalities that pattern social relationships.

In most industrialized societies, income is one of the most important divisions among people, whereas in agricultural societies kinship has a major influence on life chances. Karl Marx described stratification in different terms. He used the term social class to refer to two distinct groups: those who control the means of production and those who do not. These groups overlap extensively with the rich and poor. This section examines the life chances of the rich and the poor and of various disadvantaged groups, because they best demonstrate the crucial features of the stratification system in the United States.

The first subsection of this unit discuss the fortunes of different income classes. Daniel Huff discusses the rich, not as winners in the business competition game, but winners in the welfare game. When all government gifts, breaks, and benefits are added up, most of it goes to the upper and middle classes, not to the poor. In "The Poverty Industry," Theresa Funiciello presents a sympathetic portrayal of the hardships and vulnerability of the poor.

The next two subsections examine the social position of blacks and women. "A Crisis of Shattered Dreams" points to many impediments to the hopes of blacks. A white backlash has developed and some indicators show blacks losing ground relative to whites. Shelby Steele presents a quite different view, but his analysis pertains to the black middle class, where blacks have made real progress. Their integration has progressed so far that blacks need to reduce their defensiveness and their own prejudices. Liz Roman Gallese discusses the fact that women have risen to middle management, but they are not progressing on to the top. Both the prejudice of men and the lesser competitiveness of women contribute to this problem. In the final selection, Lori Heise details the situation of women throughout the world. The news is not good. Unfortunately, her title suggesting that there is a global war against women is not much exaggerated.

The articles in this section portray tremendous differences in wealth and life chances among Americans. Systems of inequality affect what a person does and when and how he or she does it. An important purpose of this section is to help you become more aware of how stratification operates in social life.

Looking Ahead: Challenge Questions

Will technology reduce or increase social inequalities?

Why is stratification such an important theme in sociology?

What social groups are likely to rise in the stratification system in the next decade? Which groups will fall? Why?

Upside-Down Welfare

AMERICANS SPEND VAST AMOUNTS ON "WELFARE" EACH YEAR, BUT LESS THAN 10 PERCENT GOES TO POOR PEOPLE.

Daniel D. Huff

Daniel D. Huff is a professor of social work at Boise State University in Idaho.

At this writing George Bush's "kinder, gentler nation" is still rather callous. One in four of our nation's children is now born into poverty, up from one in five a decade ago. One in six has no health insurance. Following years of progress in preventing infant deaths, improvements in infant mortality have stopped; our rate is now worse than in nineteen other nations (a black baby born in Boston or Washington, D.C., is more likely to die before his or her first birthday than a baby born in Jamaica). Twenty million Americans remain hungry; a half million children malnourished. The average American's real wages have declined since 1980. For the poor and the near poor, the drop has been more severe. Meanwhile, the share of household income of the richest fifth of the American population continues to rise. The gap between the two groups is now wider than at any time in the last fifty years.

—Robert B. Reich
The Resurgent Liberal[1]

The decade of the eighties was hard. For many of us who came of age in the sixties and early seventies, watching low-income individuals and families lose most of the meager gains won during that now dim and distant past has been frustrating. Not only have low-income people grown both in numbers and proportion of population, but also those who now find themselves economically disadvantaged are predominantly women and children, with strong representation from mentally ill and developmentally disabled people.[2] Ironically, those who should be the highest on any rational list of priorities for government assistance are receiving the least.

Our conservative friends tell us that we are now spending more of our national budget on welfare programs than at any time in our past. But how can that be? How can poverty be growing—particularly among our most vulnerable populations—at the same time that we are spending hundreds of billions of dollars for welfare?

The answer lies in our understanding of what social welfare is and who it should help. In fact, we have developed a set of extremely elaborate programs that are designed to shift income from one group of citizens to another, but need is seldom a criterion for receiving benefits. Presently, we have three types of welfare programs. First are the poverty programs, such as Food Stamps and Aid to Families with Dependent Children (AFDC), which represent a relatively small amount of money and are designed to serve only low-income people.

Second are those programs, such as Social Security and Medicare, whose benefits serve mostly middle- and upper-income individuals. The third category of welfare is a newer set of programs designed to redistribute wealth to American businesses. Unlike the traditional poverty programs, these "upside-down welfare" programs are not customarily called "welfare." Many of their benefits are funneled through obscure and "off-budget" devices that avoid the scrutiny and debate that normally accompany implementation of more conventional welfare designs. Upside-down welfare represents an immense redistribution of our national wealth and explains why so little has been done for low-income people over the past decade. While we have been redistributing our nation's wealth through a variety of benefits, most of this money has not gone to help poor people.

The upside-down welfare state is extensive and breaks naturally into two different categories. First are those schemes primarily benefiting middle- and upper-income persons. That system represents a "gilded" welfare state, which provides the nonpoor with such benefits as low-cost government insurance for their oceanside homes, tax breaks for their investments, subsidized medical care, and supplemental retirement benefits. The second is reserved for corporations, rather than individuals, and provides a redistribution system that annually transfers billions of dollars from ordinary taxpayers to the richest and largest corporations in America—a welfare program for Wall Street.

Wall Street Welfare and Business Subsidies

I live in a Northwestern city that is a hub for a large agricultural area. My rural neighbors are among the first to shout about too much government spending and are particularly angered when some big-city liberal advocates increased budgets for poverty programs. As a rule, my neighbors are

Table 1. Welfare Spending by Program

Welfare Programs for Individuals	Amount (in billions)
Means-Tested Poverty Programs	
Medicaid	$ 49
AFDC	17
SSI	13
Food Stamps	15
Other (loans, etc.)	24
Total	$ 117
Gilded Welfare Middle-Class Programs	
Social Security	247
Medicare	104
Other retirement programs	62
Miscellaneous benefits	50
Tax expenditures	300
Fringe benefits (health & retirement)	385
Total	$1,148
Grand Total	$1,265

Source: U.S. Budget, 1990; Statistical Abstracts of the United States, 1990

anti-government in attitude and intolerant of what they call "government handouts." In spite of these attitudes, my farmer friends receive immense benefits from a wide variety of government programs.

In this area of the country, almost all the farming is done under irrigation. Water is provided to farmers by the government at a rate so low that the farmers' water bills represent only a fraction of the cost of water usage. For every dollar spent by the Bureau of Reclamation to provide water, the farmer pays the government 10 cents.[3] During the course of the year, my farmer friends typically take advantage of subsidized loans to purchase various necessities and subsidized insurance to protect them from the perils of pests and weather. When harvest season arrives, the local agricultural community lines up for government loans on their crops— loans they have to repay only if the crop values are greater than the so-called target price set by the U.S. Department of Agriculture (USDA).

Many of the farms in this area are devoted to growing the sugar beet, an ugly plant that only reluctantly surrenders its sugar after extensive and expensive processing. The sole reason there is any market at all for these beets rests on a government trade policy that does not allow imports of cheaper cane sugar. This indirect subsidy to the sugar beet growers and processors costs consumers $3 billion a year.[4]

Government programs designed to increase the income of the nation's farms costs approximately $25 billion a year.[5] USDA estimated that fewer than five million Americans lived on farms in 1990.[6] We disburse $25 billion a year for five million people on farms, while spending only $15 billion a year to support 11 million women and children on AFDC. Paradoxically, most of these funds never even reach the poorer segments of rural America. Clifton Luttrell, agricultural economist for the CATO Institute, estimates that less than 20 percent of farm subsidies trickle down to the poorest farmers. He explains that if the real purpose of farm subsidies is to eliminate

farm poverty, the government could send every low-income farmer in America a check of sufficient size to pull him or her out of poverty for a cost of $2 billion to $3 billion.[7] Clearly, our current farm programs are not a very efficient means of helping the country's poorer farmers.

Unfortunately, the upside-down welfare that benefits farmers is only a small illustration of an extensive system. Local manufacturers wishing to sell their wares abroad to sometimes unstable and unreliable governments arrange for government loans at rates far below those available at commercial banks. The source of these loans, the Export-Import Bank (Ex-Im Bank), has been accused of falsifying its books in an attempt to make this subsidy appear smaller than it really is. An example of what one observer termed "creative bookkeeping" was listing loans to prerevolutionary China as fully collectible. In 1989, House Banking Committee Chair Henry Gonzales suggested that the Ex-Im Bank was so awash in red ink that even if it were liquidated, it would leave a shortfall of $4 billion to $6 billion—

Figure 1. Welfare Spending For Individuals
Total = $1.265 trillion

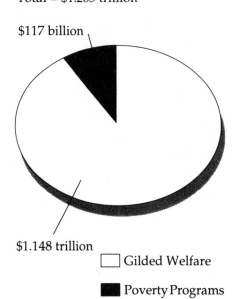

$117 billion

$1.148 trillion

☐ Gilded Welfare

■ Poverty Programs

Source: U.S. Budget, 1990; Statistical Abstracts of the United States, 1990

a loss that would be passed directly to American taxpayers.[8]

Much larger subsidies are received by the defense industry, which since World War II has enjoyed the free use of more than $100 billion worth of plants and machinery owned by the U.S. Department of Defense and has accepted gifts of more than $10 billion worth of shops and equipment.[9]

The savings and loan (S&L) debacle is a more current example of upside-down welfare. The General Accounting Office now estimates that the financial rescue of the S&L industry will cost the American taxpayer $500 billion.[10] This gigantic public relief program for the S&L industry is necessary because of deregulation policies that enriched a

> *Clearly, our current farm programs are not very efficient means of helping the country's poorer farmers.*

small number of investors and developers in a handful of states. Taxpayers from all over the country will end up paying the bill for what amounts to one of the largest transfer-of-wealth programs in American history.

Corporate welfare programs represent a huge income redistribution system, providing American business interests with more than $200 billion a year.

Gilded Welfare: Public Assistance for the Middle and Upper Classes

I have a wealthy friend who is adamant in his denunciation of government handouts. Programs for low-income people earn his special disdain, for he believes such policies sap incentive and subsidize immoral behavior. He seems to harbor no such fears for his own set of personal subsidies, however, which are substantial. My comrade enjoys flying his own airplane at our local airport, which happily

provides him services at fees representing only a fraction of their true costs. His beachfront vacation home is located in an area that is so frequently exposed to heavy weather that he cannot obtain private insurance and instead is forced to use subsidized government insurance. My friend spends many of his summer weekends camping in a neighboring national park where the fees he pays represent about one-third the actual costs of maintaining the park and its facilities. His considerable use of electricity, both at home and at his place of business, is subsidized through our regional power supplier at rates approximately one-half of those paid by consumers on the East Coast.[11]

Needless to say, my friend is hardly alone. Most of us view our personal subsidies as important benefits and just compensation for the taxes we pay. Unfortunately, while the middle- and upper-income groups have become sophisticated in lobbying and

> *Most of us view our personal subsidies as important benefits and just compensation for the taxes we pay.*

advocating for their welfare benefits, low-income Americans have proven to be less capable at seizing their share of government benefits. This fact is evident if we examine two of the largest categories of the current federal budget, Social Security and tax expenditures.

Social Security represents annual allocations of more than $240 billion.[12] Although one might imagine that the bulk of those dollars are divided among relatively low-income retirees, in fact in 1988 only 20 percent of Social Security benefits went to recipients with incomes less than 200 percent of the poverty level.[13] Although Social Security is commonly seen as an insurance program, current Social

Security benefits are heavily subsidized by current workers and are two to five times greater than those of comparable private retirement programs.[14]

Social Security, therefore, is an inelegant solution to poverty, since 96 percent of the approximately 35 million low-income Americans are not elderly. The total spending for all the programs specifically designated for low-income people of all ages is only about $100 billion, while we spend $250 billion on retirees. According to Alice Munnell of the Brookings Institute, sending every American in poverty a check large enough to raise his or her income above the poverty level would cost only $130 billion to $160 billion.[15]

In spite of Social Security's beneficence, it is not very effective as an antipoverty program. Even staunch advocates of the system, like policy analysts Merton and Joan Bernstein, admit that although more than two-thirds of Social Security recipients had incomes higher than 125 percent of the poverty level, 27 percent—almost one-third—of all beneficiaries collect so little in benefits that they are forced to live in poverty.[16] The record is even more disheartening for minorities. In 1990, more than 40 percent of all black women currently receiving Social Security benefits were living below the poverty line.[17]

The system of tax breaks for individuals highly favors the rich. Tax breaks—or, in current budgetary parlance, "tax expenditures"—represent uncollected revenues and are every bit as real as actual expenditures. Not collecting taxes has the same fiscal impact as a grant or subsidy, with the obvious advantage that tax expenditures are "off budget" and not subject to the same scrutiny as direct spending. Uncollected personal taxes made possible by the assorted tax breaks written into the 1986 tax reform bill came to a staggering $281 billion per year in 1990.[18] Obviously, the bulk of savings generated by those tax breaks is distributed among the affluent. In 1990, *Wall Street Journal* reporters David Wessel and Jeffrey Birnbaum estimated that three-quarters of all itemized deductions are taken by individuals earning $50,000 or more per year.[19] Half the benefits from the interest deductions on mortgages went to the wealthiest 10 percent of the population, and 80 percent of the benefits claimed through the deductibility of state and local taxes goes to individuals with annual incomes of more than $30,000.[20]

The $90 billion a year in tax breaks represented by the exemption granted to employer-paid health and retirement plans represents a double inequity.[21] Not only do lower-income workers benefit far less from the tax savings, but they enjoy coverage from these programs at proportionally lower rates than do upper-income workers. According to a study conducted by the U.S. Agency for Health Care Policy and Research, lower-income workers are twice as unlikely to have health insurance than their more affluent colleagues.[22] Kevin Phillips in his book, *The Politics of Rich and Poor*, notes that only four in 10 American workers even have retirement plans.[23]

Even the ostensibly benign private charity system has been accused of unfairly disbursing its largess. Most of the more than $100 billion collected every year by private nonprofits is spent on activities that only remotely affect lower-income Americans. According to Lester Solomon's Urban Institute study on private nonprofits, less than $22 billion annually is earmarked for social services, with the bulk of philanthropic spending directed to such enterprises as private hospitals, preparatory schools, universities, and a variety of cultural activities.[24] Even money spent on social services is, upon closer inspection, suspect. The highly visible United Way programs have come under attack from such organizations as the United Black Fund for underwriting mostly middle class and white "charities," such as the Boy Scouts, the Young Men's Christian Association, and the Red Cross.

Altogether, Americans spend more than a trillion dollars every year on welfare; but less than 10 percent of that is specifically earmarked for low-income people.[25] The rest, such as Social Security, private charity, tax breaks, fringe

Spending so much on the nonpoor while cutting poverty programs seems shamefully hypocritical.

benefits, and assorted subsidies for American businesses, benefit primarily those who are relatively well-to-do. Although nothing is inherently wrong or immoral about any individual component of this upside-down welfare, spending so much on the nonpoor while cutting poverty programs seems shamefully hypocritical at best, and at worst inimical to the nation's economic and social stability.

So there is the fundamental paradox of the welfare state: that it is not built for the desperate, but for those who are already capable of helping themselves. As long as the illusion persists that the poor are merrily freeloading on the public dole, so long will the other America continue unthreatened. The truth, it must be understood, is the exact opposite. The poor get less out of the welfare state than any group in America.

—Michael Harrington
The Other America[26]
PW

1. Robert Reich, *The Resurgent Liberal* (New York: Time Books, 1989), 235.

2. Robert Greenstein and Herman Leonard, *The Bush Administration Budget: Rhetoric and Reality* (Washington, D.C.: Center on Budget and Policy Practices, 1990), 1–5.

3. General Accounting Office, *Federal Charges for Irrigation Projects* (Washington, D.C.: Government Printing Office, 1981), 26–27.

4. Consumers for World Trade, "The Economic Effects of Significant Import Restraints" (Statement before the International Trade Commission: Investigation 232-263, April 5, 1989).

5. James Bovard, "Farm Policy Follies," *The Public Interest* (Spring 1989): 75–88.

6. Richard D. Hylton, "Wall Street's Latest Diversification Strategy: Down on the Farm," *New York Times*, Sept. 23, 1990, sec. F, p. 11.

7. Clifton Luttrell, *The High Cost of Farm Welfare* (Washington, D.C.: The CATO Institute, 1989), 125.

8. James Gannon, "Lawmakers' View: Export-Import Bank as a Red Ink Gusher," *The Idaho Statesman* (Boise), May 21, 1989, sec. F, p. 5.

9. Richard Stubbing and Richard Mindel, *The Defense Game* (New York: Harper & Row, 1986), 55.

10. Michael Galtner, "Biggest Robbery in History—You're the Victim," *Wall Street Journal*, Aug. 9, 1990, sec. A, p. 9.

11. Congressional Budget Office, *Charging for Federal Services* (Washington, D.C.: Government Printing Office, 1983), 66; Edward Flattan, "Federal Subsidies the Height of Folly," *The Idaho Statesman* (Boise), August 5, 1989, sec. F, p. 2; J. Peter Grace, *Burning Money* (New York: MacMillan Publishing, 1984), 174, 182.

12. Congressional Budget Office, *Special Analysis of the Budget* (Washington, D.C.: Government Printing Office, 1989), A38.

13. Pete Peterson and Neil Howe, *On Borrowing Time* (San Francisco: Institute for Contemporary Studies, KS Press, 1988), 102.

14. Howard Karger and David Stoesz, *American Social Welfare Policy* (White Plains, N.Y.: Longman, 1990), 169–172.

15. Alicia Munnell, "Lessons From the Income Maintenance Experiment: An Overview," in *Lessons From the Income Maintenance Experiment*, ed. Alicia Munnell (Washington, D.C.: Federal Reserve Board and The Brookings Institution, 1986), 4.

16. Merton C. and Joan Bernstein, *Social Security: The System That Works* (New York: Basic Books, 1987), 169–172.

17. Regina O'Grady-LeShane, "Old Women and Poverty," *Journal of Social Work* 35 (September 1990): 422–424.

18. Robert Reischauer, "The Federal Budget: Economics and Subsidies for the Rich," in *The Federal Budget: Economics and Politics*, ed. Aaron Woldauski and Michael Baskin (San Francisco: Institute for Contemporary Studies, 1989), 247.

19. Jeffrey Birnbaum and David Wessel, "Tax Breaks: Who Gets What," *Wall Street Journal*, July 20, 1990, sec. A, p. 3.

20. Reischauer.

21. Joseph Peachman, *Federal Tax Policy* (Washington, D.C.: The Brookings Institution, 1987), 361.

22. Ron Winslow, "Health Costs: Insurance Net For the Poor Frayed Badly in the 1980s," *Wall Street Journal*, Sept. 21, 1990, sec. B, p. 1.

23. Kevin Phillips, *The Politics of Rich and Poor* (New York: Random House, 1990), 42.

24. Lester Solomon, *The Non Profit Sector and the New Federal Budget* (Washington, D.C.: The Urban Institute Press, 1986), 19.

25. Congressional Budget Office, *Special Analysis of the Budget* (Washington, D.C.: Government Printing Office, 1990), A37–A39.

26. Michael Harrington, *The Other America* (New York: MacMillan Publishing, 1962), 161.

THE POVERTY INDUSTRY

DO GOVERNMENT AND
CHARITIES CREATE
THE POOR?

Theresa Funiciello

Theresa Funiciello, an activist and former welfare mother, has written "Burden of Kindness" (Atlantic Monthly, 1993), about women and welfare.

Firefighters returning from a false alarm in Queens, New York, one beautiful October day in 1989 were gazing into the sky when they passed an apartment complex. Ten stories up, a body was dangling from the window. Hector Faberlle and his coworkers yelled up front to get the rig turned around. Just as it arrived back at the building, a little girl, naked, hit the ground. Faberlle ran to resuscitate her as two other firefighters dashed in to the building.

According to Faberlle, "We tried to stabilize her. Just as she was breathing on her own, I heard people screaming. I looked up and saw another small child spinning down." Witnesses said a woman had seemed to dangle him before she let go of him. Hussein, age three, fell on his seven-year-old sister. "After that we couldn't get a pulse from her and blood was spilling from her mouth."

Ameenah Abdus-Salaam, a 32-year-old black middle-class Muslim housewife, was trying to send all five of her children back to Allah, through their apartment window. Her daughter Zainab was pronounced dead at the hospital. Hussein survived and a year later is still in rehabilitation. Just as Ms. Abdus-Salaam was about to toss out her one-year-old, firefighters burst in. As they were overtaking her, she urged the children to go quickly, as if they would go on their own. All were naked. According to one news report, she said, "We came into this world with

nothing and that's how we're going to leave." Three children and their mother, who intended to jump when she completed the task, were rescued.

Ms. Abdus-Salaam was charged with murder, attempted murder, first- and second-degree assault, reckless endangerment, and endangering the welfare of a child. Neighbors said the mother was loving and the children were always polite and clean, as if that rendered the occurrence more mysterious. And then Ameenah Abdus-Salaam and her children vanished from our collective memory.

When I was young I could not possibly have understood or forgiven (as if it were mine to forgive) the acts of Ameenah Abdus-Salaam on October 5, 1989. Some of that youth I spent as a Muslim—drapes for clothes, virtually nonstop prayers, my two feet of hair cordoned with a bolt of white cloth bound so tightly I could never forget it was there. I took this religion as seriously as those that preceded it, starting with Catholicism (I went to *that* church every day until I was 18). My religion was as solid as a rock mountain pervious only to centuries of dripping water. (Latent feminism finally crept up on me.)

In Islam, everything is ritualized, from sex to eating. That's how I know what Ameenah Abdus-Salaam was doing calmly while she held Hussein out of the window before letting go. She was praying.

Reprinted from *Ms.*, November/December 1990, pp. 32-40.

WOMEN'S AND CHILDREN'S
NEEDS ARE DETERMINED
BY THEIR PRIOR
RELATIONSHIP TO A MAN

In form and function, as in other patriarchal religions, Muslim women are buried alive in contradictions. They are equal; no, superior; no, inferior—to men, to snakes, to witches. Make no mistake: an Islamic woman without a man, especially a woman with children, isn't remotely like a fish without a bicycle.

This woman had five children, aged one to eight years, and was recently separated from her husband. She had trouble making her last month's rent. She surely feared a descent into poverty and probably homelessness. (As of this writing she is not granting interviews.) Ahead lay the streets. Welfare. Welfare hotels. Drugs, prostitution, guns, knives, gambling, drunkenness, and all manner of spiritual death. But for a woman with the option of deliverance, it wasn't inevitable.

Some years after shedding my Muslim garb, I had a baby and ended up homeless and on welfare myself. Not long after, I organized a welfare rights center, where we (the mothers trapped in this system) tried, among other things, to sort out the differences between "us" and "them" (mothers not on welfare). One subject was the stereotype of child abuse. It was something each of us understood at some terribly private gut level, but never articulated outside our circle; even then, we were cautious.

My own revelation came when my daughter was about a year old. At one point, she was sick and cried almost nonstop for a week. I was experiencing severe sleep deprivation coupled with the trauma of being unable to comfort her. For one horrible moment, I felt like hurling her against the wall. Fortunately, my mother came by unexpectedly and held the baby for a couple of hours, giving me time to gather composure. My daughter's fever broke and we both survived. But ever since, I have understood child abuse. And any parent who claims not to understand it in that context, ain't hardly trying.

I had been very close to where Ameenah Abdus-Salaam was. On another level, our circumstances were very different. A homeless mother of five (I had only one) has virtually no chance of being taken in by friends or family for more than a night or two. A homeless mother of four or more has only a 16 percent chance of keeping her children together. If she stays in an abandoned building with them and gets caught, they'll be taken away for "neglect." Still, there are commonalities shared by women of all races and religions, from rural to urban poverty. The merciless anxiety, the humiliation of being shuttled back and forth like herded animals, the stress of keeping kids in school, are constant. Only the details vary.

In New York City, if she were able to keep them together, at some point they would approach an Emergency Assistance Unit (EAU), which is obligated to shelter them in some way. This would mean waiting for hours, sometimes even days, on plastic chairs or the bare floor. If the family didn't eat pork, they'd eat nothing, since baloney sandwiches are about all they'd get for several meals. Some nights they might be moved (often after midnight) to a roach, lice, and rat infested welfare hotel for a few hours. In the morning the family would be shuttled back to wait again.

If they were lucky, after some days they would finally be placed in a welfare hotel or "transitional" shelter. These often provide less space per family member than that required for jail cells. Because the family was large, they wouldn't even get apartment referrals from city workers until after they'd been in this hell for months. (One rural homeless mother told me her family was placed in a motel with bars instead of windows and not one store or school within walking distance. She was at the mercy of a barely functional shuttle system for the homeless.)

At first, many mothers try to continue taking children to their previous schools. In New York City, this usually means traveling with them (other babies in tow) to another borough in the morning and returning for them in the afternoon. When one child is too sick to travel, none go to school. After a while, the mother might try to place the children in a school closer to the shelter. Legal, yes. Easy, no. If the mother does accomplish this, other kids in the new school will soon realize her children are "untouchables." School life will become anathema to her kids. They'll begin to adopt the coping mechanisms of other homeless kids who *will* associate with them.

Night brings scant respite. Police sirens. Gunshots from outside or down the hall. Families fighting. Too many people and too few beds, often with neither sheets nor blankets, much less pillows. The mattresses have long since burst like pastry puffs. Bedbugs pinch.

Those of us who are lucky have a little stove in the room. I'll never forget the first time I used one in a welfare hotel. I had just added eggs to the frying pan when swarms of roaches scrambled out of the lit burner in every direction—including into the frying pan. It was days before I could bring myself to try it again. All the things most people take for granted become little horrors.

LET THEM EAT OVEN BROWNER

The Cheesettes made their debut outside my window one tranquil night in January 1980. It was my birthday. Unexpectedly, I heard a megaphone outside my second-story window, "Give me a 'C,' " and a crowd shouted "C." "Give me an 'H,' " and an "H" responded. I went to the window and there were staff and members of our welfare rights organization all dressed up in cardboard boxes painted orange with green letters, shouting and dancing. When the neighbors started complaining, the Cheesettes bumbled upstairs to my living room singing a medley, beginning with, "If it says surplus surplus surplus on the label label label, you don't want it want it want it on your table table table" . . .

Gripped by a sort of fascism of kindness, do-gooders all over the country were mobilizing to bring somebody else's garbage to our tables. We jokingly dubbed it the "Table Scraps Are a Right" ("TSAR") campaign. Most of the advocates clamoring to release the warehoused cheese to the nation's poorest citizens had never even seen one of those bricks, nor, for that matter, tasted it. The labels warned it might be harmful to your health—especially for those with a tendency to high blood pressure. My mother's came with worms in it once, only she hadn't noticed them until a considerable amount had been consumed. The so-called cheese was only the beginning.

Actually, lots of what is distributed by the food banks, pantries, soup kitchens, and their conglomerates isn't food at all. Located in Chicago, the largest of the conglomerates, Second Harvest, boasts distributions to 38,000 local charities through its member banks around the nation with donated items collected from various agribusiness giants. In 1986, Second Harvest passed along (for a price) among other things:

■Over 17 million pounds of "nonfood items," but less than 2 million pounds of pasta, which is a "discard market" staple.

■More than 15 times as much "Spices/Condiments" as "Meats/Fish/Poultry."

■"Snack Foods" to the tune of over 16 million pounds; and, oddly, "Crackers and Cookies" accounted for another nearly 8 million pounds. Crackers and cookies aren't snacks?

Sara Lee's chairman and CEO keynoted Second Harvest's 1986 conference. According to their impressively multicolored annual report, "Mr. Bryan spoke of three long-term benefits to corporate social involvement, the first and most obvious being tax incentives. Another is the need for a business to support a community from which it draws its work force. Third is a concern for corporate image."

"Nonprofit" food distribution, which started as a volunteer effort, has become a megabusiness. In the aggregate, tax incentives for corporations to distribute faultily packaged goods or out-of-date ones are *uncapped*. In other words, the sky is the limit, not only on tax breaks for items that previously had to be disposed of as garbage, but also on the cost of transporting them. Where once corporations paid carters to haul this trash to dumps, now U.S. citizens pay to ship it to food bank networks.

From coast to coast poor people complain about receiving endless boxes of Hamburger Helper but no hamburger, cold cereal but no milk. One paid food pantry operator told me she was glad they got so much hair conditioner from the local food bank, because now she didn't have to purchase it for herself anymore. A potential food distributor called it quits when his operation was forced to distribute meat tenderizer. You see, if the locals won't take it, somebody else has to store it, and the conglomerates don't want to jeopardize their relationships to the producers who are getting the tax breaks, in the event that someday they deliver actual food. To poor women and kids who frequent the food pantries, the microwave browning spray that shows up month after month is ludicrous.

At the same time, these families have experienced a radical decline in cash income in recent years, in no small measure as a result of the phony claims of the discard market and the neat advantages it offers politicians who support it. It's hot to be against hunger.

When New York's City Harvest takes out full-page ads in the New York *Times* asking for donations while claiming to serve 5,000 meals a day, know a few things: 5,000 meals to nearly 2 million poor people in the city is pissing in a river, and the money you send does not buy food. It buys refrigerator trucks, the people to drive and deliver donated food, the public relations experts who market the scheme, and highly paid executives to oversee the operation; it also helps defray the cost of tens of thousands of dollars for the ads in the *Times*.

The problem in the U.S. is not a shortage of food: we are a nation of excess. To poor women, who suffer the countless indignities of feeding themselves and their children at institutionalized begging sites, who want nothing more than to purchase food they eat at a regular grocery store—the cost of the good intentions is staggering.

The discard market will never feed poor people for real. It creates the illusion of solving a problem while using up a mountain of dollars and volunteers. The President's Commission on Income Maintenance Programs examined this issue 20 years ago, reporting: "The Food Stamp and Commodity Distribution programs . . . supplement incomes but do so much less efficiently and with less consumer choice than direct cash transfer programs." Not so long ago breadlines were the shame of the U.S.A. Now we are told that they are evidence of its humanity. Sleep on that tonight.

—T.F.

THE SYSTEM DOES OFFER
INCOME DISTRIBUTION—
TO THE SOCIAL WELFARE
ESTABLISHMENT

If the Abdus-Salaam family emerged from the "temporary" shelter intact and were placed in an apartment, the world would think their problems solved. But now they would be a welfare family. Overnight she would switch from homeless victim to society's victimizer. Her living conditions would not improve nor her stress diminish, but she would join the larger class of poor women—despised abusers of the system—welfare mothers. To have come this far would have been a heroic feat, but what would be said of her is that she's a drain on national resources, has too many children she shouldn't have had if she couldn't afford to, and she doesn't "work."

On welfare, the chances of having enough money to live in a remotely decent neighborhood and pay for basic human needs are laughable—even in New York, where welfare benefits are "high." On the day when the Abdus-Salaam family almost came to total halt, the *maximum* monthly grant in New York City for a mother and five children was $814.20—or *less than three fifths of the federal poverty threshold for the same size family.* The *average* New York grant for six was $655 per month. (In January 1990 there was a slight, almost negligible increase in aggregate benefits.) Assuming the family received the maximum, the rent allotment would have been $349. Assuming the absurd—that they could find habitable housing for that price in New York or most any other U.S. city—they would be left with $465.20, or about $2.50 per person, per day, for most of their food. (Food stamps would provide less than two weeks of nutritionally adequate food for the month.) That same $2.50 must cover some of their medical expenses, and *all* their utilities, toothpaste, toilet paper, furniture, soap, baby bottles, diapers, laundry, transportation, kitchen utensils, and clothing. If Ms. Abdus-Salaam lived in South Dakota, she'd have had just about $1.88 for all those things. If she were a single mother living in California aged 25 or less, she'd have a 98 percent chance of landing on welfare. In New York, if she took one subway ride in search of an elusive job, she'd use up over 90 percent of her daily ration. If she's menstruating and needs to buy a box of sanitary napkins, she'd have to dip into her children's share. Like millions of women, she has at her disposal only one commodity guaranteed to produce sufficient income to keep her family together: her body. For some women that's unthinkable; for

example, to a devout Muslim, even survival does not justify such a damning act. Yet to kill herself—only herself—would be to act irresponsibly to her children. Had *Mr.* Abdus-Salaam died instead of leaving the family, everything would have been different.

Ameenah would have been the recipient of sympathy and support. As a widow with minor children, she would become a Social Security recipient instead of a welfare mother. (The maximum family benefit for survivor families on Social Security in 1989—$1,898.90 per month—could be enough to continue living modestly where she was. While this sum is hardly lavish, the family would remain above poverty.) No social policy experts would go nuts because she didn't have a "job." In fact, she would be thought a good mother for taking care of her children full-time, "at least while they're small." If and when she did get a paying job, she could earn thousands of dollars without a reduction in her Social Security check. (On welfare, a job would be taxed at 100 percent. Outside of minimal work-related expenses, for the most part her welfare check would be reduced one dollar for every dollar she was paid.) The message: the needs and rights of women and children are determined by the nature of their prior relationship to a man; the only difference between

WHO THE POOREST OF THE POOR ARE

As ever (and everywhere), most poor families are female-headed households. In the late 1960s—before income security for poor families was transferred to income security for mammoth charities—families on welfare in many states received benefits lifting them at least slightly above the poverty line. Now, government data regularly report the demographics of those living not just below the poverty line, but below 75 percent of the poverty line—meaning predominant-ly those on welfare. In the U.S. in 1987, people living in one-parent *female* families constituted 42.3 percent of all those living below 75 percent of the poverty line. By contrast, those living in one-parent *male* families were only 2.4 percent of all people below 75 percent of the poverty line. Even though two-parent families were still in the majority of all family groupings, they constituted a mere 26.5 percent of the population living below 75 percent of poverty.   —T.F.

4. SOCIAL INEQUALITIES: Income Classes and Welfare

"survivor" families and "welfare" families is the imprimatur of the father. How did such a cruel policy come to be?

■ *Whose* Welfare?

The Social Security Act of 1935 was the legislative blast-off point. From the start it had the aim of protecting men—and only incidentally their families—from the vagaries of the marketplace. It insured most citizens, but *not* mothers separated from living husbands. The elderly—men, by more than two to one because of their labor-force participation rates back then—were designated beneficiaries of old age insurance. It was also this bill that created unemployment insurance, intended primarily to cover males temporarily disjointed from the waged labor market. Widows (the *good* single mothers/wives) and their children were to receive survivors' benefits. (Early on, if the father divorced his wife two minutes before he died, she was not eligible for "his" Social Security benefits.) Children with living but absent fathers were almost left out, but Frances Perkins and others fought to cover them through what came to be called Aid to Dependent Children (ADC). ADC kids were presumed to live with their mothers, as in fact almost all did. But *no sum of money was designated for the women;* Perkins lost that one. It wasn't until the 1950s that the caretaker parent (mother) was added to the beneficiary unit, and ADC was changed to AFDC, or Aid to *Families* with Dependent Children.

AFDC is the program most frequently thought of today as "welfare"; 94 percent of its recipients are single mothers and their children. Conservatives, especially during the Reagan era, argued recipients opted out of the job market in favor of plentiful dollars on the dole, offered by Lyndon Johnson's Great Society legacy. In fact, for most of the post 1960s, the purchasing power of cash assistance to poor families plummeted, though aggregate social spending soared. The Great Society was a culprit—but for different reasons than those given by Reaganites. *It emphasized a service strategy to the near exclusion of income security*—with the long-term effect of eroding the income security of millions of people, thousands of whom became homeless. The conceptual framework that supported this disaster held into the 1990s, long after the nation had surrendered in the War on Poverty.

■ War (Games) on Poverty

The foundation for the Great Society was laid in the Kennedy administration. Income maintenance had been ruled out; it was thought to breed a degenerative social disease—dependency. (There was no rigorous examination of this notion, although income maintenance was really the same as Social Security payments to survivor families, and "dependency" didn't destroy *them*.)

President Johnson declared War on Poverty not only because he felt the political necessity to carry on where Kennedy left off, but because big spending programs aimed at reducing the effects of poverty had been his turf as far back as the New Deal. He liked programs that doled

out contracts across the country. Although income maintenance strategy was discussed during (and after) his administration, he too rejected it. But he did appoint an investigatory Commission on Income Maintenance Programs, which continued into the Nixon administration. Barbara Jordan, then a Texas state senator, was one of the few commission members not from the business community; still, even dominated by such stalwart capitalists as IBM's Thomas Watson and the Rand Corporation's Henry Rowen, the commission ultimately endorsed the "creation of a universal income supplement program . . . to all members of the population in need."

Why did Johnson reject income redistribution? The decline in the industrial base had limited certain jobs, and Democratic reform movements had put a stranglehold on party machines accustomed to wielding power through the jobs *they* controlled. Johnson's War on Poverty must have seemed an excellent chance to rebuild the party machine. So services emerged with regularity, each new "need" defined by the helping industry and by elected officials shagging dollars or votes. (When it works to their advantage, Republicans have shown they can also use service money to control allegiances. But generally, Republican conservatives, while railing about "big government," hand out their patronage through the military. Government spending is rarely about social remedies *or* defense; it's a contemporary form of patronage.)

The Great Society programs were the perfect vehicle for distributing patronage on a grand scale: Community Action, Vista, Model Cities. The service (plus economic development) strategy was to achieve a marriage of

THE KEY IS WOMEN'S
UNPAID, UNCOUNTED WORK
OUTSIDE THE
WAGED LABOR FORCE

otherwise feuding factions: mayors, poor people (who at first had cause for optimism), civil rights leaders, liberals, and the press. Were it not for the Vietnam war, Johnson had every reason to believe reelection in the bag. His programs were shoring up a deteriorating political machine while providing the rhetorical posture for an end to poverty.

Among the War on Poverty designers was Kennedy administration holdover Richard Boone, who repeatedly urged citizen participation in the Office of Economic Opportunity (OEO) programs, believing institutional change possible only with the "maximum feasible participation" of community (poor) people. Community Action agencies (CAAs) were hatched to do the job.

But with the exception of a few highly publicized locations, input by poor people was nonexistent. In *Betrayal of the Poor,* Stephen Rose wrote that no poor people or neighborhood representatives were involved in any of the 20 cities, although—*after* programs were designed and money budgeted—some members of groups to be served appeared on the agencies' boards of directors. In *The Great Society's Poor Law,* Sar Levitan concurred, noting that "affluent citizens who happened to live in a 'target area' could represent the poor. The law could therefore be observed without having a single low-income person on the CAA board."

CAAs genuinely committed to citizen participation were either swiftly defunded or never got out of the planning stages. Participation of poor people never took place; only the appearance of it occurred.

The mirage of participation had value, though. The impact of the civil rights, women's, and welfare rights movements was felt strongly through the 1970s, so that it was politically uncouth for advantaged parties to act in the absence of input from the disadvantaged. By manipulating the input, the social welfare establishment could appear to address poverty with the imprimatur of poor people (most commonly, women on welfare). The resulting aura of equality made it easier to get and maintain government and private foundation grants. The pretense of poor people's participation thus legitimized the social welfare institutions. The Great Society *did* offer a guaranteed income—to the social welfare establishment. By the 1980s, genuflecting to "participation" was dispensed with altogether.

Meanwhile, various other legislative events also dis-

placed income needs in favor of "service." The 1962 and 1967 Amendments to Social Security Law set the stage. First, the federal government moved to increase the states' revenue share for family services from 50 to 75 percent. Second, states were allowed to contract these services out to *nongovernmental agencies* (previously, local welfare departments were the sole service providers using federal dollars).

Those states that previously and systematically had denied welfare benefits to millions of needy families (especially black families) were now eager to qualify for the windfall revenue sharing. But first they had to find people categorically eligible for welfare. Furthermore, in order to capture services dollars from the feds, states would actually have to pay the families welfare benefits (which were also federally subsidized, but not so liberally). Not to worry. Cash assistance levels were set *by* the states, so it was (1) possible to find families eligible for welfare (to get the federal funding for services) and (2) *set AFDC levels so low that families would stay poor.*

The welfare rolls climbed so fast the phenomenon was characterized as an "explosion." This legislated windfall to states (combined with the War on Poverty strategy of delivering megabucks to state and local governments for "services" to the poor) set off a spending spree—that was peaking just when purchasing power of cash assistance began to decline.

The decrease was coupled with an increase in rhetoric about "dependency" and the necessity for women to "work." Never mind that the jobs didn't (and still don't) exist that would pay enough to lift them out of poverty. Never mind that single parenting under any circumstances *is* "work," and even harder work in poverty.

■ The Birth of an Industry

What became the professionalization of being human took off, bloating under government contracts. For every poverty problem, a self-perpetuating profession proposed to ameliorate the situation without altering the poverty. In *The Politics of a Guaranteed Income,* published in 1973, Daniel Patrick Moynihan noted the "astonishing consistency" with which middle-class professionals "improved" the condition of lower-class groups by devising schemes that would first improve their *own* condition. It doesn't take a genius to figure out that paying the administrators of a homeless shelter two or three thousand dollars a month for each family instead of providing a permanent apartment is ludicrous. Yet the most massive growth in AFDC spending in the 1980s has been for just that purpose. Furthermore, to keep the ''service'' engine stoked, every manner of failure has been ascribed to the families themselves. Laziness. Cheating. Dependency. The families lack resources to defend themselves, though the ''helping'' institutions always have government and/or foundation funds to lobby (ostensibly on the families' behalf) for *more* funding.

What has happened over the last quarter century *has* been an income redistribution scheme, the most disturbing one this country has ever seen: a redistribution from poor women and children to middle-class professionals—with men at the top calling the shots.

This has been done not only with government tax dollars but also with private charitable (and tax deducti-ble) dollars. The United Way. The American Red Cross. The Children's Aid Society. The independent federations of Protestant, Jewish, and Catholic charities. Hands Across America. . . . Each year, the New York *Times* begs its readers daily, from Thanksgiving to February, for its ''Neediest Cases Fund.'' For nearly a century the *Times* has reported that all the money goes to the poor through eight social service agencies who distribute it, with no funds spent on ''administration or fund raising.'' This is a wild exaggeration from the venerable newspaper; most of the money pays workers' salaries in the agencies, and has for years. Not to mention that the male directors of several of these already obese agencies are paid salaries in excess of $100,000 annually. Not bad for social work.

■ The ''Workfare'' Myth

In the great welfare reform debates of the late 1980s,

WHAT WE CAN DO

So where do we start?

■ Bite your tongue.

Why not extend the notion of choice from the reproductive sphere to the productive sphere? After all, it was Karl Marx who said women were not productive in an economic sense, so why does U.S. social policy seem to hinge on Marx's definition of productivity? Why shouldn't child-rearing be compensated by the society that stands to reap the benefits? Sometimes I have to bite my own tongue when referring to mothers who ''work'' and those who ''don't.'' There should be a lot more bitten tongues in the U.S.A.

■ Restrain the impulse to give money to big charities.

There is no legal obligation to report to any government entity the annual liquor bill of any given charity. Whether the fund-raiser is at Tavern on the Green or a ball at someone's plush estate, the deal is, have a party and write the shindig off. If you feel compelled to give money to someone for alcohol, hand a buck or two to your local drunk. He may not be dressed in black tie, but he buys cheaper booze.

■ Focus on justice.

One out of every four Americans experiences some poverty in a ten-year period. Some, mostly women with more than one or two children, stay poor until the children grow up. (Still, the most common family unit on welfare is a mother with only one child: *73 percent of all welfare families have two or fewer children.*) It's time to stop believing these families need to be—or for that matter can be—''fixed'' through charity. *Charity* creates a system of resource distribution that is markedly different from that used by the rest of the population. *Justice* seeks to minimize economic inequalities and unwarranted social distinctions. By establishing separate and very unequal systems of distribution, we separate ourselves in a fundamental way from poor women as equal human beings.

■ Give money directly but discreetly.

While we promote a more sane response to women's poverty, we don't have to stop giving, just because most of the charities purporting to help them are quasi-corrupt. Remember, Mother Teresa is neither the norm nor the model for the charity busi-ness. So give where it will do the most good. This holiday season, why not take a hundred dollars, put it in an envelope, and slide it under the door of a poor family? Retain your anonymity; that's least embarrassing for all concerned. Nothing could help them more (except more cash). Do it as many times as you can afford it. If you're afraid to do it yourself, find a friend you trust who will. Keep in mind that social workers, however competent, are not a reasonable substitute for income with which to purchase necessities (or a holiday dinner with gifts). Forget the tax deduction. This year give to *give.* I do.

■ Don't let 'em fool you. The money is there. It's a question of priorities.

Most other countries in the world have family or children's allowances which play a substantial role in reducing poverty rates. A one percent ''Family Security Tax'' on income would pay for it here.

■ Remember, the future isn't over yet.

The political pendulum swings wide from time to time and periods of social opportunity evolve. Put ''income security for all'' on the agenda of every organization you belong to. Social Security is welfare that works. (There is also an inverse ratio of bureaucratic bloat to the directness of cash assistance.) There is no reason other than politics that prevents the insurance from being universal. It's about time.

■ One last caveat:

It is not that services are never needed by poor women. It is that *forced* services don't serve. Affluent people vote with their pocketbooks when they do not receive adequate service. Poor women are stuck trying to balance a barely existent budget with instructions provided by people who never had to try. The women never get to participate in choosing which items they want or need: food, housing, services, etc. Services need to be on a market model, with choices made by the *women,* not the government or some well-intentioned foundation ''expert.'' Those services people choose will survive. And poverty pimping will melt away.

—T.F.

POVERTY IS THE #1 CHILD KILLER. CHILDREN ARE POOR BECAUSE THEIR MOTHERS ARE POOR.

social welfare professionals fell all over each other running after more funding (for themselves) through the jobs, training, and child care provisions of the so-called welfare reform bill, ironically presided over by Moynihan. Forgotten were the words of the President's Commission on Income Maintenance two decades earlier: "Services cannot be a substitute for adequate incomes; they cannot pay rent or buy food for a poor family." (The few surviving organizations of poor women put guaranteed income at the top of their lists, but they are rarely listened to. After all, they have no money.)

What stalled the "reform" debates for months was the issue of how much money would be allocated for those running the "reform" programs, and a turf war over whether the programs would be run by welfare departments or contracted out to private charities. (Everybody knew getting the women to "work" didn't mean getting them out of poverty.) Welfare rolls dipped slightly and briefly, but are now on the rise again nationwide. And the number and percent of single-parent female families living in profound poverty continues to climb. The relentless theme, from both the right and the left, still is to get those "nonworking" mothers to work.

In fact, the key to the tragedy of U.S. welfare policies is the notion of work—specifically, the unpaid and uncounted labor of women outside the waged labor market. About the only time the word labor is applied to women outside the wage system is in reference to the birthing process.

If any woman reading this were penniless today and went to apply for welfare to feed her children, she would not receive her first welfare check for about a month. Not because the welfare is prohibited from giving her money sooner, but because they are allowed to take 30 days to determine the obvious: that she is poor. The 30-day deadline might come and go with no relief. Or destructive policies plus bureaucratic bungling might prevent a check from ever coming. If she did make it onto the rolls, she might—like at least one million needy U.S. citizens every year—be cut off

despite being still legally entitled to welfare. This process has been given the name "churning" by the welfare department, as needy people are routinely cut off and sometimes put back on months later.

One ghastly result of such U.S. social policy is that far more children die from poverty than slip away at the hands of mothers like Ameenah Abdus-Salaam. Twelve times as many poor children die in fires than do nonpoor children. Eight times as many die of disease, according to a study done by the state of Maine—where, by the way, 98 percent of the population is white. Thirty times as many low birth weight babies die as do normal weight babies. In 1987, one in two homeless mothers in New York reported *losing* weight during pregnancy. Even at the bottom, luck plays a role: whose kid is hit by a stray bullet, whose kitchen stove explodes because it was used nonstop as the only source of heat in a frozen apartment, whose infant dies of pneumonia. Poverty is the number one killer of children in the U.S.A. Murder by malfeasance.

Children are poor because their mothers are poor.

Ameenah Abdus-Salaam's tragic acts may not be so mysterious, after all. The miracle is that more women, facing similar anguish, don't do the same.

On September 19, 1990, I attended a court hearing. Ameenah Abdus-Salaam's male attorney had pleaded her "not responsible by reason of mental disease or defect." Two court-appointed psychiatrists agreed, and recommended she be released—no longer a danger to herself or anyone else. District Attorney John Santucci's office refused to accept the recommendation until another psychiatrist, of the D.A.'s choosing, can evaluate her. The case could drag on indefinitely. The male judge has consistently refused to set bail. Ameenah herself was not "produced" for the proceedings. All four walls of the courtroom are of elaborately carved wood. Above the judge's throne, in raised gold letters, gleam the words *In God We Trust.* However misguided it may seem to outsiders, that was the one thing Ameenah Abdus-Salaam intended to do.

A Crisis of Shattered Dreams

Decades of racial progress have given way to growing resentment on both sides of the color line. A look at what divides blacks and whites—and what might be done to bridge the gap

On a Wednesday evening in early April, more than 100 blacks and Jews gathered at the Union United Methodist Church in Boston for an unusual Passover celebration. With a moving mixture of Hebrew readings and black spirituals, they retold the story of the Jewish Exodus out of slavery in Egypt. It was a heartening example of racial togetherness—unless you listened closely to the words of the two featured speakers. The Rev. Charles Stith, a prominent black minister, called for a return to the civil-rights pressure tactics of the 1950s and '60s. But Lenny Zakim, a Jewish leader, clearly rejected that strategy, calling instead for a "new coalition cognizant of new realities." Privately, he was even more blunt. Whites have grown weary of black demands for "race-conscious remedies," Zakim said, and of endless accusations of racism. "White America," he said, "got tired of being called guilty."

That bittersweet scene in Boston reflects the kind of differences that divide even the most well-meaning of whites and blacks these days. All too often, the press distorts the race issue by focusing on ugly incidents of violence: the beating of Rodney King in Los Angeles, the rape of the Central Park jogger, the Charles Stuart murder case in Boston. For the most part, today's race crisis is not the stuff of bloody headlines and cities in flames—at least not yet. The riots of the '60s were a revolution of rising expectations; blacks had tasted power and wanted more, fast. The problem today is shattered dreams. After all the high hopes and genuine progress of the past 30 years, people on both sides of the color line feel they've reached an impasse, and that things are getting worse. In a NEWSWEEK Poll three years ago, 49 percent of whites and 33 percent of blacks thought blacks were better off than they had been five years before. In a new sounding last week, the optimists had dwindled to 38 percent of whites and only 21 percent of blacks.

Is there any way to keep from losing more ground? The question is so bewildering in part because the grievances on both sides have become so complex. There's no such thing as a "white view" and a "black view" on racial problems anymore. Among whites, attitudes range from the raw fear of a Miami private-car driver who locks all his windows when he goes through the black section of Coconut Grove to the gnawing resentment of Chicago cop Jim Cosgrove, who says affirmative action made him wait seven years for a promotion to sergeant. Sources of black anger range from the utter hopelessness felt by blacks in the projects of Detroit to the subtle prejudice that rankles Denise Martin Welch, a Duke-educated attorney in Atlanta who complains about the way her legal briefs were scrutinized when she was a clerk for a superior-court judge. At stake are interests and emotions that differ from income scale to income scale and region to region; yet at some level, the sore points all come down to skin color.

The deteriorating language of racial discourse hasn't helped matters. At the height of the civil-rights movement, blacks and whites spoke to each other in the lofty words of Martin Luther King Jr.'s "I Have a Dream" speech and Lyndon Johnson's promise of a Great Society. Today those appeals to constitutional principles and

Biblical ideals have largely given way to the cheap and spiteful rhetoric of demagogues: the Louis Farrakhans and Al Sharptons, the David Dukes and Jesse Helmses. The ungainly word "quota" has become a sly way for politicians to play on white prejudices that run far deeper than opposition to the idea of setting aside jobs for blacks. Even the word underclass, the catchall term for the largely black populations of the inner cities, doesn't do justice to the depressing universe of crime, drugs and broken families it attempts to describe. It sounds more like an academic abstraction than America's gravest social problem—one that while it persists may make reconciliation between the races impossible.

Does that mean there's no hope for more progress? Far from it. Growing frustration has given rise to some stimulating, controversial new ideas about how to improve race relations, ranging from black writer Shelby Steele's appeals to African-Americans to move beyond the politics of victimization, to white journalist Nicholas Lemann's re-examination of the poverty programs of the 1960s (and conclusion that they weren't the utter failures of popular myth). In places as

opportunity. The problem isn't a lack of ideas; it's the absence of political will and public good will.

The first step has to be better communication. In private and among their own kind, blacks and whites open up about racial issues in a way they almost never do when they're brought together. If the races are going to deal with the many problems that divide them, they first must learn to understand—or at least listen to—each other's views of today's realities.

WHAT WHITES RESENT: Many whites who think of themselves as liberal, or at least socially tolerant, are baffled about why blacks are still so angry about their condition. Many whites acknowledge that there is still room for improvement, but they think things have come a long way from the days of black restrooms, Jim Crow voting laws and police dogs in the doorways of all-white universities. In fact, the National Opinion Research Center in Chicago, which since the early 1970s has been tracking racial attitudes with its General Social Survey, shows that white support for integration and racial equality (in prin-

broken into, they've been called names too many times."

For millions of more conservative, working-class whites, the issue isn't ingratitude; it's money and jobs. They resent quotas as unfair; but more to the point, they view them as coming at their own expense. Countless blue-collar whites, men in particular, share the frustration of Jim Cosgrove, the Chicago policeman. Cosgrove, 41, a 19-year veteran of the force, was made a sergeant last year. Based on his departmental-performance scores, he thinks he should have been promoted in 1983 or '84. During that time, he says, he was passed over for as many as 150 minority and women patrol officers with lower scores. Cosgrove says at first he supported affirmative action and greater diversity on the force, but that "now it's gone overboard. Historic discrimination wasn't imposed by the people being passed over for promotion today. What did I have to do with slavery? Why is the little guy paying this cost?"

Among working-class whites, that sense of being the little guy who can't afford "the cost" has grown steadily with the economic shocks of the past 20 years. At the height of the civil-rights movement the U.S. economy was still on its postwar roll. Then came the oil crises and inflation of the '70s, and the decline in the rust belt, which eliminated hundreds of thousands of jobs for blacks and whites alike. The recession of the past year has only deepened the worries about a shrinking pie. Many whites believe that they can't afford to be passed over or to pay more taxes for programs that mostly benefit blacks; besides, they suspect government will only squander that money. Keith Rush, a retired radio broadcaster from suburban New Orleans, says he's not a supporter of the Ku Klux Klan but that he planted a David Duke sign in his front yard when the former KKK leader ran for Congress in Louisiana. "I'm going to vote for David Duke," he said, "because it's the only way to let Washington know I'm pissed."

The past decade, many whites believe, has only given them more reason to be wary of blacks and their demands. The crime and drug epidemics in the inner cities have made people more afraid, even though those problems endanger far more blacks than whites. The seeming indifference of the Reagan administration sent a signal that whites didn't need to feel guilty about black concerns anymore. There are still whites who root for any form of black progress, but they are getting scarcer. Meanwhile, the number who believe the worst stereotypes of blacks is almost unwavering, even among people who have day-to-day contact with black co-workers and neighbors they like and trust. Despite the steady increase in overall white support for integration, Chicago's National Opinion

---

Is there enough legislation on the books to improve conditions for blacks in this country, with further progress coming through private efforts? Or is more legislation needed?

	WHITES	BLACKS
Enough legislation	53%	24%
More legislation needed	35%	64%

Can fairness in education, hiring and promotion be accomplished without quotas?

	WHITES	BLACKS
Yes	59%	26%
No	29%	61%

From the Newsweek Poll of April 23-25, 1991

---

different as the impoverished Dorchester section of Boston, where a group of Harvard-educated blacks have formed a religious community for street kids, and upscale black Atlanta, where a group of professionals called the Atlanta Exchange does fund raising and counseling for needy youngsters, blacks have begun to experiment with ways to help themselves without government assistance. The gulf war has held up the military as a model of an institution that can elicit loyalty and disciplined work from blacks in exchange for genuine

ciple, at least) is at a record high. The wounded feelings are particularly strong among many liberals who have worked actively for black causes. Tom Donegan is an alderman and legal-services lawyer who lives in an integrated neighborhood in Milwaukee. Among his constituents, he laments finding "so many whites who were willing to make a personal commitment to integration [but] are now saying 'I did my part. I can't resolve this. I'm not going to keep bleeding.' They've had their bicycles stolen once too often, their cars

Which categories apply to you?

	WHITES	BLACKS
Work with many members of another race	51%	84%
Uncomfortable working with members of another race	6%	17%
Worked for a boss of another race	47%	92%
Uncomfortable working for boss of another race	6%	14%
Know many members of another race well	68%	80%
Socialize regularly with members of another race	47%	63%

From the Newsweek Poll of April 23-25, 1991

Research Center has found that many whites continue to view blacks as violence-prone and lazy.

WHY BLACKS ARE STILL ANGRY: For the 31 percent of African-Americans who live in poverty, the roots of rage aren't hard to fathom. They are the sources of the grim and by now familiar litany of "black statistics": that one quarter of all African-American men are in jail or on probation or parole; that more than 60 percent of all black children are born to mothers without husbands; that almost 40 percent of black males who drop out of high school can't find jobs. Much of this underclass lives all but penned up in projects and deteriorating ghettos—what the Reverend Stith of Boston calls "our brand of apartheid"—without any realistic prospect of escaping. All these blacks can look forward to is a life of inferior schools and menial jobs (if they can get them at all), where the only real prospect for enrichment lies in crime and dealing drugs. It's not hard to see how their plight feeds the alarmingly widespread view that whites are plotting "genocide" against blacks, or creates support for the demonizing anti-white messages of Farra-khan and Sharpton. When the Rev. Bruce Wall, a black minister in Boston, takes inner-city boys out for a meal, they don't talk about girls or sports; they discuss whether they'd prefer to get shot or stabbed.

Working-class and professional blacks view the ghetto poor with mixed emotions: anger that the government won't do more to help them; but also eagerness to steer clear of that dangerous and depressing world. Yet few blacks can completely escape white fears and prejudices fed by images of the underclass. When any black man watches the tape of the Rodney King beating in L.A., he has to wonder if that could happen to him. Chicago political-scientist Gary Orfield says numerous studies show that "whites don't differentiate among blacks very well ... If an upper-middle-class black man puts on old clothes and heads for the hardware store in a mostly white neighborhood, he's likely to be seen as a threat." Recently Johnnie Roberts, a Wall Street Journal reporter, was accused of shoplifting after he bought a $600 Hugo Boss suit at the elegant Barney's men's clothing store in New York City. After Roberts produced a receipt, store officials apologized—but insisted their suspicions were "understandable."

To white charges that affirmative action is unfair, middle-class blacks respond that it was unfair for them to be starved of opportunities by 300 years of slavery and discrimination. But at a deeper level they, like whites, see jobs and money at stake. Affirmative action, enforced with quotas or not, has helped give hundreds of thousands of blacks access to colleges, graduate schools, jobs and promotions they might not have achieved otherwise. Jobs and welfare programs have created a new class of black government employees. Some blacks may have squandered those opportunities, but most believe they have done their best to take advantage of them. "I'm sure that the last two jobs I had, I got because I was a black female," says Joceyln Roy, 27, now a Howard University law student. "I do think that I was a quota, positively. [But] it's a misconception that everyone who gets in on a quota isn't qualified." Besides, most blacks believe, affirmative action rarely gets them farther than just inside the door. As Janell Byrd, a lawyer for the NAACP Legal Defense Fund, puts it: "Corporate America certainly hasn't exercised any quotas in management."

Even blacks who do make it to the management level have to live with what Christopher Edley Jr., a black law professor at Harvard, calls "the exceptions theory." They have to cope with the fact that they are often the only blacks in a meeting or at a party, and that they have to work far harder at getting along with whites than most whites ever do at getting along with blacks. They have to deal with the worry that if they fail, it will be seen as a reflection on their race. And they feel the ambivalence that comes with knowing there are thousands of talented blacks who will never get the chance to go as far. As Eula Adams, 41, the first black partner in the Atlanta office of the national accounting firm of Deloitte & Touche, puts it: "I can't accept the fact that I'm so special, and that there are so few people like me who can be successful in an organization like ours."

WHAT CAN BE DONE? Publicly, many civil-rights leaders have denounced Shelby Steele and a handful of other black "neo-conservatives" who argue that African-Americans should stop blaming whites for all their problems and do more to help themselves. But privately, an increasing number of blacks are embracing the self-help doctrine—and doing something about it. The efforts range from intensified efforts to elect black mayors and other public officials, to a return within the black middle class to the tradition of fraternities, business groups and Masonic lodges. In one intriguing experiment, Eugene Rivers, a 41-year-old ordained minister who studied at Harvard, has moved into the poor section of Dorchester, Mass., with his Radcliffe-educated wife and two children and established a full-time home for street kids called the Azura Christian Community. Conceding that it's an uphill battle, Rivers is trying to spread the notion of a "liberation theology" for the ghetto that would bring middle-class blacks into the inner cities on a full- or part-time basis to act as role models and surrogate parents for the children of the underclass.

Yet the legacy of discrimination is still far too heavy for self-help alone to bridge the gap between the races. Ultimately most blacks still need to make it in the white world, and for that they require whites' help. Affirmative action is still needed, but it doesn't have to mean rigid quotas, which are a cheap way out for both whites and blacks. What's needed is a return to the notion that John F. Kennedy had when he first used the phrase affirmative action: the most aggressive possible attempt to find minorities who are qualified, or could become qualified, to do the job. To make that happen, companies and universities have to work harder not only at recruiting but at assisting blacks who may need help fitting in or catching up—what Atlanta accountant Eula Adams calls the "mentoring" process. In Denver, for example, the police and fire departments didn't just lower their standards when they found that blacks weren't scoring as well as whites on entry tests. They instituted a program to tutor blacks—and scores improved dramatically.

At all levels, education is a key to chiseling away at racial barriers. In the long run, it offers the best hope for getting blacks to the point where they don't need affirmative action and for tackling the problems of the inner city—provided whites are willing to meet blacks halfway. None of that will be easy—but it has to be tried. The military has put so much effort into training minorities and improving race relations as a matter not of altruism but necessity: blacks make up 22 percent of its recruits. In the next decade, more and more of corporate America will face the same reality as blacks, women and other minorities actually become the majority of new entrants into the workplace. NEWSWEEK's poll shows that the races now agree overwhelmingly on this one issue: 69 percent of whites and 68 percent of blacks say that African-Americans should focus most of their energy on improving education.

The other key is integration—a once "virtuous word" that has become "highly problematic," as Randall Kennedy, a black law professor at Harvard, put it. At some level both races continue to resist it— whites with their rationales for not mixing more with blacks; blacks with the rhetoric of separatism and "community development." But ultimately prosperity in America has always resided in the mainstream, and the only way to dissolve racial differences is for more blacks to join it—and whites to welcome them in. The good news is that, despite all of their many grievances, Americans of both races still support that ideal. In NEWSWEEK's poll, 72 percent of blacks and 52 percent of whites said that they would prefer to live in a neighborhood that was racially "half and half"—more on both sides than felt that way three years ago. It's only by spending more time together that the races will learn that "workaday black people's aims and understandings aren't very different from white America's," says Kennedy. An African-American like Kennedy, who has spent his life moving between both worlds, understands that only too well; the challenge now is to get everyone else to see it.

MARK WHITAKER *with* MARK STARR *in Boston,* JOHN McCORMICK *in Chicago,* VERN E. SMITH *in Atlanta,* MARCUS MABRY *in Washington,* LYNDA WRIGHT *in Los Angeles and* GINNY CARROLL *in Houston*

THINKING BEYOND RACE

There is no question that blacks have had a harder struggle than most other groups in America. But is race still the greatest obstacle to their progress? The question itself is a sensitive one. Ten years ago, sociologist William Julius Wilson created a furor when he claimed that economics was a greater problem for blacks than race. Received wisdom dies hard. Shelby Steele here argues that the reluctance to think beyond accepted formulas is not only lazy thinking; it is a formidable obstacle to black advancement.

Shelby Steele

Shelby Steele *is professor of English at San Jose State University. Born in Chicago, Illinois, he received a B.A. (1968) from Coe College, an M.A. (1971) from Southern Illinois University, and a Ph.D. (1974) from the University of Utah.*

I am a fortyish, middle-class, black American male, with a teaching position at a large state university in California. I have owned my own home for more than ten years, as well as the two cars that are the minimal requirement for life in California. And I will confess to a moderate strain of yuppie hedonism. Year after year my two children are the sole representatives of their race in their classrooms, a fact they sometimes have difficulty remembering. We are the only black family in our suburban neighborhood, and even this claim to specialness is diminished by the fact that my wife is white. I think we are called an "integrated" family, though no one has ever used the term with me. For me to be among large numbers of blacks requires conscientiousness and a long car ride, and, in truth, I have not been very conscientious lately. Though I was raised in an all-black community just south of Chicago, I only occasionally feel nostalgia for such places. Trips to the barbershop now and then usu-

ally satisfy this need, though recently, in the interest of convenience, I've taken to letting my wife cut my hair.

I see in people's eyes from time to time, and hear often in the media, what amounts to a judgment of people like me: You have moved into the great amorphous middle class and lost your connection to your people and your cultural roots. You have become a genuine invisible man. This is a judgment with many obvious dimensions, many arrows of guilt. But, in essence, it charges me with selfishness and inauthenticity.

At one point in my life I romanticized my situation, thought of myself as a marginal man. The seductive imagery of alienation supported me in this. But in America today, racial marginality is hard to sell as the stuff of tragedy. The position brings with it an ugly note of self-insistence that annoys people in a society that is, at least officially, desegregated.

For better or worse, I'm not very marginal. In my middle-American world I see people like myself everywhere. We nod coolly at each other when we're stopped at traffic lights, our eyes connect for an awkward instant in shopping malls, we hear about one another from our white friends. "Have you met the new doctor at the hospital . . . the engineer at IBM . . . the new professor in history?" The black middle class is growing in size. We are often said to be sneaking or slipping or creeping unnoticed into the middle class, as though images of stealth best characterized our movement. I picture a kind of underground railroad, delivering us in the dead of night from the inner city to the suburbs.

But even if we aren't very marginal, we are very shy with one another, at least until we've had a chance to meet privately and take our readings. When we first meet one another, we experience a trapped feeling; it is as though we had been confronted by a set of expectations that could rob us of our individuality by reducing us to an exclusively racial dimension. We are a threat, at first, to one another's uniqueness. I have seen the same well-dressed black woman in the supermarket for more than a year now. We do not speak, and we usually pretend not to see each other. But when we turn a corner suddenly and find ourselves staring squarely into each other's eyes, her face freezes and she moves on. I believe she is insisting that both of us be more than black—that we interact only when we have a reason other than the mere fact of our race. Her chilliness enforces a priority that I agree with—individuality over group identity.

But I believe I see something else in this woman, which I also see in myself and in many other middle-class blacks. It is a kind of race fatigue, a deep weariness with things racial, resulting from the fact that our lives are more integrated than they have ever been before. Race does not determine our fates as powerfully as it once did, which means it is not the vital personal concern it once was. Before the sixties, race set the boundaries of black life. Now, especially for middle-class blacks, it is far less a factor, even though we don't always like to admit it. Because blacks still suffer from racism, we must be alert to the problem, but the imperative to be concerned with what is not personally urgent ultimately makes for race fatigue.

I have a friend who did poorly in the insurance business for years. "People won't buy insurance from a black man," he always said. Two years ago another black man and a black woman joined his office. Almost immediately both did twice the business my friend was doing, with the same largely white clientele.

Integration shock is essentially the shock of being suddenly accountable on strictly personal terms. It occurs in situations that disallow race as an excuse for personal shortcomings, and it therefore exposes vulnerabilities that previously were hidden. One response to such shock is to face up to the self-doubts that it occasions and then to act on the basis of what we learn about ourselves. After some struggle, my friend was able to do this. He completely revised his sales technique, asked himself some hard questions about his motivation, and resolved to work more diligently.

But when one lacks the courage to face oneself fully, a fear of hidden vulnerabilities triggers a fright-flight response to integration shock. Instead of admitting that racism has declined, we argue all the harder that it is still alive and more insidious than ever. We hold race up to shield us from what we do not want to see in ourselves. My friend did this at first, saying that the two blacks in his office were doing better than he was because they knew how to "kiss white ass." Here he was race-holding, using race to keep from looking at himself.

Recently I read an article in the local paper that explored the question of whether blacks could feel comfortable living in the largely white Silicon Valley. The article focused on a black family that had been living for more than a decade in Saratoga, a very well-to-do white community. The neighborhood, the children's schools, the parents' places of employment, the shopping areas and parks—the entire physical environment—were populated by affluent whites. Yet during the interview, the wife said they had made two firm rules for their children: that they go to all-black colleges back East and that they do "no dating outside the race, period."

I have pushed enough black history and culture on my own children to be able to identify with the impulse behind the first of these rules. Black children in largely white situations must understand and appreciate their cultural background. But the rigidity of these rules, not to mention the rules themselves, points to more than a concern with transmitting heritage or gaining experience with other blacks. Rigidity arises from fear and self-doubt. These people, I believed, were afraid of something.

What was striking to me about their rules, especially the one prohibiting interracial dating, was their tone of rejection. The black parents seemed as determined to reject the white world as to embrace the black one. Why? I would say because of integration shock. Their integrated lives have opened up vulnerabilities that they do not wish to face. But what vulnerabilities? In this case I think a particularly embarrassing one. On some level, I suspect, they doubt whether they are as good as the white people who live around them. You cannot be raised in a culture that was for centuries committed to the notion of your inferiority and not have some doubt in this regard—doubt that is likely to be aggravated most in integrated situations. So the rejecting tone of their rules is self-protective. "I will reject you before you have a chance to reject me." But all of this is covered over by race. The Saratoga family invokes racial pride to shield themselves from a doubt they are afraid to acknowledge. Unacknowledged, this doubt gains a negative power inside the personality that expresses itself in the rigidity and absolutism of their rules. Repressed fears tend always to escalate their campaign for our attention by pushing us further and further into irrationality and rigidity.

The refusal to see something unflattering in ourselves always triggers the snap from race fatigue to race-holding. And once that happens, we are caught, like this family, in a jumble of racial ironies. The parents in Saratoga, who have chosen to live integrated lives, impose a kind of segregation on their children. Rules that would be racist in the mouth of any white person are created and enforced with pride. Their unexamined self-doubt also leaves them unable to exploit the freedom they and their ancestors worked hard to attain. Race fatigue makes them run to a place like Saratoga, but integration shock makes them hold race protectively. They end up clinging to what they've sought to escape.

Once race-holding is triggered by fear, it ensnares us in a web of self-defeating attitudes that prevents us from taking advantage of the new freedoms we've won over the past several decades. I have seen its corrosive effects in my own life and in the lives of virtually every black person I've known. Some are only mildly touched by it, while others seem incapacitated by it. But race-holding is as unavoidable as defensiveness itself, and I am convinced that it is one of the most debilitating, yet unrecognized, forces in black life today.

I define a holding as any self-description that serves to justify or camouflage a person's fears, weaknesses, and inadequacies. Holdings are the little and big exaggerations, distortions, and lies about ourselves that prop us up and let us move along the compromised paths we follow. We develop them to defend ourselves against threats to our self-esteem, threats that make us feel vulnerable and that plant a seed of fear. This fear can work like wind on a brush fire, spreading self-doubt far beyond what the initial threat would warrant. As a result, we become even weaker and thus more needy of holdings. Since holdings justify our reticence and cowardice, they are usually expressed in the form of high belief or earthy wisdom. A man whose business fails from his own indifference holds an image

of himself as a man too honest to be a good businessman—a self-description that draws a veil over his weakness.

For some years I have noticed that I can walk into any of my classes on the first day of the semester, identify the black students, and be sadly confident that on the last day of the semester a disproportionate number of them will be at the bottom of the class, far behind any number of white students of equal or even lesser native ability. More to the point, they will have performed far beneath their own native ability. Self-fulfilling-prophesy theory says that their schools have always expected them to do poorly, and that they have simply internalized this message. But this deterministic theory sees blacks only as victims, without any margin of choice. It cannot fully explain the poor performances of these black students, because it identifies only the forces that pressure them to do poorly. By overlooking the margin of choice open to them, this theory fails to recognize the degree to which they are responsible for their own poor showing. (The irony of this oversight is that it takes the power for positive change away from the students and puts it in the hands of the very institutions that failed them in the first place.)

The theory of race-holding is based on the assumption that a margin of choice is always open to blacks (even to slaves, who had some choice). And it tries to make clear the mechanisms by which we relinquish that choice in the name of race. With the decline in racism, the margin of black choice has greatly expanded, which is probably why race-holding is so much more visible today than ever before. But anything that prevents us from exploiting our new freedom to the fullest is now as serious a barrier to us as racism once was.

Self-fulfilling-prophesy theory is no doubt correct that black students, like the ones I regularly see in my classes, internalize a message of inferiority that they receive from school and the larger society around them. But the relevant question in the 1990s is why they choose to internalize this view of themselves. Why do they voluntarily perceive themselves as inferior? We can talk about the weakened black family and countless other scars of oppression and poverty. And certainly these things have much to do with the image these students have of themselves. But they do not fully explain this self-image, because none of them entirely eliminates the margin of choice that remains open. Choice lives in the most blighted circumstances, and it certainly lives in the lives of these black college students.

I think they choose to believe in their

inferiority not to fulfill society's prophesy about them but to evade individual responsibility. Their margin of choice scares them, as it does all people. They are naturally intimidated by that eternal tussle between the freedom to act and the responsibility we must take for our actions. To some extent, all of us balk in the face of this. The difference is that these students use their race to conceal the fact that they are balking. Their "inferiority" shields them from having to see that they are afraid of all-out competition with white students. And it isn't even an honest inferiority. I don't think they really believe it. It is a false inferiority, chosen over an honest and productive confrontation with their real fears—a strategy that allows them to stay comfortably on the sidelines in a university environment that all but showers them with opportunity.

"I'm doing okay for a black student," a student once told me. "I'm doing well considering where I came from," I have told myself on many occasions. Race allows us both to hide from the real question, which is, "Am I doing what I can, considering my talents and energies?"

I see all of this as pretty much a subconscious process, fear working on a subterranean level to let us reduce our margin of choice in the name of race. Consciously, we tell ourselves that we are only identifying with our race, but fear bloats our racial identity to an unnatural size and then uses it as cover for its subversive work. The more severe the integration shock, the more cover is needed.

Doesn't race enhance individuality? I think it does, but only when individuality is nurtured and developed apart from race. The race-holder, inside the bubble of his separate self, feels inadequate or insecure; so he seeks reassurance through race. When, instead, a sense of self arises from individual achievement and self-realization, when self-esteem is established apart from race, then racial identity can only enhance, because it is no longer needed for any other purpose.

The word individualism began to connote selfishness and even betrayal to many blacks during the 1960s. Individualism was seen as a threat to the solidarity that blacks needed during those years of confrontation. Despite the decline in racism, these connotations have lingered. Race-holding keeps them alive, because they serve the race-holder's need to exaggerate the importance of race as well as to justify a fear of individual responsibility. Race-holding makes fluid the boundary between race and self, group and individual identity, allowing race to swing over at a moment's notice and fill in where fears leave a vacuum.

This is a worse problem than it at first seems, because the individual is the seat of all energy, creativity, motivation, and power. We are most strongly motivated when we want something for ourselves. When our personal wants are best achieved through group action, as in the civil-rights movement, we lend our energy to the group, and it becomes as strong as the sum of our energies. When the need for group action recedes, more energy is available to us as individuals. But race-holding intercedes here by affixing the race-holder too tightly to this racial identity and causing him to see the locus of power in race rather than in himself. In this way race-holding corrupts the greatest source of power and strength available to blacks—the energy latent in our personal desires.

One of my favorite passages in Ralph Ellison's *Invisible Man* is his description of the problem of blacks as

> not actually one of creating the uncreated conscience of [our] race, but of creating the *uncreated features of [our] face*. Our task is that of making ourselves individuals.... We create the race by creating ourselves and then to our great astonishment we will have created something far more important: We will have created a culture.

These lines hold up well close to 40 years after they were written. They seem to suggest a kind of Adam Smith vision of culture: When the individual makes himself, he makes culture. An "invisible hand" uses individual effort to define and broaden culture. In the 1990s we blacks are more than ever in a position in which our common good will best be served by the determined pursuit of our most personal aspirations.

I think the key to this pursuit, and the answer to race-holding generally, is personal responsibility, a source of great power that race-holding does its best to conceal.

S ome years ago I made a mistake at a neighbor's cocktail party that taught me something about personal responsibility. I went to the party for the thinnest of reasons, mere politeness, though the afternoon was hot and I was already in a peevish mood. The event would have been problematic even if I weren't the only black at the party. But I was, and on this afternoon I chose to make note of the fact, though it was hardly a new experience for me. As I strolled around the sun-baked patio, avoiding people more than engaging them, I held this fact more and more tightly until I came to believe it had a profound meaning I needed to understand. After a while I decided that others needed to understand it too.

During the 1960s, blacks and white liberals often engaged in something that might be called the harangue-flagellation ritual. Blacks felt anger, white liberals felt guilt, and when they came together, blacks would vent their anger by haranguing the whites, who often allowed themselves to be scourged as a kind of penance. The "official" black purpose of this rite was to "educate" whites on the issue of race, and during the '60s this purpose may sometimes have been served. But by the 1980s, after a marked decline in racism and two decades of consciousness-raising, the rite had become both anachronistic and, I think, irresponsible. Nevertheless, it suited my mood on this hot afternoon; so I retrieved it from its dusty bin and tried to make it fashionable again.

A woman at the party said how much she liked Jesse Jackson's rhetorical style. Was "style" the only thing she liked? I asked, with an edge to my voice. The woman gave me a curious and exasperated look, but I pushed on anyway. Soon I was lecturing the six or seven people around me: I told them that racism had been driven underground in the 1960s and '70s, where more insidious strategies for foiling the possibilities of black people had evolved. I pointed to the black unemployment rate, the continued segregation of many schools, housing discrimination, and many other problems. Soon I saw that the old harangue-flagellation ritual was firmly back in place. I was shaming these people, and they nodded at what I said in a way that gratified me.

But at home that night I felt a stinging shame, and even weeks later the thought of that afternoon made me cringe. Eventually I saw why. For one thing, I was trading on my race with those people, using the very thing I claimed to be so concerned with to buy my way out of certain anxieties. Like the Saratoga family, I was race-holding in response to the integration shock I felt in this integrated situation. I had begun to feel vulnerable, and I hit those people with race before they could hit me with it. My vulnerabilities, of course, were essentially the same as the Saratoga family's. On some level I doubted myself in relation to these whites, and my insecurities drove me into an offense that was really a defense. The shame I began to feel, though I could not identify it at the time, was essentially the shame of cowardice. I felt as though I'd run away from something and used race to cover my tracks.

This shame had another dimension that was even more humiliating than the cowardice I had felt. On that patio I was complaining to white people, beseeching them to see how badly blacks were still treated, and I was gratified to see their heads nod as though they understood. My voice contained no audible whine, but at least some of what I said amounted to a whine. And this is what put the sting in my shame. Cowardice was a common enough fault, but whining was quite another thing.

The race-holder whines or complains indiscriminately not because he seeks redress but because he seeks the status of victim, a status that excuses him from what he fears. A victim is not responsible for his condition, and by claiming a victim's status the race-holder gives up the sense of personal responsibility he needs to better his condition. His unseen purpose is to hide rather than fight; so the anger and, more important, the energy that real racism breeds in him are squandered in self-serving complaint. The price he pays for the false comfort of his victim's status is a kind of impotence.

The difference between the race-holder who merely complains and the honest protester is that the latter keeps the responsibility for his condition in his own hands. The honest protester may be victimized, but he is not solely a victim. He thinks of himself as fully human and asks only that the rules of the game be made fair. Fairness, rather than entitlement, is his goal. By limiting his demands to fairness, he retains his personal responsibility and the power that grows out of it. But he also understands that he must keep this responsibility, whether or not society is fair. His purpose is to realize himself, to live the fullest possible life, and he is responsible for this, like all men, regardless of how society treats him.

Personal responsibility is the brick and mortar of power. The responsible person knows that the quality of his life is something that he will have to make inside the limits of his fate. Some of these limits he can push back, some he cannot, but in any case the quality of his life will pretty much reflect the quality of his efforts. When this link between well-being and action is truly accepted, the result is power. With this understanding and the knowledge that he is responsible, a person can see his margin of choice. He can choose and act, choose and act again, without illusion. He can create himself and make himself felt in the world. Such a person has power.

I was neither responsible nor powerful when I stood on my neighbor's patio complaining about racism to people who had only the most removed interest in my racial well-being. In effect I was asking them to be responsible for something that only I and other blacks can be responsible for. Of course, whites must be fair. But they cannot be fully responsible for the well-being of blacks; they cannot actualize our lives. If I had said this to the people at the party, they might have gone away with a clearer sense of their own responsibilities. But I never considered doing so. The real goal of my complaining was to disguise a fear that I didn't want to acknowledge.

The barriers to black progress in America today are clearly as much psychological as they are social or economic. We have suffered as much as any group in human history, and if this suffering has ennobled us, it has also wounded us and pushed us into defensive strategies that are often self-defeating. But we haven't fully admitted this to ourselves. The psychological realm is murky, frightening, and just plain embarrassing. And a risk is involved in exploring it: the risk of discovering the ways in which we contribute to, if not create, the reality in which we live. Denial, avoidance, and repression intervene to save us from this risk. But, of course, they only energize what is repressed with more and more negative power, so that we are victimized as much by our own buried fears as by racism.

In the deepest sense, the long struggle of blacks in America has always been a struggle to retrieve our full humanity. But now the reactive stance we have adopted to defend ourselves against oppression binds us to the same racial views that oppressed us in the first place. Snakelike, our defense has turned on us. I think it is now the last barrier to the kind of self-possession that will give us our full humanity, and we must overcome it ourselves.

WHY WOMEN AREN'T MAKING IT TO THE TOP

Blame male managers, of course, who won't give women a fair shot. But could it also be that women don't crave power enough?

Liz Roman Gallese

LIZ ROMAN GALLESE, who writes from Wellesley, Massachusetts, is a frequent contributor to *The New York Times*, *Forbes*, and other publications. She is author of *Women Like Us: What Is Happening to the Women of the Harvard Business School, Class of '75—the Women Who Had the First Chance to Make It to the Top* (William Morrow).

In the 1970s, women first began entering managerial and professional jobs in substantial numbers. Two decades later, not one has reached the top rung of a major publicly held company by rising through the ranks. Katharine Graham, chairman of the Washington Post Company, inherited the position upon her husband's death. The retired Elisabeth Claiborne Ortenberg had founded Liz Claiborne Inc.

The prevailing wisdom holds that women aren't as ambitious or as qualified for top jobs, or that there is a point—a "glass ceiling"—beyond which discrimination hampers their advancement. But in a five-month, intensive study of 24 corporate women that I recently undertook, another theory emerged: What holds women back, at least in part, is the way they and their male peers perceive women's capacity for attaining and exercising power.

Men, say women, are ambivalent about women's ability to fight for and wield power. Women, the women themselves admit, aren't as forthright as men about doing so. And misconceptions on the part of both men and women create a vicious cycle that holds back even the most talented women.

Women's inability to get to the top "isn't inherent in the woman," asserts Christina Brown, a 53-year-old headhunter who was recently forced out of an upper-middle-level line job in finance when her former employer was taken over. "It is well accepted that women are smart," she explains. "In other words, I, Mr. Biggie Corporate, am happy for it to be a woman who handles a job that involves *thinking power*. I'm happy for it to be a woman who makes the presentation, showing me the results of the market research.

Florence Skelly gets the same respect as Daniel Yankelovich.

"But what no one has bought into yet is that women can exercise power. When it's guts-balls leverage, when it's fighting, when it's playing poker, when it's 'I bet my $4 zillion on this deal, where are you?' the world doesn't think women can do that. And I don't know how many women think women can do that."

The thesis framed by Brown's words surfaced again and again in the course of my study. The 24 women interviewed were among the most highly placed—and in some cases, highly visible—female executives in America. Two are themselves chief executive officers, albeit not of publicly held concerns. Eight hold jobs in which they report directly to the CEO; eight are in positions in which they have frequent and substantive contact with the CEO. Of the remaining six, all had held senior-level corporate jobs—and had failed to advance further. Two of these women (Brown being one) switched careers as a result. Two founded their own businesses. Two took early retirement.

During our conversations, each woman told me what had happened at each stage of her career. When taken in aggregate, their stories point to a clear pattern.

Specifically, those women who broke into the senior ranks did so because male bosses didn't allow common misconceptions about women's capacity for power to cloud their judgment, and because the women were themselves comfortable with pursuing power. The women who failed, by contrast, were held back by male superiors, and didn't scramble as aggressively for power. What follows are the stories of four of the women whom I interviewed—two who failed to reach senior positions, and two who succeeded. The names have been changed to protect their identities.

Peg Simpson: Tripped at the Finish Line

What does it mean for a woman to fail to advance because her male superiors stack the deck against her—in other words, refuse to cede power to a woman?

The answer to that question became clearer when I met 59-year-old Peg Simpson. Seated in her spacious corner office atop a brand-new building in midtown Manhattan, a spectacular silver necklace adorning her royal-blue dress, Simpson had all the trappings of the arrived corporate executive. Yet there was something awry: The big desk was devoid of paper; not a single book graced the coffee table. This was, I realized, the room where dreams die. Peg Simpson had been in the race for the presidency of this service-industry corporation, and she had lost. Now she was preparing to take early retirement.

"There are glass ceilings for women because women won't fight in the same way that a man will fight," Simpson was saying. "Women won't demand the same things. Even more importantly, the male hierarchy doesn't *expect* women to demand the same things."

On the surface, the facts were simple enough. Having risen through the ranks thanks to her superb technical skills, Simpson was named one of the firm's two executive vice presidents and was put in charge of one of the two major business lines. Both Simpson and her male peer were candidates for the presidency, she was told by the chairman.

But then came the stacked deck: Her peer was paid more than she, and was named to the board of directors. Inexplicably, Simpson wasn't—and her pleas for an explanation were stonewalled. "I was told that the board wanted to reduce the number of inside directors," she says. "I said, 'I understand that, but what are you going to do for me?'"

On paper, the firm's chairman was a forthright supporter of women's advancement. In fact, the company had been cited by women's groups as a superb employer for women. And the chairman had come to Simpson's own defense earlier in her career when she had been up against a boss who wasn't supportive.

Yet when she edged closer to a job at the very top—the presidency—the chairman had set up an unequal race. Why hadn't he met her halfway?

Simpson theorizes that he is supportive of women's advancement *intellectually,* but not *emotionally;* in other words, it's okay in theory, but not in his backyard. "In his gut, he isn't supportive," she says. "I think he didn't want me as a major contender because he was uncomfortable thinking a woman would be president of this company."

Simpson's case exemplifies a phenomenon noted by many other women interviewed: Women move easily within the lower ranks of the corporate world because men have no trouble with women displaying technical expertise, as is required at the bottom and middle rungs. It's at the higher levels, when the game becomes exercising raw power, that apprehensions arise.

Another subtlety of corporate power noted by the women in my study was that jobs at the upper middle level—which usually involve the exercise of autonomous line authority over a chunk of business—are the most typical point of derailment for women in corporations. One explanation is that jobs at the next higher level—those in the senior circle—suddenly require far different skills: that of deference to the chief executive officer, support for his goals, and the building of consensus among both the top people and the troops. A man's ability to perform these functions is highly valued by other men, say the women in the study, but in a woman, the same ability is perceived as weakness. For men, a female executive exhibiting the kind of deferential behavior that characterizes high-level jobs triggers associations with other women in their lives—wives, mothers, daughters, secretaries, and more recently, executive assistants—among whom deference often denotes powerless helpmates.

One woman in the study, for example, brought her high evaluation of a female subordinate to the attention of her male boss, telling him that the young woman was promotable because she was "smart, attractive, articulate, and presented herself well." Her boss replied: "It's interesting you speak highly of her. I always think of her as … I mean, she could be married to my brother."

By and large, the male response to women on the issue of deference remains subconscious and conflicted. As a result, female executives often receive mixed signals from men about how they are expected to behave. One woman in the study, who had recently advanced from an upper-middle-level job into the senior ranks, says she frequently runs into this problem at corporate parties. "On one hand, the men want you to be like a wife at a cocktail party and stand a half pace behind," she says. "On the other hand, they want you to be one of the boys and contribute to the conversation."

Peg Simpson's case begs an intriguing question: Was the chairman trying to test her ability to demand the power due her—her seat on the board? Simpson admits she could have done more to that end. A popular executive with underlings, Simpson says she "could have traveled around the country, making myself visible," and that she could have strengthened alliances with other powerful board members, then threatened the chairman with an appeal to the board if the two of them were unable to resolve the problem.

"A man would have done that," Simpson speculates, including the peer to whom she lost the race. ("He's a tough guy," she says.) "But I couldn't be the person saying, 'Slit that other guy's throat to give me what I want.'"

Simpson's inaction in this situation gives one pause, but backs right up against a brick wall when one considers that a man at Simpson's level wouldn't have been denied the board seat in the first place. The issue is not just deference but fairness.

For a woman, moreover, deference holds yet another subterfuge. As is the case for many women, Peg Simpson had always been promoted a step or two behind similarly able men, and so had come to believe that patience was an ally in her climb to the top. When first denied the board seat, she says, her reaction was, "In time this too will be corrected." Yet the race at this ultimate level was different. Indeed, Simpson's career was short-circuited because of a discrepancy on the part of her male superior between what was promised—a shot at a top job—and what was delivered—an unequal race. And in her spectacular empty office, Simpson is left to speculate about the reasons for the chairman's misconceptions about women and power.

Christina Brown: Outside the In-Group

In her homey Manhattan office, Christina Brown is analyzing her failure to survive at the upper-middle-level job she had held at a top financial corporation. In some respects, it's an old story: A takeover occurs, the new team comes in, and out goes the old management.

Yet for Brown there's another dimension to the tale—the issue of the way female executives are treated in the after-

Why Women Follow

The latest firestorm in the world of management is whether women's "feminine" characteristics make them better leaders than men in this era of flattening hierarchies and increasing global competition. Fanning the flames have been Sally Helgesen with her book *The Female Advantage: Women's Ways of Leadership*, held by some as the feminist doctrine of the '90s, and Judy B. Rosener with her *Harvard Business Review* article "Ways Women Lead."

Unfortunately, their fire is burning up the wrong tree. Sure, women may be more inclined to use what Rosener, a management professor at the University of California at Irvine, calls "interactive leadership," in which subordinates are empowered and group decision-making is encouraged. Similarly, men may more often employ "command-and-control" authority, in which formal authority is used to reward subordinates for deeds done or punish them for inadequate performance. But the real controversy ought not to be whether women's methods are better than men's—for the recent leadership studies, Rosener's included, show that each sex uses both interactive *and* command-and-control leadership methods, albeit to a different degree—but, rather, why so few women lead.

Last year *Fortune* found that less than 0.5 percent of the highest-paid officers and directors in America's largest public corporations are women. The question of why there are virtually no women in the top echelon of our corporations becomes even more perplexing when one looks at a study released late last fall by Russell Reynolds Associates, the executive recruiting firm. The study of 164 executives, in both line and staff positions, assessed executive success factors, leadership orientation (measured by the well-known Burke Leadership Questionnaire), and the corporate environment. Among its findings: Significantly more female executives display leadership potential than do their male counterparts.

Moreover, while men who hold staff positions are less likely than men in line positions to have leadership qualities (vision, charisma, innovativeness, and strategic ability) and more likely to have management qualities (ability to maintain momentum, balance interests, stabilize forces, and implement tactical plans), women in staff and line positions are about equally likely to have leadership potential. In fact, a greater proportion of female staff executives display leadership talent than do male executives in line jobs, the traditional breeding ground of corporate officers. Thus, as Malcolm MacKay, a managing director of Russell Reynolds Associates, puts it, female staff executives appear to suffer from a double bias: They are staff and they are women.

The Russell Reynolds Associates findings seem to dispel the popular notion that women have not broken through the glass ceiling because they don't have the same leadership abilities as men. If anything, our top corporate women show more of an aptitude to lead. Why, then, aren't they in positions of power?

The answer, supported by the accompanying article, may lie in the perceptions of the men now atop corporate America. The Russell Reynolds Associates study found that only 2 percent of leader-type men believe that executive women are subject to hostility from their superiors. In contrast, 67 percent of leader-type women say that women suffer such bias on the job. More than three quarters of leader-type men believe that women are given equal opportunities to exercise power and authority; more than half of leader-type women believe that men receive more opportunities. Three quarters of leader-type men say their firms actively encourage women's career development; two thirds of leader-type women disagree.

This dissonance in perception, says MacKay, may be because leader-type men are winning the game in the corporation, thus they have an investment in believing that success is merely the result of competence—not of maleness. **—Beth Enslow**

---

math of a power play. She speaks matter-of-factly about her demise, though her brow furrows slightly under carefully combed blond hair. For the new management team, she asserts, "maleness equaled money equaled power." The new chairman was so "uncomfortable" with women as equals that he "went out of his way to make staff meetings formal agenda-type stuff," she says. He held the real meetings on Sunday mornings at his home so that he could decide for himself whom to include.

Brown was quickly swept out of the inner circle. The revenue level for divisions to be included was upped, so that the division she ran no longer qualified. Unlike Peg Simpson's case, Brown's new superiors seemed to be treating her in the same way as her male peers. Numbers are numbers, after all.

But the kicker was that a male colleague, whose division was smaller than hers, was awarded part of another unit so that he could still be part of the circle. The male hierarchy took care of their own, Brown says, while women were left to fend for themselves. According to Brown, her male peers are still at the company, "and, for the most part, very rich now."

Brown didn't depart immediately. She hung on until she had "almost no will but to get out," she says. Indeed, she seems a bit proud when noting that the chairman himself was surprised by her tenacity. Yet given that the situation was untenable, why didn't Brown bail out sooner? Could it have been that she was ambivalent about demanding the power due her? Did she actually want peace instead? "I bought peace rather than power," she responds, "because I decided I couldn't get power."

Joan Prendergast: An Objective Appointment

Joan Prendergast is one of the few women who have achieved both peace and power in a corporate setting. Hunched over her big desk, the gray drapes in her office drawn as if to focus her attention on the task therein, Prendergast, the newly appointed president of a large Midwestern bank, appears to blend with her environment. She wears a gray banker's suit, sturdy low-heeled shoes, and a stoic can-do expression.

Why was she able to get to the top when both Simpson and Brown fell short? "The chairman of my company has a very interesting way of making decisions" about whom to appoint to top jobs, Prendergast begins.

The chairman bases his selection on criteria that are as objective as possible. To select a candidate, he draws a matrix, listing down the side the qualifications necessary for the job, and across the top the candidates. To each box on the chart, he assigns a score. When Prendergast scored highly on all, he knew he "had to consider my candidacy seriously," she says.

How simple, how right, one is compelled to think. But in the real world of corporate baton-passing at the highest levels, how rarely done. Prendergast's champion himself was no doubt aware of that, for in presenting her as his candidate to the full board, he made his case judiciously.

Asking her to wait outside, he addressed his fellow board members without naming her or in any way indicating that she was a woman. Rather, he carefully reviewed all the criteria the board had agreed were necessary for the job, then the scores he had assigned to each prospect. "The board

One woman's chairman told a subordinate that he wouldn't have to answer to her: "She's coming in, but she isn't really your boss."

went through, in a very careful way, what they had agreed were the qualifications," says Prendergast, then "they went through my candidacy relative to the requirements."

Only then did the chairman announce that his nominee for the position was a woman. Prendergast also happened to be six months pregnant at the time. "From the moment I walked in, the atmosphere was friendly and relaxed," she says. "Maybe the board was incredulous about meeting a pregnant woman—I don't know."

Other factors may also have contributed to the unbiased manner in which Prendergast was treated. For one, the bank was in trouble and needed help fast. The chairman couldn't easily afford to differentiate between male and female candidates—he simply needed to find the best possible person. On another level, the job itself was perceived by the board of directors as more technical in nature than the top jobs at most corporations. Indeed, one requirement was an advanced academic degree.

In many respects, the Prendergast case was an exception. At the highest corporate levels, the emphasis on technical

skill—which seems to make a female candidate far more acceptable to men—is downplayed, if raised at all. Technical competence has long been assumed. Typically, the issue at the upper echelon is an individual's capacity to wield power over others: Can candidate A set goals and motivate subordinates to achieve them?

Another common requirement, infrequently acknowledged, is a proper chemistry between chairman and candidate. The strictly objective way in which the chairman in the Prendergast case zeroed in on his candidate is rare.

Susan Appel: Laying Claim to Power

Susan Appel, like Joan Prendergast, was brought into her organization at a senior level rather than promoted from within. Hired by a major communications corporation to head a new venture, which was the chairman's pet project, Appel, 45, has risen swiftly to a position of even greater power. She is the only woman in the study to have been appointed to her company's board.

Like other women in the study, Appel had to fight for the power due her. The test for Appel came shortly after she arrived when a subordinate told her that the chairman had indicated he wouldn't have to answer to her. According to Appel, the chairman had said, "She's coming in, but life goes on as usual, and she isn't really your boss."

In her characteristically direct and efficient manner, Appel "fixed that pretty quickly," by having the man transferred to another department. But she was appalled that the chairman would try to undermine her in such a way. It was a "dirty trick," she maintains.

Put in the best light, the chairman might have been trying to ease tensions among the troops, she concedes. But asked whether it might also have been an oversight on his part, she refuses to let him off the hook: "There are no oversights for the chairman of this company."

Misconceptions about women's capacity to achieve and exercise power hurt women in a number of insidious ways. One surprise in the study was that women at the highest levels—like their entry-level counterparts in generations past—are underpaid relative to their male peers. Most hadn't complained, preferring to hold the inequity as a card to play when combating what they viewed as more treacherous discrimination. Besides, as one woman put it: "I like my $120,000."

Impolitic as it may be to fight the salary issue, a more disheartening finding was the lowering of expectations on the part of the most capable women. One such woman, a 45-year-old banker, spoke of being named by her boss to a senior-level line job, which would have put her in the running for the presidency in the years ahead. The day her appointment was to be announced, her boss's boss—the chairman of the company—called her into his office and asked her to decline the position. What he offered instead was a senior staff job.

Although the staff job had both visibility and influence—it came with the fillip of appointment to the bank's policy-making inner circle—it was still a staff job. It didn't involve the exercise of power. It wouldn't test her ability to run a major unit of the bank. Without such responsibility, her chances for the presidency of the company were virtually nil. "I had major misgivings about taking this role," she concedes, "but when the chairman asks you to do something, you do it."

Asked about her future, she appears a bit wistful. "I think about career achievements in terms of enrichment and enjoyment rather than just sheer power," she says.

While women with thwarted ambitions and cheated careers may now be the evident casualties of the power imbalance in corporate America, it will ultimately be American business that suffers most if the imbalance continues uncorrected. The global challenges of the 1990s require that companies choose from the full spectrum of executive talent. To those corporate officers contemplating the task of bringing women in from the cold, Susan Appel offers a few words of advice: "Go the extra mile. Take the risk. And don't let the woman executive sit out there and freeze. See to it that your support is verbal, clear, and positive."

THE GLOBAL WAR AGAINST WOMEN

Lori Heise

Lori Heise is a senior researcher at the Worldwatch Institute. She prepared a recent report on this subject for
World • Watch *magazine.*

Violence against women—including assault, mutilation, murder, infanticide, rape and cruel neglect—is perhaps the most pervasive yet least recognized human-rights issue in the world. It is also a profound health problem sapping women's physical and emotional vitality and undermining their confidence—both vital to achieving widely held goals for human progress, especially in the Third World.

Despite its invisibility, the dimensions of the problem are vast. In Bangkok, Thailand, a reported 50 percent of married women are beaten regularly by their husbands. In the barrios of Quito, Ecuador, 80 percent of women are said to have been physically abused. And in Nicaragua, 44 percent of men admit to beating their wives or girlfriends. Equally shocking statistics can be found in the industrial world.

Then there are the less recognized forms of violence. In Nepal, female babies die from neglect because parents value sons over daughters; in Sudan, girls' genitals are mutilated to ensure virginity until marriage; and in India, young brides are murdered by their husbands when parents fail to provide enough dowry.

In all these instances, women are targets of violence because of their sex. This is not random violence. The risk factor is being female.

Most of these abuses have been reported in one or another country, at one or another time. But it is only when you begin to amass statistics and reports from international organizations and countries around the world that the horrifying dimensions of this global war on women come into focus. For me the revelation came only recently after talking with scores of village women throughout the world.

I never intended to investigate violence; I was researching maternal and child health issues overseas. But I would commonly begin my interviews with a simple question: What is your biggest problem? With unnerving frequency, the answer came back: "My husband beats me."

These are women who daily have to walk four hours to gather enough wood for the evening meal, whose children commonly die of treatable illnesses, whose security can be wiped out with one failed rain. Yet when defining their own concerns, they see violence as their greatest dilemma. Those dedicated to helping Third World women would do well to listen.

More than simply a "women's issue," violence could thwart other widely held goals for human progress in the Third World. Study after study has shown that maternal education is the single most effective way to reduce child mortality—not because it imparts new knowledge or skills related to health, but because it erodes fatalism, improves self-confidence and changes the power balance within the family.

In effect, these studies say that women's sense of self is critical to reducing infant mortality. Yet acts of violence and society's tacit acceptance of them stand as constant reminders to women of their low worth. Where women's status is critical to achieving a development goal—such as controlling fertility and improving child survival—violence will remain a powerful obstacle to progress.

Measured by its human costs alone, female-focused violence is worthy of international attention and action. But it has seldom been raised at that level, much less addressed. Millions of dollars are spent each year to protect the human rights of fetuses. It is time to stand up for the human rights of women.

The Indian subcontinent is home to one of the most pernicious forms of wife abuse, known locally as "bride-burning" or "dowry deaths." Decades ago dowry referred to the gifts that a woman received from her parents upon marriage. Now dowry has become an important part of premarital negotiations and refers to the wealth that the bride's parents must pay the groom as part of the marriage settlement.

Once a gesture of love, ever-escalating dowry now represents a real financial burden to the parents of unwed daughters. Increasingly, dowry is being seen as a "get rich quick" scheme by prospective husbands, with young brides suffering severe abuse if promised money or goods do not materialize. In its most severe form, dowry harassment ends in suicide or murder, freeing the husband to pursue a more lucrative arrangement.

Dowry deaths are notoriously undercounted, largely because the husband and his relatives frequently try to disguise the murder as a suicide or an accident and the police are loathe to get involved. A frequent scam is to set the women alight with kerosene, and then claim she died in a kitchen accident—hence the term "bride-burning." In 1987 the police official recorded 1,786 dowry deaths in all of India, but the Ahmedabad Women's Action Group estimates that 1,000 women may have been burned alive that year in Gujurat State alone.

4. SOCIAL INEQUALITIES: Sex Inequalities

A quick look at mortality data from India reveals the reasonableness of this claim. In both urban Maharashtra and greater Bombay, 19 percent of all deaths among women 15 to 44 years old are due to "accidental burns." In other Third World countries, such as Guatemala, Ecuador and Chile, the same statistic is less 1 percent.

Elsewhere in the world, the marriage transaction is reversed, with prospective husbands paying "bridewealth" to secure a woman's hand in marriage. In many cultures—especially in Africa—the exchange has become so commercialized that inflated bridewealth leaves the man with the distinct impression that he has "purchased" his wife.

The notion that bridewealth confers ownership was clearly depicted during recent parliamentary debates in Papua New Guinea over whether wife-beating should be made illegal. Transcripts show that most ministers were violently against the idea of parliament interfering in "traditional family life." Minister William Wi of North Waghi argued that wife-beating "is an accepted custom and we are wasting our time debating the issue." Another parliamentarian added: "I paid for my wife, so she should not overrule my decisions, because I am the head of the family."

It is this unequal power balance—institutionalized in the structure of the patriarchal family—that is at the root of wife-beating. As Cheryl Bernard, director of Austria's Ludwig Boltzmann Institute of Politics, notes: "Violence against women in the family takes place because the perpetrators feel, and their environment encourages them to feel, that this is an acceptable exercise of male prerogative, a legitimate and appropriate way to relieve their own tension in conditions of stress, to sanction female behavior . . . or just to enjoy a feeling of supremacy."

While stress and alcohol may increase the likelihood of violence, they do not "cause" it. Rather, it is the belief that violence is an acceptable way to resolve conflict, and that women are "appropriate" and "safe" targets for abuse, that leads to battering.

Today's cultures have strong historical, religious and legal legacies that reinforce the legitimacy of wife-beating. Under English common law, for example, a husband had the legal right to discipline his wife—subject to a "rule of thumb" that barred him from using a stick broader than his thumb. Judicial decisions in England and the United States upheld this right until well into the 19th century. Only last week, a New York judge let off with only five years' probation a Chinese immigrant who admitted bludgeoning his wife to death. The judge justified the light sentence partly by reference to traditional Chinese attitudes toward female adultery.

While less overt, the preference for male offspring in many cultures can be as damaging and potentially fatal to females as rape or assault. The same sentiment that once motivated infanticide is now expressed in the systematic neglect of daughters—a neglect so severe in some countries that girls aged 2 to 4 die at nearly twice the rate of boys.

"Let it be late, but let it be a son," goes a saying in Nepal, a country that shares its strong preference for male children with the rest of the Indian subcontinent, as well as China, South Korea and Taiwan. In these cultures and others, sons are highly valued because only they can perpetuate the family line and perform certain religious rituals. Even more important, sons represent an economic asset to the family and a source of security for parents in their old age.

Studies confirm that where the preference for sons is strong, girls receive inferior medical care and education, and less food. In Punjab, India, for example, parents spend more than twice as much on medical care for boy infants as for girls.

In fact, the pressure to bear sons is so great in India and China that women have begun using amniocentesis as a sex identification test to selectively abort female fetuses. Until protests forced them to stop, Indian sex detection clinics boldly advertised it was better to spend $38 now on terminating a girl than $3,800 later on her dowry. Of 8,000 fetuses examined at six abortion clinics in Bombay, 7,999 were found to be female.

In parts of Africa and the Middle East, young girls suffer another form of violence, euphemistically known as female circumcision. More accurately, this operation—which removes all or part of the external female genitalia, including the clitoris—is a life-threatening form of mutilation. According to the World Health Organization, more than 80 million women have undergone sexual surgery in Africa alone.

While female circumcision has its origin in the male desire to control female sexuality, today a host of other superstitions and beliefs sustains the practice. Some Moslem groups mistakenly believe that it is demanded by the Islamic faith, although it has no basis in the Koran. Others believe the operation will increase fertility, affirm femininity or prevent still births. Yet ultimately what drives the tradition is that men will not marry uncircumcised women, believing them to be promiscuous, unclean and sexually untrustworthy.

The medical complications of circumcision are severe. Immediate risks include hemorrhage, tetanus and blood poisoning from unsterile and often primitive cutting implements (knife, razor blade or broken glass), and shock from the pain of the operation, which is carried out without anesthesia. Not uncommonly, these complications result in death.

The long-term effects, in addition to loss of all sexual feeling, include chronic urinary tract infections, pelvic infections that can lead to infertility, painful intercourse and severe scarring that can cause tearing of tissue and hemorrhage during childbirth. In fact, women who are infibulated—the most severe form of circumcision—must be cut open on their wedding night to make intercourse possible, and more cuts are necessary for delivery of a child.

Despite these horrific health effects, many still oppose the eradication of this practice. As late as June 1988, Muslim religious scholars in Somalia argued that milder forms of circumcision should be maintained to temper female sexuality. Others defend circumcision as an "important African tradition." But as the Kenyan women's magazine *Viva* observes: "There is nothing 'African' about injustice or violence, whether it takes the form of mistreated wives and mothers, or slums or circumcision. Often the very men who . . . excuse injustice to women with the phrase 'it is African' are wearing three-piece pin-striped suits and shiny shoes.''

Fortunately, women have not sat idle in the face of such abuse. Around the world they are organizing shelters, lobbying for legal reform and fighting the sexism that underlies violence.

Most industrial countries and at least a dozen developing nations now have shelter movements to provide refuge for abused women and their children. Brazil has established almost 30 all-female police stations for victims of rape, battering and incest. And in Africa, women are organizing education campaigns to combat sexual surgery.

Elsewhere women have organized in their own defense. In San Juan de Miraflores, a shantytown of Lima, Peru, women carry whistles that they use to summon other women in case of attack.

Yet it will take more than the dedicated action of a few women to end crimes of gender. Most important is for women worldwide to recognize their common oppression. Violence against women cuts across all cultures and all socioeconomic groups. Indeed, we in America live in our own glass house: In the United States a woman is beaten every 15 seconds, and each day four women are killed by their batterers.

Such statistics are as important as they are shocking. Violence persists in part because it is hidden. If governments and women's groups can expose violence through surveys and better documentation, then ignorance will no longer be an excuse for inaction.

Also critical is challenging the legal framework that undergirds male violence, such as unequal inheritance, discriminatory family laws and a husband's right to chastise. Especially important are the social inequities and cultural beliefs that leave women economically dependent on men. As long as women must marry to survive, they will do whatever they must to secure a husband—including tolerating abuse and submitting themselves and their daughters to sexual surgery.

Action against violence, however, must proceed from the international community down as well as from the grass roots up. Where governments tacitly condone violence through their silence, or worse yet, legitimize it through discriminatory laws and customs, international pressure can be an important impetus for reform. Putting violence against women high on the world agenda is not appeasing a "special interest" group. It is restoring the birthright of half of humanity.

Social Institutions in Crisis and Change

Social institutions are the building blocks of social structure. They represent the ways in which the important tasks of society are accomplished. The regulation of reproduction, socialization of children, production and distribution of economic goods, law enforcement and social control, and organization of religion and other value systems are examples of social tasks performed by social institutions.

Social institutions are not rigid arrangements; they reflect changing social conditions. Institutions generally change slowly. At the present time, however, many of the social institutions in the United States and many parts of the world are in crisis and are undergoing rapid change. Eastern European countries are literally transforming their political and economic institutions. Economic institutions such as stock markets are becoming truly international, and when a major country experiences a recession many other countries experience the effects. In the United States the political system is ineffective; it does not generate great leaders. The public consensus seems to be "the less government intervention, the better." American foreign policy sometimes appears to be guided more by fear than by reason. The United States economy is on shaky ground. The management of American businesses has been blamed for the decline in productivity. Medical care in some cases is uncaring. Institutional crisis is found everywhere. Even the family as an institution is under attack. Critics of the system complain that social institutions are not meeting the needs of society. Whether this is because institutions are changing too rapidly or too slowly will continue to be debated. However, in order to appreciate how social institutions endure, it is necessary to understand the development and process of such changes.

The first subsection of this unit presents two views of the state of the world and the crises of institutions in various parts of the world. Alan Durning describes the horrid conditions of the world's poor that have become poorer and more numerous even as the rich have prospered. The major hope for the poor is grass-roots organizations.

Benjamin Barber identifies two powerful forces in the world today: tribal identification and global markets. The first often leads to hatred of others and unmanageable conflicts between groups. The second leads to the weakening of parochial ties and incorporation into worldwide systems and institutions. Both, however, present problems for democracy.

The second subsection of this unit presents analyses of where national and world trends have brought the United States. Robert Reich explains how the skills of the work force are the key to a healthy balance of trade and leadership in the world economy. Kenneth Hunter explains how the United States has allowed problems to grow into uncontrollable messes through inattention.

Americans have much to be proud of in the political sphere, from human rights and civil liberties to democratic processes and the rule of law. Nevertheless, the polity also has its faults.

In "From Ouagadougou to Cape Canaveral: Why the Bad News Doesn't Travel Up," Charles Peters focuses on a major flaw of bureaucracies: the fact that within them, bad news is screened out as information is passed up to the top. The next article presents a sophisticated analysis of the way special interests influence government. Votes on specific bills are seldom bought by PACs but access is, and access is often converted to changes in the details of legislation that determines its real effects on the special interests.

In the economic sphere, dramatic changes are taking place. *Business Week* magazine describes the profound transformation that is taking place in American business. The modern corporation is being restructured away from efficiencies of scale to decentralization for flexibility and creativity. In contrast to the optimism of this article, Edward Luttwak portrays America as a declining power with increasingly malfunctioning systems.

The social sphere is in turmoil. The most contested issue is abortion and Carl Sagan and Ann Druyan try to sort out and appraise this very complex issue. There is a universal call for reform of the school system, but there is widespread disagreement about which reforms would do the most good. William Greider argues that vouchers would destroy the public schools but choice within schools improves the system. A major struggle in the religious sphere focuses on the separation of church and state. Nancy Gibbs describes how the courts are redefining just what this separation means.

Looking Ahead: Challenge Questions

Why is it important to preserve some continuity in institutions?

Can institutions outlive their usefulness?

Why are institutions so difficult to change? Cite examples where changes are instituted from the top down, and others where they are instituted from the bottom up. Do you see a similar pattern of development for these types of change?

LIFE ON THE BRINK

Grinding poverty traps millions in conditions that fall beneath any definition of human decency. The world's poor became poorer and more numerous during the 1980s.

Alan Durning

Alan B. Durning, senior researcher at the Worldwatch Institute, studies the relationship between poverty and ecological degradation. He is author of Worldwatch Paper 92, Poverty and the Environment: Reversing the Downward Spiral.

Historians of the world's fortunate class—those billion-odd people who inhabit industrial lands—have already labeled the 20th century an era of economic miracles. The poor tell a different tale. The disparities in living standards that separate them from the rich have never been greater. Indeed, they verge on the surreal.

The world has 157 billionaires and perhaps 2 million millionaires, but 100 million people around the globe are homeless, living on sidewalks, in garbage dumps, and under bridges. The concerns of the rich contrast violently with those of the poor. Americans spend $5 billion each year on special diets to lower their calorie consumption, while the world's poorest 400 million people are so undernourished they are likely to suffer stunted growth, mental retardation, or death.

As water from a single spring in France is bottled and shipped to the prosperous around the world, 1.9 billion people drink and bathe in water contaminated with deadly parasites and pathogens. More than half of humanity lacks sanitary toilets. In 1988, the world's nations devoted $1 trillion—$200 for each person on the planet—to the means of warfare, but failed to scrape together the $5 per child it would have cost to eradicate the disease that killed 14 million that year.

In the 1980s, the histories of rich and poor diverged sharply. For industrial nations, the decade was a time of resurgence and recovery after the economic turmoil of the 1970s. For the poor, particularly in Africa and Latin America, the 1980s were an unmitigated disaster, a time of falling earnings and rising debt, of contracting food supplies, and escalating death rates.

Once entered, destitution in the modern era is perpetuated by a set of mutually reinforcing factors that form a poverty trap. Locally, poor people's lack of productive assets, their physical weakness, susceptibility to illness, and powerlessness combine with rapid population growth to keep them in straitened circumstances. Nationally, government policies in many sectors favor the urban fortunate over the

From *World • Watch*, March/April 1990, pp. 20-30. *World • Watch*, published by Worldwatch Institute, Washington, D.C.

rural masses. And, at the international level, interlocking patterns of debt, trade and capital flight during the 1980s made the rich richer and the poor poorer.

Still, there is hope for prying open the poverty trap. Poor people have formed hundreds of thousands of grass-roots organizations to help themselves gain what official development programs have failed to provide. In some cases, enlightened governments and international agencies have sponsored these groups. Ultimate success, though, depends on turning these hopeful beginnings into a full-fledged mobilization to end poverty.

POVERTY IN THE EXTREME

In 1978, Robert McNamara, then-president of the World Bank, gave what stands as the classic description of absolute poverty: "A condition of life so limited by malnutrition, illiteracy, disease, squalid surroundings, high infant mortality, and low life expectancy as to be beneath any reasonable definition of human decency." As McNamara's words suggest, poverty is far more than an economic condition.

Although usually measured in terms of income, poverty's true horror extends into all aspects of an individual's life. Susceptibility to disease, limited access to most types of services and information, lack of control over resources, subordination to higher social and economic classes, and utter insecurity in the face of changing circumstances are the norm for a poor person. Flowing from these physical dimensions, poverty's psychological toll is equally severe: the erosion of human dignity and self-respect.

Unfortunately, even the most basic poverty indicator—income is hardly monitored. It is possible to know precisely how much money is in circulation in Haiti, how much steel is produced in Malaysia, and how many automobiles there are in the Congo. But the number of people living in the wretched misery of poverty is a matter largely left to conjecture, since little information is gathered. What does exist is often inconsistent, outdated or unreliable.

In this article, absolute poverty is defined as the lack of sufficient income in cash or kind to meet the most basic biological needs for food, clothing and shelter. From country to country, the income threshold for absolute poverty varies between $50 and $500 per year, depending on such factors as prices, access to subsistence resources, and availability of public services.

In the early 1980s, World Bank and U.N. Food and Agriculture Organization (FAO) estimates of the number of people living in absolute poverty ranged between 700 million and 1 billion. Since then, most indicators suggest that poverty has increased dramatically in sub-Saharan Africa, Latin America and parts of Asia, swamping reductions in China and India. The result is that approximately 1.2 billion people live in absolute poverty, at least 200 million more than in 1980 (see Table 1). World Bank figures suggest that the global poverty rate stood at 22.3 percent in 1980, after declining gradually but steadily since mid-century. The new poverty estimate of 1.2 billion people translates to a poverty rate of 23.4 percent. During the 1980s, then, the global poverty rate not only stopped falling, it rose.

Table 1.

People Estimated to be Living in Absolute Poverty, 1989

Region	Number of People[1] (millions)	Share of Total Population (percent)
Asia	675	25
Sub-Saharan Africa	325	62
Latin America	150	35
N. Africa and Middle East	75	28
World	**1,225**	**23**

[1] Ratio of share of national income of richest 20 percent of households to share of national income of poorest 20 percent of households.
[2] Estimated from average national incomes; true world income distribution is less equitable.
Source: Worldwatch Institute.

THE RICH GET RICHER

Perhaps the best way to analyze income per person, or average income, was developed by Robert Summers and Alan Heston, economics professors at the University of Pennsylvania. Their database incorporates per-capita gross domestic product figures on 130 nations compiled from two decades of reports by the United Nations, World Bank, and Organization for Economic Cooperation and Development. Their key innovation was to make systematic adjustments that reflect the widely varying purchasing power for goods and services from country to country. The result is a much more realistic picture of income levels.

Based on Summers and Heston's data, average income per person worldwide in constant 1980 U.S.

dollars has doubled to $3,300 since 1950. The fruits of global economic growth, however, have almost all gone to the fortunate. Grouping the world's nations into four classes based on their 1985 per-capita income brings the disparities into sharp focus. Wealthy nations, including those in Europe and North America, almost tripled their per-capita incomes over the last 40 years. Middle-income countries, such as Brazil, Mexico and Turkey, more than doubled theirs before entering a period of stagnation around 1980. Poor nations, including China, Egypt and the Philippines, experienced some rise, but the per-person income of the poorest countries, including much of the Indian subcontinent and Africa, has remained effectively level since mid-century.

Wide as the gap between the world's rich and poor appears when measured in average income, the real situation is worse. Averages disguise the gross disparities in income distribution that characterize the majority of countries. Between 60 and 70 percent of the people in most countries earn less than their nation's average income. Almost nowhere does the poorest fifth of households collect even 10 percent of national income, while the richest fifth commonly receives half.

Among the world's most populous nations, China, the Soviet Union and Japan have relatively equitable income distributions, with the richest fifth of households in the nation receiving between three and four times as much per year as the poorest fifth. Indonesia and India fall in the middle of the range, with the rich earning 8 to 10 times as much as the poor. Mexico is worse, with a factor of 18 separating top and bottom, while in Brazil members of the richest fifth earn 28 times as much as members of the poorest fifth (see Table 2).

Data on income distribution and average income can be combined to help reveal the extent of poverty. The poor may be fairly well off even when average income is low, or suffer greatly where average income is high. In 1985, for example, Egypt's per-capita income was about half of Peru's, but because Egypt is more equitable, poor Egyptians earned one-third more than poor Peruvians. Likewise, Brazil's average income was twice Sri Lanka's, but the Sri Lankan poor earned more than the Brazilian poor.

In terms of economic security, what different classes own is as important as what they earn. Although reliable information is scarce, the disparity in distribution of wealth appears to be wider than the disparity in distribution of income. The

situation in India is probably representative of developing countries generally. There, the richest tenth of households receive income worth 25 times as much as the poorest tenth of households, but own assets worth 250 times as much.

A CRUEL DECADE

For the poor of Africa, Latin America, and parts of Asia, the 1980s were a time of cruel reversals, a period when the global economy seemed to conspire against them. On top of the runaway population growth and accelerating environmental decline

Table 2.

Approximate Income Distribution, Selected Nations, Most Recent Available Year

Country	Equity Ratio[1]
China (cities)	3
Soviet Union	4
Japan	4
Bangladesh	7
Indonesia	8
India	10
United States	12
Mexico	18
Brazil	28
World[2]	**15**

[1]Ratio of share of national income of richest 20 percent of households to share of national income of poorest 20 percent of households.
[2]Estimated from average national incomes; true world income distribution is less equitable.
Source: Worldwatch Institute.

that were already dragging down living standards across the Third World, prices for poor nations' exports plummeted, and international debt siphoned a growing share of their income into the hands of foreign financiers. The poor, in short, earned less and paid more. Consequently, they ate less.

Developing nations' debt of $1.2 trillion caused a reversal of the flow of international capital. Today, poor nations are paying rich ones $50 billion each year in debt and interest payments beyond what they receive in new loans. Capital flight from wealthy people in poor lands may bring the exodus up to $100 billion each year. Trade protectionism in industrial countries results in annual losses on a similar scale, as Third World export prices fall and markets shrink.

This massive hemorrhage of financial resources from poor regions only augments their destruction

Figure 1: Real GNP Per Capita in China, India, Latin America, and Sub-Saharan Africa, 1960-88

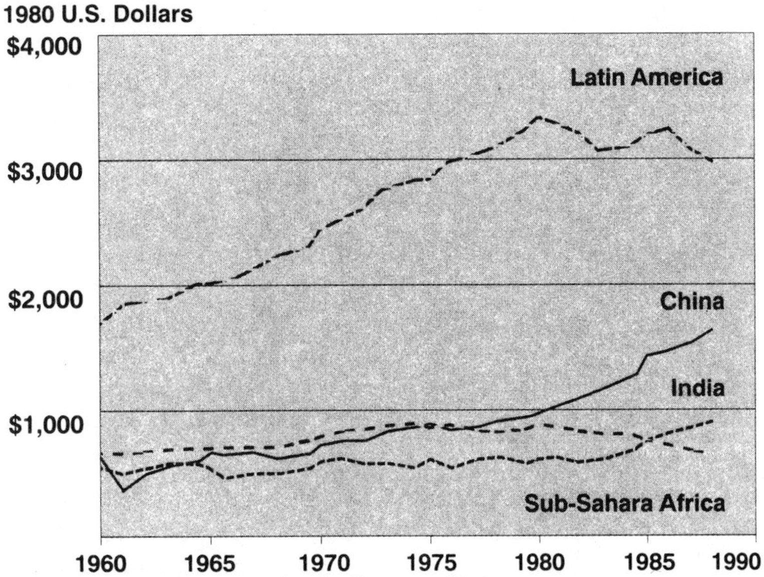

1980 U.S. Dollars

Source: Worldwatch Institute, based on Summers and Heston

of natural resources. Poor countries are forced to exploit mineral deposits, forests and fisheries to meet debt obligations. And they are left with few resources to alleviate poverty. The poor turn to the only means of survival available to them: marginal lands. They plow mountain slopes, burn plots in tropical forests, and overgraze grasslands, often knowing full-well that their actions are destructive to the environment and therefore cannot last.

Close to half of the absolute poor now live in regions of marginal agricultural productivity, where they are falling into a downward spiral of ecological and economic impoverishment. The stark choice for the dispossessed, trapped as they are in stagnant economies that are exporting precious resources to pay bank debts, is between sacrificing their environment and sacrificing their children.

ONE STEP FORWARD, TWO STEPS BACK

From 1950 to 1980, the gap between rich and poor nations has grown, mostly because the rich got richer. Since 1980, the poor in many developing countries have been getting poorer, too. More than 40 Third World nations probably finished the decade poorer, in per-capita terms, than they started it. The 14 most devastated countries—including Zambia, Bolivia and Nigeria—saw per-capita income plummet as drastically as did the United States

during the Great Depression. In fact, the term "developing nation" has become a cruel misnomer; many countries are no longer so much developing as disintegrating.

The human impact of the decade's economic backslide in Africa, Latin America, and parts of Asia has been ruinous. Malnutrition is documented to have risen in Burma, Burundi, the Gambia, Guinea-Bissau, Jamaica, Niger, Nigeria, Paraguay, the Philippines, Nicaragua, El Salvador, Peru, and undoubtedly elsewhere. The World Bank reports that from 1979 to 1983, life expectancy fell in nine African countries, and more than 100 million Africans are thought to lack sufficient food to sustain themselves in good health.

The economic turmoil of the 1980s truly wreaked havoc south of the Sahara. Income per capita peaked in 1974, stumbled along until 1980, and then plunged, dropping 25 percent by 1988 (see Figure 1). Nigeria, Zaire and Zambia, dependent on exports of mineral resources, and war-torn Angola, Ethiopia, Mozambique and Sudan saw their economies unravel more rapidly still. North African and Middle Eastern nations suffered less than most in the early 1980s, but with the drop of oil prices in mid-decade, unemployment spread and poverty rose again.

In Latin America, per-capita income stood at almost $3,400 in 1980. Sadly, skewed income distribution meant that destitution continued to be the lot of a large share of the population. The 1980s darkened the outlook across the region, but were especially gloomy for the poor. As Inter-American Development Bank President Enrique Iglesias said in September 1988, "The per-capita income of the average Latin American is 9 percent lower today than it was in 1980. This is average. In some countries the standard of living has slipped back to what it was 20 years ago. It does not take much imagination to realize that behind this statistic are plummeting real wage levels, soaring unemployment . . . increased levels of marginality, and acute poverty—in short, an erosion of every measure of social well-being."

El Salvador, Nicaragua and Peru, all torn by war, went into economic tailspins. Peruvian children are malnourished to the point that one in three has stunted growth, according to the government's National Investigation of Nutrition and Health. In El Salvador, staples like beans are now called "rich people's food" and health workers report that infant mortality is surging.

Asian economies were sharply divided during the turbulence of the last decade. In China, average income rose by more than 60 percent since 1980. India, Indonesia, Pakistan and Thailand also raised per-capita income appreciably during the 1980s, in some cases at a faster rate than in earlier decades. Bangladesh, Burma and Vietnam, by contrast, stagnated, and the Philippines experienced a sharp decline.

Asian countries that did well during the 1980s—coincidentally, among the few countries for which fairly reliable poverty estimates exist—also made strides in alleviating poverty. The extent of absolute poverty in China was cut dramatically during a period of rapid economic growth. In 1980, according to a World Bank estimate, 150 million Chinese lived in poverty; by 1988, best estimates put the number at 70 million, even though the country's population had grown by 69 million over this period.

Indonesia, meanwhile, reduced the portion of its population in poverty by between one-fourth and one-half since 1970, according to different estimates. Thailand reportedly made a 50-percent reduction since 1960. Although still controversial, indications are that the poverty rates in India and Pakistan declined by several percentage points in the 1980s.

WHO ARE THE POOR?

Poor people are not a homogeneous group. Nonetheless, a few generalizations help answer the question, Who are the poor? Despite rapid urbanization and growing urban poverty in much of the world, four-fifths of those in absolute poverty still live in rural areas. Only in Latin America do a large share of the poor—nearly one-half—live in cities. Almost all of the poor live in, and are culturally shaped by, the world's two million villages—the tightly knit social and economic institutions that have been at the center of human life since the dawn of agriculture.

Even among the absolute poor, degrees of poverty can be distinguished. Michael Lipton, director of the Food Consumption and Nutrition Program at the International Food Policy Research Institute in Washington, D.C., has demonstrated that those at the very bottom of the economic ladder form a distinct sub-class. Defined as those who spend 80 percent of their income on food but still lack sufficient calories to meet their metabolic needs, this undernourished class accounts for perhaps one-third of the absolute poor, or 400 million people. All of the poor eat boring, monotonous, and unappetizing diets of cereals, roots and legumes day after day. All may be hungry periodically.

The world's poor are overwhelmingly illiterate and therefore lack access to information and ideas that could help them escape poverty. Indeed, social scientists studying poverty through statistical analysis commonly find educational level to be the variable that correlates most closely to standard of living. Even among landless laborers, where literacy would seem to matter little, those who can read tend to earn more than those who cannot.

The poor are often distinct from dominant wealthy groups in race, tribe, or religion. In Africa, with its hundreds of different cultural groups, economic strata are often drawn along tribal lines. Indian poverty is concentrated among tribal peoples and lower castes. The hill tribes of Southeast Asia and the Philippines fall at the bottom of the economic ladder, while Latin American Indians are the poorest of that region, particularly in Guatemala, Peru and Bolivia, where they form a majority of the population.

The poor are slightly more likely to be female than male, particularly in urban areas, leading some analysts to speak of a global "feminization of poverty." Although the true extent of female poverty remains uncertain, there is no question that life is harsher for poor women than for poor men.

Women's burdens multiply endlessly. They are paid less than men—in Egypt, half as much for farm labor. But they work more—one to three additional hours each day, according to studies of villages in four countries. They are less educated—female literacy trails male literacy by 38 percentage points on average in the world's worst-off countries—but bear greater responsibility for the health of children.

Women are expected to give birth to, raise, and feed numerous (preferably male) offspring, and consequently grow weak and ailing as their bodies are exhausted by the cycle of repeated pregnancy and childbirth. They are often abused and beaten at home, but have few legal rights and fewer property rights. They cannot leave their husbands unless they are willing to lose their social standing, economic security, and their children. For poor women, as a peasant woman from the Brazilian state of Minas Geraïs says, "The only holiday . . . is when you are asleep."

The work of the poor is concentrated at the fringes of the global economy. Most are landless agricultural laborers, sharecroppers, marginal farmers, or, if they live in cities, unskilled laborers in the underground economy. Landlessness has been on the rise as small farms are divided into plots too tiny for subsistence and as agricultural commercialization pushes tenants and sharecroppers out of fertile zones. Landless and near-landless rural households probably number near 200 million in developing countries.

What work the landless can find is usually piecemeal, unstable and insecure, not to mention backbreaking and tedious, yet they work hard day in and day out. As Professor Robert Chambers of the Institute for Development Studies in Brighton, England, puts it, "People so close to the edge cannot afford laziness or stupidity. They have to work, and work hard, whenever and however they can. Many of the lazy and stupid poor are dead."

A PAINFUL INHERITANCE

Poverty's most savage toll is measured in the lives of children. As income declines, family size increases. Lipton reports that whereas 15 to 30 percent of families in developing countries have eight or more members, 55 to 80 percent of poor families are that large. Consequently, perhaps two-thirds of the world's absolute poor are under the age of 15. The prospects for these young people are even worse than for their parents.

Not surprisingly, at lower incomes, infant death rates turn sharply upward. Wracked by disease, lacking sufficient nourishment and clean water, per-

haps one-third of these youngsters die before their fifth birthday. Many of those who survive are physically stunted and mentally impaired as a result of chronic hunger during the critical age of 6 months to 2 years, foreclosing their already slim chances of escaping poverty.

In Zambia, twice as many children died from malnutrition in 1984 as in 1980. The infant mortality rate in Brazil rose in 1983 and 1984 for the first time in decades—rising most steeply in the poorest regions. Similar trends are afoot in much of the Third World, leading UNICEF to conclude in its 1989 annual report that "hundreds of thousands of the developing world's children have given their lives to pay their countries' debts, and many millions more are still paying the interest with their malnourished minds and bodies."

HUNGER IN THE LAP OF LUXURY

Absolute poverty is rare in affluent lands, yet it is worth noting that industrial countries' own, less-severe form of poverty also rose during the 1980s, particularly in the United States, the United Kingdom, and Eastern Europe. With *glasnost*, the Soviet Union and Eastern European countries have begun to reveal the extent of deprivation within their borders. One-fifth of Soviet citizens reportedly live below the official poverty line of 75 rubles ($116) a month, and many Poles have seen their livelihoods wither as their economy unravels.

In the United States, the past decade saw more people living below the poverty line—which stood at just over $12,000 per year for a family of four in 1988—than at any time since the War on Poverty was initiated in the mid-1960s. In 1979, the equity of income distribution began to deteriorate rapidly; by 1986, disparities in earnings were the worst on record. Meanwhile, the median family income was lower in 1988 than in 1973, measured in constant dollars, and average weekly earnings were lower than in 1962.

Falling real wages and greater inequality led inevitably to rising poverty: In 1988, some 32 million Americans lived below the official poverty line. Most severely affected are minorities, female-headed households, and the young. One-fifth of American children are growing up in poverty.

With widening income disparities round the globe, it will not be long before there is a Third World within the First World, and a First within the Third.

*"Between
the mortar and pestle,
the chili cannot last. We
poor are like chilies—each year
we are ground down, and
soon there will be
nothing left."*

ENDING POVERTY

To alleviate poverty worldwide will require national governments and international agencies to redefine development away from generalized aid for entire nations. True development is the struggle to help the poorest break out of the poverty trap.

The touchstone of true development was best expressed decades by Mahatma Gandhi. "Whenever you are in doubt . . . apply the following test. Recall the face of the poorest and the weakest man whom you may have seen, and ask yourself if the step you contemplate is going to be of any use to him. Will he gain anything by it? Will it restore him to a control over his own life and destiny?" Given the changing profile of poverty, the only updating Gandhi's principle needs is to substitute "poorest child" for "poorest man."

A variety of innovative grass-roots strategies from around the world have now proven that effective assaults on poverty begin by putting the poor in control. As nutrition analyst Paulus Santosa put it, "It would be very hard to find professional nutrition workers in Indonesia today who can raise a family of five with U.S. $0.50 per day and stay healthy." The only true experts on poverty are the poor.

Critical components of a grass-roots mobilization against poverty are female education, redistribution of farmland, empowerment of communities to control local natural resources, and extension of credit, clean water supplies, primary health care, and family planning services.

In West Bengal, India, "untouchables"—those at the bottom of the country's caste system—who received tiny allotments of scrub land from the state started tree farms that enabled them to buy fertile plots from absentee landlords. They helped them-

selves and the environment. In the highlands of Bolivia, home of the Quechua Indians, local efforts to start a community newspaper unleashed local knowledge and energy that has since flowed into dozens of activities, including soil and forest conservation.

The state of Kerala, India, provides a model of fighting poverty with grass-roots participation. The state's success speaks for itself. Despite per-capita income one-third below the Indian average, the state's literacy rate is almost twice the national mark, its people typically live 11 years longer, its birth-rate is one-third lower, and its infant death rate is two-thirds lower.

Yet, local and national efforts will amount to little in the absence of fundamental changes at the international level. Without accords to reduce debt dramatically, lower protectionist barriers to Third World exports, and slow the astronomical rate of capital flight, poverty will continue to rise during the 1990s.

VOICES OF THE POWERLESS

Described in numbers, poverty seems horrible enough; in the words of the poor, though, its full cruelty is revealed. A young woman from the highlands of Guatemala describes the misery and powerlessness of life, and death, on the coffee plantations

---

A Few Entry Points for Fighting Poverty

Support poor people's grass-roots organizations through:
Oxfam-America
115 Broadway
Boston, Massachusetts 02116
617/482-1211

Promote reform of international development agencies through:
Bread for the World
802 Rhode Island Avenue, NE
Washington, DC 20018
202/269-0200

and through:
The Global Tomorrow Coalition
1325 G Street, NW
Washington, DC 20005
202/628-4016

Educate yourself on a Third World study tour with:
Global Exchange
2141 Mission Street, Suite 202
San Francisco, California 94110
415/255-7269

where her family and thousands of other Indians worked as migrants:

Two of my brothers died in the plantation. The first, he was the eldest, was called Felipe. . . . They'd sprayed the coffee with pesticide by plane while we were working, as they usually did, and my brother couldn't stand the fumes and died. . . . The second one . . . his name was Nicolás . . . died when I was eight. . . . He was two then. When my little brother started crying, crying, crying, my mother didn't know what to do. . . . He lasted fifteen days. . . .

The little boy died early in the morning. We didn't know what to do. Our two neighbors were anxious to help my mother but they didn't know what to do either—not how to bury him or anything. Then the overseer told my mother she could bury my brother in the plantation but she had to pay a tax to keep him buried there. My mother said, "I have no money at all." He told her: "Yes, and you already owe a lot of money for medicine and other things, so take his body and leave." . . . It was impossible to take his body back to the highlands. . . . So my mother decided that, even if she had to work for a month without earning, she would pay the tax to the landowner, or the overseer, to bury my brother in the plantation. . . . One of the men brought a little box, a bit like a suitcase. We put my brother in it and took him to be buried. . . . That night the overseer told us: "Leave here tomorrow."

They were fired for missing work to bury Nicolás. For the Indians of Guatemala, like the rest of the poor, life is a grueling ordeal. Days before his own death, a farm laborer in Bangladesh named Hari reflected on his years: "Between the mortar and the pestle, the chili cannot last. We poor are like chilies—each year we are ground down, and soon there will be nothing left."

The poor, more than ever, are rallying to their own defense, but the global poverty trap only tightens around them. The challenge of forestalling Hari's prophecy falls largely to the rich.

Jihad vs. McWorld

The two axial principles of our age—tribalism and globalism—clash at every point except one: they may both be threatening to democracy

Benjamin R. Barber

Benjamin R. Barber is the Whitman Professor of Political Science at Rutgers University. Barber's most recent books are Strong Democracy *(1984),* The Conquest of Politics *(1988), and* An Aristocracy of Everyone.

Just beyond the horizon of current events lie two possible political figures—both bleak, neither democratic. The first is a retribalization of large swaths of humankind by war and bloodshed: a threatened Lebanonization of national states in which culture is pitted against culture, people against people, tribe against tribe—a Jihad in the name of a hundred narrowly conceived faiths against every kind of interdependence, every kind of artificial social cooperation and civic mutuality. The second is being borne in on us by the onrush of economic and ecological forces that demand integration and uniformity and that mesmerize the world with fast music, fast computers, and fast food—with MTV, Macintosh, and McDonald's, pressing nations into one commercially homogenous global network: one McWorld tied together by technology, ecology, communications, and commerce. The planet is falling precipitantly apart and coming reluctantly together at the very same moment.

These two tendencies are sometimes visible in the same countries at the same instant: thus Yugoslavia, clamoring just recently to join the New Europe, is exploding into fragments; India is trying to live up to its reputation as the world's largest integral democracy while powerful new fundamentalist parties like the Hindu nationalist Bharatiya Janata Party, along with nationalist assassins, are im-

periling its hard-won unity. States are breaking up or joining up: the Soviet Union has disappeared almost overnight, its parts forming new unions with one another or with like-minded nationalities in neighboring states. The old interwar national state based on territory and political sovereignty looks to be a mere transitional development.

The tendencies of what I am here calling the forces of Jihad and the forces of McWorld operate with equal strength in opposite directions, the one driven by parochial hatreds, the other by universalizing markets, the one re-creating ancient subnational and ethnic borders from within, the other making national borders porous from without. They have one thing in common: neither offers much hope to citizens looking for practical ways to govern themselves democratically. If the global future is to put Jihad's centrifugal whirlwind against McWorld's centripetal black hole, the outcome is unlikely to be democratic—or so I will argue.

MCWORLD, OR THE GLOBALIZATION OF POLITICS

Four imperatives make up the dynamic of McWorld: a market imperative, a resource imperative, an information-technology imperative, and an ecological imperative. By shrinking the world and diminishing the salience of national borders, these imperatives have in combination achieved a considerable victory over factiousness and particularism, and not least of all over their most virulent traditional form—nationalism. It is the realists who are now Europeans, the utopians who dream nostalgically of a resurgent England or Germany, perhaps even a resurgent Wales or Saxony. Yesterday's

wishful cry for one world has yielded to the reality of McWorld.

The market imperative. Marxist and Leninist theories of imperialism assumed that the quest for ever-expanding markets would in time compel nation-based capitalist economies to push against national boundaries in search of an international economic imperium. Whatever else has happened to the scientist predictions of Marxism, in this domain they have proved farsighted. All national economies are now vulnerable to the inroads of larger, transnational markets within which trade is free, currencies are convertible, access to banking is open, and contracts are enforceable under law. In Europe, Asia, Africa, the South Pacific, and the Americas such markets are eroding national sovereignty and giving rise to entities—international banks, trade associations, transnational lobbies like OPEC and Greenpeace, world news services like CNN and the BBC, and multinational corporations that increasingly lack a meaningful national identity—that neither reflect nor respect nationhood as an organizing or regulative principle.

The market imperative has also reinforced the quest for international peace and stability, requisites of an efficient international economy. Markets are enemies of parochialism, isolation, fractiousness, war. Market psychology attenuates the psychology of ideological and religious cleavages and assumes a concord among producers and consumers—categories that ill fit narrowly conceived national or religious cultures. Shopping has little tolerance for blue laws, whether dictated by pub-closing British paternalism, Sabbath-observing Jewish Orthodox fundamentalism, or no-Sunday-liquor-sales Massachusetts puritanism. In the context of common markets, international law ceases to be a vision of justice and becomes a workaday framework for getting things done—enforcing contracts, ensuring that governments abide by deals, regulating trade and currency relations, and so forth.

Common markets demand a common language, as well as a common currency, and they produce common behaviors of the kind bred by cosmopolitan city life everywhere. Commercial pilots, computer programmers, international bankers, media specialists, oil riggers, entertainment celebrities, ecology experts, demographers, accountants, professors, athletes—these compose a new breed of men and women for whom religion, culture, and nationality can seem only marginal elements in a working identity. Although sociologists of everyday life will no doubt continue to distinguish a Japanese from an American mode, shopping has a common signature throughout the world. Cynics might even say that some of the recent revolutions in Eastern Europe have had as their true goal not liberty and the right to vote but well-paying jobs and the right to shop (although the vote is proving easier to acquire than consumer goods). The market imperative is, then, plenty powerful; but, notwithstanding some of the claims made for "democratic capitalism," it is not identical with the democratic imperative.

The resource imperative. Democrats once dreamed of societies whose political autonomy rested firmly on economic independence. The Athenians idealized what they called autarky, and tried for a while to create a way of life simple and austere enough to make the polis genuinely self-sufficient. To be free meant to be independent of any other community or polis. Not even the Athenians were able to achieve autarky, however: human nature, it turns out, is dependency. By the time of Pericles, Athenian politics was inextricably bound up with a flowering empire held together by naval power and commerce—an empire that, even as it appeared to enhance Athenian might, ate away at Athenian independence and autarky. Master and slave, it turned out, were bound together by mutual insufficiency.

The dream of autarky briefly engrossed nineteenth-century America as well, for the underpopulated, endlessly bountiful land, the cornucopia of natural resources, and the natural barriers of a continent walled in by two great seas led many to believe that America could be a world unto itself. Given this past, it has been harder for Americans than for most to accept the inevitability of interdependence. But the rapid depletion of resources even in a country like ours, where they once seemed inexhaustible, and the maldistribution of arable soil and mineral resources on the planet, leave even the wealthiest societies ever more resource-dependent and many other nations in permanently desperate straits.

Every nation, it turns out, needs something another nation has; some nations have almost nothing they need.

The information-technology imperative. Enlightenment science and the technologies derived from it are inherently universalizing. They entail a quest for descriptive principles of general application, a search for universal solutions to particular problems, and an unswerving embrace of objectivity and impartiality.

Scientific progress embodies and depends on open communication, a common discourse rooted in rationality, collaboration, and an easy and regular flow and exchange of information. Such ideals can be hypocritical covers for power-mongering by elites, and they may be shown to be wanting in many other ways, but they are entailed by the very idea of science and they make science and globalization practical allies.

Business, banking, and commerce all depend on information flow and are facilitated by new communication technologies. The hardware of these technologies tends to be systemic and integrated—computer, television, cable, satellite, laser, fiber-optic, and microchip technologies combining to create a vast interactive communications and information network that can potentially give every person on earth access to every other person, and make every datum, every byte, available to every set of eyes. If the automobile was, as George Ball once said (when he gave his blessing to a Fiat factory in the Soviet Union during the Cold War), "an ideology on four wheels," then electronic telecommunication and information systems are an ideology at 186,000 miles per second—which makes for a very small planet in a very big hurry. Individual cultures speak particular languages; commerce and science increasingly speak English; the whole world speaks logarithms and binary mathematics.

Moreover, the pursuit of science and technology asks for, even compels, open societies. Satellite footprints do not respect national borders; telephone wires penetrate the most closed societies. With photocopying and then fax machines having infiltrated Soviet universities and *samizdat* literary circles in the eighties, and computer modems having multiplied like rabbits in communism's bureaucratic warrens thereafter, *glasnost* could not be far behind. In their social requisites, secrecy and science are enemies.

The new technology's software is perhaps even more globalizing than its hardware. The information arm of international commerce's sprawling body reaches out and touches distinct nations and parochial cultures, and gives them a common face chiseled in Hollywood, on Madison Avenue, and in Silicon Valley. Throughout the 1980s one of the most-watched television programs in South Africa was *The Cosby Show.* The demise of apartheid was already in production. Exhibitors at the 1991 Cannes film festival expressed growing anxiety over the "homogenization" and "Americanization" of the global film industry when, for the third year running, American films dominated the awards ceremonies. America has dominated the world's popular culture for much longer, and much more decisively. In November of 1991 Switzerland's once insular culture boasted best-seller lists featuring *Terminator 2* as the No. 1 movie, *Scarlett* as the No. 1 book, and Prince's *Diamonds and Pearls* as the No. 1 record album. No wonder the Japanese are buying Hollywood film studios even faster than Americans are buying Japanese television sets. This kind of software supremacy may in the long term be far more important than hardware superiority, because culture has become more potent than armaments. What is the power of the Pentagon compared with Disneyland? Can the Sixth Fleet keep up with CNN? McDonald's in Moscow and Coke in China will do more to create a global culture than military colonization ever could. It is less the goods than the brand names that do the work, for they convey life-style images that alter perception and challenge behavior. They make up the seductive software of McWorld's common (at times much too common) soul.

Yet in all this high-tech commercial world there is nothing that looks particularly democratic. It lends itself to surveillance as well as liberty, to new forms of manipulation and covert control as well as new kinds of participation, to skewed, unjust market outcomes as well as greater productivity. The consumer society and the open society are not quite synonymous. Capitalism and democracy have a relationship, but it is something less than a marriage. An efficient free market after all requires that consumers be free to vote their dollars on competing goods, not that citizens be free to vote their values and beliefs on competing political candidates and programs. The free market flourished in junta-run Chile, in military-governed Taiwan and Korea, and, earlier, in a variety of autocratic European empires as well as their colonial possessions.

The ecological imperative. The impact of globalization on ecology is a cliché even to world leaders who ignore it. We know well enough that the German forests can be destroyed by Swiss and Italians driving gas-guzzlers fueled by leaded gas. We also know that the planet can be asphyxiated by greenhouse gases because Brazilian farmers want to be part of the twentieth century and are burning down tropical rain forests to clear a little land to plough, and because Indonesians make a living out of converting their lush jungle into toothpicks for fastidious Japanese diners, upsetting the delicate oxygen balance and in effect puncturing our global lungs. Yet this ecological consciousness has meant not only greater awareness but also greater inequality, as modernized nations try to slam the door behind them, saying to developing nations, "The world cannot afford *your* modernization; ours has wrung it dry!"

Each of the four imperatives just cited is transnational, transideological, and transcultural. Each applies impartially to Catholics, Jews, Muslims, Hindus, and Buddhists; to democrats and totalitarians; to capitalists and socialists. The Enlightenment dream of a universal rational society has to a remarkable degree been realized—but in a form that is commercialized, homogenized, depoliticized, bureaucratized, and, of course, radically incomplete, for the movement toward McWorld is in competition with forces of global breakdown, national dissolution, and centrifugal corruption. These forces, working in the opposite direction, are the essence of what I call Jihad.

JIHAD, OR THE LEBANONIZATION OF THE WORLD

OPEC, the World Bank, the United Nations, the International Red Cross, the multinational corporation . . . there are scores of institutions that reflect globalization. But they often appear as ineffective reactors to the world's real actors: national states and, to an ever greater degree, subnational factions in permanent rebellion against uniformity and integration—even the kind represented by universal law and justice. The headlines feature these players regularly: they are cultures, not countries; parts, not wholes; sects, not religions; rebellious factions and dissenting minorities at war not just with globalism but with the traditional nation-state. Kurds, Basques, Puerto Ricans, Ossetians, East Timoreans, Quebecois, the Catholics of Northern Ireland, Abkhasians, Kurile Islander Japanese, the Zulus of Inkatha, Catalonians, Tamils, and, of course, Palestinians—people without countries, inhabiting nations not their own, seeking smaller worlds within borders that will seal them off from modernity.

A powerful irony is at work here. Nationalism was once a force of integration and unification, a movement aimed at bringing together disparate clans, tribes, and cultural fragments under new, assimilationist flags. But as Ortega y Gasset noted more than sixty years ago, having won its victories, nationalism changed its strategy. In the 1920s, and again today, it is more often a reactionary and divisive force, pulverizing the very nations it once helped cement together. The force that creates nations is "inclusive," Ortega wrote in *The Revolt of the Masses.* "In periods of consolidation, nationalism has a positive value, and is a lofty standard. But in Europe everything is more than consolidated, and nationalism is nothing but a mania. . . ."

This mania has left the post-Cold War world smoldering with hot wars; the international scene is little more unified than it was at the end of the Great War, in Ortega's own time. There were more than thirty wars in progress last year, most of them ethnic, racial, tribal, or religious in character, and the list of unsafe regions doesn't seem to be getting any shorter. Some new world order!

The aim of many of these small-scale wars is to redraw boundaries, to implode states and resecure parochial identities: to escape McWorld's dully insistent imperatives. The mood is that of Jihad: war not as an instrument of policy but as an emblem of identity, an expression of community, an end in itself. Even where there is no shooting war, there is fractiousness, secession, and the quest for ever smaller communities. Add to the list of dangerous countries those at risk: In Switzerland and Spain, Jurassian and Basque separatists still argue the virtues of ancient identities, sometimes in the language of bombs. Hyperdisintegration in the former Soviet Union may well continue unabated—not just a Ukraine independent from the Soviet Union but a Bessarabian Ukraine independent from the Ukrainian republic; not just Russia severed from the defunct union but Tatarstan severed from Russia. Yugoslavia makes even the disunited, ex-Soviet, nonsocialist republics that were once the Soviet Union look integrated, its sectarian fatherlands springing up within factional motherlands like weeds within weeds within weeds. Kurdish independence would threaten the territorial integrity of four Middle Eastern nations. Well before the current cataclysm Soviet Georgia made a claim for autonomy from the Soviet Union, only to be faced with its Ossetians (164,000 in a republic of 5.5 million) demanding their own self-determination within Georgia. The Abkhasian minority in Georgia has followed suit. Even the good will established by Canada's once promising Meech Lake protocols is in danger, with Francophone Quebec again threatening the dissolution of the federation. In South Africa the emergence from apartheid was hardly achieved when friction between Inkatha's Zulus and the African National Congress's tribally identified members threatened to replace Europeans' racism with an indigenous tribal war after thirty years of attempted integration using the colonial language (English) as a unifier, Nigeria is now playing with the idea of linguistic multiculturalism—which could mean the cultural breakup of the nation into hundreds of tribal fragments. Even Saddam Hussein has benefited from the threat of internal Jihad, having used renewed tribal and religious warfare to turn last season's mortal enemies into reluctant allies of an Iraqi nationhood that he nearly destroyed.

The passing of communism has torn away the thin veneer of internationalism (workers of the world unite!) to reveal ethnic prejudices that are not only ugly and deep-seated but increasingly murderous. Europe's old scourge, anti-Semitism, is back with a vengeance, but it is only one of many antagonisms. It appears all too easy to throw the historical gears into reverse and pass from a Communist dictatorship back into a tribal state.

Among the tribes, religion is also a battlefield. ("Jihad" is a rich word whose generic meaning is "struggle"—usually the struggle of the soul to avert evil. Strictly applied to religious war, it is used only in reference to battles where the faith is under assault, or battles against a government that denies the practice of Islam. My use here is rhetorical, but does follow both journalistic practice and history.) Remember the Thirty Years War? Whatever forms of Enlightenment universalism might once have come to grace such historically related forms of monotheism as Judaism, Christianity, and Islam, in many of their modern incarnations they are parochial rather than cosmopolitan, angry rather than loving, proselytizing rather than ecumenical, zealous rather than rationalist, sectarian rather than deistic, ethnocentric rather than universalizing. As a result, like the new forms of hypernationalism, the new expressions of religious fundamentalism are fractious and pulverizing, never integrating. This is religion as the Crusaders knew it: a battle to the death for souls that if not saved will be forever lost.

The atmospherics of Jihad have resulted in a breakdown of civility in the name of identity, of comity in the name of community. International relations have sometimes taken on the aspect of gang war—cultural turf battles featuring tribal factions that were supposed to be sublimated as integral parts of large national, economic, postcolonial, and constitutional entities.

THE DARKENING FUTURE OF DEMOCRACY

These rather melodramatic tableaux vivants do not tell the whole story, however. For all their defects, Jihad and McWorld have their attractions. Yet, to repeat and insist, the attractions are unrelated to democracy. Neither McWorld nor Jihad is remotely democratic in impulse. Neither needs democracy; neither promotes democracy.

McWorld does manage to look pretty seductive in a world obsessed with Jihad. It delivers peace, prosperity, and relative unity—if at the cost of independence, community, and identity (which is generally based on difference). The primary political values required by the global market are order and tranquillity, and freedom—as in the phrases "free trade," "free press," and "free love." Human rights are needed to a degree, but not citizenship or participation—and no more social justice and equality than are necessary to promote efficient economic production and consumption. Multinational corporations sometimes seem to prefer doing business with local oligarchs, inasmuch as they can take confidence from dealing with the boss on all crucial matters. Despots who slaughter their own populations are no problem, so long as they leave markets in place and refrain from making war on their neighbors (Saddam Hussein's fatal mistake). In trading partners, predictability is of more value than justice.

The Eastern European revolutions that seemed to arise out of concern for global democratic values quickly deteriorated into a stampede in the general direction of free markets and their ubiquitous, television-promoted shopping malls. East Germany's Neues Forum, that courageous gathering of intellectuals, students, and workers which overturned the Stalinist regime in Berlin in 1989, lasted only six months in Germany's mini-version of McWorld. Then it gave way to money and markets and monopolies from the West. By the time of the first all-German elections, it could scarcely manage to secure three percent of the vote. Elsewhere there is growing evidence that glasnost will go and perestroika—defined as privatization and an opening of markets to Western bidders—will stay. So understandably anxious are the new rulers of Eastern Europe and whatever entities are forged from the residues of the Soviet Union to gain access to credit and markets and technology—McWorld's flourishing new currencies—that they have shown themselves willing to trade away democratic prospects in pursuit of them: not just old totalitarian ideologies and command-economy production models but some possible indigenous experiments with a third way between capitalism and socialism, such as economic cooperatives and employee stock-ownership plans, both of which have their ardent supporters in the East.

Jihad delivers a different set of virtues: a vibrant local identity, a sense of community, solidarity among kinsmen, neighbors, and countrymen, narrowly conceived. But it also guarantees parochialism and is grounded in exclusion. Solidarity is secured through war against outsiders. And solidarity often means obedience to a hierarchy in governance, fanaticism in beliefs, and the obliteration of individual selves in the name of the group. Deference to leaders and intolerance toward outsiders (and toward "enemies within") are hallmarks of tribalism—hardly the attitudes required for the cultivation of new democratic women and men capable of governing themselves. Where new democratic experiments have been conducted in retribalizing societies, in both Europe and the Third World, the result has often been anarchy, repression, persecution, and the coming of new, noncommunist forms of very old kinds of despotism. During the past year, Havel's velvet revolution in Czechoslovakia was imperiled by partisans of "Czechland" and of Slovakia as independent entities. India seemed little less rent by Sikh, Hindu, Muslim, and Tamil infighting than it was immediately after the British pulled out, more than forty years ago.

To the extent that either McWorld or Jihad has a *natural* politics, it has turned out to be more of an antipolitics. For McWorld, it is the antipolitics of globalism: bureaucratic, technocratic, and meritocratic, focused (as Marx predicted it would be) on the administration of things—with people, however, among the chief things to be administered. In its politico-economic imperatives McWorld has been guided by laissez-faire market principles that privilege efficiency, productivity, and beneficence at the expense of civic liberty and self-government.

For Jihad, the antipolitics of tribalization has been explicitly antidemocratic: one-party dictatorship, government by military junta, theocratic fundamentalism—often associated with a version of the *Führerprinzip* that empowers an individual to rule on behalf of a people. Even the government of India, struggling for decades to model democracy for a people who will soon number a billion, longs for great leaders; and for every Mahatma Gandhi, Indira Gandhi, or Rajiv Gandhi taken from them by zealous assassins, the Indians appear to seek a replacement who will deliver them from the lengthy travail of their freedom.

THE CONFEDERAL OPTION

How can democracy be secured and spread in a world whose primary tendencies are at best indifferent to it (McWorld) and at worst deeply antithetical to it (Jihad)? My guess is that globalization will eventually vanquish retribalization.

The ethos of material "civilization" has not yet encountered an obstacle it has been unable to thrust aside. Ortega may have grasped in the 1920s a clue to our own future in the coming millennium.

Everyone sees the need of a new principle of life. But as always happens in similar crises—some people attempt to save the situation by an artificial intensification of the very principle which has led to decay. This is the meaning of the "nationalist" outburst of recent years. . . . things have always gone that way. The last flare, the longest; the last sigh, the deepest. On the very eve of their disappearance there is an intensification of frontiers—military and economic.

Jihad may be a last deep sigh before the eternal yawn of McWorld. On the other hand, Ortega was not exactly prescient; his prophecy of peace and internationalism came just before blitzkrieg, world war, and the Holocaust tore the old order to bits. Yet democracy is how we remonstrate with reality, the rebuke our aspirations offer to history. And if retribalization is inhospitable to democracy, there is nonetheless a form of democratic government that can accommodate parochialism and communitarianism, one that can even save them from their defects and make them more tolerant and participatory: decentralized participatory democracy. And if McWorld is indifferent to democracy, there is nonetheless a form of democratic government that suits global markets passably well—representative government in its federal or, better still, confederal variation.

With its concern for accountability, the protection of minorities, and the universal rule of law, a confederalized representative system would serve the political needs of McWorld as well as oligarchic bureaucratism or meritocratic elitism is currently doing. As we are already beginning to see, many nations may survive in the long term only as confederations that afford local regions smaller than "nations" extensive jurisdiction. Recommended reading for democrats of the twenty-first century is not the U.S. Constitution or the French Declaration of Rights of Man and Citizen but the Articles of Confederation, that suddenly pertinent document that stitched together the thirteen American colonies into what then seemed a too loose confederation of independent states but now appears a new form of political realism, as veterans of Yeltsin's new Russia and the new Europe created at Maastricht will attest.

By the same token, the participatory and direct form of democracy that engages citizens in civic activity and civic judgment and goes well beyond just voting and accountability—the system I have called "strong democracy"—suits the political needs of decentralized communities as well as theocratic and nationalist party dictatorships have done. Local neighborhoods need not be democratic, but they can be. Real democracy has flourished in diminutive settings: the spirit of liberty, Tocqueville said, is local. Participatory democracy, if not naturally apposite to tribalism, has an undeniable attractiveness under conditions of parochialism.

Democracy in any of these variations will, however, continue to be obstructed by the undemocratic and antidemocratic trends toward uniformitarian globalism and intolerant retribalization which I have portrayed here. For democracy to persist in our brave new McWorld, we will have to commit acts of conscious political will—a possibility, but hardly a probability, under these conditions. Political will requires much more than the quick fix of the transfer of institutions. Like technology transfer, institution transfer rests on foolish assumptions about a uniform world of the kind that once fired the imagination of colonial administrators. Spread English justice to the colonies by exporting wigs. Let an East Indian trading company act as the vanguard to Britain's free parliamentary institutions. Today's well-intentioned quickfixers in the National Endowment for Democracy and the Kennedy School of Government, in the unions and foundations and universities zealously nurturing contacts in Eastern Europe and the Third World, are hoping to democratize by long distance. Post Bulgaria a parliament by first-class mail. Fed Ex the Bill of Rights to Sri Lanka. Cable Cambodia some common law.

Yet Eastern Europe has already demonstrated that importing free political parties, parliaments, and presses cannot establish a democratic civil society; imposing a free market may even have the opposite effect. Democracy grows from the bottom up and cannot be imposed from the top down. Civil society has to be built from the inside out. The institutional superstructure comes last. Poland may become democratic, but then again it may heed the Pope, and prefer to found its politics on its Catholicism, with uncertain consequences for democracy. Bulgaria may become democratic, but it may prefer tribal war. The former Soviet Union may become a democratic confederation, or it may just grow into an anarchic and weak conglomeration of markets for other nations' goods and services.

Democrats need to seek out indigenous democratic impulses. There is always a desire for self-government, always some expression of participation, accountability, consent, and representation, even in traditional hierarchical societies. These need to be identified, tapped, modified, and incorporated into new democratic practices with an indigenous flavor. The tortoises among the democratizers may ultimately outlive or outpace the hares, for they will have the time and patience to explore conditions along the way, and to adapt their gait to changing circumstances. Tragically, democracy in a hurry often looks something like France in 1794 or China in 1989.

It certainly seems possible that the most attractive democratic ideal in the face of the brutal realities of Jihad and the dull realities of McWorld will be a confederal union of semi-autonomous communities smaller than nation-states, tied together into regional economic associations and markets larger than nation-states—participatory and self-determining in local matters at the bottom, representative and accountable at the top. The nation-state would play a diminished role, and sovereignty would lose some of its political potency. The Green movement adage "Think globally, act locally" would actually come to describe the conduct of politics.

This vision reflects only an ideal, however—one that is not terribly likely to be realized. Freedom, Jean-Jacques Rousseau once wrote, is a food easy to eat but hard to digest. Still, democracy has always played itself out against the odds. And democracy remains both a form of coherence as binding as McWorld and a secular faith potentially as inspiriting as Jihad.

*The Republicans say that the key to a strong economy is money in the
hands of rich investors. The Democrats say that we must redistribute money from
the rich to entitlement programs for the poor and middle class. According to the author, neither
model is adequate to the economy of the 1990s and beyond—a world economy in
which the true sources of national wealth are the accrued skills of the work force and the
quality of the social and material infrastructure supporting them*

THE REAL ECONOMY

ROBERT B. REICH

THE CENTRAL TENET OF REPUBLICAN ECO-nomics is that everyone benefits when the rich are allowed to keep more of their income for themselves. Ronald Reagan believed that the benefits of the 1981 tax cut for wealthy Americans would "trickle down" to everyone else. For most of his presidency thus far George Bush has claimed that a lower tax on capital gains (which would benefit the wealthy, who own most of the nation's capital assets) would give a surge of momentum to the economy, and thus help all of us. In contrast, the central tenet of Democratic economics is that this allocation of the tax burden isn't fair. Taxes on the wealthy should be raised, and government should spread the wealth directly, through a myriad of social programs.

The two sides were at a stalemate throughout the 1980s. Taxes on the wealthy stayed low *and* entitlements stayed high (while military expenditures grew), with the result that the federal budget ballooned. In last year's budget agreement both sides conceded a bit: taxes on the rich will rise somewhat (but not anywhere near as high as they were in the late 1970s), and entitlement programs will grow when there is money to finance them. But underlying the compromise—which is more like a truce in an ongoing war—the same choice remains: growth or fairness, private investment or public spending, tax cuts for the rich or entitlements for everyone else. In this contest Republicans continue to represent the brute force of American capitalism, Democrats the softer and more generous side of our natures.

But this isn't the real choice facing Americans as we approach the twenty-first century, and it creates a false picture of where the economy is heading and what must be done. Republican economics is wrong: The success of American capitalism no longer depends on the private investments of highly motivated American capitalists. Our nation's future economic success depends instead on our unique attributes—the skills and insights of our work force, and how well we link those skills and insights to the world economy. The Democratic rejoinder is equally wrongheaded: The government's role is not just to spread the wealth. It is to build our human capital and infrastructure, and to bargain with global capital on our behalf. To prepare us for twenty-first-century capitalism, American economic policy must be adapted to the new realities of the world economy.

Global Capital

AGAIN, REPUBLICANS HAVE IT WRONG. THE IN-vestments of wealthier Americans (who have the wherewithal to save and invest) no longer trickle down to the rest of the American population. Instead, they trickle out to wherever on the globe the best returns can be had. The savings of foreigners, meanwhile, trickle in to find promising projects within the United States. Foreign investments in America rose to a record $2 trillion in 1989, up 12 percent from the year before. Since 1980 foreign capital investment in the United States has increased fourfold. Capital—in the form of loans, shares of stock, and corporate factories, equipment, and research laboratories—moves around the world with scant respect for national boundaries.

Global stock trading is now commonplace. In 1989 Americans poured $13.7 billion into foreign stocks, up

Increasingly, educated brainpower—along with the roads, airports, computers, and fiber-optic cables linking it up—determines a nation's standard of living.

813 percent from 1988. All told, net cross-border equity investments soared to a record $92.3 billion—nearly triple the previous high of $31.7 billion, set in 1986. Such cross-border investments are undertaken quietly; the American investor, assigning his or her savings to a mutual fund, an insurance fund, or a pension plan, may often be unaware of lending to or buying into companies with foreign-sounding names, headquartered in exotic places. But the people who manage the funds, and who compete furiously to achieve higher returns than other fund managers, now scour the globe for investment prospects. **There's a good reason: during the 1980s overseas stocks gained an average of 22 percent a year, calculated in U.S. dollars; U.S. stocks gained 17 percent a year. In a recent survey conducted by Louis Harris & Associates, money managers, traders, and corporate finance officers predicted that nearly a quarter of their trading volume would involve foreign securities by 1995, up from 14 percent today. More than half of the 198 corporate treasurers interviewed predicted that in five years they would be selling bonds, stocks, and commercial paper in overseas markets.**

American capital also leaves the United States in the form of factories, equipment, and laboratories placed in foreign lands by American-owned corporations. Here, too, the reason is that higher profits are often available abroad. Europe is booming in anticipation of 1992's integrated European market. Many East Asian economies continue to expand at a breakneck rate (although not quite so fast as they did). Thus, although profits earned in the United States by American multinational corporations dropped by 19 percent in 1989, the overseas profits of these firms surged by 14 percent. Small wonder that American firms, having increased their capital investments abroad by 13 percent in 1989, expected to increase them still more—by a whopping 17 percent—last year, while increasing their American investments by slightly more than six percent. Hewlett-Packard now designs and makes personal computers in France; Texas Instruments makes a large percentage of its semiconductor chips in Japan; more and more of the automobiles produced by the Big Three are designed and engineered in Germany, Italy, or Japan.

Wealthy Americans may reap high returns from their worldwide investments, but the rest of us enjoy few of the beneficial consequences. With the connections between American capitalists and the American economy thus unraveling, all that remains rooted within our borders is the American *people*.

National Assets

THE ANSWER ISN'T SIMPLY TO TAKE MONEY from the wealthy and spread it around, however, as Democrats often want to do. Even though the investments of individual Americans are becoming disconnected from the American economy, there is a growing connection between the amount and kind of investments we make together as a nation and the capacity of America to attract global capital. Herein the new logic of economic nationalism: the skills and insights of a nation's work force, and the quality of its transportation and communication links to the world (its infrastructure), are what make it unique, and uniquely attractive, in the new world economy. Increasingly, educated brainpower—along with roads, airports, computers, and fiber-optic cables connecting it up—determines a nation's standard of living.

To understand why, it's first necessary to grasp what is happening to the global economy. The highest earnings in most worldwide industries are to be found in locations where specialized knowledge is brought to bear on problems whose solutions define new horizons of possibility. Whether the industry is old or new, mature or high-tech, specialized knowledge is accounting for a larger and larger portion of its revenues. The hottest sector of the tool-and-die-casting industry, for example, produces precision castings out of aluminum and zinc for computer parts. The leading textile businesses depend on the knowledge needed to produce specially coated and finished fabrics for automobiles, office furniture, rain gear, and wall coverings, among a great many other products. The fastest-growing semiconductor firms make microprocessors and customized chips that are tailored to the particular needs of buyers. As computers with standard operating systems become virtually identical, the high profits come from devising software to meet particular user needs.

Traditional services are experiencing the same rapid transformation. The fastest-growing telecommunications services involve specialized knowledge: voice, video, and information processing; the development of "smart buildings," to connect office telephones, computers, and facsimile machines; and running specialized communications networks that link employees in different locations. The fastest-growing trucking, rail, and air-freight businesses meet shippers' needs for specialized pickups and deliveries, unique containers, and worldwide integration of different modes of transportation. The leading financial businesses offer a wide range of interconnected services, including banking, insurance, and investment, tailored to the unique needs of individuals and companies.

These businesses are highly profitable both because customers are willing to pay a premium for goods and services that exactly meet their needs and, more important, because they are knowledge-intensive businesses that cannot easily be duplicated by low-cost competitors elsewhere in the world. Worldwide competition continues to compress profits on anything that is uniform, routine, and standard—that is, on anything that can be made, reproduced, or extracted in volume almost anywhere on the globe. The evidence shows that successful businesses in advanced nations respond to this dynamic by moving toward the higher ground of specialized products and services.

To be sure, successful companies have not entirely jettisoned high-volume, standardized production. Japanese companies, for example, continue to improve their synchronized systems for mass-producing automobiles, video-cassette recorders, and semiconductor chips. And there will always be a lucrative worldwide market for Coca-Cola, blue jeans, and other staples of modern society. But to maintain competitiveness even in mass-produced commodities requires continuous improvement. Japanese cars, VCRs, and computer chips appear in ever greater variety and at ever higher quality; Coca-Cola develops new formulas and products and marketing techniques. Here, as elsewhere, the barrier to entry is not volume or price; it is skill in finding new and ever-more-valuable connections between particular ideas and particular markets.

The Core Skills

LOOK CLOSELY AT THESE HIGH-VALUE BUSInesses and you see three different but related skills that drive them forward. First are the *problem-solving* skills required to put things together in unique ways (be they alloys, molecules, semiconductor chips, software codes, movie scripts, or pension portfolios). Next are the *problem-identifying* skills required to help customers understand their needs and how those needs can best be met by customized products. In contrast to marketing and selling standard commodities—which requires persuading many customers of the virtues of one particular product, taking lots of orders for it, and meeting sales quotas—the key here is to identify new problems to which customized products might be applicable. The art of persuasion is replaced by the identification of opportunity.

Third are the skills needed to link problem-solvers and problem-identifiers. Those with such skills must understand enough about specific technologies and markets to see the potential for a new product, raise whatever money is necessary to launch the project, and assemble the right personnel to solve and identify problems. They play the role of *strategic brokers*.

In the high-value businesses, profits derive not from scale and volume but from an ongoing discovery of connections between the solutions to problems and the identification of new needs. The idea of "goods" as something distinct from "services" has become meaningless, because so much of the value provided by a successful enterprise—in fact, the only value that cannot be easily replicated worldwide—entails services: the specialized research, engineering, design, and production services necessary to solve problems; the specialized sales, marketing, and consulting services necessary to identify problems; and the specialized strategic, financial, and management services necessary to broker the first two. High-value enterprises are in the business of providing such services.

Steelmaking, for example, is becoming a service business. When alloys are molded to a specific weight and tolerance, services account for a significant part of the value of the resulting product. Steel service centers help customers choose the steels and alloys they need, and then inspect, slit, coat, store, and deliver the materials. Computer manufacturers are likewise in the service business, because a larger and larger portion of every consumer dollar goes toward customizing software and then integrating and installing systems around it. The immensely successful IBM personal computer comprised a collection of services—research, design, engineering, sales, maintenance; only about 10 or 15 percent of its purchase price reflects the actual cost of manufacture.

America's arcane system of national accounting still has separate categories for manufacturing and services—classifying, for example, computer software as a service (although it is reproduced like a manufactured item), and a computer as manufactured goods (although an ever-larger portion of its cost lies in services). The pharmaceutical industry is classified under "manufacturing" although production costs represent a tiny fraction of the price of a drug; most costs derive from research and development, clinical trials, patent applications and regulatory clearances, drug marketing, and distribution. Ninety-one percent of the increase in the number of jobs since the 1982 recession was in services, and, remarkably, 73 percent of private-sector employees now work in service businesses. But as the line between services and goods blurs, such numbers are increasingly meaningless—they do not tell us what is actually going on in the economy, and where the real value lies.

A Nation's Key Exports

IT FOLLOWS THAT THE VALUE A NATION'S WORK force adds to the world economy is no longer measurable in terms of products shipped across borders. Increasingly a nation's key exports are the skills involved in solving, identifying, and brokering new problems. Products are becoming composites of global services from many different nations. Consider: A London department-store buyer of high-fashion apparel orders a line of dresses devised by a New York fashion designer. Within an hour of the order the designer sends via satellite the drawings and specifications for making the dresses to a fiber-optic link in Hong Kong, where they appear on a high-resolution computer monitor, ready for a manufacturing engineer to transform them into prototype garments. The prototypes are then reproduced in a Chinese factory. The designer, the engineer, and the factory supervisor conduct a video teleconference to work out details, and the finished garments arrive in London less than six weeks after the order was placed. Here, America "exported" a fashion design and some management services linking the design with the London buyer and the Hong Kong and Chinese technicians.

This sort of trade is hard to pin down. When, as now, traders deal repeatedly with one another across borders—exchanging services that are priced not on an open market but by agreement among divisions of the same global corporation or according to complex employment contracts, profit-sharing agreements, or long-term supply arrangements—determinations about what it is that one nation has paid out to another nation can be no better than fair approximations. Thus trade statistics are notoriously imprecise, subject to wide swings and seemingly inexplicable corrections. The truth is that these days no one knows exactly at any given time whether America's (or any other nation's) international trade is in or out of balance, by how much, or what the significance of an imbalance might be. For the same reason, it's becoming impossible for governments seeking to levy corporate taxes to tell exactly how much of a given product is made where. Peter J. Sprague, the chairman of the American-owned National Semiconductor Corporation, says, "We are using Russian engineers living in Israel to design chips that are made in America and then assembled in Asia." Is it an American product? Who can tell?

The notion that products have national origins is so deeply ingrained that governments, and the publics they represent, are often preoccupied with such things as calibrating trade imbalances and determining corporate taxes—both predicated on subtle measurements and elaborate legal definitions—when they should be concerned about a far more relevant issue: what portion of the value of any given product derives from the ability of the nation's workers to conceptualize problems and solutions?

Why Ownership Matters Less

THE KEY INDUSTRIAL STRUGGLE OF THE LATE nineteenth and the first half of the twentieth century was between those who owned the machines and those who ran them. Each side wanted a larger share of the resulting revenues. American politics reflected this tug-of-war: the Republican Party emerged as the voice of the American industrialist, the Democratic Party as that of the American blue-collar worker. The dominant images of the two parties even today owe much to this struggle.

In the emerging global economy, however, the interests both of laborers and of investors are increasingly subordinated to the interests of those who solve, identify, and broker new problems. This trend has been gathering momentum for several decades. Through the postwar era the wages of U.S. workers engaged in routine production have steadily declined as a percentage of the gross national product, from 11.6 percent in 1949 to approximately 4.6 percent in 1990. During the same interval corporate profits have also diminished as a percentage of the gross national product. In the mid-1960s corporate profits reached 10.98 percent of GNP, and then fell, to 7.48 percent in 1970. Subsequent percentages have been lower at both expansionary heights and recessionary lows. By the end of the 1980s profits claimed only 6.29 percent of GNP.

As the portions of GNP going to routine laborers and to investors have steadily dwindled, the portion going to those who solve or identify problems and those who broker solutions has steadily grown. In 1915 the wages of routine production workers in the typical American manufacturing firm accounted for about 45 percent of the cost of making the product. By 1975 they made up only 25 percent, with most of the remainder going to designers, technicians, researchers, manufacturing engineers, industrial engineers, planners, strategists, financial specialists, accountants, executive officers, lawyers, advertisers, and marketers. Almost 80 percent of the cost of a high-technology item such as a computer is attributable to conceptualizers like these.

The increasing subordination of financial capital to intellectual capital has confused investors. "Owning" a company no longer means what it once did. Members of the accounting profession, not known for public displays of emotion, have fretted openly about the difficulties of informing potential investors about the true worth of enterprises whose value rests in the brains of employees. As intellectual capital continues to displace plant and equipment as the key asset of corporations, shareholders find themselves in an ever more tenuous position, for much of the value of an enterprise can disappear with the departure of key employees. In 1986 General Electric assumed that it had acquired Kidder, Peabody, the financial-services firm. But when GE tried to exert control over its new acquisition, many of Kidder's most highly skilled employees departed for more congenial surroundings.

Certain intellectual assets will remain even after talented employees depart, of course—among them patents and copyrights. But in the emerging economy such distilled intellectual capital often loses its value quickly. After all, patents and copyrights only guard discoveries made at a particular point in time; they do not protect the identification of a specific problem that consumers are eager to solve (for example, how to record television programs for viewing at a more convenient time) or insights gained after the patenting of a given solution (such as that consumers might like a video-cassette recorder to double as a lightweight camcorder). Yet these sorts of discoveries—that a market exists, and that there are various ways to serve it—are often even more valuable than the original patented or copyrighted invention. Problem-solvers, problem-identifiers, and brokers who may have had no part in developing the original product race to exploit the new markets that have been uncovered and stimulated by the discovery. Often, greater rewards flow to quick and clever followers than to brilliant and original inventors. Although legally protected, inventions are rapidly outmoded and replaced.

The steady subordination of financial capital to intellectual capital has confused Americans who worry that foreigners are "buying up" the nation's technological assets. Such worries are usually unfounded. In fact it is often the case that without the foreign money, the intellectual capital that has already accumulated in the United States would not develop further.

Consider two typical American firms that were acquired by foreigners in 1989: Materials Research, a semiconductor-equipment manufacturer whose American owners sold it to Sony after the firm found it impossible to raise money from American investors or to borrow it from American banks; and Arco Solar, sold to Germany's Siemens by Atlantic Richfield, the giant American oil company, which was no longer willing to finance Arco's effort to become the world leader in photovoltaic technology. Superficially it appears that foreigners are running off with two of America's leading-edge technology companies. But look closely at these two firms and you find groups of American problem-solvers and problem-identifiers who have accumulated potentially valuable insights about how to produce highly efficient semiconductor equipment and solar energy, respectively. In acquiring them, the foreign firms have not destroyed this cumulative learning, nor have they enslaved these Americans and shipped them back to Japan and Germany; the American problem-solvers and problem-identifiers have no intention of leaving the United States. That some of the profits now go to investors outside the United States is no cause for great alarm; the assets with the greatest value, commanding the highest return, remain within our borders.

Such cumulative skills and insights, upon which future innovations are based, make up the nation's key technological assets. They will be lost only if insufficiently nurtured and developed, as they might have been in these cases had foreign capital not come to the rescue.

The Virtuous Cycle

IN THE EMERGING ECONOMY OF THE TWENTY-FIRST century only one asset is growing more valuable as it is used: the problem-solving, problem-identifying, and strategic-brokering skills of a nation's citizens. Unlike machinery that gradually wears out, raw materials that become depleted, and patents and copyrights that grow obsolete, the skills and insights that come from discovering new linkages between technologies and needs increase with practice.

The more complex the task, the better preparation it provides for the next, even more complex task. One puzzle leads to another. Assembling just the right combination of technical and marketing skills to develop software for assisting mechanical engineers can help strategic brokers gain insight into what's needed to develop more-complex software for aerospace engineers. Developing and marketing specialty chemicals can lead to developing and marketing high-performance ceramics and single-crystal silicon. And so forth.

Conventional economic theory assumes that a resource gets used up when it is put to work. As it becomes scarce, its price increases; the price rise in turn encourages buyers to conserve the resource and find cheaper substitutes, which ultimately brings the price down again. One of the great advantages of a price system, as all economists will quickly attest, is that it tends to balance itself automatically. But human capital operates according to a different principle. Because people learn through practice, the value of what they do tends to increase as they gain experience. This system is not self-correcting, in the sense that workers who first gain knowledge and insights do not eventually lose whatever premium in price they have commanded in world markets when others catch up with them. Rather, a work force can become steadily more valuable over time as insights lead to other insights.

Thus a virtuous cycle can be set in motion: A work force possessing a good basic education, which can efficiently bring the fruits of its labors to the global economy, can attract global capital for its performance of moderately complex tasks. The experience gained by performing these tasks generates additional on-the-job training and experience, which serve to lure global capital for more-complex activities. As skills build and experience accumulates, the nation's citizens receive more and more from the rest of the world in exchange for their services—which permits them to invest in better schools, transportation, research, and communications systems. As their problem-solving, problem-identifying, and brokering skills grow, and their links with the world steadily improve, their income rises.

But without adequate skills and infrastructure, the relationship can be the opposite—a vicious cycle in which global money and technology are lured only by low wages and low taxes. These enticements in turn make it more difficult to finance adequate education and infrastructure; the jobs available under these conditions provide little on-the-job training or experience pertinent to more-complex jobs in the future. Such a vicious cycle has no natural stopping place. Theoretically it can continue to push wages downward until the citizens of the nation (or region, or city) have a standard of living like that typical of the Third World.

The choice is rarely as stark as this, of course. Virtuous or vicious cycles gather momentum gradually, and often imperceptibly. No one would intentionally choose the vicious cycle, but in the contest for global capital such a choice is sometimes made implicitly. Politicians are everywhere trying to lure the world's capital, like traveling salesmen hawking their wares or carnival barkers pitching their special attractions. Mikhail Gorbachev tells business leaders in Minneapolis about the benefits of investing in the Soviet Union; President Gnassingbe Eyadema, of Togo, courts executives in Atlanta; Governor Bill Clinton sells Japanese business executives on the wonders of Arkansas; Mayor David Dinkins touts New York to European investors. Similar pitches must be made even to hometown investors, lest they take their savings elsewhere. "There is the greatest competition in

Are we able to make large public investments and demand sacrifices of ourselves in order to pay for them? Are we capable of bargaining with global corporations?

the last forty-five years for financial capital," William T. Archey, the international vice-president of the U.S. Chamber of Commerce, told *The Washington Post*. The U.S. Chamber of Commerce is visited every eight to ten days by some foreign delegation seeking investments by American companies.

Some carnival barkers promise skilled workers and world-class infrastructure; others promise low wages. If they want to improve the standard of living of their citizens, they will make the former kind of promise, and they will bargain for the sort of jobs that will give their workers on-the-job training in conceptualizing problems and solutions.

In virtuous cycles low wages are not the central attraction. The average worker in the former West Germany earns a higher hourly wage than the average American, but global capital is nonetheless attracted to Germany by the nation's pool of skilled workers and its first-class transportation and communications facilities. There most non-college-bound young people enter apprenticeship programs, in which they learn technical skills. Germany is already on the way to transforming its modern system of autobahns into "smart" superhighways that can regulate traffic flow by computer. France, another high-wage nation, has provided a videotext system free of charge to all telephone subscribers, has recently launched a computerized library and information bank designed to be accessible from every home, and is aggressively training scientists and engineers. Japan is building a $250 billion fiber-optic network that by the year 2000 will carry video, voice, and data around the nation up to 1,000 times faster than existing networks can. All three of these nations are spending significant sums of money on education, training, and research and development.

The National Bargain

IT IS EASIER TO FORM A VIRTUOUS RELATIONSHIP with global capital if you are a nation strongly committed to economic development—ruled by a benevolent dictator like Singapore's Lee Kuan Yew, dominated by a single political party and an "old boy" oligarchy, as in Japan, or habituated to a form of corporatist planning orchestrated by big banks and major industrial firms, as in Germany. In such countries political power is sufficiently concentrated that substantial resources can be mobilized for education, training, research, and infrastructure—and sacrifices can be elicited from the public in order to make these investments. Moreover, deals can be cut with global corporations—offering subsidies, tax breaks, or access to the national market in exchange for good jobs.

But what of a decentralized and contentious democracy like the United States, which deeply distrusts concentrated power? Apart from war emergencies, are we able to make large public investments and demand sacrifices of ourselves in order to pay for them? Are we capable of bargaining with global corporations?

Much of the responsibility for America's national economic development has fallen by default to states and cities. America bids for global capital through fifty state governments that compete against one another, and thousands of cities and townships, which also compete. Who successfully lures the jobs becomes a matter of state and local pride as well as employment; it may also bear significantly on the future careers of politicians who have pledged to win them. The possibility of establishing a factory in the region sets off a furious auction; a threat to remove one initiates equally impassioned negotiations. All too often these jurisdictions bargain for routine jobs that will be automated out of existence in years to come or else will drift to the Third World. Lacking educated workers and an up-to-date infrastructure, many of our governors and mayors have little to offer except what is euphemistically known as a "good business environment"—meaning low wages, few regulations, low taxes, and generous subsidies.

Forty-three states maintain offices in foreign capitals for the express purpose of bargaining for global capital, according to the National Association of State Development Agencies. Unlike most nations, which have a unified international economic strategy, the United States has dozens—emanating from such places as Little Rock, Arkansas, and Lansing, Michigan. When Chrysler-Mitsubishi's Diamond-Star Motors announced, in 1985, that it would begin assembling automobiles in America, four states (Illinois, Indiana, Michigan, and Ohio) entered the competition. The winner was Illinois, which offered a ten-year package of direct aid and incentives worth $276 million—or about $25,000 for every new job that Mitsubishi planned to create in the state. As the bidding has intensified during the past fifteen years, the incentives have become more generous. In 1977 the state of Ohio induced Honda to build an auto plant there by promising $22 million in subsidies and tax breaks; by 1986 it took a $100 million package from Kentucky for Toyota to create about the same number of jobs there.

The total amount of subsidies and tax breaks flowing to global firms of whatever nationality is much higher than it would be if the United States did its bargaining as a whole, through the federal government. Nations whose constituent parts refrain from internecine battles end up paying far less to lure jobs their way. Although direct comparisons between the United States and other nations are hard to come by, an analogous situation suggests the magnitude of the difference. In seeking the rights to televise the 1988 Olympic Games in Calgary, the Western European nations bid as a whole. In the United States, in contrast, each television network made its own separate bid. The Western European market contains even more people than the U.S. market, with buying power that is at least as great. Nevertheless, because Western Europe negotiated as a whole, it got the rights to televise the Olympics in Europe for $5.7 million. The winning network in the United States paid $309 million to televise the Olympics here.

Disinvestment

EVEN IF AMERICA BARGAINED FOR GLOBAL CAPital as a nation, it would still have difficulty attracting good jobs unless it could offer an educated work force and first-class transportation and communications systems. And here lies a more serious problem. For even as other nations have been increasing their public investments in people and infrastructure, the United States as a *nation* has been cutting back. As the table below shows, federal spending on infrastructure, nondefense research and development, and education has steadily dropped as a proportion of the gross national product from 1980 onward. By 1990 federal investment as a proportion of GNP was lower in each of these categories than it was in 1970. States and cities with large populations of poorer Americans have been hard pressed to make up the difference.

FEDERAL GOVERNMENT INVESTMENT SPENDING
AS A PERCENTAGE OF GNP

	1970	1975	1980	1985	1990
Physical Investment	.97	1.03	1.14	.91	.75
Education	.43	.43	.51	.40	.37
Nondefense R&D (excluding space)	.36	.39	.42	.37	.31

From "The Federal Budget and the Nation's Economic Health," by Charles L. Schultze, in Setting National Priorities *(The Brookings Institution, 1990).*

Consider infrastructure. David Aschauer, an economist at Bates College and formerly a researcher at the Federal Reserve Bank of Chicago, has shown a direct link between America's investments in infrastructure and the productivity of the nation's work force: a one-dollar increase in the stock of public infrastructure adds as much to the productivity of Americans as a four-dollar increase in the stock of business capital. His calculations imply that a one-time increase of $10 billion in the stock of public infrastructure would result in a *permanent* increase of $7 billion in the annual GNP. Aschauer's study has been criticized for being too optimistic; after all, he demonstrates only that public investment and national productivity growth have increased and decreased together, over the same interval of time—not that the one necessarily caused the other. But even accepting the possibility of other explanations for why American productivity growth has slowed, the correlation is striking. The United States began to cut back on public investments just when public investments became uniquely important in the new global economy.

In the early 1960s the United States began building a modern transportation system. Spending on infrastructure at all levels of government then absorbed almost four percent of the nation's GNP; it held that position through the 1960s. That's when we began to build the interstate highway system, for example. The productivity of the American work force soared. But the growth of public spending on the nation's transportation system declined throughout the 1970s, just as our productivity growth declined. Infrastructure spending declined even more sharply in the 1980s, to the point where the nation was spending only two percent of GNP on building and maintaining infrastructure. Hence the specter of collapsing bridges, crumbling highways, and rush-hour traffic jams extending for miles.

Although part of the decline in spending represents a failure to maintain existing infrastructure, spending on new infrastructure has fallen even more dramatically, from 2.3 percent of GNP in 1963 to only one percent in 1989. As Western Europe and Japan lay plans for "smart" roads, high-speed trains, and national information networks, America lies dormant; the nation has not even built a new airport since 1974. As of the beginning of last year Washington was annually investing about the same amount of money in infrastructure (in constant dollars) as it had invested thirty years before, although the gross national product had grown 144 percent in the interim. It is projected that physical capital investment, which accounted for 24 percent of total federal outlays in 1960, will account for less than 11 percent in 1991.

Expenditures on public elementary and secondary education have shown a similarly perverse pattern—falling short just as intellectual capital has become a uniquely important national asset. Many politicians and business leaders (and many ordinary citizens) are quick to claim that the current crisis in public education is unrelated to a lack of public funding. One premise of their argument—that there are many means of improving American schools that do not require large public outlays—is surely correct. Yes, responsibility for teaching needs to be transferred from educational bureaucracies to classroom teachers; and yes, the inculcation of basic skills must be the primary mission of the schools.

Researchers have, however, found that schools with smaller classes and better-paid teachers produce young people who command higher salaries once they join the work force. David Card and Alan Krueger, researchers at Princeton University, studied the education and incomes of a million men born from 1920 to 1949 who attended public schools. They found that even within the same socio-economic group, higher lifetime earnings correlate with smaller class size and better-paid teachers (for every year of schooling above eighth grade, students' subsequent earnings increased 0.4 percent for every five fewer students per teacher, and for every 10 percent hike in teacher salaries, subsequent earnings increased 0.1 percent). The extra tax revenues generated by these higher lifetime incomes alone would finance the smaller classes and better-paid teachers.

Controlled for inflation, public spending on primary and secondary education per student increased during the 1980s, when the nation began to fret openly about the quality of its public schools, but not appreciably faster than it did during the 1970s. From 1970 to 1980 annual spending per student grew 36 percent in real terms; since 1980 it has grown 38 percent.

Yet there are several reasons for believing that the more recent increases have been inadequate. First is the comparative measure of what other nations are spending. By the late 1980s America's per-pupil expenditures were below per-pupil expenditures (converted to dollars using 1988 exchange rates) in eight other nations—namely, Sweden, Norway, Japan, Denmark, Austria, West Germany, Canada, and Switzerland. (Even using the exchange rate from 1985, when the dollar was at its height relative to other currencies, the United States is still behind—but in fourth place rather than ninth.)

International comparisons aside, it is true that the demands on public education in the United States have grown significantly during the past fifteen years. Increasing numbers of broken homes, single-parent households, and immigrants (both legal and illegal) have placed great strains on our schools, particularly in poor inner-city and rural areas. And with one out of five American children now falling below the poverty line—a significantly higher proportion than obtained fifteen years ago—the challenges are magnified. As for today's teachers, their wages have barely risen in real terms since the early 1970s—and yet talented women today have many more lucrative career options than teaching, and we also want to attract talented men to the profession.

Ironically, the schools facing the biggest social problems have been getting the least help. The averaging of figures on per-pupil expenditures in the United States disguises growing disparities among states and school districts. As federal support for elementary and secondary education has waned and states and localities have been forced to pick up the bill, the burden has fallen especially heavily on the poorest jurisdictions with the most limited tax bases. New Trier High School, in one of Chicago's most affluent suburbs, pays its teachers 34 percent more than the average teacher in Chicago's public high schools, whose pedagogic challenges are substantially greater. Public schools in White Plains and Great Neck, two of the richest suburbs of New York, spend twice as much per pupil as schools in the Bronx. (The first set of students in each of these comparisons is on the way to a virtuous relationship with global capital, the second set to a vicious one.)

In 1965 the nation decided that all students who qualified to attend college should have access to higher education. Here again, public investment ranked high on the nation's agenda. The resulting Higher Education Act established a system of grants and loan guarantees for low-income students, thus increasing their proportion even at private universities, from 22 to 26 percent by the mid-1970s. But by 1988, with grants and loan guarantees drying up, the proportion of low-income students at private universities had fallen below 20 percent. The high costs of higher education have helped to push them out and set them on their way toward a vicious relationship with global capital. (In the compromise 1991 budget federal funds for student aid will increase 10 percent for the academic year 1991–1992, but the prospect for the following year looks grim.) Meanwhile, in an equally ominous development, the federal retreat from higher education is being replicated at the state level. The rate of increase in state support for higher education dropped to a thirty-year low in 1990, representing the smallest increment since data on this subject have been collected. State universities have long promoted mobility among children of less affluent families. These data suggest that in future there will be less mobility. Even high schoolers safely in the middle class are being squeezed out of college. From 1982 to 1989, while the proportion of American middle-income families ($40,000 to $60,000) dropped five percent, the proportion of middle-income students in public universities dropped 10 percent.

Federal support for research and development (excluding defense and space) has also languished; it now accounts for 0.31 percent of GNP, the smallest proportion in twenty years. Corporate America hasn't filled the gap. All told, nondefense R&D accounts for two percent of GNP in the United States, compared with almost three percent in Japan and 2.6 percent in the former West Germany. We have sacrificed, as a consequence, not breakthrough discoveries (which, after all, are almost immediately shared in by the scientific community and corporations worldwide) but the know-how and experience that come from *doing* current research.

While Western Europe, Japan, and many developing nations are ensuring that their scientists and engineers are ready to embrace the microelectronic and molecular technologies of the future, America is squandering its scientific and engineering brainpower. Federal funding of university research dropped 18 percent in real terms from 1967 to 1990. The National Science Foundation's 1990 budget for most small research projects in mathematics, physics, chemistry, engineering, biology, and computer science—the seed corn of science—fell below even that for 1988. Steven Younger, of the Los Alamos National Laboratory, told *The New York Times*, "The foundation of university science is dying."

Federal funding to train and retrain workers, meanwhile, dropped by more than 50 percent during the 1980s, from $13.2 billion to $5.6 billion. Most other industrialized nations—including Germany, France, Britain, and Japan—devote a much higher percentage of their GNP to workplace training. Private training, the costs of which corporations deduct from their taxable incomes, has hardly made up the difference. American companies claim to spend some $30 billion a year training their employees, but most of these funds have been used on what is euphemistically termed "executive training." College graduates are 50 percent more likely to be trained by their corporations than are high school graduates, and employees with postgraduate degrees are 30 percent more likely than college graduates. Those who lack a rudimentary educational background receive little compensatory training from the private sector.

Can We Afford It?

THE OFFICIAL REASON GIVEN FOR WHY AMERICA cannot invest more money in infrastructure, education, research, and training is that we cannot afford it. In his inaugural address George Bush noted regretfully, "We have more will than wallet." It has become a frequent lament. But only excessive politeness constrains one from inquiring, Whose will? Whose wallet?

The claim that America cannot afford to invest any more money than it does in the future productivity of its citizens is a curious one, to say the least. Americans are not overtaxed. In 1989 we paid less in taxes as a percentage of GNP (about 30 percent) than the citizens of any other industrialized country. Wealthy Americans, in particular, are not overtaxed. Their marginal income-tax rate is the lowest top tax rate in any industrialized nation. Nor does the U.S. government overspend. If defense is excluded from the calculation, the combined spending of state, local, and federal government accounts for a smaller share of GNP in America than in any other industrialized country, including Japan.

This nation was willing to dig deep into its wallet to rebuild Western Europe and Japan after the Second World War. Now, with an economy four times as large as it was

then, we should be able to rebuild America. Bush has it backward: We have the wallet. What we lack is the will. Republicans do not want taxes on the wealthy raised; Democrats do not want entitlement programs diminished for the middle class. As a result, less and less is left over for public investment.

The current debate between Republicans and Democrats over economic growth or fairness obscures the real issue, which is how much we are willing to invest in the future productivity of Americans. Each year the American economy generates about $5 trillion worth of goods and services. If we dedicated only four percent of this sum—about $200 billion a year—to public investment

In his inaugural address George Bush noted regretfully, "We have more will than wallet." Bush has it backward: We have the wallet. What we lack is the will.

during the 1990s, the nation could get ready for the twenty-first century.

Where would the money come from? First: a more progressive income tax. During each of the past few years American citizens have had about $3,500 billion to spend, after taxes. About half this sum has gone to the lower four fifths of wage earners, the other half to the top fifth. Were the personal income tax as progressive as it was even as late as 1977, in 1989 the top tenth would have paid $93 billion more in taxes than they did. At that rate, from 1991 to 2000 they would contribute close to a trillion dollars more, even if their incomes failed to rise.

Second: limiting entitlements to those who need them. If there were no cap on the income on which the pension and disability portions of Social Security payroll taxes are levied, and if all Social Security benefits were treated as taxable income, another $600 billion would be freed during the decade.

Third: defense cuts. If defense spending were to fall during the decade by 15 percent (a fairly modest, and by most accounts realistic, decrease, even considering the cost of policing regional conflicts in the Middle East and elsewhere), we would have an additional $450 billion. A strong national economy is more important to our national security than troops and weapons.

The grand total: more than $2 trillion for the 1990s—to say nothing of all the savings that could be achieved by bargaining with global capital through the federal government instead of the states and cities. This sum would constitute a significant down payment on the future productivity of *all* Americans. The $2 trillion should be spent on education (at all levels), training, research, and infrastructure. It should *not* be used to reduce the budget deficit. Contrary to what many in government and much of the public assumes, there is nothing wrong with being indebted so long as the borrowings are invested in means of enhancing our future wealth. In fact, taking on debt for this purpose is preferable to maintaining a balanced budget by deferring or cutting back on such investments. Debt is a problem only if the borrowings are squandered on consumption. Any competent business person understands the soundness of this principle: If necessary, you borrow in order to invest in the greater future productivity of your enterprise. Once the new levels of productivity are achieved, they enable you to pay back the debt and enjoy higher returns thereafter.

To be sure, we have already engaged in a consumption frenzy, in the 1980s; can we afford to embark on a new era of investment off this base of indebtedness? The question should be reversed: Can we afford not to? Our future capacity both to pay off the debt and to assure our children and grandchildren a high standard of living depends largely on the public investments we make today—a principle that we have irresponsibly neglected over the past decade. The long-term case is compelling. But even as a short-term anti-recession strategy, increasing public investment makes sense.

Politicians and business leaders are quick to concede the central importance of national economic strength, but they fail to comprehend the new basis of that strength, which is to an ever greater extent public investments in work-force skills and infrastructure. "Increased economic strength is . . . fundamental to success in the global competition with rising economic superpowers," the Bush Administration noted, correctly, in its 1991 budget submission to Congress. "Thus, there is a first-order issue for the budget (and the economic policy it represents): How can it best preserve and build upon America's strengths, while advancing the American economy toward even greater capacities for leadership and growth?" Having asked the right question, Bush's budget wizards got the answer wrong. They advocated public parsimony—sometimes outright cuts—in infrastructure, education, training, and related public endeavors, accompanied by reductions in the tax rate for capital gains. "National economic strength" was tacitly equated with the savings and investments of individual Americans. Further, the Administration has signaled that whatever savings result from smaller defense outlays should be used to cut the budget deficit and, if possible, reduce taxes, rather than be invested in good schools, roads, and other forms of public capital.

Yet the national wealth no longer depends, as it once did, on the accumulation of financial capital in American hands. It depends on the development of the skills and insights of our citizens, and on the infrastructure necessary to link them to the new world economy. The Democrats have displayed almost as little insight on this point as have the Republicans. In the final budget compromise of last October the Democrats carefully insulated Social Security benefits from future cuts by removing the entire program from budget calculations, and barely touched Medicare. As a result, these programs for the elderly will account for the only real growth in domestic spending to occur between now and the year 2000. But what about the nation's future productivity? As part of the same compromise, the total of public investments in education, training, research and development, and infrastructure will be frozen at the 1991 level, adjusted for inflation. (Slight increases for several of these programs in 1991 will be offset by cuts in 1992.) It was further agreed that any additional revenues from tax increases would be used only to expand entitlements or to reduce the budget deficit.

A message for Republicans and Democrats alike: Stop fighting over how much money government is taking from the wealthy and redistributing to everyone else. Start worrying about the capacity of Americans to add value to the emerging global economy. What we own is coming to be far less important than what we are able to do.

PROBLEMS THAT GROW BIGGER AND BIGGER

Big Messes

Kenneth W. Hunter

Kenneth W. Hunter is a senior faculty member of the Training Institute, U.S. General Accounting Office, 441 G Street, N.W., Washington, D.C. 20548. He is also treasurer of the World Future Society and co-editor of *Futures Research Quarterly*.

World War II left the United States with a storehouse of technology ready for use, an underemployed labor force, a huge pent-up economic demand, and no strong economic competitors in the global marketplace. Under these conditions, the United States was launched forward on a massive wave of economic growth that did not begin to lose its force until the 1970s. The events that signaled this turning point are all familiar: Vietnam, Watergate, the end of the Bretton Woods agreement, Nixon's opening to China, the entry of Japan Inc. into the global marketplace, and the rise of OPEC.

These events have put Americans into a state of shock and denial. U.S. leaders and citizens alike have been denying that these changes are significant and that they require changes in our own behavior. Only in the past few months have events forced the United States to examine the nature of the major shifts taking place in the world, and so far that examination has been very superficial. The majority of Americans remain focused on their own needs and desires, continuing the high-consumption lifestyle that they can now maintain only through credit and sales of assets. Little or no attention is paid to the future.

What's been going on in Washington all the while? Not much. The electorate is denying that serious problems exist, and the political consensus basically favors the policies that were created between the 1930s and the 1960s. So the nation's elected representatives have a mandate only to oversee the administration of government operations and to maintain the status quo by making the marginal changes required by external forces.

TODAY'S ISSUES HAVE BECOME "BIG MESSES," WHICH SHARE THREE COMMON CHARACTERISTICS: THEY'RE GLOBAL, CROSS-CUTTING, AND LONG TERM.

Lacking any big assignments, they have taken on many little assignments, mostly on behalf of individual constituents and special-interest groups.

From Issues to Big Messes

As the decades of denial have rolled on, the imbalances and conflicts we generally call "issues" have grown into big messes. These messes share several characteristics. One is longevity: It took years of neglect to create the big messes that exist in the environment, in drug addiction and the illegal industry that supports it, in the nation's financial institutions, in its education system, in infrastructure, and in housing. Again and again, technical analysts and auditors have reported internally on deteriorating conditions, but policy officials failed to take action at a time when the needed corrections would have been easier and cheaper to make than they are now or will be in the future.

This pattern of neglect appeared in both the savings-and-loan industry and the weapons-production industry. The thrift industry began deteriorating after the laws regulating it were changed in the early 1980s. By 1985, the U.S. General Accounting Office (GAO) had assessed the industry's condition and alerted Congress that the industry had problems with the quality of its assets as well as with interest rates. It took four more years for the situation to get bad enough that any action was taken.

In the case of the nuclear weapons production industry, by the early 1980s GAO had reported that the federal government's nuclear facilities had safety and health problems and that the Department of Energy's oversight was inadequate. GAO discovered more and more problems as the 1980s progressed; it continued to report on them and to increase its estimates of the cleanup costs. As these estimates passed the $100-billion mark — nearly a decade after GAO began examining the problems — the issue finally got onto the nation's policy agenda. The search for solutions is now under way.

I expect the same pattern of events to emerge in other areas during the 1990s. Major water-supply systems will continue to deteriorate and may collapse. The existing system of financial markets will be increasingly unable to effectively handle the global flow of transactions in stocks and commodities while at the same time serving as the primary source of capital financing. Health care in inner cities and rural communities will keep deteriorating, and there will be increased conflict among those who provide services, as well as those who finance services, consumers, and regulators, with no real mechanism for resolving these disputes. Environmental damage will continue, and it may become clear that some of this damage is not reversible and that the world must adapt to permanently deteriorated living conditions. In addition, there will be the wild cards — problems that we cannot foresee today.

Besides longevity, the big messes are alike in being global in scope. Political borders have proven almost irrelevant to the flow of pollution, communications, money and credit, technology, weapons, and migrants.

A third characteristic of the big messes is that they are also cross-cutting: Such problems as the trade deficit, the underclass, and the deterioration of the nation's infrastructure don't fit into the prescribed domains of existing legislative committees, executive departments,

> **"AMERICANS GENERALLY HAVE A BASIC OPTIMISM, A PENCHANT FOR HIGHLIGHTING GOOD NEWS AND DENYING INDICATIONS OF PROBLEMS."**

academic disciplines, industry associations, or long-established interest groups, so they are automatically kicked upstairs and become the responsibility of the leadership.

Fighting Shortsighted Optimism

Unfortunately, America's political institutions have great difficulty dealing with issues that are long term, global, or cross-cutting. Americans generally have a basic optimism, a penchant for highlighting good news and denying indications of problems. Americans also tend to be shortsighted, favoring actions that have short-term benefits and long-term costs and opposing actions whose initial costs are clearly defined but whose benefits are unclear or off in the future. For example, the compromise strategy to address the savings-and-loan crisis was crafted to fit the industry's immediate needs and the government's immediate budgetary constraints; it will be up to future generations to pay off the long-term debts that are being incurred to cover payments to individuals who had money in the failed institutions.

Similarly, a natural protectionist bias emerges in any issue that involves international relationships. Jobs for American workers automatically become a major factor to be considered. If the issue is aid to developing countries, the question is, "How much of it will be used to buy goods and services from U.S. suppliers?" If the issue is intellectual property rights, the question is, "How can we protect the rights of Americans who hold pat-

ents, trademarks, or copyrights?" If the issue is the structure of regional trade arrangements, such as those emerging in Europe and Asia, the question is, "How can U.S. companies be guaranteed access to these markets?"

The fact that the issues tend to be cross-cutting brings out the worst bureaucratic instincts of even the best-intentioned people. All the issues tend to be forced onto top leaders, who must deal with petty bickering as well as substantive problems. For instance, to address the nation's drug-abuse problem it became necessary to install a new White House official with a strong personality who could coordinate the wide array of actions under way in law enforcement, the military, foreign diplomacy, and health and social services. Each sector has its own view of the problem and its own approach — a situation that, if not handled skillfully, can become totally chaotic.

Despite these impediments to real progress on major problems, people continue to seek elected office in the United States. But they have learned to keep their campaigns free of any real examination of the big messes, which cannot be discussed in 20-second sound bites and about which people really don't want to hear anything, anyway. Not having campaigned for any substantive policy changes, elected officials have no mandate for advocating such changes or for even raising fundamental questions. Their only mandate is to seek marginal changes that will make the problems go away for now. So that's basically what Washington has been up to.

Looking to the 1990s

How long can the United States continue to avoid these unresolved issues while other countries have accepted the need for action and begun the process of reform? How might the dynamics of public policy in the United States change in the 1990s? What might trigger such a change?

It appears that America can maintain its addiction to high consumption and low investment as long as the Japanese and Germans are willing to accept U.S. credits and to defer their own consumption. Both countries have been content to do so, until recently when Japanese interest rates began rising and reunified Germany became involved in reviving the former East German economy. Certainly some change in America's relationships with those two countries now seems inevitable: Sooner or later the World-War-II residue of fear and suspicion must be confronted, and this decade seems likely to see some restructuring of global military relationships. But it's difficult to say whether such a restructuring would result in a major reduction of the U.S. share of the defense bill in the Far East and Europe, or in Japan and Germany increasing their militaries beyond narrowly defined defensive forces. Neither Japan nor Germany seems likely to force these issues anytime soon, since they are sensitive domestically and could create a great deal of conflict.

So one must look elsewhere for forces that might drive the United States to change its behavior and its policies. What about the American people? In general, there seems to be little interest in how the government operates or in the processes of change. The individuals who will have to pay the bills for the country's current excesses, and whose standard of living will as a result be lower than that of their counterparts in Germany and Japan, are now too young to vote or else don't vote in large numbers. Therefore, they are not likely to force change through the electoral process — but they would be quick to take their protests into the streets if some event pushed them beyond their threshold of tolerance.

What else might trigger change? Existing businesses and interest groups have invested so much time and energy in gaining influence in the current system that they are among the strongest advocates of maintaining the status quo. Entrepreneurs are too few and too detached from the policy process to have much impact on it. And the majority of people in political leadership positions developed their values and approaches to public

NEW YORK STOCK EXCHANGE

policy during the boom years. The president and most of the congressional leaders started their work in public office well before the major changes of the late 1960s and early 1970s. Back then, leading and legislating — designing and implementing new programs — were fun.

Today's leaders still remember the good old days and seem to resent the politics of limits and survival. They seem to be having as much trouble as the public in accepting that changes need to be made.

Stock markets seem to have become detached from the real economy. They dropped substantially in 1987 without affecting the economy in any major way, author Hunter says. A recession might be rationalized as inevitable after so many years of growth and so would not spur fundamental changes in economic policy.

Crisis as Catalyst

Major changes can always be triggered by crises. But what kind of crisis might bring such change in the 1990s? Sudden military threats still have the capacity to ef-

169

fect rapid change, as the Iraqi invasion of Kuwait has demonstrated. But in the post-Cold-War era, the conflicts that endure are increasingly being shifted to the agendas of international organizations. A stock-market crash? The stock markets seem to have become detached from the real world of investment and the economy: The market can drop substantially without affecting the economy in any major way. A severe recession? A recession as severe as that of 1982 could be rationalized as inevitable after so many years of growth. How about the collapse of a major system — such as a communications system, air-traffic control, the water supply to a major city, or an energy supply — that would cause serious economic and social disruption? These systems are so decentralized that they would deteriorate rather than collapse completely. Therefore, the impact of a system's deterioration would be local and varied.

If there is no triggering event to make the United States examine its behavior and its consequences, the nation will have great difficulty cleaning up the big messes and will miss some big opportunities. The United States will continue its slide downward relative to other nations that are conserving, saving and investing, and strengthening their long-term economic capabilities.

In addition, the consequences of long-term neglect of crucial problems will begin to mount up. Employers will continue to encounter new entrants into the labor market who lack the skills to become effective workers. Environmental damage will continue to lower living conditions. Homeless, drug-addicted, mentally ill, and unskilled individuals will continue to live below the safety net; some of them will continue to resort to drugs and crime as escapes, however temporary, from their hopeless lives.

As the decade drifts on, the American people's threshold of tolerance for relative discomfort may be approached or even passed. Parents will become troubled that they cannot be sure their children's living standard will be higher than theirs was; many will conclude that it will be lower. It will become more

---

"TODAY'S LEADERS . . . SEEM TO BE HAVING AS MUCH TROUBLE AS THE PUBLIC IN ACCEPTING THAT CHANGES NEED TO BE MADE."

Soil erosion—another long-term and avoidable problem—can permanently degrade land if not curbed and can cause silting of rivers downstream.

apparent that the entry of women into the labor market since the early 1970s was not just a matter of choice but was in many cases the only way for families to make ends meet. People will become aware that the Japanese and the Europeans are living better than Americans are — and they'll wonder how that could have happened. The United States has demonstrated a high tolerance for ineffectiveness and inefficiency, but one has to believe that at some point there's a limit.

The mounting level of concern will probably translate into a shift in voter attitudes and expectations. The campaigns for the 1992 or 1996 elections may begin to address questions about the future and about the changes that need to be implemented now to make that future better for the American people and their children. Interestingly, most of today's leaders who got their starts in the good old boom days will be out of active politics. The debates will be among candidates who entered politics during the last turning point — the 1968-1973 period — when they ran for office as environmentalists, anti-Vietnam-War advocates, and post-Watergate political reformers. They gained office because, for that very brief period, voters were hungry for real reforms. Some of these representatives fought for those reforms, but as their constituents' hunger for change has dissipated, they have settled for marginal adjustments, quick fixes, and numbers games year after year. How these politicians handle shifts in voter attitudes and shape them into mandates for real change will be one of the critical variables in this decade's political landscape. My hunch is that enough of them will take advantage of the opportunity to launch a real reform effort.

Such a grass-roots-driven modernization movement would include an array of policy changes. It could be directed at creating a government that is not just smaller, as the budget deficit dictates, but that is also smarter. In other words:

● A sharp reduction in subsidies to obsolete and inefficient producers.
● A big investment in education and training, in infrastructure, science, and technology — but with a focus on modernization.
● Revisions in accounting and financial practices that would force current producers and consumers to pay for the costs of environmental cleanup and protection rather than passing them on to future generations.
● Restructuring of organizations, simplification of computer software, and widespread training so that there will finally be some real benefits from the massive investments that have been made to bring

> ## "THE UNITED STATES [CANNOT] SAIL THROUGH THE 1990s WITHOUT BEING AFFECTED BY THE STORM OF CHANGE OCCURRING AROUND IT."

computer technology into the workplace.

● Creating information services that cut through the information glut (which makes managing more difficult than ever) and enable people to see and deal with problems effectively.
● A new social contract that reflects the realities of the two-earner family.
● A shift in the formal and continuing education of the nation's leaders that emphasizes global, long-term, and cross-cutting ways of thinking rather than the currently prevalent short-term, narrow, discipline-based approaches.
● An acceptance of the constant need to monitor changes occurring in the world so that normal problems can be dealt with before they become big messes that can be fixed only through herculean efforts.

Unfortunately, to anticipate that such a transformation could take place quickly and directly is wishful thinking. I do not believe that the United States can sail through the 1990s without being affected by the storm of change occurring around it. How would the nation respond if the Japanese and Germans really acted like its bankers (which they are) and began dictating the terms of U.S. fiscal, monetary, and industrial policies? How would it respond to widespread wars throughout Africa and the Middle East that included the use of tactical nuclear, chemical, and biological weapons? How would it respond to the accidental detonation of a single nuclear weapon? How would it respond if the AIDS virus threatened to spread broadly among the white, heterosexual, non-intrave-

nous-drug-using population? How would it respond to evidence that environmental damage in some parts of the world might take hundreds of years to reverse and that millions of people should be relocated? How would it respond to a really big earthquake — much bigger than the one that hit San Francisco in 1989?

In my opinion, the United States has not prepared well for such contingencies. So far, however, it has been exceptionally lucky, and it has become fairly good at managing crises — at least one at a time. Therefore, it seems likely that the 1990s will not see a cataclysm but rather a long, drawn-out process of gradual change. The country's bankers in Tokyo and Frankfurt will continue to support it, and over the course of the decade the nation will face several discrete and reasonably manageable crises.

This is about as optimistic as I can be. Of course, there is always the threat that the nation's luck could fail and that several crises could converge at once, overwhelming its leaders and political institutions and forcing major changes under adverse conditions, as in the 1930s.

Actions Today

The United States should follow a basic strategy of keeping the current big messes from getting totally out of hand and of acting on opportunities whenever possible. As it makes policy decisions in pursuit of this strategy, three simple, overarching ideas can serve as "guiding principles."

The first need is a way of thinking about and acting on problems that is global, long term, and crosscutting — to match the nature of the big messes. The second need is to keep in mind that education and training are the keys to success, so when in doubt the country should invest more in learning. The third need is to hold elected leaders personally accountable for managing change in society — for the results both of their actions and of their decisions not to take action.

The need to develop new ways of thinking — my first guiding principle — is critical. The solutions to problems do not lie in the traditional, narrowly defined boxes such as academic disciplines, but in the gaps between them. The flexibility, capacity, and know-how to take the ideas from one box and merge them with those from another are needed. Information systems and reporting procedures that highlight problems before they become big messes are needed. Today, America learns by trial and error — a risky and time-consuming process that requires a long-term perspective and a lot of patience.

Consider, for example, the restructuring of European political, military, and economic relationships that is now going on. This appears to be one of the most complex sets of social changes ever undertaken. One of its remarkable features is that the leaders who are guiding the reform process seem to be attempting to respond in moderation to each other and to each new phase of the situation. This contrasts sharply with the traditional process of change through war or revolution, with whoever wins getting to redesign the social and political institutions. Most individuals involved in Europe's current transition seem to understand that they have made a major shift to a new set of rules and that they are now at the very frontiers of social change, where each day's events must be evaluated to plan the next day's actions. In other words, Europeans are now fully engaged in creating their own future.

The second of my guiding principles for the 1990s — that education is of paramount importance — touches on all areas of U.S. life. Why is learning so important? For the individual, it creates more choices about what kind of work one does and for whom one works, about how one spends one's leisure time, and about how one deals with the growing complexities of everyday life. For employers and for the economy, learning determines the quality of the work force and the company's — or the nation's — relative competitiveness in the marketplace. For society, learning affects the diversity and quality of the organizations, products, and services that are available. For the polity, it sets the electorate's intellectual level and degree of participation, the quality of the candidates, and the richness of the policy choices that are laid out. My approach would be to build into all education programs not only a core of basic knowledge, but also a set of skills that would enable people to keep learning new material and solving new problems throughout their lives.

The third of my guiding principles — that the leader of any type of organization needs to know how to manage change — is likely to become more and more important as the major transitions occurring in the world continue to unfold. Leaders tend to spend most of their time juggling the many current issues — the problems and opportunities — that must be dealt with if their organizations are to operate smoothly and perform a societal function effectively. A leader's job is to understand the forces that are driving the need for change; to sort out those issues that require fundamental change from those that call for only marginal adjustments; to have a sense of the organization's capacity to tolerate shocks and stress and to respond to crises and challenges; to jettison the formula approaches — such as the indexing of benefits to inflation — that have substituted for decision making in the past few decades; and to manage both fundamental and marginal changes in such a way that the short-term and long-term strategies are consistent and mutually reinforcing and comprise a clear and coherent vision of the organization's future.

Although I'm frustrated sometimes by the slow pace at which America deals with the big messes and potential opportunities, each day I read about people and organizations that are taking outstanding and innovative actions along the lines I've advocated here. I am encouraged that, in some places at least, new strategies and techniques are being implemented. I have to hope that these developments will spread and that from the ranks of doers and thinkers will emerge the leaders needed for the nation to navigate safely into the twenty-first century.

FROM OUAGADOUGOU TO CAPE CANAVERAL:
WHY THE BAD NEWS DOESN'T TRAVEL UP

Charles Peters

Charles Peters is editor-in-chief of The Washington Monthly.

Everyone is asking why the top NASA officials who decided to launch the fatal Challenger flight had not been told of the concerns of people down below, like Allan McDonald and the other worried engineers at Morton Thiokol.

In the first issue of *The Washington Monthly*, Russell Baker and I wrote, "In any reasonably large government organization, there exists an elaborate system of information cutoffs, comparable to that by which city water systems shut off large water-main breaks, closing down, first small feeder pipes, then larger and larger valves. The object is to prevent information, particularly of an unpleasant character, from rising to the top of the agency, where it may produce results unpleasant to the lower ranks.

"Thus, the executive at or near the top lives in constant danger of not knowing, until he reads it on Page One some morning, that his department is hip-deep in disaster."

This seemed to us to be a serious problem for government, not only because the people at the top didn't know but because the same system of cut-offs operated to keep Congress, the press, and the public in the dark. (Often it also would operate to keep in the dark people within the organization but outside the immediate chain of command—this happened with the astronauts, who were not told about the concern with the O-rings.)

I first became aware of this during the sixties, when I worked at the Peace Corps. Repeatedly I would find that a problem that was well-known by people at lower and middle levels of the organization, whose responsibility it was, would be unknown at the top of the chain of command or by anyone outside.

The most serious problems of the Peace Corps had their origins in Sargent Shriver's desire to get the organization moving. He did not want it to become mired in feasibility studies, he wanted to get volunteers overseas and into action fast. To fulfill his wishes, corners were cut. Training was usually inadequate in language, culture, and technical skills. Volunteers were selected who were not suited to their assignments. For example, the country then known as Tanganyika asked for surveyors, and we sent them people whose only connection with surveying had been holding the rod and chain while the surveyor sighted through his gizmo. Worse, volunteers were sent to places where no job at all awaited them. These fictitious assignments were motivated sometimes by the host official's desire to please the brother-in-law of the president of the United States and sometimes by the official's ignorance of what was going on at the lower levels of his own bureaucracy.

But subordinates would not tell Shriver about the problems. There were two reasons for this. One was fear. They knew that he wanted action, not excuses, and they suspected that their careers would suffer if he heard too many of the latter. The other reason was that they felt it was their job to solve problems, not burden the boss with them. They and Shriver shared the view expressed by Deke Slayton, the former astronaut, when he was asked about the failure of middle-level managers to tell top NASA officials about the problems they were encountering:

"You depend on managers to make a decision based on the information they have. If they had to transmit all the fine detail to the top people, it wouldn't get launched but once every ten years."

The point is not without merit. It is easy for large organizations to fall into "once every ten years" habits. Leaders who want to avoid that danger learn to set goals and communicate a sense of urgency about meeting them. But what many of them never learn is that once you set those goals you have to guard against the tendency of those down below to spare you not only "all the fine detail" but essential facts about significant problems.

For instance, when Jimmy Carter gave the Pentagon the goal of rescuing the Iranian hostages, he relied on the chain of command to tell him if there were any problems. So he did not find out until after the disaster at Desert One that the Delta Commandos thought the Marine pilots assigned to fly the helicopters were incompetent.

In NASA's case chances have been taken with the shuttle from the beginning—the insulating thermal tiles had not gone through a reentry test before the first shuttle crew risked their lives to try them out—but in recent years the pressure to cut corners has increased markedly. Competition with the European Ariane rocket and the Reagan administration's desire to see agencies like NASA run as if they were private businesses have led to a speedup in the launch schedule, with a goal of 14 this year and 24 by 1988.

"The game NASA is playing is the maximum tonnage per year at the minimum costs possible," says Paul Cloutier, a professor of space physics. "Some high officials don't want to hear about problems," reports *Newsweek*, "especially if fixing them will cost money."

Under pressures like these, the NASA launch team watched Columbia, after seven delays, fall about a month behind schedule and then saw Challenger delayed, first by bad weather, then by damaged door handles, and then by bad weather again. Little wonder that Lawrence Mulloy, when he heard the warnings from the Thiokol engineers, burst out: "My God, Thiokol, when do you want me to launch? Next April?"

Mulloy may be one of the villains of this story, but it is important to realize that you need Lawrence Mulloys to get things done. It is also important to realize that, if you have a Lawrence Mulloy, you must protect yourself against what he might fail to do or what he might do wrong in his enthusiastic rush to get the job done.

And you can't just ask him if he has any doubts. If he's a gung-ho type, he's going to suppress the negatives. When Jimmy Carter asked General David Jones to check out the Iran rescue

plan, Jones said to Colonel Beckwith: "Charlie, tell me what you really think about the mission. Be straight with me."

"Sir, we're going to do it!" Beckwith replied. "We want to do it, and we're ready."

John Kennedy received similar confident reports from the chain of command about the readiness of the CIA's Cuban Brigade to charge ashore at the Bay of Pigs and overthrow Fidel Castro. And Sargent Shriver had every reason to believe that the Peace Corps was getting off to a fabulous start, based on what his chain of command was telling him.

With Shriver, as with NASA's senior officials, the conviction that everything was A-OK was fortified by skillful public relations. Bill Moyers was only one of the geniuses involved in this side of the Peace Corps. At NASA, Julian Scheer began a tradition of inspired PR that endured until Challenger. These were men who could sell air conditioning in Murmansk. The trouble is they also sold their bosses the same air conditioning. Every organization has a tendency to believe its own PR—NASA's walls are lined with glamorizing posters and photographs of the shuttle and other space machines—and usually the top man is the most thoroughly seduced because, after all, it reflects the most glory on him.

Favorable publicity and how to get it is therefore the dominant subject of Washington staff meetings. The minutes of the Nuclear Regulatory Commission show that when the reactor was about to melt down at Three Mile Island, the commissioners were worried less about what to do to fix the reactor than they were about what they were going to say to the press.

One of the hottest rumors around Washington is that the White House had put pressure on NASA to launch so that the president could point with pride to the teacher in space during his State of the Union speech. The White House denies this story, and my sources tell me the denial is true. But NASA had—and this is fact, not rumor—put pressure on *itself* by asking the president to mention Christa McAuliffe. In a memorandum dated January 8, NASA proposed that the president say:

"Tonight while I am speaking to you, a young elementary school teacher from Concord, New Hampshire, is taking us all on the ultimate field trip as she orbits the earth as the first citizen passenger on the space shuttle. Christa McAuliffe's journey is a prelude to the journeys of other Americans living and working together in a permanently manned space station in the mid-1990s. Mrs. McAuliffe's week in space is just one of the achievements in space we have planned for the coming year."

The flight was scheduled for January 23. It was postponed and postponed again. Now it was January 28, the morning of the day the speech was to be delivered, the last chance for the launch

When NASA's George Hardy told Thiokol engineers that he was appalled by their verbal recommendation that the launch be postponed and asked Thiokol to reconsider and make another recommendation, he was telling them, "Don't tell me," or "Don't tell me officially so that I won't have to pass bad news along to my bosses."

to take place in time to have it mentioned by the president. NASA officials must have feared they were about to lose a PR opportunity of stunning magnitude, an opportunity to impress not only the media and the public but the agency's two most important constituencies, the White House and the Congress. Wouldn't you feel pressure to get that launch off this morning so that the president could talk about it tonight?

NASA's sensitivity to the media in regard to the launch schedule was nothing short of unreal. Here is what Richard G. Smith, the director of the Kennedy Space Center, had to say about it after the disaster:

"Every time there was a delay, the press would say, 'Look, there's another delay. . . . here's a bunch of idiots who can't even handle a launch schedule.' You think that doesn't have an impact? If you think it doesn't, you're stupid."

I do not recall seeing a single story like those Smith describes. Perhaps there were a few. The point, however, is to realize how large even a little bit of press criticism loomed in NASA's thinking.

Sargent Shriver liked good press as much as, if not more than, the next man. But he also had an instinct that the ultimate bad press would come if the world found out about your disaster before you had a chance to do something to prevent it. He and an assistant named William Haddad decided to make sure that Shriver got the bad news first. Who was going to find it out for them? Me.

It was July 1961. They decided to call me an evaluator and send me out to our domestic training programs and later overseas to find out what was really going on. My first stop was the University of California at Berkeley where our Ghana project was being trained. Fortunately, except for grossly inadequate language instruction, this program was excellent. But soon I began finding serious deficiencies in other training programs and in our projects abroad.

Shriver was not always delighted by these reports. Indeed, at one point I heard I was going to be fired. I liked my job, and I knew that the reports that I and the other evaluators who had joined me were writing were true. I didn't want to be fired. What could I do?

I knew he was planning to visit our projects in Africa. So I prepared a memorandum that contrasted what the chain of command was saying with what I and my associates were reporting. Shriver left for Africa. I heard nothing for several weeks. Then came a cable from Somalia: "Tell Peters his reports are right." I knew then that, however much Shriver wanted to hear the good news and get good publicity, he could take the bad news. The fact that he could take the bad news meant that the Peace Corps began to face its problems and do something about them before they became a scandal.

NASA did the opposite. A 1983 reorganization shifted the responsiblity for monitoring flight safety from the chief engineer in Washington to the field. This may sound good. "We're not going to micromanage," said James M. Beggs, then the NASA administrator. But the catch is that if you decentralize, you must maintain the flow of information from the field to the top so that the organization's leader will know what those decentralized managers are doing. What NASA's reorganization did, according to safety engineers who talked to Mark Tapscott of *The Washington Times*, was to close off "an independent channel with authority to make things happen at the top."

I suspect what happened is that the top NASA administrators, who were pushing employees down below to dramatically increase the number of launches, either consciously or unconsciously did not want to be confronted with the dangers they were thereby risking.

This is what distinguishes the bad leaders from the good. The good leader, realizing that there is a natural human tendency to avoid bad news, traps himself into having to face it. He encourages whistleblowers instead of firing them. He visits the field himself and talks to the privates and lieutenants as well as the generals to find out the real problems. He can use others to do this for him, as Shriver used me, or as Franklin Roosevelt used his wife Eleanor and Harry Hopkins, and as they in turn used Lorena Hickock* to find out what the New Deal was really accomplishing. But he must have some independent knowledge of what's going on down below in order to have a feel for whether the chain of command is giving him the straight dope.

What most often happens, of course, is that the boss, if he goes to the field at all, talks only to the colonels and generals. Sometimes he doesn't want to know what the privates know. He may be hoping that the lid can be kept on whatever problems are developing, at least until his watch is over, so that he won't be blamed when they finally surface. Or he may have a very good idea that bad things are being done and simply wants to retain "deniability," meaning that the deed cannot be traced to him. The story of Watergate is filled with "Don't tell me" and "I don't want to know."

When NASA's George Hardy told Thiokol engineers that he was appalled by their verbal recommendation that the launch be postponed and asked Thiokol to reconsider and make another recommendation, Thiokol, which Hardy well knew was worried about losing its shuttle contract, was in effect being told, "Don't tell me" or "Don't tell me officially so I won't have to pass bad news along and my bosses will have deniability."

In addition to the leader himself, others must be concerned with making him face the bad news. This includes subordinates. Their having the courage to speak out about what is wrong is crucial, and people like Bruce Cook of NASA and Allan McDonald of Thiokol deserve great credit for having done so. But it is a fact that none of the subordinates who knew the danger to the shuttle took the next step and resigned in protest so that the public could find out what was going on in time to prevent disaster. The almost univer-

sal tendency to place one's own career above one's moral responsibility to take a stand on matters like these has to be one of the most depressing facts about bureaucratic culture today.

Even when the issue was simply providing facts for an internal NASA investigation after the disaster, here is the state of mind Bruce Cook describes in a recent article in *The Washington Post*:

"Another [NASA employee] told me to step away from his doorway while he searched for a document in his filing cabinet so that no one would see me in his office and suspect that he'd been the one I'd gotten it from."

It may be illuminating to note here that at the Peace Corps I found my most candid informants were the volunteers. They had no career stake in the organization—they were in for just two years—and thus had no reason to fear the results of their candor. Doesn't this suggest that we might be better off with more short-term employees in the government, people who are planning to leave anyway and thus have no hesitation to blow the whistle when necessary?

Certainly the process of getting bad news from the bottom to the top can be helped by institutionalizing it, as it was in the case of the Peace Corps Evaluation Division, and by hiring to perform it employees who have demonstrated courage and independence as well as the ability to elicit the truth and report it clearly.

Two other institutions that can help this process are the Congress and the White House. But the staff they have to perform this function is tiny. The White House depends on the OMB to tell it what the executive branch is doing. Before the Challenger exploded, the OMB had four examiners to cover science and space. The Senate subcommmittee on Space, Science and Technology had a staff of three. Needless to say, they had not heard about the O-rings.

Another problem is lack of experience. Too few congressmen and too few of their staff have enough experience serving in the executive branch to have a sense of the right question to ask. OMB examiners usually come aboard straight from graduate school, totally innocent of practical experience in government.

The press shares this innocence. Only a handful of journalists have worked in the bureaucracy. Like the members of Congress, they treat policy formulation as the ultimate reality: Congress passed this bill today; the president signed that bill. That's what the TV reporters on the Capitol steps and the White House lawn tell us about. But suppose the legislation in question concerns coal mine safety. Nobody is going to know what it all adds up to until some members of Congress and some members of the press go down into the coal mine to find out if conditions actually are safer or if only more crazy regulations have been added.

---

*See Political Booknotes, May 1981, page 58. Other articles concerned with the issues raised here: "The Shriver Prescription: How Government Can Find Out What It's Doing," November 1972; "How Carter Can Find Out What the Government Is Doing," January 1977; "Blind Ambition in the White House," March 1977; "The Prince and His Courtiers," March 1971; "Why the White House Press Didn't Get the Watergate Story," July/August 1973. The latter two are included in the fourth edition of Inside the System (Holt Rinehart), the foreword of which, by Richard Rovere, describes evaluation in the Peace Corps. More about Peace Corps evaluation can be found in A Moment in History, by Brent Ashabranner (Doubleday) and The Bold Experiment, by Gerard Rice (Notre Dame). Blowing the Whistle (Praeger) is a collection of Washington Monthly articles dealing with employees who speak up. Also see The Culture of Bureaucracy, (Holt Rinehart) and How Washington Really Works (Addison-Wesley).

Unfortunately, neither the congressmen nor the press display much enthusiasm for visits to the mines. Yet this is what I found to be the key to getting the real story about the Peace Corps. I had to go to Ouagadougou and talk to the volunteers at their sites before I could really know what the Peace Corps was doing and what its problems were. I wasn't going to find out by asking the public affairs office.

But that's where most reporters go and sit all day—outside Larry Speakes's office or its equivalent throughout the government.

Because the reporters don't know any better, they don't press the Congress to do any better. What journalists could do is make the public aware of how little attention Congress devotes to what is called "oversight," i.e., finding out what the programs it has authorized are actually doing. If the press would publicize the nonperformance of this function, it is at least possible that the public would begin to reward the congressmen who perform it consistently and punish those who ignore it by not reelecting them.

But the press will never do this until it gets itself out of Larry Speakes's office. Woodward and Bernstein didn't get the Watergate story by talking to Ron Ziegler, or, for that matter, by using other reportorial techniques favored by the media elite, like questioning Richard Nixon at a press conference or interviewing other administration luminaries at fancy restaurants. They had to find lower-level sources like Hugh Sloan, just as the reporters who finally got the NASA story had to find the Richard Cooks and Allan McDonalds.

Eileen Shanahan, a former reporter for *The New York Times* and a former assistant secretary of HEW, recently wrote "of the many times I tried, during my tenure in the Department of Health, Education and Welfare, to interest distinguished reporters from distinguished publications in the effort the department was making to find out whether its billion-dollar programs actually were reaching the intended beneficiaries and doing any good. Their eyes glazed over."

I have had a similar experience with reporters during my 25 years in Washington. For most of that time they have seemed to think they knew everything about bureaucracy because they had read a Kafka novel and stood in line at the post office. In their ignorance, they adopted a kind of wise-guy, world-weary fatalism that said nothing could be done about bureaucratic problems. They had little or no sense about how to approach organizations with an anthropologist's feel for the interaction of attitudes, values, and institutional pressures.

There are a couple of reasons, however, to hope that the performance of the press will improve. The coverage of business news has become increasingly sophisticated about the way institutional pressures affect executive and corporate behavior, mainly because the comparison of our economy with Japan's made the importance of cultural factors so obvious. And on defense issues, visits to the field are increasingly common as reporters attempt to find out whether this or that weapon works.

But these are mere beachheads. They need to be radically expanded to include the coverage of all the institutions that affect our lives, especially government. This may seem unlikely, but if the press studies the Challenger case, I do not see how it can avoid perceiving the critical role bureaucratic pressure played in bringing about the disaster. What the press must then realize is that similar pressures vitally influence almost everything this government does, and that we will never understand why government fails until we understand those pressures and how human beings in public office react to them.

MONEY CHANGES EVERYTHING

Daniel Clawson, Alan Neustadth, and Denise Scott

In the past twenty years political action committees, or PACs, have transformed campaign finance. The chair of the PAC at one of the twenty-five largest manufacturing companies in the United States explained to us why his corporation has a PAC:

> The PAC gives you access. It makes you a player. These congressmen, in particular, are constantly fundraising. Their elections are very expensive and getting increasingly expensive each year. So they have an on-going need for funds.
>
> It profits us in a sense to be able to provide some funds because in the provision of it you get to know people, you help them out. There's no real quid pro quo. There is nobody whose vote you can count on, not with the kind of money we are talking about here. But the PAC gives you access, puts you in the game.
>
> You know, some congressman has got X number of ergs of energy, and here's a person or a company who wants to come see him and give him a thousand dollars, and here's another one who wants to just stop by and say hello. And he only has time to see one. Which one? So the PAC's an attention getter.

Most analyses of campaign finance focus on the candidates who receive the money, not on the people and political action committees that give it. PACs are entities that collect money from many contributors, pool it, and then make donations to candidates. Donors may give to a PAC because they are in basic agreement with its aims, but once they have donated they lose direct control over their money, trusting the PAC to decide which candidates should receive contributions.

Corporate PACs have unusual power that has been largely unexamined. In this book we begin the process of giving corporate PACs, and business-government relations in general, the scrutiny they deserve. By far the most important source for our analysis is a set of in-depth interviews we conducted with corporate executives who direct and control their corporations' political activity. The insight these interviews provide into the way corporate executives think, the goals they pursue, and the methods they use to achieve those goals is far more revealing than most analyses made by outside critics. We think most readers will be troubled, as we are, by the world view and activities of corporate PAC directors. . . .

WHY DOES THE AIR STINK?

Everybody wants clean air. Who could oppose it? "I spent seven years of my life trying to stop the Clean Air Act," explained the PAC director for a major corporation that is a heavy-duty polluter. Nonetheless, he was perfectly willing to use his corporation's PAC to contribute to members of Congress who voted for the act:

> How a person votes on the final piece of legislation often is not representative of what they have done. Somebody will do a lot of things during the process. How many guys voted against the Clean Air Act? But during the process some of them were very sympathetic to some of our concerns.

In the world of Congress and political action committees things are not always what they seem. Members of Congress want to vote for clean air, but they also want to receive campaign contributions from corporate PACs and pass a law that business accepts as "reasonable." The compromise solution to this dilemma is to gut the bill by crafting dozens of loopholes inserted in private meetings or in subcommittee hearings that don't receive much (if any) attention in the press. Then the public vote on the final bill can be nearly unanimous: members of Congress can assure their constituents that they voted for the final bill and their corporate PAC contributors that they helped weaken the bill in private. We can use the Clean Air Act of 1990 to introduce and explain this process.

The public strongly supports clean air and is unimpressed when corporate officials and apologists trot out their normal arguments: "corporations are already doing all they reasonably can to improve environmental quality"; "we need to balance the costs against the benefits"; "people will lose their jobs if we make controls any stricter." The original Clean Air Act was passed in 1970, revised in 1977, and not revised again until 1990. Although the initial goal of its supporters was to have us breathing clean air by 1975, the deadline for compliance has been repeatedly extended—and the 1990 legislation provides a new set of deadlines to be reached sometime far in the future.

Because corporations control the production process unless the government specifically intervenes, any delay in government action leaves corporations free to do as they choose. Not only have laws been slow to come, but corporations have fought to delay or subvert implementation. The 1970 law ordered the Environmental Protection Agency (EPA) to regulate the hundreds of poisonous chemicals that are emitted by corporations, but as William Greider notes, "in twenty years of stalling, dodging, and fighting off court orders, the EPA has managed to issue regulatory standards for a total of seven toxics."

Corporations have done exceptionally well politically, given the problem they face: the interests of business often are diametrically opposed to those of the public. Clean air laws and amendments have been few and far between, enforcement is ineffective, and the penalties for infractions are minimal. On the one hand, corporations have had to pay billions; on the other hand, the costs to date are a small fraction of what would be needed to clean up the environment.

This corporate struggle for the right to pollute takes place on many fronts. One front is public relations: the Chemical Manufacturers Association took out a two-page Earth Day ad in the Washington Post to demonstrate its concern for the environment; coincidentally many of the corporate signers are also on the EPA's list of high-risk producers. Another front is research: expert studies delay action while more information is gathered. The federally funded National Acid Precipitation Assessment Program (NAPAP) took ten years and $600 million to figure out whether acid rain was a problem. Both business and the Reagan administration argued that no action should be taken until the study was completed. The study was discredited when its summary of findings minimized the impact of acid rain—even though this did not accurately represent the expert research in the report. But the key site of struggle has been Congress, where for years corporations have succeeded in defeating environmental legislation. In 1987 utility companies were offered a compromise bill on acid rain, but they "were very adamant that they had beat the thing since 1981 and they could always beat it," according to Representative Edward Madigan (R-Ill.). Throughout the 1980s the utilities defeated all efforts at change, but their intransigence probably hurt them when revisions finally were made.

The stage was set for a revision of the Clean Air Act when George Bush was elected as "the environmental president" and George Mitchell, a strong supporter of environmentalism, became the Senate majority leader. But what sort of clean air bill would it be? "What we wanted," said Richard Ayres, head of the environmentalists' Clean Air Coalition, "is a health-based standard— one-in-1-million cancer risk." Such a standard would require corporations to clean up their plants until the cancer risk from their operations was reduced to one in a million. "The Senate bill still has the requirement," Ayres said, "but there are forty pages of extensions and exceptions and qualifications and loopholes that largely render the health standard a nullity." Greider reports, for example, that "according to the EPA, there are now twenty-six coke ovens that pose a cancer risk greater than 1 in 1000 and six where the risk is greater than 1 in 100. Yet the new clean-air bill will give the steel industry another thirty years to deal with the problem."

This change from what the bill was supposed to do to what it did do came about through what corporate executives like to call the "access" process. The main aim of most corporate political action committee contributions is to help corporate executives attain "access" to key members of Congress and their staffs. Corporate executives (and corporate PAC money) work to persuade the member of Congress to accept a carefully predesigned loophole that sounds innocent but effectively undercuts the stated intention of the bill. Representative Dingell (D-Mich.), chair of the House Committee on Energy and Commerce, is a strong industry supporter; one of the people we interviewed called him "the point man for the Business Roundtable on clean air." Representative Waxman (D-Calif.), chair of the Subcommittee on Health and the Environment, is an environmentalist. Observers of the Clean Air Act legislative process expected a confrontation and contested votes on the floor of the Congress.

The problem for corporations was that, as one Republican staff aide said, "If any bill has the blessing of Waxman and the environmental groups, unless it is totally in outer space, who's going to vote against it?" But corporations successfully minimized public votes. Somehow Waxman was persuaded to make behind-the-scenes compromises with Dingell so members didn't have to publicly side with business against the environment during an election year. Often the access process leads to loopholes that protect a single corporation, but for "clean" air most special deals targeted entire industries, not specific companies. The initial bill, for example, required cars to be able to use strictly specified cleaner fuels. But the auto industry wanted the rules loosened, and Congress eventually modified the bill by incorporating a variant of a formula suggested by the head of General Motors' fuels and lubricants department.

Nor did corporations stop fighting after they gutted the bill through amendments. Business pressed the EPA for favorable regulations to implement the law: "The cost of this legislation could vary dramatically, depending on how EPA interprets it," said William D. Fay, vice president of the National Coal Association, who headed the hilariously misnamed Clean Air Working Group, an industry coalition that fought to weaken the legislation. An EPA aide working on acid rain regulations reported, "We're having a hard time getting our work done because of the number of phone calls we're getting" from corporations and their lawyers.

Corporations trying to convince federal regulators to adopt the "right" regulations don't rely exclusively on the cogency of their arguments. They often exert pressure on a member of Congress to intervene for them at the EPA or other agency. Senators and representatives regularly intervene on behalf of constituents and contributors by doing everything from straightening out a social security problem to asking a regulatory agency to explain why it is pressuring a company. This process—like campaign finance—-usually follows accepted etiquette. In addressing a regulatory agency the senator does not say, "Lay off my campaign contributors, or I'll cut your budget." One standard phrasing for letters asks regulators to resolve the problem "as quickly as possible within applicable rules and regulations." No matter how mild and careful the inquiry, the agency receiving the request is certain to give it extra attention; only after careful consideration will they refuse to make any accommodation.

The power disparity between business and environmentalists is enormous during the legislative process but even larger thereafter. When the Clean Air Act passed, corporations and industry groups offered positions, typically with large pay increases, to congressional staff members who wrote the law. The former congressional staff members who work for corporations know how to evade the law and can persuasively claim to EPA that they know what Congress intended. Environmental organizations pay substantially less than Congress and can't afford large staffs. They are rarely able to become involved in the details of the administrative process or influence implementation and enforcement.

Having pushed Congress for a law, and the Environmental Protection Agency for regulations, allowing as much pollution as possible, business then went to the Quayle Council for rules allowing even more pollution. Vice President J. Danforth Quayle's Council, technically the Council on Competitiveness, was created by President Bush specifically to help reduce regulations on business. Quayle told the *Boston Globe* "that his council has an 'open door' to business groups and that he has a bias against regulations." The Council reviews, and can override, all federal regulations, including those by the EPA setting the limits at which a chemical is subject to regulation. The council also recommended that corporations be allowed to increase their polluting emissions if a state did not object within seven days of the proposed increase. Corporations thus have multiple opportunities to win. If they lose in Congress, they can win at the regulatory agency; if they lose there, they can try again at the Quayle Council. If they lose there, they can try to reduce the money available to enforce regulations, tie up the issue in the courts, or accept a minimal fine.

The operation of the Quayle Council probably would have received little publicity, but reporters discovered that the executive director of the Council, Allan Hubbard, had a clear conflict of interest. Hubbard chaired the biweekly White House meetings on the Clean Air Act. He owns half of World Wide Chemical, received an average of more than a million dollars a year in profits from it while directing the Council, and continues to attend quarterly stockholder meetings. According to the *Boston Globe*, "Records on file with the Indianapolis Air Pollution Control Board show that World Wide Chemical emitted 17,000 to 19,000 pounds of chemicals into the air last year." The company "does not have the permit required to release the emissions," "is putting out nearly four times the allowable emissions without a permit, and could be subject to a $2,500-a-day penalty," according to David Jordan, director of the Indianapolis Air Pollution Board.

In business-government relations attention focuses on scandal. It is outrageous that Hubbard will personally benefit by eliminating regulations that his own company is violating, but the key issue here is not this obvious conflict of interest. The real issue is the *system* of business-government relations, and especially of campaign finance, that offers business so many opportunities to craft loopholes, undermine regulations, and subvert enforcement. Still worse, many of these actions take place outside of public scrutiny. If the Quayle Council were headed by a Boy Scout we'd still object to giving business yet another way to use backroom deals to increase our risk of getting cancer. In *Money Talks* we try to analyze not just the exceptional cases, but the day-to-day reality of corporate-government relations. . . .

MYTH ONE: KEY VOTES ARE THE ISSUE

Many critics of PACs and campaign finance seem to feel that a corporate PAC officer walks into a member's office and says, "Senator, I want you to vote against the Clean Air Act. Here's $5,000 to do so." This view, in this crude form, is simply wrong. The (liberal) critics who hold this view seem to reason as follows: (1) we know that PAC money gives corporations power in relation to Congress; (2) power is the ability to make someone do something against their will; (3) therefore campaign money must force members to switch their votes on key issues. We come to the same conclusion about the outcome—corporate power in relation to Congress—but differ from conventional critics on both the understanding of power and the nature of the process through which campaign money exercises its influence.

The debate over campaign finance is frequently posed as, "Did special interests buy the member's vote on a key issue?" Media accounts as well as most academic analyses in practice adopt this approach. With the question framed in this way, we have to agree with the corporate political action committee directors we interviewed, who answered, "No, they didn't." But they believed it followed that they have no power and maybe not even any influence, and we certainly don't agree with that. If power means the ability to force a member of Congress to vote a certain way on a major bill, corporate PACs rarely have power. However, corporations and their PACs have a great deal of power if power means the ability to exercise a field of influence that shapes the behavior of other social actors. In fact, corporations have effective hegemony: some alternatives are never seriously considered, and others seem natural and inevitable; some alternatives generate enormous controversy and costs, and others are minor and involve noncontroversial favors. Members of Congress meet regularly with some people, share trust, discuss the issues honestly off the record, and become friends, while other people have a hard time getting in the door much less getting any help. Members don't have to be forced; most of them are eager to do favors for corporations and do so without the public's knowledge. If citizens did understand what was happening their outrage might put an end to the behavior, but even if the favors are brought to light the media will probably present them as at least arguably good public policy.

High-Visibility Issues

Corporate PAC officers could stress two key facts: First, on important highly visible issues they cannot determine the way a member of Congress votes; second, even for low-visibility issues the entire process is loose and uncertain. The more visible an issue, the less likely that a member's vote will be determined by campaign contributions. If the whole world is watching, a member from an environmentally conscious district can't vote against the Clean Air Act because it is simply too popular. An April 1990 poll by Louis Harris and Associates reported that when asked, "Should Congress make the 1970 Clean Air Act stricter than it is now, keep it about the same, or make it less strict?" 73 percent of respondents answered, "Make it stricter"; 23 percent, "Keep it about the same"; and only 2 percent, "Make it less strict" (with 2 percent not sure). Few members could risk openly voting against such sentiments. To oppose the bill they'd have to have a very good reason—perhaps that it would cost their district several hundred jobs, perhaps that the bill was fatally flawed, but never, never, never that they had been promised $5,000, $10,000, or $50,000 for doing so.

The PAC officers we interviewed understood this point, although they weren't always careful to distinguish between high- and low-visibility issues. (As we discuss below, we believe low-visibility issues are an entirely different story.) Virtually all access-oriented PACs went out of their way at some point in the interview to make it clear that they do not and could not buy a member's vote on any significant issue. No corporate official felt otherwise; moreover, these opinions seemed genuine and not merely for public consumption. They pointed out that the maximum legal donation by a PAC is $5,000 per candidate per election. Given that in 1988 the cost of an average winning House campaign was $388,000 and for the Senate $3,745,000, no individual company can provide the

financial margin of victory in any but the closest of races. A member of Congress would be a fool to trade 5 percent of the district's votes for the maximum donation an individual PAC can make ($5,000) or even for ten times that amount. Most PACs therefore feel they have little influence. Even the one person who conceded possible influence in some rare circumstances considered it unlikely:

> You certainly aren't going to be able to buy anybody for $500 or $1,000 or $10,000. It's a joke. Occasionally something will happen where everybody in one industry will be for one specific solution to a problem, and they may then also pour money to one guy. And he suddenly looks out and says, "I haven't got $7,000 coming in from this group, I've got $70,000." That might get his attention: "I've got to support what they want." But that's a rarity, and it doesn't happen too often. Most likely, after the election he's going to rationalize that it wasn't that important and they would have supported him anyway. I just don't think that PACs are that important.

This statement by a senior vice president at a large *Fortune* 500 company probably reflects one part of the reality: most of the time members' votes can't be bought; occasionally a group of corporations support the same position and combine resources to influence a member's vote even on a major contested issue. Even if that happens, the member's behavior is far from certain.

Low-Visibility Issues and Nonissues

This is true only if we limit our attention to highly visible, publicly contested issues. Most corporate PACs, and most government relations units, focus only a small fraction of their time, money, and energy on the final votes on such issues. So-called access-oriented PACs have a different purpose and style. Their aim is not to influence the member's public vote on the final piece of legislation, but rather to be sure that the bill's wording exempts their company from the bill's most costly or damaging provisions. If tax law is going to be changed, the aim of the company's government relations unit, and its associated PAC, is to be sure that the law has built-in loopholes that protect the company. The law may say that corporate tax rates are increased, and that's what the media and the public think, but section 739, subsection J, paragraph iii, contains a hard-to-decipher phrase. No ordinary mortal can figure out what it means or to whom it applies, but the consequence is that the company doesn't pay the taxes you'd think it would. For example, the 1986 Tax "Reform" Act contained a provision limited to a single company, identified as a "corporation incorporated on June 13, 1917, which has its principal place of business in Bartlesville, Oklahoma." With that provision in the bill, Philips Petroleum didn't mind at all if Congress wanted to "reform" the tax laws.

Two characteristics of such provisions structure the way they are produced. First, by their very nature such provisions, targeted at one (or at most a few) corporations or industries, are unlikely to mobilize widespread business support. Other businesses may not want to oppose these provisions, but neither are they likely to make them a priority, though the broader the scope the broader the support. Business as a whole is somewhat uneasy about very narrow provisions, although most corporations and industry trade associations feel they must fight for their own. Peak business associations such as the Business Roundtable generally prefer a "clean" bill with clear provisions favoring business in general rather than a "Christmas tree" with thousands of special-interest provisions. Most corporations play the game, however, and part of playing the game is not to object to or publicize what other corporations are doing. But they don't feel good about what they do, and if general-interest business associations took a stand they would probably speak against, rather than in favor of, these provisions.

Second, however, these are low-visibility issues; in fact, most of them are not "issues" at all in that they are never examined or contested. The corporation's field of power both makes the member willing to cooperate and gets the media and public to in practice accept these loopholes as noncontroversial. Members don't usually have to take a stand on these matters or be willing to face public scrutiny. If the proposal does become contested, the member probably can back off and drop the issue with few consequences, and the corporation probably can go down the hall and try again with another member. . . .

What Is Power?

Our analysis is based on an understanding of power that differs from that usually articulated by both business and politicians. The corporate PAC directors we interviewed insisted that they have no power:

> If you were to ask me what kind of access and influence do we have, being roughly the 150th largest PAC, I would have to tell you that on the basis of our money we have zero. . . . If you look at the level of our contributions, we know we're not going to buy anybody's vote, we're not going to rent anybody, or whatever the cliches have been over the years. We know that.

The executives who expressed these views used the word *power* in roughly the same sense that it is usually used within political science, which is also the way the term was defined by Max Weber, the classical sociological theorist. Power, according to this common conception, is the ability to make someone do something against his or her will. If that is what power means, then corporations rarely have power in relation to members of Congress. As one corporate senior vice president said to us, "You certainly aren't going to be able to buy anybody for $500 or $1,000 or $10,000. It's a joke." In this regard we agree with the corporate officials we interviewed: a PAC is not in a position to say to a member of Congress, "Either you vote for this bill, or we will defeat your bid for reelection." Rarely do they even say, "Vote for this bill, or you won't get any money from us." Therefore, if power is the ability to make someone do something against his or her will,

then PAC donations rarely give corporations power over members of Congress.

This definition of power as the ability to make someone do something against his or her will is what Steven Lukes calls a *one-dimensional view of power*. A *two-dimensional view* recognizes the existence of nondecisions: a potential issue never gets articulated or, if articulated by someone somewhere, never receives serious consideration. In 1989 and 1990 one of the major political battles, and a focus of great effort by corporate PACs, was the Clean Air Act. Yet twenty or thirty years earlier, before the rise of the environmental movement, pollution was a nonissue: it simply didn't get considered, although its effects were, in retrospect, of great importance. In one Sherlock Holmes story the key clue is that the dog didn't bark. A two-dimensional view of power makes the same point: in some situations no one notices power is being exercised—because there is no overt conflict.

Even this model of power is too restrictive, however, because it still focuses on discrete decisions and nondecisions. Tom Wartenberg . . . argues instead for a *field theory of power* that analyzes social power as similar to a magnetic field. A magnetic field alters the motion of objects susceptible to magnetism. Similarly, the mere presence of a powerful social agent alters social space for others and causes them to orient to the powerful agent. One of the executives we interviewed took it for granted that "if we go see the congressman who represents [a city where the company has a major plant], where 10,000 of our employees are also his constituents, we don't need a PAC to go see him." The corporation is so important in that area that the member has to orient himself or herself in relation to the corporation and its concerns. In a different sense, the mere act of accepting a campaign contribution changes the way a member relates to a PAC, creating a sense of obligation and need to reciprocate. The PAC contribution has altered the member's social space, his or her awareness of the company and wish to help it, even if no explicit commitments have been made.

Business Is Different

Power therefore is not just the ability to force people to do something against their will; it is most effective (and least recognized) when it shapes the field of action. Moreover, business's vast resources, influence on the economy, and general legitimacy place it on a different footing from other so-called special interests. Business donors are often treated differently from other campaign contributors. When a member of Congress accepts a $1,000 donation from a corporate PAC, goes to a committee hearing, and proposes "minor" changes in a bill's wording, those changes are often accepted without discussion or examination. The changes "clarify" the language of the bill, perhaps legalizing higher levels of pollution for a specific pollutant or exempting the company from some tax. The media do not report on this change, and no one speaks against it. . . .

Even groups with great social legitimacy encounter more opposition and controversy than business faces for proposals that are virtually without public support. Contrast the largely unopposed commitment of more than $500 billion for the bailout of savings and loan associations with the sharp debate, close votes, and defeats for the rights of men and women to take *unpaid* parental leaves. Although the classic phrase for something non-controversial that everyone must support is to call it a "motherhood" issue, and it would cost little to guarantee every woman the right to an unpaid parental leave, nonetheless this measure generated intense scrutiny and controversy, ultimately going down to defeat. Few people are prepared to publicly defend pollution or tax evasion, but business is routinely able to win pollution exemptions and tax loopholes. Although cumulatively these provisions may trouble people, individually most are allowed to pass without scrutiny. *No* analysis of corporate political activity makes sense unless it begins with a recognition that the PAC is a vital element of corporate power, but it does not operate by itself. The PAC donation is always backed by the wider range of business power and influence.

Corporations are different from other special-interest groups not only because business has far more resources, but also because of this acceptance and legitimacy. When people feel that "the system" is screwing them, they tend to blame politicians, the government, the media—but rarely business. Although much of the public is outraged at the way money influences elections and public policy, the issue is almost always posed in terms of what politicians do or don't do. This pervasive double standard largely exempts business from criticism. We, on the other hand, believe it is vital to scrutinize business as well. . . .

The Limits to Business Power

We have argued that power is more than winning an open conflict, and business is different from other groups because of its pervasive influence on our society—the way it shapes the social space for all other actors. These two arguments, however, are joined with a third: a recognition of, in fact an insistence on, the limits to business power. We stress the power of business, but business does not feel powerful. As one executive said to us,

I really wish that our PAC in particular, and our lobbyists, had the influence that is generally perceived by the general population. If you see it written in the press, and you talk to people, they tell you about all that influence that you've got, and frankly I think that's far overplayed, as far as the influence goes. Certainly you can get access to a candidate, and certainly you can get your position known; but as far as influencing that decision, the only way you influence it is by the providing of information.

Executives believe that corporations are constantly under attack, primarily because government simply doesn't understand that business is crucial to everything society does but can easily be crippled by well-intentioned but unrealistic government policies. A widespread view among the people we interviewed is that "far and away the vast majority of things that we do are literally to protect ourselves from public policy that is poorly crafted and nonresponsive to the needs and realities and circumstances of our company." These misguided policies, they feel, can come from many sources—labor unions, environmentalists, the pressure of unrealistic public-interest groups, the government's constant need for money, or the weight of its oppressive bureaucracy. Simply maintaining equilibrium requires a pervasive effort: if attention slips for even a minute, an onerous regulation will be imposed or a precious resource taken away. To some extent such a view is an obvious consequence of the position of the people we interviewed: if business could be sure of always winning, the government relations unit (and thus their jobs) would be unnecessary; if it is easy to win, they deserve little credit for their victories and much blame for defeats. But evidently the corporation agrees with them, since it devotes significant resources to political action of many kinds, including the awareness and involvement of top officials. Chief executive officers and members of the board of directors repeatedly express similar views. . . .

Like the rest of us, business executives can usually think of other things they'd like to have but know they can't get at this time or that they could win but wouldn't consider worth the price that would have to be paid. More important, the odds may be very much in their favor, their opponents may be hobbled with one hand tied behind their back, but it is still a contest requiring pervasive effort. Perhaps once upon a time business could simply make its wishes known and receive what it wanted; today corporations must form PACs, lobby actively, make their case to the public, run advocacy ads, and engage in a multitude of behaviors that they wish were unnecessary. From the outside we are impressed with the high success rates over a wide range of issues and with the lack of a credible challenge to the general authority of business. From the inside they are impressed with the serious consequences of occasional losses and with the continuing effort needed to maintain their privileged position.

THE 21ST CENTURY CORPORATION

PARADIGMS FOR POSTMODERN MANAGERS

THE ACCENT IS ON ADAPTABILITY

The modern corporation is a thing of the past. The 20th century enterprise was defined by Alfred P. Sloan, the legendary chairman of General Motors Corp. and the most influential professional manager of our time. His classic opus, *My Years with General Motors,* articulated a management philosophy that has dominated American corporations for decades. The success of the vast modern company, he argued, was based on efficiency and economies of scale—he never once mentioned the words creativity or flexibility. Large, efficient organizations, Sloan theorized, must decentralize manufacturing while centralizing corporate policy and financial controls in hierarchical structures.

For decades, that model remained intact—even as managers ranging from the brash conglomerateurs of the 1960s to the nimble entrepreneurs of the 1980s challenged, debated, and refined it. But by now, so many management gurus and corporate executives have abandoned Sloan's tenets that they're increasingly speaking of a "paradigm shift" in management thought—a dramatic change in the way we think about business problems and organizations.

KEY VALUES. This new paradigm values teamwork over individualism, seeks global markets over domestic ones, and focuses on customers, not short-term profits. It views time, rather than a single-minded focus on costs, as the key competitive advantage. It recognizes the value of a multicultural work force in an increasingly diverse labor pool and customer base. The new form of organization is based on a network of alliances and partnerships, not Sloan's self-sufficient hierarchy. And it is governed by an independent board with a broad view of the company's constituents, who include not just shareholders, but also employees, suppliers, customers, and the local community (table).

If GM once defined the shape of the old model, no existing organization serves as the prototype of this 21st century corporation. And no company is likely to assume the ideal shape, because the successful company of the future will be an adaptive one, in which change replaces stability as a key trait. What's right today isn't likely to be right tomorrow or the next day.

Global forces have spurred rapid changes in the marketplace, making it more difficult to establish systems that can be depended upon for years on end. It's a world Sloan would have had trouble competing in, a world that his stumbling descendants at GM are still trying to figure out. "There's an awareness that the reinvention of the corporation is going to go on forever," says Daniel Valentino, a managing director with Gemini Consulting. "That's a new feeling. Not long ago, executives thought this thing called change was an event."

If no one corporation does it all, certain innovators have come up with exceptionally effective approaches to managing some aspects of change. These are the strategies that will help their practitioners to thrive in the global economy of the 21st century. When it comes to employee empowerment, for example, it is Saturn Corp.—a GM division, ironically enough—that's leading the way. Saturn's teams of workers manage everything from budgets to inventory control, often without direct oversight from top management. Levi Strauss & Co. is demonstrating that a culturally diverse work force is a precious asset in serving culturally diverse markets.

As for the global focus that will be needed in a worldwide economy, it is Loctite Corp., a small maker of adhesives and sealants, that's showing all companies why they should never define their markets narrowly. Long a fierce overseas player, Loctite earns $8 of every $10 of profit outside its U.S. base. For focus on the customer, 7-Eleven Japan Co. has few rivals. It took an American concept, the convenience store, and made it an overwhelming success in Japan. Now it's setting its sights on using customer service to remake the moribund U.S. chain. And one of America's most progressive corporations, Dayton-Hudson Corp., is writing new rules for corporate governance by distributing power more evenly between directors and top officers.

Each of these companies has mastered at least one of the attributes of the organization of tomorrow. What many of them have found, however, is that even a single change poses new challenges to management and has implications that reach far beyond the concept itself.

Take the notion of the customer-driven company. Organizations that have, in today's parlance, "reintroduced themselves to their customers" have discovered that this newfound focus affects how they think about everything from corporate organization and strategy to inventory and governance. "The command-and-control structure of many companies made managers responsible to each other instead of to customers," says John W. Humphrey, chief executive of Forum Corp., a consulting and training firm. "The rediscovery of the customer is changing the shape of work. Managers are spending more time developing more connected relationships with their customers than ever before."

TEST OF TIME. Many of the new ideas are interconnected, too. Time-based competition, for example, is often a powerful tool to deliver superior customer service. That turned out to be the case at Wausau Paper Mills Co. Wausau didn't have $600 million to buy the new, high-volume equipment it needed to compete against bigger, wealthier rivals. Instead, it sought ways to differentiate itself with customers on the basis of speed. Today, some 95% of the company's orders are filled in less than 24 hours, instead of several days or weeks, eliminating customers' need to carry expensive inventory. "It adds a whole new dimension to competition," says CEO Arnold M. Nemirow. "It provides a way of competing that offsets our disadvantages."

Similarly, the idea of giving the customer what he or she wants also hooks up with the growing emphasis on flat organizations, teamwork, and employee empowerment. "We're going to see a lot more power given to the folks on the firing-line level," believes Jack Zenger, chairman of Zenger-Miller Inc., which consults on quality and work teams. "We'll see it because executives are recognizing it's embarrassing to make decisions at the top when those down below know far more about what's needed."

Zenger is among those who say that management will focus much more on process than on function in the organization of the future. Bell Atlantic Corp., for example, learned that lesson after a close look at what it took to fill an order for telephone lines from a long-distance carrier. Because of its function-based organization, in which each department performed its own discrete task before passing the job on to the next department, Bell Atlantic found that the order passed through 28 hands before it was filled. All those steps added costs, slowed the order down, and introduced opportunities for errors.

PROCESS-DRIVEN. To speed things up, the company focused on the process: It ruthlessly eliminated less relevant duties and assigned teams to follow a single order through to completion. Today, it can fill in hours some orders that once took 15 to 25 days. This shift from function to process is part of the reengineering movement headed by management guru Michael Hammer, who urges that companies fundamentally change the way work is performed—often by shifting to teams that can outthink and outperform individuals. And many believe teamwork will help to restore a sense of community within the corporation, a feeling of belonging shattered by waves of restructurings and downsizings.

A critical element of the new paradigm is Total Quality Management (TQM). Many managers once saw quality in terms of what they could afford. Now they see it as an issue in which they can't afford to make compromises. But despite this transformation of thought, quality may be less a competitive tool today than an absolute necessity to compete. "Quality is your ticket into the stadium," says Nemirow of Wausau Paper Mills. "You can't even come to the game unless you have a quality product and process in place. You have to compete on other dimensions today."

Alfred Sloan would surely be proud that at least a piece of GM is competing in new dimensions and helping to reinvent the modern corporation. But he would just as surely be shocked that some of his ideas, adhered to for too long in a changing world, contributed to the erosion of one of the great capitalist empires.
By John A. Byrne in New York

Is America on the Way Down?

The idea that the United States is in decline might itself have been expected to decline with the collapse of the Soviet Union and our emergence as the only remaining superpower. But declinism, instead of disappearing, has now shifted its focus from the political, ideological, and military conflict with the Soviet Union to the issue of economic competition, especially (though not exclusively) with Japan. Unlike the declinism of the late 80's, moreover, this latest mutation has found support not only among liberals, for whom it served as a weapon against the arms build-up sponsored by Ronald Reagan, but also among conservatives like EDWARD N. LUTTWAK *(who had been critical of the old school).*

Mr. Luttwak, who holds the Arleigh Burke Chair in Strategy at the Center for Strategic and International Studies in Washington, D.C., is working on a book that will develop the themes he explores here.

Edward N. Luttwak

When will the United States become a third-world country? One estimate would place the date as close as the year 2020. A more optimistic projection might add another ten or fifteen years. Either way, if present trends simply continue, all but a small minority of Americans will be impoverished soon enough, left to yearn hopelessly for the lost golden age of American prosperity.

Nor can American decline remain only economic. The arts and sciences cannot flower and grow without the prosperity that pays for universities, research centers, libraries, museums, the theater, orchestras, ballet companies. It was the ample earnings of Italian traders and bankers that fed the scholars, painters, sculptors, architects, and poets who gave us the Renaissance. When Italy was by-passed by the new flows of oceangoing trade, its impoverished merchants and bankrupt financiers could no longer commission artists or keep scholars at their work, so that economic decline was followed in short order by the bleak downfall of Italian art and scholarship.

Finally, democracy too must become fragile once better hopes are worn away by bitter disappointment. What Americans have in common are their shared beliefs, above all in equality of opportunity in the pursuit of affluence. It would be too much to expect that democratic governance would long survive the impoverishment of all Americans except for a small privileged minority of inheritors, agents of foreign interests, and assorted financial manipulators.

When Buenos Aires was still a leading world metropolis, when the people of Argentina still enjoyed their famous steak-at-every-meal abundance that lasted into the 1950's, they would never have believed that their future would be a 40-year slide into poverty. Equally, the citizens of the U.S., still today by far the richest country in the world, steadfastly refuse to recognize what future is in store for them unless they can alter the course they are now on. Yet the simplest numbers confirm the slide, and suggest the chilling forecast.

In 1970, Americans were two-and-a-half times as productive as the Japanese, and twice as productive as the citizens of the European Community on average.[1] By 1980, the pattern of decline had already set in. The United States was still well ahead of the European Community and Japan, but its edge had been cut in half in a mere ten years, while West Germany had actually overtaken it.[2]

At that point, in 1980, a simple straight-line projection of the sort that professional economists deplore as much too simplistic would have suggested that in one more decade the United States would be overtaken by the richer Europeans and by Japan. And that is exactly what happened.[3]

This being a 20-year trend and not just a brief

downturn, it is perfectly reasonable to calculate what the future numbers would be if the United States were to remain on its present path. Already in the year 2000, Japan's gross national product per person would be twice that of America, while the richer European countries would have a 50-percent edge over the United States. Ten years after that, Japan would be more than three times as productive per person as the United States, and the richer European countries would be almost twice as productive per person as the United States.

Finally in 2020, when the children of today's middle-aged Americans will themselves be middle-aged, the richest Europeans would be more than twice as productive, while the gap between Japanese and Americans at 5-to-1 would be just about the same as the 1980 gap between Americans and Brazilians. At that point, the United States would definitely have become a third-world country—at least by Japanese standards. Certainly Americans would no longer be in the same class as West Europeans.

Actually, this particular trend is already well-established. In the 1950's, even young Americans traveling to Europe on student budgets could stay at the best hotels and eat in the best restaurants. Coming from a far more productive society, they found that the pocket money of summer jobs or minor parental handouts was quite enough to pay for European luxury. Today American students still travel to Europe, though they now complain that the high prices keep them out of all but the cheapest lodgings. As for the luxury hotels that once depended on American customers, they are now filled with Japanese and European tourists, with only a few Americans still able to afford their rates. If the 2020 projection holds true, none but the wealthiest Americans could travel to Europe unless there were a demand for casual labor, more or less as the poor of Latin America and Caribbean peasants now come to California and Florida for the harvest.

As of now, tens of thousands of young Americans live in Japan as illegal immigrants at any one time. Many teach English to pay their way, but many others work in bars and night clubs or as models of various kinds. American girls serving as bar hostesses and part-time prostitutes are now so common in Tokyo that their services no longer command a premium—though there is still a fair demand for blondes. When a country is in economic decline, not only its currency but also its flesh is cheapened.

THERE is no doubt that to project the future by simply extending the past is a procedure truly simplistic, because unexpected changes can always outweigh continuities. But so far, at least, the path seems straight enough—and straight downhill. It is also true that international comparisons can easily be distorted by abrupt exchange-rate fluctuations: one reason Switzerland reached the astounding gross national product of $30,270 per person in 1989 was that the Swiss franc happened to be very high during that year. Moreover, all fluctuations aside, exchange rates routinely deform comparisons because they reflect only the *international* supply and demand for capital, goods, and services denominated in any particular currency (as well as speculation and central-bank manipulations), and not the much greater amount of purely domestic transactions. Hence currencies can be greatly overvalued or undervalued as compared to their purchasing power at home.

Because the United States has chosen to open its markets to imports to a much greater extent than most other countries, let alone famously import-phobic Japan and Korea, the great outflow of dollars reduces the exchange rate far below the dollar's purchasing power at home. If we rely on a measure based on purchasing-power parities, we find that the United States scores much higher in international comparisons.[4] Yet while purchasing-power values can depict living standards more or less realistically, it is only comparisons based on straight exchange rates that determine the "who-does-what-to-whom" of the international economy—including the little matter of which parties can buy attractive pieces of other (open-door) economies, and which parties can only sell them off. And that, of course, can make the enjoyment of even splendid living standards somewhat ephemeral.

Finally, if we switch to the purchasing-power plus gross-domestic-product criterion, we find that although the United States is still ahead, the trend is just as unfavorable as it is with other measures, and the pattern of relative decline just as evident.[5]

To be sure, both the gross national product and the gross domestic product are indeed gross measures: a car accident increases both of them by the amount of ambulance, hospital, and bodyshop bills, while a healthy drop in cigarette smoking reduces them as sales and excise taxes go down. Nor can any international comparison be free of all sorts of distortions, large and small, no matter what criterion is employed, if only because the different consumption preferences prevalent in different countries are hard to equate. And yet, after all possible objections and all proper reservations are listed, it cannot finally be denied that the totality of all the relevant numbers contains irrefutable evidence that the American economy has long been in severe decline by world standards—and still is.

MANY observers would reach the same verdict without need of any numbers. Follow a traveler from Tokyo to New York—though it would be much the same if he came from Zurich, Amsterdam, or Singapore. After leaving his taxi at Tokyo's downtown City Air Terminal—a perfectly ordinary Tokyo taxi and therefore shiny clean, in perfect condition, its neatly dressed driver in white gloves—our traveler will find himself aboard an equally spotless airport bus in five minutes flat, with his baggage already checked in, boarding card issued, and passport stamped by the seemingly effortless teamwork of quick, careful porters who refuse tips, airline clerks who can actually use computers at computer speed, passport officers who act as if it were their job to expedite travel, and bus crews who sell tickets, load baggage, and courteously help the encumbered while strictly keeping to departure schedules timed to the exact minute.

Then, after an hour's bus ride over the crowded expressway to the gleaming halls of Tokyo's Narita international airport, and after the long trans-Pacific flight, when our traveler finally arrives, he will be confronted by sights and sounds that would not be out of place in Lagos or Bombay. He has landed at New York's John F. Kennedy airport.

Instead of the elegance of Narita, or Frankfurt, or Amsterdam, or Singapore, arriving travelers at one of the several JFK terminals that belong to near-bankrupt airlines will find themselves walking down dingy corridors in need of paint, over frayed carpets, often struggling up and down narrow stairways alongside out-of-order escalators. Those are JFK's substitutes for the constantly updated facilities of first-world airports. The rough, cheap remodeling of sadly outdated buildings with naked plywood and unfinished gypsum board proclaims the shortage of long-term money to build with, of invested capital. Equally, the frayed carpets, those defective escalators, and the pervasive minor dirt reveal how day-to-day money is being saved: by deferred maintenance—the most perfect sign of third-world conditions, the instantly recognizable background of South Asian, African, and Latin American street scenes, with their potholed streets, dilapidated buildings, crudely painted signs, and decrepit buses.

If the sheer lack of capital to provide proper facilities is the first third-world trait, the second is undoubtedly the lack of skill and diligence in the labor force. This phenomenon will be brutally obvious as soon as our traveler arrives in the customs hall, where baggage is contemptuously thrown off the incoming belts in full view of the hapless passengers. By then he will be too exhausted to complain: after a long flight, he is likely to have waited for hours to have his passport examined.

In due course, if our traveler transfers to a domestic flight, he may well encounter airline porters already paid to place suitcases on conveyor belts who nevertheless ask for tips in brusque undertones, just as in Nairobi or Karachi, sometimes hinting that the baggage might not arrive safely if no money changes hands. And he will in all probability then be trapped in slow lines while imminent flight departures are called out, waiting to be checked in by untrained clerks who tap on computer keyboards very slowly, with one finger.

Here, then, is the final trait typical of the third world—the chronic disorganization of perfectly routine procedures.

If our traveler is headed for a Manhattan hotel, he can choose between a dirty, battered, and possibly unsafe bus, or a dirtier and more battered taxi, usually driven by an unkempt lout who resembles his counterparts in Islamabad or Kinshasa rather than in London or Tokyo, where licensing requirements are strict and dress codes are enforced. At that point, a first-time visitor may still believe that both airport and taxi are glaring exceptions to the America he had always ima-gined—clean, modern, efficient. If so, he will immediately be disillusioned by the jolting drive over potholed highways and crumbling bridges, through miles of slums or miserable public housing.

Not as colorful as in Jakarta or Madras, the passing scene will still amaze those who come from the many European and even Asian cities where slums are now reduced to isolated survivals in remote parts of town (New York tour guides report a growing demand for the thrills of the South Bronx from European tourists quite uninterested in its pleasant greenery or the zoo, but eager to see open-air drug dealing at street corners, and the rows of burned-out buildings). After this unsettling encounter with an America already in full third-world conditions, an affluent tourist will next reach the luxurious glitter of a Manhattan hotel, but even there beggars may be standing near the door, just as in New Delhi or Lima.

IT SEEMS only yesterday that the professional optimists among us were still pointing to the continued American dominance of the world's entertainment, biotechnology, and aviation industries to reassure us that all was well, in spite of the virtual extinction of the U.S. consumer-electronics industry, the steady retreat of the auto industry, the drastic decline of the steel industry, and the widespread collapse of the machine-tool industry, still very much the foundation of all other industries.

Since then, Columbia Pictures has been sold to Sony, which had already purchased CBS Records in a previous transaction; the multimedia industry leader MCA has been sold off to Matsushita; Time-Warner, which includes HBO, has been partly sold to Toshiba and C. Itoh for $1 billion; and other notable names now belong to French and Italian interests. Word has it that it is only a matter of time before the remaining entertainment giants will go on the block in full or in part. Even hugely successful Disney, long the toast of Wall Street, chose to sell off the ownership of the hugely profitable Disneylands in France and Japan to local investors, in a typical exercise of capitalism-without-capital in the new American style.

Thus, Michael Jackson records may still sell by the millions all over the world, and American films may continue to dominate the global market, but the profits and the resulting opportunity for further capital accumulation now accrue to foreign owners.

Then there is the biotechnology industry, the *locus classicus* of the dynamic creativity and bold entrepreneurship that are supposed to compensate for all the other weaknesses of the American economy. The names of both buyers and sellers are far more obscure than in the Hollywood pairings, and the deals are much smaller (e.g., Chugai's $100 million purchase of Gen-Probe), but the great sell-off is under way just the same.

The pattern is by now well established. Americans still do most of the inventing, but because they cannot find capital at home to build the required facilities, they sell out to Japanese and European companies, receiving millions in license fees for products whose sales can eventually earn billions. Unfortunately, it is only those millions—and not the billions that will be earned mainly by foreign companies—that can be taxed to pay for basic research as well as all other government expenditures. As it is, the United States spent $5 billion on biotechnology research in 1990 as compared with only $1.7 billion for Japan, and less for Europe, but it is the Japanese and Europeans who are prospering, in great part by selling products originally developed in the U.S., mostly at the taxpayers' expense.

Now it is the turn of the aviation industry, which contributed $23.6 billion of exports to alleviate the U.S. trade imbalance at the last count. For all its success, it too is desperately short of capital. Boeing's only U.S. competitor, the McDonnell Douglas Corporation, recently announced that its commercial division, maker of the familiar DC-9, among other aircraft, is to become a separate company, so that 40 percent of it can be sold to the Taiwan Aerospace Corporation for $2 billion. Of that, only half a billion is for fresh investment—much less than the cost of engineering a single new airliner nowadays—while the remaining $1.5 billion is to reduce the company's crushing burden of debt, amounting to $2.6 billion at the last count.

T HAT places McDonnell Douglas in a very crowded field. For it is not only our public and private finance that is already in third-world conditions, with the federal government,[6] many state governments, and most large municipalities hugely in debt. Nor is it only a multitude of banks and insurance companies as well as the notorious S & L's that are badly under-

capitalized, if not actually insolvent—with another 400 expected to fail in 1992. Many industrial and commercial enterprises of seemingly solid standing are also afflicted with the McDonnell Douglas disease of excessive debt; they too are surviving on bankers' doles ("unscheduled refinancing"), just like the much more colorful real-estate tycoons who once bought everything in sight with money recklessly borrowed and recklessly lent. And every day another great name among our major corporations falls below even that minimal standard, with bankruptcies that leave pension funds short, medical benefits cut off, and customers as well as suppliers abruptly stranded, often with large invoices unpaid. Because many of them are in turn badly undercapitalized, they too can easily be dragged down into bankruptcy, spawning still further insolvencies.

But to return to the airline industry: some time before the McDonnell Douglas sale was announced, even Boeing decided that it could not afford the investment needed to engineer and produce its next airliner on its own. Having failed to find partners in the capital-starved U.S. aircraft industry, it turned to a Japanese consortium which now has a 20-percent risk-sharing partnership in the future Boeing 777.

As in the case of biotechnology, therefore, a leading industry, whose advancement owes much to basic research and specific technologies that U.S. taxpayers have funded in one way or another, is selling pieces of itself to foreign buyers, instead of only selling them its products.

When a farmer is reduced to selling off his broad acres rather than only his crops, his ultimate fate is not in doubt. Of course the analogy should be false because instead of a waning stock of acres, there is the unending flow of new technology that comes from the constantly celebrated creativity of our pluralist, multi-ethnic, undisciplined but ever-dynamic society.

Note, however, the small print that accompanied the dramatic announcement of the very latest example of that famous creativity. As soon as the suitably Korean-born chief developer of digital High-Definition (HD) TV revealed that the suitably small company he works for had totally overtaken the Japanese giants and their merely analog HD-TV, the company's owner, General Instrument, let it be known that it would not even try to raise the capital needed to produce and market the new invention, preferring to license production to established TV manufacturers, i.e., the Japanese TV giants.

In a manner literally pathetic, for pathos is the emotion evoked in the spectators to an inevitable downfall, a company spokesman hopefully speculated that if 20 million HD-TV sets were sold annually, its royalties at $10 per set could amount to as much as $200 million a year, a nice bit of change as they say—but truly mere change as compared to the $20-25 *billion* that the actual producers would earn each year, largely, no doubt, by exports to the United States.

But that is by now standard operating procedure, given our bootless capitalism-without-capital. It was Ampex, a U.S. company, which first developed the video-recorder technology that was then licensed for mere change to Matsushita, Sony, and the rest of those vigorous exporters—though of course their VCR export earnings did come back to the United States, through the purchase of CBS Records, Columbia Pictures, and MCA.

It is all very well to speak of the "globalization of industry" and to deride concerns for the nationality of production in an era of "transnational manufacturing," but when Taiwan acquires 40 percent of Douglas, or Japan's consortium has 20 percent of the next Boeing airliner, they assume no such responsibility for funding future U.S. aviation research, or Medicare for that matter—and the future earnings from those efforts will accrue to their balance of payments, and not ours.

WHAT is happening to the U.S. aviation industry in particular exposes the embarrassingly wide gap between the realities of what I have labeled geo-economics, and the free-trade-plus-globalization fantasy that remains unchallenged dogma for so many Americans, not least in the Bush White House.

To begin with, the American aviation industry's only significant foreign competitor is the European consortium Airbus Industrie, which has been very successful of late even against Boeing, by selling its government-subsidized aircraft with the aid of government-subsidized loans at low interest. Similarly, Taiwan Aerospace is a government-guaranteed company, no more exposed to the vagaries of the free market than the Vatican; as such, it will always be able to count on government subsidies to underbid Douglas subcontractors, thereby taking over specialized manufactures conducive to its own planned growth into an independent maker of civilian airliners.

The wider meaning of such narrowly-aimed industrial subsidies and "national technology programs" is plain enough. Just as past generations were put in uniform to be marched off in pursuit of geopolitical schemes of territorial conquest, today's taxpayers in Europe and elsewhere have been persuaded to subsidize geo-economic schemes of industrial conquest. The free-trade true believers smile at such foolish generosity, and invite us to enjoy the resulting subsidy of our own consumption. Thus they safeguard the interests of the citizen-as-consumer, while ignoring the interests of the citizen-as producer, but of the two roles it is only the latter that comports with the satisfactions of achievement and the dignity of employment. Moreover, the benefits of subsidized consumption that displaces our own production can only last so long as we still have acreage,

famous buildings, golf courses, industries, and new technologies to sell off.

As for globalization, while 40 percent of Douglas can freely be bought by Taiwan, or 40 percent of Boeing could be bought by Japan at any time, a U.S. buyer would have rather greater chances of being allowed to acquire 40 percent of the Sistine Chapel than 40 percent of Mitsubishi Industries.

It is this flat refusal of reciprocity that justifies concerns over the scope of Japanese direct investment in U.S. manufacturing and research companies—far more consequential acquisitions than Rockefeller Center or any number of golf courses. At the last count, total European direct investment in the U.S. was still very much larger, at $262 billion, than Japan's $69.7 billion. But it is not racism that accounts for the widespread concern over the latter and not the former, as even well-informed Japanese sincerely believe. Almost all European countries positively encourage almost all U.S. acquisitions and almost all forms of U.S. investment, while in Japan, as in Korea, only the likes of soft-drink bottling plants can be established or acquired without hindrance.

For free-trade-plus-globalization true believers, this entire discussion of foreign investment in the U.S., and of the barriers to U.S. investment in Japan and Korea, misses the point entirely. Foreign investment, they ceaselessly point out, brings jobs, thereby neatly offsetting the consequence of their other article of faith: import-caused unemployment. Equally, U.S. investment abroad exports jobs, and if other countries are foolish enough to keep it out, the loss of optimal earnings for capital is compensated by the retention of employment within the United States. Both claims are perfectly valid, but to leave it at that, as many do, ignores the wider implications of foreign investment on both sides.

In the first place, when U.S. auto production, for example, is displaced by the output of foreign-owned "transplants," the complete employment pyramid of technical designers, development engineers, stylists, corporate managers, and sundry ancillary professionals is decapitated, leaving only the base of assembly-line workers with a few junior-executive positions thrown in.

And this is precisely the object of the geo-economic competition that is increasingly dominating the main arena of world affairs, now that geopolitics is being provincialized to the unfortunate lands where armed conflict is still plausible, if not actually under way. The goal of geo-economics is not to accumulate gold, as in mercantilism, for it is not kings in need of coin to pay their regiments who are the protagonists, but rather corporate executives and their bureaucratic allies. Their aim is not territorial security or territorial expansion but its geo-economic equivalent: the conquest of the more desirable roles in the world economy.

Thus geo-economics is the very appropriate expression of meritocratic ambitions projected onto the world scene, just as geopolitics once expressed quintessentially aristocratic ambitions. Transplants do replace some of the jobs lost to imports, but what jobs? Are they the jobs that we would want for our children?

NONE of this is to say that Japanese corporate expansionism, or foreign interests in general, are responsible for the woes of the American economy. Decades of unilateral market access have undoubtedly weakened American businesses and contributed to their decapitalization. But it would obviously be foolish to blame foreigners for our own policies, and our own delusions. I do not recall any commandos from Japan's Ministry of International Trade and Industry (MITI) descending on Washington to impose unreciprocated Japanese access to American markets and American technology. Nor can Toyota or Hyundai be blamed if the U.S. government simply fails to insist on reciprocity, trusting instead in the gentle conduct of interminable negotiations that yield insignificant results.

Certainly neither our European competitors nor the Japanese can be blamed for the long list of self-inflicted wounds that have been engendering the third-worldization of America.

They did not arrange the regulatory and business-culture changes that brought the mores and urgencies of Las Vegas to Wall Street and corporate boardrooms across the land, to subordinate both future growth and current employment to immediate payoffs for well-placed principals.

They had no say in the most original invention of American statecraft: representation without taxation to extract "entitlements" galore, so that savings, already scant, have been absorbed in Treasury paper, instead of modern factories or updated infrastructure.

They did not seize control of our classrooms, to discredit the discipline and absolute standards that are the prerequisites of all education, nor lately appoint the "multiculturalism" inspectors who equate arithmetic with racism, and who annex the study of history to group therapy.

Nor did foreigners devise our spectacularly antisocial "social" programs, by now most nefariously entangled in both racial politics and the crudest racism. There are very few Afro-Swedes, yet because Sweden is very generous to unmarried mothers, such mothers account for 50.9 percent of all births, as opposed to 25.7 percent in the less generous United States, and only 1 percent in notably ungenerous Japan, where 99 percent of all children are still compelled to grow up with both fathers and mothers. That, no doubt, is yet another of those exotic Japanese practices devised by the sinister MITI—certainly nothing enhances a country's competitive position more than a population properly brought up in stable families.

The list is by no means complete. The many new perversions of the administration of justice could add an entire list of their own, from ruinous product-liability awards against the manufacturers of 50-year-old machinery for one-year-old accidents, to the abandonment of the loitering laws, which leaves policemen powerless against urban predators. But even the few dysfunctions listed above would have been sufficient to propel our rapid slide into third-world conditions, complete with an entire generation of children as doomed as the street waifs of Rio de Janeiro. The newborn son of a long-gone teenage father and a fifteen-year-old mother, with a grandmother in her thirties and a great-grandmother in her forties—all of them unmarried, uneducated, and unemployed—has become a rather common American type, destined from birth to roam the streets in between episodes of casual labor, crime, addiction, and imprisonment.

A search for the deeper sources of all the blatantly obvious diseases of American society would take us very far—though it might be said in passing that Anglo-Saxon style individualism could only be successful so long as there was still enough Calvinism to go around. But at least the immediate causes of our third-worldization are simply economic, a matter of capital and labor. And while the inadequate diligence of our labor force obviously has no simple cause, the immediate reason for our disastrous shortage of capital is plain enough. Americans have little to invest because they save so little.[7]

Obviously, it is possible to invest without saving, if others lend the necessary money. And of course the United States has borrowed hugely in recent years, and also absorbed a vast amount of foreign investment.[8] Yet given the size of the American economy, even the huge inflow of money from abroad could not possibly remedy the disastrous difference between our rate of savings and those of our competitors.[9]

IN ANY case, the relentless erosion of the entire economic base of American society is revealed by undisputed statistics that have none of the flaws of international comparisons. During the last 20 years—half a working lifetime—American "non-farm, non-supervisory" employees actually earned slightly less, year by year. As a matter of fact, by 1990 their real earnings (corrected for inflation) had regressed to the 1965 level.[10] Will they regress further—perhaps to the 1960 level by 1995, and then to the 1955 level by the year 2000? It seems distinctly possible. Given the lack of invested capital, it is only with ever-cheaper labor that we can compete internationally. Therein lies our own path to Bangladesh.

Who are these poor unfortunates whose real earnings have been declining since 1965? Are they perhaps some small and peculiar minority?

5. SOCIAL INSTITUTIONS: Economic Sphere

Not so. In November 1990, the last month for which those statistics are complete, they numbered 74,888,000, or just over 81 percent of all non-farm employees—that is, more than eight out of ten of all Americans who are not self-employed, from corporate executives earning hundreds or even thousands of dollars per hour, to those working at the minimum wage.

Far from being a minority whose fate cannot affect the base of American society, then, they *are* the base of American society, the vast majority of the labor force of manufacturing, mining, construction, transport, utility, wholesale and retail trade, finance, insurance, real estate, all other service enterprises, and government employees.

How can the entire structure of American affluence and advancement from luxurious living to scientific laboratories *not* decline when the vast majority of all working Americans are earning less and less? And how can the U.S. not slide toward third-world conditions if this absolute decline continues while in both Western Europe and East Asia real earnings continue to increase?

Inevitably, the most telling comparison is with Japan. In 1970, Japanese manufacturing employees earned only just over a quarter (or more precisely 27 percent) as much as their American counterparts. In 1988, they earned 7 percent more. If the trend were to continue straight on both sides, in 18 more years American earnings would be reduced to less than a quarter (23 percent) of the Japanese level, almost the same proportion as now obtains between Brazilian and American hourly wages in manufacturing.

It stands to reason that by then the United States would become Japan's Brazil, an amusing, sometimes unsettling country of vast expanses with a cheerful but impoverished third-world population. The casual banter that nowadays greets errors of blatant incompetence in American offices, factories, and shops; the patient silence evoked even by acts of willful negligence and aggressive apathy; the learned ability to ignore unkempt urban vagrants and all their importunings; and generally our increasing acceptance of breakdowns, delays, and all forms of physical decay—all this shows that we are indeed adapting to our fate, by acquiring the necessary third-world traits of fatalistic detachment. But they, of course, ensure that the slide will continue.

---

[1] As measured by the gross national product per capita, which was $4,950 for the United States; $2,360 for the European Community; and $1,950 for Japan.

[2] The 1980 figures were: for the U.S., $12,000; for Japan, $9,870; and for the European Community, $9,760 (but West Germany came in at $13,340).

[3] The 1989 GNP per capita for the United States was $21,000, while Japan's had soared to $23,810. Distorted by the entry of three poor countries, Greece, Portugal, and Spain, the figure for the European Community was $15,980, or 76 percent of the American level, but Germany at $20,750 was substantially even, while Switzerland, Europe's top performer, was well ahead at $30,270.

[4] In 1988, the last year for which those particular figures are available, the gross *domestic* product (all factor costs plus indirect taxes minus subsidies, and excluding net factor income from abroad, which is included in the GNP) per person was $19,558 for the United States; $14,161 for West Germany as it then still was; $16,700 for Europe's champion, Switzerland; and only $14,288 for Japan (as opposed to the straight exchange-rate GNP comparison for that same year, in which Japan's $20,960 per person already exceeded the $19,820 figure for the U.S.).

[5] In 1970, the figures for the United States, West Germany, Italy, and Japan were $4,922, $3,380, $2,848, and $2,765, respectively. Because there was so much inflation in the years that followed, all those figures had greatly increased by 1988. The U.S. figure for 1988 was just under four times greater (x 3.97, to be exact); the West German increase was somewhat greater (x 4.18); the Italian increase was greater still (x 4.55), in spite of the notorious undercounting caused by the explosion of Italy's underground economy during those very years; while Japan's figure was more than five times greater (x 5.16).

[6] The latest official estimate of the fiscal 1992 deficit is $340 billion—a catastrophic number *five times* larger than early 1991 White House estimates.

[7] From 1970 to 1989, total U.S. savings fluctuated between 12.1 percent and 14.1 percent of the gross domestic product, as opposed to 22.9 percent and 22.7 percent for the European Community average, and 38.9 percent and 34.9 percent for Japan.

[8] As late as 1982, our net international investments, holdings, and claims amounted to $136.7 billion, but by the end of 1989 (it is worse now), our net position was *minus* $663.7 billion, very much more than the combined debt of Brazil, Korea, Mexico, Indonesia, Algeria, Turkey, Portugal, Argentina, India, Malaysia, Greece, and China—most of them countries still poor but developing quite rapidly, for which foreign borrowing is perfectly appropriate, and the entry of foreign investment a clear mark of progress.

[9] In 1989, the numbers stood at $7,000 per person for Japan; $3,190 per person for the European Community (by then depressed by the admission of Greece, Portugal, and Spain); and $3,000 per person for the U.S. That miserable number is readily explained by the increase in personal consumption, from $8,650 in 1970 to $12,760 in 1989 (in constant 1987 dollars), as compared to $11,800 for Japan, and $8,830 for the European Community average in 1989.

[10] Average hourly earnings in constant 1982 dollars were $8.03 in 1970, $7.78 in 1980, and $7.53 in 1990. Averages conceal many tales, of course, from the rising earnings of federal, state, and municipal employees no matter what, to the degradation of $18-per-hour industrial workers into $10-per-hour janitors, or even their desperate poaching of minimum-wage jobs, once the stepping stones of underclass achievement.

Is It Possible To Be Pro-Life and Pro-Choice?

Carl Sagan and Ann Druyan

Carl Sagan teaches and does research at Cornell University. The idea that fetal brain activity might help provide a rational compromise in the abortion debate was raised in his 1977 book "The Dragons of Eden," for which he received the Pulitzer Prize.

Ann Druyan is secretary of the Federation of American Scientists—founded in 1945 by the original atomic scientists to combat the misuse of science and technology. A member of the board of directors of the Children's Health Fund in New York City, she is also a writer and television producer whose most recent work includes two worldwide television specials on the Voyager 2 encounter with the planet Neptune.

They are married and have one child.

The issue had been decided years ago. The court had chosen the middle ground. You'd think the fight was over. Instead, there are mass rallies, bombings and intimidation, arrests, intense lobbying, legislative drama, Congressional hearings, Supreme Court decisions and clerics threatening politicians with perdition. Partisans fling accusations of hypocrisy and murder. The intent of the Constitution and the will of God are equally invoked. Doubtful arguments are trotted out as certainties. The contending factions call on science to bolster their positions. Families are divided, husbands and wives agree not to discuss it, old friends are no longer speaking. Politicians check the latest polls to discover the dictates of their consciences. Amid all the shouting, it is hard for the adversaries to hear one another. Opinions are polarized. Minds are closed.

Is it wrong to abort a pregnancy? Always? Sometimes? Never? How do we decide? We wrote this article to understand better what the contending views are and to see if we ourselves could find a position that would satisfy us both. We had to weigh the arguments of both sides for consistency and to pose test cases, some of which are purely hypothetical. If in some of these tests we seem to go too far, we ask the reader to

be patient with us—we're trying to stress the various positions to the breaking point to see their weaknesses and where they fail.

In contemplative moments, nearly everyone recognizes that the issue is not wholly one-sided. Many partisans of differing views, we find, feel some disquiet, some unease when confronting what's behind the opposing arguments. (This is partly why such confrontations are avoided.) And the issue surely touches on deep questions: What are our responsibilities to one another? Should we permit the state to intrude into the most intimate and personal aspects of our lives? Where are the boundaries of freedom? What does it mean to be human?

Testing "Freedom of Choice"

Of the many actual points of view, it is widely held—especially in the media, which rarely have the time or the inclination to make the fine distinctions—that there are only two: "pro-choice" and "pro-life." This is what the two principal warring camps like to call themselves, and that's what we'll call them here. In the simplest characterization, a pro-choicer would hold that the decision to abort a pregnancy is to be made only by the woman; the state has no right to interfere. And a pro-lifer would hold that, from the moment of conception, the embryo or fetus is alive; that this life imposes on us a moral obligation to preserve it; and that abortion is tantamount to murder. Both names—pro-choice and pro-life—were picked with an eye toward influencing those whose minds are not yet made up: Few people wish to be counted as being against freedom of choice or as opposed to life. Indeed, freedom and life are two of our most cherished values, and here they seem to be in fundamental conflict.

Let's consider these two absolutist positions in turn. A newborn baby is surely the same being it was just before birth. There is good evidence that a late-term fetus responds to sound—including music, but especially its mother's voice. It can suck its thumb or do a somersault. Occasionally, it generates adult brain wave patterns. Some people say they remember being born, or even the uterine environment. Perhaps there is thought in the womb. It's hard to maintain that a transformation to full personhood happens abruptly at the moment of birth. Why, then, should it be murder to kill an infant the day after it was born but not the day before?

As a practical matter, this isn't very important: less than one percent of all tabulated abortions in the United States are listed in the last three months of pregnancy (and, on closer investigation, most such reports turn out to be due to miscarriage or miscalculation). But third-trimester abortions provide a test of the limits of the pro-choice point of view. Does a woman's "innate right to control her own body" include the right to kill a near-term fetus who is, for all intents and purposes, identical to a newborn child?

We believe that many supporters of reproductive freedom are troubled at least occasionally by this question. But they are reluctant to raise it because it is the beginning of a slippery slope. If it is impermissible to abort a pregnancy in the ninth month, what about the eighth, seventh, sixth . . . ? Once we acknowledge that the state can interfere at *any* time in the pregnancy, doesn't it follow that the state can interfere at all times?

This conjures up the specter of predominantly male, predominantly affluent legislators telling poor women they must bear and raise alone children they cannot afford to bring up; forcing teenagers to bear children they are not emotionally prepared to deal with; saying to women who wish for a career that they must give up their dreams, stay home and bring up babies; and, worst of all, condemning victims of rape and incest to carry and nurture the offspring of their assailants. Legislative prohibitions on abortion arouse the suspicion that their real intent is to control the independence and sexuality of women. Why should legislators have any right at all to tell women what to do with their bodies? To be deprived of reproductive freedom is demeaning. Women are fed up with being pushed around.

And yet, by consensus, all of us think it proper that there be prohibitions against, and penalties exacted for, murder. It would be a flimsy defense if the murderer pleads that this is just between him and his victim and none of the government's business. If killing a fetus is truly killing a human being, is it not the *duty* of the state to prevent it? Indeed, one of the chief functions of government is to protect the weak from the strong.

If we do not oppose abortion at *some* stage of pregnancy, is there not a danger of dismissing an entire category of human beings as unworthy of our protection and respect? And isn't that dismissal the

hallmark of sexism, racism, nationalism and religious fanaticism? Shouldn't those dedicated to fighting such injustices be scrupulously careful not to embrace another?

Testing the "Right to Life"

There is no right to life in any society on Earth today, nor has there been at any former time (with a few rare exceptions, such as among the Jains of India): We raise farm animals for slaughter; destroy forests; pollute rivers and lakes until no fish can live there; kill deer and elk for sport, leopards for their pelts and whales for fertilizer; entrap dolphins, gasping and writhing, in great tuna nets; club seal pups to death; and render a species extinct every day. All these beasts and vegetables are as alive as we. What is (allegedly) protected is not life, but *human* life.

And even with that protection, casual murder is an urban commonplace, and we wage "conventional" wars with tolls so terrible that we are, most of us, afraid to consider them very deeply. (Tellingly, state-organized mass murders are often justified by redefining our opponents—by race, nationality, religion or ideology—as less than human.) That protection, that right to life, eluded the 40,000 children under 5 who died on our planet today—as every day—from preventable starvation, dehydration, disease and neglect.

Those who assert a "right to life" are for (at most) not just any kind of life, but for—particularly and uniquely—human life. So they too, like pro-choicers, must decide what distinguishes a human being from other animals and when, during gestation, the uniquely human qualities—whatever they are—emerge.

Despite many claims to the contrary, life does not begin at conception: It is an unbroken chain that stretches back nearly to the origin of the Earth, 4.6 billion years ago. Nor does *human* life begin at conception: It is an unbroken chain dating back to the origin of our species, tens or hundreds of thousands of years ago. Every human sperm and egg is, beyond the shadow of a doubt, alive. They are not human beings, of course. However, it could be argued that neither is a fertilized egg.

In some animals, an egg develops into a healthy adult without benefit of a sperm cell. But not, so far as we know, among humans. A sperm and an unfertilized egg jointly comprise the full genetic blueprint for a human being. Under certain circumstances, after fertilization, they can develop into a baby. But most fertilized eggs are spontaneously miscarried. Development into a baby is by no means guaranteed. Neither a sperm and egg separately, nor a fertilized egg, is more than a *potential* baby or a *potential* adult. So if a sperm and an egg are as human as the fertilized egg produced by their union, and if it is murder to destroy a fertilized egg—despite the fact that it's only *potentially* a baby—why isn't it murder to destroy a sperm or an egg?

Hundreds of millions of sperm cells (top speed with tails lashing: 5 inches per hour) are produced in an average human ejaculation. A healthy young man can produce in a week or two enough spermatozoa to double the human population of the Earth. So is masturbation mass murder? How about nocturnal emissions or just plain sex? When the unfertilized egg is expelled each month, has someone died? Some lower animals can be grown in the laboratory from a single body cell. If such cloning technology were ever developed for humans, would we be committing genocide by shedding a drop of blood?

All human sperm and eggs are genetic halves of "potential" human beings. Should heroic efforts be made to save and preserve all of them, everywhere, because of this "potential"? Is failure to do so immoral or criminal? Of course, there's a difference between taking a life and failing to save it. And there's a big difference between the probability of survival of a sperm cell and that of a fertilized egg. But the absurdity of a corps of high-minded semen-preservers moves us to wonder whether a fertilized egg's mere "potential" to become a baby really does make destroying it murder.

Opponents of abortion worry that, once abortion is permissible immediately after conception, no argument will restrict it at any later time in the pregnancy. Then, they fear, one day it will be permissible to murder a fetus that is unambiguously a human being. Both pro-choicers and pro-lifers (at least some of them) are pushed toward absolutist positions by parallel fears of the slippery slope.

Another slippery slope is reached by those pro-lifers who are willing to make an exception in the agonizing case of a pregnancy resulting from rape or incest. But why should the right to live depend on the *circumstances* of conception? If the same child were to result, can the state ordain life for the offspring of a lawful union but death for one conceived by force or coercion? How can this be just? And if exceptions are extended to such a fetus, why should they be withheld from any other fetus? This is part of the reason some pro-lifers adopt what many others consider the outrageous posture of opposing abortions under any and all circumstances—only excepting, perhaps, when the life of the mother is in danger.

By far the most common reason for abortion is birth-control. So shouldn't opponents of abortion be handing out contraceptives? That would be an effective way to reduce the number of abortions. Instead, the United States is far behind other nations in the development of safe and effective methods of birth control—and, in many cases, opposition to such research (and to sex education) has come from the same people who oppose abortions.

When Do We Become Human?

The attempt to find an ethically sound and unambiguous judgment on when, if ever, abortion is permissible has deep historical roots. Often, especially in Christian tradition, such attempts were connected with the question of when the soul enters the body—a matter not readily amenable to scientific investigation and an issue of controversy even among learned theologians. Ensoulment has been asserted to occur in the sperm before conception, at conception, at the time of "quickening" (when the mother is first able to feel the fetus stirring within her) and at birth. Or even later.

Different religions have different teachings. Among hunter-gatherers, there are usually no prohibitions against abortion, and it was common in ancient Greece and Rome. The Assyrians impaled women on stakes for attempting abortions. The Jewish Talmud teaches that the fetus is not a person and has no rights. The Old and New Testaments—rich in detailed prohibitions on dress, diet and permissible words—contain not a word specifically prohibiting abortion. The only passage that's remotely relevant (*Exodus* 21:22) decrees that if there's a fight and a woman bystander is accidentally injured and made to miscarry, the assailant must pay a fine. The Catholic Church's first and long-standing collection of canon law (according to the leading historian of the Church's teachings on abortion, John Connery, S.J.) held that abortion was homicide only after the fetus was already "formed"—roughly, the end of the first trimester. It was not until 1869 that abortion at any time for any reason became grounds for excommunication.

If you deliberately kill a human being, it's called murder. If you deliberately kill a chimpanzee—biologically, our closest relative—whatever else it is, it's not murder. To date, murder uniquely applies to killing human beings. Therefore, the question of when personhood (or, if we like, ensoulment) arises is key to the abortion debate. When does the fetus become human? When do distinct and characteristic human qualities emerge?

We recognize that specifying a precise moment will overlook individual differences. Therefore, if we must draw a line, it ought to be drawn conservatively—that is, on the early side. There are people who object to having to set some numerical limit, and we share their disquiet; but if there is to be a law on this matter, and it is to effect some useful compromise between the two absolutist positions, it must specify, at least roughly, a time of transition to personhood.

Every one of us began from a dot. A fertilized egg is roughly the size of the period at the end of this sentence. The momentous meeting of sperm and egg generally occurs in one of the two fallopian tubes. One cell becomes two, two become four, and by the sixth day the fertilized egg has become a kind of hollow sphere wandering off to another realm: the womb. It destroys tissue in its path. It sucks blood from capillaries. It establishes itself as a kind of parasite on the walls of the uterus.

• By the third week, around the time of the first missed menstrual period, the forming embryo is about 2 millimeters long and is developing various body parts. But it looks a little like a segmented worm.

• By the end of the fourth week, it's approximately 5 millimeters (about ⅕ inch) long. It's recognizable as a vertebrate, its tube-shaped heart is beginning to beat, something like the gill arches of a fish or an amphibian have become conspicuous, and there is a pronounced tail. It looks something like a newt or a tadpole. This is the end of the first month after conception.

• By the fifth week, the gross divisions of the brain can be distinguished. What will later develop into eyes is apparent, and little buds appear—on their way to becoming arms and legs.

• By the sixth week, the embryo is 13 millimeters (about ½ inch) long. The eyes are still on the side of the head, as in most animals, and the reptilian face has connected slits where the mouth and nose eventually will be.

• By the end of the seventh week, the tail is almost gone, and sexual characteristics can be discerned (although both sexes look female). The face is mammalian but somewhat piglike.

• By the end of the eighth week, the face resembles a primate's but is still not quite human. Most of the human body parts are present in their essentials. Some lower brain anatomy is well-developed. The fetus shows some reflex response to delicate stimulation.

• By the tenth week, the face has an unmistakably human cast. It is beginning to be possible to distinguish males from females. Nails and major bone structures are not apparent until the third month.

• By the fourth month, you can tell the face of one fetus from that of another. Quickening is most often first felt in the fifth month. The bronchioles of the lungs do not begin developing until approximately the sixth month, the alveoli still later. Recognizably human brain activity begins intermittently around the middle of the seventh month.

So, if only a person can be murdered, when does the fetus attain personhood? When its face becomes distinctly human, near the end of the first trimester? When the fetus becomes responsive to stimuli—again, at the end of the first trimester? When the fetus becomes active enough to be felt as quickening, typically in the middle of the second trimester? When the lungs have reached a stage of development sufficient that the fetus might, just conceivably, be able to breathe on its own in the outside air?

The trouble with such developmental milestones is not just that they're arbitrary. More troubling is the fact that none of them involves *uniquely human* characteris-

tics—apart from the superficial matter of facial appearance. All animals respond to stimuli and move of their own volition. Large numbers are able to breathe. But that doesn't stop us from slaughtering them. Reflexes and motion and respiration are not what makes us human.

Other animals have advantages over us—in speed, strength, endurance, climbing or burrowing skills, camouflage, sight or smell or hearing, mastery of the air or water. Our one great advantage, the secret of our success, is thought—characteristically human thought. We are able to think things through, imagine events yet to occur, figure things out. That's how we invented agriculture and civilization. Thought is our blessing and our curse, and it makes us who we are.

Thinking occurs, of course, in the brain—principally in the top layers of the convoluted "gray matter" called the cerebral cortex. The roughly 100 billion neurons in the brain constitute the material basis of thought. The neurons are connected to each other, and their linkups play a major role in what we experience as thinking. But large-scale linking up of neurons doesn't begin until the 24th to 27th week of pregnancy—the sixth month.

By placing harmless electrodes on a subject's head, scientists can measure the electrical activity produced by the network of neurons inside the skull. Different kinds of mental activity show different kinds of brain waves. But brain waves with regular patterns typical of adult human brains did not appear in the fetus until about the 30th week of pregnancy—near the beginning of the third trimester. Fetuses younger than this—however alive and active they may be—lack the necessary brain architecture. They cannot yet think.

Acquiescing in the killing of any living creature, especially one that might later become a baby, is troublesome and painful. But we've rejected the extremes of "always" and "never," and this puts us—like it or not—on the slippery slope. If we are forced to choose a developmental criterion, then this is where we draw the line: when the beginning of characteristically human thinking becomes barely possible. It is, in fact, a very conservative definition: Regular brain waves are rarely found in fetuses. More research would help. If we wanted to make the criterion still more stringent, to allow for precocious fetal brain development, we might draw the line at six months. This, it so happens, is where the Supreme Court drew it in 1973—although for completely different reasons.

Viability and the Court

Its decision in the case of *Roe v. Wade* changed American law on abortion. It permits abortion at the request of the woman without restriction in the first trimester and, with some restrictions intended to protect her health, in the second trimester. It allows states to forbid abortion in the third trimester except when there's a serious threat to the life or health of the woman. In a recent reassessment, the Supreme Court declined explicitly to overturn *Roe v. Wade* but in effect invited the 50 state legislatures to decide for themselves.

What was the reasoning in *Roe v. Wade*? There was no legal weight given to what happens to the children once they are born, or to the family. Instead, a woman's right to reproductive freedom is protected, the court ruled, by constitutional guarantees of privacy. But that right is not unqualified. The woman's guarantee of privacy and the fetus's right to life must be weighed—and when the court did the weighing, priority was given to privacy in the first trimester and to life in the third. The transition was decided not from any of the considerations we have been dealing with so far in this article—not when "ensoulment" occurs, not when the fetus takes on sufficient human characteristics to be protected by laws against murder. Instead, the crite-

rion adopted was whether the fetus could live outside the mother. This is called "viability" and depends in part on the ability to breathe. The lungs are simply not developed, and the fetus cannot breathe—no matter how advanced an artificial lung it might be placed in—until about the 24th week, near the start of the sixth month. This is why *Roe v. Wade* permits states to prohibit abortions in the last trimester. It's a very pragmatic criterion.

If the fetus at a certain stage of gestation would be viable outside the womb, the argument goes, then the right of the fetus to life overrides the right of the woman to privacy. But just what does "viable" mean? Even a full-term newborn is not viable without a great deal of care and love. There was a time before incubators, only a few decades ago, when babies in their seventh month were unlikely to be viable. Would aborting in the seventh month have been permissible then? After the invention of incubators, did aborting pregnancies in the seventh month suddenly become

---

Abortion In American History

From colonial times to the 19th century, the choice was the woman's until "quickening" (when she is first able to feel the fetus stirring within her). An abortion in the first or even second trimester was at worst a misdemeanor. Convictions were rarely sought and almost impossible to obtain, because they depended entirely on the woman's own testimony of whether she had felt quickening, and because of the jury's distaste for prosecuting a woman for exercising her right to choose. In 1800 there was not, so far as is known, a single statute in the U.S. concerning abortion. Advertisements for drugs to induce abortion could be found in virtually every newspaper and even in many church publications—although the language used was suitably euphemistic, if widely understood.

But by 1900, abortion had been banned at *any* time in pregnancy by every state in the Union, except when necessary to save the woman's life. What happened to bring about so striking a reversal? Religion had little to do with it. Drastic economic and social changes were turning this country from an agrarian to an urban-industrial society. America was in the process of changing from having one of the highest birthrates in the world to one of the lowest. Abortion certainly played a role and stimulated forces to suppress it.

One of the most significant of these forces was the medical profession. Up to the mid-19th century, medicine was an uncertified, unsupervised business. Anyone could hang up a shingle and become

a doctor. With the rise of a new, university-educated medical elite, anxious to enhance the status and influence of physicians, the American Medical Association was formed. In its first decade, the AMA began lobbying against abortions performed by anyone except licensed physicians. New knowledge of embryology, the physicians said, had shown the fetus to be human even before quickening.

Their assault on abortion was motivated not by concern for the health of the woman but, they claimed, for the welfare of the fetus. You had to be a physician to know when abortion was morally justified, because the question depended on scientific and medical facts understood only by physicians. At the same time, women were effectively excluded from the medical schools, where such arcane knowledge could be acquired. So, as things worked out, women had almost nothing to say about terminating their own pregnancies. It was also up to the physician to decide if the pregnancy posed a threat to the woman and was entirely at his discretion to determine what was and was not a threat. For the rich woman, it might be a threat to her emotional tranquillity or even to her lifestyle. The poor woman was often forced to resort to the back alley or the coat hanger.

This was the law until the 1960s, when a coalition of individuals and organizations, the AMA now among them, sought to overturn it and to reinstate the more traditional values that were to be embodied in *Roe v Wade*.

immoral? What happens if, in the future, a new technology develops so that an artificial womb can sustain a fetus even before the sixth month by delivering oxygen and nutrients through the blood—as the mother does through the placenta and into the fetal blood system? We grant that this technology is unlikely to be developed soon or become available to many. But *if* it were available, does it then become immoral to abort earlier than the sixth month, when previously it was moral? A morality that depends on, and changes with, technology is a fragile morality; for some, it is also an unacceptable morality.

And why, exactly, should breathing (or kidney function, or the ability to resist disease) justify legal protection? If a fetus can be shown to think and feel but not be able to breathe, would it be all right to kill it? Do we value breathing more than thinking and feeling? Viability arguments cannot, it seems to us, coherently determine when abortions are permissible. Some other criterion is needed. Again, we offer for consideration the earliest onset of human thinking as that criterion.

Since, on average, fetal thinking occurs even later than fetal lung development, we find *Roe v. Wade* to be a good and prudent decision addressing a complex and difficult issue. With prohibitions on abortion in the last trimester—except in cases of grave medical necessity—it strikes a fair balance between the conflicting claims of freedom and of life.

Stand and deliver

*To ensure equality, we need to
provide alternatives within public schools*

WILLIAM GREIDER

The radically democratic idea that America bequeathed to the world nearly two centuries ago—the common school, where children of all classes come together to learn society's shared knowledge—is now in jeopardy.

Powerful interests have concluded that the nation's struggling public schools are beyond repair and incapable of reforming themselves. These interests propose instead to divert public financing—that is, tax money—to private schools, which will presumably do a better job of preparing kids for the high-tech future. George Herbert Walker Bush, Andover '42, Yale '48, is leading the assault.

This year, Bush staged a photo op on the White House lawn, surrounded by school kids, to announce his own "GI bill for children"—federal tuition vouchers of $1,000 that families of modest means (up to $40,000 income) could use to send their children to private schools. The idea has a natural constituency among Catholic parents and others who are already footing the bill for parochial or private schools, but it also appeals to many aspiring ghetto families whose kids are trapped in the worst urban schools.

The concept (euphemistically labeled "school choice") also has some political heavyweights behind it. The Catholic Church—whose own parochial-school system has been steadily shrinking for decades—is, not surprisingly, enthusiastic about securing a new source of revenue. So are many Protestant Evangelicals on the Christian right, who support Christian schools.

Choice is also being promoted by the Business Roundtable, the lobbying front for the 200 largest corporations, as well as by the *New York Times* and conservative think tanks from the Brookings Institution to the Heritage Foundation. Their argument is that "competition" will be good for public schools, driving them toward self-improvement.

Those opposed to vouchers, of whom I am one, argue that diverting public money to private schools—schools that can pick and choose among the most desirable students and ignore the undesirables—will inevitably doom the public-school system. The ultimate effect would be to create a two-tiered system: elite private schools for the most promising students, underfinanced public ones for the remaining masses.

In time, as elites divert resources to their schools and starve the public sector, we may well see the rise of gross inequalities and divisive class conflicts—the worst features of educational systems in societies like Great Britain and Japan. Disassembling the common school means, in effect, giving up on the democratic idea itself.

Bill Clinton and the Democratic party forthrightly staked out their opposition. The party's 1992 platform declared: "We oppose the Bush administration's efforts to bankrupt the public school system—the bedrock of democracy—through private school vouchers." Critics dismiss the Democrats' position as special-interest politics, since the teachers' unions are a major constituency. But in fact the Democrats are defending the long-term interests of most American families. Despite conservative propaganda to the contrary, 89 percent of the country's 48 million elementary and secondary students are in public schools. And the overwhelming majority want to stay there.

Like most political issues in this era, school reform has a subtext of private profit: Certain commercial enterprises will reap huge returns if public money can be channeled into private schools. The most visible of these is Whittle Communications, the same company that has taken Channel One TV news and commercials into classrooms. Chris Whittle, a creative publishing entrepreneur, has announced grandiose plans to launch 200 private, tuition-supported schools by 1996 and 1,000 by the year 2005. He promises to revolutionize schooling in America while also turning a profit.

Business discovered education in a big way in the past decade. Scores of corporations are now contributing valuable ideas and real money to improving public education. In the next round of reform, however, the danger is that businesses will turn our children into commodities—lunch-box-toting profit centers.

My prejudices on education run deep. It's not just that my wife and I and our children attended public schools but that we come from families closely tied to public education. Beyond that, I feel a sense of personal debt to the common school because I cherish the story of my own grandfather's rise from poverty. He ran away from home when he was 15—escaping from a tyrannical, no-account father who worked his sons on a marginal farm in northern Indiana and wouldn't let them go to school. My runaway grandfather made his way across the Midwest as an itinerant farmhand, then landed in Kansas and somehow managed to complete his schooling while laboring in the fields. I have this image of him as an earnest teenager, sitting among smaller children in a country schoolhouse as he caught up with the education he missed as a boy. By his mid-20s, he had become a teacher himself. His family secured the comfortable life of the middle class; his thirst for learning was passed on to his descendants.

My grandfather's is the classic American story of public schools helping a bright, ambitious kid to find his way out of poverty. This possibility is the pride of the nation.

But as we all know, America's schools today rarely deliver on this possibility. Public-school students and parents are painfully familiar with teachers who are stupid louts, textbooks that are drivel, and the brain-deadening regimen of public schooling. Anyone who reads newspapers knows the grim tales of gun-toting students in big-city schools and the documented ignorance of many recent graduates.

But there is a parallel reality that has been forgotten in the current debate: Public schools have actually improved over the past generation, at least in terms of serving poor blacks and other minorities. However terrible the present failures are, the system is not sliding downward, as critics claim. Hopes for equal opportunity are still flagrantly disappointed, but conditions have improved substantially during the past three decades.

The statistics on blacks' growing educational achievement are dramatic although seldom noted. In 1964 only 45 percent of young blacks aged 25 to 29 had finished high school. By 1987, 83 percent had. The dropout rate among blacks, though still severe in some

---

Diverting public money to private schools via vouchers will doom the public schools.

---

inner cities, has been declining steadily since the '60s and is approaching overall parity with whites'.

In terms of basic skills—reading and writing and arithmetic—black students have also gained significant ground, narrowing the gap with white students, though they still lag far behind. In 1971, 18 percent of black 17-year-olds could not read at even a basic level; by 1988 the number had shrunk to 3 percent. Black students' math skills, likewise, rose sharply over the past two decades. "These findings are obviously at odds with the widespread view that inner-city schools have deteriorated over the past generation," concludes social scientist Christopher Jencks, author of *Rethinking Social Policy.*

In other words, the problem of reforming public schools is not quite what the headlines suggest. Poor kids who were routinely pushed out of the system a generation ago are now generally included. But that raises a new point: What do these kids actually learn? They are better educated than their parents or grandparents, but not well enough to cope with a much more complicated world. This reality poses a different question for the reform debate: If public schools have been improving rather than deteriorating, why give up on them now?

A new pink-and-aquamarine building in Miami Beach is Dade County's answer to the question. South Pointe Elementary School had 2,000 visitors in its initial year of operation—educators, school-board members, reporters—because the word got out that something truly original was happening there. The first public school in the nation designed and operated by a private corporation—Education Alternatives Inc. of Minneapolis—South Pointe is very different from Grade School, U.S.A.

For one thing, there are three IBM PCs in every classroom, plus a media center with networks of IBMs and Macintoshes. All the kids use them routinely, and every teacher also has a computer of his or her own to design and coordinate the highly individualized teaching plans for each of the school's 620 children.

But South Pointe is also awash in books—it spent $100,000 on learning materials, several times what's spent at other Dade County elementary schools. Kids get half an hour of "free choice" time each day to read whatever they choose or noodle around with their own projects.

Most important of all, the pupil-teacher ratio at South Pointe is only 15 to 1—less than half the national average and comparable with the best private schools. This is possible because the school hired 15 teaching assistants from the University of Miami—student teachers who work alongside the professionals and help supervise the continuous swirl of small-group activity and individual instruction.

If South Pointe works, it will provide a powerful model of reform because it is not avoiding the hardest cases. Sixty-six percent of its students are Hispanic, 13 percent are black; 80 percent come from the poorest families in town. A third are not up to speed in English. The school must also cope with the high transient rate—57 percent student turnover each year—that's typical of inner-city schools. A small percentage of students also come from some of Miami Beach's wealthiest families, attracted by the idealism and innovations of the experiment.

It will be two or three years before anyone can prove definitively that student performance has been altered by South Pointe's changes. In the meantime, Principal Pat Parham is confident of the results: "After 32 years in the public schools, it's beautiful to see a school where the kids really are the focus. To see them learning to take responsibility for their own education and learning their academic material and being excited about it—it's just been awesome."

Baltimore officials were so impressed by what they saw that they hired Education Alternatives Inc. to refashion and manage nine of the city's schools next fall. Duluth, Minnesota, has brought to EAI to manage its entire school system through temporary difficulties. Other cities are studying the same public-private option. [*Editor's note: EAI is hired by a school district on a contract basis just as any other consultant or supplier is. It is not funded directly by tax-based school assessments.*]

In a sense, EAI is the counterpoint to Whittle's experiment. As EAI president David A. Bennett says, "One circumvents public schools, and one reinvents them." Bennett, a former school superintendent in St. Paul, Minnesota, thinks the idea of using vouchers to build a new private-school system alongside the $200 billion public system will be vastly wasteful for taxpayers but also inequitable to the kids who lack social and economic advantages.

"We can fairly well predict that a tremendous sorting-out process will go on under vouchers," Bennett says. "If a private school has only one seat and two kids are at the door—one well scrubbed and one smelling of poverty—you tell me which one will be chosen. The remnant of the public-school system will become the debtor schools, and that's intolerable for democracy."

In contrast, EAI's profit potential is based on the conviction that public schools themselves can change—given adroit leverage from outside business managers. "We don't want to be in a situation of selecting our clientele, as you always do in private schools," Bennett says. "We'll take all the children, all the employees. We don't have broken people—we have a broken governance system that just doesn't work."

As Pat Parham explains, EAI's approach is a synthesis of different strategies that conscientious reformers have always known were necessary, including smaller classes and teaching plans tailored to each child. The core concept, however, will offend those hard-nosed conservatives who want tougher discipline in public education. "We don't stress competition at all," Parham says. "We don't reward children for doing what they're supposed to do. We tell children to take charge of their own growth."

South Pointe does not hand out A's, B's, or C's. The kids are given the answer sheets and grade their own tests. Instead of regular report cards, teachers write four- or five-page progress reports discussing a child's strengths and weaknesses. Parents are required to meet with teachers at least four times a year to go over these reports and to make their own analysis of the children's progress.

In sum, this school is aimed at breaking out of the "factory" mold that has dominated American education in this century and deadened lots of young minds with its repetition and cookie-cutter tedium. Creating a new model means changing lots of bureaucratic rules—including union work rules—and the involvement of a prestigious outside contractor helps give school administrators the leverage to do this.

But here is the most audacious part: EAI claims it can accomplish all this without spending more money. At South Pointe, per-pupil spending is the same as elsewhere in Dade County, despite all the extras and the low teacher-pupil ratio. But in order to make its point, EAI has agreed to cover any cost overruns. The financial trick, according to Bennett, lies in applying stern business practices to the other things that schools spend so much money on—from bus fleets to cafeterias, from administrative staffs to janitors.

Still, Principal Parham isn't worried about the prospect of spending exceeding current levels: "If you have a program that works for high-risk children and these children are having success beyond their wildest dreams, we think the public will be willing to pay more for it."

In any case, the much-publicized alternative—creating new private schools—is bound to cost taxpayers much more in the long run. Bennett suspects that the Whittle venture is counting on tax-supported vouchers, even though Whittle denies it.

For the next few years, these different corporate approaches will be competing fiercely with one another—both for the allegiance of parents and for political favor in state legislatures and the federal government.

Powerful interests have concluded that the public schools are beyond repair.

Education is big business and a promising growth sector for private enterprise.

But in the end, money is the least of it. What Americans decide about public schools will either accelerate the deep fracturing of society already under way or help to reverse it. Public schools cannot themselves overcome these divisive forces. But restoring the vitality of the common school would make an important statement about ourselves—that, as Americans, we are all in this together.

America's Holy War

For the past generation, the courts have fenced God out of the country's public life, but has the separation of church and state gone too far? The Supreme Court must decide.

NANCY GIBBS

To say that God is everywhere in American life is as much a statement of fact as of faith. His name appears on every coin, on every dollar bill and in the vast majority of state constitutions. Schoolchildren pledge allegiance to one nation, under him. The President of the United States ends his speeches with a benediction. God bless America.

In a country born of a pilgrim's dream, a country that exalts freedom of worship as a sacred right, perhaps none of that is surprising. What *is* surprising is that for most of the ensuing 200 years, Americans have not stopped arguing about God. In the past decade alone, the Supreme Court has decided more religion cases than ever before, and each day brings a fresh crusade.

At issue is the meaning of the basic principle enshrined in the First Amendment: that Congress, and by later extension the states, "shall make no law respecting an establishment of religion, or prohibiting the free exercise thereof." The modern Supreme Court has taken that to mean that government cannot do anything that promotes either a particular faith or religion in general. The backlash was a long time coming, but now it is here with a vengeance.

The fight is not so much over what people ought to believe; it is over what they can say, and where, and to whom. The battleground spreads from the courtroom to the schoolroom to the town square:

▶ Last month the Pennsylvania Supreme Court threw out the sentence of a murderer who killed a 70-year-old woman with an ax, on the ground that the prosecutor had unlawfully cited biblical law to the jury in his summation urging the death penalty.

▶ In Decatur, Ill., a primary-school teacher discovered the word God in a phonics textbook and ordered her class of seven-year-olds to strike it out, saying that it is against the law to mention God in a public school.

▶ The town of Oak Park, Ill., blocked a private Catholic hospital from erecting a cross on its own smokestack because, councilors say, some local residents would be offended.

This is not simply a struggle between believers and nonbelievers, or between liberals and conservatives. The conflict is far more subtle, a product of centuries of legal evolution. It gets to the very heart of America's identity, for it is about a clashing of rights and responsibilities: Should Christian Scientist parents be allowed, on religious grounds, to reject medical treatment for a dying child? Should Mormon parents be allowed to claim a tax deduction for the money they spend sending their children out as missionaries? Like so many other issues—abortion, the right to die, the right to bear arms—the issue of religion's place in American life is at once deeply personal and yet highly public. It falls to the courts to find a way to preserve freedom of conscience while protecting individuals from the imposition of other people's beliefs.

THE TWO SIDES

In the broadest terms, there are two main camps in this holy war. On one side are the "separationists," who argue that church and state must remain clearly apart and that government should not be in the business of endorsing one faith or another. Some members of the camp make their case on practical grounds: they insist that in a country with nearly 1,200 different religious bodies, the only way to keep the peace is to keep them all out of the shared public sphere. Too many wars have been fought, too many freedoms crushed in God's name, for a democracy to try to integrate theology into its public life.

Other separationists argue on religious grounds; they want to protect their own churches and their private beliefs from exploitation by politicians or demagogues. "Religious beliefs worthy of respect are the product of free and voluntary choice by the faithful," Justice John Paul Stevens, the Supreme Court's most ardent separationist, wrote in 1985. "Government must pursue a course of complete neutrality toward religion."

In opposition are the "accommodationists," who believe that the "wall of separation" between church and state has grown too thick and costs too much. By isolating God from public life, they argue, the courts have replaced freedom of religion with freedom *from* religion. A nation's identity is informed by morality, and morality by faith. How can people freely debate issues like nuclear arms or the death penalty, how can children be educated, without any reference to spiritual heritage? As Justice Antonin Scalia observed in 1987, "Political activism by the religiously motivated is part of our heritage." The accommodationists deny that their agenda is to enforce conformity; all they want is for their positions to get a fair hearing.

For the past 40 years or so, because of a lengthy series of Supreme Court rulings, the tide has generally favored the separationists. In this nation of spiritual paradoxes, it is legal to hang a picture in a public exhibit of a crucifix submerged in urine, or to utter virtually any conceivable blasphemy in a public place; it is not legal, the federal courts have ruled, to mention God reverently in a classroom, on a football field or at a commencement ceremony as part of a public prayer.

The debate has now arrived at a crossroads. Last month the Supreme Court heard arguments in a case that invites it to rewrite the canons of church-state law. *Lee v. Weisman* involves a Rhode Island rabbi whose bland prayer at a middle-school graduation was later ruled unconstitutional. The rabbi gave thanks to God for "the legacy of America, where diversity is celebrated and the rights of minorities are protected." The district court suggested that the invocation would have been fine if the rabbi had just left out all the references to God. The school board is arguing that so long as the prayer was not coercive, it did not violate the establishment clause of the First Amendment.

Various courts around the country have already wrestled with the same issue. California earlier this year ruled against the constitutionality of graduation prayers, as have Iowa and Rhode Island. Virginia and Pennsylvania permit them; it falls to the Supreme Court to decide which is right.

This may turn out to be the first accommodationist court in years. "The wall of separation between church and state is a metaphor based on bad history," declared Chief Justice William Rehnquist in 1985. "It should be frankly and explicitly abandoned." The *Lee* case is also the first major test of Justice Clarence Thomas, who remarked in 1985, "My mother says that when they took God out of the schools, the schools went to hell. She may be right." Were Thomas and his colleagues to agree with Rehnquist, it could change dramatically the role that religion plays in America's marketplace of ideas—and ultimately, in every citizen's private life.

If ever there was an issue cast in shades of gray, this is it. Faith is often a matter of given truths and absolute beliefs, but once it becomes entangled in law and politics, its certainties begin to blur. One of the primary fears of the separationists is that if government gets too involved with religion, the result will resemble the bloodless, lifeless state-backed churches in Europe. Many of the supporters of the church-state wall fear that politicians, bent on compromise more than conversion, would try to invent some inoffensive brand of faith—the crèche encircled by reindeer hauling Santa's sleigh. "What you are tending to see is a new secular state religion," says Lee Boothby, a Seventh-day Adventist who is general counsel with Americans United for Separation of Church and State. "It's not really religion."

Other separationists are most concerned with protecting atheists or members of minority faiths from pressure to conform. This is a far more diverse country than it was in 1892, when the Supreme Court declared, "This is a Christian nation." Millions of Americans attend worship services each week, but the locales range from Hindu temples in California to churches of snake-handling Pentecostalists in Appalachia. Baptist parents might like

their child's school day to start with a Bible reading, but could a Muslim teacher choose a passage from the Koran instead? Do Satanists have the right to distribute materials at school? Would a *santero* football coach be allowed to sacrifice a chicken before the big game?

If only the Christian God is allowed to make public appearances, non-Christians fear they will be unprotected in many subtle ways. "The danger," notes Harvard law professor Laurence Tribe, a noted liberal constitutional expert, "is that those who are not part of the locally dominant culture will be reduced to a sort of second-class citizenship. Though they may not have to wear yellow stars on their sleeves, they will be given a message that they are outsiders."

On the other side, accommodationists make many of the same arguments with a different twist. It is religious people who have been ostracized, argues lawyer John Whitehead, founder of the Rutherford Institute, a not-for-profit religious-liberty advocacy organization backed by conservative Protestants. Whitehead entered the church-state fray in 1976 when he defended a fourth-grade girl in California whose teacher said she could not wear a cross on her necklace. "Society has been secularized, and the religious person finds he's the odd person out," Whitehead says. "In public schools, religion is something to be avoided, obsolete. I see kids expressing their beliefs as healthy."

To accommodationists, previous Supreme Court decisions appear to be sending the message that religion is acceptable so long as it is not too public. It is a strange definition of free speech and religious liberty, they note, that prohibits mention of God. "Angela Davis, a communist, was the speaker at my son's high school graduation," says Berkeley law professor Phillip Johnson. "People have to listen to the most heavy-handed dogmatism. Then suddenly the Constitution is violated if an agnostic hears the word God. This is absurd. If we have to put up with things we don't agree with, why is only God excluded?"

The issues involved are not mere differences of philosophy; in the inner cities especially, the debate is deeply practical. Religious groups contend that moral and spiritual teaching can strengthen their efforts in prevention of teen pregnancy and drug abuse, as well as health services, tutoring and other social services, and that such groups can perform those tasks more cheaply and humanely than government agencies.

THE LEGAL DEBATE

At the heart of the legal debate is the clashing of two constitutional principles enshrined in the First Amendment. The idea of guaranteeing "free exercise" of religion while shunning any "establishment" of religion was designed to protect liberty and keep the peace. Anyone could worship

however he or she pleased, the framers said, but the government was forbidden to install a monopoly state church along the lines of the Church of England.

These were radical notions at the time, born of a commitment to moral self-improvement and an Enlightenment faith in the power of free inquiry and tolerance. The task of the Founding Fathers—some of them quite devout, others much less so—was to identify some vision of the common good that could be shared by citizens with very different priorities. They constructed a system of government and law in which freedom and equality were both essential, and religion was neither too close a friend nor the enemy.

During those years and beyond, churches enjoyed fairly free access to the public sphere. Before the Revolution, the Anglican church in Georgia was supported by a tax, and under the state's first constitution, only Protestants were allowed to sit in the legislature. When the Bill of Rights took effect, five of the 13 states had government-sponsored churches, and most schools were church-run. For literally centuries, until 1961, Maryland required officeholders to declare their belief in God. The problem is that as the nation's religious life grew more varied and its public life more complex, it became nearly impossible to uphold both constitutional principles—free exercise and nonestablishment—with equal consistency.

The modern debate over church-state separation dates back to 1947, when the Supreme Court first set strict limits on the use of state funds that benefit religious institutions or activities. Justice Hugo Black, a Baptist, wrote that neither federal nor state governments "can pass laws which aid one religion, aid all religions or prefer one religion over another." That ruling marked a sharp separationist turn in court thinking. It unleashed a torrent of litigation that continues to flood courtrooms 44 years later. And in a succession of cases, the court drew the line ever more strictly.

In the landmark 1962 case *Engel v. Vitale,* the high court threw out a brief non-denominational prayer composed by state officials that was recommended for use in New York State schools. "It is no part of the business of government," ruled the court, "to compose official prayers for any group of the American people to recite." The following year the court outlawed mandatory daily Bible readings in public schools.

But as the court became increasingly concerned about government support for religious expression, opponents began speaking up. It was one thing to outlaw state-written prayers, they said, but what about a moment of silence? Perhaps reading the Bible as part of a morning devotional was inappropriate, but what about recognition of extracurricular religious clubs? Justice Potter Stewart, writing in 1963, foreshadowed the debates of the 1980s and '90s when he warned that the court was hardly being neutral in its school-prayer decisions. A ban on noncoercive religious exercises in school placed religion "at an artificial and state-created disadvantage," he said.

The case that crystallized church-state separation doctrine, *Lemon v. Kurtzman*, came in 1971, when the court struck down Pennsylvania and Rhode Island laws that set subsidies for the salaries of parochial school teachers. Referring to earlier cases, the Justices proposed a threefold test to determine the permissibility of government activities that touched the religious realm. First, state action must have a secular purpose. Second, the primary effect of the action must neither advance nor inhibit religion. And finally, there should be no "excessive entanglement" between church and state.

In the 20 years since that ruling, the *Lemon* test has come under accommodationist fire. With the birth of the Moral Majority in 1979 and the political rise of the religious right, clashes over religious issues that had once been quiet and philosophical became loud and politically explosive. Then, as the composition of the Supreme Court became more conservative in the Reagan and Bush years, expectations began to rise that the accommodationists might get a more sympathetic hearing. Yet many major issues remain in dispute, such as whether voluntary prayer should be allowed in schools, whether government bodies can mount religious displays and whether public funding should be used for church-sponsored social programs.

The most pure and abstract battles remain to be fought over the use of religious symbols in the public arena—an issue rife with irony in a country that stamps its coins with the words "In God We Trust." Later this year the Supreme Court will decide whether to hear an appeal from the city of Zion, Ill., which was ordered by a lower court to scrap the city seal, consisting of a ribbon with the words "God Reigns" and a shield containing a dove, sword, crown and Latin cross. The device was adopted in 1902. The city argues that the seal is mainly a historical artifact, recalling the founding of the city by the Christian Catholic Church.

THE PUBLIC SCHOOLS

The symbolic issues pale, however, compared with the heated debates about what can take place in the nation's public schools. This has always been the central battleground for church-state conflict in America. On the one hand, children are viewed as more impressionable and vulnerable to peer pressure than adults and so should be protected from anything resembling religious indoctrination.

But on the other hand, many devout parents are eager to instill in their children the moral strength that they hope will deliver them from evil, whether it is sex, drugs or secular humanism. Such families also believe that faith is central to serious intellectual activity and should not be relegated to Sunday school. So the debate over what teachers can teach, what books may be used, what songs sung, even what clothes children may wear at school strikes at the heart of many families' sense of spiritual freedom.

The content of curriculum and textbooks has been closely examined on both sides. Fundamentalists are often criticized for wanting to teach creationism or for incorporating Christian "propaganda" into history and literature classes. But they respond that the intrusions and distortions can cut both ways. One 1985 government-funded study of public school textbooks found that social-studies textbooks rarely mentioned religion at all, even when discussing events in which churches were a driving force, such as the abolition of slavery. Many books omitted the deep religious motivation of Martin Luther King Jr. Others failed to say to whom the Pilgrims gave thanks on Thanksgiving.

Over time, many schools have come to avoid mentioning religion at all, fearing that the subject was too controversial and invited lawsuits. But in recent years the balance has shifted in areas where accommodationist sentiment has grown. Two years ago, North Carolina's board of education launched a revision of the state curriculum to include religious references in classes on history, social studies and culture. Other states, such as Arizona and California, have introduced similar programs, though all have been careful to distinguish between exposing students to the history and beliefs of various religions and advocating any creed.

Strict separationists have worked not only to keep religious practices out of the classroom; they also want to prevent religious activity anywhere on school grounds. Frequently under litigation is the issue of what religious materials may be distributed on those precincts. Earlier this year, a federal judge ruled that school officials in Wauconda, Ill., could stop a junior high school student, Megan Hedges, from distributing copies of an evangelical Christian newspaper, *Issues and Answers*. The court agreed with school administrators who did not want to appear to endorse the publication, which includes articles with headlines like SATANISM BRED IN SECULAR SCHOOL SYSTEM.

"We're probably the most suppressed newspaper in America," says Dan Rodden, whose Caleb Campaign publishes *Issues and Answers*. "In the schools today there is definitely a religious and philosophical bent that is anti-Christian. Little children,

by the time they're in second grade, know that God is illegal." The issue of prayer in the classroom arouses even greater passions. If public schools allow teachers to lead students in prayer, it looks very much like an endorsement of religion, and it is hard to imagine that a child would not feel pressured into joining in. Particularly in deeply religious communities, atheist and agnostic families are often afraid to protest. "In many areas no one complains when the church starts creeping into public life," says Jay Jacobson, executive director of the Arkansas affiliate of the ACLU. "We get calls at the beginning of the school year against a generic prayer at football games, but no one is willing to file an official complaint. The Bill of Rights is not self-enforcing."

The fears may not be unfounded. Two Little Axe, Okla., families that brought suit against morning prayers in school in 1981 became targets of relentless harassment. The children were repeatedly asked by teachers why they didn't believe in God, and one youngster found an upside-down cross hung on his locker. One evening while members of one of the families were at a football game, their house was fire bombed and burned down.

But on the other hand, when fifth-grader Monette Rethford, in Norman, Okla., is told that she cannot get together with other students on school property to pray or read the Bible, it looks very much like a restriction of her freedom to worship. To publicize their own fervor, tens of thousands of students gathered around their school flagpoles to pray last Sept. 11. "I don't want a government church or a teacher opening class with prayer," says Jay Sekulow of Christian Advocates Serving Evangelism, a conservative organization specializing in church-state litigation. "But the First Amendment protects individual speech, even religious speech, and even on public property."

The popular compromise proposal of recent years is a moment of silence. Douglas Laycock, associate dean of the University of Texas School of Law, who favors strict government neutrality toward religion, finds it hard to believe that it could be unconstitutional merely to tell a classroom of kids to keep quiet for a minute. He says, however, that "it's beastly hard to implement it in a fair way. Teachers do deliver messages, and the children do have understandings."

There are still other religion cases pending before the court, and in light of its recent rulings, no one can predict which way the Justices will decide. Many accommodationists were encouraged last year when the court, by an 8-to-1 vote, approved a federal law that allows voluntary student religious clubs to meet in public schools after hours on the same basis as other noncurricular student clubs.

But one of the most important religion cases in years, *Employment Division, Department of Human Resources of Oregon v. Smith,* confounded partisans on all sides and for once has united the forces that usually disagree on most church-state issues. Unlike the most controversial recent cases, *Smith* did not involve "establishment" issues, of the government getting too involved in some religious activity. Instead it focused on the free-exercise clause, which protects the right of individuals to adhere to their private religious beliefs. The case involved Alfred Smith and Galen Black, two members of the Native American Church who chewed peyote as part of their church's religious ceremonies. They were fired from their jobs as drug counselors and were refused unemployment benefits.

The challenge to the court in *Smith* was to decide when the government's interest in law enforcement should take priority over someone's private religious practices. The first major ruling on that issue came in 1879, when Mormons were forbidden to practice polygamy. One of the leading precedents was fixed in 1963 in *Sherbert v. Verner,* when the Supreme Court ruled that a worker who refused to work on Saturdays because it was a day of worship was still entitled to unemployment compensation. In that opinion, the court stated that government had to demonstrate a "compelling interest" in order to justify an infringement of religious liberty.

In their *Smith* ruling last year, the Justices could have used many rationales against accepting the use of peyote for religious reasons—for instance, that the government has a compelling interest in keeping the workplace free of illegal drugs. But instead, by a 5-to-4 vote, they discarded precedent and decided against Smith and Black on entirely different grounds. Writing for the majority, Justice Scalia declared that "the right of free exercise does not relieve an individual of the obligation to comply with a 'valid and neutral law of general applicability.'" There was no need to use the compelling-interest test in such a situation, he said, because that would permit every person "to become a law unto himself."

For all the rifts among religious and civil-libertarian groups, this decision brought a choir of outrage singing full-voice. A whole clause of the Bill of Rights had been abolished, critics charged, and the whole concept of religious freedom was now imperiled. "On the really small and odd religious groups," said the University of Texas' Laycock, "it's just open season." The court itself was deeply split. In a spirited dissent, Justice Sandra Day O'Connor said the majority's stance "is incompatible with our nation's fundamental commitment to individual religious liberty." As a result of the uproar, Congress is considering a law to restore the compelling-interest test.

THE CHALLENGE

There is no predicting which way this court will go in a case like *Lee v. Weisman.* The basic split is not only between those who want to accommodate religion and government and those who want to keep the two separate. There is also a split on the court between those who defer to the government and those who continue to emphasize individual liberty.

If the court's conservative majority is taking its cues from the Bush Administration, it promises to go much further to usher in a new era of accommodation. Solicitor General Kenneth Starr argued the Administration's position in the *Lee* case. He maintained that the government promotion of religion through civic ceremonies does not violate the Constitution if coercion is not involved. Students who did not want to pray at graduation, Starr implied, could sit without joining in prayer or skip the exercises.

If the Supreme Court agrees with that position and decides to apply it across the board, the new test of the separation of church and state would not consider whether an action favors religion or whether it entangles church and state but rather whether it forces people to join in expressions of a religious belief. The implications of such a change are radical and would call

into question hundreds of settled cases. "This will tear the country and each county apart," says Seventh-Day Adventist Boothby. "The unfortunate result would be to create more religious controversy, discontent and disharmony." Says Laycock: "All sorts of astonishing things become O.K. The Constitution then means a lot less than we've thought." Theoretically, Congress could decide, for example, that it would pay the salaries of preferred members of the clergy. Even less outrageous consequences, such as requiring that all public functions begin with a nondenominational prayer, could be highly divisive.

A country already wrestling with a new tribalism, with racial tensions and cultural clashes that set language and law on edge, cannot afford to slip further into religious contention. Some yardstick of moderation, and perhaps a measure of common sense, is necessary. What is too often missing from all the talk of religious and secular rights is any mention of mutual respect. When people claim the right to pray or not to pray, to worship or not to worship, as they choose, they must also respect the right of others to choose differently. For government to arbitrate in such intensely personal matters invites insurrection; but if the court and the Congress decided to distance themselves from religious disputes, they must also keep the playing field level.

For God to be kept out of the classroom or out of America's public debate by nervous school administrators or overcautious politicians serves no one's interests. That restriction prevents people from drawing on this country's rich and diverse religious heritage for guidance, and it degrades the nation's moral discourse by placing a whole realm of theological reasoning out of bounds. The price of that sort of quarantine, at a time of moral dislocation, is—and has been—far too high. The courts need to find a better balance between separation and accommodation—and Americans need to respect the new religious freedom they would gain as a result.

—*Reported by David Aikman/Washington and Richard N. Ostling/New York*

Social Change and the Future

- **New Population Issues (Articles 40 and 41)**
- **Technology and the Environment (Articles 42 and 43)**
- **The Future (Article 44)**

Fascination with the future is an enduring theme in literature, art, poetry, and religion. Human beings are anxious to know if tomorrow will be different from today and in what ways it might differ. Coping with change has become a top priority in the lives of many. One result of change is stress. When the future is uncertain and the individual appears to have little control over what happens, stress can be a serious problem. On the other hand, stress can have positive effects on people's lives if the changes can be perceived as challenges and opportunities.

Any discussion of the future must begin with a look at basic demographic trends and consideration of their impacts. Robert McNamara describes the world population picture under the graphic title "The Population Explosion." Explosion suggests a situation that is out of control and has damaging consequences. His analysis supports this image.

Another demographic issue that worries many Americans is the influx of immigrants who compete for scarce jobs with citizens. *Business Week* magazine, however, argues that immigrants contribute far more to America than they cost America. In fact, immigrants are helping America to be competitive in many world markets.

The next section deals with technology and the environment. David Pimentel focuses on the pressure of population on resources and the environment and underlines McNamara's conclusion that population must be controlled. In light of the current degradation of the environment, destruction of natural resources, and widespread poverty, Pimentel believes that sustainability of adequate standards of living would require a U.S. population of only about 200 million and a world population of under two billion.

The major technological revolution that is now under way is the data/communications revolution. It promises great benefits in greater productivity and many new and improved consumer goods and services. It also creates many serious risks and problems that Scott Cunningham and Alan Porter discuss. For example, it presents threats to individual privacy and liberty, could increase inequalities, and could undermine national loyalties.

Finally, Peter Drucker assesses the future world that current students will experience. It will be both postcommunist and postcapitalist. It will be based on knowledge as its primary resource, and this resource shift is transforming institutions, values, and life-styles. He pegs the beginning of the new era to the G.I. Bill of Rights that enabled millions to go to college and started the shift to the knowledge society. The current period is one of transformation, a troubled and exciting time when all institutions are shaken and reshaped. It is also a time of opportunity for those with knowledge.

Looking Ahead: Challenge Questions

What are the significant factors bringing about social change at the present time?

In what ways will social change accelerate? How can it slow down?

What are some ways to deal with social change?

Unit 6

The Population Explosion

HIGH POPULATION GROWTH IS MAKING POOR PEOPLE POORER, THE HUNGRY HUNGRIER, AND AN ALREADY-FRAGILE ENVIRONMENT TOO WEAK TO SUPPORT ITS PROLIFERATING INHABITANTS.

Robert S. McNamara

Robert S. McNamara is former president of the World Bank and former U.S. secretary of defense. His address is 1455 Pennsylvania Avenue, N.W., Washington, D.C. 20004.

For thousands of years, the world's human population grew at a snail's pace. It took over a million years to reach 1 billion people at the beginning of the last century. But then the pace quickened. The second billion was added in 130 years, the third in 30, and the fourth in 15. The current total is some 5.4 billion people.

Although population growth rates are declining, they are still extraordinarily high. During this decade, about 100 million people per year will be added to the planet. Over 90% of this growth is taking place in the developing world. Where will it end?

The World Bank's latest projection indicates that the plateau level will not be less than 12.4 billion. And Nafis Sadik, director of the United Nations Population Fund, has stated that "the world could be headed toward an eventual total of 14 billion."

What would such population levels mean in terms of alleviating poverty, improving the status of women and children, and attaining sustainable economic development? To what degree are we consuming today the very capital required to achieve decent standards of living for future generations?

More People, Consuming More

To determine whether the world—or a particular country—is on a path of sustainable development, one must relate future population levels and future consumption patterns to their impact on the environment.

Put very simply, environmental stress is a function of three factors: increases in population, increases in consumption per capita, and changes in technology that may tend to reduce environmental stress per unit of consumption.

Were population to rise to the figure referred to by Sadik—14 billion—there would be a 2.6-fold increase in world population. If consumption per capita were to increase at 2% per annum—about two-thirds the rate realized during the past 25 years—it would double in 35 years and quadruple in 70 years. By the end of the next century, consumption per capita would be eight times greater than it is today.

Some may say it is unreasonable to consider such a large increase in the per capita incomes of the peoples in the developing countries. But per capita income in the United States rose at least that much in this century, starting from a much higher base. And today, billions of human beings across the globe are now living in intolerable conditions that can only be relieved by increases in consumption.

A 2.6-fold increase in world population and an eightfold increase in consumption per capita by 2100 would cause the globe's production output to be 20 times greater than today. Likewise, the impact on non-renewable and renewable resources would be 20 times greater, assuming no change in environmental stress per unit of production.

On the assumptions I have made, the question becomes: Can a 20-fold increase in the consumption of phys-

From *The Futurist*, November/December 1992, pp. 9-13. Reproduced with permission from *The Futurist*, published by the World Future Society, 7910 Woodmont Ave., Suite 450, Bethesda, Maryland 20814.

ical resources be sustained? The answer is almost certainly "No." If not, can substantial reductions in environmental stress—environmental damage—per unit of production be achieved? Here, the answer is clearly "Yes."

Reducing Environmental Damage

Environmental damage per unit of production can—and will—be cut drastically. There is much evidence that the environment is being stressed today. But there are equally strong indications that we can drastically reduce the resources consumed and waste generated per unit of "human advance."

With each passing year, we are learning more about the environmental damage that is caused by present population levels and present consumption patterns. The superficial signs are clearly visible. Our water and air are being polluted, whether we live in Los Angeles, Mexico City, or Lagos. Disposal of both toxic and nontoxic wastes is a worldwide problem. And the ozone layer, which protects us all against skin cancer, is being destroyed by the concentration of chlorofluorocarbons in the upper atmosphere.

But for each of these problems, there are known remedies—at least for today's population levels and current consumption patterns. The remedies are costly, politically difficult to implement, and require years to become effective, but they can be put in place.

The impact, however, of huge increases in population and consumption on such basic resources and ecosystems as land and water, forests, photosynthesis, and climate is far more difficult to appraise. Changes in complex systems such as these are what the scientists describe as nonlinear and subject to discontinuities. Therefore, they are very difficult to predict.

A Hungrier Planet?

Let's examine the effect of population growth on natural resources in terms of agriculture. Can the world's land and water resources produce the food required to feed 14 billion people at acceptable nutritional levels? To do so would require a fourfold increase in food output.

Modern agricultural techniques have greatly increased crop yields per unit of land and have kept food production ahead of population growth for several decades. But the costs are proving to be high: widespread acceleration of erosion and nutrient depletion of soils, pollution of surface waters, overuse and

---

"MORE AND MORE BIOLOGISTS ARE WARNING THAT THERE ARE INDEED BIOLOGICAL LIMITS TO THE NUMBER OF PEOPLE THAT THE GLOBE CAN SUPPORT AT ACCEPTABLE STANDARDS OF LIVING."

---

contamination of groundwater resources, and desertification of overcultivated or overgrazed lands.

The early gains of the Green Revolution have nearly run their course. Since the mid-1980s, increases in worldwide food production have lagged behind population growth. In sub-Saharan Africa and Latin America, per capita food production has been declining for a decade or more.

What, then, of the future? Some authorities are pessimistic, arguing that maximum global food output will support no more than 7.5 billion people. Others are somewhat more optimistic. They conclude that if a variety of actions were taken, beginning with a substantial increase in agricultural research, the world's agricultural system could meet food requirements for at least the next 40–50 years.

However, it seems clear that the actions required to realize that capacity are not now being taken. As a result, there will be severe regional shortfalls (e.g., in sub-Saharan Africa), and as world population continues to increase, the likelihood of meeting global food requirements will become ever more doubtful.

Similar comments could be made in regard to other natural resources and ecosystems. More and more biologists are warning that there are indeed biological limits to the number of people that the globe can sup-

port at acceptable standards of living. They say, in effect, "We don't know where those limits are, but they clearly exist."

Sustainability Limits

How much might population grow and production increase without going beyond sustainable levels—levels that are compatible with the globe's capacity for waste disposal and that do not deplete essential resources?

Jim MacNeil, Peter Winsemaus, and Taizo Yakushiji have tried to answer that question in *Beyond Interdependence*, a study prepared recently for the Trilateral Commission. They begin by stating: "Even at present levels of economic activity, there is growing evidence that certain critical global thresholds are being approached, perhaps even passed."

They then estimate that, if "human numbers double, a five- to ten-fold increase in economic activity would be required to enable them to meet [even] their basic needs and minimal aspirations." They ask, "Is there, in fact, any way to multiply economic activity a further five to ten times, without it undermining itself and compromising the future completely?" They clearly believe that the answer is "No."

Similar questions and doubts exist in the minds of many other experts in the field. In July 1991, Nobel laureate and Cal Tech physicist Murray Gell-Mann and his associates initiated a multiyear project to try to understand how "humanity can make the shift to sustainability." They point out that "such a change, if it could be achieved, would require a series of transitions in fields ranging from technology to social and economic organization and ideology."

The implication of their statement is not that we should assume the outlook for sustainable development is hopeless, but rather that each nation individually, and all nations collectively, should begin now to identify and introduce the changes necessary to achieve it if we are to avoid costly—and possibly coercive—action in the future.

One change that would enhance the prospects for sustainable development across the globe would be a reduction in population growth rates.

6. SOCIAL CHANGE AND THE FUTURE: New Population Issues

Population and Poverty

The developing world has made enormous economic progress over the past three decades. But at the same time, the number of human beings living in "absolute poverty" has risen sharply.

When I coined the term "absolute poverty" in the late 1960s, I did so to distinguish a particular segment of the poor in the developing world from the billions of others who would be classified as poor in Western terms. The "absolute poor" are those living, literally, on the margin of life. Their lives are so characterized by malnutrition, illiteracy, and disease as to be beneath any reasonable definition of human dignity.

Today, their number approaches 1 billion. And the World Bank estimates that it is likely to increase further—by nearly 100 million—in this decade.

A major concern raised by poverty of this magnitude lies in the possibility of so many children's physical and intellectual impairment. Surveys have shown that millions of children in low-income families receive insufficient protein and calories to permit optimal development of their brains, thereby limiting their capacity to learn and to lead fully productive lives. Additional millions die each year, before the age of five, from debilitating disease caused by nutritional deficiencies.

High population growth is not the only factor contributing to these problems; political organization, macroeconomic policies, institutional structures, and economic growth in the industrial nations all affect economic and social advance in developing countries. But intuitively we recognize that the immediate effects of high population growth are adverse.

Our intuition is supported by facts: In Latin America during the 1970s, when the school-age population expanded dramatically, public spending per primary-school student fell by 45% in real terms. In Mexico, life expectancy for the poorest 10% of the population is 20 years less than for the richest 10%.

Based on such analyses, the World Bank has stated: "The evidence points overwhelmingly to the conclusion that population growth at the rates common in most of the developing world slows development. . . . Policies to reduce population growth can make an important contribution to [social advance]."

A Lower Plateau for World Population?

Any one of the adverse consequences of the high population growth rates—environmentally unsustainable development, the worsening of poverty, and the negative impact on the status and welfare of women and children—would be reason enough for developing nations

---

"THE FUNDS REQUIRED ARE SO SMALL, AND THE BENEFITS . . . SO LARGE, THAT MONEY SHOULD NOT BE ALLOWED TO STAND IN THE WAY OF REDUCING FERTILITY RATES."

---

across the globe to move more quickly to reduce fertility rates. Taken together, they make an overwhelming case.

Should not every developing country, therefore, formulate long-term population objectives—objectives that will maximize the welfare of both present and future generations? They should be constrained only by the maximum feasible rate at which the use of contraception could be increased in the particular nation.

If this were done, I estimate that country family-planning goals might lead to national population-stabilization levels that would total 9.7 billion people for the globe. That is an 80% increase over today's population, but it's also 4.3 billion fewer people than the 14 billion toward which we may be heading. At the consumption levels I have assumed, those additional 4.3 billion people could require a production output several times greater than the world's total output today.

Reducing Fertility Rates

Assuming that nations wish to reduce fertility rates to replacement levels at the fastest possible pace, what should be done?

The Bucharest Population Conference in 1974 emphasized that high fertility is in part a function of slow economic and social development. Experience has indeed shown that as economic growth occurs, particularly when it is accompanied by broadly based social advance, birth rates do tend to decline. But it is also generally recognized today that not all economic growth leads to immediate fertility reductions, and in any event, fertility reduction can be accelerated by direct action to increase the use of contraceptives.

It follows, therefore, that any campaign to accelerate reductions in fertility should focus on two components: (1) increasing the pace of economic and social advance, with particular emphasis on enhancing the status of women and on reducing infant mortality, and (2) introducing or expanding comprehensive family-planning programs.

Much has been learned in recent years about how to raise rates of economic and social advance in developing countries. I won't try to summarize those lessons here. I do wish to emphasize, however, the magnitude of the increases required in family planning if individual countries are to hold population growth rates to levels that maximize economic and social advance.

The number of women of childbearing age in developing countries is projected to increase by about 22% from 1990 to 2000. If contraception use were to increase from 50% in 1990 to 65% in 2000, the number of women using contraception must rise by over 200 million.

That appears to be an unattainable objective, considering that the number of women using contraception rose by only 175 million in the past *two* decades, but it is not. The task for certain countries and regions— for example, India, Pakistan, and almost all of sub-Saharan Africa—will indeed be difficult, but other nations have done as much or more. Thailand, Indonesia, Bangladesh, and Mexico all increased use of contraceptives at least as rapidly. The actions they took are known, and their experience can be exported. It is available to all who ask.

Financing Population Programs

A global family-planning program of the size I am proposing for 2000 would cost approximately $8 billion, with $3.5 billion coming from the developed nations (up from $800 million spent in 1990). While the additional funding appears large, it is very, very small in relation to the gross national products and overseas development assistance projected for the industrialized countries.

Clearly, it is within the capabilities of the industrialized nations and the multilateral financial institutions to help developing countries finance expanded family-planning programs. The World Bank has already started on such a path, doubling its financing of population projects in the current year. Others should follow its lead. The funds required are so small, and the benefits to both families and nations so large, that money should not be allowed to stand in the way of reducing fertility rates as rapidly as is desired by the developing countries.

The developed nations should also initiate a discussion of how their citizens, who consume seven times as much per capita as do those of the developing countries, may both adjust their consumption patterns and reduce the environmental impact of each unit of consumption. They can thereby help ensure a sustainable path of economic advance for all the inhabitants of our planet.

THE IMMIGRANTS

HOW THEY'RE HELPING TO REVITALIZE THE U.S. ECONOMY

Give me your tired, your poor,
Your huddled masses yearning to breathe free. . . .

These words carved into the base of the Statue of Liberty speak to America's vision of itself. We were, and still are, a nation of immigrants. In the 1980s alone, a stunning 8.7 million people poured into the U.S., matching the great immigration decade of 1900–10. But with the country facing difficult economic and social problems, is it time to put aside our romantic past and kick away the immigrant welcome mat?

A lot of Americans feel the answer is "yes." In a BUSINESS WEEK/Harris poll, 68% of respondents said today's immigration is bad for the country, even though most thought it was good in the past. President Bush has found it politically expedient to refuse refugees from Haiti. And in areas like recession-weary Southern California, immigrants are being blamed for everything from rising unemployment to a rocketing state budget deficit. "I understand, in the past, 'give me your tired, your poor.' Today, the U.S. has to look at our own huddled masses first," says former Colorado Governor Richard D. Lamm, who is running for the U.S. Senate.

This rising resentment against immigrants is no surprise. The million or so immigrants—including 200,000 illegals—that will arrive in the U.S. this year are coming at a time when unemployment is high and social services strained. Unlike past waves of immigration, the new immigrants are mainly from Asia and Latin America. And just like the American work force, these immigrants are split between the highly skilled and well-educated and those with minimal skills and little education. Hungry for work, the newcomers compete for jobs with Americans, particularly with the less skilled. The large number of untrained immigrants, especially those from Mexico, are finding it harder to move up the employment

ladder than did past generations of newcomers. And in the cities, the new immigrants seem to inflame racial and ethnic conflicts.

But on balance, the economic benefits of being an open-door society far outweigh the costs. For one thing, the U.S. is reaping a bonanza of highly educated foreigners. In the 1980s alone, an unprecedented 1.5 million college-

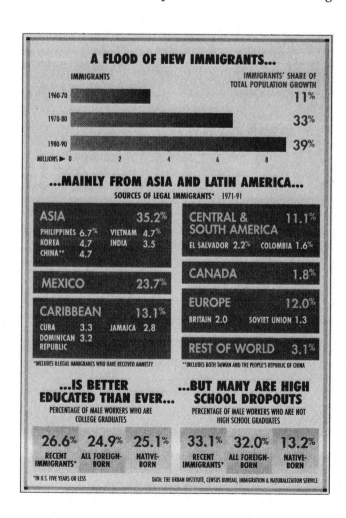

A FLOOD OF NEW IMMIGRANTS...

IMMIGRANTS | IMMIGRANTS' SHARE OF TOTAL POPULATION GROWTH
1960-70 | 11%
1970-80 | 33%
1980-90 | 39%
MILLIONS ► 0   2   4   6   8

...MAINLY FROM ASIA AND LATIN AMERICA...
SOURCES OF LEGAL IMMIGRANTS* 1971-91

ASIA 35.2%	CENTRAL & SOUTH AMERICA 11.1%
PHILIPPINES 6.7% VIETNAM 4.7% KOREA 4.7 INDIA 3.5 CHINA** 4.7	EL SALVADOR 2.2% COLOMBIA 1.6%
MEXICO 23.7%	CANADA 1.8%
CARIBBEAN 13.1% CUBA 3.3 JAMAICA 2.8 DOMINICAN REPUBLIC 3.2	EUROPE 12.0% BRITAIN 2.0 SOVIET UNION 1.3
	REST OF WORLD 3.1%

*INCLUDES ILLEGAL IMMIGRANTS WHO HAVE RECEIVED AMNESTY   **INCLUDES BOTH TAIWAN AND THE PEOPLE'S REPUBLIC OF CHINA

...IS BETTER EDUCATED THAN EVER...
PERCENTAGE OF MALE WORKERS WHO ARE COLLEGE GRADUATES

26.6%	24.9%	25.1%
RECENT IMMIGRANTS*	ALL FOREIGN-BORN	NATIVE-BORN

...BUT MANY ARE HIGH SCHOOL DROPOUTS
PERCENTAGE OF MALE WORKERS WHO ARE NOT HIGH SCHOOL GRADUATES

33.1%	32.0%	13.2%
RECENT IMMIGRANTS*	ALL FOREIGN-BORN	NATIVE-BORN

*IN U.S. FIVE YEARS OR LESS   DATA: THE URBAN INSTITUTE, CENSUS BUREAU, IMMIGRATION & NATURALIZATION SERVICE

educated immigrants joined the U.S. work force. More and more, America's high-tech industries, from semiconductors to biotechnology, are depending on immigrant scientists, engineers, and entrepreneurs to remain competitive. And the immigrants' links to their old countries are boosting U.S. exports to such fast-growing regions as Asia and Latin America.

Even immigrants with less education are contributing to the economy as workers, consumers, business owners, and taxpayers. Some 11 million immigrants are working, and they earn at least $240 billion a year, paying more than $90 billion in taxes. That's a lot more than the estimated $5 billion immigrants receive in welfare. Immigrant entrepreneurs, from the corner grocer to the local builder, are creating jobs—and not only for other immigrants. Vibrant immigrant communities are revitalizing cities and older suburbs that would otherwise be suffering from a shrinking tax base. Says John D. Kasarda, a sociologist at the University of North Carolina at Chapel Hill: "There is substantial evidence that immigrants are a powerful benefit to the economy, and very little evidence that they are negative."

In 1965, when Congress overhauled the immigration laws, nobody expected this great tide of new immigrants. But that law made it easier to bring close relatives into the country and, influenced by the civil-rights movement, eliminated racially based barriers to immigration. Prior to that, it was difficult for anyone who was not European or Canadian to settle here. The result: a surge of immigrants from Asia and Latin America, especially from countries like South Korea and the Philippines that had close economic and military ties to the U.S. And once a group got a foothold in the U.S., it would continue to expand by bringing over more family members.

NEW WAVE. The aftermath of the Vietnam War provided the second powerful source of immigrants. Over the last 10 years, the U.S. granted permanent-resident status to about 1 million refugees, mostly from Vietnam, Cambodia, and Laos. And now the end of the cold war is tapping another immigrant stream: Over the last three years, the fastest-growing group of new settlers has been refugees from Eastern Europe and the former Soviet Union.

Throughout the 1970s and 1980s, a total of some 5 million illegal immigrants from Mexico and other countries settled in the U.S., drawn by opportunity here and fleeing economic troubles at home. Many settled in Southern California and Texas. In 1986, Congress passed the Immigration Reform & Control Act (IRCA), which imposed penalties on employers who hired illegal immigrants but also gave amnesty to many illegal immigrants. About 2.5 million people have become permanent residents under the amnesty program. And the pending North American Free Trade Agreement, by strengthening economic ties between Mexico and the U.S., might very well increase illegal immigration in the short run rather than diminish it.

Opening the gates to Asians and Latin Americans dramatically altered the face of immigration. In the 1950s, 68% of legal immigrants came from Europe or Canada. In the 1980s, that percentage fell to only 13%. Conversely, the proportion of legal immigrants coming from Latin America and Asia rose from 31% to 84%, including illegal aliens granted amnesty under the 1986 law.

As the ethnic mix of the new immigrants changed, so did their levels of skill. At the low end, the plethora of low-wage service-sector jobs drew in a large number of unskilled, illiterate newcomers. About one-third of immigrant workers are high school dropouts, and one-third of those entered the U.S. illegally.

But the number of skilled immigrants has been increasing as well. "The level of education of recent immigrants has definitely increased over the last 10 years," says Elaine Sorensen, an immigration expert at the Urban Institute. About one-quarter of immigrant workers are college graduates, slightly higher than for native-born Americans. Some groups, such as Indians, are on average much better educated than today's Americans. Observes Steven Newman, an executive at the New York Association for New Americans, which will resettle about 20,000 immigrants from the former Soviet Union this year, including many engineers, computer programmers, and other skilled workers: "The only thing they lack is English skills."

TALENT BASE. Even immigrants who were doing well in their home countries are being drawn to the U.S. Take Subramonian Shankar, the 43-year-old president of American Megatrends Inc., a maker of personal-computer motherboards and software based in Norcross, Ga. He was director of personal-computer R&D at one of India's largest conglomerates. Then in 1980, he came to the U.S. In 1985, he and a partner founded AMI, which last year had sales of $70 million and employed 130 workers, both immigrants and native-born Americans. "I couldn't have done this in India," says Shankar. "That's one good thing about America. If you're determined to succeed, there are ways to get it done."

IMMIGRATION'S NEW LOOK

The 1990 Immigration Act took effect this year. The new law boosts legal immigration by 40%. It still favors family members of U. S. citizens and permanent residents, but it more than doubles the slots available for skilled workers. Political refugees come under a different act. Here's the likely pattern of immigration in 1992:

■ Close relatives of U. S. citizens, and spouses and children of permanent residents	520,000
■ Skilled workers and their families	140,000
■ Citizens of countries with relatively few immigrants in recent years, such as Argentina and Ireland	40,000
■ Political refugees, including those from the former Soviet Union	141,000
■ Illegal immigrants	200,000*
TOTAL	**1,041,000**

*Estimate   DATA: IMMIGRATION & NATURALIZATION SERVICE, BW

And U.S. industry has been eager to take advantage of the influx. About 40% of the 200 researchers in the Communications Sciences Research wing at AT&T Bell Laboratories were born outside the U.S. In Silicon Valley, the jewel of America's high-tech centers, much of the technical work force is foreign-born. At Du Pont Merck Pharmaceutical Co., an $800 million-a-year joint venture based in Wilmington, Del., losartan, an antihypertensive drug now in clinical trials, was invented by a team that included two immigrants from Hong Kong and a scientist whose parents migrated from Lithuania. People from different backgrounds bring a richness of outlook, says Joseph A. Mollica, chief executive of Du Pont Merck, "which lets you look at both problems and opportunities from a slightly different point of view."

The next generation of scientists and engineers at U.S. high-tech companies will be dominated by immigrants. While about the same number of Americans are getting science PhDs, the number of foreign-born students receiving science doctorates more than doubled between 1981 and 1991, to 37% of the total. In biology, the hot field of the 1990s, the number of non-U.S. citizens getting doctorates tripled over the last 10 years. And about 51% of computer-science doctorates in 1991 went to foreign-born students. "We are getting really good students—very, very smart people," says Victor L. Thacker, director of the office of international education at Carnegie Mellon University, which has doubled its foreign enrollment since 1985.

UP THE LADDER. Attracted by the research opportunities and the chance to use what they know, about half of them stay in the U.S. after graduation, estimates Angel G. Jordan, a professor and former provost at Carnegie Mellon, who himself emigrated from Spain in 1956. And the 1990 changes to the immigration law, by increasing the number of visas for skilled immigrants, will increase the number of foreign graduates who remain in the U.S.

Besides boosting the nation's science and engineering know-how, the latest wave of immigrants is loaded with entrepreneurs. Korean greengrocers and other immigrant merchants are familiar sights in many cities, but the entrepreneurial spirit goes far beyond any one ethnic group or single line of business. Almost by definition, anyone who moves to a new country has a lot of initiative and desire to do well. Says Dan Danilov, an immigration lawyer based in Seattle: "They're willing to put in more hours and more hard work."

And do they work. Paul Yuan, for example, left Taiwan with his wife in 1975, seven days after their marriage, eventually settling in Seattle with several thousand dollars in life savings and no work visas. For two years Yuan, a college graduate, worked in Chinese restaurants. Then, in 1978, he became a legal resident and opened his own travel agency while working nights as a hotel dishwasher. Today, at age 43, Yuan owns a thriving Seattle travel business, and he and his family live in a $4 million house. In 1965, 21-year-old Humberto Galvez left Mexico City for Los Angeles. He started pumping gas and busing tables, working his way up the ladder, with a lot of bumps along the way. After starting, then selling, the chain of 19 "El Pollo Loco" charbroiled chicken restaurants in the Los Angeles area, he now owns six Pescado Mojado (wet fish) seafood diners, employing 100 workers.

Immigrant entrepreneurs have also made big contributions to the U.S. export boom. Businesses run by immigrants from Asia, for example, have ready-made connections overseas. Immigrants bring a global perspective and international contacts to insular American businesses. And it is not just Asians. From Poles to Mexicans, "the utility of the immigrant groups is that they bring their fearless spirit of competing globally," observes Michael Goldberg, dean of the University of British Columbia's business school.

That's certainly true for Benjamin and Victor Acevedo,

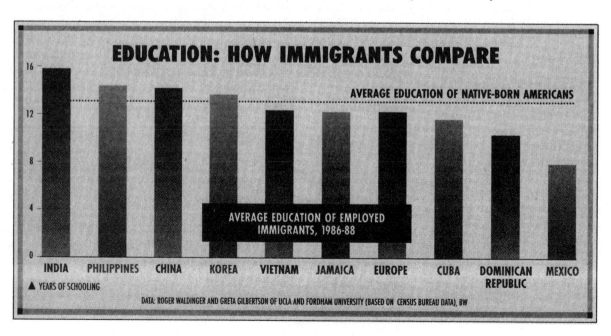

EDUCATION: HOW IMMIGRANTS COMPARE

AVERAGE EDUCATION OF NATIVE-BORN AMERICANS

AVERAGE EDUCATION OF EMPLOYED IMMIGRANTS, 1986-88

INDIA   PHILIPPINES   CHINA   KOREA   VIETNAM   JAMAICA   EUROPE   CUBA   DOMINICAN REPUBLIC   MEXICO

▲ YEARS OF SCHOOLING

DATA: ROGER WALDINGER AND GRETA GILBERTSON OF UCLA AND FORDHAM UNIVERSITY (BASED ON CENSUS BUREAU DATA), BW two brothers whose family moved from Tijuana, Mexico, to California in 1960, when they were 3 and 8. In 1984, the Acevedos started up a wood-products company in the south San Diego community of San Ysidro, just across the U.S.–Mexico border. Cal-State Lumber Sales Inc. now commands 10% of the architectural molding market in the U.S. and had 110 employees and $147 million in sales last year. And as long-term trade barriers with Mexico crumbled over the past few years, the Acevedos have been able to take advantage of their bicultural heritage. "My brother and I started shipping all over Mexico, and our export business boomed," says Ben Acevedo.

URBAN BOOSTERS. Perhaps the least-appreciated economic benefit from the new immigrants is the contribution they are making to American cities. Immigrants have been drawn to the major metropolitan areas. They are invigorating the cities and older suburbs by setting up businesses, buying homes, paying taxes, and shopping at the corner grocery. In the past decade, population in the nation's 10 largest cities grew by 4.7%, but without new immigrants it would have shrunk by 6.8%, according to calculations done by BUSINESS WEEK based on the 1990 census. Almost a million immigrants came to New York City in the 1980s, more than offsetting the 750,000 decline in the rest of the city's population. Indeed, about a third of adults in New York, 44% of adults in Los Angeles, and 70% of adults in Miami are now foreign-born, according to the 1990 census.

Immigrants have turned around many a decaying neighborhood. Ten years ago, Jefferson Boulevard in south Dallas was a dying inner-city business district filled with vacant storefronts. Today, there are almost 800 businesses there and on neighboring streets, and about three-quarters of them are owned by Hispanics, many of them first- and second-generation immigrants. "They were hungry enough to start their own businesses," says Leonel Ramos, president of the Jefferson Area Assn. And sociologist Kasarda adds: "There is a whole multiplier effect throughout the community."

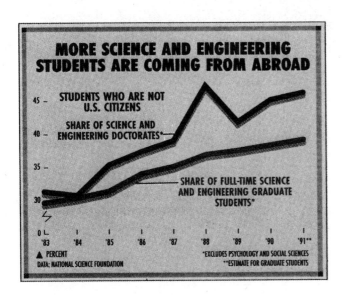

MORE SCIENCE AND ENGINEERING STUDENTS ARE COMING FROM ABROAD

45 — STUDENTS WHO ARE NOT U.S. CITIZENS

40 — SHARE OF SCIENCE AND ENGINEERING DOCTORATES*

35 —

SHARE OF FULL-TIME SCIENCE AND ENGINEERING GRADUATE STUDENTS*

30 —

0 L

'83 '84 '85 '86 '87 '88 '89 '90 '91**

▲ PERCENT
DATA: NATIONAL SCIENCE FOUNDATION

*EXCLUDES PSYCHOLOGY AND SOCIAL SCIENCES
**ESTIMATE FOR GRADUATE STUDENTS

Moreover, immigrants provide a hardworking labor force to fill the low-paid jobs that make a modern service economy run. In many cities, industries such as hotels, restaurants, and child care would be hard-pressed without immigrant labor. At the Seattle Sheraton, 28% of the hotel's staff of 650 is foreign-born, and most work in housekeeping, dish-washing, and other low-paying jobs. "We don't have American-born people apply for those positions," says Carla Murray, hotel manager for the Seattle Sheraton.

MARGIN DWELLERS. But all the economic vitality immigrants add comes at a price. While economists and employers may celebrate industrious immigrants, many barely survive on the economy's margins. "They don't go to the doctor, don't buy insurance, don't buy glasses, don't buy anything you or I are used to," says Hannah Hsiao, head of the Employment Program at the Chinese Information & Service Center in Seattle. A firing, unpaid wages, a deportation, or some other calamity is always threatening. And racial discrimination makes their lot even harder, especially those who don't speak English. Some, like economist George J. Borjas of the University of California at San Diego, worry that these poor and unskilled immigrants are condemned to years of poverty.

In many cities, newcomers and longtime residents struggle over jobs and access to scarce government resources. Immigrants are straining health and education services in some cities and suburbs. And many African-Americans believe the apparent success of immigrants is coming at their expense. In New York City, blacks picketed a number of Korean greengrocers. According to the BUSINESS WEEK/Harris poll, 73% of blacks said businesses would rather hire immigrants than black Americans.

The people hurt worst by immigrants are native-born high school dropouts, who already face a tough time. They compete for jobs against a large number of unskilled immigrants, including illegals from Mexico and the Caribbean who are poorly educated, unable to start their own businesses, and willing to work harder for lower wages than most longtime residents.

For Americans who have at least a high school education, however, the influx of immigrants hasn't had much negative impact. High school graduates, for example, saw their real wages decline by 10% in the 1980s. But almost all of that drop came from import competition and rising skill requirements of many jobs, and only a fraction from immigrant competition, according to a study by Borjas of UC, San Diego, and Richard Freeman and Lawrence Katz of Harvard University. "It is extremely convenient to point a finger at immigrants," says Muzaffar Chishti, director of the Immigration Project for the International Ladies' Garment Workers' Union in New York. "But the problems of black employment are outside the immigrant domain."

Moreover, for all their struggles, most immigrants are hardly wards of the state. Illegals are not eligible for welfare, and even many legal immigrants shun it, fearing

Business Week/Harris Poll

AMERICA'S WELCOME MAT IS WEARING THIN

Most Americans are uneasy about immigrants. While a majority think immigration was once a good thing, they now believe it's harming the country. The public worries that new arrivals take away jobs, drive down wages, and use too many government ser-  vices. But forget the conventional wisdom about black resentment of immigrants: Even though 73% of blacks believe businesses would rather hire immigrants, blacks in general feel more positively toward immigrants than do nonblacks.

FEELING THE INFLUX

■ Compared to other times in our history, would you say there are more immigrants coming to the U.S. now, fewer immigrants, or about the same number as before?

All respondents	
More	64%
Fewer	11%
Same	21%
Not sure	4%

PAST BENEFITS

■ Overall, over our history, do you think immigration has been good or bad for this country?

All respondents	
Good	59%
Bad	35%
Neither	3%
Not sure	3%

PRESENT DANGERS

■ Right now, do you think immigration is good or bad for this country?

	Nonblacks	Blacks
Good	26%	40%
Bad	69%	53%
Neither	2%	6%
Not sure	3%	1%

LESSEN THE FLOW

■ In the 1990s, would you like to see this country admit more, fewer, or about the same number of immigrants as were admitted in the 1980s?

	Nonblacks	Blacks
More	3%	12%
Fewer	62%	47%
Same	31%	34%
Not sure	4%	7%

BOON OR BURDEN?

■ Now I'd like to read you a series of statements about immigration in this country. For each statement, please tell me if you agree or disagree.

	Nonblacks			Blacks		
	Agree	Disagree	Not sure	Agree	Disagree	Not sure
New immigrants take jobs away from American workers	62%	37%	1%	63%	34%	3%
A lot of immigrants bring needed skills to this country	49%	49%	2%	60%	34%	6%
New immigrants joining the labor force drive down wages	66%	32%	2%	61%	36%	3%
Many new immigrants are very hard-working	83%	15%	2%	87%	10%	3%
Immigrants use more than their fair share of government services, such as welfare, medical care, and food stamps	62%	32%	6%	59%	34%	7%

	Nonblacks			Blacks		
	Agree	Disagree	Not sure	Agree	Disagree	Not sure
A lot of immigrants start new businesses, which helps the U.S. economy grow	55%	40%	5%	67%	29%	4%
Immigration makes race relations in our cities worse	61%	35%	4%	43%	52%	5%

ON THE HIRING LINE

■ Which do you think businesses prefer to hire—immigrants or black Americans?

	Nonblacks	Blacks
Immigrants	49%	73%
Black Americans	30%	15%
Makes no difference	6%	5%
Not sure	15%	7%

BILINGUAL DILEMMA

■ In areas where there are a lot of non-English-speaking immigrants, do you think public schools should or should not offer education in their language?

	Nonblacks	Blacks
Should offer	43%	77%
Should not offer	56%	20%
Not sure	1%	3%

PRICE OF ADMISSION

■ Should immigrants who have education and skills be favored for admission to this country over those immigrants with less education and skills or not?

	Nonblacks	Blacks
Immigrants with education and skills should be favored for admission	47%	36%
Not favored	48%	59%
Not sure	5%	5%

THE DREAM LIVES ON

■ Is the American dream of middle-class prosperity still a realistic goal for new immigrants or not?

All respondents	
American dream still realistic	56%
Not realistic	39%
Not sure	5%

Edited by Christopher Power

Survey of 1,418 adults, including 246 blacks, conducted June 10-14, 1992, for BUSINESS WEEK by Louis Harris & Associates Inc. Results should be accurate to within 3 percentage points, except that results for the smaller sample of blacks should be accurate to within 7 percentage points.

that it will make it harder to become a citizen in the future. A study by Borjas shows that in 1980—the latest national data available—only 8.8% of immigrant households received welfare, compared to 7.9% of all native-born Americans. And with the education and skill levels of immigrants rising in the 1980s, the expectations are that the spread between the two hasn't worsened, and may have even narrowed. In Los Angeles County, for example, immigrants amount to 16% of the 722,000 people on Aid to Families with Dependent Children, the government's main welfare program. Yet immigrants are more than 30% of the county's population. "Immigrants benefit natives through the public coffers by using less than their share of services and paying more than their share of taxes," says Julian L. Simon, a University of Maryland economist.

SCHOOL DAZE. One real concern is whether urban school systems can handle the surge of immigrant children. "The public school is the vehicle through which the child of immigrants becomes Americanized," says Jeffrey S. Passel, a demographer for the Washington-based Urban Institute. But in many cities, the task of educating immigrant students has become an enormous burden. In Los Angeles, 39% of the city's students don't speak English well, and in Seattle, 21% come from homes where English is not the family's first language. In the nation's capital, the school system is nearly overwhelmed by a huge number of Vietnamese, Haitians, and Salvadorean children. "If the school system is inadequate, then it's much more difficult to help immigrants move up the economic ladder," says Robert D. Hormats, vice-chairman of Goldman, Sachs International and head of the Trilateral Commission's working group on immigration.

City schools, despite the constraint of tight resources, are finding innovative ways to reach immigrant children. In Seattle, about half the immigrant students speak such limited English that they qualify for a program where they are taught subjects in simplified English. The Los Angeles schools offer dual language classes in Spanish, Korean, Armenian, Cantonese, Filipino, Farsi, and Japanese. Other organizations, such as unions, are also teaching immigrants English. In New York, the Garment Workers Union, often called the immigrant union, offers English classes to its members and their families.

In the coming decade, it won't be easy to assimilate the new immigrants, whether they come from Laos or Russia. But the positives far outweigh any short-term negatives. In today's white-hot international competition, the U.S. profits from the ideas and innovations of immigrants. And by any economic calculus, their hard work adds far more to the nation's wealth than the resources they drain. It is still those "huddled masses yearning to breathe free" who will keep the American dream burning bright for most of us.

By Michael J. Mandel and Christopher Farrell, with Dori Jones Yang in Seattle, Gloria Lau in Los Angeles, Christina Del Valle in Washington, S. Lynne Walker in San Diego, and bureau reports

Rural Populations and the Global Environment

David Pimentel

Cornell University

INTRODUCTION

Rural populations are feeling the impact of the rapid changes that are occurring throughout the environment more intensely than their urban neighbors. Their life activities put them into close contact with the land, water, biological resources and indeed the entire natural ecosystem. Most of the observed changes are being caused by the rapidly expanding world population that is currently at 5.5 billion and is projected to reach nearly 8.4 billion by the year 2025 and possibly reach 15 billion by 2100 (PCC, 1989). Each day a quarter million humans are being added to the world! Approximately 75% of the world population live in developing countries which are experiencing the highest rate of growth.

As the human population increases, so does its needs for food, wood, shelter, and fuel, to mention a few of the essentials. Even now from 1.2 to 2 billion humans are severely disadvantaged including those living in poverty, those malnourished, those living with a heavy disease burden, and those with shortened life-spans (Durning, 1989; V. Abernathy, Vanderbilt University, PC, 1992). Furthermore, substantial losses of fertile soil, forests, fresh water, and biodiversity escalate, while our fossil energy supply dwindles (Worldwatch, 1992; WRI, 1992). The problem that we now face is how to balance the size of the human population with the carrying capacity of the earth's resources.

Aspects of the global environment that all humans depend on for maintaining the quality of their lives and, in some instances, for their survival are discussed in this paper. Priorities are suggested for protecting natural resources essential for continued socio-economic development.

THREATS TO THE GLOBAL ENVIRONMENT

The explosive expansion of the world population is occurring even though serious shortages of arable land, water, and fossil energy already exist in many regions of the world (WRL, 1992; Worldwatch, 1992). Because these resources function interdependently, each can be manipulated to some extent to make up for a partial shortage in one or more of the other resources. To date such substitutions have lessened the impact of the population explosion and masked the seriousness of the problem that exists. The degradation of the environmental resources, however, affects all future development, especially in rural communities.

Land Resources

Land is a basic resource for the survival of all humans because it supplies their food as well as some sources of renewable energy. More than 98% of the world food supply comes from the terrestrial environment, while the remaining small percentage comes from ocean, lake, and other aquatic ecosystems (Pimentel and Hall, 1989). Worldwide, food and fiber crops are cultivated on 12% of the earth's land mass (Buringh, 1989). Another 24% of the land is used as pasture to graze the livestock that provide meat and milk products, while forests cover another 31% (Buringh, 1989).

All arable land that is currently in crop production, particularly marginal land, is highly susceptible to degradation. Extensive degradation of land which threatens most crop and pasture areas in the world, includes soil erosion, salinization, water-logging, and other types of land mismanagement (Mabbutt, 1989; Lal and Pierce, 1991).

Each year more than 10 million hectares [ha] of productive arable land become unsuitable for continued crop production because of agricultural mismanagement, like replacing crop rotations with extensive monocultures (Pimentel et al., 1992a). Also, each year an additional 5 million hectares must be found and brought into production to help feed the 92 million humans added to the world population annually. To compensate for the additional 15 million ha needed, land is being taken from the world's forests. In fact, the pressing need to augment agriculture accounts for 80% of the deforestation that is now occurring throughout the world (Myers, 1990).

Reprinted by permission from *The Rural Sociologist*, October 1992, pp. 12-26.

Of all causes of soil degradation, soil erosion is the single most serious. Erosion adversely affects crop productivity by reducing water availability, water holding capacity, nutrient content, soil organic matter, and soil depth. Worldwide, soil erosion on cropland ranges from about 16 t/ha/yr in the USA to 40 t/ha/yr in China (USDA, 1991; Wen, 1992). In Africa during the past 30 years, the rate of soil loss has increased 20 times (Tolba, 1989). Erosion is now so intense in China that its soil particles are detected in the Hawaiian atmosphere when planting starts in China (Parrington et al., 1983). High rates of soil erosion are of particular concern because the pace of soil reformation is extremely slow. It takes approximately 500 years to reform 2.5 cm (1 inch) of topsoil under agricultural conditions (OTA, 1982; Elwel, 1985; Troeh et al., 1980). Thus, in many regions topsoil is being lost 20 to 40 times faster than its formation rate. Predictions are that agricultural land degradation is expected to depress food production about 20% during the next 25-year period (Buringh, 1989). Meanwhile, fossil energy inputs for fertilizer and pesticide production and for irrigation are being increased in an effort to offset the reduced productivity caused by land degradation (OTA, 1982; Follett and Stewart, 1985; Pimentel, 1992).

Water Resources

As with land resources, adequate water supplies are a necessity and one often taken for granted. All vegetation requires and transpires massive amounts of water. For example, a corn crop that produces about 7,000 kg/ha of grain will take up and transpire about 4.2 million liters/ha of water during just one growing season (Layton, 1983). To supply this much water to the crop, not only must 10 million liters (1,000 mm) of rain fall per hectare, but it must be evenly distributed during the year and especially during the growing season.

To supplement or substitute for inadequate rainfall, water is pumped from surface and groundwater sources for irrigation. Agricultural irrigation "consumes" more freshwater than any other human activity (Falkenmark, 1989). Worldwide, about 87% of the water is "consumed" (non-recoverable) by agriculture (S. Postel, Worldwatch Institute, PC, 1992), while in the United States this figure reaches almost 85% (NAS, 1989). Not only is a major portion of irrigation water lost by evapotranspiration and thus irrecoverable but its use is also frequently wasteful.

Throughout the world, surface water and groundwater each supply one-half of the needed fresh water (Wolman, 1986; Falkenmark, 1989). Groundwater resources are renewed but at an extremely slow rate of only about 1% per year (CEQ, 1980). Because of this slow recharge rate, groundwater resources must be carefully managed to prevent overdraft. However, groundwater resource overdraft is now a serious problem worldwide. For example, in Tamil Nadu, India groundwater levels declined 25 to 30 m during the 1970s because of over pumping for irriga-

tion (Postel, 1984; UNFPA, 1991). Also, in China the Beijing groundwater table is declining at a rate of 1 m/yr and in Tianjin the decline is 4.4 m/yr (Postel, 1984). Overdraft of groundwater in the United States is also common, averaging a 25% greater rate of decline than replacement (USWRC, 1979). In some locations, like the Ogallala Aquifer, the pumping is so great that the overdraft is 130% to 160% above the replacement rate (Beaumont, 1985).

A current and on-going future problem is the equitable sharing of surface water supplies of rivers and lakes between states, regions, and countries. As fresh water use increases to meet the needs of expanding agriculture, industry, and individuals, the distribution of this limited water will come into dispute, especially in arid regions. Furthermore, if rainfall patterns alter, and/or rainfall decreases, the crops typically grown in some areas will have to be changed.

Another major threat to future supplies of water is the pollution imposed by the activities of individuals and their diverse industries. Indeed, water pollution is a rising problem in the United States (USBC, 1990), and it is even more serious in developing countries.

Clearly, as the world's population grows, so does its water needs. During the next decade when the world's population is projected to increase 20%, the need for water is expected to double (Veltrop, 1991). One solution is to curtail population growth and also establish strategies to conserve water supplies.

Biological Resources

In the United States there are approximately 500,000 species of natural plants, animals, and microbes that provide many essential functions for humans, including recycling manure and other organic wastes, degrading chemical pollutants, and purifying water and soil (Pimentel et al., 1992a).

Humans clearly cannot survive by depending only on relatively few livestock and crop species. The millions of natural species, although less obvious, are equally vital. For example, the activities of honey bees and wild bees are essential in pollinating about $30 billion worth of U.S. crops annually as well as pollinating natural plant species. Honey bees and wild bees in New York State on a bright, sunny day in July pollinate approximately one trillion blossoms (Pimentel, 1992). Humans have found no technology to substitute for this natural service or for the many others supplied by wild biota.

As valuable as our biological resources are, the world is losing about 150 species per day because of the human activities of deforestation, pollution, applying pesticides, urbanization, and the encroachment of human activities throughout our ecosystem (Reid and Miller, 1989). All our biological species, both microscopic and larger, must be preserved in order to carry out their beneficial activities. Of equal import is the fact that they are a vital reservoir of genetic material for the continuous development of agriculture, forestry and medicine.

Energy Resources

Energy resources, and especially the availability of expensive fossil energy, have made it possible to expand agricultural food production, develop the agricultural industry, and benefit the health and quality of human life even as our environment has been degraded. For example, vast amounts of energy are used to power irrigation. It also purifies and pumps water for human consumption, thereby preventing the spread of disease. Energy is the basis for pesticides and fertilizers that have enhanced crop productivity, and energy powers machinery and transportation.

Worldwide, the use of energy, especially fossil energy, is about 369 quads (quad = 10^{15} BTU) per year and is increasing as the world population escalates (Pimentel et al., 1992b). The by-product of this energy use is responsible for increasing environmental degradation, particularly chemical pollution of soils, waterways and even the atmosphere.

Developed nations, which have about 25% of the world population, currently consume about 80% of the fossil energy worldwide while the developing nations with 75% of the world population utilize only 20% (UNEP, 1985; DOE, 1991). Each year the United States alone consumes about 25% of the world's fossil fuel.

Energy usage continues to escalate throughout the world and particularly in developing countries, like China, where rapid population growth necessitates increased food supplies. Since 1955, there has been a 100 fold increase in the use of fossil energy in Chinese agriculture (Wen and Pimentel, 1984).

Projections of the availability of fossil energy resources are discouraging. In fact, a recent report published by the U.S. Department of Energy (DOE, 1991), based on the current oil-drilling reports, states that the estimated amount of national oil reserves has plummeted. This means that instead of the 35-year supply of U.S. oil reserves that DOE projected about four years ago, the current known and discoverable potential oil reserves are now limited to a mere 10- to 13-year supply (DOE, 1990; Lawson, 1991). Because the United States is now importing more than half of its oil, a serious energy problem already exists here (Gibbons and Blair, 1991). Although the world supply of oil is more ample than that of the United States, it is estimated to last only about 35 years (Matare, 1989).

In both the United States and the world, the natural gas supply is considered ample for about 35 years and the coal reserves should be ample for about 100 years (Matare, 1989). Other supply estimates range as high as 150 years for total energy, but these are based primarily on coal (BP, 1991). However, all these estimates are based on current consumption rates and current population numbers. If the human population continues to expand, energy supplies will be depleted more rapidly than estimated and this will have a negative impact on the expansion of agricultural production. Thus, increased energy efficiency is mandated now as is a substantial research investment in the development of sustainable sources of energy.

FOOD, AGRICULTURE, AND THE ENVIRONMENT

China, with its population of 1.2 billion and a land area similar to that of the United States, illustrates the direction developing countries and the United States are headed in both agricultural production and environmental degradation. At present, China is experiencing diminished per capita supplies of food and other essential resources, plus a deteriorating natural environment as evidenced by the loss of forests, intense soil erosion, and mining of groundwater resources (Wen, 1992; McLaughlin, 1992). Although soil loss and other environmental problems are probably not as serious worldwide as in China, they are more intense than ever before in history and demand action to halt these losses (Pimentel, 1992; Pimentel and Hall,. 1989; WRI, 1991).

To provide a nutritious diet of diverse plant and animal products, about 0.5 ha of cropland per capita is required (Lal, 1989). The supply of productive cropland in the United States is at this point now, while worldwide the average is only 0.28 ha per capita or nearly one-half available in the United States. This shortage of productive cropland is in part the cause of the food shortages and poverty that humans in some regions are experiencing.

Another important factor causing food shortages is the maldistribution of the resources necessary to grow food crops, namely land and capital. Within many nation-states and regions, sufficient resources exist to produce plentiful food supplies, but the ownership of huge amounts of land and capital by the privileged prevents access to these resources by small farmers.

To compensate for the scarcity of arable agricultural land, large amounts of fossil energy in the form of fertilizers, pesticides, and irrigation are being used to substitute for and extend the productivity of land resources. Analyzing the approximate 1,000 liters of oil equivalents that industrialized nations now expend to produce food per hectare of land suggests strategies that could be employed to decrease the fossil-based energy expenditure, stop waste and at the same time make agriculture more environmentally sound. For example, the plant nutrients in fertilizers lost or wasted in U.S. agricultural production totals about $18 billion per year in fertilizer nutrients as they are eroded along with soils (Troeh et al., 1980). Consider that in the United States livestock manures contain an amount of nitrogen fertilizer equal to the amount applied to U.S. agriculture each year. Manures are underutilized, wasted, and/or allowed to erode along with the soil. Also, a return to more extensive use of crop rotations with legume crops would enhance soil fertility and lessen reliance on costly commercial fertilizers. Significant amounts of fossil energy could be saved if effective soil conservation methods were implemented, manures were used more extensively, and legume crops were used in rotations whenever possible (Pimentel et al., 1989).

Another major and costly waste now occurring in industrialized agriculture is the heavy application of pesticides. Since 1945 the use of synthetic pesticides in the United States has grown 33 fold, yet crop losses to pests continue to increase (Pimentel et al., 1991). For example, corn losses to insects have risen nearly 4 fold, despite a 1,000-fold increase in the use of insecticides on corn (Pimentel et al., 1991). Certainly pesticides have helped in controlling some pest species, yet they contribute to the pollution of soil and water resources, eliminate numerous beneficial species, and cause resistance to develop in major pests (Pimentel et al., 1992).

Also, since 1945 agricultural technologies have drastically changed and these have caused more pest problems to arise. For example, vast acreages of monocultures have replaced crop diversity. Crop rotations have been abandoned for many major crops, like corn, with the result that about half of U.S. corn is now grown continuously as corn. These changes have resulted in an increased number of corn pests because with continuous culture the growth cycles of pests are not interrupted and they increase with each growing season of the same food resource for the pests in the same land.

However, for most crops it is possible to reduce pesticide use by about 50% by substituting various nonchemical alternatives—like crop rotations, crop diversity, and biocontrol—for pesticidal controls (Pimentel et al., 1991). Adopting these and other sustainable agricultural technologies would help stem soil erosion, conserve fertile land, reduce water requirements for irrigation, and decrease pesticide and fertilizer use. Together these would conserve fuel, soil, and water resources (Pimentel et al., 1989). If land mismanagement and soil and nutrient losses were substantially decreased, current yields of food on the available land could be maintained but with about half the energy inputs now used in developed-country agriculture. The added benefit would be the preservation of natural resources and an environmentally sound agricultural system (Pimentel et al., 1989; NAS, 1989; Paoletti et al., 1989).

CONCLUSION

Along with the explosive expansion of the human population, evidence of stark poverty, malnutrition, starvation, and disease is increasing. Meanwhile, prime agricultural land is being lost by erosion and urban spread while pure water and fossil energy resources are being depleted at an ever-increasing rate. Worldwide pollution of air and water is escalating, prime forest areas are being clearcut and burned, and our valuable resource of diverse biological species is being lost forever. Now the resources in many regions are unable to support the adequate production of food and forest products, retain a healthy environment, and provide a decent standard of living for inhabitants within the region.

Americans have to decide whether to continue to support uncontrolled population growth, increased destruction of natural resources, degradation of the environment, and widespread poverty or begin to reduce human numbers and move toward an adequate standard of living for an optimum U.S. population of about 200 million and a world population of 1 to 2 billion humans. With this number, a quality life is sustainable. This would include our being self-sufficient in solar (renewable) energy and in arable land for food. In addition, there would be adequate in fresh water and forests, and we would have a quality, functioning environment. Making the adjustment of population numbers from 5.5 billion to 1 to 2 billion will be slow and probably take about a century, but it is entirely possible.

Starting to deal with natural resources and the future before it reaches a crisis level is the only way to avert a real tragedy for rural and urban people alike. Hopefully, Americans and other people of the world will be able to face the future knowing that they are all working toward achieving an optimum population that will ensure freedom from poverty and a quality global environment. The standard of living of future generations, indeed their survival, depends on the thoughtful decision we are willing to make during this decade.

REFERENCES

Beaumont, P.
1985 Irrigated agriculture and groundwater mining on the High Plains of Texas, USA. Environ. Cons. 12:11.
B.P.
1991 British Petroleum Statistical Review of World Energy. London: British Petroleum Corporate Communications Services.
Brewster, J.A.
1987 World Resources 1987. A Report by the International Institute for Environment and Development and The World Resources Institute. New York: Basic Books, Inc.
Buringh, P.
1989 Availability of agricultural land for crop and livestock production. Pp. 69–83 in D. Pimentel and C. W. Hall (eds.), Food and Natural Resources. San Diego: Academic Press.
CEQ.
1980 The Global 2000 Report to the President of the U.S. Entering the 21st Century. New York: Pergamon Press.
Demeny, P.G.
1986 Population and the Invisible Hand. New York: Paper No. 123. Center for Policy Studies, Population Council.
DOE.
1990 Annual Energy Outlook. Washington, DC: U.S. Department of Energy.

DOE.
1991 Annual Energy Outlook With Projections to 2010. Washington, DC: U.S. Department of Energy, Energy Information Administration.

Elwell, H.A.
1985 An assessment of soil erosion in Zimbabwe. Zimbabwe Sci. News 19:27–31.

Falkenmark, M.
1989 Water scarcity and food production. Food and Natural Resources. 164–191 in D. Pimentel and C. W. Hall (eds.), San Diego, CA: Academic Press.

Follett, R.F., and B.A Stewart
1985 Soil Erosion and Crop Productivity. Madison, WI: American Society of Agronomy, Crop Science Society of America.

Gibbons, J.H., and P.D. Blair
1991 U.S. energy transition: On getting from here to there. Am. Inst. of Physics July:21–30.

Hardin, G.
1986 Cultural carrying capacity: a biological approach to human problems. BioScience 36:599–606.

Keyfitz, N.
1984 Impact of trends in resources, environment and development on demographic prospects. 97–124. Population, Resources, Environment and Development. New York: United Nations.

Lal, R.
1989 Land degradation and its impact on food and other resources. 85–140 in D. Pimentel (ed.), Food and Natural Resources. San Diego: Academic Press.

Lal, R., and F.J. Pierce
1991 Soil Management for Sustainability. Ankeny, Iowa: Soil and Water Conservation Soc. in Coop. with World Assoc. of Soil and Water Conservation and Soil Sci. Soc. of Amer.

Lawson, R.L
1991 The U.S. should increase its use of coal. 41–45 in C.P. Cozic and M. Polesetsky (eds.), Energy Alternatives. San Diego: Greenhaven Press.

Leyton, L.
1983 "Crop water use: principles and some considerations for agroforestry" in P. A. Huxley (ed.), Plant Research and Agroforestry. Nairobi, Kenya: International Council for Research in Agroforestry.

Mabbutt, J.A.
1989 Impacts of carbon dioxide warming on climate and man in the semi-arid tropics. Climatic Change 15:191–221.

Matare, H.F.
1989 Energy: Fact and Future. Boca Raton, FL: CRC Press.

McLauglin, L.
1992 Soil erosion and conservation in Northwestern China. in D. Pimentel (ed.), World Soil Erosion and Conservation. Cambridge: Cambridge University Press.

Moore-Lappe, F., and J. Collins
1986 World Hunger: Twelve Myths. New York: Grove Press.

Myers, N.
1990 Mass extinctions: What can the past tell us about the present and future? Global and Planetary Change 2:82.

NAS.
1989 Alternative Agriculture. Washington, DC: National Academy of Sciences.

OTA
1982 Impacts of Technology on U.S. Cropland and Rangeland Productivity. Washington, DC: Office of Technology, U.S. Congress.

Paoletti, M.G., B.R. Stinner, and G.G. Lorenzoni
1989 Agricultural Ecology and the Environment. Agr. Ecosyst. and Environ. 27 (1–4)

Parrington, J.R., W.H. Zoller, and N.K. Aras

1983 Asian dust: seasonal transport to the Hawaiian Islands. Science 246:195–197.

PCC.
1989 Population. Washington, DC: Population Crisis Committee.

Pimentel, D.
1990 Environmental and social implications of waste in U.S. agriculture and food sectors. J. Agr. Ethics 3:5–20.

Pimentel, D.
1992 World Soil Erosion and Conservation. Cambridge: Cambridge University Press.

Pimentel, D., T.W. Culliney, I.W. Butler, D.J. Reinemann, and K.B. Beckman
1989 "Ecological resource management for a productive, sustainable agriculture." 301–323 in D. Pimentel and C.W. Hall (eds.), Food and Natural Resources. San Diego: Academic Press.

Pimentel, D., and C.W. Hall
1989 Food and Natural Resources. San Diego: Academic Press.

Pimentel, D., U. Stachow, D.A. Takacs, H.W. Brubaker, A.R. Dumas, J.J. Meaney, J. O'Neil, D.E. Onsi, and D. B.Corzilius
1992a Conserving biological diversity in agricultural/forestry systems. BioScience 42: 354–362.

Pimentel, D., M. Herdendorf, S. Eisenfeld, L. Olander, M. Carroquino, C. Corson, J. McDade, Y. Chung, W. Cannon, J. Roberts, L. Blumen, and J. Gregg
1992b Environmental and economic benefits of alternative energy. Cornell University.

Pimentel, D., L. McLaughlin, A. Zepp, B. Lakitan, T. Kraus, P. Kleinman, F. Vancini, W.J. Roach, E. Graap, W.S. Keeton, and G. Selig
1991 "Environmental and economic impacts of reducing U.S. agricultural pesticide use." in D. Pimental (ed.), Handbook on Pest Management in Agriculture. Boca Raton, FL: CRC Press.

Postel, S.
1984 Water: Rethinking Management in an Age of Scarcity. Washington, DC: Worldwatch paper no. 62. Worldwatch Institute.

Postel, S.
1989 Water for Agriculture: Facing the Limits. Washington, DC: Worldwatch Institute.

PRB.
1991 World Population Data Sheet. Washington, DC: Population Reference Bureau.

Reid, W.V., and K.R. Miller
1989 Keeping Options Alive: The Scientific Basis for Conserving Biodiversity. Washington, DC: World Resources Institute.

Tolba, M.K.
1989 Our biological heritage under siege. BioScience 39: 725–728.

Troeh, F.R., J.A. Hobbs, and R.L. Donahue
1980 Soil and Water Conservation for Productivity and Environmental Protection. Englewood Cliffs, N.J.: Prentice-Hall.

UNEP
1985 Energy Supply Demand in Rural Areas in Developing Countries. Nairobi: United Nations Environment Program, Report of the Executive Director.

UNFPA.
1991 Population and the Environment: The Challenges Ahead. New York: United Nations Fund for Population Activities, United Nations Population Fund.

USBC.
1990 Statistical Abstract of the United States 1990. Washington, DC: U.S. Bureau of the Census, U.S. Government Printing Office.

USDA.
1991 Agricultural Resources: Cropland, Water, and Conservation Situation and Outlook Report. Washington, DC: Economic Research Service, AR-23, U.S. Department of Agriculture.

Veltrop, J.A.
1991 There is no substitute for water. Water International 16:57.

Wen, Dazong
1992 "Soil erosion and conservation in China." in D. Pimentel, World Soil Erosion and Conservation. Cambridge: University of Cambridge Press.

Wen, D., and D. Pimentel
1984 Energy inputs in agricultural systems of China. Agr. Ecosyst. Environ. 11:29–35.

Wolman, MG.
1986 "Consensus, conclusions, and major issues in water resources." in J. Cairns and R. Patrick (eds.), Managing Water Resources. New York: Praeger.

Worldwatch
1992 State of the World. Washington, DC: Worldwatch Institute.

WRI
1991 World Resources 1990–91. New York: Oxford University Press.

Communication Networks

A DOZEN WAYS THEY'LL CHANGE OUR LIVES

Scott Cunningham and Alan L. Porter

Scott Cunningham is a graduate student in industrial and systems engineering at the Georgia Institute of Technology, Atlanta, Georgia 30332-0205.

Alan L. Porter directs the Technology Policy Assessment Center at Georgia Tech and serves as professor of industrial and systems engineering and of public policy. He is the senior author of *Forecasting and Management of Technology* (John Wiley & Sons, 1991).

Over the next few decades, communication networks will trigger a host of social changes affecting people and institutions worldwide. A better understanding of the possible implications of these networks can help us foster positive change and reduce undesirable impacts.

The medium of choice for the innovations in telecommunications is the optical fiber. Such a fiber, roughly the diameter of a human hair, can transmit as many as 1 billion bits of information per second, in the form of digitized pulses of

Communication networks offer the promise of more-personalized media and widespread telecommuting, but they also threaten individual privacy and increase the potential for information discrimination.

light. That's almost a million times faster than most modems available on the market today. In addition, fiber optics promise superior fidelity, protection from electrical disturbances and security breaches, and a lower cost than copper wire.

Data "superhighways," utilizing the power and speed of fiber-optic networks, will provide the infrastructure for standardized communications protocols such as ISDN (Integrated Services Digital Network). ISDN allows users to interface with others regardless of equipment or data type. ISDN also permits simultaneous voice and data transmission and interactive graphics. Potential applications include information and database services, catalog shopping, and two-way video interactions.

The key hurdle for connecting users to such fiber networks is the cost of replacing copper wire with fiber-optic cable to homes. However, by the turn of the century the vast majority of American homes are expected to be part of an extensive digital network, though not generally via fiber. In the year 2000, fully 85% of American homes will subscribe to a cable service, and nearly 70% of those subscribing will have access to ISDN or two-way cable ser-

From *The Futurist*, January/February 1992, pp. 19-22. Reproduced with permission from *The Futurist*, published by the World Future Society, 7910 Woodmont Ave., Suite 450, Bethesda, Maryland 20814.

vices. These interactive services will provide a wide variety of educational and entertainment offerings that will vary from home shopping and banking to on-line databases.

Control of these new networks will be a heated issue in the coming decade. Both cable and telephone companies could offer similar services through the next 15 years or so. Eventually, the telephone companies will win out, based upon sheer size and momentum. Telephone companies are implementing digital and ISDN services at a rapid pace, and these services will eventually outstrip even cable television. Opponents of fiber optics insist that the owners of such networks will be positioned to monopolize the information economy. The telephone companies, however, contend that offering information services is only a natural and needed extension of their current business.

A Dozen Social Impacts

The following 12 social impacts are likely to result from the widespread use of digital information networks over the next 30 years. These relatively direct impacts will also spawn further indirect effects.

1 Demassed media. The "mass media" show signs of decay. The three main TV networks are losing audience share. Radio stations fill niche markets. Newspapers are losing influence, in both readership and advertising revenue.

Communication networks are accelerating these trends by facilitating several highly personalized and increasingly interactive media. These "demassed" media, which allow the user greater freedom to select and to schedule, include cable TV, compact discs, computer bulletin boards, electronic mail, electronic newspapers, fax, hypermedia, music synthesizers, on-line databases, remote classrooms via satellite, video games, and videocassettes.

A darker side of demassed media is "narrowcasting." Advertisers and politicians are now capable of addressing highly specific consumer and political interests. Media analysts have a variety of tools for subtly tailoring messages to each target audience and analyzing the wants and desires specific to each group. While narrowcasting may benefit particular constituencies, it could also promote cultural factionalism and a heightened elitism, with the underclasses being largely ignored.

2 Digital footprints. The interconnection of diverse databases provides a continually expanding amount of information about the affairs of the average citizen. These databases may result in the loss of individual privacy and personal liberty, offering the potential for discrimination on a scale never seen before.

However, the positive aspects of these interconnected databases must not be ignored. They offer the potential for the quick and easy indexing of massive amounts of medical, demographic, political, and social data. Such databases may allow rapid apprehension of criminals, careful control of epidemic disease, and the accurate collection of extensive sociological data. Careful management will be required to ensure that this information is handled properly and that individual rights are preserved.

3 Digital tampering. Cheap transmission and reproduction of all sorts of information opens the door to reengineering selected data. Computer editing allows one to make changes in numerical and text data, as well as audio and video data. Data tampering poses troubling security issues, making it impossible to ensure the veracity of information. A proliferation of such tampering could foster suspicious audiences.

In a well-publicized example of digital tampering, *National Geographic* magazine slightly altered the position of Egypt's Great Pyramid on its cover photo for the sake of aesthetics. When incensed readers complained, the editor replied that such changes were insignificant when compared with the license already given to photographers in presenting visual information.

An issue linked with visual tampering is ownership. It becomes increasingly difficult to define ownership and intellectual authorship when information can be revised and resold in infinite permutations.

4 Computer crime. Losses to computer theft are already valued in billions of dollars, yet both corporations and the public are curiously ambivalent about these new crimes. The public sheds few tears over theft from large corporations, even though corporate losses revert back to the consumer as higher prices. Likewise, despite the vehemence with which many corporations condemn computer crime, some corporations reward apprehended computer criminals with choice positions in computer-security divisions.

Expanded networks with increasingly complex interconnections boost criminal opportunities. Society is coming to a rapid, if difficult, understanding of the nature of computer and communications crime, yet the punishment for such offenses is not yet fully formulated within existing law.

Sabotage poses another concern. Today, computer viruses and worms are largely taken as pranks. Yet, some artificial-life enthusiasts insist that these viruses have already acquired some characteristics of biological species, including the capacity of breeding and mutating on resident networks to produce ever more virulent and resistant bugs. On the other hand, Lotus 1-2-3 software creator Mitch Kapor rails against government prosecution and solicits contributions to a sizable defense fund for those ingenious hackers at play. In affairs of computing, especially, there can be a fine line between innovation and destruction.

5 Reduced freedom of information. Communication networks would seem by their very nature to increase access to information, but this is not necessarily the case. Banking, credit, and insurance companies collect extensive databases on customers and potential customers and sometimes sell these databases to others. "Information embargoes" may well emerge as possessors of prized information recognize its value and act for economic gain. Whether through dramatic cutoffs or mere price increases, the result is apt to be restricted information access to poorer individuals, institutions, and nations.

Information is valuable; marketing, sales, and technical data are becoming more and more salable. Although, for instance, scientists would like free and open channels of cooperation and collaboration, corporate sponsors often choose to limit this prerogative. As a result, public access to information suffers.

As Ithiel de Sola Pool worried in *Technologies of Freedom: On Free Speech in an Electronic Age* (Harvard University Press, 1983):

> Videodisks, integrated memories, and databases will serve functions that books and libraries now serve, while information retrieval systems will serve for what magazines and newspapers do now. . . . Speech will not be free if these are not also free.

6 **Information discrimination.** A new form of segregation is occurring in our society. The "information poor" are limited in their access to occupations by a lack of information-manipulation skills. The telecommunications revolution may be bad news for the poor and the uneducated, note futurist Marvin Cetron and science writer Thomas O'Toole in *Encounters with the Future: A Forecast of Life into the 21st Century* (McGraw-Hill, 1982):

> As technological training and higher education become more and more important to the use of things like the two-way cable, as life grows more abstract for the middle-class people enjoying the benefits of the computer, the division between the haves and the have-nots will deepen.

7 **Hyperpolitics.** Communication networks are accelerating the pace of political change. For example, student protests in China were propagated using fax machines, acquiring new urgency with the attention of the international press. The leaders of the failed Soviet coup badly misjudged the sufficiency of control of the official media and the docility of the people after years of exposure to democratic ideas through various media.

A new political order is on the rise in which geographical locale is no longer as important as shared cultural interests. It will be interesting to see how the new European democracies fashion their governments in recognition of the immense power of media and communications.

8 **Transnationality.** Just as information transcending national borders will alter political structures, it will also change corporate, religious, and cultural institutions. What are the geographical loyalties of a corporation such as IBM, which produces and sells in scores of countries, with its multinational stockholders also widely dispersed? Can national boundaries withstand broadband bonding of groups with strong common interests (e.g., German peoples)? Minorities and oppressed groups, if able to gain access to telecommunication networks, could translate information to power. Certainly, multinational corporations are well positioned to take advantage; perhaps a variety of others will be able to do so as well.

9 **Banana dollars.** Communication networks make possible the electronic transfer of enormous amounts of money all around the world. International electronic funds transfers amounted to $114 *trillion* in 1990, up from $72 trillion in 1985. As Peter Schwartz, president of Global Business Network, puts it, "Finance is not one of the biggest customers of communication services; it is *by FAR* the biggest customer."

These electronic funds bear a resemblance to the imaginary dollars charged for time on many computer systems, nicknamed bananas. Like bananas, electronic funds transactions are based less on tangible values than on fluctuations in demand on international markets. The massive flows of such "banana" dollars can rapidly destabilize all but the largest national economies.

In addition, the international transfer process is poorly regulated because national financial regulatory agencies and even international organizations have little authority over such a diffuse process.

10 **Telecommuting.** A sizable portion of American workers could do their work at home through the screens of their personal computers. Clerical and professional workers are coming to dominate the work force, and many of their tasks can be done at home. Author Hugh B. Stewart notes a growing reliance on small, flexible, specialized service companies, which are especially well-suited to employ home-based workers.

Telecommuting could provide several benefits:

• Reduced transportation and energy requirements.

• Greater community stability, since employees don't have to move every time they change jobs.

• Deepening of emotional relationships in the home and the neighborhood.

On the other hand, several costs loom large:

• Decreased benefits for a large class of workers, as corporations "contract" clerical and other work at home and from cheap labor pools abroad, raising concerns about who provides medical insurance and pensions.

• Urban decay as office work moves out, plus reduced job opportunities for the urban poor.

• Strain on familial relationships and increased divorce.

• Isolation and alienation as workers lose the social interaction of the office.

11 **Telecommunity.** Increased network communication implies less face-to-face interaction. This would degrade our social lives, suggests political scientist Langdon Winner in *The Whale and the Reactor: A Search for Limits in an Age of High Technology* (University of Chicago Press, 1986):

> Many practical activities once crucial to even a minimal sense of community life are rendered obsolete [by

computers]. One consequence of these developments is to pare away the kinds of face-to-face contact that once provided important buffers between individuals and organized power.

However, the quality of networked interaction is improving with the advent of higher-resolution, more-interactive video. This could enhance familial bonds and friendship circles, often sundered by current job-based moving. A concern is whether videophone-type services would be largely restricted to the corporate world and the rich consumer.

12 **Technification.** Communication networks already define users and their needs in ways that fit the networks' mechanical means. For ease and convenience of storing information, humans are reduced to a series of numbers by many networks: Social Security, addresses, telephone and fax numbers. Yet, we have also benefited immeasurably from our tools.

People should and will resist having politics, family life, and the arts bow down to the dictates of information technologies. The challenge in managing these volatile technologies is the preservation of the best of our existing culture, while still encouraging new forms to flourish. It can be difficult to accommodate human concerns in the face of the overwhelming momentum exhibited by much of modern communications technology.

Managing the Impacts

Some of these dozen impacts are likely to be more manageable than others. The impacts can be divided into four categories according to their potential magnitude and their amenability to corrective policy action:

• High impact and high potential action: information discrimination, reduced freedom of information, and telecommuting. These impacts all deal with the equitable distribution

"It can be difficult to accommodate human concerns in the face of the overwhelming momentum exhibited by much of modern communications technology."

of the costs and benefits of new communications technology. Thoughtful policy by legislators can ensure that communication is used to relieve rather than heighten discrimination based upon education and social class.

• High impact and low potential action: hyperpolitics, banana dollars, and transnationality. These impacts deal with the reshaping of society on a massive scale. National identity, political power, and even economic wealth lie in the balance. Although these impacts are beyond the power of institutions, or even nations, to shape consistently, all organizations and institutions must make themselves flexible to these new forces of change. These impacts bring disconcerting challenges, but they also offer great opportunities for institutions farsighted enough to take advantage of them.

• Low impact and low potential action: demassed media, computer crime, and technification. These impacts involve new adaptations of society to emerging technology. All three of these impacts have an open-ended feel to them, with society shaping and being shaped by these new technologies. Careful study and thoughtful exploration are needed for those who wish to gauge the extent and future of these changes.

• Low impact and high potential action: digital footprints, telecommunity, and digital tampering. These impacts involve the interaction of existing societal trends with new communications technology. While these issues were not created by communication networks, such networks lend them a new speed and urgency. These problems may require rethinking, to better adapt to an age of heightened communication.

The technological "push" provided by the emerging telecommunications technologies is reinforced by a tremendous societal "pull." Beyond the pull of their immediate applications lies the concern that the United States had better implement these technologies — and quickly — or risk another blow to its international competitiveness. The nation dare not take its time in implementing ISDN, high-definition television, and so on. Yet, these technologies will markedly alter the country's social fabric; they warrant careful consideration even in the rush to develop them.

The Post-Capitalist World

Peter F. Drucker

Peter F. Drucker is Clarke Professor of Social Science and Management at the Claremont Graduate School.

Every few hundred years in Western history there occurs a sharp transformation. Within a few short decades, society—its world view, its basic values, its social and political structure, its arts, its key institutions—rearranges itself. Fifty years later there is a new world. And the people born then cannot even imagine the world in which their grandparents lived and into which their own parents were born. We are currently living through such a transformation.

One such transformation occurred in the thirteenth century, when the Western world suddenly, almost overnight, became centered on the new city. There was the emergence of the city guilds as the dominant social class; the revival of long-distance trade; the appearance of the Gothic, that eminently urban new architecture; the new painting of the Sienese; the shift to Aristotle from theology as the foundation of new wisdom; the new urban universities replacing the monasteries in their rural isolation, as the centers of culture; the new urban religious orders, the Dominicans and Franciscans, the carriers of religion, of learning, of spirituality; and within a few decades, the shift from Latin to the vernacular, with Dante creating a European literature.

Two hundred years later, the next transformation took place. It happened in the sixty years between Gutenberg's invention of printing with movable type and with it the printed book in 1455, and Luther's Protestant Reformation in 1517. These were the years of the blossoming of the Renaissance (peaking between 1470 and 1500 in Florence and Venice); of the rediscovery of Antiquity; of the discovery of America; of the first standing army (the Spanish Infantry) since the Roman Legions; of the reinvention of the study of anatomy and with it of scientific inquiry in general; and of the widespread adoption of Arabic numerals in the West, providing a new ease of computation. And again, no one living in 1520 could easily have imagined the world in which his grandparents had lived and into which his parents had been born.

The next transformation began in 1776—the year of the American Revolution, of Watt's perfected steam engine, and of Adam Smith's *Wealth of Nations*. It came to a conclusion forty years later, at Waterloo—forty years during which all modern "isms" were born. During these years capitalism, communism, and the Industrial Revolution emerged. These forty years produced, in effect, a new European civilization. Again, no one living in 1820 could easily imagine the world in which his grandparents had lived and into which his parents had been born. One had to read novels to learn about that world.

A NEW ERA

Our time, 200 years later, is again such a period of transformation. Only this time it is not confined to Western society and Western history. Indeed, one of the fundamental changes is that there is no longer a "Western" history or a "Western" civilization. There is only world history and world civilization—the creation, to be sure, of Western history and Western civilization. Whether this transformation began with the emergence of the first non-Western country, Japan, as a great economic power (that is, around 1960) or with the first computer (that is, with information becoming central) is debatable. My own candidate would be the American G.I. Bill of Rights after World War II, which gave every returning American soldier the money to attend a university—something that would have made absolutely no sense only thirty years earlier at the end of World War I. The G. I. Bill of Rights, and the enthusiastic response to it on the part of America's veterans, signaled the shift to the knowledge society. We are still in the middle of this transformation—indeed, if history is any guide, it will not be completed until 2010 or 2020. But already it has changed the political, economic, social, and moral landscape of the world. No one born in 1990 will easily imagine the world in which his grandparents (i.e., my generation) grew up, or the world into which his own parents were born.

The first successful attempt to understand the transformation that began in 1455 and turned the Middle Ages and Renaissance into the Modern World was not even attempted until fifty years later, with the *Commentaries* of Copernicus (written between 1510 and 1514), Machiavelli's *The Prince* (written in 1513), Michaelangelo's synthesis and transcendence of all Renaissance art in the ceiling of the Sistine Chapel (painted between 1510 and 1512), and the reestablishment of the Catholic Church in the Tridentine Council of the 1530s. Similarly, the next transformation—the one that occurred 200 years ago, ushered in by the American Revolution—was first understood and analyzed sixty years afterward, in Alexis de Tocqueville's *Democracy in America*, written between 1835 and 1840.

We are today far enough advanced into the new post-capitalist society—because the post-industrial society is really that—to review and revise the social, economic, and political history of the age of capitalism and of the nation-state. To foresee what the post-capitalist world itself will look like is, however, still very risky. What new questions will arise and where the big new issues will lie, we can, I believe, already discover with a high degree of probability. We can also, in many areas, describe what will not work. But "answers" are in most cases still hidden in the future. The one thing we can be sure of is that the world that will emerge from the present rearrangement of values, of beliefs, of social and economic structures, of political concepts and systems, of world views, will be different from anything anyone today imagines. But in some areas—and especially in society and its structure—basic shifts have already happened. That the new society will be both a non-socialist and a post-capitalist society is practically certain. And it is certain also that its primary resource will be knowledge and that, therefore, it will have to be a society of organizations. In politics we have already shifted from the 400 years of the sovereign nation-state to a pluralism in which the nation-state will be one rather than the unit of political integration. It will be a component—although still a key component—in what I call the "post-capitalist polity," a system in which transnational, regional, nation-state and local, indeed tribal, structures compete and coexist.

These things have already occurred. They can therefore be described.

Only twenty years ago "everybody" knew that a post-capitalist society would be of a Marxist complexion. Now we all know that a socialist society is the one thing the next society is not going to be. But most of us also know—or at least sense—that the developed countries are moving away from anything that could be called "capitalism." The market will surely remain the effective integrator of economic activity. But as a society the developed countries have also already moved into post-capitalism with new "classes" and a new central "resource."

Capitalist society, as it peaked in the nineteenth century, was dominated by two social classes: the "capitalists," who owned and controlled the means of production, and the "workers." The "workers" eventually became the "affluent" middle class as a result of what has been called the "productivity revolution"—the revolution that began at the very time of Marx's death in 1883, and reached its climax in every developed country shortly after World War II. Around 1950, the industrial worker—no longer a "proletarian" but still "labor"—seemed to dominate politics and society in every developed country. But then,

with the onset of the "management revolution," blue-collar workers in manufacturing industry rapidly began to decline both in numbers and even more in power and status. By the year 2000 there will be no developed country in which traditional workers making and moving goods account for more than one-sixth or one-eighth of the work force.

The capitalist probably reached his peak even earlier—by the turn of the century, and surely no later than World War I. At least no one since has been able to match in power and visibility the likes of Morgan, Rockefeller, Carnegie, and Ford in the United States; of Siemens, Thyssen, Rathenau, and Krupp in Germany; of Mond, Cunard, Lever, Vickers, and Armstrong in England; of de Wendel and Schneider in France; or of the families that owned the great *zaibatsu* of Japan—Mitsubishi, Mitsui, and Sumitomo. By the time of World War II they had all been replaced by "professional managers." There are still a great many very rich people around, of course, and they are still prominent in the newspapers' society pages. But they have become "celebrities." Economically they have almost ceased to matter. The head of a corporation who retires with $50 million, or even double that amount, is an economic non-entity.

Today it is the well-established pension funds that increasingly control the supply and allocation of money in developed countries. In the U.S. in 1991 these funds owned half the capital of the country's largest businesses and held almost as much of these companies' fixed debts. The beneficiary owners of the pension funds are, of course, the nation's employees. If "socialism" is defined as ownership of the means of production by the employees, then the U.S. has become the most "socialist" country around—while still being the most "capitalist" one as well. And the pension funds are run by a new breed of "capitalists"—the faceless and anonymous employees who run the pension funds as investment analysts and portfolio managers.

But equally important: The real and controlling "resource" and the absolutely decisive "factor of production" today is neither capital, nor land, nor labor. It is knowledge. And instead of "capitalists" and "proletarians," the relevant "classes" of the post-capitalist society are "knowledge workers" and "service workers."

THE SHIFT TO THE KNOWLEDGE SOCIETY

The move to the post-capitalist society began shortly after World War II. But only with the collapse of Marxism as an ideology and of communism as a system did it become clear that we have already moved into a new and different society.

The moral, political, and economic bankruptcy of Marxism, and the collapse of the communist regimes, were not "The End of History." Even the staunchest believers in the free market surely hesitate to trumpet its triumph as the Second Coming. But 1989 and 1990 did indeed signify the end of one kind of history. They brought to a close 250 years that were dominated by a secular religion—what I have called "belief in salvation by society." Its first prophet was Jean-Jacques Rousseau. The Marxist utopia was its ultimate distillation and apotheosis.

But the same forces that destroyed Marxism as an ideology and communism as a social system are also rapidly making capitalism as a social order obsolescent. For 250 years, from the second half of the eighteenth century on, capitalism was the dominant social ideology. Both are rapidly being superseded by a new and very different society and way of thinking about the world.

Whatever this new society will be, it will not be a socialist one. It surely—to say it again—will use the free market as the one proven mechanism of economic integration. It surely will not be an "anti-capitalist society." It will not even be a "non-capitalist society"; the institutions of capitalism will survive, though some (e.g., banks) may play quite different roles. But the new society—and it is already here—is a "post-capitalist" society. Its center of gravity, its structure, its social and economic dynamics, its social classes, and its social problems are different from those that characterized the last 250 years, dominated them, informed them, and defined the issues around which political parties, social groups, social value systems, and personal and political commitments crystallized.

The basic economic resource is knowledge. The wealth-creating activities will be neither the allocation of capital to productive uses nor "labor"—the two poles of nineteenth- and twentieth-century economic theories whether classical, Marxist, Keynesian, or neo-classical. They will center around "productivity" and "innovation," both applications of knowledge to work. The representative social groups of the knowledge society will be neither the "capitalist" nor the "worker," the two groups which characterized society since the Industrial Revolution 250 years ago. The ruling group will be knowledge workers, knowledge executives, knowledge professionals, and knowledge entrepreneurs who have the insight to allocate knowledge to productive use, the way the "capitalists" knew how to allocate capital to productive use. Practically all of them will be employed, either originally or eventually, in organizations. Yet unlike traditional employees, these knowledge workers own their knowledge, the new "means of production," and can take it with them wherever they go. The economic challenge of the post-capitalist society will therefore be the productivity of knowledge work and the knowledge worker.

But there will also be a second representative group—I call them "service workers"—who will lack the necessary education to be knowledge workers. And in every country, even the most highly advanced ones, they will constitute a majority. The social challenge of the post-capitalist society will thus be to ensure the dignity of service work and the service worker.

The post-capitalist society will also be divided by a new dichotomy of values and of aesthetic perceptions. It will not be the "Two Cultures"—the humanist, literary culture and the scientific culture of which the English novelist, scientist, and government administrator C. P. Snow wrote—though that split is real enough. It will be a dichotomy between "literati" and "managers," the former being concerned with words and ideas, the latter with people and work. To transcend this dichotomy in a new synthesis will be a central philosophical and educational challenge for the post-capitalist society.

OUTFLANKING THE NATION-STATE?

The late 1980s and early 1990s also marked the end of another era, another "kind of history." If the fall of the Berlin Wall in 1989 was the climactic event that symbolized the fall of Marxism and communism, the formation of a transnational coalition opposing Iraq's invasion of Kuwait was the climactic event that marked the end of the 400 years of history in which the sovereign nation-state was the main—and often the only—actor on the political stage. Future historians will surely rank January 1991 among the "big dates." There is no precedent for such transnational action, no earlier occasion where nations, without a single dissenter of consequence (and almost without dissent altogether), put the common interest of the world community in putting down terrorism ahead of their own national sentiments and, in many cases, ahead even of their own national interests. There is no precedent for the all-but-universal realization that terrorism is not a matter of "politics" to be left to individual national governments, but rather a threat that requires non-national, transnational action.

In the 400 years since the French lawyer-politician Jean Bodin invented it (in his 1576 book *Six Livres de la Republique*), the nation-state had become the sole organ of political power, internally and externally. And since the French Revolution it had also become the carrier of the secular religion, the belief in "salvation by society." Totalitarianism—communist as well as Nazi—was the ultimate distillation and apotheosis of the doctrine of the sovereign nation-state as the one and only organ of power.

Political theory and constitutional law still know only the sovereign state. And in the last one hundred years it has steadily become more powerful and more dominant. It has mutated into the "mega-state." It is also the one political structure we so far understand, are familiar with, and know how to build out of prefabricated and standardized parts—an executive, a legislature, courts, a diplomatic service, a national army, and so on. Every one of the 200-odd new countries that have been carved out of the former colonial empires has been set up as a sovereign nation-state. And this is what every one of the various parts of the last of the colonial empires, the Soviet empire, aspires to become.

Yet since the end of World War II the sovereign nation-state has steadily been losing its position as the one organ of power. It is fast becoming instead one among many such organs. Internally, developed countries are fast becoming pluralist societies of organizations. Externally, some governmental functions are becoming transnational, others regional (i.e., the European Economic Community), others are being tribalized.

The nation-state is not going to "wither away." It may remain the most powerful political organ around for a long time to come. But it will no longer be the indispensable one, and will increasingly share power with other organs, other institutions, other policymakers. We are moving fast toward the "post-capitalist" polity. And the division of power, the division of tasks, the division of responsibilities and accountabilities between the various levels of this post-capitalist polity are still to be defined: What is to remain the domain of the nation-state? What is to be carried out within the state by autonomous institutions? What is to be "supernational"? What is to be "transnational"? What is to be "separate and local"? Resolving these questions will be the central political agenda for decades to come. In its specifics, the outcome is quite unpredictable. But whatever it will be, the political order fifty years hence will look different from the political order of the last centuries, when the actors differed in size, wealth, constitutional arrangements, and political creed but were uniform as nation-states, each sovereign within its territory, and each defined by its territory.

The last of what might be called the "pre-modern" philosophers, Gottfried Leibnitz (1646–1716), spent much of his life in a futile attempt to restore the unity of Christendom. His motivation was not the fear of religious wars between Catholics and Protestants or between Protestant sects—that danger was already past when Leibnitz was born. But he feared that without a common belief in a supernatural God, secular religions would emerge. And a secular religion, he was convinced, would—almost by definition—have to be a tyranny and suppress the freedom of the individual.

A century later Jean-Jacques Rousseau proved Leibnitz right by asserting that society could and should control the individual human being. It could and should create a "New Adam." It could and should create universal human perfection. But it also could and should subordinate the individual to the impersonal, super-personal "general will" (*volonté générale*)—what Marxists later came to call the "objective laws of history." Since then salvation by society has been the dominant creed of Western Man. And however much it pretends to be "anti-religious," it is a religious belief. The means are, of course, non-spiritual: banning liquor; killing all Jews; universal psychotherapy; abolition of private property. The goal, however, is religious: to establish the Kingdom of God on earth by creating the "New Man."

And for more than one hundred years the most powerful, the most pervasive and near-universal of these secular creeds, with their promise of salvation through society, was, of course, Marxism. Indeed it was the religious promise of Marxism—far more than its convoluted ideology and its increasingly unrealistic economic theory—that constituted its tremendous appeal, especially to intellectuals.

Communism collapsed as a system. It collapsed economically. Its material promises proved hollow. Instead of creating wealth it created misery. Instead of creating economic equality it created a nomenklatura of functionaries enjoying greater economic privileges than the world had ever seen. But as a creed, Marxism collapsed because it did not create the "New Man." Instead it brought out and strengthened all the worst in the "Old Adam": corruption, greed, and lust for power; envy and mutual distrust; petty tyranny and secretiveness; lying, stealing, and denunciation; and, above all, cynicism. Communism, the system, had its heroes. But Marxism, the creed, never had any saints.

The human being may well be beyond redemption. The Latin poet may have been right: Basic human nature always returns through the back door no matter how many times the pitchfork tosses it out the front door. Maybe the cynics are right who asset that there is no virtue, no goodness, no selflessness, only self-interest and hypocrisy (though there are enough witnesses to the contrary, as I remind myself in my darkest hours).

But surely the collapse of Marxism as a creed signifies the end of the belief in salvation by society. What will emerge we cannot know—we can only hope and pray. Perhaps nothing beyond stoic resignation? Perhaps a rebirth of traditional religion addressing itself to the needs and challenges of the person in the knowledge society? The explosive growth of what I call "pastoral" Christian churches in America—Protestant, Catholic, non-denominational—might be a portent. But so might the resurgence of fundamentalist Islam. For the young people in the Moslem countries who now so fervently embrace Islamic fundamentalism would, forty years ago, have been equally zealous Marxists. Or will there be new religions? In any event, redemption, self-renewal, spiritual growth, conversion, goodness, and virtue—the "New Man," to use the traditional term—will be seen as existential, i.e., as applying to a person with an inner nature and commitment and experience, rather than as raw material for a social goal and political ideology. In that sense, too, we are seeing the end of one kind of history.

WHAT ABOUT THE THIRD WORLD?

The Third World houses two-thirds of the world's population; and by the time the present period of transition comes to an end—around 2015 or 2020—the Third World will house three-quarters of the world's population. I consider it highly probable that within the next decade or two there will be new and startling "economic miracles" in which poor, backward countries transform themselves virtually overnight into highly developed, fast-growing economic powers. It is even possible that there will be far more such transformations than there have been in the last forty years, that is, since we first began to talk about "economic development." There is the vast potential of the coastal, urbanized areas of Mainland China—from Tsienstin in the North to Canton in the South. All the economic elements for rapid growth are present there: a huge domestic market; a highly educated population with tremendous respect for learning; an old entrepreneurial tradition; close ties to the "overseas Chinese" in Singapore, Hong Kong, and Taiwan, with access to their capital, trading networks, and knowledge workers. All this might be released in an explosion of entrepreneurial growth if only Beijing's political and economic tyranny could be removed, and removed peacefully. There is India, with enormous untapped potential. There is Latin America, and especially Latin America's larger countries, which offer an adequate domestic market—Mexico may already be in the "take-off" stage. Brazil might surprise everybody by the speed of its turnaround once it has mustered the political courage to follow Mexico's recent example and abandon the suicidal policies into which it plunged itself fifteen years ago. And no one could possibly foretell what surprises the former communist countries of Eastern Europe might produce.

But the developed countries also have a tremendous stake in the Third World. Unless there is rapid development there—both economic and social—the developed countries will be inundated by Third-World immigrants, far beyond their economic, social, or cultural capacity to absorb, assimilate, and integrate. But the forces that are creating a post-capitalist society and a post-capitalist polity originate in the developed world; indeed, they are the product and result of its development. The answers to the challenges of a post-capitalist society and a post-capitalist polity will not be found in the Third World. If anything has been totally disproven it is the promises of the Third World leaders of the 1950s and 1960s—Nehru in India, Mao in China, Castro in Cuba, Tito in Yugoslavia, the apostles of Negritude in Africa and such neo-Marxists as Che Guevara—that the Third World would find new and different answers. The Third World has not delivered on the promises made in its name. The challenges, opportunities, and problems of post-capitalist society and the post-capitalist polity can only be dealt with where they originated. And that is in the developed world.

SOCIETY, POLITY, KNOWLEDGE

I am often asked whether I am an optimist or a pessimist. For any survivor of this century to be an optimist would be fatuous. And we do know that we are nowhere near the end of the turbulence, the transformations, the sudden upsets that have made this century one of the meanest, cruelest, bloodiest in human history. Anyone who deludes himself that we are anywhere near the "End of History" is in for very unpleasant surprises—the kind of surprises that afflicted President Bush when he first bet on the survival of the Russian Empire under Mr. Gorbachev, and then on the success of Mr. Yeltsin's "Commonwealth of Independent States."

But surely this is a time to make the future. Nothing "post" is permanent or even long-lived. Ours is a transition period. And what the future society will look like, let alone whether it will indeed be the "knowledge society" some of us dare to hope for, depends on how the developed countries—their intellectual leaders, their business leaders, their political leaders, but above all, each of us in his own life and sphere—respond to the challenges of this transition period, the post-capitalist period.

This glossary of sociology terms is included to provide you with a convenient and ready reference as you encounter general terms in your study of sociology that are unfamiliar or require a review. It is not intended to be comprehensive, but taken together with the many definitions included in the articles themselves, it should prove to be quite useful.

Absolute Poverty A condition in which one lacks the essentials of life such as food, clothing, or shelter. *See* Relative Poverty.

Achieved Status The position of an individual within a system of social stratification based on changeable factors such as occupations, high income, or marriage into higher social strata. *See* Ascriptive Status.

Agents of Socialization The people, groups, and organizations who socialize the individual. *See* Socialization.

Alienation A sense of separation from society. In the context of the bureacracy, one's feeling of not having control over or responsibility for one's own behavior at work. *See* Bureaucracy.

Altruism Behavior motivated by a desire to benefit another individual, or sacrifice by individuals for the benefit of the group as a whole.

Androgyny A combination of male and female characteristics. The term may be used in a strictly physical sense or it may apply to a wider, social ideal.

Anomie The loosening of social control over individual behavior that occurs when norms become ineffective.

Ascriptive Status The position of an individual within a system of social stratification based on factors such as sex, age, race, over which the individual has no control. *See* Achieved Status, Social Stratification, Status.

Assimilation The absorption of a subordinate group into the dominant culture.

Authority Power that people recognize as just, legitimate, and necessary; the basis for compliance with a government's laws.

Authority Systems Systems by which authority is legitimated. According to Max Weber, in a traditional system, positions of authority are obtained by heredity. In a charismatic system, leaders are followed because of some extraordinarily appealing personal quality. In a legal-rational system, the office is the source of authority, rather than the officeholder.

Autocratic Leader The type of group leader who is authoritarian and impersonal and who does not participate in group projects. *See* Democratic Leader, Laissez-Faire Leader.

Awareness Context The "total combination of what each interactant in a situation knows about the identity of the other and [about his or her] own identity in the eyes of the other."

Belief System Groups of basic assumptions about general concepts such as the existence and nature of God, the meaning of life, or the relationship of the individual and the state held by a culture.

Bilineal Kinship Kinship system in which descent is traced through both parents and all grandparents. *See* Kinship, Lineal Kinship.

Biological Determinism The view of behavior as a product of genetic makeup.

Biological-Instinctual Theories Theories of behavior that stress the importance of instinct. *See* Environmental Theories.

Biosocial Interaction The ways in which interrelationships with society influence and are influenced by biological factors. *See* Biosociologists.

Biosocial Systems Systems of social organization such as those among insects, which survive because behavior patterns are biologically controlled.

Biosociologists Sociologists who are concerned with the implications of biology in the study of society. They study the genotype-environment interactions in the production of behavior. *See* Genotype/Phenotype, Sociobiology.

Birth Rate (Crude) The number of people born in a single year per 1,000 persons in the population.

Bourgeoisie The class that owns the means of production. *See* Proletariat.

Bureaucracy An authority structure arranged hierarchically for the purpose of efficient operation.

Case Study A research method which involves intensive examination of a particular social group over time. *See* Sample Survey, Participant Observation, Research.

Caste A rigid form of social stratification, rooted in religious standards, in which individuals spend their lives in the stratum into which they were born. *See* Class, Estate, Social Stratification.

Census A periodic count and collection of demographic information about an entire population. *See* Demography.

Central City The core unit of a metropolitan area. The term is also used to mean "inner city" or "ghetto," with its urban problems of poverty, crime, racial discrimination, poor schools and housing, and so on.

Centrality of the Leader A concept of group interaction formulated by Sigmund Freud which considers the group leader's power and authority to be centrally important to the group.

Charisma Exceptional personal leadership qualities which command authority as contrasted to legal or formal authority. A driving, creative force that attaches both to individuals and to social movements.

Clan A lineal kinship group. *See* Kinship, Lineal Kinship.

Class A form of social stratification in which groups are divided primarily by economic positions. According to Weber, people with the same amount of property belong to the same class. *See* Caste, Estate, Social Stratification.

Class Conflict According to Marxist theory, the dynamics for change created by the conflict between ruling classes and subordinate classes in society.

Class Consciousness According to Marxist theory, the awareness of what it means to be a member of a certain class.

Classless Society According to Marxist theory, the goal of socialism and the state in which all social stratification on the basis of class is eliminated. *See* Class, Social Stratification.

Cliques Tight clusters of friends and acquaintances who share relatively intense feelings of belonging. Cliques are primary groups. *See* Primary Groups.

Closed Community A type of community in which families within tight kinship groups cooperate closely and are closed to non-relatives. *See* Open Community.

Closed System A social stratification system which offers an individual no way to rise to a higher position; based on ascriptive status. *See* Ascriptive Status, Open System.

Coercion The power to compel people to act against their will, by using force or the threat of force. The constraint of some people by others. According to conflict theorists, it is that glue that binds society together. *See* Conflict Model, Power.

Coercive Organization According to Amitai Etzioni, an organization in which force is the major means of control. Examples include prisons and custodial mental hospitals. *See* Normative and Utilitarian Organizations, Compliance Patterns.

Cognitive Category Category of knowledge and experience into which people organize their perceptions of the world.

Cognitive Development A theory of psychology which states that cognitive processes such as thinking, knowing, perceiving, develop in stages although they function and influence even newborns' behavior. *See* Behaviorist.

Collective Behavior The behavior of a loosely associated group which is responding to the same stimulus. The concept embraces a wide range of group phenomena, including riots, social movements, revolutions, fads, crazes, panics, public opinion, and rumors. All are responses to as well as causes of social change. Elementary forms of collective behavior (panics, rumors) are relatively spontaneous and unstructured, but longer-lasting activities (social movements) require more planning and coordination. *See* Social Aggregate.

Communalism The need for scientific discoveries to be made available to the whole community. *See* Universalism.

Communism A political-economic system in which wealth and power are shared harmoniously by the whole community. The concept today refers mainly to the revolutionary socialism of Karl Marx and to the political systems that adhere to his principles. *See* Socialism.

Community The spatial, or territorial, unit in social organization; also the psychological feeling of belonging associated with such units. *See* Metropolis.

Competitive Social System A social system in which the dominant group views the subordinate group as aggressive and dangerous and thereby in need of suppression. *See* Paternalistic Social System.

Compliance Patterns According to Amitai Etzioni, the (three) ways in which formal organizations exercise control over members. *See* Coercive, Normative, Utilitarian Organizations.

Comte, Auguste (1798-1857) French philosopher who coined the term "sociology" and is considered the founder of the modern discipline.

Concentric Zone Theory A proposal by the Chicago School founders, Park and Burgess, saying that cities grew from a central business district outward in a series of concentric circles. Each zone was inhabited by different social classes and different types of homes and businesses. *See* Multiple-Nuclei Theory, Sector Theory.

Conflict Model The view of society that sees social units a sources of competing values and norms. See Equilibrium Model.

Conforming Behavior Behavior that follows the accepted standards of conduct of a group or society. See Deviance.

Conjugal Family A family type in which major emphasis is placed on the husband-wife relationship. See Consanguine Family.

Consanguine Family The family type in which the major emphasis is on the blood relationships of parents and children or brothers and sisters.

Contagion Theory A theory of collective behavior, originated by Gustave LeBon, which states that the rapid spread of a common mood among a large number of people is what forms a crowd.

Conventional Morality According to Lawrence Kohlberg, the second level of moral development, at which most adults remain. This level involves conformity to cultural or family norms, maintenance of, and loyalty to, the social order. See Preconventional, Postconventional Morality.

Convergence Theory A theory of collective behavior which states that people with certain tendencies are most likely to come together in a crowd. This theory assumes that crowd behavior is uniform.

Core of the Aggregate People in a particularly visible location within a social aggregate who may induce action by the aggregate. See Social Aggregate.

Crimes Without Victims Violations of criminal law, such as homosexuality, drug addiction, prostitution, or abortion, which raise questions about the enforcement of morality by legal controls. See Crime, Sin.

Criminal Justice System Authorities and institutions in a society concerned with labeling and punishing criminals according to formal social sanctions.

Criminality Deviant behavior that is punishable through formal sanctions, or penalties, applied by political authorities. See Crime, Deviance.

Criminalization The labeling of individuals as criminals, especially by the criminal justice system. See Criminal Justice System, Stigmatization.

Criminology The social science that analyzes crime as a social occurrence; the study of crime, criminality, and the operation of the criminal justice system. See Crime.

Crowd A type of social aggregate in which all participants are in the same place at the same time, and they interact in a limited way. See Social Aggregate.

Cults Small groups whose teachings stress ritual, magic, or beliefs widely regarded as false by the dominant culture. See Religion.

Cultural Adaptation The flexibility of a culture that allows it to change as the environment changes.

Cultural Diffusion The adaptation of a culture as it encounters another and undergoes social change.

Cultural Lag The condition that exists when values or social institutions do not change as rapidly as social practices.

Cultural Relativism The principle of judging a culture on its own terms. See Ethnocentrism.

Culture The knowledge people need to function as members of the particular groups they belong to; our shared beliefs, customs, values, norms, language, and artifacts.

Culture of Poverty As defined by Oscar Lewis, "an effort to cope with the feelings of hopelessness and despair that arise [when the poor realize] the improbability of their achieving success in terms of the prevailing values and goals."

Death Traditionally defined as the end of all vital functions. Some states define the cessation of breathing and absence of heartbeat as death. Others say death occurs when brain activity stops.

Death Rate (Crude) The number of deaths in a single year per 1,000 persons in the population. See Demography.

Democratic Leader A type of group leader who encourages group decision-making rather than giving orders. See Autocratic and Laissez-faire Leader.

Democratization The process of making something democratic. According to Max Weber, political democratization is related to the growth of the bureaucratic state.

Demographic Transition The pattern in which death rates fall with industrialization, causing a rise in population and ensuing drop in birth rate which returns the rate of population growth to nearly the same level as before industrialization.

Demography The study of human population, focusing on birth rate, death rate, and migration patterns.

Dependent Variable The factor that varies with changes in the independent variable. See Independent Variable.

Desegregation Elimination of racial segregation in a society. See Discrimination.

Determinism The view of social change proposing that an inevitable pattern of change occurs in societies because of a universal principle, or dynamic, of the historic process. See Deterministic.

Deterministic Any theory that sees natural, social, or psychological factors as determined by preceding causes.

Deterrence Theory A theory held by some criminologists that punishment will prevent as well as control crime.

Deviance The label for all forms of behavior that are considered unacceptable, threatening, harmful, or offensive in terms of the standards or expectations of a particular society or social group. See Conforming Behavior, Norm, Secondary Deviance.

Dewey, John (1859-1952) American philosopher and educator, a functionalist, whose ideas about education had a strong effect on schooling. He pressed for a science of education and believed in learning by doing. Individualized instruction and experimental learning can be traced to his theories.

Dialectical Materialism The philosophical method of Karl Marx, who considered knowledge and ideas as reflections of material conditions. Thus the flow of history, for example, can be understood as being moved forward by the conflict of opposing social classes. See Communism.

Discrimination Unfavorable treatment, based on prejudice, of groups to which one does not belong. See Prejudice.

Disinterestedness The quality of not allowing personal motives or commitments to distort scientific findings or evaluations of scientific work. See Communalism, Organized Skepticism.

Division of Labor The separation of tasks or work into distinct parts that are to be done by particular individuals or groups. Division of labor may be based on many factors, including sex, level of technology, and so on. See Task Segregation.

Double Standard A moral judgment by which sexual activity of men is considered appropriate or excused while that of women is considered immoral. See Sex Role.

Doubling Time The time it takes a population to double its size.

Dramaturgical Perspective The point of view, favored by Erving Goffman, that social interaction can be compared to a dramatic presentation.

Durkheim, Emile (1858-1917) French sociologist and one of the founders of modern sociology. Deeply influenced by the positivism of Auguste Comte, Durkheim's major concern was with social order, which he believed to be the product of a cohesion stemming from a common system of values and norms.

Dying Trajectory A graph that plots the time span from the terminally ill patient's hosptial admission until the moment of death, and the course of the patient's physical deterioration. See Thanatology.

Ecological Determinism The point of view stressing how environment affects behavior. See Urbanism.

Economic Determinism The doctrine, supported by Karl Marx, that economic factors are the only bases for social patterns.

Economic Modernization Shift from an agricultural-based economy to an industrial one.

Education The social institution by which a culture is transmitted from one generation to the next. See Institutions, Sociology of Education.

Egalitarianism Emphasis within a society on the concept of equality among members of social systems.

Egocentricity The characteristic quality of very young children, their awareness of only their own point of view.

Elaborated Code According to Basil Bernstein, the formal type of language available to the middle class only. See Restricted Code.

Elements of Culture Factors such as customs, language, symbols, and values shared by members of a cultural group.

Elite Those at the top of a hierarchy based on status and on economic, social, or political power. See Hierarchy.

Elite Groups Members of the top ranks of society in terms of power, prestige, and economic or intellectual resources. See Power Elite.

Emergent Norm Theory A theory of collective behavior stating that social aggregates form in response to specific problems that cannot be solved through institutionalized action. See Crowd, Social Aggregate.

Encounter Groups Groups of individuals who meet to change their personal lives by confronting each other, discussing personal problems, and talking more honestly and openly than in everyday life. See Group Therapy.

Endogamy Marriage within one's social group. See Exogamy.

Environmental Theories Theories of behavior that stress the influence of learning and environment. See Biological-Instinctual Theories.

Equilibrium Model A view of society as a system of interdependent parts which function together to maintain the equilibrium of the whole system. *See* Conflict Model, Functionalism.

Erikson, Erik (1902-) Danish-born psychoanalytic theorist who lives in the United States. He supplemented Freud's theory of psychosexual development with a separate theory of psychosocial development. He theorized that individuals move through a series of psychosocial stages throughout life, with the integrity of the personality depending largely on the individual's success in making appropriate adaptations at previous stages.

Estate A form of social stratification based on laws, usually about one's relationship to land. *See* Social Stratification.

Ethnic Group A social group distinguished by various traits, including language, national or geographic origin, customs, religion, and race.

Ethnicity The act or process of becoming or being a religious, racial, national, cultural, or subcultural ethnic group. *See* Ethnic Group.

Ethnocentrism The tendency to judge other groups by the standards of one's own culture and to believe that one's own group values and norms are better than others'. *See* Cultural Relativism.

Ethology The comparative study of animal behavior patterns as they occur in nature.

Eugenics The science of controlling heredity.

Evolution A process of change by which living organisms develop, and each succeeding generation is connected with its preceding generation.

Evolutionary Change A gradual process of social change. *See* Revolutionary Change.

Exchange Theory The viewpoint that stresses that individuals judge the worth of particular interactions on the basis of costs and profits to themselves.

Exogamy Marriage outside one's social group. *See* Endogamy.

Experiment A research method in which only one factor is varied at a time and efforts are made to keep other variables constant in order to isolate the causal or independent variable. *See* Research, Independent Variable.

Extended Family A family type consisting of two or more nuclear families. Also characterized as three or more generations who usually live together. *See* Modified Extended Family System.

Facilitating Conditions In a model of suburban growth, those factors that make movement from city to suburb possible. Such factors include commuter transportation systems and communications technology. *See* Motivating Conditions.

Family A set of people related to each other by blood, marriage, or adoption. Family membership is determined by a combination of biological and cultural factors that vary among societies.

Family Life Cycle The process of characteristic changes that a family's task (such as child-rearing) undergo over time.

Family Planning The theory of population control that assumes that parents should be able to determine and produce the number of children they want, spaced at the intervals they think best. *See* Population Control.

Fashioning Effect The tendency for role categories to determine people's behavior and thus to help shape their self-concepts. *See* Role Selection.

Feral Children Children who are not socialized because they have been, according to unconfirmed reports, brought up by wild animals. *See* Social Isolates.

Fertility Rate The number of births in relation to the number of women of childbearing age in a population.

Folk Taxonomy Classification system used by a culture to organize its cognitive categories.

Formal Organization A large social unit purposely set up to meet specific, impersonal goals. *See* Informal Organization.

Freud, Sigmund (1856-1939) Viennese founder of modern psychology and originator of psychoanalysis. Basic to Freud's theories are the beliefs that much of human behavior is unconsciously motivated and that neuroses often have their origins in early childhood wishes or memories that have been repressed. He developed an account of psychosexual development in which he said that sexuality was present even in infants, although the nature of this sexuality changed as the individual progressed through a sequence of stages to mature adult sexuality.

Freud also proposed a division of the self into the *id* (instinctual desires), the *ego* (the conscious self), and the *superego* (conscience). The ego mediates between the pressures of the other two parts in an effort to adapt the individual to the demands of society, and personality formation is largely the result of this process. *See* Psychoanalytic Theory.

Functionalism A dominant school in modern sociology which assumes that each part of the social structure functions to maintain the society and which views social change according to the equilibrium model; also called structural-functionalism. *See* Equilibrium Model.

Game Theory The study of situations in which the outcome of interaction depends on the joint action of the partners.

Gemeinschaft/Gesellschaft Simple, close-knit communal form of social organization/impersonal bureaucratic form. Typology of social organization devised by Tönnies and used to understand variety and changes in societies' social structure. *See* Tönnies.

Gender Identity A child's awareness of being either male or female. *See* Sex Role.

Gene Pool The total of genes present in the population.

Generalized Others According to George Herbert Mead, the developmental stage in which children adopt the viewpoint of many other people or, in short, of society in general. *See* Significant Others.

Genetic Engineering Altering the reproductive process in order to alter the genetic structure of the new organism.

Genetic Load The presence of genes in a population that are capable of reducing fitness. *See* Adaptive.

Genocide Deliberate destruction of a racial or ethnic group.

Genotype/Phenotype Genotype is the entire structure of genes that are inherited by an organism from its parents. Phenotype is the observable result of interaction between the genotype and the environment.

Gerontology The study of the problems of aging and old age.

Group Two or more people who know each other, interact regularly or systematically, share ideas or goals, and think of themselves as a unit.

Group Marriage Marriage among two or more women and two or more men at the same time.

Group Processes The dynamics of group functioning and decision-making and of the interactions of group members.

Group Space A concept of Robert Bales, from his research on social groups. Bales correlated many factors and then constructed dimensions, such as dominance, likeability, task orientation, along which group members could be placed. When these dimensions are combined in three dimensions, they form the group space.

Group Therapy A form of psychotherapy in which interaction among group members is the main therapeutic mode. Group therapy takes many forms but essentially requires a sense of community, support, increased personal responsibility, and a professionally trained leader.

Hierarchy The relative positions of individuals or groups within a body or society and their relationship to power and control. *See* Social Sciences.

Hobbes, Thomas (1588-1679) British philosopher and writer who theorized about social order and social confict. He was the first social conflict theorist.

Hobbesian Question The term referring to the question of the 17th-century philosopher Thomas Hobbes, who asked how society could establish and maintain social order. Today, sociologists apply this question to the problem of conformity within the social order.

Human Ecology Term used by geographers to define the impact of changes in human populations in the broader environment; refers to the relationship between humans and their environment.

Hypothesis An "educated guess," a statement of a probable relationship between variables in a research design. *See* Research, Scientific Method, Theory.

Ideal Type A conceptual model or tool used to help analyze social occurrences. It is an abstraction based on reality, although it seldom, if ever, occurs in exactly that form.

Identity According to Erik Erikson, a person's sense of who and what he or she is.

I/Me According to George Herbert Mead, the I is the spontaneous, natural, self-interested aspect of the self. The me is the socialized part that has adopted the norms of the community.

Imperialism According to Lenin, a nation's policy of building empires by extending its power and domination.

Independent Variable The causal variable, or factor that changes. *See* Dependent Variable.

Individuation The development and recognition of the individual as a distinct being in the group.

Industrialization The systematic organization of production through the use of machinery and a specialized labor force.

Industrial Society Society characterized by mechanized means of production for its goods and services, a high degree of economic development, and a specialized labor force. *See* Postindustrial Society, Traditional Society.

Infant Mortality Rate The number of children per 1,000 dying in the first year of life.

Influence A subtle form of power involving the ability to sway people to do what they might not otherwise do. *See* Power.

Informal Norms The rules governing behavior generally set by an informal group instead of the formal requirements of an organization. *See* Informal Organization.

Informal Organization In contrast to and within a formal organization, those groups of people or roles they play that cut across the official bureaucratic pattern. *See* Formal Organization.

Instinct An unlearned fixed action pattern that occurs in response to specific stimuli as a result of complex hormonal and neurological processes.

Institutions Complex and well-accepted ways of behaving aimed at meeting broad social goals. The major social institutions are government, family, religion, education, and the economy. *See* Organization.

Intelligence A capacity for knowledge. There is not agreement on a precise definition, although intelligence has come to refer to higher-level abstract processes.

Intelligence Quotient (IQ) A measurement of intelligence, defined as a relation between chronological and mental ages. Measured IQ is a good indicator of school performance. Relative contributions of genetic inheritance and environment are not known.

Interest Groups Political factions made up of citizens who associate voluntarily and who aim to influence communal action. *See* Pluralism.

Intergenerational Learning Learning by one generation from another. It is found generally among nonhuman primates as well as among humans.

Intergenerational Status Transmission The passing of the parents' socioeconomic status onto their children.

Internalization In the process of socialization, the taking into oneself of attitudes, values, and norms so that they are part of one's personality. *See* Socialization.

Interpersonal Space The physical distance between people. Cultures vary in the amount of space people leave between themselves when they interact in various ways.

Iron Law of Oligarchy According to Robert Michels, the tendency of formal organizations to give their officers a near monopoly of power. *See* Formal Organization.

Kin Selection A process in which individuals cooperate, sacrifice themselves, or do not reproduce so that their kin can survive and reproduce.

Kinship A system of organizing and naming relationships that arise through marriage (affinal kinship) and through birth (consanguine kinship). *See* Lineal Kinship, Bilineal Kinship.

Kinship Networks Family systems.

Labeling Theory The school of thought that sees deviance or criminality as a status imposed by societal reaction. *See* Criminality, Opportunity Theory, Secondary Deviance, Status.

Laissez-faire Leader A type of group leader who makes few suggestions and allows the group great freedom to do what it wants. *See* Autocratic Leader, Democratic Leader.

Language A means of communication using vocal sounds that make up units of meaning (words) and arranged according to rules of usage and order (grammar and syntax).

Leisure Class The social stratum which exists on inherited wealth. *See* Social Stratification.

Level of Interaction The way in which people relate to one another. Interactions may be subtle and nearly undetectable, or they may be clear and obvious. People may relate on a number of different levels with each statement or gesture. *See* Group Processes.

Lineal Kinship Kinship traced through one parent only. *See* Clan, Kinship, Bilineal Kinship.

Linguistic Relativity The concept that different languages analyze and portray the universe in different ways.

Locke, John (1632-1700) British philosopher and political theorist who put forward a social contract theory of government, which saw people as rational and dignified and entitled to overthrow any government that grew tyrannical. *See* Social Contract.

Macrosociology The sociological study of relations between groups. Some sociologists consider it the study of the entire society or social system. *See* Microsociology.

Malthus, Thomas (1766-1834) British economic and demographic theorist who predicted that population increases would outrun increases in food production, with starvation as a result.

Malthusian Theory Pessimistic pronouncements by Thomas Malthus (1766-1834) about population growth outstripping increases in food production, thus resulting in starvation. *See* Demography, Thomas Malthus.

Marriage The social institution that sanctions, or gives approval to, the union of husband and wife and assumes some permanence and conformity to social custom. Marriage patterns differ among societies.

Marx, Karl (1818-1883) The German-born economic, political, and social thinker whose ideas provided the inspiration for modern communism. Marx's social theory is based on a determinist view of history: according to the "materialist method" that Marx elaborated, the mode of production in any particular society determines the character of the economy of the society and hence the society's cultural characteristics. The economic base constitutes the substructure of society, and all other social and cultural phenomena, such as law, religion, or art, form a superstructure that is ultimately conditioned by the economic base. Social change comes about through a dialectical process of conflict between opposing classes; all history is but the history of class conflict. In capitalist society, class conflict reaches its most antagonistic form; the struggle between the bourgeoisie and proletariat will result ultimatley in the creation of a classless society. In such a society people will finally realize their own potential, no longer feeling themselves alien in the social world they have created.

Mass A type of social aggregate in which separate individuals respond to a common stimulus, but with little or no communication or interaction. For example, all of the people who watch the same television program constitute a mass. *See* Mass Society, Social Aggregate.

Mass Communications Those forms of communication, including especially the mass media, which involve the transmission of ideas and attitudes from a communications center to a diverse mass of people. *See* Mass, Mass Media.

Mass Media The press (newspapers and magazines) and broadcasting (radio and television). The mass media are important agents of socialization. *See* Agent of Socialization.

Mass Society The complex, industrialized society that displays a basic uniformity of material goods, ideas, roles, and lifestyles. Also used in the sense of those at the bottom of the social scale who produce a nation's goods and perform its services. *See* Mass, Mass Media.

Matrilineal Kinship The tracing of one's descent through the mother and her side of the family. *See* Patrilineal Kinship.

Matrilocal A pattern of residence in which a married couple lives with or near the wife's family. *See* Patrilocal.

Mead, George Herbert (1863-1931) American social psychologist and philosopher whose theories of mind, self, and society had a major influence on sociological approaches such as role theory and symbolic interactionism. *See* I/Me, Significant Others.

Measures of Central Tendency Descriptive statistical techniques used to measure the central tendency of distribution of group scores or results.

Mechanisms of Perpetuation In a model of suburban growth, factors that assure that successive generations of target populations will exist and will be drawn to the suburbs. Such factors include movement of industry from city to suburbs and cheaper land, taxes, and facilities in the suburbs. *See* Target Population.

Median Age The age that divides the population in half. Half of the population is older and half younger than the median age.

Megalopolis Urban areas made up of more than one metropolis, "supercities." The area between New Hampshire and nortnern Virginia is one megalopolis. *See* Metropolis.

Methodology The logic of applying the scientific perspective and the set of rules for conducting research. *See* Scientific Method.

Metropolis Urban area made up of separate cities, towns, and unincorporated areas which are interrelated. *See* Standard Metropolitan Statistical Area.

Microsociology The sociological study of interaction between individuals. *See* Macrosociology.

Migration The movement of people, a variable affecting the size and composition of population. Migration may be internal, within a country, or international, between countries. *See* Demography.

Milling The physical moving about of people in a crowd who spread emotions as their contact increases. Milling is an important factor in the escalation of excitement in collective behavior. *See* Collective Behavior.

Mills, C. Wright (1916-1962) The leader of mid-20th-century American sociological thought, who attempted to develop a radical sociological critique of capitalist society. His social-interactionist position, derived from Max Weber and Herbert Spencer, also influenced his thinking.

Miscegenation Mingling of races, particularly marriage or cohabitation between whites and other races. *See* Race.

Modernization The process of gradual change in a society from traditional social, economic, and political institutions to those characteristic of modern urban, industrial societies. *See* Industrialization, Social Modernization.

Modified Extended Family System A middle-class urban family pattern of related nuclear families participating in a kinship structure based on ties of affection rather than ties demanded by tradition. *See* Extended Family.

Monasticism An organized system of withdrawal from everyday life and devotion to religous principles.

Monogamy Marriage of one woman and one man. *See* Polygamy.

Moral Absolutism The idea that one's own moral values are the only true ones and that they are the proper basis for judging all others. *See* Cultural Relativism.

Moral Development The growth of a child into an adult who is willing to make the sacrifices necessary for social living. Study of moral development has focused on how people come to adopt their culture's standards of right and wrong and how they resist the temptation to defy the rules of acceptable conduct.

Mores Folkways or customs to which group members attach social importance or necessity; standards of behavior that carry the force of right and wrong. *See* Socialization.

Motivating Conditions In a model of suburban growth, factors that stimulate the shift of population from city to suburb. Such factors include deteriorating conditions in the cities and rising economic productivity. *See* Facilitating Conditions.

Multiple-Nuclei Theory Theory of urban development stating that a city grows from a number of centers rather than from a single point. *See* Concentric Zone Theory, Sector Theory.

Natural Increase Births minus deaths per 1,000 population.

Natural Selection The evolutionary process by which those individuals of a species with the best-adapted genetic endowment tend to survive to become parents of the next generation. *See* Evolution.

Negative Rites According to Emile Durkheim, rites which maintain taboos or prohibitions. *See* Piacular Rites.

Neoidealism A philosophy that rejects the positivist approach to social phenomena as inadequate. Neoidealists believe that a full explanation must take into account the experience and subjective values of the social actors. *See* Positivism, *Verstehen.*

Non-participant Observations A research method used in case studies by social scientists who come into contact with others but do not interact and behave primarily as a trained observer. *See* Participant Observation.

Nonperiodic Assemblies Gatherings that occur sporadically and whose membership is rarely the same over a period of time. Parades, protest demonstrations, and rallies are examples. *See* Periodic Assemblies.

Norm A shared standard for judging the behavior of an individual. Norms are elements of culture.

Normative Organization According to Amitai Etzioni, a formal organization to which people belong because of personal interest or commitment to the organization's goals. Examples include religious, political, and professional organizations. *See* Coercive and Utilitarian Organizations.

Nuclear Family The smallest family type, consisting of parents and their children. In Western society, custom has broadened the basic definition to include childless couples and single parents.

Open Community A type of community in which families interact with relatives and friends and have selective attachments to a variety of associations and secondary social groups which offer relatively impersonal relationships. *See* Closed Community.

Open System A social stratification system which allows an individual to rise to a higher position; based on achieved status. *See* Achieved Status, Closed System.

Opportunity Theory The school of criminology that sees criminality as conduct. It is based on the writings of Robert Merton, who reasoned that deviance results from pressures within the social structure. *See* Criminology, Labeling Theory.

Organization A deliberately formed group of people who achieves the aims of a social institution. For example, the aims of the educational institution are carried out by organizations such as schools and colleges. *See* Institution.

Organization Development A field of endeavor that seeks to help organizations adapt to a difficult and changing environment by techniques such as sensitivity training, and which aims to humanize and democratize bureaucracies. *See* Formal Organization, Sensitivity Training.

Organized Skepticism The suspension of judgment until all relevant facts are at hand and the analysis of all such facts according to established scientific standards. *See* Communalism, Disinterestedness.

Parsons, Talcott (1902-1979) An American sociologist and one of the most controversial and influential of social theorists. Although clearly identified with the functionalist approach to social analysis, Parsons avoided becoming personally involved in the debates surrounding that concept. His career has passed through a number of phases, ranging from a substantive approach to social data involving a moderate level of abstraction to an analytic approach of almost metaphysical abstraction. *See* Functionalism.

Participant Observation A research method used in case studies by social scientists who interact with other people and record relatively informal observations. *See* case study, Non-Participant Observations.

Party According to Max Weber, made up of people who share political interests. Parties are goal-oriented, and they aim to acquire social power.

Passive Euthanasia The practice of letting a very ill person die naturally when there is no hope of recovery.

Paternalistic Social System A social system in which people or groups are treated in the manner in which a father controls his children. *See* Competitive Social System.

Pathological Behavior Conduct that results from some form of physical or mental illness or psychological problem. *See* Deviance.

Patrilineal Kinship The tracing of one's descent through the father and his side of the family. *See* Matrilineal Kinship.

Patrilocal A pattern of residence by which married couples reside with or near the husband's family. *See* Matrilocal.

Pecking Order A hierarchical relationship of dominance and submission within a flock, herd, or community.

Peer Group Group of people with whom one has equal standing.

Periodic Assemblies Gatherings that are scheduled in advance, have a preset time and place, and draw repeated attendance if they are part of a series. *See* Nonperiodic Assemblies.

Personality The individual's pattern of thoughts, motives, and self-concepts.

Phenomenology A scientific method that attempts to study an individual's awareness of experience without making assumptions, theories, or value judgments that would prejudice the study. *See* Relativism.

Piacular Rites According to Emile Durkheim, religious rites which comfort or console individuals, help the community in times of disaster, and ensure the piety of the individual. *See* Negative Rites.

Piaget, Jean (1896-1980) Swiss biologist and psychologist who has demonstrated the developmental nature of children's reasoning processes. He believes that humans pass through a universal, invariant development sequence of cognitive stages. Intelligence is at first a purely sensorimotor phenomenon. But it develops through a hierarchical process until it can finally be applied to formal, hypothetical thinking.

Pluralism A state of society in which a variety of groups and institutions retain political power and distinctive cultural characteristics.

Pluralistic Society A society in which power is distributed among a number of interest groups which are presumed to counterbalance each other.

Political Modernization The shift in loyalty or administrative structure from traditional authorities, such as tribal and religious leaders, to large-scale government organizations or from regional to national government. *See* Social Modernization.

Political Socialization The social process by which political values are acquired, particularly by young children. *See* Socialization.

Political Sociology The sociological study of politics, which, in turn, involves the regulation and control of citizens; closely related to political science. Traditionally, politcal scientists have been concerned with the abstract qualities of the political order and the formal behavior of citizens, especially in voting and political party participation. Sociologists generally claim that they are more inclined to focus on the actual power relations cloaked by the formal political structure. *See* Political Science.

Polyandry The marriage of one woman to several men. *See* Polygamy, Polygyny.

Polygamy The marriage of one woman to several men. *See* Monagamy.

Polygyny The marriage of one man to several women. *See* Polygamy, Polyandry.

Population Control Lowering the rate of natural increase of population. *See* Natural Increase.

Population Explosion A sudden, dramatic growth in the rate of natural increase of population. *See* Natural Increase.

Positivism A philosophy that rejects abstract ideas in favor of a factual, scientific orientation to reality. *See* Neoidealism.

Postconventional Morality According to Lawrence Kohlberg, the final level of moral development, which few people ever attain. This level is concerned with the moral values and individual rights apart from the group or society. *See* Conventional, Preconventional Morality.

Postindustrial Society A "service" economy of relatively recent development, in which the principal economic activity has advanced from industrial production to services that depend on significant inputs of knowledge. *See* Industrial Society.

Power The ability of people to realize their will, even against others' opposition. *See* Coercion, Influence.

Power Elite According to C. Wright Mills, the leaders in an organization or society who have a near monopoloy on policy making. *See* Elite Groups.

Preconventional Morality According to Lawrence Kohlberg, the first level of moral development. At this level, children know cultural labels of good and bad, although they judge behavior only in terms of consequences. *See* Conventional, Post Convention Morality.

Prejudice A biased prejudgment; an attitude in which one holds a negative belief about members of a group to which one does not belong. Prejudice is often directed at minority ethnic or racial groups. *See* Stereotype.

Primary Groups Groups such as the family, work group, gang, or neighborhood, which are characterized by face-to-face contact of members and which are thought to significantly affect members' personality development. *See* Secondary Group.

Products of Culture Religion, art, law, architecture, and all the many material objects used and produced by a given cultural group.

Projection According to Sigmund Freud, the tendency for people to attribute to others beliefs or motives that they have but cannot bring themselves to recognize or admit consciously. *See* Prejudice.

Proletariat According to Karl Marx, the working class. *See* Bourgeoisie.

Protestant Ethic According to Max Weber, the belief that hard work and frugal living would ensure future salvation.

Psychoanalytic Theory A theory of personality development, based on the work of Sigmund Freud, which maintains that the personality develops through a series of psychosexual stages as it experiences tension between demands of society and individual insticts for self-indulgence and independence. *See* Personality.

Public A loose, heterogenous social aggregate held together for a specific period by a shared interest in a public event or issue. Participants are not usually in the same physical location. *See* Social Aggregate.

Public Opinion Open verbal or nonverbal expressions by members of a social aggregate who are giving attention to a particular controversial point at a particular time. *See* Collective Behavior, Public, Social Aggregate.

Race Biologically, the classificiation of people by observed physical characteristics; culturally, the meaning we give to physical characteristics and behavior traits when identifying in- and outgroups.

Race Relations Social interactions among members of different groups that are based on, or affected by, an awareness of real or imagined racial or ethnic differences. *See* Race.

Racial Group As defined sociologically, any collection of people that other groups treat as a distinct race. *See* Race.

Racism A belief in racial superiority that leads to discrimination and prejudice toward those races considered inferior. *See* Discrimination, Prejudice, Race.

Rationalization According to Max Weber, the systematic application of impersonal and specific rules and procedures to obtain efficient coordination within modern organizations. *See* Formal Organization.

Recidivism The return to criminal behavior after punishment has been administered. *See* Deterrence Theory.

Relative Poverty Poverty of the lower strata of society as compared to the abundance enjoyed by members of higher strata. *See* Absolute Poverty.

Relativism The idea that different people will have different experiences and interpretations of the same event. *See* Phenomenology.

Reliability A criterion for evaluating research results that refers to how well the study was done. A reliable study can be duplicated and its results found by other researchers. *See* Validity.

Religion A communally held system of beliefs and practices that are associated with some transcendent supernatural reality. *See* Sect.

Replacement Level The rate of population increase at which individuals merely replace themselves. *See* Zero Population Growth.

Research In the application of scientific method, the process by which an investigator seeks information to verify a theory. *See* Scientific Method, Theory.

Resocialization Major changes of attitudes or behavior, enforced by agents of socialization, that are likely to occur in institutions in which people are cut off from the outside world, spend all day with the same people, shed all possessions and identity, break with the past, and lose their freedom of action. *See* Socialization.

Restricted Code According to Basil Bernstein, the kind of ungrammatical, colloquial speech available to both middle-class and working-class people. *See* Elaborated Code.

Revolutionary Change Violent social change, most likely to occur when the gap between rising expectations and actual attainments becomes too frustrating for people to bear. *See* Evolutionary Change, Rising Expectations.

Rising Expectations The tendency of people to expect and demand improved social, economic, and political conditions as social change progresses within a society.

Rite of Passage A ceremony that dramatizes a change in an individual's status. Weddings and funerals are examples.

Role The behavior of an indivdiual in relations with others. Also, the behavior considered acceptable for an individual in a particular situation or in the performance of a necessary social function. *See* Role Allocation, Role Label, Role Performance.

Role Allocation Assignment of people to separate jobs, such as cook, table setter, and dishwasher. *See* Division of Labor.

Role Convergence A growing similarity in roles that were formerly segregated and distinct. As men and women come to share domestic tasks, for example, their roles converge. *See* Sex Role.

Role Label The name assigned to an individual who acts in a particular way. Role labels may be broad ("laborer") or specific ("people who get colds easily").

Role Performance The actual behavior of individuals in a particular role.

Role Portrayal The adapting of roles to fit one's style of interaction. *See* Fashioning Effect, Role Selection.

Role Selection The process of choosing a role that allows one to fulfill one's self-concept. *See* Fashioning Effect, Role Portrayal.

Rumor Unconfirmed stories and interpretations. They are the major form of communication during the milling process in collective behavior. *See* Collective Behavior, Milling.

Rural Areas Settlements of fewer than 2,500 residents or areas of low population density, such as farmlands. *See* Urban Areas.

Salience The degree of importance of a group to its members; its impact on members. Generally, the smaller the group, the more salient it can become. *See* Small Groups.

Sample Survey A research method in which a representative group of people is chosen from a particular population. Sample surveys may be conducted by interview or questionnaire. *See* Case Study, Experiment.

Scapegoat A person or community that is made the undeserving object of aggression by others. The aggression derives from the need to allocate blame for any misfortune experienced by the aggressors. *See* Prejudice.

Scientific Method The process used by scientists to analyze phenomena in a systematic and complete way. It is based on an agreement that criteria must be established for each set of observations referred to as fact and involves theory, research, and application. *See* Research, Theory.

Secondary Group A social group characterized by limited face-to-face interaction, relatively impersonal relationships, goal-oriented or task-oriented behavior, and possibly formal organization. *See* Primary Group.

Sect A relatively small religious movement that has broken away from a larger church. A sect generally is in opposition to the larger society's values and norms.

Sectarianism Having characteristics of sects, such as opposition to and withdrawal from, the larger society. *See* Sect.

Sector Theory Theory of urban development which states that urban growth tends to occur along major transportation routes and that new residential areas are created at the edges of older areas of the same class. These developments produce more or less homogeneous pie-shaped sectors. *See* Concentric Zone Theory, Multiple-Nuclei Theory.

Secularization The displacement of religious beliefs and influences by worldly beliefs and influences.

Segmental Roles Specialized duties by people in a bureaucratic society and over which they have little control. *See* Role, Specialization.

Segregation Involuntary separation of groups, on the basis of race, religion, sex, age, class, nationality, or culture.

Sex Role The culturally determined set of behavior and attitudes considered appropriate for males and females. *See* Gender Identity.

Shaman The individual in a tribal or nonliterate society who is priest, sorcerer, and healer all in one. The shaman treats diseases, exorcizes evil spirits, and is considered to have supernatural powers.

Significant Others According to George Herbert Mead, parents and other relatives or friends whose viewpoints children learn to adopt. *See* Generalized Others.

Simmel, Georg (1858-1918) German sociologist and conflict theorist who proposed that a small number of stable forms of interaction underlie the superficial diversity of manifest social occurrences. *See* Conflict Model.

Small Group An interaction system in which members have face-to-face contact and which tend to have important effects on members' behavior. *See* Primary Group.

Social Aggregate A relatively large number of people who do not know one another or who interact impersonally. Aggregates have loose structures and brief lives. There are basically three types of aggregates: the crowd, the mass, and the public. *See* Collective Behavior, Crowd, Mass, Public.

Social Bonding The quality of forming relatively permanent associations, found in both human and some animal and insect societies.

Social Change An alteration of stable patterns of social organization and interaction, preceded or followed by changes in related values and norms.

Social Conflict Disagreement over social values and competing interests. *See* Conflict Model.

Social Constraints Factors that produce conformity to the behavioral expectations of society, such as ridicule, expulsion from a group, or punishments. Knowledge of social constraints is taught during socialization. *See* Socialization.

Social Contract An agreement binding all parties that sets up rights, responsibilities, powers, and privileges and forms a basis for government.

Social Control Techniques and strategies for regulating human behavior.

Social Darwinism The view which sees society as an organism that grows more perfect through the natural selection of favored individuals. In this view, the wealthier and better-educated classes are more "fit" because they have competed their way to success. Social Darwinism applies Darwin's theory of biological evolution to social groups. *See* Evolution, Natural Selection.

Social Disorganization The breakdown of institutions and communities, which results in dislocation and breakdown of ordinary social controls over behavior.

Social Distance The relative positions of members or groups in a stratified social system; the degree of social acceptance that exists between certain social groups in a society.

Social Dynamics All the forces and processes involved in social change.

Social Engineering Systematic planning to solve social problems.

Social Epidemiology The study of illness rate in a population within a specific geographic area. *See* Sociology of Medicine.

Social Group A collection of interrelating human beings. A group may consist of two or more people. The interaction may involve performing a complex task—a surgical team—or simple proximity—all the drivers on a road during rush hour. Groups may be classified as primary or secondary. *See* Primary Group, Secondary Group, Small Groups.

Social Interaction The effect that two or more people have on each other's behavior, thoughts, and emotions through symbolic and nonsymbolic modes of expression.

Social Isolates Children who have had minimal human contact because of abandonment or parental neglect. Also refers to people cut off from social contact voluntarily or involuntarily. *See* Feral Children.

Social Mobility The movement of people up or down a social hierarchy based on wealth, power, and education.

Social Modernization A process of change in social institutions, usually viewed as a movement from traditional or less-developed institutions to those characteristic of developed societies. *See* Economic Modernization.

Social Movement A long-term collective effort to resist or to promote social change. See collective behavior.

Social Organization A general term used in different ways in different contexts, but usually referring to organizational aspects of societies, communities, institutions, and groups. Perhaps the most basic aspect of social organization is a common understanding among members of the organization about the interpretation of social reality.

Social Relations Perspectives A view which emphasizes factors other than intelligence, such as family, in determining an individual's economic positions. *See* Technocratic Perspective.

Social Sciences Branches of learning concerned with the institutions of human societies and with human behavior and interrelationships. Social sciences draw their subject matter from the natural sciences.

Social Stratification A system of social inequality in which groups are ranked according to their attainment of socially valued rewards.

Social System The arrangement or pattern of organization of any social group. A system is a whole made up of interacting parts.

Socialism An economic system in which means of production (land, equipment, materials) are collectively owned and controlled by the state rather than by private individuals. *See* Capitalism, Communism.

Socialization The complex process by which individuals learn and adopt the behavior patterns and norms that enable them to function appropriately in their social environments. *See* Agents of Socialization, Personality.

Society A social group that is relatively large, self-sufficient, and continues from generation to generation. Its members are generally recruited through the process of socialization. *See* Conflict Model, Functionalism, Socialization, Sociology.

Sociobiology A realtively new field which is a branch of behavioral biology that studies the biological bases of the social behavior and social organization of all animal species. *See* Biosociology.

Sociocultural Social organization in which patterns of behavior are largely governed by a network of learned values, norms, and beliefs. *See* Culture, Norm.

Sociogram A diagram showing the interaction among group members. A sociogram of a group might show, for example, who is most liked and who is least liked. *See* Group Processes.

Sociological Perspective The point of view of the sociologist. It aims at precision and objectivity through the scientific method. *See* Scientific Method.

Sociology The social science concerned with the systematic study of human society and human social interaction. *See* Society.

Sociology of Death The inquiry into the impact of dying on a patient's relationship to self, to others, and to the social structure as a whole. *See* Thanatology.

Sociology of Education The scientific analysis of both formal and informal learning in a society. *See* Education.

Sociology of Medicine The study of the definition, causes, and cure of disease in different societies and social groups. The sociology of medicine also studies the social organization of modern medical care and the social roles of staff and patients at various medical facilities.

Sociology of Work A study of the relations of production and consumption and the influence of work on social organization and social change. *See* Social Change.

Specialization A concentration of work in a specific area. According to Max Weber, specialization is a characteristic of an ideal type of bureaucratic organization. *See* Bureaucracy, Ideal Type.

Spencer, Hebert (1820-1913) British philosopher whose descriptive sociology was very influential and formed the basis for Social Darwinism. *See* Social Darwinism.

Standard Metropolitan Statistical Area (SMSA) A Census Bureau concept for counting population in core cities, their suburbs, satellite communities, and other closely related areas. SMSAs ignore usual political divisions, such as state boundaries. *See* Metropolis.

State The political-legal system that represents a whole country, its territory, and people. A state is a more formal legal and technical entity than the broader concept, "society." *See* Society.

Statistics A method for analyzing data gathered from samples of observations in order to: describe the amount of variation in each of the variables; describe hypothetical relationships among variables; to make inferences from the results to the larger population from which the sample was drawn.

Status The position of the individual (actor) in a system of social relationships. *See* Achieved Status, Ascribed Status.

Status Group According to Max Weber, people with similar lifestyles and social standing.

Stereotype An exaggerated belief associated with some particular category, particularly of a national, ethnic, or racial group. *See* Racial Group, Sex Role.

Stigmatization The labeling of individuals in such a way that they are disqualified from full social acceptance and participation. Criminalization is part of this process. *See* Criminalization, Deviance.

Structural Differentiation The specialization of institutions, social roles, and functions that accompanies social change.

Structural-functionalism *See* Functionalism.

Structuralism An intellectual approach which emphasizes studying the underlying structures of human behavior rather than obvious, surface events.

Subcultures Various groups within the society who share some elements of the basic culture but who also possess some distinctive folkways and mores. *See* Culture.

Surrogate Religion A belief system that substitutes for a traditional religion. Communism is an example.

Symbol Anything that stands for something else. For example, words may be symbols of objects, ideas, or emotions.

Symbolic Interactionism A theory in academic sociology founded by George Herbert Mead that says humans communicate through symbols—words and gestures—and develop self-images through others' responses.

Symbolic Interactions Interactions conducted through the use of symbols.

Target Population In a model of suburban growth, a group of people who are affected both by facilitating and motivating conditions. This population consisted of young to middle-age white married couples. *See* Facilitating and Motivating Conditions.

Task Segregation A division of labor based on a feature such as the sex or age of the participants. Task segregation is common in most societies. *See* Division of Labor.

Taxonomy A classification system of cognitive categories. *See* Folk Taxonomy.

Technocracy The domination of an industrial society by a technical elite. *See* Elite Groups, Technocratic Perspective.

Technocratic Perspective The view which sees the hierarchical division of labor as a result of the need to motivate the ablest individuals to undertake the most extensive training, which will allow them to perform the most difficult and important occupations in a society. *See* Technocracy.

Thanatology The study of theories, causes, and conditions of death.

Theory A set of generalized, often related, statements about some phenomenon. A theory is useful in generating hypotheses. Middle-range theories interrelate two or more empirical generalizations. Grand theory organizes all concepts, generalizations, and middle-range theories into an overall explanation. *See* Hypothesis, Research.

Tönnies, Ferdinand (1855-1936) Classical German sociologist who was the first to recognize the impact of the organic point of view on positivism. He identified the social organization concepts of *Gemeinschaft* and *Gesellschaft*. *See* Gemeinschaft/Gesellschaft.

Totemism Religious belief in which a totem—a representation of some natural object in the environment—figures prominently. Totems serve as symbols of clans and sacred representations. *See* Clan.

Traditional Society Rural, agricultural, homogeneous societies characterized by relatively simple means of production. *See* Industrial Society.

Tylor, Sir Edward Burnett (1832-1917) British pioneer anthropologist upon whose central ideas about culture all modern definitions are based.

Typology A classification system of characteristics. An example is *Gemeinschaft/Gesellschaft,* two types of social organization.

Universalism A rule for scientific innovation, according to Robert Merton. It refers to an objectivity which does not allow factors such as race, religion, or national origin to interfere with scientific inquiry. *See* Communalism, Disinterestedness, Organized Skepticism.

Urban Area According to Census Bureau definitions, a settlement of 2,500 or more persons. *See* Rural Area.

Urban Society A form of social organization in which: (1) economic exchange and markets are very important; (2) social roles are highly specialized; (3) centralized administrative and legal agencies provide political direction; and (4) interaction tends to be impersonal and functional. *See* Urbanization.

Urbanism The ways in which the city affects how people feel, think, and interact.

Urbanization The movement of people from country to city as well as the spread of urban influence and cultural patterns to rural areas. Also refers to the greater proportion of the population in urban areas than in rural areas. *See* Urban Society.

Utilitarian Organization According to Amitai Etzioni, a formal organization that people join for practical reasons, mainly jobs and salaries. Examples include blue-collar and white-collar industries. *See* Coercive and Normative Organizations.

Validity A criterion for evaluating research results that refers to how well the data actually reflect the real world. *See* Reliability, Research.

Value-added Theory Neil Smelser's theory which postulates five stages in the development of collective behavior. *Social conduciveness* describes situations that permit collective behaviors to occur. *Structural strain* refers to problems in the social environment. The growth of a *generalized belief* involves the interpretation of structural conduciveness and strain in a way that favors collective behavior. *Precipitating factors* are events that trigger collective behavior. *Mobilization for action* is the ''organizational'' component and usually involves explicit instruction and/or suggestions. *See* Collective Behavior.

Values Individual or collective conceptions of what is desirable. This conception usually has both emotional and symbolic components. *See* Norm.

Variables Factors that can change. Reserachers must state the specific variables they intend to measure. An independent variable is causal. A dependent variable changes according to the independent variable's behavior. *See* Research, Scientific Method.

Verstehen Subjective understanding which, according to Max Weber, must be employed in sociological investigation. *See* Neoidealism, Positivism.

Weber, Max (1864-1920) German sociologist whose work profoundly influenced Western sociological thought and method. The key to Weber's analysis of the modern world is his concept of *rationalization*—the substitution of explicit formal rules and procedures for earlier spontaneous, rule-of-thumb methods and attitudes. The result of this process was a profound ''disenchantment of the world,'' which had been carried to its ultimate form in capitalist society, where older values were being subordinated to technical methods. The prime example of the rationalized insitution was bureaucracy.

Weber's writings on methodology have been singularly influential. He argued that the social sciences were inherently different from the natural sciences, for a full understanding of social action must involve *Verstehen* (empathetic understanding). He firmly believed that, although true objectivity was impossible, the sociologist should attempt to remain value-free. *See* Rationalization, *Verstehen*.

Woman Suffrage The right of women to vote. *See* Women's Movement.

Women's Movement A social movement by women to gain equal social, economic, and legal status with men. *See* Feminists, Social Movement.

Zero Population Growth The point at which population stops increasing. *See* Population Control, Replacement Level.

Source for the Glossary:

This glossary of terms is reprinted from *The Study of Society, Second Edition.* © The Dushkin Publishing Group, Inc., Guilford, CT 06437.

Credits/
Acknowledgments

Cover design by Charles Vitelli
Introduction photo—United Nations.

1. Culture

Facing overview—United Nations photo. 37-40—Photos by Colin
M. Turnbull.

2. Socialization, Biology, Social Control, and Deviance

Facing overview—United Nations photo by Christina D. Sagona.

3. Groups and Roles in Transition

Facing overview—United Nations photo.

4. Stratification and Social Inequalities

Facing overview—United Nations photo by Gaston Guarda.

5. Social Institutions in Crisis and Change

Facing overview—United Nations photo by Maggie Steber. 175—
NASA.

6. Social Change and the Future

Facing overview—United Nations photo by John Isaac.

PHOTOCOPY THIS PAGE!!!*

ANNUAL EDITIONS ARTICLE REVIEW FORM

■ NAME: _____ DATE: _____

■ TITLE AND NUMBER OF ARTICLE: _____

■ BRIEFLY STATE THE MAIN IDEA OF THIS ARTICLE: _____
_____
_____
_____
_____

■ LIST THREE IMPORTANT FACTS THAT THE AUTHOR USES TO SUPPORT THE MAIN IDEA:
_____
_____
_____
_____
_____
_____

■ WHAT INFORMATION OR IDEAS DISCUSSED IN THIS ARTICLE ARE ALSO DISCUSSED IN YOUR
TEXTBOOK OR OTHER READING YOU HAVE DONE? LIST THE TEXTBOOK CHAPTERS AND PAGE
NUMBERS:
_____
_____
_____
_____
_____
_____
_____

■ LIST ANY EXAMPLES OF BIAS OR FAULTY REASONING THAT YOU FOUND IN THE ARTICLE:
_____
_____
_____
_____
_____

■ LIST ANY NEW TERMS/CONCEPTS THAT WERE DISCUSSED IN THE ARTICLE AND WRITE A
SHORT DEFINITION:
_____
_____
_____
_____
_____

*Your instructor may require you to use this Annual Editions Article Review Form in any number of ways:
for articles that are assigned, for extra credit, as a tool to assist in developing assigned papers, or simply
for your own reference. Even if it is not required, we encourage you to photocopy and use this page;
you'll find that reflecting on the articles will greatly enhance the information from your text.

We Want Your Advice

ANNUAL EDITIONS: SOCIOLOGY 93/94
Article Rating Form

Here is an opportunity for you to have direct input into the next revision of this volume. We would like you to rate each of the 44 articles listed below, using the following scale:

1. **Excellent: should definitely be retained**
2. **Above average: should probably be retained**
3. **Below average: should probably be deleted**
4. **Poor: should definitely be deleted**

Your ratings will play a vital part in the next revision. So please mail this prepaid form to us just as soon as you complete it.
Thanks for your help!

Annual Editions revisions depend on two major opinion sources: one is our Advisory Board, listed in the front of this volume, which works with us in scanning the thousands of articles published in the public press each year; the other is you—the person actually using the book. Please help us and the users of the next edition by completing the prepaid article rating form on this page and returning it to us. Thank you.

Rating	Article	Rating	Article
	1. Invitation to Sociology: A Humanistic Perspective		24. The Poverty Industry: Do Government and Charities Create the Poor?
	2. Real Patriots Ask Questions		25. A Crisis of Shattered Dreams
	3. The Tyranny of Choice		26. Thinking Beyond Race
	4. Workers of the World, Unwind		27. Why Women Aren't Making It to the Top
	5. The Fragmenting of America		28. The Global War Against Women
	6. The Upbeat Generation		29. Life on the Brink
	7. Blame It on Feminism		30. Jihad vs. McWorld
	8. The Mountain People		31. The REAL Economy
	9. Tribal Wisdom		32. Big Messes: Problems That Grow Bigger and Bigger
	10. Childhood Through the Ages		33. From Ouagadougou to Cape Canaveral: Why the Bad News Doesn't Travel Up
	11. Guns and Dolls		34. Money Changes Everything
	12. Is TV Ruining Our Children?		35. Paradigms for Postmodern Managers
	13. Crime Pays, But So Does Imprisonment		36. Is America on the Way Down?
	14. The Nature of the Beast		37. Is It Possible to Be Pro-Life and Pro-Choice?
	15. A Way Out of the Morass		38. Stand and Deliver
	16. Breakup of the Family: Can We Reverse the Trend?		39. America's Holy War
	17. Can We Talk?		40. The Population Explosion
	18. A Time for Men to Pull Together		41. The Immigrants
	19. The Second Coming of the Small Town		42. Rural Populations and the Global Environment
	20. 'They Can't Stop Us Now'		43. Communication Networks
	21. Further Thoughts on a "Sociology of Acceptance" for Disabled People		44. The Post-Capitalist World
	22. Dignity, Choice, and Care		
	23. Upside-Down Welfare		

(Continued on next page)

ABOUT YOU

Name_____ Date_____

Are you a teacher? ☐   Or student? ☐

Your School Name _____

Department _____

Address _____

City_____ State _____ Zip _____

School Telephone #_____

YOUR COMMENTS ARE IMPORTANT TO US!

Please fill in the following information:

For which course did you use this book? _____

Did you use a text with this Annual Edition?   ☐ yes   ☐ no

The title of the text? _____

What are your general reactions to the Annual Editions concept?

Have you read any particular articles recently that you think should be included in the next edition?

Are there any articles you feel should be replaced in the next edition? Why?

Are there other areas that you feel would utilize an Annual Edition?

May we contact you for editorial input?

May we quote you from above?

ANNUAL EDITIONS: SOCIOLOGY 93/94

BUSINESS REPLY MAIL

First Class   Permit No. 84   Guilford, CT

Postage will be paid by addressee

The Dushkin Publishing Group, Inc.
Sluice Dock
DPG **Guilford, Connecticut 06437**

No Postage
Necessary
if Mailed
in the
United States